LIMITATION PERIODS

LITIGATION LIBRARY

LIMITATION PERIODS

SIXTH EDITION

by

Andrew McGee, B.A., B.C.L., (Oxon.), F.R.S.A.
of Lincoln's Inn, Barrister

Professor of Business Law, Manchester University
Barrister, Kings Chambers, Leeds and Manchester

SWEET & MAXWELL

 THOMSON REUTERS

First edition published in 1990
Second edition published in 1994
Third edition published in 1998
Fourth edition published in 2002
Fifth edition published in 2006

Published in 2010 by
Thomson Reuters (Legal) Limited
(Registered in England & Wales, Company No 1679046.
Registered Office and address for service: 100 Avenue Road,
London, NW3 3PF) trading as Sweet & Maxwell

For further information on our products and services, visit
www.sweetandmaxwell.co.uk

Typeset by YHT Ltd, London
Printed in Great Britain by CPI William Clowes, Beccles, NR34 7TL

No natural forests were destroyed to make this product;
only farmed timber was used and replanted

A CIP catalogue record for this book is available from the
British Library

ISBN 978 0 414 042988

For Judith

PREFACE

It is now twenty years since the publication of the first edition of this book (and more like thirty years since I first became interested in the subject). In that time the law of limitation has certainly not become any easier or any simpler. We have seen new rules on latent damage in 1986 and amendments in relation to defamation. There have been more cases, reported and unreported, than I could possibly count. There has been time for the House of Lords to make at least one absurd decision on limitation (*Stubbings v Webb*) and then rather shamefacedly correct it in *A v Hoare*. There has also been a Law Commission Report proposing reforms which presently have no real prospect of being enacted.

All of this reflects the fact that the fundamental questions of limitation are really very difficult and do not yield to a purely intellectual analysis. When should time start to run? How long should the limitation period be? Should there be any discretion to extend time? And what happens when time expires? All these questions raise deep issues about the role of the legal and judicial process in a sophisticated society. The answers given by the law are necessarily compromises; moreover, English law, here as elsewhere, has developed piecemeal and would surely benefit from some rationalisation, which it is not immediately likely to get.

The law on accrual of action in tort has seen further development and clarification, not least in *Axa Insurance v Akther & Darby*, whilst the CPR provisions of addition of parties and causes of action after the expiry of the limitation period have perhaps been the area of purely domestic law which has seen most development since the last edition. Another very important development has been the growth of cases involving matters of European Union law and human rights law. This has led to the splitting of Chapter 27 into two chapters, with the new Chapter 28 concentrating on European and International law.

These developments suggest that there will be plenty of scope for future editions of this work. They also suggest that they are likely to go on getting steadily larger—so far each edition has been longer than its predecessor, despite my best efforts to cull redundant material (notably in Chapter 22, where much obsolete material on dismissal for want of prosecution has been removed). I retain, however, the original aim of giving the most comprehensive account of the subject to be found anywhere, while focussing on the important and trying to bring clarity to the area.

As ever, various acknowledgements are due. Colleagues, both academic and professional, have raised many interesting points and have been very patient in listening to me discussing limitation. Litigants have contributed many interesting cases, though they may not have realised it at the time. The editorial staff of Sweet & Maxwell have done their usual excellent job of turning my manuscript into something publishable.

My family have, as always, provided essential support in all sorts of practical ways, not least by tolerating with good humour my interest in this (to them) arcane area of law. I continue to nurse the hope that Grace will one day take over responsibility for future editions of the text.

The law is stated as at 1 July 2010.

Andrew McGee
September 2010

TABLE OF CONTENTS

TABLE OF CASES

li

TABLE OF STATUTES

TABLE OF STATUTORY INSTRUMENTS

TABLE OF CIVIL PROCEDURE RULES

CHAPTER 1

Definition, Background and Policy

DEFINITION

For present purposes, a limitation period is construed as including any **1.001**
provision which specifies a time-limit within which legal proceedings of a
particular kind must be brought or, exceptionally, within which notice of a
claim or dispute must be given to another party. This differs from the
practice adopted in some of the earlier texts on this subject,[1] and disregards
the dictum of Pickford J. in *Gregory v Torquay Corporation*[2] that a statute
of limitation is "any statute which imposes a limit of time upon an existing
right of action" in that it extends also to statutes which create a new right
and at the same time impose a time-limit upon its exercise.[3] The justification for this rather broader view of the subject is that a book aimed
essentially at the busy practitioner needs to consider any possible statutory
time-limit, and cannot therefore confine itself by reference to artificial
divisions such as that proposed by Pickford J.

At the same time, the consideration of enactments which do not deal
principally with limitation is restricted almost entirely to Public General
Acts,[4] and such enactments are for the most part treated only briefly.
Consequently, the effects of both the Consumer Protection Act 1987[5] and
the Carriage by Air Act 1961[6] will be dealt with in this work, though the
former will receive much closer attention than the latter. The European
dimension of English law (including that arising from the semi-incorporation

---

[1] See, e.g., preface to Preston and Newsom, *Limitation of Actions* (1st edn, 1940). The third
edn of this work (1953) remains the most thorough and scholarly account of the major
cases under the Limitation Act 1939.
[2] [1911] 2 K.B. 556 at 559.
[3] Perhaps the best example is the Consumer Protection Act 1987: see Ch.7.
[4] Also included is a Measure of the General Synod of the Church of England, the Patronage
(Benefices) Measure 1986 (No. 3), whose effect on the law relating to advowsons is considered at paras 17.010–17.012.
[5] See Ch.7.
[6] See paras 26.024–26.031.

into English law of the European Convention of Human Rights by the Human Rights Act 1998) is also increasingly important, and the role of limitation periods in European law will be considered in Ch.28.

BACKGROUND

1.002　Limitation of actions is entirely a matter of statute, there being no principle of limitation at common law. The first statute was the Statute of Limitations 1623, and over the succeeding centuries a number of other relevant statutes were passed. The principal ones before the twentieth century were the Civil Procedure Act 1833, the Real Property Limitation Acts 1833 and 1874 and the Public Authorities Protection Act 1893. These were consolidated, with amendments, in the Limitation Act 1939 (the 1939 Act), which came into force on July 1, 1940 and which was, until the Limitation Act 1980 (the 1980 Act), the principal enactment.[7] Its predecessors are now largely of no more than historical interest, though some knowledge of earlier case law may be useful when dealing with principles developed by the courts in the period 1623–1939. The more important of these areas covered by the 1980 Act are s.36, dealing with equitable remedies,[8] and s.32, dealing with fraud, concealment and mistake.[9] In addition, some familiarity with the 1939 Act is useful since many cases of great importance were decided under it.

1.003　Important amendments were introduced by the Limitation Act 1963 (the 1963 Act) and the Limitation Act 1975 (the 1975 Act), and the legislation was again consolidated in the 1980 Act,[10] which came into force on May 1, 1981.[11] Since then a further major change of principle has been enacted in the Latent Damage Act 1986, which came into force on September 18, 1986.[12] The Consumer Protection Act 1987, which came into force on March 1, 1988,[13] follows the same principle.[14] Since 1980 the limitation period applicable to actions for defamation has twice been reduced. Section 57 of the Administration of Justice Act 1985 reduced it from six years to three, and s.5 of the Defamation Act 1996 reduced it to one year.

　　The increased attention given to limitation of actions by the legislature in

---

[7] Although amendments were made by the Law Reform (Limitation of Actions) Act 1954, the Limitation Act 1963 and the Limitation Act 1975.

[8] On s.36, see Ch.3.

[9] See Ch.20.

[10] The Limitation Amendment Act 1980 introduced minor reforms as a preparation to the consolidation process.

[11] 1980 Act, s.41(2). This did not apply to s.35, which was, however, brought into force on the same day by Commencement Order SI 1981/588.

[12] Latent Damage Act 1986 s.5(3).

[13] SI 1987/1680.

[14] Though the relevant provisions of that Act are framed in obedience to EC Directive 85/374.

the past 30 years has to some extent been matched by the specialist literature, and a number of books on the whole topic or on particular aspects of it are now in print.[15] In 1995 the question of limitation of actions generally was referred to the Law Commission, which produced a working paper[16] in 1998 and a final report[17] in 2000.

Scheme of the Limitation Act 1980

The 1980 Act is considered in detail in the following chapters of this work, but a brief outline is appropriate at this point. Part I of the 1980 Act sets out the basic periods of limitation applicable. Essentially these are categorised according to the cause of action which is under consideration; they vary from two years in the case of contribution action to 60 years in the case of certain actions by the Crown for the recovery of land. Part II of the 1980 Act then deals with situations in which the periods provided by Pt I may be extended. In the case of acknowledgments, part payments,[18] disability,[19] fraud, concealment and mistake[20] these extensions are automatic. In addition, s.33 of the Act confers upon the court a limited discretion to override the Pt I rules in the case of personal injuries.[21] Part III contains a number of supplemental provisions, of which s.34, relating to arbitration awards,[22] and s.35, relating to counterclaims and third party claims,[23] are perhaps the most important. **1.004**

Three basic issues

The law of limitations may be divided into three questions as follows: **1.005**

(1) When does time start to run?

(2) How long is the limitation period?

(3) What happens when time expires?

---

[15] Ruth Redmond-Cooper, *Limitation of Actions* (1992), Terry Prime and Gary Scanlan, *The Modern Law of Limitation* (2nd edn, 2001), Rodney Nelson-Jones and Frank Burton, *Personal Injury Limitation Law* (1994), R.D. James, *Limitation* (1996), David Oughton, *Limitation of Actions* (1998).
[16] No.151.
[17] No.252.
[18] See Ch.18.
[19] See Ch.19.
[20] See Ch.20.
[21] See Ch.8.
[22] See Ch.16.
[23] See Ch.23.

When does time start to run?

1.006 A consequence of the categorisation of limitation periods according to the basis of the cause of action is that time may start to run at different points in different types of action. Thus it was settled in the nineteenth century that in contract actions time runs from the date of the breach of contract,[24] even though the breach may cause the plaintiff no more than nominal loss. The decision of the House of Lords in *Cartledge v E. Jopling Ltd*[25] established that under the 1939 Act time, in cases of personal injury, began to run as soon as the injury was suffered even though the plaintiff was not, and could not reasonably have been, aware of it at that time. This rule was altered by the 1963 Act, and the rules on personal injuries, which still embody the principle of discoverability, though the details are different, are now found in ss.11–14 and 33 of the 1980 Act. Outside the area of personal injuries it was only with the decision of the House of Lords in *Pirelli General Cable Works v Oscar Faber & Partners*[26] that the universal applicability of the date of accrual rule was firmly established. This case was decided under the 1939 Act, but the relevant provisions were reproduced without material change in the 1980 Act. The 24th Report of the Law Reform Committee[27] led to the passage of the Latent Damage Act 1986, which greatly extends the scope of the principle that in actions for negligence time does not start to run until the cause of action is discoverable. The Consumer Protection Act 1987 follows the same approach, and it is now clear that a major revolution in the English law of limitations, at least with regard to actions in tort, has taken place since 1980. It is no exaggeration to say that the Pirelli principle applies to only a minority of actions in tort, even leaving aside personal injuries cases, to which it never applied. The present state of the law in these areas is analysed in Chs 5–8.

Length of the period

1.007 The length of the limitation period varies from one cause of action to another. Periods of one, two, three, six, 12, 30 and 60 years are found. These are dealt with in the appropriate chapters of this work.

Expiry of the period

1.008 The effect of the expiry of the period again varies. Generally the result is that no action[28] may be brought in respect of the time-barred claim. It is said, though, that the expiry of time bars the remedy but does not extinguish the right. By contrast, in cases involving real property the expiry of

---

[24] *Gibbs v Guild* (1882) 8 Q.B.D. 296.
[25] [1963] A.C. 758.
[26] [1983] 2 A.C. 1.
[27] Cmnd. 9390.
[28] The meaning of the term "action" is considered at para.2.002.

the limitation period can serve to deprive a person of title to property and to confer it upon another. These issues are discussed in Ch.2.

Transitional provisions

It is in the nature of limitation provisions to be concerned with time, and to have to deal with cases where considerable time has elapsed. Consequently, changes in the law relating to limitation cause particular problems. Both the 1980 Act and the Latent Damage Act 1986 contain elaborate transitional provisions to deal with the situation where a cause of action, for which the 1980 Act introduces new rules, has arisen, but not become time-barred before the passing of the 1980 Act. This problem does not arise in the case of the Consumer Protection Act 1987, since the cause of action created by that Act is entirely new. The transitional provisions under the Latent Damage Act 1986 are considered in Ch.6,[29] whilst those under the 1980 Act and earlier provisions are examined in paras 1.029 et seq. These provisions are now virtually obsolete in view of the lapse of time since the enactment of the statute. **1.009**

Cause of action

All the provisions of the 1980 Act use the concept of the cause of action. Usually the date on which a cause of action accrues is at least one of the possible starting dates for the limitation period. The concept of accrual varies according to the nature of the action, and is therefore examined separately in each of the chapters where it is relevant. The term "cause of action" is not defined in the 1980 Act, though "action" is partially defined by s.38(1) as including any proceedings in a court of law, including an ecclesiastical court. In addition, s.34(1) makes the provisions of the 1980 Act applicable to arbitrations in the same way as they apply to an action in the High Court. It can thus be seen that "actions" includes both arbitrations and proceedings, and the term "cause of action" must be regarded as also encompassing a cause of arbitration and a cause of proceedings. Thus, in *China v Harrow Urban DC*[30] it was held that a claim for arrears of rates was an action for limitation purposes, since it was undeniably a proceeding, the cause of proceeding being the ratepayer's failure to pay on demand, as he was legally obliged to do. At the same time it must be remembered that not all actions fall within the scope of the 1980 Act. For a good example of this see *Bray v Stuart A. West & Co*,[31] considered in paras 1.042 and 2.002. **1.010**

---

[29] See paras 6.040–6.041.
[30] [1954] 1 Q.B. 178, DC.
[31] (1989) 139 New L.J. 753, Warner J.

1.011   Although the term "cause of action" is not defined in the statute, it has received some consideration in the case law. The classic definition is that given by Lord Esher M.R. in *Coburn v Colledge*[32]:

> "Every fact which it would be necessary for the plaintiff to prove, if traversed, in order to support his right to the judgment of the court."

In other words the plaintiff must prove that the defendant has owed him a duty and has committed a breach of that duty. In most cases, he will also have to show that he has suffered damage as a consequence of that breach of duty, but there are some wrongs which are actionable per se without proof of damage. Most of the difficulties that have arisen in regard to this definition concern the question of whether the necessary elements have been fulfilled, i.e. whether the cause of action has accrued. These are dealt with under each of the separate causes of action.

1.012   A further problem arises from the rule[33] that only one action may be brought in respect of any cause of action. This rule may require the cause of action in a given case to be identified with some care. One of the earliest authorities is *Darley Main Colliery Co v Mitchell*,[34] the facts of which require careful explanation. The defendants caused subsidence on the plaintiff's land by working coal under it. They were sued, and in 1868 paid compensation for the damage. Thereafter they ceased to work this coal, but in 1882 further subsidence occurred. This could have been prevented if either an adjoining owner had not worked coal under his own land or the defendants had left adequate support under the plaintiff's land. A further action was brought, and the defendants relied on the "one action" rule, and contended that the cause of action had accrued in the 1860s. The majority of the House of Lords held that the cause of action accrued in 1882. In effect this is a decision that there are two separate causes of action, and the decision is not at all easy to understand. It seems clear that there was only one breach of duty by the defendants, which continued until 1868. At first sight this looks like a case where the same breach of duty has caused damage on two separate occasions but the inevitable result of that analysis would be that there is only one cause of action. It is submitted that the decision can be justified, but only if the facts are interpreted as showing that there are really two breaches of duty, the first being the mining and the second being the failure to support the land adequately. This is admittedly a strained interpretation, and it may be preferable to regard the case as wrongly decided. In any event the case neatly illustrates the difficulties of

---

[32] [1897] 1 Q.B. 702, CA.
[33] *Fitter v Veal* (1701) 12 Mod.Rep.542, also reported at (1701) 1 Ld. Raym. 339 sub nom. *Fetter v Beal*; *Henderson v Henderson* (1843) 3 Hare 100.
[34] (1886) 11 App.Cas.127, HL.

applying the "one action" rule. The same basic issue has been canvassed in a number of more modern decisions.

In *Post Office v Official Solicitor*,[35] a postman was injured by the defendant's negligent driving. The Post Office successfully sued the driver for the loss of the postman's services. They also gave the postman a disability pension, and later sought to sue the driver's estate for the amounts they had paid out by way of pension. It was held (though without any clear reasoning on the point) that this was a separate cause of action from that relating to the loss of services, so that the plaintiff was not precluded from bringing the action. Given that both claims arose from the same breach of duty by the defendant, it is hard to understand why the one action rule did not apply in this case. That case may be contracted with more modern cases on economic loss, such as *Forster v Outred & Co*,[36] and *D.W. Moore & Co Ltd v Ferrier*,[37] where the same breach of duty gave rise to an immediate diminution of the plaintiff's estate, coupled with the risk of subsequent further diminution, in which risk has later materialised. The courts have consistently held that there is only one right of action in such cases. It is true that in *Post Office v Official Solicitor* the two claims might be said to be in respect of different "kinds" of damage,[38] but there is no indication in any of the reported cases that this is a relevant factor. In addition, the authorities cannot be reconciled on the basis that in *Post Office v Official Solicitor* the two claims required proof of different facts. In all three cases there was only one breach of duty, and in all three the problem was that the damage had accrued in stages rather than all at once. Given that *Post Office v Official Solicitor* is a case at first instance, whilst *Forster v Outred* and *Moore v Ferrier* are both appellate decisions, it may be possible to resolve the conflict by saying that the Post Office case was incorrectly decided. The absence of reasoning in that case supports this approach, and this would have the advantage of allowing a rather clearer definition on this point, namely that "cause of action" must be regarded as covering all the relief which can be claimed by any one plaintiff in respect of any one breach of duty by the defendant.

An alternative approach to these difficulties is to be found in *Smith Stone & Knight Ltd v City of Birmingham DC*.[39] This was a claim for compensation for subsidence under the Public Health Act 1936.[40] The difficulty was that subsidence had happened on more than one occasion, and the question before the court was when the cause of action accrued. The judge held that there was a fresh cause of action on each occasion of subsidence.

1.013

1.014

---

[35] [1951] 1 All E.R. 522, Barry J.
[36] [1982] 1 W.L.R. 86, CA.
[37] [1988] 1 W.L.R. 267, CA.
[38] *The Wagon Mound* [1961] A.C. 361.
[39] March 30, 1988, Judge Bowsher as Official Referee, Unreported.
[40] This is arguably a case of claiming a sum due under an enactment, but the principles applicable to accrual appear to be the same. See further paras 11.012–11.015.

He explained this decision on the basis that this was a case of continuing breach of duty and as such was to be compared with the cases of continuing nuisance, where it is accepted that a fresh cause of action accrues every day. He treated the *Darley Main Colliery* case as being in the same category,[41] and therefore distinguishable from *Pirelli*. It is submitted, however, that this solution gives rise to a number of difficulties. In the continuing nuisance cases there is a continuing breach of duty, and fresh damage occurs every day: it is for these reasons that there is a fresh cause of action every day. In cases like *Pirelli* there is normally only one breach of duty, though damage may arise on a number of separate occasions. It can therefore be seen that the vital element in the distinction is that of continuing breach, not that of repeated damage. It is not at all clear that in the *Smith Stone & Knight Ltd* case (or in the *Darley Main Colliery* case) there is really a continuing breach of duty. Certainly in the latter case there appears to be only one breach, and it may well be that the same is true in the former. On this basis, the reconciliation of the authorities presented in *Smith Stone & Knight Ltd v City of Birmingham DC* is unconvincing.

1.015   The *Henderson*[42] rule was considered again in *Stanway v Attorney-General*,[43] where the question was whether a claimant should be allowed to pursue an action, having discontinued a counterclaim in a related action against, among others, the same defendants. The issues raised in the counterclaim were broadly similar to those in the action which the claimant wished to pursue. In this respect *Stanway* differs from the cases considered in the preceding paragraphs. There is no suggestion that there could have been two distinct causes of action. It is apparent that both claims arise out of broadly the same facts, but there are associated procedural factors which explain why the actions proceeded as they did. From a procedural point of view the matter was somewhat complicated by the provisions of CPR 38.7, which provides:

"A claimant who discontinues a claim needs the permission of the court to make another claim against the same defendant if—

(a) he discontinued the claim after the defendant filed a defence; and
(b) the other claim arises out of facts which are the same or substantially the same as those relating to the discontinued claim."

1.016   It was argued for the defendants that the words "make another claim" applied to the present case, even though the present action was started before the discontinuance. The defendants contended that that this must be so because otherwise the effect of the rule could easily be avoided by

---

[41] Relying on *Crumbue v Wallsend Local Board* [1891] 1 Q.B. 503, CA.
[42] See fn.33, above, and para.1.012.
[43] *The Times*, November 25, 1999, Lloyd J.

starting any new claim just before serving notice of discontinuance. Lloyd J. rejected that argument, holding that this rule only applies where the second proceedings have not been commenced at the time of the discontinuance.[44]

That left a separate argument based on *Henderson v Henderson*. Lloyd J. **1.017** observed that it is a principle of fairness, which allows the court to prevent misuse of its procedure in a way that would be manifestly unfair to a party to litigation.[45] The basis of the principle was the desirability that a defendant should not be oppressed by successive suits when one would be enough.[46] It is based on the court's power to prevent the abuse of its process: only if the new proceedings do amount to an abuse are they to be stopped on this ground.[47]

As the principle was first formulated, it did not apply except where the first action had been brought to judgment. It presupposed that a party should not be allowed to embark on one set of proceedings, pursue them to judgment and then start another set of proceedings raising different issues which could (and in the court's view should) have been raised in the first action. In *Johnson v Gore Wood & Co.*[48] the House of Lords extended the principle to a case where the first action had been compromised, and the second action was brought by the director and sole shareholder of the company that had brought the first action. Both claims, however, were in negligence against the same solicitors, claiming damages arising (for the most part) out of identical circumstances. The Court held that it was sufficient that the first claim had been brought to finality by compromise and that the proper approach was to look at substance not form. On the facts of *Stanway* it was held that the issues raised in the claimant's action were wider than the issues arising in the previous counterclaim. The claimant had not been guilty of abuse of process in limiting the issues pleaded in the counterclaim, which did not involve exactly the same parties as the later claim. Consequently, *Henderson v Henderson* could not properly be used as a basis for striking out the claim.[49]

It is clear that *Stanway* is the culmination of a reformulation of what had **1.018** previously been regarded as the *Henderson* rule. There is now no blanket rule that it is impossible to bring two actions on the same cause of action. Rather, the court will look at all the circumstances in order to decide whether the second action is an abuse of process. It does not matter whether the two actions are simultaneous or sequential, nor does it matter that the

---

[44] Reference was also made to the definitions of "claim" in CPR Pt 20 and CPR 3.4(4).
[45] See Lord Diplock in *Hunter v Chief Constable of West Midlands Police* [1982] A.C. 529; [1981] 3 All E.R. 727 at 536 of the former report.
[46] *Barrow v Bankside Members Agency Ltd* [1996] 1 All E.R. 981; [1996] 1 W.L.R. 257 at 260 of the latter report, per Sir Thomas Bingham M.R.
[47] *Brisbane City Council v Attorney-General for Queensland* [1979] A.C. 411; [1978] 3 All E.R. 30.; *Basso v Estry* [2005] All ER (D) 44 (Nov), Mark Cawson QC.
[48] [2001] 1 All E.R. 481.
[49] See also *Bradford & Bingley Building Society v Seddon, Hancock (Third Parties)* [1999] 4 All E.R. 217; [1999] 1 W.L.R. 1482.

first action has ended (whether by judgment or by compromise) or that it is still going on. That is not to say that there will be many cases where the result will be any different from what might previously have been expected, but a more flexible and merits-based approach to the reasoning will need to be adopted.

1.019   The most recent cases on abuse of process in relation to limitation is *Good Challenger Navegante*.[50] In January 1993, the claimants obtained an order without notice in the English courts that they be at liberty to enforce an award made in arbitration proceedings in Romania. On advice from the Romanian lawyers, the claimants did not serve the order on the defendants whilst the Romanian proceedings were continuing. The Romanian proceedings were protracted; they were ultimately concluded in March 1998 with the result that the claimants succeeded in having the award recognised in Romania but failed in their attempts to have it enforced.

After an unsuccessful attempt to found a cause of action in England on the basis of the judgment of the Romanian courts, the claimants obtained an order lifting the automatic stay (imposed by virtue of the Civil Procedure Rules, CPR) on the 1993 order and granting permission to serve it on the defendants. In the event, service was not effected on the defendants until August 2001. The Court of Appeal applied the principles set out in *Johnson v Gore Wood* in relation to abuse of process by relitigating a question which had already been litigated. On the facts it was held that there was no abuse in seeking to have the stay lifted, because the claimants had always intended to enforce the 1993 order and had delayed doing so on legal advice because it was thought that enforcement would have prejudicial consequences for the Romanian proceedings. The Court of Appeal considered that in the circumstances this was a good explanation and showed that there was no abuse.

Concurrent causes of action

1.020   The decision of the House of Lords in *Henderson v Merret Syndicates*[51] settles authoritatively the controversy[52] over the possibility of concurrent rights of action in contract and tort. In that case it was held that an assumption of responsibility by a person providing professional services, coupled with a reliance by the person to whom the services were rendered, could give rise to a tortious duty of care even if there was also a contract between the parties. Such concurrent duties would normally exist in the absence of a provision in the contract to exclude them. However, as a

---

[50] [2003] EWCA Civ 1668; [2003] All ER (D) 320 (Nov).
[51] [1994] 3 All E.R. 506.
[52] See, e.g., *Midland Bank v Hett, Stubbs & Kemp* [1979] Ch.384, Oliver J.; *Tai Hing Cotton Mills Ltd v Liu Chong Hing Bank Ltd* [1986] A.C. 80, PC.

matter of general principle it is clear that a plaintiff is still not allowed to bring separate actions in respect of the tort claim and the contract claim, if only because it would be an abuse of the process of the court to do so. The point may be of importance in a limitation context because the tort limitation period will in some cases expire later than the contract limitation period.

Application to the Crown

It should be observed that s.37 of the 1980 Act makes the provisions of that Act applicable in actions involving the Crown in the same way as they apply to actions between subjects. This principle is subject to specified exceptions. Section 37(2) disapplies the Act in the case of proceedings for any tax or duty (or interest thereon), forfeiture proceedings under the Customs and Excise Acts[53] and proceedings for the forfeiture of a ship. It is to be noted that the taxing statutes normally include their own time-limits. In addition there are special rules relating to actions by the Crown for the recovery of land.[54]   1.021

Effect of repeal of limitation provisions

The long period of time over which limitation provisions necessarily operate can give rise to difficulties where Parliament repeals an enactment which protected a particular class of defendant. The point is well illustrated by the decision of the House of Lords in *Arnold v Central Electricity Generating Board*.[55] The plaintiff in this case sued an executrix of a man who had worked in a power station from 1938 to 1943. The liabilities of his then employers had devolved on the CEGB. In 1981 the deceased was diagnosed as suffering from an asbestos-related disease, from which he died the following year. The writ against the CEGB was issued in 1984. Limitation was pleaded as a defence, based on s.21 of the 1939 Act, which provided a limitation period of one year from the date when the cause of action accrued in the case of actions against public authorities (which this admittedly was). Section 21 was repealed by the Law Reform (Limitation of   1.022

---

[53] The Customs and Excise Management Act 1979 is the principal statute in this area.
[54] Sch.1, Pt II. The position of the Crown and of certain other privileged bodies is examined in Ch.9.
[55] [1988] A.C. 228; (1988) *Statute Law Review* 130. See also *Marsal v Apong* [1998] 1 W.L.R. 674, PC where a Brunei enactment that lengthened limitation periods was held to be effective to extend time in the case of causes of action which had accrued but not become time-barred, but not effective to revive causes of action which were already time-barred when the new enactment took effect.

Actions, etc.) Act 1954 (the 1954 Act), though s.7(1) of that Act expressly preserved the right to plead any accrued time-bar as a defence.

1.023   The Limitation Act 1963 effected a further relaxation in the rules in personal injury cases by removing the three-year limit where the plaintiff could show that he had neither actual nor constructive knowledge of his right to sue, but s.1(4)(a) of that Act preserved any defence "available by virtue of any enactment". The Limitation Act 1975 then further amended the law in this area by making the three-year period run from the later of two dates either the date when the cause of action accrued or the date when the plaintiff could reasonably have discovered it (the 1963 Act was accordingly repealed so far as necessary to introduce this rule). The 1975 Act was expressed to apply to cases of action which had accrued before its passing as well as to those which accrued afterwards. It contained no provision expressly saving defences that had already accrued prior to its coming into effect. In the speech of Lord Bridge of Harwich in Arnold, with whom the remainder of the House[56] agreed, it is possible to discern three strands of reasoning, all of which are of significance in considering the general problem of the effect of repeal of limitation provisions. These may be denominated as the legislative purpose approach, the strict construction approach and the Interpretation Act approach.

The legislative approach

1.024   One of the arguments on behalf of the plaintiff in this case was that the 1963 Act had been intended to remedy the injustice disclosed in *Cartledge v E. Jopling & Sons Ltd*,[57] namely that a plaintiff in a personal injuries case might find his cause of action barred even before its existence became reasonably discoverable. The decision at first instance in that case[58] led to the formation of the Committee on Limitation of Actions in Cases of Personal Injury, and its subsequent report[59] was the background to the 1963 Act. Given that the causes of action in *Cartledge v Jopling* accrued not later than September 1950, a decision against the plaintiff in Arnold would mean that the 1963 Act had failed to reverse the effect of the decision in *Cartledge*. Lord Bridge was not persuaded that the apparent undesirability of this result could be a sufficient reason for rejecting it. Although his Lordship was prepared to look at the report of that Committee, he did not find it conclusive, particularly in the light of the statement[60] that:

> "We have, therefore, approached our task as one involving a duty to seek a balance between the interests of each litigating party and we appreciate

---

[56] Lords Fraser, Brightman, Ackner and Oliver.
[57] [1963] A.C. 758, HL.
[58] Glyn-Jones J., Unreported.
[59] Cmnd. 1829.
[60] See para.17 of the Report.

that, whatever solution to the problem may eventually be adopted, there are bound to be hard cases."

Accordingly, the argument based upon purposive interpretation of the statute was rejected, and it may be surmised that the same approach will be taken to arguments of this type should other points concerning transitional provisions arise.

The strict construction approach

The most important limb of Lord Bridge's judgment was a careful construction of the provisions of the 1954, 1963 and 1975 Acts. The 1954 Act applied (by ss.2(1) and 7(1)) a limitation period of three years to actions for personal injuries against public authorities. This period was made applicable to actions which had accrued within one year before the passing of that Act, but this did not operate to revive any cause of action that was already barred. **1.025**

The 1963 Act This statute had a more radical effect. If the conditions imposed by that Act (which related to the discoverability of the cause of action) were satisfied, the result of ss.1 and 6 of that Act was to deprive defendants in personal injury actions where the cause of action accrued after June 4, 1954 (the date when the 1954 Act came into force) of time-bars accrued under the 1939 Act, as amended by the 1954 Act. However, this leaves unresolved the effect of the 1963 Act on a claim for personal injuries that accrued before June 4, 1954, as was the case in *Arnold*. In resolving this issue, Lord Bridge found it necessary to compare the position where the defendant is a public authority with that of other defendants. There was Court of Appeal authority in *Knipe v British Railways Board*[61] that in the latter instance the 1963 Act operated to revive causes of action which were already time-barred. Lord Bridge, having held that it would be undesirable to differentiate between these two classes of defendant, went on to reject the view adopted by the Court of Appeal in *Knipe*. The basis of Lord Bridge's view is perhaps the central point of the entire case. **1.026**

Section 1(1) of the 1963 Act provides: **1.027**

"Section 2(1) of the Limitation Act 1939 (which, in the case of certain actions, imposes a time-limit of three years for bringing the action) shall not afford any defence to an action to which this section applies . . . in respect of which . . . the requirements of subsection (3) of this section are fulfilled."

---

[61] [1972] 1 Q.B. 371, CA.

Section 1(3) provides, so far as material:

"The requirements of this subsection are fulfilled in relation to a cause of action if it is proved that the material facts relating to that cause of action were or included facts of a decisive character which were at all times outside the knowledge (actual or constructive) of the plaintiff until a date which (a) either was after the end of the three-year period relating to that cause of action or was not earlier than 12 months before the end of that period . . . "

Lord Bridge relied on two aspects of these provisions. First, the words in parentheses in s.1(1) imply that the reference to s.2(1) of the 1939 Act is a reference to that provision as amended by the 1954 Act, rather than to the original version of the provision, since the original form of the 1939 Act imposed a limit of six years, not three. Lord Bridge deduces from this that the 1963 Act is not intended to have any effect on causes of action which accrued before June 4, 1954, to which the 1954 Act would have applied. Secondly, the language of s.1(3)(a) is incapable of sensible application to any case involving a limitation period of six years, such as would have applied to a personal injuries action (not against a public authority) which accrued before June 4, 1954. It would then, according to Lord Bridge, be extraordinary if the Act had affected accrued time-bars under s.21 of the 1939 Act. This view is further reinforced by s.1(4)(a) of the 1963 Act, which provides:

"Nothing in this section shall be construed as excluding or otherwise affecting (a) any defence which, in any action to which this section applies, may be available by virtue of any enactment other than s.2(1) of the Limitation Act 1939 (whether it is an enactment imposing a period of limitation or not) or by virtue of any rule of law or equity."

Section 21 of the 1939 Act is an enactment other than s.2(1) of that Act, and the validity of a defence under it is thus not affected by the 1963 Act.

1.028 **The 1975 Act** The plaintiff in *Arnold* relied heavily on the 1975 Act, and in particular on the new s.2A which it introduced into the 1939 Act. This section is expressed to apply to "any action". Lord Bridge's response to this provision is perhaps the least satisfactory aspect of his speech. He deals with it by referring to the legislative history and to the 20th Report of the Law Reform Committee[62] which led to the enactment of the 1975 Act. This report did not express any dissatisfaction with the retrospective operation of the 1963 Act, and on this basis Lord Bridge concludes that the 1975 Act

---

[62] Cmnd. 5630.

cannot have been intended to sweep away the rules introduced by the 1963 Act in relation to pre-1963 (and pre-1954) causes of action. Accordingly, his Lordship reached the conclusion that the 1975 Act does not retrospectively revive the plaintiff's time-barred action.

Unfortunately, this line of reasoning is far from convincing. First, the use of the Report of the Law Reform Committee is questionable, both as a matter of principle and because it neither approves nor disapproves the operation of the 1963 Act on this point—silence here can hardly be taken to denote approval. Secondly, even if the Committee had been wholeheartedly in favour of the operation of the 1963 Act, that fact would have no direct bearing on the question of what the words of the 1975 Act mean. It is submitted that the words "any action" mean exactly what they say: they apply to any action, whenever it accrued. It must be recognised, though, that the present opinion of the House of Lords is against this construction. Further, the decision in Arnold is undeniably convenient and has recently been followed.

In *McDonnell v Christian Brothers*, the claimant sought to recover damages against both defendants for physical, emotional and sexual abuse which he claimed to have suffered at various times between 1941 and 1951. Under the statutory law in force at the time, his claims became statute-barred on January 6, 1963, but the claimant did not issue proceedings until August 2000. He argued that the effect of the Limitation Act 1963 or of the Limitations Acts 1975 and 1980 was retrospectively to remove the statutory bar to his claims. The leading judgment in the House of Lords was given by Lord Bingham of Cornhill, who acknowledged that *Arnold* had been subjected to criticism[63] and that it might have been decided differently. Despite this, their Lordships declined to depart from it and the claimant's action was dismissed in limitation grounds.

It is a cause of regret that the House of Lords should more or less acknowledge that their earlier decision was wrong and yet decline the opportunity to correct it. There would without doubt have been serious difficulties in conducting a fair trial of the action after so long a lapse of time, but that is a point which could potentially have caused difficulties for both sides. In any event, it cannot be a proper ground for ignoring the correct construction of an Act of Parliament.

The Interpretation Act approach

A further point made by Lord Bridge concerned what is now s.16(1) of the Interpretation Act 1978 (formerly s.38(2) of the Interpretation Act 1889). This states that: 1.029

---

[63] In, among other places, this book. At para.24 he said "The decision has been the subject of measured but penetrating criticism by McGee in the *Statute Law Review* 1988, pp.130-134 and *Limitation Periods*, 3rd edn (1998), pp.8-13."

"the repeal of an enactment does not, unless the contrary intention appears . . . (c) affect any right, privilege, obligation or liability acquired, accrued or incurred under that enactment".

Lord Bridge approved the approach adopted by the Privy Council in *Yew Bon Tew v Kenderaan Bas Mara*,[64] namely regarding a right to plead the Limitation Act as an accrued right, and, as such, protected by the Malaysian enactment corresponding to the Interpretation Act from removal by the repeal of the relevant limitation provision. His Lordship was unable to discover any contrary intention expressed in the relevant legislation, and would therefore apparently have been prepared to hold on this ground alone, had not the matters of construction discussed in the previous paragraph pointed to the same conclusion, i.e. that the repeal of the special one-year period of limitation for public authorities could not allow the revival of a cause of action which had already become time-barred.

The position after *Arnold*

1.030 Although the point at issue in *Arnold* was a narrow one, the dicta of the House of Lords range widely over the general issue of the retrospective effect of statutes of limitation. It is to be expected that these dicta will carry considerable weight in future cases in this area, and it is therefore appropriate to summarise the position as it appears to stand in the light of these dicta.

The 1980 Act

1.031 The possible effect on the cause of action in *Arnold* of the 1980 Act was not considered by the House of Lords. The relevant provision is in Sch.2, which contains the transitional provisions. Paragraph 9(1) of that Schedule states that nothing in the 1980 Act shall allow the bringing of any action which was barred by the 1939 Act before August 1, 1990.[65] The reference to the 1939 Act must be understood as a reference to that Act in the form in which it was in force on August 1, 1980. Therefore, it includes the provisions introduced by the 1975 Act, which added new sections to the 1939 Act. It follows from this that any action which was not barred under those provisions is not barred by para.9(1) of Sch.2. Also, the provisions of the 1980 Act on personal injuries are in all material respects identical to those of the 1975 Act. In considering the retrospective operation of the 1980 Act it is

---

[64] [1982] 3 All E.R. 833.
[65] Sch.2, para.9(2) to the 1980 Act; the date is that on which the Limitation Amendment Act 1980 came fully into force.

16

therefore necessary to distinguish between personal injury actions and all other causes of action.

Personal injuries

If the decision in *Arnold v CEGB*[66] is correct, then these causes of action were not retrospectively revived by the 1975 Act (in so far as they were barred at the coming into force of that Act). Further, any cause of action barred as at August 1, 1980 is not revived by the 1980 Act.[67] This provision is perhaps not strictly necessary, since in this context the 1980 Act effects no material change in the law, and therefore could not revive such causes of action. Alternatively, if Arnold is wrong, for the reasons given in paras 1.019–1.024, so that the 1975 Act did retrospectively revive pre-1975 causes of action, the effect of the 1980 Act is to preserve those causes of action after 1980 (since para.9(1) of Sch.2 does not apply to them). Section 11 of the 1980 Act is similarly expressed to apply to "any action" for personal injuries, and this anomaly, if such it is, has therefore been carried forward into the present law.

1.032

Other claims

The difficulties discussed in the previous paragraph do not apply outside the area of personal injuries, since these cases quite clearly do not suffer from the uncertainty generated by the 1975 Act, which applied only to personal injury cases. Consequently, neither the 1980 Act nor the 1975 Act has any retrospective application to them, and it can safely be said that any cause of action within this class which was barred before August 1, 1980 has not been revived by the 1980 Act.

1.033

Position outside England and Wales

The Limitation Act 1980 (as amended) and the Latent Damage Act 1986 apply only to England and Wales. In Northern Ireland the relevant statute is the Limitation (Northern Ireland) Act 1958, as amended. The provisions of this Act are substantially similar to those of the 1980 Act. In Scotland the law is governed by the Prescription and Limitation (Scotland) Act 1973, as amended by the Prescription and Limitation (Scotland) Act 1984 and the Consumer Protection Act 1987. The scheme contained in this Act is significantly different from that which prevails in English law, but the details of Scots law in this area are beyond the scope of the present work.[68]

1.034

---

[66] [1988] A.C. 228, HL.
[67] 1980 Act, Sch.2, para.9(1).
[68] For a general guide see R. Walker, *The Law of Prescription and Limitation of Actions in Scotland* (4th edn, 1989).

POLICY

1.035 Policy issues[69] arise in two major contexts. The first concerns the justification for having statutes of limitation at all and the particular limits that presently exist.[70] The second concerns the procedural rules that apply after an action has been commenced. Arguments with regard to the policy underlying statutes of limitation fall into three main types. The first relates to the position of the defendant. It is said to be unfair that a defendant should have a claim hanging over him for an indefinite period and it is in this context that such enactments are sometimes described as "statutes of peace". The second looks at the matter from a more objective point of view. It suggests that a time-limit is necessary because with the lapse of time, proof of a claim becomes more difficult—documentary evidence is likely to have been destroyed and the memories of witnesses will fade. The third relates to the conduct of the plaintiff, it being thought right that a person who does not promptly act to enforce his rights should lose them. All these justifications have been considered by the courts.

1.036 In *A'Court v Cross*[71] Best C.J. said:

> "It has been supposed that the Legislature only meant to protect persons who had paid their debts, but from length of time had destroyed the proof of payment. From the title of the Act to the last section, every word of it shows that it was not passed on this narrow ground. It is, as I have often heard it called by great judges, an Act of peace. Long dormant claims have often more of cruelty than of justice in them. Christianity forbids us to attempt enforcing the payment of a debt which time and misfortune have rendered the debtor unable to discharge. The Legislature thought that if a demand was not attempted to be enforced within six years, some good excuse for non-payment might be presumed, and took away the legal power of recovering it."[72]

It may be doubted whether as a general rule the law forbids the enforcement of a debt merely on the ground that the debtor is unable to pay it.

A further justification for statutes of limitation was stated by Lord Atkinson in *Board of Trade v Cayzer, Irvine & Co.*[73]

> "The whole purpose of the Limitation Act is to apply to persons who have good causes of action which they could, if so disposed, enforce, and

---

[69] For a general critical analysis of the English law of limitation periods, see (1990) 9 C.J.Q. 366; Mullaney [1993] L.M.C.L.Q. 34.
[70] For a critical review of this area of the law see (1990) 9 C.J.Q. 366.
[71] (1825) 3 Bing. 329.
[72] (1825) 3 Bing. at 332–333.
[73] [1927] A.C. 610, HL.

to deprive them of the power of enforcing them after they have lain for a number of years respectively and omitted to enforce them. They are thus deprived of the remedy which they have omitted to use."[74]

In *Chagos Islanders v AG*[75] arguments were advanced which, if accepted, would have had fundamental implications for the law of limitation. This was a claim by the islanders for damages arising from the circumstances in which they had been resettled many years previously. Many complex arguments arose, including limitation issues. The limitation issues which are of relevance here concern a general attack mounted against the limitation defence on the ground that it did not apply to any person who had a good cause of action but was unable to enforce it. Not surprisingly, the claimant was unable to refer to any provision of the Act itself for this proposition. Instead reliance was placed on a dictum of Lord Atkinson in *Board of Trade v Cayzer, Irvine and Co Ltd*[76], who said that the whole purpose of the applicable Limitation Act

> "is to apply to persons who have good causes of action which they could, if so disposed, enforce, and to deprive them of the power of enforcing them after they have lain by for the number of years. . . and omitted to enforce them. They are thus deprived of the remedy which they have omitted to use".

Inevitably, this argument failed. There is no relevant provision to that effect within the Act and this dictum does not constitute a rule of interpretation.

The claimant next made a general argument that the court could suspend the effect of the Act where it would be unconscionable to allow the Defendants to rely upon it. This argument was also bound to fail. There is no basis upon which a court could decide that a statute could be removed from the arena to which its language made it apply, simply because a court thought that it would be unconscionable to allow a party to rely upon the rights which Parliament had given him. The 1980 Act is quite explicit in prohibiting the bringing of a cause of action after the relevant time limit, and has made varied and explicit provision for the circumstances in which time should not run against a claimant or should be extended. That represents the Parliamentary view of where it would be wrong to allow a defendant to take advantage of the passage of time and marks the balancing of the interests of finality in litigation and fairness to a claimant.

1.037

1.038

---

[74] [1927] A.C. 610 at 628.
[75] [2003] EWHC 2222 (Q.B.); [2003] All ER (D) 166 (Oct) Ouseley J.
[76] [1927] AC 610 at 628.

1.039   *Awoyomi v Radford*[77] considered the consequences for limitation purposes of a decision by the House of Lords which apparently changed the
law. In *Arthur J S Hall & Co (a firm) v Simons, Barratt v Ansell (trading as
Woolf Seddon (a firm)); Harris v Scholfield Roberts & Hill (a firm)*[78] the
House of Lords departed from previous decisions[79] holding that advocates
could not be sued for negligence in the conduct of proceedings. That
decision was given in 2000, but related to an alleged act of negligence in
1991. In the present case the alleged negligence occurred in 1995. The
question was whether time ran from 1995 or from 2000. Lloyd Jones J.
held that the decision of the House of Lords in *Hall v Simons* proceeded on
the basis that the change in the law should operate retroactively to the
conduct which formed the subject of those proceedings; the defendants as
advocates therefore did not enjoy immunity from suit in relation to criminal
or civil proceedings in 1995. In the *Hall* case the House of Lords had held
that the immunity of advocates in respect of the conduct of civil proceedings could in 1991 no longer be justified on grounds of public policy. Thus
the defendants had no immunity in 1995, and time ran from that date.

1.040   To this point the reasoning cannot be faulted. It is an inevitable consequence of the well-established (albeit somewhat artificial) doctrine that
common law courts merely declare what the law is[80] (even when they
depart from the views expressed on the same point by an earlier court). In
the present case Lloyd Jones J approached the matter slightly differently
because the reasoning of the majority in *Hall* was not that *Rondel v
Worsley* was wrong when it was decided, but that in the time since it was
decided circumstances had changed, with the result that the immunity was
no longer justified. Nevertheless, upon an analysis of the speeches in *Hall*,
he concluded that that decision had been meant to have retrospective effect.

1.041   The judge added that even if the rule of advocates' immunity had sub-
sisted in 1995 it would not have prevented the accrual of a cause of action
and would not have prevented the running of time for the purposes of
limitation. In reaching this conclusion he relied on a number of the cases
cited at paras 5.054-5.058 as well as *Thomson v Lord Clanmorris*[81] and
Douglas v Forrest[82]; *Re Russo-Asiatic Bank, Re Russian Bank for Foreign
Trade* [1934] Ch.720; and *Musurus Bey v Gadban*,[83] as well as more recent
cases on diplomatic immunity, including *Dickinson v Del Solar*[84] and

---

[77] [2007] All E.R. (D) 183 (Jul); [2007] EWHC 1671 (Admin) Lloyd Jones J.
[78] [2000] 3 All E.R. 673.
[79] Notably *Rondel v Worsley* [1967] 1 A.C. 191.
[80] See for example para.14 of this judgment, though in para.15 there is an apparent acceptance
that prospective overruling would exceptionally be available to English courts, relying on *In
Re Spectrum Plus Ltd.* [2005] UKHL 41; [2005] 2 A.C. 680.
[81] [1900] 1 Ch.718 at pp.728, 729.
[82] (1828) 4 Bing. 686 at p.704.
[83] [1894] 1 Q.B. 533.
[84] [1930] 1 K.B. 376.

Empson v Smith.[85] He reiterated the established distinction between an immunity from suit (sometimes also called a procedural bar) and a non-liability. The latter prevents the cause of action from accruing and thus prevents time from running, whereas the latter does not.

Although that analysis is uncontroversial, it is open to much greater **1.042** doubt whether it is correct to describe the rule in *Rondel v Worsley* as relying on an 'immunity'. The point in *Musurus Bey v Gadban* was that the ambassador could not be sued while he was ambassador (because of diplomatic immunity) nor while he was, or was deemed to be, beyond the seas (because that was the law under the Limitation Act 1623, which was the statute then in force). That immunity would have ended if he had been within the jurisdiction and not the ambassador. It is surely a distortion of reality to suggest that the position of the advocate before *Hall* was comparable to that. He did not have a personal immunity to suit which could somehow be lost. He simply was not liable for negligence in the conduct of proceedings because, up until 2000, the law had taken the view that compelling reasons of public policy precluded the imposition of such liability.

Regrettably, the approach taken in this case does not really address the **1.043** issues. The question of the relationship between judge-made changes in the law and the running of time raises questions of policy which were briefly alluded to by Lord Hoffmann in *Kleinwort Benson*[86], when he said 'the Limitation Act. . . as presently drafted is inadequate to deal with the problem of retrospective changes in law by judicial decision' but which do not otherwise appear to have been addressed in any previous case. Those questions have to do with how seriously the fiction of judicial 'declaration' of law should be taken, and whether it is fair to hold that time runs against a claimant at a time when the law is—or appears to be—that the facts of his case give rise to no right of action. Although the particular problem of the removal of advocates' immunity is unlikely to arise again in a limitation context, the general question may well recur at some future point. It is submitted that as a pragmatic solution to the problem, it would be better to hold that time does not run against a claimant for as long as the perceived state of the law is that he has no remedy. There is really no compelling analogy in the law of limitation periods which mandates the opposite conclusion, and the solution proposed here is surely the fairest answer.

General principles of equitable remedies

A plaintiff who seeks an equitable remedy must come to court quickly if the **1.044** remedy is not to be lost.[87] This principle coexists with the specific time-

---

[85] [1966] 1 Q.B. 426.
[86] [1999] 2 A.C. 349 at 401D-E.
[87] *Lindsay Petroleum Co. v Hurd* (1874) L.R. P.C. 221.

limits laid down by the statutes of limitation. Section 36 of the 1980 Act provides that many of the time-limits laid down by that Act shall not apply to claims for equitable relief, "except in so far as any such time-limit may be applied by the court by analogy in like manner as the corresponding time-limit under any enactment repealed by the Limitation Act 1939 was applied before 1st July 1940". Section 36(2) goes on to provide that the 1980 Act shall not affect any equitable jurisdiction to refuse relief on the grounds of acquiescence or otherwise.[88]

1.045　　In *Nomura International plc v Granada Group Ltd*[89] Cooke J. held that it is an abuse of process to issue proceedings, even for the purpose of preventing the running of time, where the claimant has no present intention to prosecute proceedings and is not aware of valid grounds for a claim. Such proceedings are liable (and likely) to be struck out.

1.046　　In *Boake Allen Ltd v Revenue and Customs Commissioners*[90] the House of Lords commented on the operation of limitation provisions in the context of GLOs, and in particular the rules in GLO's requiring individual claims to be registered and brief details to be given of them. At para.33 it was said that for limitation purposes in the case of a GLO the individual claims should be construed in conjunction with the applications for the claims to be registered and, from the time of registration, the register.

Application by analogy

1.047　　Two points require analysis in the context of application by analogy. The first is the reference in s.36(1) of the 1980 Act to the use of analogy, whilst the second, considered in the previous paragraph, is the reference to enactments by the 1939 Act. The point of s.36(1) is that strict limitation periods are considered to be inappropriate to those remedies which had their origin in courts of equity. With regard to the use of analogy, a court of equity has a discretion to take account of the expiry of any statutory period of limitation when considering whether to grant an equitable remedy. It might, for example, be a relevant consideration that the plaintiff's common law remedy was time-barred, and that the application for an equitable remedy was an attempt to circumvent this problem. In practice, however, it seems likely that the action in this case can be dismissed on the similar ground of laches. It is a principle of equity that the plaintiff must come to court quickly[91] and it seems unlikely that there will be many cases where the statutory limitation period has expired but the court is prepared to grant an equitable remedy. An exceptional case might occur where, under the Latent Damage Act 1986, the plaintiff's action is time-barred because of

---

[88] For equitable remedies generally, see Ch.3.
[89] [2007] EWHC 605 (Comm).
[90] [2007] 3 All E.R. 205 HL.
[91] *Milward v Earl of Thanet* (1801) 5 Ves.Jr.720n.

the longstop provisions of that Act, but he was not in fact aware of the existence of the cause of action. In a case of this kind the drafting of s.36 produces a curious result. The court is empowered to apply the statutory rules in a similar manner as it did under any enactment repealed by the 1939 Act but since longstop provisions were unknown before the Latent Damage Act 1986 there can be no appropriate analogy on which to draw. The effect is apparently that the expiry of the longstop period cannot be used as a ground for refusing the equitable relief, though the plaintiff's unawareness of the existence of the cause of action may be a ground for refusing to apply the doctrine of laches.[92]

Present trends

Although the policy arguments above can all be presented as justifications for a system of limitation periods, the question of policy in this area of the law has not traditionally been an important one in determining cases. Policy questions have most commonly been left to the legislature, which has been increasingly active in the past 40 years, often as a result of decisions in particular cases which have highlighted anomalies in the existing system.[93] It is important to be aware that the trend in limitation periods is away from a rigid system of time-limits that take no account of the claimant's own position of knowledge. This trend may be seen as having started with the 1963 Act, which first made the discoverability of the cause of action a relevant factor in personal injury cases. These rules were amended by the 1975 Act, which also gave the court, for the first time, a discretion to allow an action to proceed notwithstanding that the limitation period had in fact expired. The rules of the 1975 Act were consolidated in the 1980 Act. The Latent Damage Act 1986 has now introduced a further fundamental change by providing that in actions for negligence the plaintiff is generally entitled to measure time from the date of discoverability rather than from the date of accrual where it is more advantageous for him to do so. The quid pro quo for this relaxation has been a shortening in the time-limits as measured from discoverability. It has been a common feature of the law of limitations over the past 200 years to shorten limitation periods, and in the context of personal obligations three years is the relevant period in an increasing number of cases.[94]   1.048

The interrelationship between limitation and human rights has generated   1.049

---

[92] For the application of the doctrine of laches see further paras 3.014–3.016.
[93] The 1963 Act was a direct result of the decision of the House of Lords in *Cartledge v E. Jopling & Co. Ltd* [1963] A.C. 758, whilst the controversy created by the decision of the House of Lords in *Pirelli General Cable Works Ltd v Oscar Faber & Partners Ltd* [1983] 2 A.C. 1 led to the passing of the Latent Damage Act 1986.
[94] This now covers personal injuries and defamation (Ch.8), latent damage (Ch.6) and actions under the Consumer Protection Act 1987 (Ch.7).

some signficiant litigation since the last edition of this book, no doubt an inevitable consequence of the incorporation into English law of the European Convention on Human Rights.[95] It is easy to see that limitation provisions are capable of barring a person's access to the courts (a potential Art.6 violation) and, at least in the case of real property, taking away a person's title to land (a potential expropriation of property and thus a potential Art.2 violation. In a series of cases English courts have begun to work through these arguments, and their conclusions are considered in detail in the relevant Chapters.[96]

Procedural questions

1.050 The law of limitation periods inevitably overlaps with the rules governing the procedural conduct of an action, especially those relating to delay after proceedings have been commenced. These rules are found in the Civil Procedure Rules.[97] One conspicuous feature of these rules is that they generally impose much shorter time-limits than do the limitation acts, but at the same time confer much greater discretion upon the court to override the limits when it appears just to do so. The choice between generous limits strictly enforced and stricter limits generously applied is a fundamental one in the administration of justice. The former are simpler to administer, but are more capable of producing injustice.

1.051 Now that the CPR have been in force for some years, it is possible to make some comment on their effectiveness and on their relationship to issues involving limitation periods. The introduction in 1999 of the Civil Procedure Rules 1998 was intended to mark a radical departure in the conduct of civil actions.[98] Of particular relevance in the present context is the ambition to reduce delays in the bringing and concluding of proceedings. However, the CPR do not shorten any limitation period. So far as delay after the commencement of proceedings is concerned, Pts 17 and 19 of the CPR largely reproduce the effects of the former RSC Orders 15 and 20.[99] If the CPR have any significant effect on the pace at which proceedings are conducted, it must be through the changes in litigation culture which they seek to promote rather than through detailed provisions affecting the running of time. One area where the modern culture can be seen to have had some effect is that of applications to dismiss claims for

---

[95] Effected by the Human Rights Act 1998, with effect from October 2, 2000. Although the Act does not fully incorporate the Convention (since the dualist tradition of English law has been maintained to the extent that Convention provisions do not override English law) English courts are nevertheless required to consider whether substantive legal provisions are compatible with the Convention.

[96] principally paras 28.034-28.037.

[97] The detailed provisions in this area are considered in Chs 22 and 23.

[98] See the Interim and Final "Access to Justice" Reports, which led to the introduction of the CPR.

[99] See further Ch.22.

want of prosecution. These have now largely vanished, principally because more active case management means that actions are not left to go stale, and the question of want of prosecution can scarcely arise any more. Instead, the focus in relation to the validity of claim forms is now on the exercise of the court's discretion to extend time for service[100]. These may be regarded as beneficial developments, but they do emphasise the limits of the CPR's impact on limitation of actions.

No limitation at common law

The concept of limitation of actions had no place in the common law,[101] **1.052** though equity developed the doctrine of laches at a fairly early stage. Limitation provisions are normally in the form "no action shall be brought after the expiry of . . .". This form of wording does not say expressly that the action may be brought at any time until the expiry of the limitation period, and there have been occasional suggestions that an action for common law relief can be dismissed before the expiry of the limitation period if the plaintiff has been guilty of inordinate and inexcusable delay. It is accepted, in the light of the decision of the House of Lords in *Birkett v James*,[102] that this may very occasionally be appropriate where proceedings have been commenced within the limitation period but there has then been a very long delay.[103] It was for a long time thought that delay before the issue of the claim form but within the limitation period can never be regarded as inordinate and inexcusable for these purposes[104] and that such a delay could never make the eventual action an abuse of the process of the court. However, a wholly exceptional situation occurred in *Hogg v Hamilton and Northumberland HA*,[105] where the plaintiff was under irreversible disability as a result of a surgical operation. Consequently, his action would never have become time-barred. One writ was issued and not proceeded with, then after a long delay a second writ was issued. Although the action was certainly not time-barred, the Court of Appeal struck the action out as an abuse of process.[106]

---

[100] See Ch.22.
[101] Logically, the consequence of this ought to be that any action for which no limitation period is provided by statute has no limitation period, but judges are sometimes inclined to stretch the statutory categories to catch as many cases as possible see, e.g., *Kleinwort Benson Ltd v S. Tyneside MBC* [1994] 4 All E.R. 972 where the problem of categorisation is extensively discussed in Ch.4.
[102] [1978] A.C. 297.
[103] See also *Department of Transport v Chris Smaller (Transport) Ltd* [1989] 2 W.L.R. 578; this category of case has now largely disappeared as a result of the more active approach to case management under the CPR.
[104] [1989] 2 W.L.R. 578. The position is different in actions for judicial review: see para.9.004.
[105] April 1, 1992, CA, Unreported.
[106] On the procedural aspects of this case, see para.19.019.

Cause of action not covered by statute

1.053   The 1980 Act, together with the Latent Damage Act 1986 and the various specialised statutes dealt with in this book, covers most causes of action. Nevertheless, it follows from the absence of any common law concept of limitation that in the event of a lacuna in the statutory provisions, no limitation period will apply. This rule was clearly illustrated in *Bray v Stuart A. West & Co*[107] The plaintiff asked the court to order the defendant solicitor to perform an undertaking which he had given seven years previously, and the defendant pleaded limitation. Warner J. reviewed the authorities on the exercise of the court's inherent jurisdiction over solicitors[108] and held that the 1980 Act had no application to such cases, since the cause of action is not mentioned anywhere in that Act. Nevertheless, the making of the order against the solicitor being a matter of discretion, the court was entitled to take the delay into account by means of the doctrine of laches. On the facts the solicitor was ordered to perform his undertaking despite the delay. In *Fisher v Brooker*[109] the House of Lords commented that no statutory limitation period applies to an action for breach of copyright.

REFORM

1.054   The Law Commission some years ago produced a consultation paper[110] and a Final Report[111] on Limitation Periods in Civil Proceedings. These recommend a fundamental reconsideration of the law on limitation periods. Individual recommendations are considered throughout the book in the chapters to which they relate,[112] but the following[113] provides a concise summary of the recommendations.

- A primary limitation period of three years starting from the date on which the claimant knows, or ought reasonably to know (a) the facts which give rise to the cause of action; (b) the identity of the defendant; and (c) if the claimant has suffered injury, loss or damage or the defendant has received a benefit, that the injury, loss, damage or benefit was significant.

---

[107] (1989) 139 New L.J. 753, Warner J.
[108] The major cases are *Geoffrey Silver & Drake v Baines* [1971] 1 Q.B. 396, CA; *John Fox v Bannister, King & Rigbeys* [1988] Q.B. 925, CA; and *Udall v Capri Lighting Ltd* [1988] Q.B. 907, CA.
[109] [2009] UKHL 41.
[110] Law Com. No. 151.
[111] L.C. Rep. No. 270.
[112] Although the author had a consultative role in the preparation of this Paper, the views expressed in it are those of the Law Commission alone. The author has accordingly felt at liberty to take issue with specific arguments or proposals contained in the Paper or the Final Report where appropriate.
[113] Taken from the Executive Summary in LC Rep No 270.

- A long-stop limitation period of 10 years, starting from the date of the accrual of the cause of action or (for those claims in tort where loss is an essential element of the cause of action, or claims for breach of statutory duty) from the date of the act or omission which gives rise to the cause of action (but for personal injuries claims see below).

- The core regime should apply without any qualification to the following actions: the majority of tort claims, contract claims, restitutionary claims, claims for breach of trust and related claims, claims on a judgment or arbitration award, and claims on a statute.

- The core regime will be modified in its application to claims in respect of personal injuries. The court should have a discretion to disapply the primary limitation period, and no long-stop limitation period will apply. All personal injury claims will be subject to this modified regime, whether the claim concerned is made in negligence or trespass to the person.

- Claims to recover land and related claims, though not subject to the core regime, should be subject to a limitation period of the same length as the long-stop limitation period, running from the date on which the cause of action accrues.

- The core regime should extend, but with some qualifications, to the following claims: claims under the Law Reform (Miscellaneous Provisions) Act 1934, the Fatal Accidents Act 1976 and the Consumer Protection Act 1987; claims for conversion; claims by a subsequent owner of damaged property; claims in relation to mortgages and charges; and claims under the Companies Act 1985 and in insolvency proceedings.

- Where the core regime applies to common law remedies for a cause of action, it should also apply to equitable remedies for that cause of action; but that delay may still bar a remedy before the limitation period under the core regime has expired. We recommend that the core regime should apply to all claims unless excluded by another provision of the proposed Bill (or any other enactment).

- During the claimant's minority the initial limitation period should not run. The long-stop limitation period should run during minority, but not so as to bar an action before the claimant reaches the age of 21. Adult disability (including supervening disability) should suspend the initial limitation period, but will not affect the long-stop limitation period.

- However, the protection given to the adult claimant suffering from a disability will not be unlimited. Where the claimant under a disability has suffered personal injury (to which no long-stop period will apply) and is in the care of a responsible adult ten years after the later of: (a) the act or omission giving rise to the claim and (b) the onset of disability, the primary limitation period should run from the date the responsible adult knew or ought to have known the relevant facts unless the responsible adult is a defendant to the claim.

- The long-stop limitation period should not run where the defendant has concealed relevant facts, but only if the concealment was dishonest.

- Acknowledgments and part payments should start time running again, but not once the initial or long-stop limitation period has expired.

- The parties may agree that the limitation regime we recommend should not apply to disputes between them, or should only apply in modified form. They will not however be able to reduce the protection afforded by the provisions on concealment, minority or other disability nor to modify the application of the long-stop limitation period to claims under the Consumer Protection Act 1987.

1.055   In many ways these proposals may be considered to represent an improvement on the present law. A uniform limitation period would certainly be a welcome simplification, whilst the shortening of that period to three years would be in line with modern trends and would help to resolve cases more quickly. The author very much regrets that in the Final Report the Law Commission did not feel able to accept the proposal in the Consultation Paper to remove the pernicious power currently given to judges in certain cases to extend the limitation period. It is also to be regretted that the Law Commission felt it necessary to accept the arguments in favour of a long-stop. It is also unfortunate that the Law Commission accepted the idea that in considering the significance of a loss, courts should continue to be required to make the (in most cases) counterfactual assumption that the defendant will not deny liability.

1.056   It seems increasingly unlikely that Parliament will find the time to implement any or all of these proposals in the foreseeable future. The prospects do not look good. The Final Report appeared some years ago, and nothing has yet been done. This is perhaps not surprising. Limitation of actions is hardly to be regarded as a vote-winner, and it is understandable that the Report has been left to gather dust. At the time of writing the present edition of this text it might also be thought that government has more pressing priorities. Nevertheless, it is to be hoped that some legislative space can be found to deal with a number of problems which, though undeniably technical in character, are capable of having unfortunate and unjust effects in a number of cases.

CHAPTER 2

The Running and Expiry of Time

THE RUNNING OF TIME

Once time has begun to run it will run continuously, except in the situations discussed at paras 2.011 et seq. This general rule is of very wide application, and it is only in rare cases that the clock can be stopped once it has started. Time ceases to run when the plaintiff commences legal proceedings in respect of the cause of action in question. It is a general principle of some importance that the bringing of an action stops the running of time for the purposes of that action only. Therefore, in *Manby v Manby*[1] the bringing of a creditor's petition in an administration action did not save the debt from becoming statute-barred for other purposes.[2] In *Lefevre v White*[3] the plaintiff brought a personal injuries action, which was successful. When the defendant became bankrupt the plaintiff sought to sue the defendant's liability insurers under the 1930 Act. The writ against the insurers was issued more than six years after the injury was suffered. The plaintiff argued that the writ against the defendant saved the running of time for the purposes of this action, but this argument was rejected—commencing proceedings against one defendant does not stop time from running in favour of other defendants.[4] In *Virgo Steamship Co. v Skaarup Shipping Corporation*,[5] the plaintiffs had begun separate actions against each of two

2.001

---

[1] (1876) 3 Ch.101, Malins V.-C.
[2] Part of the difficulty in this case arose from the fact that the actions were commenced before the Judicature Acts 1873–1875 came into force, and one was in the Common Pleas whilst the other was in Chancery. This distinction is wholly obsolete, but the reasoning in the case proceeds on the more general principle stated in the text.
[3] [1990] 1 Lloyd's Rep. 569, Popplewell J.
[4] The Law Commission's proposals on this topic (contained in the Draft Bill annexed to Law Com. 272) would have the effect that in an action for a declaration by a third party against an insurer, the insurer would not be able to rely on a limitation defence against the third party unless the insured could also rely on it against the third party. This would be relevant where proceedings were started after the expiry of a limitation period applicable to an action against the insured, but while such an action was in progress.
[5] June 21, 1988, Hobhouse J., Unreported.

defendants. After the expiry of the limitation period they sought to add the first defendants in the action against the second defendants. At first sight, s.35 of the 1980 Act would seem to preclude this,[6] but the plaintiffs argued that the running of time had been suspended by the bringing of the action against the first defendants. Hobhouse J. rejected this argument, holding that the action brought against the first defendants was effective to stop the running of time only for the purposes of that particular action.[7] This decision goes further than that in *Manby v Manby*, since the plaintiffs here were merely seeking a different way of enforcing the same claim against the same person, whereas in *Manby v Manby* the enforcement of different claims (and claims against different persons) was in issue. The position is also often different in cases to which the Hague-Visby Rules apply and in which suit is validly brought in another jurisdiction.[8]

MEANING OF "ACTION"

2.002 "Action" is partially defined in s.38(1) of the 1980 Act as including proceedings in any court of law, including an ecclesiastical court. Section 34 of the 1980 Act extends the effect of this by providing that the limitation rules apply to arbitrations as they apply to actions in the High Court. It can be seen that the definition is a very broad one, but *Lowsley v Forbes*[9] establishes beyond doubt that the enforcement of a judgment is not an action for these purposes. It must be remembered that the time-limits do not apply to an action which is not governed by the 1980 Act at all, such ascertain actions for equitable relief[10] or an action asking the court to exercise its inherent jurisdiction over a solicitor.[11]

COMMENCING ACTION AND NOTIFYING CLAIMS

2.003 A few of the more specialised limitation provisions in English law draw a distinction between notifying claims and bringing proceedings. The most common examples are to be found in the International Carriage statutes, discussed in Ch.26. In these cases the usual result appears to be that the

---

[6] For s.35, see Ch.23.
[7] See also *The Kapetan Markos* [1986] 1 Lloyd's Rep. 211, CA. The position is now governed by CPR 17.4 and 19.5, as to which see Ch.23.
[8] *The Nordglimt* [1988] Q.B. 183, Hobhouse J.; for the Hague-Visby Rules, see paras 26.002–26.016.
[9] [1999] A.C. 329 HL, affirming principles laid down in *W.T. Lamb & Sons Ltd v Rider* [1948] 2 K.B. 331, CA and *Natwest Bank v Powney* [1991] Ch.339, CA; see also Ch.17 for discussion of points about interest arising in these cases.
[10] 1980 Act, s.36; see Ch.3.
[11] *Bray v Stuart A. West & Co.* (1989) 139 New L.J. 753, Warner J.

notifying of a claim to the prospective defendant may be a condition precedent to the bringing of a claim.[12] However, a time-limit of this kind is not
properly to be regarded as a limitation period, since it is not a limit within
which proceedings must be brought.[13]

COMPUTATION OF TIME

A system of law which adopts limitation periods must also have rules for **2.004**
determining exactly when time expires in any given case. A number of
difficulties arise in measuring time, and the response of English law to these
is discussed in the following paragraphs.

Parts of a day are ignored

The general rule in calculating the expiry of a limitation period is usually **2.005**
expressed as being that parts of a day are ignored. This formulation is
ambiguous, and needs to be clarified by example. In *Gelmini v Moriggia*[14]
the defendant had given a promissory note. The time for payment of this
expired on September 22, 1906. The plaintiff's writ on the note was issued
on September 23, 1912. Channell J. held that the cause of action was
complete at the beginning of September 23, 1906, since that was the earliest
moment at which proceedings could have been commenced, notwithstanding that the court office obviously would not have been open at
midnight. Consequently the six-year limitation period expired at the end of
September 22, 1912, and the writ issued on the following day was out of
time. This is the simplest possible example, since the cause of action was
held to accrue at the very beginning of a day. Greater complexities arise
where the cause of action accrues during the course of a day. In *Radcliffe v
Bartholomew*[15] the relevant statute required an action against justices to be
brought "within one month" of the commission of the wrong. The alleged
wrong occurred on May 30 and the action was commenced on June 30. It
was held that this action was in time, since the day of commission of the
wrong was to be excluded from the calculation.

That case may be contrasted with *Dorber v London Brick Co.*[16] This was **2.006**
an unfair dismissal case, and it was held that the day of dismissal was

---

[12] As was apparently the case under the Workmen's Compensation Act 1897–1925; see *Leivers v Barber Walker & Co. Ltd* [1943] 1 All E.R. 386, CA; see further para.27.002.
[13] See also para.1.001 for the definition of limitation period for the purposes of this work.
[14] [1913] 2 K.B. 549, Channell J.
[15] [1892] 1 Q.B. 161, DC.
[16] [1974] I.C.R. 270, NIRC.

included in the calculation of the time period allowed.[17] Perhaps the most satisfactory of the authorities on this point is *Marren v Dawson Bentley & Co.*[18] The plaintiff was injured in an accident at 1.30 p.m. on November 8, 1954, and the writ was issued on November 8, 1957. The question was whether time had expired at the end of November 7, 1957, and Havers J. held that it had not. The day on which the cause of action accrues is to be disregarded in calculating the running of time. It therefore followed that time began to run at the first moment of November 9, 1954 and expired at the end of November 8, 1957. Havers J. expressly declined to follow *Gelmini v Moriggia*, but it is not clear whether his decision is inconsistent with that in *Gelmini*. The latter case deals with one very specific situation, namely where the cause of action must accrue on the stroke of midnight. It is arguable that here there is no question of disregarding any part of a day; the cause of action was in existence throughout September 23, 1906. Consequently, it may be argued that on those very special facts the decision is still good law.

2.007　　The alternative is to say that time did not begin to run until the start of September 24, which seems a very odd conclusion, given that the time for payment expired at the end of September 22. It is submitted that the cases are reconcilable and that both are correct on this point. The rule is that any part of a day (but not a whole day) happening after the cause of action accrues is excluded from the calculation of the limitation period. Strictly speaking this will normally lead to the extension of the limitation period by a few hours, but it could equally be argued that the contrary rule would lead to the shortening of that period.

Where process cannot be issued on the last day

2.008　　A difficult practical problem arises when it is impossible to issue process on the last day of the limitation period because the court offices are closed on that day. In two cases, *Morris v Richards*[19] and *Gelmini v Moriggia*,[20] it was held that time could not be extended until the next day on which the court was open. There has, of course, long been a power in rules of court to extend the time for doing any act which those rules required,[21] but the acts involved here are required to be done by a statute, and rules of court cannot

---

[17] Though it may be possible to explain this case as applying only to the particular wording of the statute in question.

[18] [1961] 2 Q.B. 135, Havers J.

[19] (1881) 45 L.T. 210.

[20] [1913] 2 K.B. 549 Channell J.

[21] Formerly RSC Ord.3, r.5. CPR 3.10 now gives a general power to remedy any procedural error, imposing such sanctions as are appropriate. For guidance on the application of this new provision see *Cala Homes (South) Ltd v Chichester D.C., The Times*, October 15, 1999; *Hannigan v Hannigan* May 18, 2000, Unreported, CA.

and do not purport to extend the time for these. These cases relied on the absence of any corresponding rule in the Limitation Act as a ground for holding that time could not be extended. In *Hodgson v Armstrong*[22] a different view was taken of a provision which required the plaintiff to give notice to the court by a certain time. It was held that this situation, which required the court actively to do something, could properly be distinguished from those in the two earlier cases.

Error by court staff

Although the general rule is that proceedings are started when the court issues a claim form at the request of the claimant,[23] it may happen that the form as issued is received in the court office on a date earlier than that on which it is issued (where, for example, the claimant sends the form by post). In these circumstances the claim is 'brought' for limitation purposes on the date when the form is received in the court office, not on the later date when it is issued.[24]   **2.009**

There are two important recent authorities on the question of what happens when documents for the issuing of process are received in the court office before the expiry of the limitation period, but the proceedings are not issued until after the end of the limitation period. In *St Helens Metropolitan BC v Barnes*[25] the Court of Appeal considered para.5 of CPR 7PD, which so far as presently relevant reads: **2.010**

> "5.1 Proceedings are started when the court issues a claim form at the request of the Claimant (see r.7.2) but where the claim form as issued was received in the court office on a date earlier than the date on which it was issued by the court, the claim is 'brought' for the purposes of the Limitation Act 1980 and any other relevant statutes on that earlier date.
>
> 5.2 The date on which the claim form was received by the court will be recorded by a date stamp either on the claim form held on the court file or on the letter that accompanied the claim form when it was received by the court."

---

[22] [1967] Q.B. 299, CA.
[23] CPR 7.2.
[24] CPR 4PD 5.1. Under the old rules the same position was reached, without benefit of a corresponding express provision, in *Riniker v University College London*, March 31, 1999, Unreported. For the earlier authorities see *Clarke v Smith* (1858) 2 H. & N. 753 (157 E.R. 311); *Campbell v Smart* (1847) 5 C.B. 196 (136 E.R. 851); *Carr v Morice* (1873) 16 Equity 125; *Chanoch v Hertz* (1888) 4 T.L.R. 331; re N [1967] 1 Ch.512; *Harrison v Touche Ross*, *The Times*, February 14, 1995.
[25] [2006] EWCA Civ 1372.

In this case, the day before the limitation period expired, the claimant's solicitor attended the court office with the claim form in triplicate and a cheque for the issue fee. The solicitor handed these and a covering letter to a clerk. The clerk date stamped the solicitor's copy of the letter with the court's official stamp to record the fact that the letter and its enclosures had been received on that day. The following day (a Friday) the court offices were open but a number of its staff were taking industrial action. When the solicitor phoned the court that day he was told that there was nobody working in the new issue section but they would be back to work on Monday. So it was that the claim form was not issued and dated until three days after time had expired.

The question for the Court of Appeal was when is a claim "brought" for the purpose of the 1980 Act under the procedural regime introduced by the CPR? Is it on the date which appears on the claim form when the court issues it and the proceedings are started as provided by r.7.2, or is it when the court receives the request to issue it? The Court of Appeal held that proceedings start on the date entered on the claim form by the court which is their date of issue, but are "brought" for the purposes of the Limitation Act when the claimant's request for the issue of a claim form (together with the court fee) is delivered to the court office.

The same principle was followed in *Secretary of State for Trade and Industry v Vohora*,[26] a case concerning s.7(2) of the Company Directors Disqualification Act 1986 which provides:

> "Except with the leave of the court, an application for the making under that section of a disqualification order against any person shall not be made after the end of the period of 2 years beginning with the day on which the company of which that person is or has been a director became insolvent".

It was held that the application is made when the form is received in the court office and is recorded by a date stamp either on the claim form held on the court file or on the letter that accompanied the claim form when it was received by the court, even if it is not issued until a later date.[27]

2.011   This distinction is a somewhat uncomfortable one, since the court must take an active step when issuing a claim form, but in the light of the two recent cases, and of the express provisions of the CPR, this point must for the time being be regarded as settled.[28]

---

[26] [2007] EWHC 2656 (Ch) Evans-Lombe J.
[27] For a similar point arising under the Magistrates Court Act 1980 see para.27.028.
[28] Earlier cases, in particular *Pritam Kaur v S. Russel & Sons Ltd* [1973] QB 336 Willis J., must now be regarded as having been superseded.

Suspension of running of time

As a general rule it may be said that the English law of limitations does not **2.012**
permit the running of time to be suspended once it has started. Thus in
Prideaux v Webber[29] it was held that not even the suspension of the King's
law during the period of the Commonwealth could prevent time from
running in a case where it had started to do so before the Commonwealth
began. Five exceptions to this principle may be mentioned. The first is
found in s.34(5) of the 1980 Act. This provides that where the High Court
orders that an arbitration award should be set aside or that an arbitration
agreement should cease to have effect, the court may also order that the
period between the commencement of the arbitration and the making of the
order shall not count for the purposes of calculating the time within which
proceedings may be commenced.[30] The second is contained in s.33 of the
Limitation Act 1980. This is the section that allows the court to extend the
normal three-year limitation period in the case of actions for personal
injuries. In exercising this discretion the court may take account of any
disability of the plaintiff which arose after the cause of action accrued. In
both cases it is a matter for the court's discretion whether to rely on these
matters, and only in the former case can the running of time be stopped.
Under s.33 the court is merely empowered to allow the bringing of the
action notwithstanding that time has expired.

The position is, of course, quite different where time has not already **2.013**
started to run. In such cases, Pt II of the 1980 Act contains a number of
provisions which may delay the date at which time starts to run in the event
of disability,[31] acknowledgment[32] or fraud.[33] The third exception arises
under the statutes relating to the carriage of goods (and in some cases
persons), which are dealt with in Ch.26. Most of these provide that the
running of time is suspended if a plaintiff makes a written claim to the
carrier, even though no proceedings are started. This suspension lasts until
the carrier rejects the claim, after which time starts to run again (if the
carrier admits the claim, the problem of timing clearly does not arise). The
fourth exception arises from the decision of the House of Lords in *Sheldon
v Outhwaite*,[34] where it was held that a deliberate concealment by the
defendant of a material fact after the cause of action has accrued operates
to reset the limitation clock to zero. The final exception is to be found in the
Limitation (Enemies and War Prisoners) Act 1945.[35] This statute suspends
the running of time where any person who is a necessary party to the action

---

[29] (1661) 1 Lev. 31.
[30] See further para.16.029.
[31] 1980 Act, ss.28, 28A; see Ch.19.
[32] 1980 Act, ss.29–31; see Ch.18.
[33] 1980 Act, ss.32, 32A; see Ch.20.
[34] [1995] 2 All E.R. 558 for a detailed discussion of this case see Ch.20.
[35] See also para.27.004.

is an enemy[36] or is detained in enemy territory. In these circumstances time cannot expire until at least one year after the party ceases to be an enemy or to be detained, and this provision is capable of suspending the running of time where the cause of action has already accrued. Time will be suspended if any necessary party to the action meets the requisite conditions. Therefore, this Act, uniquely among limitation provisions, will suspend the running of time because of the unavailability of the defendant. However, it is only parties whose absence can have this effect—the absence under the same circumstances of a necessary witness in the case does not bring the statute into operation. Clearly this provision is of very little practical importance at the present day.

Dual capacity

2.014   The general rule explained in the preceding paragraph is clearly capable of giving rise to injustice. One problematic situation is that of the person who occupies two capacities at once. He is not allowed to use one capacity to bring an action against himself in the other capacity, and it may therefore be necessary to decide whether the running of time can be suspended so long as the two capacities coexist. An example of this occurred in *Bowring-Hanbury's Trustee v Bowring-Hanbury*[37] where a husband lent money to his wife, who died without repaying it. He became her executor, but was then made bankrupt. His trustee in bankruptcy sought to sue the wife's estate. In the Court of Appeal[38] the case turned on whether the running of time could be suspended so long as the husband was both the creditor and the personal representative of the debtor. The Court of Appeal held that the running of time is not suspended in these circumstances, but suggested that the position might be different where the creditor is the administrator of the estate.[39]

2.015   The position may be different where a debtor of the deceased becomes the personal representative. Where the debtor becomes the administrator it appears that time ceases to run. Where the debtor becomes the executor the rule is that time continues to run until the will is proved, but on proof of the will the debt is treated as having been paid at the time of death, so that the original obligation ceases to exist. However, the debtor is obliged

---

[36] Within the meaning of the Trading with the Enemy Act 1939.

[37] [1942] 1 All E.R. 516, Bennett J.; [1943] 1 All E.R. 48, CA.

[38] At first instance the plaintiff had rested his case on acknowledgment; see para.14.039.

[39] See *Re Benzon* [1912] 1 Ch.196; *Seagram v Knight* (1867) 2 Ch.App. 628; *Rhodes v Smethurst* (1938) 4 M. & W. 42. See also (1943) 59 L.Q.R. 117 for an argument that time continues to run where the creditor becomes the personal representative, whether as executor or as administrator.

to account for the sum due out of the estate[40]; consequently, a new obligation arises on death, and time will presumably run from the date of death.

Protective claims

A claimant may issue proceedings in order to prevent the limitation period from expiring, even though he has no present intention of pursuing the litigation. However, it is likely to be an abuse of process to issue proceedings where the claimant has no present awareness of proper grounds for bringing the action, but is aware that such grounds may come into existence at a later date.[41] A defendant has some limited tactical riposte to the issue of a protective claim form by calling for it to be served within fourteen days[42]. If the claimant does not comply, the defendant may apply to court, which may dismiss the claim or make such other order as it thinks fit. It seems unlikely that a court would do more than order prompt service of the claim form.   **2.016**

Service of process

The preceding paragraphs have dealt with calculation of time in connection with the issuing of process. In *Trow v Ind Coope (West Midlands) Ltd*[43] the Court of Appeal had to resolve similar problems in connection with the service of a writ. The writ in this case was issued on September 10, 1965 and was served on September 10, 1966. The majority of the Court of Appeal, Lord Denning M.R. dissenting, held that the service was out of time. For the purpose of calculating the duration of a writ, the day on which the writ is issued is included. This is obviously in direct contradiction to the rule for the issuing of a writ, and it is easy to sympathise with Lord Denning's view that there is no rational justification for the distinction. It nevertheless appears still to be good law.   **2.017**

When considering the effect of the expiry of a limitation period in English law there are essentially two possible results. The first is that the plaintiff's remedy is barred, but his right is not extinguished. The second is that the plaintiff's right is itself extinguished.[44]   **2.018**

---

[40] *Ingle v Richards (No.2)* (1860) 28 Beav. 366.
[41] *West Bromwich Building Society v Mander Hadley & Co.*, The Times, March 9, 1998, *The Independent*, March 10, 1998, CA.
[42] CPR 7.7.
[43] [1967] 2 Q.B. 899, CA.
[44] On the history of this distinction, see *Sanders v Sanders* (1881) 19 Ch.D. 373; *Re Alison* (1879) 11 Ch.D. 284; *Re Clifden* [1900] 1 Ch.774; *Harvey v Wynn* (1905) 22 T.L.R. 93, and *Unger* (1940) 4 M.L.R. 45.

WHERE REMEDY BARRED

2.019 The barring of the remedy has been regarded as the usual response of the law to the expiry of the limitation period. Therefore, in an action founded on contract[45] (simple or special) or on tort[46] the effect of the expiry of the limitation period is generally said to be that the remedy is barred, but the plaintiff's right is not extinguished.

Theft and conversion

2.020 The general principle stated in the previous paragraph was significantly modified by the enactment of ss.3 and 4 of the 1980 Act. These sections, which are extensively considered in Ch.12, deal with the time-limits applicable in cases of theft and conversion of property.[47] They provide that upon the expiry of the limitation period which they stipulate, the property rights of the original owner shall be extinguished. This is in addition to the barring of the original owner's judicial remedy.[48] Consequently, the general principle stated above will not apply in tort cases involving rights to personal property[49].

The Latent Damage Act 1986

2.021 It appears that the Latent Damage Act 1986 follows the general rule for tort cases. Thus, the expiry of any limitation period prescribed by this Act serves only to bar the remedy, not to extinguish the plaintiff's right.

The Merchant Shipping Act 1995

2.022 The Merchant Shipping Act 1995,[50] which is considered extensively in Ch.24, applies to claims arising out of damage caused by the fault of a ship. It does not deal expressly with the question of the effect of expiry of time, but judges have assumed that it follows the traditional patterns for non-

---

[45] *Royal Norwegian Government v Constant & Constant* [1960] 2 Lloyd's Rep. 431, Diplock J.

[46] *C. & M. Matthews Ltd v Marsden Building Society* [1951] Ch.758.

[47] This is necessarily limited to personal property, since real property can be neither stolen nor converted.

[48] The Law Commission's Consultation Paper proposes reversing this rule.

[49] See also section 27A, inserted by the Proceeds of Crime Act 2002 and considered at para.27.034.

[50] Section 190 of this Act replaces the former s.8 of the Maritime Conventions Act 1911, though for present purposes the two provisions are materially identical.

property-based claims by merely barring the plaintiff's remedy.[51] This conclusion would appear to be sound as a matter of principle, and it is submitted that it is correct.

Effect of barring of remedy

A number of potentially significant consequences follow from holding that the plaintiff's right is not extinguished. First, limitation is a matter which must be specifically pleaded by the defendant if he wishes to take advantage of it,[52] and the plaintiff's cause of action is not regarded as time-barred until that plea is made.[53] A defendant who considers it unconscionable to take advantage of the lapse of time need not do so,[54] though it is possible that this rule does not apply to trustees defending an action relating to the trust property.[55] Secondly, if the plaintiff is able to assert his right in some way other than by the bringing of an action (and which does not involve any other unlawful act) then his right will be recognised by the law: all that is taken away is the possibility of obtaining a judicial remedy to enforce his right.[56] Thirdly, a mortgagee is entitled to retain arrears of mortgage interest on the redemption of a mortgage, even though his action for those arrears has become time-barred.[57]

2.023

WHERE RIGHT EXTINGUISHED

In a number of cases the effect of the expiry of the period of limitation is to extinguish entirely the plaintiff's right. It is not clear how this affects the principles discussed in the previous paragraph. Logically, it might be thought that limitation would not have to be pleaded in such cases, but CPR 16PD-014[58] draws no distinction of this kind, and it therefore appears that an express plea is still required. It may be suggested, however, that in these cases leave to amend the pleadings to include a limitation plea will more readily be given, subject, of course, to an appropriate order for costs.

2.024

---

[51] *The Preveze* [1973] 1 Lloyd's Rep. 202, Mocatta J.
[52] CPR 16PD-014. Although it is in the discretion of the court whether to allow limitation to be relied upon where it has not been pleaded, it is thought that courts continue to be reluctant to allow limitation defences which have not been clearly set up.
[53] *Kennett v Brown* [1988] 1 W.L.R. 582, CA.
[54] *Unger* (1940) 4 M.L.R. 45.
[55] See paras 14.023–14.025.
[56] *C. & M. Matthews Ltd v Marsden Building Society* [1951] Ch.758; see also *Allen v Waters & Co.* [1935] 1 K.B. 200.
[57] See paras 12.019-12.020.
[58] The former rule was RSC, Ord.18, r.8, but the position was the same.

The following paragraphs consider a number of cases falling into this category.

Land

2.025 The most important class of case where the expiry of time extinguishes the plaintiff's right is that relating to land. Section 17 of the 1980 Act provides that, subject to specified exceptions on the expiry of the limitation period for bringing any action for the recovery of land (within the extended meaning given to that phrase by s.38 of the Act[59]), the title of the person whose action is barred shall be extinguished.

Personal property

2.026 As is explained in Ch.12, the expiry of the limitation period for an action for conversion will normally have the effect of extinguishing the title of the person deprived to the chattel. This rule is subject to exceptions in the case of stolen property.

The Consumer Protection Act 1987

2.027 Section 11A(3) of the 1980 Act[60] provides that the expiry of the 10-year long-stop period for the bringing of an action under the Consumer Protection Act 1987 shall operate to extinguish the plaintiff's right of action, even where that right has not accrued at the time. However, this rule does not apply to the expiry of the basic three-year period laid down by the Act, and it is therefore to be assumed that this operates merely to bar the remedy.

The Hague-Visby Rules

2.028 These Rules, considered extensively at paras 26.002–26.016, govern many contracts for the international carriage of goods by sea. In *Aries Tanker Corporation v Total Transport Ltd*[61] the House of Lords held that the expiry of the one-year time-limit applied under those rules extinguishes the rights of the plaintiff, as well as barring his remedy.

---

[59] See para.13.003.
[60] As added by Sch.1 to the Consumer Protection Act 1987.
[61] [1976] 2 Lloyd's Rep. 256.

CHAPTER 3

The Relevance of the Remedy

Section 36 of the Limitation Act 1980 disapplies some of the general pro-   **3.001**
visions of the Act in the case of equitable remedies.[1] It is necessary therefore
to know which time-limits also apply to equitable remedies, as well as
which remedies originate at common law and which in equity. In addition
there is some authority[2] on the question of how to characterise the remedy
being claimed in a particular case. To some extent this issue can overlap
with the characterisation problems that are the subject of Ch.4. This
chapter will then go on to consider briefly the question of time-limits in
connection with seeking equitable remedies.

AMBIT OF SECTION 36

Section 36(1) provides that seven specified time-limits contained in the   **3.002**
1980 Act do not apply to claims for equitable relief. These are:

(a) the six-year limit under s.2 for actions founded on tort;

(b) the one-year time-limit under s.4A for actions for libel or slander[3];

(c) the six-year time-limit under s.5 for actions founded on simple
     contract;

(d) the six-year time-limit under s.7 for actions to enforce awards where
     the submission is not by an instrument under seal;

(e) the 12-year time-limit under s.8 for actions on a specialty;

---

[1] 1980 Act, s.36(1).
[2] See Ch.4.
[3] The 1980 Act s.4A was added by the Administration of Justice Act 1985, s.57 and amended
by the Defamation Act 1996 s.5; see also paras 8.071–8.078.

(f) the six-year time-limit under s.9 for actions to recover a sum due under an enactment;

(g) the six-year time-limit under s.24 for actions on a judgment.

None of the time-limits imposed in respect of actions to recover land or in relation to mortgages or trust property (ss.15–21) is caught by s.36. Nor does the section apply to actions in respect of personal injuries, whether on behalf of the injured person (s.11) or under the fatal accidents legislation (s.12). The exclusion of ss.11 and 12 is unlikely to be of great practical significance, since actions under these sections will invariably be actions for common law damages, but the exclusion of ss.15–21 is likely to be of more significance, since equitable remedies such as foreclosure, orders for sale and specific performance are much more commonly sought in this area of the law. Of the claims included in s.36, those relating to recovery of sums due under enactments, and actions on awards, are unlikely to be of major significance since these will not be claims for equitable relief. By far the most important provisions are those relating to actions in tort (including defamation) and contract. In these cases the considerations will differ fundamentally according to whether the remedy sought lies at common law or in equity.

COMMON LAW REMEDIES

3.003 The most important of the common law remedies is damages. This was the major remedy developed by the courts of common law in the years preceding the Judicature Acts. It should be noted, however, that after the Chancery Amendment Act 1858 (also known as Lord Cairns' Act) it was possible for the courts of equity to award damages in certain cases, and it is therefore necessary to look carefully at the right which has been violated. The common law also developed the action for an account of profits, which could be used in cases where the defendant had wrongfully made a profit at the expense of the plaintiff, and was liable to account to him for it. However, equity also recognised this concept, and the equitable action for an account was the proper procedure in cases where the defendant's wrong amounted to the breach of a fiduciary duty (since only equity recognised the concept of breach of fiduciary duty). Furthermore, the procedure in equity was considerably simpler and more efficient than that at common law.[4] The consequence of this was that the common law procedure fell into disuse, equity being prepared to lend its procedures to assist in the common law action. The distinction between common law account and equitable

---

[4] See *Tito v Waddell* (No.2) [1977] Ch. 106, per Megarry V.-C.

account was abolished by s.23 of the 1980 Act. That section lays down the rule that the period of limitation applicable to an action for an account shall be the same as that for an action in respect of the breach of duty which is the basis of the action. Therefore, actions for an account no longer exist as a separate category for limitation purposes.

Declarations

In *National Bank of Commerce v National Westminster Bank*[5] the plaintiff **3.004** sought a declaration in respect of alleged breaches of contract. The issues as to accrual of cause of action are considered under Ch.10, below. Webster J. also discussed the treatment of declarations in a limitation context. He said that, although such actions do not become time-barred, because a declaration is not an independent cause of action, it would rarely, if ever, be appropriate to grant a declaration of a right which could not be enforced in the English courts because it was time-barred. It is submitted that these observations by Webster J. display some confusion. It is not correct to say that an action for a declaration cannot become time-barred. The vital question for limitation purposes is as to the basis of the action. The remedy sought is relevant only in the context of equitable remedies, where s.36 of the Limitation Act 1980 may apply. The present action was an action founded on simple contract, and any action for a common law remedy became barred after six years. This includes an action for a declaration.

Further, the court retains a discretion to refuse to make a declaration on **3.005** the grounds of delay, acquiescence and/or laches—*Fisher v Brooker*[6].

EQUITABLE REMEDIES

Equitable remedies are those which before the Judicature Acts 1873–1875 **3.006** would have been available only in the court of equity. The 1623 Act never applied to them, and this general principle is still preserved in the 1980 Act.[7] The most important of these remedies historically was the injunction, an order to the defendant to do or (more often) to refrain from doing some act. In the present context attention is drawn expressly to injunctions restraining the continuance of a nuisance and injunctions (including quia timet injunctions) restraining the publication of an allegedly defamatory statement pending the trial of the action. Related to the injunction is the order for specific performance, which is available only where there is a

---

[5] *Financial Times*, March 18, 1990, Webster J.
[6] [2008] EWCA Civ 287; the subsequent appeals to the Court of Appeal and the house of Lords do not appear to affect this point, being concerned with other issues in the case.
[7] 1980 Act s.36.

contract between the parties: it is an order to one of those parties requiring him to carry out his obligations under the contract. A plea seeking to set off arrears of rent against a claim for breaches of a landlord's covenant for quiet enjoyment is an equitable set-off, to which s.36 applies.[8] A mortgagee's duty to obtain a proper price when selling the mortgaged property is an equitable duty, but the content of the duty is the same as that of a duty in negligence, so s.36 applies and the limitation period for such an action is six years.[9]

STATUTORY REMEDIES

3.007   A category of remedies which is of increasing importance in the modern law is that of remedies which exist only under statute. In the present context, a significant group of these remedies relate to the winding-up of a company. At first sight these may not appear to be covered by any of the provisions of the Limitation Act. This point was considered by Mervyn Davies J. in *Re Karnos Property Co. Ltd*,[10] where it was held that a petition for the compulsory winding-up of a company was an action to recover a sum of money due under a statute (since that was the petitioner's ultimate aim), notwithstanding that the immediate result of the action could only be a winding-up order, which would not of itself give the petitioner any money. It is wholly unclear to what extent this approach, namely of looking behind the form of action to see what the plaintiff is really trying to achieve, can be applied to the more general question of the categorisation of remedies. In any case the approach may well be inappropriate even when dealing with winding-up petitions, which are, at least in theory, a class remedy for the benefit of creditors generally rather than a debt-collection mechanism.[11]

MODERN REMEDIES

3.008   Remedies such as search orders[12] and freezing orders,[13] which did not exist at the time of the Judicature Acts, should for these purposes be treated in the same way as equitable remedies, since they are by their nature discretionary, and it is usually important that they should be sought promptly and

---

[8] *Filross Securities Ltd v Midgeley* [1998] 43 E.G. 134; [1998] 3 E.G.L.R. 43; (1998) 31 H.L.R. 465, CA.

[9] *Raja v Lloyds TSB Bank plc*, August 22, 2000, Unreported, CA.

[10] (1989) 5 B.C.C. 14.

[11] See paras 17.023–17.026. In some cases it would be possible to argue that the claim was to recover a sum due under an enactment, so that the 1980 Act s.9 applied: see Ch.11.

[12] Formerly Anton Piller orders.

[13] Formerly Mareva injunctions.

on the basis of full and frank disclosure by the plaintiff of all relevant circumstances.

THE PROVISO TO SECTION 36(1)

The proviso to this subsection is of great importance. Before the consolidation of the law in the 1939 Act there was no comparable rule in the statute. The 1623 Act did not apply to equitable remedies, although the provisions of the Real Property Limitation Act 1833 and the Trustee Act 1888 related, inter alia, to at least some actions for equitable remedies. However, the courts had developed a more general principle whereby limitation periods could be applied to equitable remedies.[14] This principle is preserved by s.36(2) of the 1980 Act, which provides that statutory periods of limitation may be applied to cases of equitable remedies in so far as they would have been so applied by the courts before 1939 (a date chosen because it was the date of the first major consolidation of the law on limitation periods since the original Act of 1623). This naturally invites consideration of the circumstances in which this analogy was adopted before 1939.

3.009

The pre-1939 position

The courts made fairly extensive use of the principle of analogy[15] before the 1939 Act came into force. For example, a claim against beneficiaries to whom an estate had wrongly been distributed was treated as being analogous to a common law claim for money had and received.[16] The same rule was applied to an action against beneficiaries under a trust to whom money had been paid under a common mistake of fact.[17] More generally there was authority that the periods applicable to common law actions should normally be applied in an analogous way to claims for equitable relief.[18] This,

3.010

---

[14] See, e.g., *Knox v Gye* (1872) L.R. 5, H.L. 656; *Gibbs v Guild* (1882) 8 Q.B.D. 296. L. Spry, *Principles of Equitable Remedies* (6th edn, 2001), pp.224–244. The Real Property Limitation Acts of 1833 and 1874 also made limited use of this principle.

[15] Spry, *Principles of Equitable Remedies*, pp.224–244 criticises the wording of the proviso for failing to distinguish between acting by analogy to the statute and acting in obedience to it. However, it is submitted that at the present day nothing turns on this distinction, the phrase "by analogy" covering both concepts.

[16] *Re Blake* [1932] 1 Ch. 54; *Re Mason* [1929] 1 Ch. 1; see now 1980 Act s.22 and *Re Diplock's Estate* [1948] 2 All E.R. 318, CA.

[17] *Re Robinson* [1911] 1 Ch. 502, Warrington J.; see also *Re Mason* [1928] Ch. 385 and *Re Blake* [1932] 1 Ch. 54.

[18] *Bulli Coal Mining Co. v Osborne* [1899] A.C. 357, PC—although this is a Privy Council case, the advice proceeds on the assumption that in this respect the principles are the same in English law.

however, leaves open the question of what is truly "analogous". The most authoritative consideration of this point is now to be found in *P&O Nedlloyd BV v Arab Metals Co and Others (The "UB Tiger")*[19], where Colman J. held that the limitation period in s.5 of the Limitation Act 1980 applies by analogy to a claim for specific performance and held that claims for that relief were on the facts time-barred, and that none of the new claims which were sought to be advanced arose out of the same, or substantially the same, facts as the existing claims and so refused permission to amend. The Court of Appeal[20] subsequently took a different view, holding that the new claims did arise out of same facts as the original claims and that therefore, even if the new claims were time-barred, it had jurisdiction to allow the amendment. In reaching that conclusion the court found it unnecessary to consider the question of limitation and declined to express any view on it. When the new claims were properly pleaded the defendant served an amended defence raising the defence of laches in response to all the claims for specific performance. Tomlinson J. dismissed an application for summary judgment in favour of the claim for specific performance, though without deciding whether the defence of laches was available, and the claimants appealed on the basis that the defence of laches is unsustainable as a matter of law where the statutory limitation period has not expired (in effect relying on the views expressed in the earlier hearing by Colman J.) The Court of Appeal, having held that Colman J.'s earlier judgment did not give rise to an issue estoppel, went on to consider afresh the question whether the statutory limitation should apply by analogy. Having reviewed the existing authorities, the court held[21] that if a statutory limitation provision, properly interpreted, applies to the claim under consideration, equity will apply it in obedience to the statute, as indeed it must. However, even if the limitation period does not apply because the claim is for an exclusively equitable remedy, the court will nonetheless apply it by analogy if the remedy in equity is "correspondent to the remedy at law". In other words, where the suit in equity corresponds with an action at law a court of equity adopts the statutory rule as its own rule of procedure. The Court added[22] that it is not surprising that equity should apply by analogy the limitation periods applicable to claims at law for an account and for damages for breach of duty, whether in contract or tort, to claims for an account and for equitable compensation. In each case the same facts give rise to a claim, whether at law or in equity, and the same kind of relief is obtainable. By contrast, a claim for specific performance raises different considerations, however, both because relief comparable to that available from the courts of equity was not available from the common law courts

---

[19] [2005] EWHC 1276 (Comm) Colman J.; [2006] EWCA Civ 1300. See also Ch.23.
[20] [2006] EWCA Civ 1300; see Ch.23.
[21] at para.38.
[22] at para.43.

and because the facts needed to support a claim for specific performance are not in all respects the same as those necessary to support a claim for breach of contract[23]. The fact that the common law courts could not grant a coercive remedy comparable to a decree of specific performance suggests that there is no case in which "the remedy in equity is correspondent to the remedy at law" or "the suit in equity corresponds with an action at law". Although most claims for specific performance are made in response to an existing breach of contract, *Hasham v Zenab* demonstrates that an accrued right of action for breach of contract is not a necessary precondition to obtaining relief of that kind. It is therefore wrong in principle to treat specific performance as merely an equitable remedy for an existing breach of contract. Moreover, since a claim for specific performance may be made as soon as the contract has been entered into, it is very arguable that, if the limitation period were to be applied by analogy, it would be necessary to regard the cause of action as accruing at that moment with the unfortunate result that the claim could become time-barred before any need for relief had arisen. This lends further support to the conclusion that the application of the limitation period by analogy is not appropriate in relation to claims for specific performance.[24] More fundamentally, the absence of a corresponding legal remedy makes it impossible to say either that the remedy in equity is "correspondent to the remedy at law" or that "the suit in equity corresponds with an action at law". Consequently, no limitation period applies to a claim for specific performance (i.e. the statutory six-year period in contract is not to be applied by analogy).

In *Raja v Lloyds TSB Bank plc*[25] it was held that the duty of a mortgagee **3.011** in possession to obtain a proper price on the sale of a property was owed in equity rather than in contract or in tort. However, the six-year limitation period was applied by analogy. This seems to undermine still further the somewhat restrictive rule proposed by Judge Baker.

In recent years some claimants have brought actions which might most **3.012** naturally have been expressed as contractual or tortious and have attempted to evade the provisions of the Limitation Act 1980 by pleading their cases on the basis of breach of fiduciary duty. Examples include *Companhia de Seguros Imperio v Heath*,[26] *Coulthard v Disco Club Mix Ltd*,[27] *Paragon Finance Plc v D B Thakerar & Co. (a firm)*[28] and *UCB Home Loans Corporation Ltd v Carr*.[29] Such an argument would succeed if

---

[23] *Hasham v Zenab* [1960] A.C. 316; [1960] 2 W.L.R. 374.
[24] at para.47.
[25] [2001] 19 E.G. 143, Michael Tugendhat Q.C.
[26] [1999] L.R.I.R. 571, Langley J; affirmed [2000] L.R.I.R. 109, CA, where *Kershaw v Whelan* (No. 2), *The Times*, February 10, 1997, Ebsworth J., was overruled.
[27] [1999] 2 All E.R. 457, Jules Sher Q.C.
[28] [1999] 1 All E.R. 400, CA. The account of the distinction between the two types of constructive trust given in the text is taken principally from the judgment of Millett L.J. in that case.
[29] [2000] 1 Lloyd's Rep. 754, Crane J.

the plea of breach of fiduciary duty were effective to bring the case within s.21(1) of the Limitation Act 1980.[30] In all cases the attempts to do this have failed. A distinction has been drawn between two types of constructive trust. The first arises where the constructive trustee really is a trustee in the sense that it is intended from the outset by disponor and disponee that the property shall be impressed with a trust.[31] These cases fall within s.21(1). The second case arises where the defendant is implicated in a fraud and becomes liable to account to the claimant for benefits which he has received. Although it is commonly said that he is liable to account "as constructive trustee", in reality he is never a trustee at all.[32] In such a case either the matter is not really a claim for an equitable remedy at all, or, if it is such a claim, the common law period is to be applied by analogy. The approach taken by the courts here is to be welcomed as a matter of logic and as a matter of principle. These cases involved obviously inappropriate attempts to circumvent the relevant limitation rules, and the courts were rightly astute to resist those attempts.

3.013   A further point should be noted. In the context of personal obligations the effect of expiry of the limitation period is often merely to bar the plaintiff's remedy rather than to extinguish his right.[33] In cases where the common law remedy is barred even though the plaintiff could not reasonably have known of its existence,[34] there must remain at least the possibility that the court will be prepared to grant an equitable remedy, applying the principle that for the purposes of equitable remedies time does not begin to run until the plaintiff knows or should have known of the facts which entitled him to the remedy.[35]

EQUITABLE REMEDIES

3.014   The subject of equitable remedies is extensive.[36] In the context of limitation periods a few areas of the subject may be isolated as being of importance. Clearly, the major area is that of acquiescence or laches, i.e. the principle that the plaintiff who seeks an equitable remedy must come to court

---

[30] Examined more fully in Ch.14.

[31] Examples include *McCormick v Grogan* (1869) L.R. 4 H.L. 82 and *Rochefoucauld v Boustead* [1897] 1 Ch.196 and *Pallant v Morgan* [1952] 2 All E.R. 951.

[32] See, for example, *Hovenden v Lord Annesley* (1806) 2 Sch. & Lef. 607; *Burdick v Garrick* (1870) L.R. 5 Ch.App. 233; *Friend v Young* [1897] 2 Ch. 421; *North American Land and Timber Co. Ltd v Watkins* [1904] 1 Ch. 242.

[33] See paras 2.017–2.021.

[34] In the modern law this situation, in the context of personal obligations, appears to be limited to contract cases, since in cases of negligence the position would now be governed by either the personal injuries provisions of the 1980 Act or by the Latent Damage Act 1986.

[35] *Lindsay Petroleum Co. v Hurd* (1874) L.R. 5, P.C. 221.

[36] See, e.g. Spry, *Principles of Equitable Remedies* (6th edn, 2001) and Snell (ed J. McGhee), *Principles of Equity* (30th edn, 2000), for very detailed accounts of the whole topic.

quickly. It has been held that for the purpose of the doctrine of acquiescence time cannot run until the plaintiff has a clear idea of his rights.[37] The difficult matter in the context of laches is to know how long a plaintiff will be allowed before he is considered to have lost his remedy. The usual answer to this is that the plaintiff must come to court quickly,[38] but what amounts to coming to court quickly is a question of fact to be determined on a case-by-case basis. The overall effect of this is that a plaintiff who seeks an equitable remedy may have a longer or a shorter time in which to proceed than a plaintiff who seeks a common law remedy.

Laches

The equitable principle of laches requires that a plaintiff seeking an equi- 3.015
table remedy must come to court quickly once he knows that his rights are being infringed. The classic statement is in the judgment of Lord Selborne L.C. in *Lindsay Petroleum Co. v Hurd*[39]:

> "Now the doctrine of laches in courts of equity is not an arbitrary or a technical doctrine. Where it would be practicably unjust to give a remedy, either because the party has by his conduct done that which might fairly be regarded as equivalent to a waiver of it, or where by his conduct and neglect he has, though perhaps not waiving that remedy, yet put the other party in a situation in which it would not be reasonable to place him if the remedy were afterwards to be asserted, in either of these cases lapse of time and delay are most material, but in every case if an argument against relief which otherwise would be just is founded upon mere delay, that delay, of course, not amounting to a bar by any statutory limitations, the validity of that defence must be tried upon principles substantially equitable.
>
> Two circumstances always important in such cases are: the length of the delay and the nature of the acts done during the interval which might affect either party and cause a balance of justice or injustice in taking the one course or the other so far as relates to the remedy."

---

[37] *Re Howlett, Howlett v Howlett* [1949] Ch. 767, Danckwerts J.
[38] *Milward v Earl of Thanet* (1801) 5 Ves. 720n, where it was held that the plaintiff must be "ready, desirous, prompt and eager".
[39] (1874) L.R. 5 P.C. 221 at 239, 240. See also *Nelson v Rye* [1996] 2 All E.R. 186 at 201–204, per Laddie J. The observations in the latter case on this point may still be regarded as good law despite the disapproval of other aspects of the decision in *Paragon Finance v D B Thakerar & Co.* (a firm) [1999] 1 All E.R. 400, CA. And see *Schulman v Hewson*, May 3, 2002, Blackburne J., Unreported, where Laddie J.'s observations were cited with approval.

The Court of Appeal in *P&O Nedlloyd BV v Arab Metals Co*[40] also considered the relationship between laches and limitation. The court observed (although this was not necessary to the decision of the matter before it) that if and to the extent that a limitation period is applicable to a claim, it is difficult to see why mere delay (as distinct from delay which can be shown to have prejudiced the defendant) should defeat the claim until the limitation period has expired. The question for the court in each case is simply whether, having regard to the delay, its extent, the reasons for it and its consequences, it would be inequitable to grant the claimant the relief he seeks.[41]

More recently still, in *Fisher v Brooker*[42] Lord Neuberger commented, relying on *Lindsay Petroleum Co v Hurd*: ". . . laches is an equitable doctrine, under which delay can bar a claim to equitable relief." In the Court of Appeal, Mummery LJ said that there was "no requirement of detrimental reliance for the application of acquiescence or laches"—[2008] EWCA Civ 287, para.85. Although I would not suggest that it is an immutable requirement, some sort of detrimental reliance is usually an essential ingredient of laches, in my opinion.

3.016   In *Kuppusami v Kuppusami*[43] Rimer J. found that a son had since 1977 been holding the legal title to a house on a resulting trust for his father. It was argued for the son that the father's claim was barred by laches[44]. Rimer J. observed that the mere passage of time would not enable the son to succeed. The son would have to show that the father could be said to have so acted as to have waived his claim to the house, or at least that he had so acted that it would not be reasonable to require the son to re-transfer the house—in short, that it would be "practically unjust to give a remedy"[45]. In *Humphreys v Humphreys*[46] the elderly claimant sought to set aside a trust deed in favour of her son on the basis of undue influence, but the claim was not issued until 13 years after the date of the deed. Rimer J. held that the Limitation Act did not apply to the claim, and added:

"I prefer the view that, so long as the undue influence persists, claims can be brought whatever the period since the transaction;[47] but that once the

---

[40] [2005] EWHC 1276 (Comm).

[41] Cases considered in relation to this point include *Rochdale Canal Co v King* (1851) 2 Sim NS 78, 20 LJ C 675, 15 Jur 962; *Archbold v Scully* (1861) 9 HL Cas 360, 7 Jur NS 169, 5 LT 160; *Redgrave v Hurd* (1881) 20 Ch D 1, 57 LJ Ch 113, 30 WR 251 and *Re Pauling's Settlement Trusts* [1961] 3 All ER 713, [1964] 1 Ch 303, [1962] 1 WLR 86.

[42] [2009] UKHL 41 at para.64.

[43] [2002] EWHC 2758.

[44] No period of limitation could apply because of s.21(1) of the Limitation Act 1980.

[45] *Lindsay Petroleum Co v Hurd* (1874) LR 5 PC 221, at 239, 240.

[46] [2004] EWHC 2201 (Ch), [2005] 1 FCR 712.

[47] See also *Kent v M&L Management & Legal Ltd and another* [2005] EWHC 2546 (Ch), [2005] All ER (D) 251 (Nov) Park J.

complainant is no longer under the defendant's influence, a claim to set the transaction must be brought within a reasonable time."

It is important to note here the suggestion that even a defence of laches cannot be available so long as the undue influence persists.

In *Schulman v Hewson*[48] the opposite result was reached in a case where there had been a delay of fifteen years in bringing proceedings (though time had arguably not expired because of s.21(1) and there had been no intimation of any intention to bring proceedings and no adequate explanation for the delay could be put forward. On the more general question of the approach to be adopted in laches cases Blackburne J., after citing *Lindsay Petroleum Co v Hurd*, went on to approve the comments of Laddie J in *Nelson v Rye*[49] that: **3.017**

"It can be misleading to approach the equitable defences of laches and acquiescence as if they consisted of a series of precisely defined hurdles over each of which a litigant must struggle before the defence is made out."

Blackburne J added that in *Frawley v Neill*[50] Aldous LJ said that a modern approach to laches and acquiescence should not require an exhaustive inquiry into whether the circumstances could fit within the principles established in previous cases. Instead, a broader approach should be adopted, namely whether it was unconscionable for the party concerned to be permitted to assert his beneficial rights. In *Garcia v De Aldama*[51] Peter Smith J. emphasised the importance of the prejudice caused to the defendant by lapse of time when considering a defence of laches.[52]

This passage was considered again in *Patel and others v Shah and others*[53] in the particular context of a laches defence by a trustee. Mummery LJ observed: **3.018**

"[33] The effect of conduct by the Claimants, which may properly be described as unconscionable, is to release a Defendant trustee from the equitable trust obligation, which binds his conscience as the holder of the legal title for the benefit of others. In the case of an ordinary trust by way of gift to trustees for the benefit of the beneficiaries, where the beneficiary is not required or expected to do more than receive what has been given for his benefit, it will obviously be extremely rare for laches and delay on

---

[48] [2002] EWHC 855.
[49] [1996] 2 All ER 186, [1996] 1 WLR 13778 at 1392.
[50] *The Times* 5 April 1999 C.A.
[51] [2002] EWHC 2087 (Ch); [2002] All ER (D) 180 (Oct).
[52] see also *Nelson v Rye* [1996] 1 W.L.R. 1378 and *Lynch v Lynch Transport* [CHANF/1998/06563] 8/3/02 CA.
[53] [2005] EWCA Civ 157.

the part of the beneficiary to make it unconscionable for that beneficiary to assert his claim to the beneficial interest, or for the trustee to claim that he has been released from the equitable obligations that bind his conscience."

However, on the facts of that case, where the trust arose in a commercial context and not by way of gift, the Court of Appeal went on to hold that laches did apply to the claims against the trustees.

3.019   An action for relief against forfeiture of a lease by peaceable re-entry is a claim for an equitable remedy[54], but common law principles may be applied by analogy[55]. The matter is complicated because of s.139 (2) of the County Courts Act 1984, which applies a six-month limitation period to an application in the County Court, whereas there is no statutory time limit for an application to the High Court, which exercises the ancient equitable jurisdiction to relieve against forfeiture[56]. In either court the remedy is still equitable and may be refused even if an application is promptly made, since promptness is not the only criterion.

3.020   One important consequence of the cases cited above is that it is impossible to set any fixed time-limit for the operation of the principle—everything must depend on the damage caused in the particular case. It may also be possible to circumvent the operation of laches if the plaintiff is prepared to accept a suitably restricted remedy. The principle applies, though, only where the plaintiff knows of the wrong, and, despite the considerable changes in this area in the past 30 years, there are still very many provisions of the 1980 Act which do not require any knowledge in order to start time running.[57] The question which therefore arises is whether the doctrine of laches can be applied against the plaintiff in those cases of equitable remedies for which a statutory limitation period is specified. The answer must depend upon the remedy which is being sought. In the case of common law remedies, the 1980 Act does not say that an action may be brought at any time within the statutory period, but merely that no action may be brought outside that period. Nevertheless, the clear intention is that the period provided by statute shall be available for the bringing of an action, subject only to the possibility that an action might be regarded as

---

[54] whereas a claim for relief in an action for forfeiture by the court proceeds upon the basis of the relevant statute.
[55] *Vision Golf Ltd v Weightmans (a firm)* [2005] EWHC 1675 (Ch); [2005] All ER (D) 379 (Jul), Lewison J.
[56] See *Thatcher v CH Pearce & Sons (Contractors) Ltd* [1968] 1 WLR 748 Sir Jocelyn Simon P., referring also to *Lovelock v Margo* [1963] 2 QB 786 C.A.
[57] The exceptions appear to be s.4A (defamation), s.14 (personal injuries), s.14A (latent damage) and s.11A (Consumer Protection Act cases) of the 1980 Act. The Maritime Conventions Act 1911 also provides an exception to this principle. The remaining provisions are to some extent qualified by s.32, which postpones the running of time in certain cases of fraud and mistake (on this section see Ch.20). This is, however, of limited ambit.

an abuse of the process of the court. This view is supported by an obiter dictum of Wilberforce J. in *Re Pauling's Settlement Trusts Ltd.*[58]

The Limitation Acts are the only general provision[59] which require that an action be brought within a given time. There is no such thing as a common law limitation period and it would be quite inappropriate at the present time for the courts to attempt to develop such a common law doctrine. In the case of equitable remedies, by contrast, it is clear that lapse of time amounting to much less than the statutory limitation periods can cause such prejudice to the defendant as to render the granting of the remedy inappropriate.   3.021

Inconsistent remedies

It is a general principle of law that where a plaintiff has available to him two mutually inconsistent remedies he must choose between them, and that his choice of one excludes him from the other.[60] The significance of this rule for limitation purposes was considered in *Lakshmijit v Sherani.*[61] In 1948 the vendor sold land to the purchaser, the price to be paid by quarterly instalments with interest. The contract provided that in the event of default the vendor could either declare the whole purchase price due immediately or rescind the contract. There was repeated default on the instalments, but only in 1967 did the vendor seek to rescind the contract. The defence was limitation, and the Privy Council therefore had to consider when the vendor's right accrued. It was held that this occurred only when he gave notice to rescind the contract (in 1967) so that the limitation defence failed. Effectively this amounts to holding that the right of action accrued only when the vendor made his choice between the two inconsistent remedies.   3.022

The decision has been criticised[62] on the ground that the vendor could have claimed immediately for the purchase price without giving notice. This criticism is misplaced as this is a decision which turns entirely on the terms of the particular contract. Whichever remedy the plaintiff wanted, he had   3.023

---

[58] [1962] 1 W.L.R. 86, affirmed [1964] Ch. 303, but without consideration of this point. In *Securum Finance Ltd v Ashton* [2001] Ch. 291 it was suggested that where the first action had been struck out for delay, a second action on the same facts could be struck out as an abuse, although the limitation period had not expired. As to this, see further Ch.22. The occasional suggestions by Lord Denning that the plaintiff does not necessarily have the time allowed by the Act must be regarded as being expressed far too broadly and as embodying a wish for what the law ought to be rather than a proper explanation of what it is. These suggestions have been made even in the context of claims for common law remedies, where they are most clearly misplaced; see paras 3.003–3.004.

[59] In the present context this includes the statutes of specialised application which are dealt with at various places in this work.

[60] *Johnson v Agnew* [1980] A.C. 367, HL.

[61] [1973] 3 All E.R. 737, PC. Although this was a case on the Indian limitation rules, the English rules do not appear to differ in any material particular.

[62] (1974) 90 L.Q.R. 2.

first to make a decision, either declaring the purchase price outstanding or giving notice of rescission, and it is for this reason that his cause of action is correctly regarded as not accruing until he had made his choice. Of course, it follows from this that the case is not authority for a general proposition that the plaintiff's cause of action does not accrue until he has chosen between inconsistent remedies. Indeed, in the general case the opposite is true. The choice between remedies is effectively made by commencing proceedings claiming one remedy rather than the other, so that the point cannot arise directly. Further, if for any reason the plaintiff makes an effective choice at an earlier stage, for example by telling the defendant which remedy will be chosen in such circumstances as to waive his right to the other remedy, it will still be the case that the cause of action accrued on the breach. The making of the choice will not be sufficient to stop time from running, since it will not amount to the commencement of proceedings. A point which does not appear to have been addressed at all in this case is that both the possible remedies available to the plaintiff were equitable, namely specific performance of the contract or rescission of it. In an English law context this would raise the question of the application of s.36 of the 1980 Act, but it may be that this problem can be satisfactorily resolved by saying that the provisions of the Act would be applied by analogy.[63]

MULTIPLE ACTIONS

3.024 Difficult problems may arise where the plaintiff issues more than one claim form in respect of the same cause of action.[64] In *Joyce v Joyce*[65] the plaintiff commenced the first action in 1974 claiming specific performance of and/or damages for breach of a contract to transfer shares. In 1977 the defendant applied to have this action dismissed for want of prosecution. Before that application could be heard the plaintiff began a second action, this time claiming a declaration of beneficial entitlement to the shares and/or repayment of the purchase price, on the grounds of total failure of consideration. The defendant applied to have this second action struck out as an abuse of process, and his two applications were heard together. The first action was clearly a claim for equitable relief, and Megarry V.-C. held that it was therefore up to the plaintiff to show that he had a prima facie case for avoiding the operation of laches if he began a second action claiming the same relief. This principle, which appears to apply irrespective of whether a second action has in fact been started, is an attempt to apply the principles

---

[63] See paras 3.009–3.013. Alternatively, this aspect of the case might be dealt with by pointing out that it is not strictly an English law case.

[64] The relationship between this and the general rules on dismissal for want of prosecution is considered at paras 22.008–22.009.

[65] [1978] 1 W.L.R. 1170, Megarry V.-C.

laid down by the House of Lords in *Birkett v James*[66] relating to claims for common law relief. It appears to be an accurate and appropriate modification of those principles, i.e. where a second action can still be brought there is generally little point in dismissing the first action. In this case the plaintiff was compelled to accept that he had been guilty of inordinate and inexcusable delay. He was also unable to show that a second action for the same relief would not be barred by laches. Accordingly, the correct course would be to dismiss the first action. The second action, however, was not to be regarded as an abuse of process, and the defendant was unable to show that it was bound to fail. There was therefore no good reason to strike it out. It is to be observed that in this case the second writ claimed common law relief, presumably because the plaintiff feared that a claim for equitable relief would by that time quite clearly have been barred by laches.

There is apparently no authority on the correct treatment of the situation   3.025
where both actions are for equitable relief. It is submitted that such a case need cause no serious difficulty: the question of dismissing the first action can be decided on the ordinary principles of want of prosecution cases. The duty to prosecute the action expeditiously after the issue of process is the same whatever the nature of the relief sought, though the *Birkett v James* principle has to be applied by asking whether the second action is likely to be barred on the ground of laches. It follows from this that in the great majority of cases where the first action is dismissed the second will also fail on the ground of laches, though this is not inevitable. Where only one action has been started and the defendant seeks to have this action dismissed, such application may be granted in the expectation that a second action will fail. If that second action is subsequently commenced, the judge who tries it may take a different view of the application of the doctrine of laches.

THE LAW COMMISSION'S PROPOSALS

In *Companhia de Seguros Imperio v Heath*[67] Sir Christopher Staughton   3.026
observed:

"It is not obvious to me why it is still necessary to have special rules for the limitation of claims for specific performance, or an injunction, or other equitable relief. And if it is still necessary to do so, I do not see any merit in continuing to define the circumstances where a particular claim will be time-barred by reference to what happened, or might have happened, more than 60 years ago. If a distinction still has to be drawn

---

[66] [1978] A.C. 297.
[67] Above, fn. 26.

between common law and equitable claims for limitation purposes, I would hope that a revised statute will enact with some precision where that distinction should be drawn, rather than leave it to the product of researches into cases decided long ago."

The good sense of this observation appears quite indisputable.

3.027   The Law Commission's Report[68] proposes that a limitation period applying to common law remedies for a cause of action should apply also to equitable remedies for that cause of action. A consequence of this would be that laches and acquiescence would cease to be available in such cases (save in respect of interlocutory remedies). This appears a desirable simplification of the law, though it cannot be denied that it will have the effect of making equitable remedies available for a longer period than at present.

---

[68] Law Com. 272.

CHAPTER 4

Categorisation

SIGNIFICANCE

The statutes of limitation provide a number of different periods of limita-   **4.001**
tion, ranging from two years in the case of contribution actions[1] to 12 years
in the case of actions relating to land[2] and as much as 100 years in some of
the more obscure provisions dealing with advowsons.[3] In addition, the
starting point for the running of time may be the accrual of the cause of
action or the date of discoverability.[4] The consequences of the expiry of the
period may also differ. It is therefore essential to identify exactly which type
of action is in issue in a particular case. Unfortunately, the provisions of the
1980 Act do not generally offer definitions or even guidance as to what falls
within the ambit of each. Some of the more difficult borderline cases are
considered in this chapter, though issues of categorisation are also examined in the chapters on the various causes of action throughout this work.

TIME OF CATEGORISATION

In *Gulf Shipping Lines Ltd v Jadranska Slobodna Plovidba*[5] Neill J. held   **4.002**
that the vital time for determining which section of the Limitation Act 1980
applies to a particular claim is the time when the action is brought, i.e.
when process is issued,[6] rather than the time when the cause of action

---

[1] 1980 Act, s.10.
[2] 1980 Act, s.15.
[3] 1980 Act, s.25. This period was reduced to 30 years on the coming into force of the
Patronage (Benefices) Measure 1986 (No.3), which introduced a system of registration for
patronage within the Church of England.
[4] As in cases of personal injury (1980 Act s.11), latent damage (Latent Damage Act 1986)
and cases under the Consumer Protection Act 1987.
[5] [1981] 1 Lloyd's Rep. 31.
[6] On the concept of "bringing" an action, see para.2.003.

accrues or the time when the court's decision is given.[7] This point does not appear to be of general practical significance, since it will not normally be possible for the category to change, though amendments to the pleadings may affect the nature of the cause of action on which the plaintiff seeks to rely.

ACTION IN TORT

4.003 It may be suggested that a cause of action is founded on tort where it is brought for the breach of some personal obligation owed by the defendant to the plaintiff, that obligation not being one which arises out of any agreement between the parties. In *R. v Secretary of State for Transport, ex p. Factortame Ltd and Others (No. 6)*[8] a claim for damages was made by fishing-vessel owners who had successfully challenged the legality under European Community law of the enactment by the United Kingdom of provisions in the Merchant Shipping Act 1988 which discriminated against non-U.K., and particularly Spanish, vessel owners who sought licences to fish in UK waters. The European Court of Justice held that the applicants were entitled to damages for loss and injury caused by the UK government's breaches of Community law and their claims were transferred to the Technology and Construction Court. Preliminary issues were raised as to whether applications made between May and September 2000 to add additional parties to the proceedings were statute-barred under s.2 of the 1980 Act. It was held that an action for damages for an infringement, contrary to s.2 of the European Communities Act 1972, of rights conferred by Community law amounted to a breach of statutory duty and could therefore be considered "an action founded on tort" for the purposes of s.2. The term "an action founded on tort" should be widely construed as including any claim in respect of the breach of a non-contractual duty (including one under Community law) which gave a private law right to recover compensatory damages at common law. In general it is no doubt fair to say that the concept is well understood in practice, but there are a number of borderline cases that may give rise to difficulty.

Bailment

4.004 Bailment is the relationship that subsists when the chattels of one party come into the possession of another. Often there will be a deliberate entrusting of those chattels, with the anticipation that they will at some

---

[7] Although this case turned on a now obsolete provision of the 1939 Act (s.2(6)), this change in the law does not appear to affect the general principle laid down in this case.
[8] Queen's Bench Division (Technology and Construction Court) [2001] 1 W.L.R 942, Judge Toulmin Q.C.

future stage be returned to the owner.[9] Bailment is of a hybrid nature, having in some cases elements of a contract, but being also a status recognised by law to which incidents are attached irrespective of the will of the parties. The non-contractual aspects are obviously of particular importance in the case of involuntary bailment.

In *Chesworth v Farrar*[10] the defendant was the plaintiff's landlord. He took possession of the plaintiff's goods under a court order, thereby becoming a bailee of those goods. The plaintiff sued him for wrongfully selling the goods, and the claim was pleaded on the basis, inter alia, of bailment. It became necessary to decide whether, for the purposes of the Law Reform (Miscellaneous Provisions) Act 1934, this action was founded on tort. Edmund-Davies J. held that it was. It is necessary to look at the substance of the matter, and in this case the obligation owed by the defendant did not depend upon any contract between the parties.[11] It must therefore be regarded as a tortious obligation. The decision must be understood subject to two qualifications. The first is that it is not a decision on the Limitation Act, and Edmund Davies J. makes the point that the line between contract and tort may be drawn in different places for different purposes.[12] It is submitted, nevertheless, that the approach of Edmund Davies J. is correct also in relation to limitation periods, so that this difficulty ought not to stand in the way of using this case in the present context. Secondly, the reasoning of Edmund Davies J. will not necessarily produce the same result in every case of bailment. This was a case of involuntary bailment, and it would indeed have been odd to hold that the obligation was contractual in nature.[13] However, there are many cases of bailment where there is a contract between the parties. In these cases there is clearly an action in contract if the bailee breaks the terms of the bailment. The decision of the House of Lords in *Henderson v Merrett Syndicates*[14] establishes that there will also be an action in tort on the same facts.

4.005

Money had and received

In *Chesworth v Farrar*[15] the plaintiff's claim was alternatively pleaded as an action for money had and received, and Edmund Davies J. had to decide

4.006

---

[9] For an exhaustive treatment of this topic, see Norman Palmer, *Bailment* 3rd edn (2010).
[10] [1967] 1 Q.B. 407.
[11] cf. *Turner v Stallibrass* [1898] 1 Q.B. 56.
[12] Other cases on this distinction have arisen in the context of the County Courts Acts, where the rules as to jurisdiction and costs were at one time different according to the basis of the action. See further paras 4.006–4.007.
[13] See also *R. v McDonald* (1885) 15 Q.B.D. 323, where an infant to whom goods had been hired under a void contract of hire was nevertheless held to be a bailee of them for the purposes of the now obsolete offence of larceny as a bailee.
[14] [1994] 3 All E.R. 506; see further para.4.011.
[15] [1967] 1 Q.B. 407; see also para.4.005.

whether such a claim was founded on tort. He held that it was not, at least in this case, since it could be brought only if the plaintiff chose to waive the tort. His Lordship described the action as being quasi-contractual in nature, but the course which the case took did not oblige him to go on to decide where, if at all, such an action fits into the scheme of the Limitation Act. The question of the correct categorisation of such claims was considered by the Privy Council in *John v Dodwell & Co. Ltd.*[16] This was an appeal from Ceylon, and turned on the wording of the 1871 Ordinance in Ceylon. The defendant received money which the plaintiff's employee had fraudulently converted from the plaintiff, though it was accepted that the defendant had not been fraudulent. If this was an action to recover "money received to the use of the plaintiff" then it was out of time, but there were longer limitation periods for actions for "any loss, injury or damage" and for "trust". The Privy Council held that the action could properly be brought under either of the latter two heads. In other words, this type of action may simultaneously fall under other categories. This decision needs to be treated with some caution. First, it is a decision on a piece of foreign legislation, which does not appear to correspond with the provisions of the Limitation Act in England. Secondly, it is to be noted that under the Ceylon Ordinance it was to the plaintiff's advantage to show that money had and received was not the only possible category.

4.007   The most recent consideration of this question in English law was by Hobhouse J. in *Kleinwort Benson Ltd v S. Tyneside MBC,*[17] a case arising out of the making of ultra vires interest-rate swap contracts by local authorities.[18] Lenders of money under these schemes brought actions against local authorities for the recovery of these sums as money had and received. Hobhouse J. held that such actions fall within s.5 of the Limitation Act 1980 as actions founded on simple contract. In reaching this conclusion, his Lordship was influenced by the fact that there would otherwise have been no applicable period of limitation, an outcome which he regarded as unacceptable. It is submitted that this view should be treated with caution. In the first place, the principle clearly is that in the absence of a statutory limitation period the action never becomes barred. There is no reason to strain the construction of the statute, as appears to have happened here, in order to avoid such a consequence. It is interesting to observe that in another case arising out of the same situation, *Kleinwort Benson Ltd v City of Glasgow DC,*[19] it was held that for private international law purposes these claims were neither tortious nor contractual. In the second place, this case should not be regarded as establishing that every action for

---

[16] [1918] A.C. 563.
[17] [1994] 4 All E.R. 972.
[18] For the decision of the House of Lords on the validity of these contracts see *Hazell v Hammersmith & Fulham LBC* [1992] 2 A.C. 1.
[19] [1997] 4 All E.R. 641, HL.

money had and received is a contractual action for limitation purposes. Here the parties had purported to enter into a contract, so there was at least some contractual aspect to the case, but in other cases of money had and received (such as money paid under mistake of fact) it would be quite implausible to argue for s.5. Unless these actions are to be regarded as tort actions—surely an equally implausible outcome—it will have to be accepted that no period of limitation is applicable. Of course, once this principle is conceded, there is no longer any good reason why it should not apply equally to all cases of money had and received. In *Jim Ennis Construction Ltd v Premier Asphalt Ltd*[20] Judge Stephen Davies expressed the view, obiter, that the arguments made in this paragraph are incorrect. He preferred the view of *Goff & Jones*[21] that s.5 applies to such claims. It is submitted, nevertheless, that as a matter of ordinary construction an action for money had and received cannot be an action founded on simple contract. Frequently the action is based on an argument that there is in fact no contract, which is the antithesis of what s.5 covers.

Quasi-contract[22]

Most developed systems of law recognise certain obligations that do not fit   4.008
neatly into the common classification of tort and contract. These are variously described as quasi-contractual or as restitutionary. Among the many problems to which they give rise is that of classifying them for the purposes of limitation. It has been suggested that these obligations are properly classified under contract,[23] since they depend upon an implied or fictitious contract between the parties.[24] It is submitted, however, that this theory does not command wide acceptance, and that English law has moved some way in the direction of accepting these obligations as forming a third branch of the law of obligations.[25] The consequence of this is that few lawyers today would accept that such obligations are founded on contract. However, it may be, though the point has never been directly decided, that these obligations will be treated as founded on contract for the very specific

---

[20] [2009] EWHC 1906 (TCC).
[21] Para.43-002.
[22] For an analysis of the law of limitation of actions in relation to restitutionary claims, a type of claim which does not exist as a separate category within the Limitation Act 1980, see McLean (1989) 48 C.L.J. 472.
[23] C.H.S. Preston and G.N. Newsom, *Limitation of Actions* (3rd edn, 1953), pp.33–35.
[24] *Sinclair v Brougham* [1914] A.C. 398 at 415, per Lord Haldane.
[25] See, e.g., *B.P. Exploration Co. (Libya) Ltd v Hunt (No. 2)* [1979] 1 W.L.R. 783, Robert Goff J. affirmed without reference to this point [1983] 2 A.C. 352, HL. In this particular case it is at least arguable that the 1980 Act s.9 (recovery of sums due under an enactment) applies. See Ch.11.

purposes of the Limitation Act. If they are founded neither on contract nor on tort, the apparent result is that no period of limitation applies to them.[26] In the light of *Kleinwort Benson Ltd v S. Tyneside MBC*[27] it is doubtful whether a court would be prepared to reach this admittedly inconvenient result.[28]

Libel and slander

4.009 It should be noted that an action for defamation, although normally regarded as an action founded on tort, is not now governed by s.2 of the 1980 Act. Instead, s.4A[29] imposes a time-limit of one year from the date of accrual for the bringing of such an action, though this is subject to extension in certain circumstances.[30]

ACTION FOUNDED ON SIMPLE CONTRACT

4.010 The Limitation Act does not define the expression "simple contract". It was defined by Blackstone[31] as:

"where the contract upon which the obligation arises is neither ascertained by matter of record, nor yet by deed or special instrument, but by mere oral evidence, the most simple of any; or by notes unsealed, which are capable of more easy proof, and (therefore only) better than a verbal promise."

This definition may be accepted as useful for distinguishing simple contracts from special contracts. The distinction between simple contractual obligations and obligations in tort is considered in the following paragraph.

CONCURRENT RIGHTS IN CONTRACT AND TORT

4.011 The question whether a plaintiff could have concurrent rights of the same content against the same defendant in both contract and tort has been a

---

[26] This assumes that the remedies are of a common law character. In the case of equitable remedies the doctrine of laches would apply. See further para.3.014.

[27] [1994] 4 All E.R. 972.

[28] See also *West Sussex Properties Ltd v Chichester District Council*, June 28, 2000, Unreported, CA, for support for the proposition that claims based on unjust enrichment will fall within s.5 of the Limitation Act 1980.

[29] As inserted by the Administration of Justice Act 1985, s.57 and amended by the Defamation Act 1996, s.5. From 1985 to 1996 the limit was three years.

[30] See paras 8.071–8.078.

[31] 2 Blackstone's Commentaries 465.

vexed one over the past century, and has become more important as the ambit of tort has successively been widened and then narrowed by judicial decision-making. For the moment the definitive answer is to be found in the decision of the House of Lords in *Henderson v Merrett Syndicates*,[32] where it was held that a voluntary assumption of responsibility under a contract will normally create a concurrent duty in tort, unless the terms of the contract exclude the existence of such a tortious duty.[33]

Action for devastavit

"*Devastavit*" is the term used to describe a breach of duty by a personal representative in dealing with the estate of the deceased. Perhaps the most common example is the distribution of the estate to the beneficiaries without taking proper steps to pay the creditors. Such conduct leaves the personal representative liable to meet the debts out of his own pocket. It has been suggested that this action against the personal representative is properly to be regarded as founded upon contract,[34] but it is submitted that this is incorrect—there is no contract between the parties, nor is there any justification for implying one, and consequently the action should be treated as founded on tort.[35] The action for *devastavit* should not be confused with an action against the estate of a deceased person. This is dealt with in Ch.14.[36]   **4.012**

Action on a specialty

A specialty has been said to be: **4.013**

> "an archaic word of somewhat imprecise meaning; it includes contracts and other obligations in documents under seal, and also, traditionally, obligations arising under statutes".[37]

Section 8 of the 1980 Act provides that the time-limit for an action on a specialty is 12 years from the date of accrual. As this is a contract action, the cause of action is treated as accruing at the date of the breach. It should be observed that s.8(2) of the 1980 Act provides that the 12-year time-limit does not apply to any action for which a shorter period of limitation is

---

[32] [1994] 3 All E.R. 506.
[33] The earlier authorities are analysed at pp.46–47 of the 2nd edn of this book.
[34] Preston and Newsom, *Limitation of Actions*, p.25.
[35] See further paras 4.008–4.011.
[36] See paras 14.028–14.031.
[37] G. Franks, *Limitation of Actions* (3rd ed., 1959), p.188, approved by Potter J. in *Aiken v Stewart Wrightson Members" Agency Ltd* [1994] 3 All E.R. 449 at 459.

expressly provided by the Act. This point is of importance in considering the relationship between specialties and obligations under statute.[38]

Action to recover a sum of money due under statute

4.014   Section 9 of the 1980 Act imposes a time-limit of six years from the date of accrual for the bringing of actions under this head. As this is the same as the limits in respect of actions in tort and simple contract, the distinctions between these categories will be significant only if it can be shown that the cause of action accrues at a different time.[39] A long-standing problem of categorisation in this area has been that statutes are sealed. It has therefore been argued that an action upon a statute is an action on a specialty, so that the period of limitation is 12 years. The simple answer to this point is that s.8(2) of the 1980 Act disapplies the general 12-year rule where any shorter period of limitation is provided for by another section, and that s.9 is just such a section.[40] Some earlier authorities have suggested a distinction between an action "upon" a statute and an action on a cause of action given by statute. *Brueton v Woodward*[41] is perhaps the best example of this. The plaintiff sued for the recovery of gaming debts, pursuant to the Gaming Acts 1835 and 1922. Singleton J. held that this was an action on the statute rather than on a cause of action given by the statute, so that the period was 12 years. Singleton J. relied on some earlier authorities,[42] but it must be said that the distinction sought to be drawn in this case is a very difficult one.

4.015   By contrast, in *Pegler v Railways Executive*[43] the House of Lords affirmed the view of the lower courts[44] that an action to enforce a railwayman's right, conferred by statute, to compensation for loss of seniority suffered when two railway companies were merged was an action to recover a sum of money due under a statute, so that the period of limitation was six years. The point was further considered by the House of Lords in *Central Electricity Generating Board v Halifax Corporation*.[45] The CEGB was sued for a sum of compensation pursuant to the nationalisation of the electricity industry in 1948. The right to recover this sum was conferred by statute, and one[46] of the issues before the court was whether the period of

---

[38] See paras 4.022–4.024.
[39] As to accrual of a cause of action under statute, see paras 11.012–11.015.
[40] See *Leivers v Berber Walker & Co. Ltd* [1943] 1 All E.R. 386, CA; *Rowan Companies Inc. v Lambert Eggink Offshore Transport Consultants VOF* [1999] 2 Lloyd's Rep. 443, David Steel J.
[41] [1941] 1 K.B. 680.
[42] Notably, *Gutsell v Reeve* [1936] 1 K.B. 272, though it should be observed that the decision in this case went the other way.
[43] [1948] A.C. 332.
[44] [1947] 1 All E.R. 355, sub nom. *Pegler v Great Western Railway.*
[45] [1963] A.C. 785.
[46] For other issues in the case, see para.11.012.

limitation in respect of the claim was six years or 12 years. The House of Lords held that six years was the appropriate period, endorsing the argument suggested above that the provisions on sums due under statute are an express exception to the principle that the period of limitation for an action on a specialty is 12 years. It is by no means easy to see how this can be reconciled with *Pratt v Cook, Son & Co. (St Paul's) Ltd*,[47] where the House of Lords held that an action to recover deductions from wages which were forbidden by the Truck Act 1896 was an action upon a specialty. It is perhaps necessary to admit that the law in this area is now in an almost irretrievable state, since it appears that no satisfactory distinction can be drawn between cases, all of the highest authority, whose rationes decidendi appear to be in fundamental conflict.

Careful attention to the nature of the action is needed in order to resolve 4.016 this and some other related problems. There is room for a distinction between actions upon a statute and actions to recover a sum of money due under an enactment. Statutes may create a variety of rights, and not all of them will be rights to recover a sum of money. It is only those provisions which do confer such a right that are affected by s.9 of the 1980 Act. Other rights under statute, it is submitted, fall under s.8 as being actions upon a specialty, and the appropriate period of limitation is 12 years.[48] An excellent illustration of this distinction is provided by *Saif Rahman v Sterling Credit Ltd*.[49] In that case it was held that where a lender has obtained a possession order under a loan agreement secured on the borrower's property, but the order has not been executed, the borrower's application to reopen the agreement as an extortionate credit bargain under s.139 of the Consumer Credit Act 1974 in order to relieve himself from the obligation to make future payments is an action on a specialty (since no sum of money is claimed), to which a 12-year limitation period applies. By contrast, if the borrower were to seek repayment of sums already paid, that would be an action to recover a sum of money due under an enactment, and the limitation period would be six years. In the later case of *Nolan v Wright*[50] it was argued that *Saif Rahman* had proceeded on the basis of an incorrect concession by counsel, and that the decision was wrong. Judge Hodge held that the decision in *Saif Rahman* was correct, and the point should now be regarded as settled.

Similarly, in *Re Priory Garage (Walthamstow) Ltd*[51] and again in *Re* 4.017 *Nurkowski (A Bankrupt); Hill v Spread Trustee Company Limited And*

---

[47] [1940] A.C. 437, HL.
[48] *Rowan Companies Inc v Lambert Eggink Offshore Transport Consultants VOF*, [1999] 2 Lloyd's Rep. 443, David Steel J. For a further discussion of these issues see paras 4.033–4.038.
[49] July 20, 2000, Unreported CA.
[50] [2009] EWHC 305 (Ch) Judge Hodge QC.
[51] [2001] B.P.I.R. 202, John Randall QC.

Warr[52] it was held that applications to set aside transactions under the Inolvency Act 1986 are normally actions on a specialty (the statute) and subject to a 12-year limitation period. However, where the application involves seeking to recover a sum of money, that will be subject to s.9 of the Limitation Act 1980 as a claim to recover money due under a statute, and the limitation period will be six years.

4.018   An apt example of a non-monetary right under a statute was seen in the case of *Collin v Duke of Westminster*.[53] The plaintiff was the defendant's tenant, and sought to have his leasehold title enfranchised under the Leasehold Reform Act 1967. One of the questions before the Court of Appeal was the period of limitation applicable to such a claim. It was held that the tenant's rights arose not from the contract contained in his lease but from the relevant section of the statute. At the same time this is clearly not a case of suing to recover a sum of money due—the tenant's claim was for the freehold title rather than for money: consequently s.9 of the 1980 Act did not apply. As the tenant's claim was brought within 12 years of the accrual of the cause of action, it was unnecessary to decide whether the correct period was 12 years or longer, and the Court of Appeal contented itself with expressing the view that either this was an action on a specialty, so that the period was 12 years, or there was no applicable section of the 1980 Act, so that the claim was not liable to be time-barred. It is submitted that the former of these two possibilities is the correct one. This is an instance of a right under statute which is not caught by s.9. A further area of difficulty is illustrated by the decision of Lord Goddard C.J. in *West Riding of Yorkshire CC v Huddersfield Corporation*.[54] This was a claim for compensation under s.151 of the Local Government Act 1933 in respect of a boundary change made in 1937. The section provided that any dispute between the parties as to the appropriate sum payable should be referred to arbitration. The arbitration was eventually commenced in 1953, and the question was whether this was out of time. The Lord Chief Justice held that it was, rejecting an argument that the cause of action was the parties' failure to agree on compensation. The substance of the matter was that the right to compensation arose from the boundary change and was given by the statute. Consequently this must be regarded as an action to recover money due under a statute.

Meaning of "due under an enactment"

4.019   The theory advanced in the previous paragraph makes it necessary to consider what is meant in s.9 by the phrase "due under an enactment". A

---

[52] [2005] BPIR 842 Judge Weeks QC.
[53] [1985] Q.B. 581.
[54] [1957] Q.B. 540.

statute may, as in *Pegler v Railway Executive*,[55] confer a right to receive compensation, either of a set sum, or of a sum to be assessed according to a formula. In such a case it is submitted that s.9 clearly applies (and that the dicta in *Brueton v Woodward*[56] are wrong to the extent that they say otherwise). The matter has proved more controversial where the statute merely confers a right as against another private citizen and provides that damages or compensation may be recovered for the breach of that right. Three important examples here are the Patents Act 1977, the Misrepresentation Act 1967 and the Insolvency Act 1986. The Patents Act allows the grantee of a patent to recover damages from anyone who infringes that patent,[57] whilst the Misrepresentation Act provides that a person who makes a misrepresentation in pre-contractual negotiations shall, subject to conditions which are not material in this context, be liable in damages to the misrepresentee.[58] Section 214 of the Insolvency Act allows the court to require a director of an insolvent company, in certain circumstances, to contribute to the assets of the company at the suit of the liquidator. It might be thought that none of these actions falls within s.9, as no sum of money is made payable by the statute, i.e. all the claims arising under these provisions are for unliquidated damages. In *Sevcon Ltd v Lucas CAV Ltd*[59] the House of Lords said, obiter, that an action in respect of patent infringement is an action in tort for the purposes of the 1980 Act. Thus, the same six-year period applies as would apply if the case fell within s.9.

The idea that actions under the Misrepresentation Act 1967 are founded neither on tort nor on contract is supported by a dictum of Bridge L.J. in *Howard Marine and Dredging Co. v Ogden*,[60] though this would still leave open the possibility of holding that the case falls within s.9. In relation to this Act there is the further point that damages in this action are assessed on either the contractual[61] or the tortious[62] basis, and there may seem to be something odd about holding that damages are assessed on a basis which is

4.020

---

[55] [1948] A.C. 332.
[56] [1941] 1 K.B. 680.
[57] Patents Act 1977 s.13(4).
[58] Misrepresentation Act 1967 s.2(1).
[59] [1986] 1 W.L.R. 462.
[60] [1978] Q.B. 574 at 596.
[61] The contractual measure of damages is supported, to a greater or lesser extent, by *Gosling v Anderson* [1972] E.G.D. 709, Graham J., CA; *Jarvis v Swan Tours* [1973] 1 Q.B. 233, CA; *Davis & Co. (Wines) Ltd v Afa-Minerva (EMI) Ltd* [1974] 2 Lloyd's Rep. 27, Judge Fay as High Court Judge; *Watts v Spence* [1976] Ch.165 (the strongest and clearest authority on this side of the argument).
[62] The tortious measure receives support from *F. & H. Entertainments Ltd v Leisure Enterprises Ltd* (1976) 240 E.G. 455, Walton J.; *Andre et Cie SA v Ets Michel Blanc et Fils* [1977] 2 Lloyd's Rep. 166, Ackner J.; *McNally v Welltrade International* [1978] I.R.L.R. 497, Sir Douglas Franks Q.C. as High Court Judge; *Sharneyford Supplies Ltd v Edge* [1986]. Ch. 128, Mervyn Davies J. (the strongest and clearest authority on this side of the case). It is noticeable that the more recent trend is strongly in favour of the tort measure, and this is now generally accepted as being the correct approach.

apparently not appropriate to the basis of the action. The general issue of the ambit of s.9 was considered at length in *Moore v Gadd*,[63] a case concerned with s.214 of the Insolvency Act 1986, where the liquidators argued for the application of s.8(1) of the Act.[64] The Court of Appeal rejected these arguments, holding that the sum of money which became payable did so by virtue of s.214, rather than by virtue of the exercise of any discretion by the court. Although s.214 clearly does involve an exercise of discretion, it is the section which makes the money payable. It is immaterial that there is discretion both as to liability, i.e. whether the director should pay anything, and as to quantum, i.e. how much the director should pay. Although it is accepted by the Court of Appeal in *Moore v Gadd* that the action is an action on a specialty—the statute—it must be remembered that, by virtue of s.8(2) of the 1980 Act, the 12-year period for an action on a specialty applies only where no other provision of the Act specifies a different period.

4.021   It seems to follow from the previous paragraph that the result will be different in cases where a statute imposes on a public body an obligation to do some act, and the plaintiff's claim is not for damages. The 1980 Act time-limits will not apply if the claim is for equitable relief,[65] such as an injunction, or for a public law remedy by way of judicial review. However, it is submitted that an action for a declaration in respect of failure to perform a duty under a statute (assuming that the duty is one which can be enforced by a private citizen) must be subject to the 12-year limit of s.8.

Relevance of the remedy

4.022   The applicability of the provisions relating to enactments may depend upon the remedy that is sought. This proposition is supported by the confusing case of *Moody v Mayor of Poole*.[66] The plaintiff was responsible for carrying out street works in front of the defendant's premises, and claimed to be statutorily entitled to recover a proportion of the cost of the works from the defendant. When the defendant failed to pay that money, the plaintiff sought a declaration that he was entitled to a charging order on the defendant's premises under the relevant statute. The defendant argued that the action was barred as being one to recover a sum of money due under an enactment (for which the limitation period is six years). The Court of Appeal held the action was in substance one for equitable relief, namely an order for the sale of the property, so that s.2(7) of the 1939 Act (now s.36 of the 1980 Act) disapplied the rules relating to limitation periods and the

---

[63] (1997) 141 S.J.L.B. 45; *The Times*, February 17, 1997, CA.
[64] The arguments presented by the liquidators bear a distinct resemblance to those in para.4.019.
[65] 1980 Act, s.36.
[66] [1945] K.B. 350, CA.

action was not time-barred. This is a striking example of the Court looking to what it perceives as the substance of the action rather than to the specific relief claimed by the plaintiff. No doubt the ultimate step in this dispute would have been an application for an order for sale, but it is clear that the plaintiff had not yet reached that stage, and therefore it is very difficult to understand how the Court of Appeal can legitimately apply the limitation period appropriate to a different form of claim.

CONTRACT OR STATUTE

In *Cork & Bandon Railway Co. v Goode*[67] the company sued a shareholder **4.023** for unpaid calls on his shares. The action was based on the company's private Act of Parliament and on the Companies Clauses Consolidation Act 1845. It was held that the action was one upon a specialty,[68] to which a 20-year period applied. By contrast, in *Aylott v West Ham Corporation*[69] the defendant corporation passed a resolution in 1914 that they would make up the pay of any employee who lost salary through joining the armed services. At the time this resolution was unlawful, but it was retrospectively validated by an Act of 1916. Disputes arose as to the amount to which the plaintiff was entitled under the resolution, and this action was brought. Because of the lapse of time it became necessary to decide whether the action was founded on simple contract or on specialty. The Court of Appeal held that the basis of the action was the contract of employment, which had been varied by the resolution of 1914.

One difficulty with this analysis was that the variation was made effective **4.024** only by the 1916 Act,[70] but the Court of Appeal nevertheless held that this was an action upon a right of action given by the statute, rather than upon the statute itself.[71] Similarly, in *Gutsell v Reeve*[72] a farm labourer who had been paid less than the statutory minimum wage sued for arrears of pay, as the statute permitted him to do. The Court of Appeal held that this was an action based on contract, since the statute merely modified the existing contract of employment rather than creating a new one. The three decisions may be reconciled by saying that in *Bandon* there could have been no contract without the statute, whereas in *Aylott* and *Gutsell* there clearly

---

[67] (1853) 13 C.B. 826 see also *Re Cornwall Minerals Rly Co.* [1897] 2 Ch. 74, Vaughan Williams J.
[68] i.e. the Acts of Parliament. As to the effect of this see now paras 4.034–4.036. *R. v Williams* [1942] 2 All E.R. 95, PC, which appears to hold the contrary, is perhaps best explained as relating only to the question of the situs of the debt on the shares.
[69] [1927] 1 Ch. 30, Romer J., CA.
[70] The Local Government (Emergency Provisions) Act 1916, 6 & 7 Geo. 5, c.12.
[71] See *Re Cornwall Minerals Rly Co.* [1897] 2 Ch. 74; *Salford Corp. v Lancashire C.C.* (1890) 25 Q.B.D. 384; *Thomson v Lord Clanmorris* [1900] 1 Ch. 718.
[72] [1936] 1 K.B. 272, CA.

was a contract independently of the statute. However, a comparison of the two cases shows that the categorisation adopted may depend upon which element of the facts the court chooses to emphasise.[73]

TORT OR STATUTE

4.025　The distinction between actions in tort and actions under statute has occasionally fallen for consideration, though it does not appear to have arisen directly in a limitation of action context. In *Post Office v Official Solicitor*[74] Barry J. had to decide whether the Post Office's right under the Workmens' Compensation Acts 1906–1925[75] to recover from a tortfeasor who had injured one of their postmen the amount of the disability pension which they were thereby obliged to pay to him was an action founded on tort for the purposes of the Law Reform (Miscellaneous Provisions) Act 1934. His Lordship said[76]:

> "In my view a claim of this description is clearly not a claim in tort. It is a claim for indemnity, payable under the provisions of a statute, and is in no sense an action founded on tort."

By contrast, in *Sevcon Ltd v Lucas CAV Ltd*[77] the House of Lords assumed that an action under the Patents Act for patent infringement was an action founded on tort for the purposes of limitation. It is submitted that the decision of Barry J. is to be preferred. However, the point is of importance only where, as in *Collin v Duke of Westminster*,[78] the choice is between the six-year tort period and the 12-year specialty period. In the more common case the period will be six years whichever result is reached, since the choice is between tort (the 1980 Act s.2) and recovery of sum due under enactment (the 1980 Act s.9).

---

[73] See also Salford Corp. v Lancashire C.C. (1890) 25 Q.B.D. 384; Re Cornwall Minerals Rly Co. [1897] 2 Ch. 74.

[74] [1951] 1 All E.R. 522.

[75] But see also *Leivers v Berber Walkers & Co. Ltd* [1943] 1 All E.R. 386, where the Court of Appeal held that the 1939 Act had no application to the Workmens' Compensation Acts 1906–1925, since those statutes had their own system of limitation periods: see further paras 26.005–26.019.

[76] *Post Office v Official Solicitor* [1951] 1 All E.R. 522 at 527.

[77] [1986] 1 W.L.R. 462.

[78] [1985] Q.B. 581, CA.

ACTION FOR PERSONAL INJURIES

There are special rules as to limitation periods where the action is for damages for personal injuries.[79] This term is partially defined in s.38(1) of the 1980 Act: **4.026**

"Personal injuries" includes any disease and any impairment of a person's physical or mental condition, and "injury" and cognate expressions shall be construed accordingly.

Unfortunately, this definition is largely unhelpful in resolving questions of difficulty in categorisation. Some points of construction in respect of s.11 and the 1980 Act are worthy of comment.

Mixed causes of action

First, the special personal injury rules apply to cases where the damages claimed consist of or include damages for personal injuries.[80] Therefore, an action in which the plaintiff wishes to claim damages for personal injury and for some other cause of action must be brought within the period provided for personal injury actions.[81] If that period has expired, an action may still be brought for the other items of damage, since the personal injury rules will not apply if the damages claimed do not include anything in respect of personal injuries. It should also be stressed that the personal injuries period will apply even where the personal injuries are caused by a breach of contract. **4.027**

Economic loss

In *Pattison v Hobbs*[82] the plaintiffs sued the doctor who had purportedly performed a vasectomy on the male plaintiff. The claim was for the economic loss resulting from the female plaintiff's subsequent pregnancy, the operation having proved ineffective. The Court of Appeal said that this was not an action for personal injuries within the meaning of the 1980 Act, since the only damage alleged to have been caused was the extra expense of bringing up an additional child. By contrast it has been held in similar circumstances that a claim by the mother for wrongful birth is a claim for **4.028**

---

[79] See Ch.8.
[80] 1980 Act s.11(1).
[81] *Bennett v Greenland Houchen & Co.*, January 28, 1998, Unreported, CA.
[82] *The Times*, November 11, 1985.

personal injuries within the meaning of the 1980 Act.[83] The cases are clearly distinguishable, since the father certainly suffers no bodily impairment, even of a temporary kind, whereas the mother does.

Cause of personal injuries

4.029   The special rules apply to cases of personal injury caused by "negligence, nuisance or breach of duty".[84] The expression "breach of duty" has given rise to certain difficulties. It extends to cases of unintentional trespass to the person,[85] but not to cases of intentional trespass to the person,[86] though an action for damages for failing to prevent another from causing deliberate physical injury is within the notion of "breach of duty" so that s.11 does apply.[87]

4.030   The case of *Ackbar v C.F. Green & Co. Ltd*[88] illustrates the limits of the rules on personal injuries. The plaintiff instructed the defendant insurance brokers to obtain insurance cover protecting him against personal injury. They failed to do so and, on suffering injury, the plaintiff found himself uninsured. He sued the brokers, who pleaded limitation on the basis that this was an action for personal injuries. Croom-Johnson J. reiterated the basic rule that the essential task in categorisation is to identify the true basis of the action, and went on to hold that in this case the essence of the action was the brokers' breach of duty, rather than the plaintiff's personal injuries. Consequently the action must be regarded as being founded on simple contract, so that the limitation period was six years. It should be observed, however, that the limitation period for a breach of contract that causes personal injuries is three years, since a breach of contract is also a breach of duty within s.11. Ackbar was distinguished by the Court of Appeal in *Norman v Ali and MIB*,[89] where the action was against the owner of a vehicle who had allowed it to be driven without insurance.[90] The Court of Appeal said that in such a case the breach of duty by the owner of the car arises only when the accident is caused, and the victim of the accident is in effect suing for damages for personal injuries.

4.031   In *Lefevre v White*[91] the plaintiff brought a successful personal injuries action against the defendant, and the latter became bankrupt. The plaintiff therefore sought to sue the defendant's liability insurers under the 1930

---

[83] *Walkin v s.Manchester HA* [1995] 4 All E.R. 132, CA.
[84] 1980 Act s.11.
[85] *Letang v Cooper* [1964] 2 Q.B. 53, Elwes J.; [1965] 1 Q.B. 232, CA. See further paras 27.002 et seq.
[86] *Stubbings v Webb* [1993] 1 All E.R. 332, HL.
[87] *S v W* [1995] 1 F.L.R. 862.
[88] [1975] Q.B. 538.
[89] [2000] L.R.I.R. 395, CA.
[90] Based on *Monk v Warbey* [1935] 1 K.B. 75, CA.
[91] [1990] 1 Lloyd's Rep. 569, Popplewell J.

Act, but the writ against the insurers was issued out of time, assuming the action to be based on simple contract and therefore not subject to discretionary extension by the court. The plaintiff's action under the 1930 Act takes its classification from the nature of the defendant's rights against his own liability insurers, since it is those rights which are transferred to the plaintiff when the defendant becomes bankrupt. The rights are therefore contractual in nature, and in most cases the ordinary limitation period of six years will apply. This will be so even where, as here, the damages which the plaintiff originally claimed were damages for personal injuries, since the defendant's action against his own liability insurers is not a claim for personal injuries, but for the insurers' breach of contract in not paying the claim.

The Alnwick[92] considered a point about personal injuries in a maritime **4.032** context. Actions against ships are in general governed by s.190 of the Merchant Shipping Act 1995,[93] which includes a special two-year time-limit for the bringing of actions under it (subject to a judicial discretion to extend that time). The *Alnwick* confirms that the provisions of the Merchant Shipping Act still apply when the action is one for personal injuries.

ACTIONS IN RESPECT OF LATENT DAMAGE

The importance of actions in respect of latent damage as a separate cate- **4.033** gory of actions dates only from the Latent Damage Act 1986,[94] which introduces a new set of limitation rules for them. The effect of s.14A of the Limitation Act 1980, as inserted by the Latent Damage Act, is that the new rules apply to any action for damages for negligence (other than a personal injuries action) where the plaintiff does not know of the existence of the cause of action until a day later than that on which it accrued. This will cover a great many negligence actions,[95] but it should be noted that it does not apply to an action for the breach of any stricter duty, whether imposed by law or arising out of an agreement between the parties. Thus, it does not apply to actions in contract.[96]

---

[92] [1965] p.357, CA.
[93] Replacing the former Maritime Conventions Act 1911 s.8. See Ch.24.
[94] This statute is considered in detail in Ch.6.
[95] The ambit of the Act is not restricted to claims for latent property damage: *Kecskemeti v Rubens Rabin & Co., The Times*, December 31, 1992, McPherson J. See further para.6.003.
[96] *Iron Trades Mutual Insurance Co. Ltd v J.K. Buckenham Ltd* [1990] 1 All E.R. 808, Kenneth Rokison Q.C.; *Islander Trucking Ltd v Hogg Robinson* [1990] 1 All E.R. 826, Evans J.

ACTION TO RECOVER LAND

4.034   Most dispositions of land are required to be under seal, but the 1980 Act contains special provisions to deal with dispossession from land,[97] actions to recover the proceeds of sale of land[98] and mortgages.[99] These provisions override the general rule in s.8, and the special problems which they create are dealt with in Ch.13.

SIMPLE CONTRACT OR SPECIALTY?

4.035   The period of limitation for an action based on simple contract is six years[100] whereas for an action on a specialty it is 12 years.[101] In either case, time runs from the breach of the contract.[102] The 1980 Act does not define either type of contract, and the meanings of the two expressions have been considered above.[103] Some problems can arise in commercial contracts and in conveyancing practice. Where a commercial agreement under hand is entered into with the intention that it will in due course be replaced by a deed, it is a question of fact whether the deed is intended to have retrospective effect, so that it applies to causes of action arising between the execution of the agreement under hand and the execution of the deed.[104] There is no rule of law that a deed cannot be retrospective. Where a purchase of property takes place by the traditional method of exchange of contracts followed by the execution of a transfer,[105] which will take the form of a deed, the question may arise whether the limitation period in respect of physical defects in the property is six years or 12. There does not appear to be any authority bearing on this point, but it is submitted that the vital question is whether the vendor's obligation on which the action is based exists from the time of the contract, i.e. is contained in a provision of the contract. If so, then the action is based on simple contract; if not, it must be an action on a specialty. In the great majority of cases this approach will lead to the action being treated as an action of simple contract.

4.036   An obligation may be specifically declared by statute to be a specialty. The best-known example is that contained in s.14 of the Companies Act

---

[97] 1980 Act, s.15.
[98] 1980 Act, s.20
[99] 1980 Act, s.18.
[100] 1980 Act, s.5.
[101] 1980 Act, s.8.
[102] *Gould v Johnson* (1702) 2 Salk. 422; *Gibbs v Guild* (1881) 8 Q.B.D. 296. See para.10.002.
[103] See paras 4.006–4.014.
[104] *Tameside Metropolitan B.C. v Barlow Securities Group Services Ltd* (1999) 75 Con. L.R. 112, TCC, Judge Gilliland Q.C.
[105] Or a conveyance in the diminishing number of cases where title is not already registered.

1985, which declares that the obligations of the members of a company under its memorandum and articles to pay money to the company to be of the nature of a specialty. The same rule applies to the obligations of a contributory in a winding-up.[106] An action by a creditor against the liquidator or receiver of a company is, for limitation purposes, an action in tort.[107] There is conflicting authority on the extent to which a company's obligations to its members are to be regarded as specialties. In the most recent authority on this point, *Re Compania de Electricidad de la Provincia de Buenos Aires Ltd*,[108] Slade J. held that an action by a shareholder to recover dividends due from the company is an action in simple contract, rather than an action upon a specialty. Section 14 of the Companies Act, which creates the contract among the members, does not expressly make the company a party to that contract. It has been held that the company must be treated as a party,[109] but it does not follow from this that the company must be deemed to have executed the contract as a deed. This point is further reinforced by the fact that s.14(2) makes debts payable to the company specialties, but omits to do the same thing for debts payable by the company. In reaching this conclusion Slade J. refused to follow the decision in *Re Artisans Land & Mortgage Corporation*.[110] It is submitted that he was right to do so, for the reasons set out in this paragraph.

The decision in *Re Art Reproduction Ltd*[111] shows that the different periods of limitation in ss.5 and 8 of the 1980 Act may make it necessary to identify carefully which contract is the basis of the action. The plaintiff had been a company director employed under a sealed contract. Shortly before that contract was due to expire, the company passed a resolution to the effect that "the present arrangements shall continue". The question was whether the plaintiff was employed under a special contract after the term of the sealed contract had expired.Wynn-Parry J. held that he was not, it being impossible to retain the special character of the arrangement other than by executing a further deed. Consequently the effect of the resolution was to create a new and simple contract, to which the provisions of s.5 applied.

Where a contract is under seal the 12-year period applies to an action for general damages for breach of any obligation arising under it.[112]

4.037

---

[106] Companies Act 1985, s.508.

[107] *Westminster City Council v Haste* [1950] Ch. 442, Danckwerts J.

[108] [1980] Ch. 146.

[109] *Wood v Odessa Waterworks Co.* (1889) 42 Ch.D. 636, CA.

[110] [1904] 1 Ch. 796; see also *Re Cornwall Minerals Rly Co.* [1987] 2 Ch. 74, where Vaughan Williams J. held that the obligation to pay interest on debentures whose issue was authorised by statute was a liability on the statute. This case also appears unsupportable.

[111] [1952] Ch. 89, Wynn-Parry J.

[112] *Aiken v Stewart Wrightson Members' Agency Ltd* [1994] 3 All E.R. 449, Potter J.

SUING ON A JUDGMENT

4.038   An action may be brought on a judgment at any time within six years of the date of that judgment.[113] An important distinction in this area is illustrated by *Lowsley v Forbes*,[114] where it was held that the enforcement of a judgment is not the same as bringing an action on it. The latter involves bringing an action and is subject to the 1980 Act, whereas the latter is a purely procedural matter, to which the 1980 Act has no relevance.

JUDGMENT OR CONTRACT

4.039   In *Re Compania de la Electricidad de Buenos Aires Ltd*[115] one of the questions before Slade J. concerned the correct classification of the company's obligation to repay capital to shareholders pursuant to a reduction of capital scheme which had been sanctioned by the court. It was held that this is either a case of recovering money due under an enactment (the power to authorise such reductions being conferred by the Companies Act) or an action on a simple contract: it was unnecessary to decide between these two, since in either event the period of limitation would be six years. Slade J. held that this is not a case of an action on a judgment, a decision that appears to limit the scope of the term "judgment" as used in the Act. The precise limits of the term are unclear, but it may be suggested that there will only be a judgment for these purposes where there is a contested issue between a number of parties. However, this suggestion leaves open the position where creditors exercise their right to object to a proposed reduction, which is nevertheless confirmed by the Court.

TRUST AND FIDUCIARY DUTY

4.040   *Gwembe Valley v Koshy*[116] was a complex case in which there were claims for an account of profits against a company director. From a limitation point of view one crucial issue was what limitation period applied. The Court of Appeal said that having regard to settled principle, the starting point when considering the application of the 1980 Act to claims against fiduciaries[117] was the assumption that a six-year limitation period would

---

[113] 1980 Act s.24; see also paras 17.003–17.005.
[114] [1999] A.C. 329, HL, affirming principles laid down in *W.T. Lamb & Sons v Rider* [1948] 2 K.B. 331, *CA and Natwest Bank v Powney* [1991] Ch. 339, CA; see also para.2.002.
[115] [1980] Ch. 146.
[116] [2003] EWCA Civ 1478, [2003] All ER (D) 465 (Jul).
[117] See also Ch.14.

apply, either directly or by analogy under one or other provisions of the 1980 Act, unless the limitation period was specifically excluded by the Act or established case law. However, where a director had trustee like responsibilities in the exercise of the powers of management of the property of a claimant, the claim for an account, if based on a failure in the exercise of those responsibilities, fell within the scope of s.21 of the 1980 Act, and was in principle subject to the six-year period under s.21(3). If the defendant acted fraudulently, then that would bring s.21(1) into operation, and no limitation period would apply[118].

This approach may be regarded as being in line with other cases in recent years where the attempt to bring actions against fiduciaries generally within s.21 has been rejected.

SUBROGATION

Subrogation is the right of a person who has given indemnity to another under a contractual obligation, to stand in the shoes of that other in respect of any right which the other has that may go to diminish the loss for which the indemnity has been given.[119] The right cannot be exercised until the indemnity has been given, but for limitation purposes the vital point is that the indemnifier stands in the shoes of the indemnified. In *Orakpo v Manson Investments*[120] the Court of Appeal held that the right of the indemnifier to sue is synonymous with the right of the indemnified. It therefore follows that there is no separate category of subrogation rights for limitation purposes.   **4.041**

THE LAW COMMISSION'S PROPOSALS

Much of this chapter would become obsolete if the Law Commission's proposals were adopted, since many of the different categories of action for limitation purposes would be merged into the single core regime. A few issues would remain, however, notably that of actions arising from personal injuries. Given that cases within this category would have the possibility of discretionary extension of time, it would obviously be important to have case law defining what the term means.   **4.042**

---

[118] See also *Paragon Finance Plc v DB Thackerer & Co* [1999] 1 All ER 400 C.A.
[119] For a detailed treatment of subrogation, see A. McGee, *The Modern Law of Insurance*, 2nd edn (2006), Ch.22.
[120] [1978] A.C. 95.

CHAPTER 5

Actions Founded on Tort

Section 2 of the 1980 Act prohibits the bringing of an action founded on **5.001** tort[1] more than six years[2] (one year in the case of an action for defamation[3]) after the date on which the cause of action accrued. This rule is modified in those cases to which the Latent Damage Act 1986 applies,[4] but even under that Act the date of accrual of action is one of the dates from which time may run. It is therefore vital in all tort cases to be able to identify accurately the date on which the cause of action accrues.

GENERAL PRINCIPLES

In the absence of statutory guidance it has been left to the courts to establish **5.002** the test for deciding when a cause of action in tort accrues. The specific issues which have arisen are considered below, but it is appropriate to begin with a restatement of the general principles in this area. For this purpose torts may conveniently be divided into three categories, as follows:

(1) torts actionable per se: cause of action accrues on commission of wrong[5];

(2) continuing torts: a fresh cause of action accrues every day,[6] but the right to bring an action is restricted to that part of the wrong committed in the past six years[7];

---

[1] For the meaning of "an action founded on tort", see Ch.4.
[2] In the case of an action against the Post Office in respect of postal packets, the Post Office Act 1969 s.30(1) substitutes a period of 12 months.
[3] 1980 Act s.4A, as substituted by the Defamation Act 1996, s.5.
[4] See Ch.6.
[5] *Hipperson v Chief Constable of Ministry of Defence Police*, June 26, 1996, CA, Unreported.
[6] *Darley Main Colliery v Mitchell* (1886) 11 App.Cas. 127, HL.
[7] *Hardy v Ryle* (1829) 9 B. & C. 603.

(3) single torts requiring proof of damage: cause of action accrues when damage happens, and this rule applies in both negligence[8] and nuisance.[9]

(1) Torts actionable per se

5.003 Relatively few torts fall into the category of torts actionable per se. Perhaps the most important example is certain forms of defamation, namely libel and those classes of slander that do not require proof of special damage.[10] It may be observed that defamation, though not a continuing tort, is one which is capable of being repeated. Indeed, there is a fresh cause of action on every new publication of the defamation.[11] Consequently, an action can be brought in respect of any publication which happened within the preceding year.[12] False imprisonment[13] is also actionable per se,[14] as is trespass to land, though only at the instance of the person in possession[15]; so also is the wrong committed by an innkeeper who refuses accommodation to a traveller.[16]

(2) Continuing torts

5.004 Perhaps the most common example of continuing torts is a continuing nuisance. In these cases the right of action accrues afresh every day, but damages can be recovered only for that part of the loss which arose within the relevant period before the commencement of proceedings. This rule may also be important in certain personal injury cases, notably those cases of employers' liability which arise from failure to provide a safe system of

---

[8] *Pirelli General Cable Works v Oscar Faber and Partners Ltd* [1983] 2 A.C. 1, HL; the possible effect on English law of the decision in *Invercargill City Council v Hamlin* [1996] 1 All E.R. 756, PC, is considered below.

[9] Although proof of damage is normally required in nuisance, it appears that damage will readily be inferred: *Fay v Prentice* (1845) 1 C.B. 828. Note also that damage need not be proved where the nuisance is to an easement or profit à prendre: *Nicholls v Ely Beet Sugar Factory Ltd* [1936] Ch. 343.

[10] Allegation of offence punishable by imprisonment in the first instance, allegation of unfitness of profession, allegation of communicable disease and imputation of unchastity to any woman or girl (Slander of Women Act 1891).

[11] *Duke of Brunswick v Harmer* (1849) 14 Q.B. 185.

[12] The limit of one year in cases of defamation was substituted in s.4A of the 1980 Act by the Defamation Act 1996 s.5.

[13] Though in malicious prosecution the cause of action does not accrue until the prosecution is ended—*Dunlop v H.M. Customs & Excise* (1998) 142 S.J. L.B. 134, *The Times*, March 17, 1998, CA.

[14] *Coventry v Aspley* (1691) 2 Salk. 420.

[15] *Wordsworth v Harley* (1830) 1 B. & Ad. 391, where it was held that the reversioner was obliged to sue in case, which necessitated the proof of actual damage.

[16] *Constantine v Imperial Hotels* [1944] K.B. 693.

work. In such cases, difficulties have arisen in ascertaining exactly what damage has accrued within the limitation period.[17] Passing off is also a continuing tort, and a fresh cause of action accrues each day.[18] Another possible situation in this category is that of some omissions by professional advisers, where the wrong continues so long as the omission continues. For the effects of this see below, para.5.030. *In Phonographic Performance Ltd v Department of Trade and Industry and another*[19] the claimant brought an action for breach of statutory duty in the form of failure to comply by the deadline with Council Directive (EEC) 92/100 (the rental directive), which provided that member states were to provide a right in order to ensure that a single equitable remuneration was paid by the user, if a phonogram published for commercial purposes, or a reproduction of such a phonogram, was used for broadcasting by wireless means or for any communication to the public, and to ensure that this remuneration was shared between the relevant performers and phonogram producers. Morritt V-C, held that this claim was correctly characterised as a claim for breach of statutory duty and that this was a case of continuing breach, so that a fresh cause of action accrued every day while the Directive was not properly implemented. This appears correct in principle, since every day there must have been fresh instances where performers did not become entitled to royalties for the performance of music. By contrast, in *Aurangzeb Iqbal & Co (in liquidation) v Legal Services Commission*[20] the Defendant had stopped further payments to the claimant firm and had deducted amounts from sums already accrued due. It was held that the imposition of these measures was a single cause of action accruing on the date when they were first imposed.

Damage after the claim form

Another difficulty that is of relevance here arises where the damage continues after the writ has been issued. The general rule is that the plaintiff's cause of action must exist at the time when proceedings are commenced. Otherwise the action has been commenced prematurely, and is liable to be struck out under CPR 3.4 as disclosing no cause of action.[21] However, a distinction must be drawn here between cases where the cause of action has not accrued and cases where the cause of action has accrued but loss is continuing. A good example of the latter category is the personal injuries cases where at the time the writ is issued the plaintiff is still unable to work (with consequent loss of income) and is still experiencing pain and suffer-

5.005

---

[17] See further paras 8.061–8.062; see also *Masters v Brent LBC* [1978] Q.B. 841.
[18] *Global Projects Management Ltd v Citigroup Inc* [2005] EWHC 2663 (Ch) Park J.
[19] [2004] EWHC 1795 (Ch); [2005] 1 All ER 369; [2004] 1 WLR 2893; [2005] RPC 8; [2004] EMLR 647 Sir Andrew Morritt V-C.
[20] [2004] EWHC 1963 (QB), [2004] All ER (D) 54 (Aug) Judge Behrens.
[21] See further paras 21.003–21.005.

ing. In these cases it is possible to recover damages for both loss of income and pain and suffering occurring between the issue of the writ and the trial. The reason is that all the loss in question arises from the same cause of action, namely the original breach of duty by the defendant. By contrast, it would not be possible to amend the pleading so as to claim in respect of an entirely new cause of action arising after the issue of the original writ. Further, the date of trial is the latest date to which the continuing damage can be pleaded in this way. If it appears that the damage will continue after the date of trial, the court must either make a once and for all assessment of the total loss or make an award of provisional damages under s.116 of the Senior Courts Act 1981. If the plaintiff had suffered both damage to property and injury to his person arising out of the same wrong these would, however, be two separate causes of action, and could be prosecuted in separate actions with judgment in the first being no bar to the bringing of the second.[22]

(3) Single wrongs

5.006　It is in the area of single wrongs that the major difficulties have arisen in recent years. The basic rule is that the cause of action accrues when damage is suffered, and this may be said to follow from the principle[23] that the cause of action is complete only when there is a plaintiff who can sue and a defendant who can be sued, and when the ingredients of duty, breach and damage are all satisfied.[24] As is explained below,[25] the task of determining this date has proved extremely complex—matters are made more difficult still by the current controversy over the nature and extent of the losses that can be recovered in an action in tort.[26] Where there are two quite separate breaches of duty by the same defendant towards the same claimant at different times, there may be two different causes of action. In *Birmingham Midshires Building Society v J.D. Wretham*[27] the defendant firm of solicitors acted both for the purchaser of a property and for the plaintiff as mortgagee. The borrower had bought the property jointly with another for £44,500 and was borrowing £70,000 from the plaintiff, of which £42,000 was to be used to pay off his co-purchaser and the balance was to be applied elsewhere. The third defendants were aware of this and were also aware

---

[22] Thus in cases of bankruptcy, e.g. a right of action for damage to the bankrupt's property passes to the trustees in bankruptcy, whereas a right of action for personal injury to the bankrupt does not: *Boddington v Castelli* (1853) 1 E. & B. 879; *Wilson v United Counties Bank Ltd* [1920] A.C. 102.

[23] Apparent exceptions to this general principle are discussed at paras 5.048–5.056.

[24] *Coburn v Colledge* [1897] 1 Q.B. 702, CA.

[25] See paras 5.009–5.017.

[26] The relevance of this in a limitation context is considered at paras 5.016–5.017.

[27] November 30, 1998, Unreported, Judge Hicks Q.C.

that the plaintiff mistakenly thought that the borrower was buying the property for £100,000 and was providing the balance of the purchase price of £100,000 out of his own funds. However, the third defendants did not inform the plaintiff of those facts. The plaintiff did not become aware of those facts until 1995 and a writ was not issued until February 1997, alleging negligence on the part of the third defendants. At the time of the original mortgage transaction, the local search revealed that the property was subject to a demolition order, but the third defendants failed to reveal this to the plaintiff, who was informed of the existence of the demolition order in 1991. The third defendants argued that the limitation period in respect of their negligence had now expired. Since the plaintiff was aware of the admitted negligence concerning the demolition order, the fact that it did not discover the negligent failure to reveal the way in which the funds were being disbursed until 1995 was irrelevant. Hicks J. held that the negligent failure to disclose the existence of the demolition order was of a different kind from the negligent failure to disclose the nature of the transaction and gave rise to a different cause of action, so that the plaintiff was entitled to the benefit of s.14A since he had not been aware of the second breach.

Establishing the date of damage

The rule that time runs from the date of damage inevitably focuses attention on the problems of determining that date in any given case. The problems have been extensively explored in the case law. The traditional analysis of the law of tort has been in terms of duty, breach and damage, and these have normally been regarded as the elements which must be present to found a cause of action in tort for the purposes of the Limitation Acts.[28] The two major difficulties have been, first, an argument that the cause of action does not accrue until the plaintiff discovers or could with reasonable diligence discover the existence of the damage (the date at which this occurs is commonly referred to as the "date of discoverability")[29] and, secondly, some doubt over exactly when damage does occur, especially in cases of economic loss.[30] In fact this doubt arises principally from some uncertainty as to what exactly the law now means by the term "damage".

5.007

---

[28] *Cooke v Gill* (1873) L.R. 8, C.P. 107; *Coburn v Colledge* [1897] 1 Q.B. 702, CA. See also Ch.4.

[29] See *Dutton v Bognor Regis UDC* [1972] 1 Q.B. 373, CA; *Sparham-Souter v Town & Country Developments* [1976] Q.B. 858; *Pirelli General Cable Works v Oscar Faber and Partners* [1983] 2 A.C. 1, HL.

[30] *Forster v Outred* [1982] 1 W.L.R. 86; 98 L.Q.R. 514; *Baker v Ollard & Bentley* (1982) 126 S.J. 593; *D.W. Moore & Co. Ltd v Ferrier* [1988] 1 W.L.R. 267; 104 L.Q.R. 376; *Lee v Thompson* (1989) 40 E.G. 89, CA. See also paras 5.025 et seq.

The "date of discoverability" issue

5.008   In *Cartledge v E. Jopling & Sons Ltd*[31] the House of Lords rejected an argument that in cases of personal injury time ran only from the date of discoverability, holding instead that the commencement date for the period of limitation was the earliest date at which the plaintiff had suffered more than minimal damage as a result of the defendant's breach of duty. This result was reversed, for personal injury cases only, by the Limitation Act 1963 (the 1963 Act),[32] but it was for many years unclear whether the same rule applied to tort cases not involving personal injuries.[33] A fundamental decision on this matter was taken in *Pirelli General Cable Works v Oscar Faber and Partners*.[34] The case took the form of the trial of a preliminary issue[35] on the following assumed facts. The defendants were architects who were engaged to design a new factory for the plaintiffs. On their recommendation the chimneys were lined with Lytag, a material that subsequently proved unsuitable for the purpose. The work was completed in 1969, and the following year cracks developed in the chimneys, although these were not reasonably discoverable by the plaintiffs before October 1972. They were not in fact discovered until much later, and the plaintiffs' writ was not issued until October 1978. The defendant pleaded limitation, and the issue before the House of Lords was when the cause of action accrued. It was unanimously held that the vital date was the date when the cracks in the chimneys came into existence, and that it was irrelevant that the plaintiffs could not reasonably have been expected to discover these cracks until some time later. All the members of the House accepted that this was an unsatisfactory result, but felt impelled as a matter of logic to reach it.

The decision in *Pirelli* prompted a reference of the problems of undiscoverable causes of action to the Law Reform Committee, and their 24th Report[36] recommended a number of important changes. These changes were enacted in the Latent Damage Act 1986 (see Ch.6), but it should be observed that in applying that Act it will still frequently be essential to decide when the cause of action accrued, so that *Pirelli* should not be treated as having been overruled by the Act. As appears below, the decision in *Pirelli* has not been free of criticism, and the Canadian[37] and New Zealand[38] courts in particular have refused to follow it.

---

[31] [1963] A.C. 758, HL.
[32] Subsequently replaced by the Limitation Act 1975 (the 1975 Act), which is now consolidated in the Limitation Act 1980 (the 1980 Act).
[33] See the cases cited at fn.30, above.
[34] [1983] 2 A.C. 1, HL.
[35] For the details of this procedure see paras 21.007–21.009 and CPR 3.4.
[36] Cmnd. 9930.
[37] *Kamloops v Nielsen* (1984) 10 D.L.R. (4th) 641, Can. SC.
[38] *Invercargill City Council v Hamlin* [1996] 1 All E.R. 756, PC. See also (1995) 111 L.Q.R. 285; (1996) 112 L.Q.R. 369.

WHAT IS "DAMAGE"?

The difficulties surrounding the concept of damage may conveniently be   **5.009**
divided into two groups. First, there is the question of the difference
between damaged property and defective property. Secondly, there is the
question of whether particular items of loss are recoverable as a matter of
law. Problems of the first kind arise only in the context of damage to
property, whilst those of the second kind can occur also in cases of pure
economic loss. Further difficult questions arise in those cases where the
plaintiff suffers loss on two or more separate occasions.

"Damaged" or "defective"

The idea expressed in *Pirelli* that the cause of action accrues when damage   **5.010**
is suffered leads to serious problems in distinguishing a product that is
damaged from one that is merely defective. This point is explored further in
the context of the now discredited decision in *Junior Books v Veitchi Co.
Ltd*,[39] but it may be noted here that in so far as a merely defective product
gives rise to no right of action, it must follow that time does not begin to
run so long as the product is merely defective.

Buildings

In relation to buildings the matter has proved to be more complicated. It   **5.011**
has been argued[40] that the owner of a defective building suffers no loss until
the defect is discovered, or at least discoverable, since until that time the
building can be sold for its full value as if free of defect. This argument in
effect characterises the loss suffered by the owner of a defective building as
essentially economic, since it focuses on the price which could be obtained
for the building rather than on the cost of repair. The argument is, of
course, inconsistent with the reasoning underlying the decision in *Pirelli*,
and for this reason it might be supposed that it could not be accepted in
English law. In *Invercargill City Council v Hamlin*[41] the New Zealand
courts accepted this argument, declining to follow *Pirelli*. When the case
reached the Privy Council it was held that this was a correct view of the law
of New Zealand, at least in relation to defective buildings. The Privy
Council expressly restricted its expression of opinion to cases of defective

---

[39] See paras 5.021 et seq.
[40] See Jones (1984) 100 L.Q.R. 413; Duncan Wallace (1989) 105 L.Q.R. 46; Todd (1982–
83) 10 N.Z. Univ. L.R. 311; Mullaney [1993] L.M.C.L.Q 34.
[41] [1996] 1 All E.R. 756, PC.

buildings and declined to comment on whether the law of England on the point was the same. The status of *Pirelli* is thus left uncertain and the decision has of course no binding force in any English court. The difficulties surrounding *Pirelli* were well analysed by Dyson J. in *New Islington and Hackney Housing Association Ltd v Pollard Thomas & Edwards Ltd*,[42] but His Lordship was in the end compelled to admit that the decision must be treated as still being good law in an English context. More recently in *Abbott v Will Gannon & Smith Ltd*[43] the Court of Appeal has reiterated that *Pirelli* is not affected by the decision of the House of Lords in *Murphy v Brentwood DC*.[44]

"Doomed from the start"

5.012 A further point, which has given rise to considerable difficulty in the case law, concerns the possibility that a defect in a product may be so major and so obvious that the product can be said to be doomed from the start. In *Pirelli General Cable Works v Oscar Faber & Partners*[45] Lord Fraser, in considering the general problem arising from the defendant's argument based on *Junior Books*, suggested that there might be cases where the defect in a product was so great that it could be said to be "doomed from the start", and implied that in this situation the cause of action might possibly be considered to accrue as soon as the product was completed. It is to the advantage of the defendant if such a defect can be found to have existed, since this will cause time to run from an earlier stage, and it is therefore not surprising that defendants in subsequent cases have been very ready to argue for the existence of such a defect. The courts, however, have been most reluctant to uphold such arguments. In *Ketteman v Hansel Properties*[46] Lawton L.J., giving the judgment of the Court of Appeal, emphasised that Lord Fraser intended the concept of "doomed from the start" to apply only in exceptional cases, and went on to suggest that this possibility should be treated as a cautionary dictum to deal with unforeseen problems. The same approach was adopted by the Court of Appeal in *London Congregational Union v Harriss & Harriss*,[47] where Ralph Gibson L.J. said that there is no established category of case which can be excepted from the general rule in *Pirelli* merely by analysis and application of the phrase "doomed from the start".[48]

---

[42] [2001] B.L.R. 74; [2001] 3 Lloyd's Rep. PN 243; see also McKendirck (1991) 11 L.S. 326.
[43] [2005] EWCA Civ 198; 103 ConLR 92.
[44] (1990) 21 ConLR 1.
[45] [1983] 2 A.C. 1, HL.
[46] [1987] A.C. 189, CA.
[47] [1988] 1 All E.R. 15.
[48] [1988] 1 All E.R. 15 at 27.

In *Jones v Stroud DC*[49] the Court of Appeal expressed the view that the 5.013
"doomed from the start" exception cannot apply where the defect, although serious, may not lead to any danger to health or safety for many years. Indeed, it appears that there are only three cases in which the court has upheld a submission that a defective product was doomed from the start, and in one of these the running of time was postponed on a different ground. The first case is *Tozer Kemsley & Millbourn (Holdings) Ltd v J. Jarvis & Sons Ltd.*[50] The product in that case was an airconditioning plant, and the defect in it was such that it did not work at all, nor could it be made to work. The second is *Chelmsford DC v T.J. Evers Ltd,*[51] where the defendants were responsible for putting roofs on buildings, and the evidence was that these were liable to blow off at any minute. It is easy to see that the defect in these two cases are of a much greater order of magnitude than those in the other cases discussed in this paragraph. In *Junior Books,* in *Pirelli* itself, in *Ketteman and in London Congregational Union* the various products or buildings were all useable although defective, and it is tempting to use this as a basis for distinguishing all these cases from *Tozer Kemsley* and from *Chelmsford DC v Evers.* At this point, however, a cautionary note must be sounded. This was the approach adopted by Judge Newey at first instance in *London Congregational Union v Harriss & Harriss.*[52] When that case reached the Court of Appeal, Lawton L.J. said:

"It seems to me that the explanation of the limits of Lord Fraser's dictum which Judge Newey proposed in his judgment cannot be supported. In particular I cannot accept that a case is to be treated as within an exception to the general rule if it can be shown that 'nothing practicable could be done' to save the building or that part of the building which is the subject of the action nor can I accept that a case must be treated as outside any exception on the ground only that the repair or correction of the defect is practicable."[53]

Lawton L.J. does not, however, propose any alternative test for estab- 5.014
lishing whether a building or other item is doomed from the start. His observations do strongly suggest that the defendant cannot succeed by arguing that the item was bound to fail sooner or later. In view of this it is necessary to approach with some caution the third case where a building was held to be doomed from the start. This is *Kaliszewska v John Clague & Partners.*[54] The defendant firm had designed a bungalow for the plaintiff, but had failed to take due account of the fact that the site was on London

---

[49] [1986] 1 W.L.R. 1141, CA.
[50] (1983) 1 Const.L.J. 79, Judge Stabb Q.C.
[51] (1983) 1 Const. L.J. 65, Judge Newey Q.C.
[52] [1988] 1 All E.R. 5.
[53] [1988] 1 All E.R. 5 at 27.
[54] [1984] C.I.L.L. 131.

clay and was surrounded by trees. Because of these factors the land was subject to extensive subsidence caused by changes in moisture level. The bungalow was built in 1970, and the first cracks came into existence in 1974. The drought of 1975–1976 made matters much worse and eventually extensive repairs had to be carried out. Proceedings were not commenced until 1982. There was evidence that some cracks in the ceiling had been filled in by the builders during the maintenance period, which expired in January 1971. Judge White held that the bungalow was doomed from the start—it had never complied with the building regulations, had had cracks from the very earliest stages and was bound eventually to subside so as to require extensive and fundamental repairs. Consequently, the cause of action must be regarded as having accrued at the latest by January 1971, the end of the maintenance period. The doubt which must surround this case concerns the question of whether the defects were really sufficiently gross and obvious to merit a finding that the building was doomed from the start. It may be suggested that the vital evidence here was that which related to the repair work by the builders in 1970. This pointed strongly to the fact that the building was, even at the time of completion, so defective as to give rise to an immediate cause of action.

5.015   Another way of testing the matter in the case of a building might be to ask whether the defect was such as to cause imminent danger to the health or safety of the inhabitants, in other words to adopt the Anns test,[55] and Lawton L.J. does imply in *London Congregational Union*[56] that this may be a satisfactory explanation of *Chelmsford DC v Evers*. Unfortunately, this method is unlikely to work where the item in question is not a building. It does not even operate adequately for part of a building (as in *Pirelli*) or for something incorporated into a building (as in *Tozer Kemsley*). In these cases it is suggested that the only workable approach is to ask whether the item is so grossly defective as to be obviously unworkable and beyond repair. This solution appears to provide acceptable explanations of nearly all the cases in this area. A case which remains difficult even on this analysis is *Dove v Banham's Patent Locks*.[57] In one sense it might be said that the security gate in that case was useable as such, and it is arguable that it served to deter burglars for some 12 years. On the other hand, it became apparent in 1979 that it could not do its job of repelling burglars who attempted to enter, and it might be argued from this that it was never sufficient for its purpose and was therefore bound to fail at some point. Further, on reading Hodgson J.'s description of the defects in the work done, it is hard to avoid the conclusion that a fairly rudimentary inspection would have revealed the problem. Probably the answer to this depends upon identifying exactly what the function of the gate was, and on this approach it is hard to deny

---

[55] *Anns v London Borough of Merton*, but see paras 5.019 et seq.
[56] [1988] 1 All E.R. 15 at 28.
[57] [1983] 1 W.L.R. 1436, Hodgson J.; (1984) 47 M.L.R. 732.

that deterrence is at least part of the function. Given that in the cases already discussed here the courts have not been prepared to apply "doomed from the start" except where the product was entirely and obviously useless, it must be expected that this defence would fail in a case like *Dove*. It should be added that the importance of this concept in the law would be significantly reduced if the *Invercargill* case[58] were to be adopted as part of English law. In that event the question would have to be whether the defect was so serious and so obvious as to be immediately apparent, in which case time would run immediately. If the defect were not on this scale, then time would not run. Thus, there would be no need for a separate category of buildings "doomed from the start" since the date of damage would be determined on the same principles as those applicable in any other case.

Is the loss recoverable?

Another important point in determining whether the plaintiff's cause of action has accrued is to determine whether any loss which has been suffered is recoverable as a matter of law. This is conceptually separate from the question of whether damage has in fact been suffered, though the two issues are very likely to become confused. The point may be illustrated by reference to *Junior Books*. One of the reasons why that case represented a landmark was that it appeared to allow recovery for merely defective products[59]—this is the point about what constitutes damage. The other significant development in that case was that it allowed damages for loss of profits in a purely tortious action—this is the point about what loss is recoverable, and it is this latter point which is under consideration here. This aspect of the decision in *Junior Books* has been much criticised, and it must be very doubtful whether the case would be decided in the same way were the same facts to come before the courts at the present day. In *The Aliakmon*[60] the House of Lords refused to extend the principle so as to allow an action in tort for economic loss suffered by the buyer of steel arising from damage to the steel at a time when he had neither a proprietary nor a possessory interest in it. In *Simaan General Contracting Co. v Pilkington Glass Ltd*[61] the Court of Appeal declined to apply the principle to an action against a sub-contractor on the ground that the subcontractor had not voluntarily assumed a duty of care to the plaintiff. More remarkably still, in *Greater Nottingham Co-operative Society v Cementation Piling and Foundation Ltd*,[62] the Court of Appeal held that the *Junior Books* principle

5.016

---

[58] [1996] 1 All E.R. 756, PC.
[59] For a further analysis of this aspect of the case, see paras 5.021 et seq.
[60] [1986] A.C. 785, HL.
[61] [1988] Q.B. 758, CA.
[62] [1988] 3 W.L.R. 396, CA.

had no application to a case where there was a contractual relationship between the parties, the reasoning being that it was to be assumed that the parties had exhaustively defined their obligations to each other in that contract. If these decisions are correct, the result is undeniably to restrict the *Junior Books* principle more or less to its own facts. Perhaps the strongest authority on this point is *D. & F. Estates Ltd v Church Commissioners*,[63] where the House of Lords chose to reaffirm the traditional principle that the cost of repairing a defect in a chattel or structure which is discovered before it has caused personal injury or damage to other property is not recoverable in negligence. Therefore, where a defect is discovered, but only later causes personal injury or damage to other property, the date of accrual must now be that later date, whilst in the event that no such injury or damage is ever caused there will never be a right of action and the limitation question can never arise.

5.017   A noticeable feature of the cases so far discussed here is that they make no attempt to link the general question of what loss is recoverable with the Limitation Act question of when the cause of action accrues. A rare exception to this is to be found in *Department of Environment v Thomas Bates & Son Ltd*,[64] one of the first reported cases to consider the effect of the decision in *D. & F. Estates*. The plaintiffs were the under-lessees of a building built by the defendants in 1970–1971. In 1980 it was discovered that the pillars supporting the building contained only low-strength concrete, inadequate to support the design load of the building. Reinforcement was therefore carried out, and the plaintiffs claimed the cost of this from the defendants. The Court of Appeal held that this damage was not recoverable, since the work was carried out not to avert imminent danger to the occupants, but in order to upgrade the building to its full design load. To allow the recovery of this loss in tort would be to enforce the contractual standard in a tortious situation. Consequently, no cause of action accrued until the state of the building was such as to give rise to this imminent danger. It must, of course, follow from this that for the purposes of the action in tort, time could not run until that date was reached. It is interesting to note that arguments based on *Pirelli* and on *London Congregational Union* were advanced by the defendants. In this case, though, the plaintiffs contended that these were misplaced, since there was no limitation point in the present case. The Court of Appeal did not find it necessary to decide whether the limitation cases were of any relevance, but it is to be hoped that in future the courts will show greater willingness to consider the limitation implications of decisions of this kind.

---

[63] [1988] 3 W.L.R. 368, HL.
[64] (1989) 139 New L.J. 39, CA.

Subsequent owners

Where the owner of a damaged building sells the property to a purchaser **5.018** for full value (i.e. without any abatement for the defect) he apparently suffers no loss from the defect and will therefore have no cause of action against the person responsible for the damage. At common law no cause of action is acquired by the purchaser[65] in the absence of express assignment. It should be noted that s.3 of the Latent Damage Act 1986 contains provisions that address this problem for cases within that Act.[66]

LOCAL AUTHORITIES

In *Murphy v Brentwood DC*[67] the House of Lords held, overruling *Anns v* **5.019** *Merton LBC*,[68] that local authorities which approve building plans owe no duty of care to owners or prospective purchasers of the property concerned to ensure that the plans have been properly drawn, nor to ensure that the works are correctly carried out, since the cost of remedying such defects is purely economic loss and not recoverable in tort. This removes from English law some difficult issues[69] as to the time at which the cause of action against the authority arose. It may be noted that defects which do in fact cause physical injury or damage to other property are apparently still capable of giving rise to an action against the local authority. The ordinary principles of accrual of actions in tort, discussed elsewhere in this chapter, would seem to apply to such cases.

THE TWO LOSS PROBLEM

The problems arising when the claimant suffers loss on two different **5.020** occasions have been known to the law at least since 1826,[70] though they originally arose in connection with pure economic loss. Recent developments have raised the same issues in an acute form in connection with damage to property.

---

[65] *R.L. Polk & Co. (Great Britain) Ltd v Edwin Hill and Partners* (1988) 41 Build.L.R. 84, Judge Lewis Hawser Q.C.
[66] For the Latent Damage Act, see Ch.6.
[67] [1991] 1 A.C. 398.
[68] [1978] A.C. 728, HL.
[69] Discussed at pp.70–71 of the 1st edn of this book.
[70] *Howell v Young* (1826) 5 B. & C. 259.

PHYSICAL DAMAGE

5.021 After the decision in *Junior Books Ltd v Veitchi Co. Ltd*,[71] it appeared that the law was moving towards accepting that in some circumstances there could be recovery of lost profits in tort. The acceptance of such a claim would also give rise to issues about when the relevant cause of action arose (though that was not in issue in *Junior Books* itself).

In *Dove v Banham's Patent Locks Ltd*[72] the plaintiffs owned a house. Their predecessors in title had in 1967 engaged the defendants to fit a security gate for them as an aid to deterring burglars. The gate was defectively installed, and in 1979 a burglary took place, access being gained via the security gate. The plaintiffs' action was necessarily brought in tort, since they had no contract with the defendants. Hodgson J. held that the cause of action accrued in 1979. The decision has been criticised[73] on the ground that there would appear to have been a *Junior Books* action available against the defendants in 1967, as soon as the gate was installed. It is, of course, true that further damage was sustained in 1979, but it is axiomatic that only one action can be brought on each cause of action.[74] It might be argued that the Doves themselves suffered no loss until 1979, or at the earliest when they bought the house, but to accept that argument involves allowing a conveyance of a damaged property to start time running afresh and it is clear that this does not happen,[75] at least for the purposes of determining when the cause of action accrues. The case may therefore be regarded as an illustration of the apparent conflict between *Junior Books* and *Pirelli*.

5.022 The same point arose in a more acute form in *London Congregational Union v Harriss & Harriss*.[76] The defendants were a firm of architects employed by the plaintiffs to design a church hall. Practical completion took place in January 1970 and final completion was achieved by the end of 1970. In August 1971 the building was damaged by flooding when heavy rainfall caused the adjacent sewer to overflow. This flooding recurred on a number of occasions and in 1978 the plaintiffs ceased to use the hall. Their writ against the architects, alleging negligence in the design of the building, was issued in February 1977, i.e. more than six years after the completion of the building but within six years from the first flooding. One of the arguments for the defendants in that case was that the plaintiffs' action

---

[71] [1983] A.C. 520, HL.
[72] [1983] 1 W.L.R. 1436, Hodgson J.
[73] See (1984) 47 M.L.R. 732.
[74] *Fetter v Beale* (1701) 1 Ld.Raym. 339, 692.
[75] *Polk v Hill* (1988) 41 Build.L.R. 84, Judge Lewis Hawser Q.C. The position in this respect is now altered by s.3 of the Latent Damage Act 1986; see paras 6.027–6.035.
[76] [1985] 1 All E.R. 335, Judge Newey Q.C.; [1988] 1 All E.R. 15, CA. For an instructive analysis of some of the problems raised by this case see (1989) 52 M.L.R. 395.

must be considered, in accordance with *Junior Books*, to have accrued at the latest upon practical completion of the building. The majority of the Court of Appeal rejected that argument, treating *Junior Books* as a case where the plaintiff had suffered damage to his property.[77] A further recurrent theme in this context has been the argument that *Junior Books* can be of no relevance in a limitation context since the case itself was not concerned with limitation. This point was first raised by Lawton L.J. in *Ketteman v Hansel Properties*,[78] whose observations were subsequently cited with approval by Ralph Gibson L.J. in *London Congregational Union v Harriss & Harriss*.[79]

Although it is correct to say that *Junior Books* was not a limitation case, **5.023** this does not justify the conclusion that the case has no relevance in the present context. The argument is that *Junior Books* recognised a cause of action which had not previously been thought to exist in English law.[80] On this assumption it becomes necessary for limitation purposes to ask when that cause of action accrued. Two answers appear to be possible: the first is that the cause of action accrued when the laying of the floor was completed,[81] whilst the second is that the cause of action accrued only when the condition of the floor had deteriorated so much that it was unsuitable for its purpose and had to be relaid. The earlier of these dates was contended for by the defendants in *Pirelli* and in the cases presently under discussion. If that date were correct, this would clearly have considerable implications for a plea of limitation; if the second date were correct, the implications would be less drastic, though it is still arguable that in *Dove v Banham's Patent Locks Ltd*[82] the gate was unsuitable as soon as it was installed, so that the cause of action accrued at that time. It might also be said that in the light of subsequent developments much will depend on whether *Junior Books* is to be treated as a case of physical damage or as a case of economic loss. This in turn may depend on whether English law adheres to the principle adopted in *Pirelli* or whether it adopts the view of the Privy Council in *Invercargill*. In the latter event there is the additional point that the decision of the

---

[77] [1988] 1 All E.R. 15 at 25, per Ralph Gibson L.J. and citing Robert Goff L.J. in *Muirhead v Industrial Tank Specialities Ltd* [1985] 3 All E.R. 705 at 714 and Lord Templeman in *Tate & Lyle Industries v Greater London Council* [1983] 1 All E.R. 1159 at 1165; see also para.5.015.

[78] [1985] 1 All E.R. 352 at 363 (the subsequent decision of the House of Lords [1988] 1 All E.R. 38 has no bearing on the issues under discussion here).

[79] [1988] 1 All E.R. 15 at 25.

[80] It is submitted that this remains correct even if *Junior Books* is regarded as a case where the plaintiff had suffered damage to his property.

[81] The suggestion has also been made that the cause of action accrues at the latest when the buyer pays for the product. It is difficult to see how this can be correct. Surely the loss is effectively suffered as soon as the buyer is committed to paying, even though the payment has not yet been made.

[82] [1983] 1 W.L.R. 1436, Hodgson J. See also *Imperial College v Norman & Dawnbarn* (1985) 8 Con.L.R. 107, Judge Smout, where it was held that significant damage was suffered by a building when wall tiles fell off rather than at any earlier time.

House of Lords in *Murphy v Brentwood DC*[83] appears to impose severe restrictions on the recoverability of any damages in cases of purely defective buildings.

Action by solicitor for fees

5.024 *Byatt v Nash*[84] establishes that where a solicitor sues for fees in respect of a purported transaction which never reaches completion, and where the solicitor's retainer was an entire contract, the cause of action accrues when it is first reasonably clear that the matter will not be completed.

ECONOMIC LOSS

5.025 The question of the recoverability of economic loss in tort is, of course, a vexed one. Some of the complexities added to this area by the decisions in *Junior Books* and *Invercargill* have been discussed above,[85] but other significant problems have arisen in the area of liability for negligence in the giving of professional advice, most notably by solicitors. It is in the nature of such advice that when it proves to be inaccurate the usual consequence is financial loss unaccompanied by any form of physical damage, and it is, of course, well settled that there can be liability for negligently given advice. At present that liability may be founded on either contract or tort where the claimant is the client[86] and is founded on tort in those rare cases where a third party is allowed to sue.[87] In the past forty years there have been many attempts to analyse when the cause of action accrues. The following account seeks to summarise the current state of the law by reference to the most important cases[88]

The solicitors' negligence cases—action by client

5.026 The limitation issue in the context of solicitors' negligence surfaced as early as 1826 in *Howell v Young*,[89] where an attorney was sued for advising a

---

[83] [1991] 1 A.C. 398, HL.

[84] 28 June 2002 John Crowley Q.C. as High Court judge, Unreported.

[85] See paras 5.009 et seq.

[86] *Midland Bank v Hett, Stubbs & Kemp* [1979] Ch. 384, Oliver J.; for the current state of the law on concurrent duties in contract and tort see para.4.011.

[87] *Ross v Caunters* [1980] Ch. 297, Megarry V.-C.; *Clarke v Bruce Lance & Co.* [1988] 1 W.L.R. 881, CA.

[88] A number of cases dealt with in detail in earlier editions have been greatly abridged here in order to make space for the most important recent cases.

[89] (1826) 5 B. & C. 259.

client to grant a mortgage on a security which eventually proved insufficient. This case has been much relied upon in the late twentieth century, but it is submitted that this reliance is greatly to be regretted. *Howell v Young* was decided at a time when it was assumed that such actions had to be founded on assumpsit, and it was always clear that in assumpsit time ran from the date of the breach. This is still the rule in the modern law of contract,[90] but, as this chapter has made clear, it is not the position in the modern law of tort. Consequently, the reliance that has been placed on *Howell v Young* is in fact misplaced.

One of the first modern cases where the point arose was *Forster v Outred & Co.*[91] In 1973 Mrs Forster mortgaged her house to secure the debts of her son's business. In 1975 the mortgagee called in Mrs Forster's guarantee. In 1980 she issued a writ against Outred & Co., her solicitors in 1973, for negligently advising her to enter into the mortgage. The defendants pleaded limitation, and the question was whether the cause of action accrued in 1973 when she entered into the mortgage or only in 1975 when she was required to honour the guarantee. The Court of Appeal, relying on *Howell v Young*, held that the cause of action accrued in 1973, so that Mrs Forster was out of time. If *Howell v Young* were truly in point, then it would indeed appear to decide the case, but on the alternative basis that *Howell v Young* is distinguishable, it is instructive to consider what the result of this case should have been. In 1973, when she signed the mortgage, Mrs Forster acquired a sum of money, the loan, and in return accepted the obligation to repay the mortgage and a contingent risk of being deprived of her house in the event that payments were not made on the mortgage.

On the face of it this looks to be an equal bargain, in which her estate is neither increased nor diminished. The additional fact which alters that appearance is that the son whose business she was supporting was not a good businessman. Presumably an estimate at that stage of the likely outcome of this transaction would have shown that she was more likely to lose than to gain by it. On this assumption it is possible to say that the value of her estate was diminished by the transaction, though the quantification of that loss might well have been a very difficult matter. There must also have come some later time, probably after 1973 but before 1977, when the net value of the son's business was for the first time less than the amount outstanding on the loan. This would have been the first moment at which the bank would have needed to exercise their security in order to recoup themselves, and it might be argued that this was the earliest moment at which Mrs Forster suffered actual loss.[92] Undeniably, she suffered further loss in 1977: what had been a possibility then became a certainty, and any chance she ever had of redeeming the mortgage was lost. If it is accepted

5.027

---

[90] See Ch.10.
[91] [1982] 1 W.L.R. 86, CA.
[92] cf. *First National Commercial Bank v Humberts (A Firm)* [1995] 2 All E.R. 673, CA.

that she suffered some loss which was more than minimal in 1973, the result appears inevitably to be that her cause of action accrued then. The consequences of this are plainly very unfortunate. Had she sued immediately, she could have recovered only on the basis of an actuarial estimate of her loss, and would in the event have been under-compensated. By waiting until the mortgagee foreclosed she eventually lost the right to sue at all. It would surely have been preferable in this case to take the view that no damages could have been awarded since the loss was speculative and not capable of being quantified. In this way the accrual of the cause of action could have been postponed at least until the value of the son's business was less than the amount outstanding on the loan.[93]

5.028   Two significant questions arise from these observations. First, in what circumstances will the cause of action not accrue on the execution of the document? Secondly, what will be the position where no document is in fact executed? A possible answer to the first of these questions is suggested by *First National Commercial Bank v Humberts (A Firm)*.[94] The plaintiff bank made loans in reliance on a negligently prepared over-valuation of property, and the question was when their cause of action against the valuers accrued. It was held that the loss in such a case is prima facie the amount of the loan less any recovery there might be. Here, for some time after the loan was made, the value of the mortgaged property exceeded the loan and other outlay; thus the bank was fully secured, had suffered no loss and had no cause of action until the loan plus other outlays exceeded the value of the security.[95] Although this is obviously not a case of solicitors' negligence, the reasoning adopted might allow a different result to be reached, at least in *Forster v Outred*. It is less likely that this approach will be of general value in solicitors' negligence cases, since it is only relatively rarely that solicitors will be involved in advising on whether (as distinct from how) to enter into speculative transactions of this kind. Consequently, it is submitted that in the overwhelming majority of cases the cause of action will accrue when the negligent advice is acted upon, and that this will usually be when the plaintiff executes a document.

5.029   The second question opens up a range of possibilities for consideration. The client's response to the advice may take a number of forms. He may take some other step, or he may refrain from acting. Suppose that in *Moore* the defendants' advice had been that it was unnecessary to enter into a restraint of trade contract because the third party could effectively be restrained at common law, such advice would manifestly have been negligent, but when would the cause of action have accrued? The answer to this may be that a document would still have been executed, and that the date of

---

[93] Other early cases on the same lines include *Baker v Ollard & Bentley* (1982) 126 S.J. 593 C.A. and *D.W. Moore & Co. Ltd v Ferrier* [1988] 1 WLR 267 C.A.
[94] [1995] 2 All E.R. 673, CA.
[95] cf. *UBAF Ltd v European American Banking Corporation* [1984] Q.B. 713.

execution is again vital. Alternatively, suppose the advice to have been that there was no legal means of effecting such restraint, and that the plaintiffs thereupon decided not to employ the third party at all. This by itself might depress their profits, assuming the third party to be skilful in the profession, but again one must ask when the cause of action would have accrued. A further alternative is that the third party immediately set up in competition with the plaintiffs: in this event, perhaps the cause of action accrues as soon as his activities have a discernible effect on the profitability of their business. All these points remain open, but can all be satisfactorily resolved if it is remembered that the cause of action cannot accrue until the plaintiff has suffered damage,[96] and that this damage must be something more than merely trivial. It must also be capable of being measured with sufficient accuracy to enable the court to award damages.[97] Where the plaintiff's loss is caused by the solicitor's failure to act, time will run from the latest date at which the solicitor could effectively have taken the omitted step.[98]

Sins of omission

Where the solicitor's negligence takes the form of failing to do something, the cause of action may not accrue until the latest date when it could properly have been done. In *Midland Bank v Hett, Stubbs & Kemp (A Firm)*[99] the defendants had failed to register an interest in land, and it was held that the cause of action accrued only when it was too late to register it. To put the matter another way, there was a continuing breach of duty, so that a fresh cause of action accrued each day. In *Bell v Peter Browne & Co.*[100] the negligence took the form of failure to cause the execution of a declaration of trust in respect of the matrimonial home on the plaintiff's divorce and/or failure to register a caution at the Land Registry against dealings with the property. As a result the plaintiff lost the one-sixth interest in the proceeds of sale which had been agreed as part of the divorce settlement. The settlement happened in 1978, but the action was not commenced until 1987. It was held that the tort action accrued in 1978, since damage was immediately suffered. Although the damage arising from the failure to lodge a caution could have been remedied, that did not alter the fact that it had happened.

5.030

---

[96] See also *Gold v Mincoff Science & Gold* (A Firm), December 21, 2000, unreported, Neuberger J.
[97] *Lee and Another v Thompson* [1989] 40 E.G. 89 C.A.
[98] See *Midland Bank v Hett, Stubbs & Kemp* [1979] Ch. 384, Oliver J.; *Mathew v Maughold Life Assurance Co., The Times*, January 23, 1984 and *Lewis v Osborne* (November 28, 1995, Dyson J.), in which a number of earlier authorities are reviewed, including *Hopkins v McKenzie* [1995] 6 Med.L.R. 26, CA, *Melton v Walker & Stanger* (1981) 125 S.J. 861, *Baker v Ollard & Bentley* (1982) 126 S.J. 593.
[99] [1979] Ch. 384, Oliver J.
[100] [1990] 3 All E.R. 124, CA.

Nicholls L.J. distinguished the decision in the *Midland Bank* case on the ground that the solicitors there had never treated themselves as functi officio in relation to their client's affairs, but had continued to correspond with him, whereas the defendants in the latter case had had no dealings with their client since the conclusion of the divorce proceedings, and should not therefore be regarded as having had a continuing duty to him. This distinction is unconvincing, for the argument for Mr Bell was not that his solicitors had had a general continuing duty to him, but that they had been under a duty to correct their earlier omission, or, to put it another way, a duty to complete the task for which they had originally been engaged. However *Bell v Peter Browne* must now be regarded as firmly established.

Loss of a chance

5.031   In many professional negligence cases, especially those against legal advisers, the essence of the claimant's case is that the defendant's negligence has cost him the chance (but not the certainty) of bringing successful legal proceedings. The leading case from a limitation point of view is *Khan v Falvey*[101], which develops and amends the principles laid down in *Hopkins v McKenzie*.[102] It now appears that the position in the strike out cases may depend on what loss the claimant alleges he has suffered. If he claims only for the loss caused by the strike out, then by definition that loss cannot accrue until the strike out; but if he claims more generally for loss caused by the failure to bring proceedings promptly, then this loss starts to accrue at an earlier stage, as time goes on and the risk of a strike out becomes greater. It may therefore appear that the prudent claimant should claim only for the loss caused by the strike out. The difficulty with this approach surely is that where strike out has already become irresistible, the marginal loss caused by the fact of the order is very small, so that most of the loss becomes irrecoverable. Two further observations may be made. The first is that the distinction between the two cases does not really make sense. The reality is that *Hopkins v McKenzie* cannot stand with *Nykredit*, and the decision in *Khan v Falvey* represents the future in this area. The second is that the point is likely to be of diminishing importance because of the great reduction in striking out for want of prosecution as a result of the introduction of the CPR. In *Hatton v Chafes*[103] the claimant brought proceedings against his former solicitors for their alleged negligence in failing to pursue properly an earlier professional negligence claim against accountants. That claim was struck out in 1999, and these proceedings were commenced in 2000. The Court of Appeal held that by a date six years before the commencement of

---

[101] [2002] EWCA Civ 400; [2002] Lloyd's Law Rep PN 369; 146 SJ LB 108
[102] 23 B.M.L.R. 132; [1995] P.I.Q.R. 43, CA.
[103] [2003] EWCA Civ 341 13 March 2003.

proceedings the claimant already had no arguable defence to an application to strike out the claim against the accountants for want of prosecution. His claim against the solicitors, if any, had therefore accrued at the latest by that date, and the claim was time barred.

Inheritance Tax

Daniels v Thompson[104] reveals an odd quirk in relation to negligent advice 5.032
when it concerns inheritance tax schemes. The defendant firm in that case had given advice to a testator on a scheme to minimise inheritance tax liability on her death. The scheme was ineffective because the firm had overlooked a statutory provision. The scheme did not make her position worse, but it failed to make it better. She died some nine years after the scheme was executed, and proceedings were started on behalf of the estate a further four years later. At first sight it might appear that this case is on a par with *Forster v Outred*, so that the cause of action accrues when the scheme is executed. However, Inheritance Tax is not a liability of the estate but of the personal representatives.[105] Consequently, a testator who enters into a defective IHT saving scheme does not suffer any loss, since his estate is not at that point diminished. The personal representatives may suffer a contingent loss in that they stand to incur greater IHT liability than they otherwise would, but it is not at all clear that they can show that any duty is owed to them in their capacity as personal representatives (if they are also beneficiaries, they may of course have an action on the principles of *White v Jones*, discussed below). The Court of Appeal observed that if the testator in a case such as this did have any right of action, then it would have to accrue on the execution of the document. This decision is therefore not inconsistent with the principles laid down in *Forster v Outred*, and the different outcome results solely from the quirk of the Inheritance Tax Act which puts liability for the tax on the personal representatives.[106]

Solicitor's negligence—action by third party

In general a solicitor is not liable to be sued for breach of duty by anyone 5.033
other than his client, since it is to the client that his duties are primarily owed. There are, however, a few exceptional cases where such actions may succeed. The most important is where solicitors are negligent in procuring the execution of a will and as a result persons whom the testator intends to

---

[104] [2004] EWCA Civ 307.
[105] Inheritance Tax Act 1984 s.200(1)(a).
[106] See also *Macaulay and Farley v Premium Life Assurance Co Ltd* (Unreported, April 29 1999). Park J.

benefit are deprived of that benefit. The right of the disappointed beneficiary to sue has been confirmed by the House of Lords in *White v Jones*,[107]
approving earlier decisions in the lower courts.[108] In *Al-Kandari v Brown*[109]
it was held that solicitors could owe a duty of care to the opposing party in
a case when they obtained possession of his passport subject to an undertaking for safe-keeping. The third party's cause of action in these cases will
necessarily be in tort, but the question of when the cause of action arises
does not appear to have been considered judicially.

5.034   The choice in *White v Jones* would appear to be between the date when
the will is executed and the date of the testator's death. It may be argued
that the former date cannot be correct because the testator might change his
mind and because the will creates no more than an expectancy. The
weakness in this argument is that it resembles the argument for saying that
Mrs Forster's cause of action did not accrue when she signed the mortgage
deed. She, too, could still have escaped without loss, though this would
have required a course of events which she could not control (just as is the
case with the defectively drawn will). It is obviously unattractive to say that
the cause of action accrues immediately, for the consequence would be that,
subject to ss.14A[110] and 32 of the 1980 Act,[111] time would begin to run,
and could possibly expire, even before the testator died.[112] Nevertheless, it
is submitted that these cases cannot properly be distinguished from *Forster
v Outred* and *Moore v Ferrier*; a strict application of logic would produce
the result that the cause of action accrues as soon as the will is executed. It
may be doubted, however, whether the courts will be prepared to accept so
absurd an outcome. One way of resisting this result would be to say that the
plaintiff's position is not made worse by the drafting of the will, since he
was never entitled to anything anyway. Unfortunately, this argument
proves too much, for the same can equally be said of the testator's death,
and this would lead to the conclusion that the beneficiary's action should
not be allowed to succeed at all. A further complication arises where the
solicitor's negligence takes the form of failing to bring about the execution
of any will at all. In *Bacon v Howard Kennedy (A Firm)*[113] it was held that
in such a case the cause of action is not complete until the putative testator
dies. Although the solicitor is obviously negligent at an earlier stage in
failing to have the will executed within a reasonable time of receiving
instructions, this appears to be the only possible date for limitation pur-

---

[107] [1995] 1 All E.R. 691, HL.
[108] *Ross v Caunters* [1980] Ch. 297 and *Clarke v Bruce Lance & Co.* [1988] 1 W.L.R. 881,
CA.
[109] [1988] Q.B. 665, CA.
[110] See Ch.6.
[111] See Ch.20.
[112] The unattractive character of this argument was alluded to by Nicholls V.-C. in *White v
Jones* in the Court of Appeal [1993] 3 All E.R. 481 at 492.
[113] May 22, 1998, Unreported, Judge Bromley Q.C.

poses. The decision may therefore be regarded as a sensible resolution of a logical dilemma arising from the unfortunate decision in *White v Jones*.

INSURANCE

In *Iron Trades Mutual Insurance Co. Ltd v J.K. Buckenham*[114] the defendants had failed in their duty to procure effective reinsurance contracts for the plaintiffs, the contracts obtained being voidable for nondisclosure of material facts. It was held, in accordance with the authorities discussed above, that the cause of action accrued as soon as the contracts were executed, notwithstanding that at that stage the reinsurers had not repudiated liability and were indeed unaware of their right to do so. Similarly, in *Islander Trucking Ltd (In Liquidation) v Hogg Robinson & Gardner Mountain (Marine) Ltd*[115] the plaintiffs in 1980 asked the defendant broker to obtain liability insurance for them. When faced with claims in respect of the insured risks they sought indemnity, but in 1985 the insurers avoided the policies on the ground of non-disclosure. An action against the brokers was commenced in 1986, within the limitation period, but the defendants pleaded that they had acted as agents for other brokers, and were therefore not liable to the plaintiffs in contract. The other brokers were joined as parties to the action in January 1989, but sought to be released from the action on the ground that the limitation period had expired before they were joined. It was therefore necessary to decide when any cause of action against them accrued. Evans J. held that the cause of action against brokers in respect of a voidable insurance policy accrues when the policy is effected, since that is when damage is suffered, notwithstanding that the damage is not discovered until a later date.[116]

5.035

In *Martin and Another v Britannia Life Ltd*[117] a company representative missold a life-assurance policy to a customer. There was a short period between the date when the policy was issued and the date when the first premiums were paid. It was held that the action against the insurance company accrued when the policy was issued, rather than on the date when the first premiums were paid. On the particular facts of the case the difference was crucial for limitation purposes. The claimant's argument was that no detriment was in fact suffered until the premiums were paid, because in practice he was not obliged to pay them—had the chosen not to do so, the company would not have sued him; rather, the policy would simply have been allowed to lapse. This argument was rejected—his legal

5.036

---

[114] [1990] 1 All E.R. 808, K.S. Rokison Q.C. as Deputy High Court Judge.
[115] [1990] 1 All E.R. 826.
[116] See also *Knapp v Ecclesiastical Insurance Group plc* [1998] P.N.L.R. 172 where the rule was reiterated.
[117] [2000] Lloyd's Rep. PN 412, Jonathan Parker J.

obligation to pay the premiums was sufficient detriment to start time running.

Surveyors

5.037   In *Kitney v Jones Lang Wootton*[118] the defendant surveyor had failed to ensure the plaintiff's compliance with the repairing covenants in a lease, with the result that the plaintiff lost his right to a renewal of the lease. Nolan J. held that the plaintiff's right of action against the surveyor accrued on the expiry of the lease, rather than on the much later date when a court held that the right to renewal had been forfeited. In *Secretary of State for the Environment v Essex, Goodman & Suggitt*,[119] the Department of Environment had commissioned the defendant surveyors to prepare a survey report on an office block. In reliance on that report the Department took a lease of the building. It transpired that the surveyors had negligently failed to notice a number of defects, and the Department sued them. It became necessary to decide when the cause of action against the surveyors arose, and Judge Hawser Q.C. held that the vital date was that when the Department relied on the surveyors' report, i.e. when it irrevocably committed itself to the lease. This was when the loss was suffered, because until that time the Department might have avoided the expense of repairing the building. Clearly, this approach relates closely to that suggested above in the context of solicitors' negligence. However, the judge went on to say that a different result would be reached in the case of engineers, architects and builders. The reason for this lies again in the proper application of the traditional duty, breach and damage test.

The obligation of all the various professionals considered here is to provide a proper product, but the exact nature of the product in issue differs from one profession to another. In the case of the surveyor the product is a survey report. This is likely to be produced before the building is entirely finished. Further, by its nature, it can only describe the condition of the building at the date of the survey, whereas the engineer, architect and builder have an obligation to provide a sound building which will last for some considerable time. The breach of the latter duty may happen at almost any stage of the construction process, but the damage resulting from that breach may well not occur until a much later stage. In summary, it can be said that the analysis of duty, breach and damage applies to all these cases, but that its application will not always produce the same result.

---

[118] *The Times*, January 20, 1989, Nolan J.
[119] [1986] 1 W.L.R. 1432, Judge Hawser Q.C.

Valuers

This is an area of law which has seen significant activity in recent years. The 5.038
leading authority now is the decision of the House of Lords in *Nykredit v
Edward Erdman Ltd.*[120]

The emergence of cases in this category is the most recent development in
the saga of determining the date of accrual. The cases appear to fall into
two categories, those involving purchasers of property in reliance on the
survey and those involving lenders who have lent money on the basis of the
survey.

(a) Purchasers

The idea that purchasers who have bought property in reliance on a survey 5.039
can sue in tort is not new, having been established in *Smith v Eric S.
Bush.*[121] What is new is the emergence of the question about the date when
the cause of action accrues. It may, of course, happen that the purchasers do
not become aware of their loss until they come to try to sell the property, at
which time a properly conducted survey reveals the problems that the first
survey should have revealed. Cases of this kind appear very similar to *Pirelli*
in that they are cases of damaged property where the damage is not
immediately apparent. It is therefore perhaps not surprising that the discovery or discoverability of the damage should be regarded as irrelevant.
An interesting refinement of these cases is seen in *Byrne v Hall Pain and
Foster,*[122] where the writ was issued more than six years after the exchange
of contracts for the purchase of the property but less than six years after the
completion of the purchase. The Court of Appeal held that the vital date
was the date of exchange, since that was the date when the purchasers were
irrevocably bound to complete and when the loss became inevitable. The
decision is obviously correct. *Sweetman v Nathan*[123] raised similar points
to *Nykredit*. The claimant sued his former solicitors for their alleged
negligence in allowing him to purchase for £1.5 million a property which
was subsequently discovered to lack necessary planning permission, without which it was subsequently valued at £12,750. It was held that the cause
of action accrued when the purchase was completed (in the light of *Byrne v
Pain Hall Foster*[124] that probably should be when contracts were exchanged, if that happened on an earlier date).

---

[120] [1997] 1 W.L.R. 1627.
[121] [1989] 2 All E.R. 514.
[122] [1999] 1 W.L.R. 184, CA.
[123] [2002] EWHC 2458 (QB), [2002] All ER (D) 330 (Nov).
[124] [1999] 1 W.L.R. 1849 CA.

(b) Lenders

5.040   In this area two important and difficult cases have cast doubt on much of the formerly accepted wisdom about accrual of cause of action. The two cases are *FNCB v Humberts*[125] and *Nykredit v Edward Erdman*.[126] The essential facts of the two cases are identical. In both, lenders were asked to lend money on the security of commercial property. Surveys were carried out by the defendants, which suggested that the value of the property was significantly in excess of the proposed loans. This excess was important, since commercial lenders will normally not lend more than a certain percentage of the apparent value of the property. This cushion is required in order to provide a margin of error against the imprecision inherent in valuation, possible market fluctuations and the possible costs of proceedings to enforce the security. In both cases the borrowers defaulted on the loans immediately, and it then became apparent that the valuations were grossly excessive. The lenders argued that they would never have lent money on the security of the property had they known the true position. The question was when the cause of action against the negligent valuers arose. By analogy with earlier cases of reliance on advice, or even by analogy with *Byrne v Hall Pain and Foster*, the answer would at first sight appear to be that the cause of action accrues when the loan is made, or, if earlier, when the lenders enter into a binding commitment to make the loan. However, that was not the result in either of these cases. It was pointed out that the losses which could be recovered in tort were limited to the amount of the loan, plus lost interest plus the costs of enforcing the security, less any recovery made by means of that enforcement. The question to be asked was, therefore, what was the earliest date at which the recovery to be expected was less than the total costs to the lenders, i.e. the date on which they would actually be certain to make a loss. In *Law Society v Sephton & Co*[127] Lord Hoffman commented:

> "[20] The Nykredit case therefore decides that in a transaction in which there are benefits (covenant for repayment and security) as well as burdens (payment of the loan) and the measure of damages is the extent to which the lender is worse off than he would have been if he had not entered into the transaction, the lender suffers loss and damage only when it is possible to say that he is on balance worse off. It does not discuss the question of a purely contingent liability."

This statement can be accepted if it means that Nykredit does not deal with the case where the claimant incurs a contingent liability as distinct

---

[125] [1995] 2 All E.R. 673.
[126] [1998] 1 All E.R. 305.
[127] [2006] UKHL 22; [2006] 3 All E.R. 401.

from incurring the risk of a loss. However, it is not at all clear why this distinction should make any difference to the result. The issue is whether any quantifiable loss which is more than minimal has been sustained.

Nykredit is perhaps the most interesting and potentially most important of the cases considered here. Two important strands may be discerned. The first is to work through in detail how the test in this case would have been applied to the facts of individual cases. The second is to consider whether the reasoning in the case should be regarded as having in any way undermined that adopted in the earlier cases, especially *Forster v Outred*.[128] It is to be observed that all these valuation cases involve the execution of documents—not the valuation report itself, but the documents effecting the transaction entered into in alleged reliance on the valuation report. A reading of the earlier cases might therefore lead to an expectation that the execution of the document would mark the accrual of the cause of action, yet, as has been seen above, this was not the view adopted by the courts.

5.041

Lord Nicholls' deceptively simple test for determining the accrual of the case of action in *Nykredit* conceals some significant difficulties. First, it is necessary to be able to draw a comparison between the value of what the lender has at any given time (the security on the property and the borrower's personal covenant) and the amount outstanding on the mortgage. The latter can, of course, be calculated, exactly, on a day-by-day basis if necessary, but the former is more difficult, since both elements are matters of judgment. Yet the day-by-day calculation is necessary because the cause of action does not accrue until the first time when the lender's asset is worth less than the sum outstanding. Lord Nicholls seeks to dismiss these points as matters of evidence rather than of principle, but it should be said that they are matters of evidence which are in danger of making the determination of the date of accrual almost impossible in some cases. Secondly, it is dangerous to assume that the relationship between the two figures can move only in one direction. If the property market fluctuates, or if the borrower's circumstances improve, so that his covenant is worth more or so that he is able to make some repayments on the mortgage, then the position may change so that overall the lender is back in credit. Suppose that the position then deteriorates again, so that the lender is in debit overall. It is submitted that this cannot amount to the accrual of a fresh cause of action—the action must accrue once and for all when first the lender goes into debit. Yet this may produce the result that by the time of trial the lender is back in credit and has no right of recovery, yet is unable to sue again when the position later deteriorates. This problem appears logically insoluble, yet it is an inevitable result of the decision in *Nykredit*.

5.042

---

[128] Accepted in *Law Society v Sephton* as being in effect the starting point of the modern law in this area.

Valuing the borrower's covenant

5.043 Although in *Nykredit* it was accepted that the borrower's covenant has to be valued, little attention was given to the problem of how to perform that valuation. The matter was more fully considered in *DNB Mortgages v Bullock & Lees*.[129] The task is not one of exact science, and there is an important question about whether the valuation should be taken on the basis of the position as it appeared at the time or with the benefit of hindsight, which will usually involve taking account of the subsequent bankruptcy/insolvency of the borrower. The Court of Appeal inclined to the view that the proper course was to attempt a valuation as matters would have appeared at the relevant time. It is submitted that this is the correct approach—the position as it then appeared gives a better guide to the amount for which the lender might have expected to be able to assign the benefit of the loan.

Falling market

5.044 A further difficulty in *Nykredit* cases is that the defendant may seek to argue that some or all of the claimant's loss is caused by a fall in the market. It is obvious that the defendant can be liable only for the loss caused by his breach of duty. Although the claimant may say that he would not have entered into the transaction if the valuation had been competently done, this cannot alter the fact that the fall in the market is not caused by the defendant, who therefore cannot be liable for such losses.[130] It is of course a question of fact in each case how much of the loss is caused by the falling market and how much by the negligent valuation.

Relationship with *Forster v Outred*

5.045 In *Havenledge Ltd v Graeme John & Partners (A Firm)*[131] the claimants had in 1987 bought a nursing home, which had prospered until 1990 when various structural defects were discovered. The claimants alleged that the defendants, who had been their solicitors, were negligent in failing to advise them to obtain a mining engineer's report, which, they said, would have revealed the risk of damage from past coal-mining operations. It was the claimants' case that they would then not have bought the property. However, it was accepted that at the time of purchase the property was worth at least as much as they paid for it. This apparently odd finding rests on the

---

[129] [2000] 17 E.G. 168; [2000] 1 E.G.L.R. 92, CA.
[130] *South Australia Asset Management Corporation v York Montague Ltd* [1997] A.C. 191, HL.
[131] December 18, 2000, Unreported, CA.

very specific circumstance that British Coal was liable to compensate the owners of the property for any damage resulting from coal-mining activities. It makes this case one which is likely to be confined to its own facts, taking it out of the normal run of *Nykredit* cases and approximating it much more closely to the *Forster v Outred* line of cases. Consequently, the claimants sought to recover the expenditure which they had incurred in converting and renovating the property. The Court of Appeal, by a majority, held that the cause of action was time-barred before 1996, when proceedings were issued, but even the majority were unable to agree when the cause of action accrued. Buxton L.J. thought that it was on the purchase of the property, because, by analogy with *Moore v Ferrier*[132] and *Forster v Outred*[133] that was the point at which the claimants did not get what they had paid before, whereas Pill L.J. thought that no actual loss was incurred until the claimants spent substantial sums on renovating the property. It is suggested that it is only in unusual cases such as this that *Forster v Outred* is likely to be relevant in this area. That case should be regarded as establishing when the loss happened in particular circumstances, but it does not help us to understand the answer in the typical *Nykredit* case.

Accountants

In *Moon v Franklin*[134] the defendant accountant had involved the plaintiff (his client) in a large additional charge to tax by wrongly advising him to allow a partnership to discontinue its previous trade, an action which under s.118 of the Income and Corporation Taxes Act 1988 amounted to the cessation of the partnership and therefore brought into play the closing year rules of assessment. It was held that the cause of action accrued on the cessation, since that was when the increased charge became inevitable, rather than on the later date when the accounts for the relevant period were signed. Similarly, in *Cotterell (Executrix of Reece Deceased) v Leeds Day (A Firm)*,[135] where an accountant failed to give prompt notice of a deed of variation of a will, with the result that the right to effect the variation for inheritance tax purposes was lost, the cause of action accrued on the date when an effective election ceased to be possible. Where a professional adviser gives negligent advice about Inheritance Tax planning, with the result that the liability to IHT on death is greater than it otherwise would have been, the loss is suffered by the estate and not by the testator.

5.046

---

[132] [1988] 1 All E.R. 400.
[133] [1982] 1 W.L.R. 86, CA.
[134] December 19, 1991, CA, Unreported.
[135] December 21, 1999, Unreported, Buckley J.

Accordingly, it does not accrue until death, and the cause of action in tort accrues only on that date.[136]

Frankovich Claims

5.047 A claim against the government for damages for failure to implement a Directive correctly is a claim in tort for limitation purposes. In *Poole v HM Treasury*,[137] the claimants were Lloyd's names who sued the government for failing to implement a European Directive, as a consequence of which it was contended that the Government had failed to ensure that there was an appropriate system in place whereby the reserves of Lloyd's syndicates were adequate to meet liabilities. The Government argued that any cause of action in tort was time barred because that cause of action accrued when the particular claimant became a Lloyd's name or remained a name or increased his or her underwriting limit. In contrast, the claimants argued that the cause of action only accrued at the earliest when they first became liable to pay a contribution to syndicate underwriting liabilities, or received reduced profits by reason of syndicate underwriting liabilities, as a result of the defendant's failure to implement the Directive. Langley J. found in favour of the Government, distinguishing *Sephton* on the basis that the liabilities in *Sephton* were contingent because the misappropriations by the solicitor might have been made good and a claim on the Law Society Compensation Fund had to be made in proper form. In the event that the misappropriations were made good or the claim on the Fund was not in proper form, obviously there would be no valid claim on the Fund. By contrast, in the case of the Lloyds names the claimants on joining a syndicate were immediately committed to the liabilities of that syndicate under Reinsurance to Close "RITC" it had written and on all business (including RITC) it did write in the course of his membership.[138]

5.048 In *Spencer v Secretary of State for Work and Pensions*[139], another decision of the Court of Appeal, the claimant suffered personal injury and brought a claim against his former employers. He alleged that this failed by reason of the Government's failure properly to implement European law which required a remedy to be provided in the circumstances. A claim was then brought for *Francovich* damages against the Government. The issue was when the claimant's cause of action against the Government arose, the alternative contentions being when the personal injury was suffered, in which event the claim was time barred or only when the claim for damages

---

[136] *Daniels v Thompson* [2004] EWCA Civ 307 18 March 2004 unreported, following *Macaulay and Farley v Premium Life Assurance Co Ltd* (Unreported, April 29 1999) Park J.
[137] [2006] EWHC 2731 (Comm), [2007] 1 All ER (Comm) 255, [2007] Lloyd's Rep IR 114.
[138] Per Langley J. at para.239.
[139] [2008] EWCA Civ 750; [2009] 1 All E.R. 314; [2009] 2 W.L.R. 593.

for personal injury failed by reason of the deficiency in the law, in which event it was not time-barred. The Court of Appeal held that the cause of action against the Government arose when the claimant suffered his personal injury, because although he had a claim against his former employers that claim was not as valuable as the claim he contended that he should have had if the Government had implemented European law as it should have done, so that it was at that point that the claimant suffered actual damage for the purposes of the accrual of his cause of action against the Government.

Modern Reconciliations of Principle

Two twenty-first century cases have provided detailed and authoritative examination of the principles of accrual in economic loss cases, and any approach to the law as it currently stands must take due account of them. In *Law Society v Sephton*[140] the court had to consider, apparently for the first time, the question of accrual of action in a claim by the Law Society against an accountant who had negligently certified a solicitor's accounts under s.34 of the Solicitors Act. In fact the solicitor had been committing numerous breaches of the Solicitors Accounts Rules in misappropriating money from client accounts, and in due course substantial grants were made to clients from the Compensation Fund. Before the Court of Appeal seven different possible accruals dates were proposed: **5.049**

   (i) the date of reliance by the Society on each of the Reports;

  (ii) (if different) the date subsequent to each Report when the solicitor's practising certificate was granted or renewed;

(iii) the various dates subsequent to each of the Reports upon which the solicitor first misappropriated clients' money;

 (iv) the date when the Society resolved to intervene in the solicitor's practice;

  (v) the date when the Society did intervene in the solicitor's practice;

 (vi) the date when a claim was first made on the Compensation Fund by a victim of a relevant misappropriation by the solicitor;

(vii) the date when the first payment to such a victim was first made out of the Compensation Fund.

---

[140] [2004] EWHC 544 (Ch) Michael Briggs QC.

5.050   The matter was further is complicated by the fact that the Law Society relied upon a series of successive Reports, and that misappropriations took place over a substantial period of time. The case had certain particular features of this case which distinguished it from the existing authorities:

(a) The Society's conduct in reliance on the Reports consisted merely of its not taking steps available to it to prevent the solicitor's depredations upon his clients' funds.

(b) The Society never incurred a legal liability to make payments out of the Fund to his clients, since payments out of the fund are always discretionary.

(c) There are reasons why the Society may decline to make a grant in favour of a claimant apparently within one of the statutory classes, for example if the claimant's loss is otherwise insured, or if the claimant has caused or contributed to his loss by his own carelessness.[141]

The relevant principles are those set out by Clarke LJ in *Polley v Warner Goodman & Street*[142]:

(i) A cause of action in negligence does not arise until the claimant suffers damage as a result of the defendant's negligent act or omission;

(ii) The damage must be 'real' as distinct from minimal;

(iii) Actual damage is any detriment, liability or loss capable of assessment in money terms and includes liability which may arise on a contingency;

(iv) The loss must be relevant in the sense that it falls within the measure of damages applicable to the wrong in question;

(v) A claimant cannot defeat the statute of limitations by claiming only in respect of damage which occurs within the limitation period if he has suffered damage from the same wrongful act outside that period.

The House of Lords held that the correct date was the date when a claim was first made on the Compensation Fund, that being the date when the Law Society first suffered an actual, as distinct from contingent, loss.[143]

---

[141] See for example *R (on the application of Ingman Foods) v The Law Society* [1997] 2 All E.R. 666.

[142] [2003] EWCA Civ. 1013; [2003] PNLR 40.

[143] In reaching this conclusion doubt was cast on the decision in *Gordon v J B Wheatley & Co (a firm)* [2000] Lloyd's Rep PN 605.

Lord Hoffman's observations on many of the earlier cases have been cited above. It may be observed in relation to this particular decision that it is not at all obvious why the loss is suffered when the claim is made, since there is no obligation to accede to the claim. It might have been better to say that the crucial date was when the Society resolved to make the payment. However, the more general observations of their Lordships are clearly of considerable interest in trying to reconcile the various cases on the date of damage.

The second of the cases is *Axa Insurance Ltd v Akther & Darby Solicitors*.[144] The Court of Appeal had to consider the date of accrual in a case arising from the claimant's[145] provision of After the Event "ATE" Legal Expenses Insurance to clients of the defendant firm of solicitors in order to support the bringing of various forms of legal proceedings. Part of the role performed by the defendant solicitors was the vetting of claims. Claims accepted under the scheme had to have prospects of success of at least 51 per cent and be for a minimum amount of £1000. The claimant argued that panel solicitors had owed a duty to vet and only take on scheme claims that had a greater than 50 per cent prospect of success and a likelihood of damages of £1000 or more and to conduct cases with reasonable care and skill after they were taken on. It was alleged that the defendants had breached these duties with the result that claims had failed and/or that greater costs liabilities had been incurred. There were thus two categories of breach, referred to respectively as the vetting breaches and the conduct breaches, and these will be considered separately. The panel solicitors contended that the claims in respect of those policies were time-barred, and limitation was tried as a preliminary issue, the question being when time started to run for the purposes of claims in tort under Limitation Act 1980 s.2. The claimants argued that in each case the damage could not be said to have occurred until the date when the underlying claim had failed. The panel solicitors contended that actual damage was first suffered when each ATE policy was entered. Each side sought to invoke the decision in *Law Society v Sephton*[146] in aid of its case.

5.051

The Vetting Breaches

5.052

It might be thought that the claimant had the more difficult task, at least on the basis of *Forster v Outred & Co*[147] and it is not surprising that the defendant argued that *Sephton* does not change the previous law in this

---

[144] [2009] All ER (D) 285 (Mar); [2009] EWHC 635 Comm Flaux J.; [2009] EWCA Civ 1166.
[145] In fact the Claimant's assignor, but for present purposes nothing turns on this.
[146] [2006] UKHL 22; [2006] 2 A.C. 543; [2006] 3 All E.R. 401.
[147] [1982] 2 All E.R. 753; [1982] 1 W.L.R. 86 CA.

area, and that the decision in *Sephton* is to be approached with caution and to be given a narrow interpretation limited to its own special facts. Thus actual damage was first suffered when each ATE policy was entered. This argument depends not only on an analysis of the case law but on the nature of ATE insurance. Under an ATE policy, there is no gap between the receipt of the premium and the claim arising. The relevant event has already occurred and the ATE insurer's meter starts running the moment it agrees to fund the particular claim. It takes on the risk of funding proceedings that have already arisen. As soon as an ATE policy incepts, the insurer is exposed to immediate transactional commitments, which is why it essential from the outset for the insurer to exercise control over the handling of proceedings.

The claimants inevitably sought to advance an analysis of cases of this kind and especially of the decision in *Sephton* which would lead to the opposite conclusion. The claimant's contention was that, loss and damage cannot be said to have occurred until the date when the underlying claim has "failed" (either when the insurer withdrew indemnity in respect of the claim or there was a settlement or judgment which meant that the claimant was liable for the other side's costs or had recovered less than the amount that the insurer would have to pay out under the relevant ATE policy). Until then any liability NIG was under was wholly contingent. Thus, applying the principle in *Sephton*[148] that contingent liabilities are to be disregarded, the claim would not accrue until that moment.

5.053   The Court of Appeal, by a majority rejected the claimant's arguments. The question whether or not actual damage has been suffered is, in each case, fact specific. Moreover, *Sephton* does not support the conclusion that the date when "actual damage" occurred as a consequence of vetting breaches in the present case should be suspended until any claim has actually "failed" in the sense defined above. The crucial point is that this is in fact not a case of a purely contingent liability standing alone. Third, if the claimant's tripartite analysis were accepted, the present case would rightly belong in category 2 case in the sense that the duty which the defendant solicitors are alleged to have been under in tort was on analysis a duty "to bring about a transaction with particular characteristics or features". This does not of course imply that the solicitors were warranting that the cases would succeed, but they were warranting that on a fair analysis there was at least a 51% chance of success.[149] Thus even that approach analysis would result in a finding that the cause of action accrued when the policies incepted.

5.054   The possible analogy with *Nykredit*[150] also deserves consideration. It will be recalled that in *Nykredit* it was held that the cause of action against the

---

[148] See in particular paras 18, 20, 22, 30, 31, 48, 51, 76, 77.
[149] Para.36.
[150] *Nykredit v Edward Erdman* [1998] 1 All E.R. 305; [1997] 1 W.L.R. 1627.

valuers accrued only when the property was worth less than the amount outstanding on it, even though it cannot be denied that the lenders were supposed to get a reliable valuation and did not do so. The answer to this rests on the view that in *Nykredit* there was no immediate loss at all, so that the loss could properly be regarded as purely contingent in the *Sephton* sense, whereas in the present case there was some loss as soon as the policy was taken out, so that the case falls into the line of authorities with *Forster v Outred*. *Nykredit* is of course a case where it was said that the lenders would not have entered into the transaction at all if they had had proper valuations, but this characteristic of *Nykredit* is not the basis of the decision, which rests instead on the fact-specific question of when damage was suffered.

The Conduct Breaches   5.055

The second category of breaches alleged against the defendants was the conduct breaches, i.e. the failure to conduct the cases properly after they had been taken on. This was either because the chances of success were subsequently seen to be below 50% or because the defendants conducted the cases without due care and attention, thereby prejudicing the client's chances of successfully advancing a good claim. The first of these is on a par with the initial failure to vet the case properly—the loss happens when the insurer is exposed to a greater risk than it should face, which is when the defendants wrongly fail to notify the insurer that the chances have declined. The second category is closer to the case where, as a consequence of a solicitor's negligence, a claim becomes doomed to fail in the sense of being struck out. In *Hatton v Chafes*[151], a case of this kind, Clarke LJ said[152]:

> "It seems to me that there are three possibilities as to when damage is caused by negligence in such a case so that the Claimant's cause of action has accrued and time begins to run against him. The first is when the Claimant has no arguable basis for avoiding the claim being struck out, the second is when it is more probable than not that the claim will be struck out and the third is when there is a real (as opposed to a minimal or fanciful) risk of the claim being struck out. The reason why it is not necessary to determine which of those possibilities is correct here is that, in my opinion, this is an example of the first class of case on the facts."

The House of Lords in *Sephton* appeared inclined to the view that the   5.056
cause of action would not accrue until the action was certain to be struck

---

[151] [2003] PNLR 24.
[152] At para.17.

out, though their observations were not part of the *ratio*.[153] In this case it was held that the cause of action in this category of conduct breach case will have accrued when, as a consequence of the breach, there has been a material diminution in the prospects of success.[154] However, this aspect of the case received rather less attention than did the conduct breaches, though the conclusion reached seems to be based on the same principle, namely that the cause of action accrues as soon as the claimant suffers more than trivial damage—that is why the diminution in chances of success has to be 'material' in order to set time running.

5.057   Taken together, *Sephton* and *Axa* provide detailed and definitive guidance on the approach to be adopted to accrual of cause of action in economic loss cases. *Forster v Outred* has been firmly upheld, and it does not seem excessive to say that there will be far more cases governed by it than by *Sephton*, which increasingly appears an interesting but somewhat exceptional case.

PROCEDURAL QUESTIONS

5.058   In addition to the substantive points already considered, there are a number of procedural issues arising in connection with actions in tort. These are considered in the following paragraphs.

The cause of action and the right to sue

5.059   It was stated above[155] that the cause of action is complete only when there is a plaintiff who can sue. The validity of this as a general proposition cannot be doubted, but there are a few cases where it has been held that the cause of action is complete, so that time runs against the plaintiff, notwithstanding that for some reason no action can be brought. In *Sevcon Ltd v Lucas CAV Ltd*[156] the plaintiff alleged patent infringement by the defendant. Such infringement began after the application for the patent had been filed but before the patent had been granted. Section 13(4) of the Patents Act 1949[157] provides that no proceedings for infringement may be commenced before the patent has been granted, though after the grant the plaintiff may sue in respect of infringements occurring between application

---

[153] And see Silber J. in *Jessup v Wetherell* [2007] PNLR 10 at para 42, where he seems to assume that it is still open to argument which is the correct formulation of the test.
[154] At para.108.
[155] See para.5.006.
[156] [1986] 1 W.L.R. 462, HL; (1986) 49 M.L.R. 650.
[157] Now s.69(2) of the Patents Act 1977.

and grant. The House of Lords treated the case as being an action in tort[158] and held that the cause of action accrued as soon as there was infringement, notwithstanding that the plaintiff could not have sued at that time. The decision was reached by analogy with a similar decision[159] in the context of the awarding of interest. It is submitted that the decision in *Sevcon v Lucas* was neither necessary nor desirable. Quite apart from the question of whether this was really an action in tort at all, it is surely objectionable in principle to hold that time runs against the plaintiff although he cannot yet bring an action. Their Lordships admitted that no earlier case was directly in point, and it is very regrettable that they should have come to this decision.

A case which was apparently not cited in *Sevcon v Lucas*, but which 5.060 might have had some relevance to it, is *O'Connor v Isaacs*.[160] In 1942 magistrates made a maintenance order against the plaintiff in the mistaken belief that they had jurisdiction to do so. On a number of subsequent occasions between 1942 and 1945 the plaintiff was imprisoned for non-payment of the instalments under this order. In 1954, the lack of jurisdiction to make the original order having been discovered, the order was quashed by the court. The plaintiff sought to sue the magistrates who had made the original order as well as those who had from time to time committed him to prison for disobedience to it. The limitation question was when the cause of action arose, the choice being between 1945 and 1954. The argument for the former was that this was the date of the last wrongful action, whilst the argument for the latter was that this was the date when the order of 1942 was quashed, and the plaintiff could not sue until then, since the quashing was an essential element in his case for false imprisonment. Diplock J., whose decision and reasoning were upheld by the Court of Appeal,[161] delivered a lengthy and learned judgment analysing the history of the action against magistrates for excess of jurisdiction and drawing a distinction between those cases where the later event is an integral part of the cause of action,[162] and those cases where the later event merely removes a procedural bar to the bringing of the action.[163] Diplock J. held that this case fell into the latter category, so that the last cause of action for the plaintiff accrued in 1945 and his action was therefore out of time. This is a

---

[158] See further para.4.024.
[159] *General Tire and Rubber Co. v Firestone Tyre and Rubber Co. Ltd* [1975] 1 W.L.R. 819, HL.
[160] [1956] 2 Q.B. 288, Diplock J.
[161] [1956] 2 W.L.R. 585, CA.
[162] Such as *Board of Trade v Cayzer, Irvine & Co.* [1927] A.C. 616, HL; *Musurus Bey v Gadban* [1894] 2 Q.B. 352, CA (see below).
[163] These include *Coburn v Colledge* [1897] 1 Q.B. 702, CA. *Read v Brown* (1888) 22 Q.B.D. 128, CA and *Cooke v Gill* (1873) L.R. 8, C.P. 107, which are also mentioned in this context, are really cases on other aspects of the ingredients of the cause of action, and are not really relevant for present purposes.

somewhat difficult distinction and examination of the relevant cases may be helpful.

Later event an integral element of cause of action

5.061   In *Board of Trade v Cayzer, Irvine & Co.*[164] it was held that an arbitration clause, providing that no cause of arbitration should accrue until the arbitrator's award was made, was effective to prevent time from running until that event happened. The decision in the case itself must be regarded as being overruled by what is now s.34(2) of the 1980 Act,[165] but the principle that express agreement can delay the accrual of the cause of action may still be regarded as good law. In *Musurus Bey v Gadban*[166] the defendant had been the Turkish ambassador to London. As such he was protected by diplomatic immunity from an action in tort. The plaintiff sued after the defendant had ceased to be ambassador, and the question was whether time ran from the commission of the wrong or only from the date when the defendant was no longer immune. The Court of Appeal held that the latter was the relevant date, and that the immunity continued for a reasonable time after he ceased to be ambassador so as to allow him time to wind up his affairs in this country.

More recently, in *Baker v Commissioner of Police for the Metropolis*[167] it was held that the cause of action in a case of malicious prosecution does not accrue until the prosecution has finally been dismissed, since this is a fact which the plaintiff must prove in order to have any chance of succeeding in such an action. The judge distinguished *O'Connor v Isaacs* on the basis that historically the action for false imprisonment was an action on the case, requiring proof of special damage, whereas an action for false imprisonment is an action for trespass to the person and as such does not require proof of special damage.

Later event merely removes procedural bar

5.062   In *Coburn v Colledge*[168] the plaintiff was a solicitor suing on a bill of costs. Then, as now, the law forbade the bringing of an action on such a bill until the expiry of one month from the delivery of the bill to the client. The question was whether the cause of action accrued on the delivery of the bill

---

[164] [1927] A.C. 616, HL.
[165] For consideration of s.34(2), see paras 16.026–16.028.
[166] [1894] 2 Q.B. 352, CA.
[167] June 24, 1996, Sir John Wood, Unreported; see also *Wenlock v Shinwell* (April 27, 1996, CA, Unreported). See also *Dunlop v H.M. Customs & Excise* (1998) 142 S.J. L.B. 134, *The Times* March 17, 1998, CA.
[168] [1897] 1 Q.B. 702, CA.

or on the expiry of the month. The Court of Appeal held that it accrued at the earlier date, on the ground that the expiry of the month was purely a procedural point, which did not affect the existence of the right of action, and, in particular, did not affect the solicitor's right to retain client money in his hands for the purpose of meeting the bill.

Evidential aspects

A further matter that may give rise to confusion in this context is the distinction between matters which are part of the cause of action and matters which are merely relevant to proving the existence of the cause of action. In making this distinction it may be helpful to bear in mind the definition of cause of action given by Lord Esher M.R. in Read v Brown[169]:

5.063

> "Every fact which it would be necessary for the plaintiff to prove, if traversed, in order to support his right to the judgment of the court."

The point here is that once those facts exist, it is irrelevant that the plaintiff will have great difficulty in proving them. He cannot claim that time does not run against him until he has all the evidence he requires.[170]

Another case along the same lines is *Hipperson v Chief Constable of Ministry of Defence Police*.[171] The plaintiff had been arrested numerous times while taking part in the Greenham Common protest in the 1980s. At the time it was assumed that these arrests were lawful, but at a later date it was held in *Director of Public Prosecutions v Hutchinson*[172] that the relevant RAF Greenham Common byelaws were ultra vires the enabling power and thus invalid. The plaintiff argued that her cause of action for wrongful imprisonment did not arise until that decision was made, but the Court of Appeal held that it arose on the making of each arrest. The decision that the byelaws were invalid merely removed a defence which would otherwise have been available. The same point may perhaps be made about *O'Connor v Isaacs*, where the plaintiff suffered all the relevant wrongs immediately he was imprisoned, even though his action could not succeed until the order of the justices had been set aside. If the order of 1942 was void, then it would presumably follow that the plaintiff could

---

[169] (1888) 22 Q.B.D. 128, CA. Although this is not a limitation case, the definition which it gives is of general relevance and was approved by the Court of Appeal in *Coburn v Colledge* [1897] 1 Q.B. 702, CA.

[170] Slightly different considerations may apply in cases of personal injury and latent damage, where time does not run until the cause of action is reasonably discoverable. This, however, is separate from the question whether the cause of action has accrued, and is dealt with in Ch.6 (Latent Damage) and Ch.8 (Personal Injuries).

[171] June 26, 1996, CA, Unreported.

[172] [1990] 2 A.C. 783; [1990] 2 All E.R. 836.

have sued immediately, and that the decision that the order was void was merely a matter of evidence, which could not affect the existence of the cause of action. Although Diplock J. does not explain his decision in these terms, this rationale probably provides the best possible support for the case.

5.064 Whatever the merits of the decisions in *O'Connor v Isaacs* and *Hipperson v Chief Constable of Ministry of Defence Police*, the approach adopted appears to be a sound one. However, the foregoing discussion has shown the need for a rather fuller description of the two categories of case than Diplock J. gave (or needed to give) in that case. Consequently, the following classification is suggested:

(a) cases where the later event is an essential ingredient in the cause of action, including cases where the parties have agreed to postpone the cause of action;

(b) cases of procedural bar, including cases where the plaintiff is entitled to enforce his right by other means and, possibly, cases where the plaintiff's difficulty is merely a matter of evidence.

This classification appears to leave problems surrounding one of the cases discussed in this context. *Musurus Bey v Gadban*[173] appears to be a case where the cause of action had accrued, but the plaintiff was subject to a procedural bar (namely the defendant's diplomatic immunity) which prevented him from bringing his claim. On the other hand, *Sevcon v Lucas*[174] seems to fit well with this analysis. The wrong had clearly been committed, and the only obstacle to the bringing of the action was the procedural rule in the Patents Act 1977 forbidding the institution of proceedings before the grant of the patent.

5.065 The final point in this context is to inquire whether the basic distinction drawn in these cases is either desirable or necessary. In cases which are held to fall into the category of procedural bar, the inevitable consequence is that time runs against the plaintiff before his action could possibly succeed, and it is very difficult to understand how that can be a just result. It is submitted that there was no need for the law to go down this path. The major wrong step appears to have been taken in *Coburn v Colledge*,[175] where the decision in *Read v Brown*,[176] which related to the situs of the cause of action and had nothing to do with limitation, was misapplied in a limitation context without taking account of the special problems which arise when questions of limitation are in issue. *Coburn v Colledge* is also the principal authority relied upon by Diplock J. in *O'Connor v Isaacs* for the notion of

---

[173] [1894] 2 Q.B. 352, CA.
[174] [1986] 1 W.L.R. 462, HL. See para.4.025.
[175] [1897] 1 Q.B. 702, CA.
[176] (1888) 22 Q.B.D. 128, CA.

procedural bar, and this too could have been avoided had the Court of Appeal acted differently in *Coburn v Colledge*. *Sevcon v Lucas* may be regarded as being similar to *Coburn v Colledge* for this purpose, since it concerns a statutory bar. The case is very unsatisfactory for its failure to consider these earlier authorities and for its reliance on a case which was clearly distinguishable from it. Although it is a decision of the House of Lords, it is submitted that it would be better to regard it as being confined to its own facts. It is to be hoped that, should the opportunity arise again, the House of Lords will be prepared to confine *Sevcon v Lucas* in this way, whilst overruling *Coburn v Colledge*, *O'Connor v Isaacs* and *Hipperson v Chief Constable of Ministry of Defence Police*. The law would then have reached the eminently sensible position that time does not run against a plaintiff until he can bring an action.

THE LAW COMMISSION'S PROPOSALS

The Law Commission Report would have significant effects in relation to this chapter, since the basic six-year limitation period of s.2 would be abolished in favour of the uniform three-year period. Chapters 5 and 6 of this book would then for most practical purposes be merged under a single set of rules, which would be very similar to the rules currently considered in Ch.6. **5.066**

CHAPTER 6

The Latent Damage Act 1986

BACKGROUND

The decision of the House of Lords in *Pirelli General Cable Works v Oscar Faber & Partners*[1] resolved a controversy, which had continued throughout the 1970s, as to the date of accrual of a cause of action in tort not involving personal injuries. The issue was whether the cause of action accrued as soon as the plaintiff suffered damage, or only when he discovered, or could with reasonable diligence have discovered, that damage. *Pirelli* decided in favour of the former alternative. The rule is clearly capable of operating harshly on claimants who, through no fault of their own, are unable to discover the existence of a cause of action until after the limitation period has expired, and the decision has not been followed in Canada[2] or New Zealand.[3] So far as English law is concerned, s.33 of the 1980 Act deals with the problem in the context of personal injuries cases by giving the court discretion to allow an action to be brought, notwithstanding that the primary limitation period has expired. Section 4A of the Act, as inserted by s.5 of the Defamation Act 1996,[4] also allows a limited discretion to extend time in actions for defamation.[5] Following the decision in *Pirelli* the general issue of what is commonly referred to as "latent damage", i.e. damage which is not reasonably discoverable until some time after it occurs, was referred to the Law Reform Committee. The 24th Report of that Committee[6] recommended a number of significant changes in the law, and these were subsequently enacted as the Latent Damage Act 1986 ("the LDA 1986"). This chapter therefore begins with a detailed examination of the provisions of that Act.

6.001

---

[1] [1983] 2 A.C. 1.
[2] *Central Trust Co. v Rafuse* [1986] 2 S.C.R. 147: (1986) 31 D.L.R. (4th) 481.
[3] *Invercargill C.C. v Hamlin* [1996] 1 All E.R. 756, PC.
[4] Replacing the original s.4A inserted by s.57 of the Administration of Justice Act 1985.
[5] 1980 Act, s.33, and the Defamation Act 1996 s.5, are examined in Ch.8.
[6] Cmnd. 9390.

THE LATENT DAMAGE ACT 1986

6.002 The Latent Damage Act 1986 operates principally by inserting additional sections into the 1980 Act. The major conditions are ss.14A and 14B, though it is necessary to consider also the new s.28A as well as a number of minor amendments to other sections. Further, s.3 of the LDA 1986, which is considered at paras 6.027–6.035 below, stands on its own.

Ambit of sections 14A and 14B

6.003 Section 14A of the 1980 Act, as inserted by s.1 of the LDA 1986, applies to any action for damages for negligence, other than one to which ss.11, 11A or 12 of the 1980 Act applies.[7] A number of points need to be made about this definition. It has been decided that s.14A has no application to an action based on contract. The term "negligence" is not defined by either the 1980 Act or the LDA 1986. Obviously it covers actions for tortious negligence, but the wording leaves it unclear whether it covers the breach of a duty to take care arising from a contract. The first case on this point was *Iron Trades Mutual Insurance v J.K. Buckenham.*[8] This was an action arising out of the alleged failure of the defendants over a number of years to obtain valid reinsurance contracts covering the primary liability of the plaintiffs, and the action was initially brought in both contract and tort. The tort claim was rejected on grounds which are not relevant for present purposes, and it therefore became necessary to consider whether the contract action was statute-barred. The dates of the various contracts were such that the contract for one of the years could possibly have fallen within the ambit of the LDA 1986, and the issue was whether the Act had any application to an action founded on contract. The learned judge held that it did not. Section 14A speaks only of "negligence"; this may be contrasted with s.11 of the 1980 Act, which creates a similar regime for personal injuries, but which speaks of "negligence, nuisance or breach of duty". The plaintiffs were driven to contend that the omission of any reference to breach of duty was an oversight on the part of the draftsman, but this argument, too, was rejected.

6.004 The same conclusion was reached in *Islander Trucking Ltd v Hogg Robinson & Gardner Mountain (Marine) Ltd,*[9] another case involving duties of insurance brokers, where the question of concurrent duties in contract and tort was again in issue. These decisions were approved by the Court of Appeal in *Société Commerciale de Reassurance v ERAS Interna-*

---

[7] i.e. an action for personal injuries.
[8] [1990] 1 All E.R. 808, K.S. Rokison Q.C. as a deputy High Court judge.
[9] [1990] 1 All E.R. 826, Evans J.

tional Ltd,[10] and the point is now beyond argument. The reasoning behind these decisions is convincing, even though the apparent result is that a claimant who derives his rights against the defendant from contract is unable to rely on the LDA 1986. It may seem odd that a claimant who sues in tort is in a stronger position than a claimant with privity of contract,[11] but that is the effect of the statute.

In *Laws v Lloyds*[12] the Court of Appeal held that actions for mis-representation under s.2 of the Misrepresentation Act 1967 do not fall within ss.14A because they are not claims for damages for negligence, but that claims for negligent misrepresentation at common law do fall within the section.

    6.005

Actions in nuisance

Another point of uncertainty is whether the LDA 1986 is available to a claimant whose action is based on nuisance. It must be accepted that negligence and nuisance have a substantial degree of overlap in the modern law, but there may still be cases where the action must be framed in nuisance because the claimant cannot otherwise show the necessary breach of duty. In such a case, it is submitted that s.14A has no application. An action where it is not necessary to show any want of care on the part of the defendant cannot properly be described as an action for negligence. The argument adopted in *Iron Trades Mutual Insurance v J.K. Buckenham*[13] may again be invoked in support of this conclusion.

    6.006

Other duties

The principle explained in the previous paragraph must apply equally to any case where the liability is strict[14] and to any case of breach of statutory duty where the duty requires something more than the taking of reasonable care. It will also apply to cases of deliberately caused damage. The decision of the House of Lords in *Stubbings v Webb*[15] establishes that an action for intentional trespass to the person is not within s.11 of the 1980 Act because it is not an action for negligence. For the same reason, it is not within the

    6.007

---

[10] [1992] 2 All E.R. 82, CA.
[11] Though of course the differing starting dates for the running of time under ss.2 and 5 of the 1980 Act can already produce a result of this kind.
[12] [2003] EWCA Civ 1887, [2003] All ER (D) 392 (Dec).
[13] [1990] 1 All E.R. 808.
[14] Such as liability for wild animals under the Animals Act 1971 or liability for some forms of trespass: see also para.6.001.
[15] [1993] 1 All E.R. 332.

LDA 1986, nor is an action for deliberately caused damage to property. For all tort actions based on deliberate wrongdoing the appropriate limitation period is six years from the date of accrual, as provided in s.2 of the 1980 Act. The 1986 Act has no application to actions within s.9 of the 1980 Act to recover a sum of money due under an enactment,[16] even where the sum is due in respect of what is considered to amount to negligence.

Defective premises

6.008 The great majority of the cases in which the problem of latent damage has arisen have been cases involving defective buildings.[17] The LDA 1986 is not limited to cases of this kind, but extends to any case of negligence where the damage is not immediately discoverable.[18] It appears that the LDA 1986 does not apply to claims brought under the Defective Premises Act 1972.[19]

The extended limitation period

6.009 Where s.14A applies, s.2 of the 1980 Act does not apply. Instead, time for the bringing of the action expires at the later of six years from the date when the cause of action accrues and three years from the "starting date". It has been held that this provision creates a single limitation period rather than two alternative limitation periods.[20]

Accrual of cause of action

6.010 The date of accrual is not defined, but since s.14A is part of the 1980 Act, it is to be assumed that the expression is to be construed in accordance with that Act. Further, since the gist of the action under consideration here is damage, it is submitted that the *Pirelli* test remains the appropriate one for determining the date of accrual under s.14A.

The starting date

6.011 The phrase "date of discoverability" has become a convenient piece of shorthand in this area of the law, but it is not the term used by s.14A, which

---

[16] *Martin v Britannia Life* [2000] L.R.P.N. 412, Jonathan Parker J.

[17] Although the Defective Premises Act 1972 is capable of applying to at least some cases of this kind, it appears that it has only rarely been relied upon. This Act is considered at para.27.013.

[18] *Berg v Glentworth Bulb Co. Ltd*, September 30, 1988, CA, Unreported.

[19] *Warner v Basildon Development Corp.* (1991) 7 Const.L.J. 146.

[20] *Busby v Cooper*, (1996) 52 Con.L.R. 94; [1996] E.G.C.S. 64; *The Times*, April 15, 1996, CA.

speaks instead of "the starting date".[21] This term is defined by s.14A(5) as:

"the earliest date on which the claimant or any person in whom the cause of action was vested before him first had both the knowledge required for bringing an action for damages in respect of the relevant damage and a right to bring such an action".

The reference to the right to bring such an action is apparently an allusion to the possibility that the claimant may acquire the knowledge before he acquired an interest in the damaged property. In such a case time will not start to run against him until he acquired that interest.

Relevant knowledge

Section 14A(6)–(8) goes on to define what is meant by "the relevant knowledge". This convoluted definition requires close attention. The relevant knowledge is such facts about the damage as would lead a reasonable person who had suffered such damage to consider it sufficiently serious to justify his instituting proceedings for damages against a defendant who did not dispute liability and was able to satisfy a judgment, together with the fact that the damage was attributable in whole or in part to the act or omission which is alleged to constitute negligence, the identity of the defendant and, if it is alleged that the act or omission was that of a person other than the defendant, the identity of that person and the additional facts supporting the bringing of an action against the defendant. At the outset it is appropriate to remember what Bingham L.J. said in *Spencer-Ward v Humberts*[22]:

6.012

"It is, I think, necessary that issues on this section [14A] should be approached in a broad common-sense way, bearing in mind the object of the section and the injustice that it was intended to mitigate. There is a danger of being too clever and it would usually be possible to find some fact of which a plaintiff did not become sure until later. It would be a pity if a desire to be indulgent to plaintiffs led the court to be unfair to defendants."

It has also been held that, for the purposes of s.14A, a claimant need not:

"know for certain and beyond the possibility of contradiction. It does, however, mean 'know with sufficient confidence to justify embarking on

---

[21] This may be compared with the concept of the "date of knowledge" in personal injury cases; see paras 8.015–8.022.

[22] [1995] 1 E.G.L.R 123; [1995] 06 E.G. 148, at p.151 of the latter report.

the preliminaries to the issue of a writ, such as submitting a claim to the proposed defendant, taking legal and other advice and collecting evidence. Suspicion, particularly if it is vague and unsupported, will indeed not be enough, but reasonable belief will normally suffice.' "[23]

The following paragraphs consider the definitional problems arising out of these subsections. The definition of the starting date may readily be recognised as bearing many similarities to that of the date of knowledge for the purposes of personal injury actions as given in s.14 of the 1980 Act, and in at least two cases[24] the Court of Appeal has been prepared to cite cases on the date of knowledge under s.14 of the 1980 Act as aids to interpreting the meaning of s.14A. There are, however, some minor differences in wording.

"Sufficiently serious"

6.013   It is not at first sight easy to understand why a claimant would consider any damage not sufficiently serious to justify the bringing of an action if the (frequently unrealistic and counterfactual) assumption is made that the defendant does not deny liability and has the money to meet a judgment.[25] An important point here is that only one action may be brought on any cause of action.[26] If the damage which immediately flows from the cause of action is only slight, but there is a clear risk that further, more substantial damage will follow at a later date, it may seem reasonable to delay the bringing of the action until more damage has occurred. It therefore seems that the LDA 1986 has significantly altered the former rule that time ran as soon as the plaintiff suffered damage that was more than minimal. In *Hallam-Eames v Merrett* Syndicates there was a suggestion at first instance,[27] not pursued on appeal, that some Lloyd's Names might be so rich that even a letter advising them of very substantial losses might not make them think the matter sufficiently serious to justify instituting proceedings. It is not relevant that the claimant is not yet in a position to quantify his loss, so long as he knows that the loss is sufficiently serious.[28]

---

[23] per Lord Donaldson M.R. in *Halford v Brookes* [1991] 3 All E.R. 559; [1991] 1 W.L.R. 428, at 443E of the latter report.

[24] *Spencer-Ward v Humberts*, n. 21 above, Unreported; *Hallam-Eames v Merrett Syndicates*, *The Times*, January 25, 1995, CA.

[25] In *Horbury v Craig Hall & Rutley*, May 24, 1991, Judge Bowsher Q.C., it was said that damage costing only £132 to repair was "sufficiently serious" as here defined, although the judge expressly admitted that a claimant might well not have been prepared to sue a defendant who disputed liability.

[26] See also *Darley Main Colliery v Mitchell* (1886) 11 App.Cas. 127, HL. For the effect of any continuing tort see also paras 5.004–5.005.

[27] October 14, 1994, Gatehouse J., Unreported.

[28] *Mortgage Corporation v Lambert & Co.* [2000] Build. L.R. 265, CA.

"Attributable"

The requirement that the claimant must know that the damage suffered is **6.014** attributable to the act or omission which is alleged to cause negligence has an exact counterpart in s.14 of the 1980 Act, and the extensive case law on that provision[29] may usefully be referred to as an aid to understanding attributability in this context. In addition, there is now a slowly emerging body of case law on the particular problems that arise in latent damage cases not involving personal injury. In *Wilson v Le Fevre Wood and Royle*[30] the plaintiff unsuccessfully argued that he did not have this knowledge because the defendant, a professional adviser whom he later sued, was continuing to represent that the problems were not caused by negligence. By contrast, in *Campbell v Meacocks (A Firm)*[31] plaintiffs who had received a letter from loss adjusters about the possible need to have their house underpinned were held not to be fixed with knowledge that there was damage attributable to the defendants. These two decisions may at first sight appear to be in conflict, but in fact they are merely applications of the general principle that it is necessary in each case to look carefully at what information was available to the claimant and consider what conclusions a reasonable person would have drawn from that information. Where the claimant is a large organisation such as a mortgage lender, the court is likely to expect it to have in place efficient systems for detecting commonly encountered problems such as mortgage fraud.[32]

However, 'attributable . . . to' does not necessarily embrace any factor which might be said to have played some part in the events which are alleged to have led to 'the relevant damage'.[33] Thus, in the example given by Hoffmann LJ in *Hallam-Eames* (in the passage from his judgment quoted in para.103 above), the fact that it could be said that a Lloyd's Name suffered losses because some members' agent took him to lunch and persuaded him to join Lloyd's would not be sufficient. As Hoffmann LJ says in that passage:

". . . the act or omission of which the plaintiff must have knowledge must be that which is causally relevant for the purposes of an allegation of negligence."

Or, as Hoffman LJ expressed it in *Hallam-Eames v Merrett*,[34] the fact that it could be said that a Lloyd's Name suffered losses because some

---

[29] See para.8.021.
[30] (1995) 16 Con.L.R. 74.
[31] [1993] C.I.L.L. 886; [1995] E.G.C.S. 143 CA.
[32] *Abbey National Plc v Sayer Moore (A Firm)*, *The Times*, August 30, 1999, Jacob J.
[33] *Haward v Fawcetts (a firm)* [2004] EWCA Civ 240 at para.160 per Jonathan Parker L.J.; the subsequent decision of the House of Lords appears to be to the same effect.
[34] (1995) 7 Med LR 122.

members' agent took him to lunch and persuaded him to join Lloyd's would not be sufficient.

It is clear that there are difficult issues about how much aware of causation issues the claimant must have. The Act does not refer to the claimant knowing what caused his loss, and the standard must be lower than one which would require such knowledge. At the same time the claimant must be aware, actually or constructively, of at least some facts which are causally relevant and which should therefore lead him to 'attribute' the loss to the Defendant's negligent acts or omissions.

"The identity of the defendant"

6.015   This creates a further exception to the general rule that time runs once the damage is suffered even though the claimant can neither trace nor identify the defendant.[35] No writ can be issued unless the defendant has been identified, and this provision (s.14A(8)(b)) ensures that, at least for the purposes of the three-year period, time will not run until the defendant has been identified.

Negligence of another

6.016   The reference to acts or omissions of another covers the situation where there is vicarious liability. It may not be immediately obvious to the claimant that the act or omission in question is one for which another person is vicariously responsible. For the purposes of the action against that other (though not, of course, for the purposes of the action against the actual wrongdoer) the three-year period will not run until the claimant knows both that there is vicarious responsibility and the identity of the person who bears that responsibility.

Fact and law

6.017   Section 14A(9) provides that knowledge that any act or omission did or did not, as a matter of law, involve negligence is irrelevant for the purpose of determining the starting date.[36] This is a difficult provision. The intention presumably is to make the determination of the starting date a matter of factual, rather than legal, knowledge, and it is easy to see how this rule might operate against a claimant. If he is in possession of all the relevant facts, then time will run against him even though he did not appreciate their legal significance. The distinction between matters of fact and matters of law was considered in *HF Pension Trustees Ltd v Ellison*.[37] This was an action by trustees of a pension fund against a solicitor for alleged negligence

---

[35] R.B. Policies at *Lloyd's v Butler* [1950] 1 K.B. 76, Streatfield J.
[36] *Fennon v Anthony Hodari & Co. (A Firm)* [2001] L.R.P.N. 183, CA.
[37] [1999] L.R.P.N. 489, Jonathan Parker J.

in advising that a proposed transfer of assets out of the fund would be lawful. The Pensions Ombudsman subsequently held that it was unlawful, and Knox J. upheld that conclusion. The question was whether s.14A could postpone the starting date beyond the date when the unlawful payments were made. Jonathan Parker J. held that the claimant had the necessary knowledge as soon as the payment has been made, because it knew that it had suffered loss, even though it could not know that the payment would later be held to be unlawful. The distinction is between causation, which the claimant must recognise, and negligence, which he need not recognise.[38] It is, of course, always a matter of fact whether the events which have happened are sufficient to make a reasonable claimant aware of the possibility of the facts on which he later seeks to rely. In deciding that question a judge can legitimately consider the circumstances of the claimant, and his relationship with the defendant.[39] *Haward v Fawcetts (a firm)*[40] was a claim for professional negligence against accountants for business advice given. It was held that time ran from the date when the advice was given because the claimant was aware that it had been given and what it said immediately. As a general proposition this must be too broad, though it may well be that in particular cases the claimant has enough knowledge of the matters in question to be fixed with knowledge immediately. The case may be contrasted with *Brown v Bird & Lovibond*[41], where it was said that a claimant had no reason to check what her solicitor had done in mortgaging her house to a bank until the bank started possession proceedings. *Haywards v Fawcett* was also considered and applied in *Harris Springs Ltd v Howes*[42] where cracks had developed in a property but the defendant had written to the claimant's architect in terms which suggested that the cracks should simply be monitored. It was held that on these facts the claimant had not been on notice of the cause of action and was not expected to seek alternative expert advice. The crucial point appears to be that the claimant reasonably relied on a letter from the defendant, and that letter suggested that there was no cause of action at that time. However, it must surely always be a question of fact whether it is reasonable for a claimant to refrain from further investigation on the basis of representations from the defendant.

A more difficult issue is whether s.14A(9) can ever serve to protect a claimant. The only way in which this can happen is where the claimant is in possession of only some of the material facts but does appreciate their legal significance. In such a case it cannot be argued that the starting date has

---

[38] See also *Bradstock Trustee Services Ltd v Nabarro Nathanson (A Firm)* [1995] 4 All E.R. 888; [1995] 1 W.L.R. 1405, Paul Baker Q.C.
[39] For an example, see *Gold v Mincoff Science & Gold* [2001] L.R.P.N. 423, Neuberger J.
[40] [2004] EWCA Civ 240.
[41] [2002] EWHC 719 (QB), Robin Moxon-Browne QC
[42] [2007] EWHC 3271 (TCC) Judge Raynor Q.C.

arrived. In all other cases this subsection can only operate to the detriment of the claimant.

Meaning of "knowledge"

6.018　Section 14A(10) provides that a person's knowledge for s.14A includes knowledge which he might reasonably have been expected to acquire from facts observable or ascertainable by him, or from facts ascertainable by him with the help of appropriate expert[43] advice which it is reasonable for him to seek. This subsection extends the concept of knowledge to include constructive knowledge, i.e. matters of which the claimant ought reasonably to have been aware, even though he was in fact ignorant of them. In *Manotaan Ltd v Rose and Birn (A Firm)*[44] it was held that an experienced businessman was justified in not reading every word of a draft lease sent to him by the defendant solicitor. Although he probably could have discovered the defect in the lease (a break clause) if he had read it with sufficient care, he was entitled to rely on the solicitor to draw his attention to any clauses which might cause particular problems. On the other hand, in *Webster v Cooper & Burnett (A Firm)*[45] it was held that a wfie who signed a guarantee of the debts of her husband's business must be treated as having knowledge at least of the general nature of the document which she had signed, even if she had not read it. In *Finance for Mortgages Ltd and Another v Farley and Company (A Firm)*[46] it was said that a mortgage company ought to have sought a prompt retrospective valuation on a mortgaged property once it became apparent that the borrowers were defaulting on the mortgage and had disappeared.

Section 14A(10) then adds a further proviso, to the effect that a person is not fixed with constructive knowledge of facts ascertainable only with the help of expert advice, so long as he has taken all reasonable steps to obtain and, where appropriate, to act on that advice. In *Coban v Allen*[47] P was an illegal immigrant, and D had threatened to report him to the immigration authorities if he attempted to instigate legal proceedings in relation to their dispute. It was held that this was not a sufficient reason for P to fail to seek legal advice, since his excuse was in effect the direct consequence of his own wrongdoing in being in the country illegally. A claimant who properly seeks advice will not be fixed with knowledge which his chosen expert should have provided him, but in fact did not.[48] However, the expert must be someone independent of the parties—even where the defendant professes

---

[43] In the context of the similar provision in personal injuries it has been held that a solicitor is not an "expert" for these purposes: see *Farrell v N.C.B.*, *The Times*, May 28, 1986 and see para.8.022.

[44] July 20, 1995.

[45] [2000] L.R.P.N. 167, CA.

[46] [1998] P.N.L.R. 145, Maurice Kay J.

[47] *The Times*, October 14, 1996, CA.

[48] *Gravgaard v Aldridge and Brownlee* [2009] EWCA Civ.1529 at para.9 per Arden L.J.

expertise in the subject-matter, it is not possible to rely on advice from the defendant.[49]

McCarroll v Statham Gill Davies[50] provides a reminder that under s.14A once the claimant knows the relevant facts, the running of time cannot be suspended or reset by the concealment and/or later discovery of further facts which may be regarded as strengthening the case.

In *Graham v Entec Europe Ltd (t/a Exploration Associates)*[51] the Court   6.019
of Appeal considered the imputation to a claimant of knowledge acquired by the loss adjuster acting for his insurers. The context of this was that the subsequent proceedings, although brought in the name of the policyholder, were in fact conducted by the insurers in the exercise of their subrogation rights. It was held that the adjuster's knowledge could be imputed to the policyholder. It is clear that this rests on the specific point that this was a subrogated claim. As a general rule the loss adjuster acts for the insurers, by whom he is paid. He does not act for and is not the agent of the policy-holder. However, in subrogation cases the position is different because the insurer is the party which has the real and effective interest in the pro-ceedings. The Court of Appeal went so far as to draw an analogy here between subrogation and assignment, whilst correctly admitting that the two things are by no means the same. It is submitted that this decision must be regarded as taking a very robust view of the imputation of knowledge, for at the time when the knowledge was first acquired by the adjuster, the insurer's subrogation rights had not arisen. At the same time the observa-tion that the insurer is the party with the real and effective interest is obviously correct, and the decision may be defended on that pragmatic ground.

The wording of the proviso to s.14A(10) also calls for examination; the   6.020
vital words are "so long as". If there is a fact ascertainable only with expert advice, then the claimant has a reasonable time (and what is reasonable must surely vary from case to case) in which to seek that advice. Until that reasonable time expires, he is not deemed to know the fact. If he seeks the advice within the reasonable time, then his date of knowledge is postponed until he receives the advice (even if this does not happen until after the expiry of the reasonable time for seeking the advice). If the first piece of expert advice which he received indicates the need to take further steps to obtain the facts (including, it is submitted, the taking of further expert advice), then the date of knowledge is postponed further, since the claimant must be allowed a reasonable time in which to take the further steps. So long as all steps are taken within the reasonable time, the date of knowledge for these purposes will be the date of actual knowledge. It appears that this rule applies even where the advice which the claimant receives is negligent,

---

[49] *Williams v Lishman Sidwell* [2009] EWHC 1322 (QB) Judge Reddihough.
[50] [2003] EWCA Civ 425, [2003] Lloyd's Rep PN 167.
[51] [2003] EWCA Civ 1177 August 6, 2003.

so that the date of actual knowledge is later than it might otherwise have been. Thus in *Oakes v Hopcroft*[52] the claimant had suffered personal injury. On the basis of a negligent diagnosis and prognosis she was advised to settle the claim for personal injury for a modest sum. Only later did it become apparent that her injury was relatively serious. It was held that the starting date for the purposes of her action against the doctor responsible for the negligent advice could not arrive until the later date when she obtained a second medical report which identified the errors in the first report. A curious case in this regard is *Mortgage Corporation v Lambert*,[53] where the claimant lenders had obtained a number of retrospective valuations of a mortgaged property from their debt-collection agents, and it was held that because these were valuations from persons not qualified as valuers they were not sufficient to fix the claimants with knowledge of the true valuation. The oddity is that the claimants were clearly aware that there was a problem with the mortgage and that issues of retrospective valuation might become relevant, yet the judge regarded the case as distinguishable from *Finance for Mortgages Ltd v Farley*.[54]

If the claimant at any stage allows the reasonable time for the taking of the next fact-finding step to expire without taking that step, he is thereupon fixed with knowledge of that fact, and no amount of subsequent diligence can change that.

The longstop

6.021   Section 14B of the 1980 Act, which is also inserted by s.1 of the LDA 1986, imposes a further restriction on the right to bring actions conferred by the 1986 Act. No action for damages for negligence (except one to which the 1980 Act, s.11 or 11A applies, i.e. a personal injuries action or an action under the Consumer Protection Act 1987) may be brought more than 15 years after the date of the last act which is alleged to constitute negligence to which the damage in question is wholly or partially attributable. Therefore, in a case where there have been successive acts of negligence, each separate act will effectively set the 15-year longstop running afresh. In extreme cases this may result in the longstop operating only at a point very much more than 15 years later than the date of the original act of negligence. This is perhaps an unsatisfactory state of affairs, but its practical importance is likely to be small: the longstop is of significance only where the periods of limitation provided for by s.14A have not expired by the time the 15-year limit is reached. These cases will obviously be rare; they presuppose, for example, that the starting date has not arrived within 12 years

---

[52] [2000] L.R.P.N. 946, CA.
[53] [1999] L.R.P.N. 947, David Oliver QC.
[54] See above, para.6.017.

of the accrual of the cause of action, and the longer the expiry of the 15-year period is postponed, the less likely it is that the longstop will be of relevance. The date of the last act of negligence is conceptually different from the date when the cause of action accrues, since there is no cause of action until there is damage as well as duty and breach.[55]

In those cases where the longstop does apply, its effect is drastic. It bars the right of action notwithstanding that the cause of action has not accrued and/or that the starting date for the purposes of s.14A has not arrived. As with s.14A it is important to observe that this provision is not limited to cases of what is commonly described as latent damage. It applies to all actions for damages for negligence except personal injury cases. Therefore, in cases where the damage occurs some considerable time after the relevant breach of duty,[56] the limitation period available to the claimant may be less than the six years allowed by ss.2 and 14A of the 1980 Act. Section 14B therefore, in some cases, reduces the limitation period that would be available under the present law. What is not at all clear from s.14B is whether the expiry of the longstop period extinguishes the underlying right of the claimant or whether, like other limitation periods in English law, it merely bars the remedy. It is submitted that the answer ought to be that it extinguishes the underlying right, given that the longstop is properly to be regarded as the trade-off for the introduction of the concept of the starting date, and given that the longstop can apply even where the cause of action has not yet accrued. In *Financial Services Compensation Scheme Ltd v Larnell (Insurances) Ltd*[57] the Court of Appeal, in the context of a claim affected by insolvency, disagreed with this statement, suggesting that the language used was not sufficient to achieve this drastic effect.[58] It is of ocurse true that the language is not so explicit as that used in, for example, s.15 of the Limitation Act 1980, but it is submitted that this is not conclusive of the point, and that the arguments set out above ought to be given weight in coming to the conclusion that the right is extinguished. The point is more fully considered at para.15.004 in the context of contribution claims, which appear to be the only other area where the question is likely to be of practical importance.

6.022

Fraud and the longstop

The one important situation to which s.14B will not apply is that where s.32(1)(b) (concealment of material fact by defendant) does apply.[59] In such cases the limitation period is six years from the date on which the cause of

6.023

---

[55] *Lewis v Osborne*, November 28, 1995, Dyson J.
[56] Or the last such breach, where there is more than one.
[57] [2005] EWCA Civ 1408 CA.
[58] See in particular per Lloyd L.J. at para 48.
[59] 1980 Act, s.32(5) as inserted by LDA 1986, s.2; see para.2.033. For a further discussion of fraud, see para.6.028.

action was discovered or could with reasonable diligence have been discovered by the claimant.

The longstop and adding new parties

6.024 The discretion under s.35 of the 1980 Act and CPR 19.5 to add new parties after the expiry of a relevant limitation period extends to a case where the longstop has expired.[60]

Disability

6.025 Section 2 of the LDA 1986 makes a number of consequential provisions necessitated by s.1. A new s.28A is introduced to the 1980 Act. Section 28A, like s.28 of the 1980 Act, deals with persons under a disability, and aims at the situation where the claimant is under disability and ss.14A and 14B apply. However, it is essential to understand that s.28A does not apply if s.28 does. Therefore s.28A is limited to the case where the claimant is under a disability at the starting date, but was not under a disability when the cause of action accrued. Clearly, this can only occur where the claimant becomes of unsound mind in the period between the date of accrual and the starting date. In this case the period of limitation expires three years after the claimant dies or ceases to be under a disability. On the other hand, if the claimant was under a disability when the cause of action accrued, then, irrespective of the position at the date of knowledge, the limitation period expires six years after the claimant dies or ceases to be under disability. The rationale for this curious distinction is difficult to fathom, although the application of a three-year period is one of the basic features of the LDA 1986. A possible explanation would be that the date of knowledge will always be somewhat later than the date of accrual, and that the need to restrict the bringing of stale actions mandates a shorter time-limit. One further point here is that under s.28A the claimant is apparently restricted to the three-year period from the end of the disability, whereas in cases under s.14A of the 1980 Act the period is the longer of six years from accrual and three years from end of disability. In those cases where the date of knowledge follows quite closely after the date of accrual, careful attention to the wording of the statute is required. The following example may be found illuminating:

A's cause of action accrues in June 2002. In December 2002 A becomes of unsound mind. The starting date is found to be May 2003. A ceases to be of unsound mind in October 2004. The period of three years from the end

---

[60] *Horne-Roberts (A Child) v Smithkline Beecham plc, The Times*, January 10, 2002, CA. Although this case is on the longstop under CPA 1987 (Ch.7), the principle appears equally applicable to cases under s.14A.

of disability expires in October 2007. If A had not become of unsound mind time would have expired in June 2008, since this is later than May 2006, the date produced by allowing three years from the starting date.

It would, however, be wrong to conclude that time expires in October 2007. This odd consequence is, however, prevented by s.28A(1)(a), which provides that s.28A is to apply only when the relevant period of limitation is three years from the starting date. Reference back to s.14A(4) shows that this will occur only when the three-year period expires later than the six-year period. Section 28A therefore has no application to the above example, and A's time would expire in June 2008. To bring s.28A into operation it is necessary to modify the example as follows:

A's cause of action accrues in June 2002. He becomes of unsound mind in December 2002. The starting date is found to be May 2006. A ceases to be of unsound mind in November 2007. Without s.28A time would expire in May 2009 (three years from the starting date) but the application of s.28A extends that to November 2010 (three years from the end of disability).

Therefore, s.28A can extend the claimant's time for bringing an action, but can never shorten it.

Disability and the longstop

A restriction on the availability of s.28A is found in s.28A(2), which provides that the section cannot be used to allow the claimant to bring an action after the expiry of the 15-year longstop period provided for by s.14B of the 1980 Act.

Fraud

Section 2 of the LDA 1986 also adds a new s.32(5) to the 1980 Act. Section 32(5) is clumsily worded, but should not cause great problems in practice. It deals with the case where the date of discoverability is later than the date of damage and the claimant's right of action has been concealed from him by the defendant. Under s.32(1)(b) of the 1980 Act, the rule for this has previously been that the period is six years measured from the date of discoverability, and the effect of s.32(5) is to preserve that rule rather than importing the ss.14A and 14B provisions into this situation. Two important consequences follow from this rule. The first is that the three-year period from the starting date is irrelevant. The second is that the 15-year longstop from the date of the last act of negligence has no application. This is the only situation on an action for damages for negligence not including personal injuries where the longstop provision does not apply. This rule is restricted to cases under s.32(1)(b) of the 1980 Act and does not operate in relation to cases under s.32(1)(a) or (c).

6.026

6.027

6.028

Successive owners

6.029 Section 3 of the LDA 1986 deals with the position of successive owners of property that has suffered latent damage. Section 3(1) sets out the basic conditions for applying the section. These are that a cause of action has accrued to a person because of negligence causing (wholly or partly) damage to property in which he has an interest and another person acquires an interest in that property after the date when the cause of action accrued but before the material facts about the damage became known to any person who, at the time when he acquired that knowledge, also had an interest in the property. In these circumstances a fresh cause of action accrues to the person acquiring an interest in the property on the date on which he acquires that interest. A number of points about this definition call for comment.

Acquisition of interest

6.030 Section 3 does not require that the interest shall be outright ownership,[61] nor that the previous owner shall have divested himself of all interest in the property. Therefore, in the case of land (which will be the most common case to which this section will apply) a person who acquires a leasehold or reversionary interest in the property will fall within this part of the definition. In the case of personal property it appears that any interest will suffice, even if it is no more than the special property acquired by a bailee. In practice, though, the effect of this will be limited by the fact that persons with limited interests in personal property are relatively unlikely to suffer loss as a result of any defects in the property and are therefore less likely to want to sue.

Material facts

6.031 Section 3(5) defines the material facts referred to in s.3(1) as such facts about the damage as would lead a reasonable person who has an interest in the damaged property at the time when those facts become known to him to consider the damage sufficiently serious to justify his instituting proceedings for damages against a defendant who did not dispute liability and was able to satisfy a judgment. Section 3(6) further amplifies this by providing that for these purposes a person's knowledge includes knowledge which he might reasonably have been expected to acquire from facts observable or ascertainable by him or from facts ascertainable by him with the help of appropriate expert advice which it is reasonable for him to seek. However, a person is not to be fixed with knowledge or matters ascertainable by him

---

[61] Nor, indeed, that the interest acquired shall be a legal one. On the wording, an equitable interest would be sufficient.

only with the help of expert advice so long as he has taken all reasonable steps to obtain that advice and, where appropriate, to act on it.

This definition of material facts is very similar to the definition of "knowledge required for bringing an action for damages" under s.14A of the 1980 Act,[62] but there are some significant differences. The first is that the knowledge must be possessed by a person who has an interest in the property at that time. Therefore, the requirements of the definition are not satisfied by a person who first acquires the knowledge after disposing of the interest or before obtaining it. However, where a person has the knowledge and subsequently acquires the interest this part of the definition is satisfied. It is not necessary that the information be first acquired at a time when the person has an interest in the property. The coincidence of knowledge and interest is not expressly required under s.14A, but any claimant who seeks to rely on this section will necessarily have both the knowledge and the interest, since he will be the original owner of the property. Secondly, the concept of constructive knowledge of facts here refers to knowledge acquired or acquirable from facts ascertained by the owner of the interest, whereas the definition in s.14A refers to knowledge acquired or acquirable from facts ascertainable by the claimant. If this very slight difference of wording is to be construed strictly, the result will apparently be that under s.3 the claimant is fixed with knowledge obtainable with expert advice only where he has actually ascertained those facts, whereas under s.14A of the 1980 Act, he may be treated as having knowledge which he does not in fact have because of his own failure to seek the expert advice when it was reasonable for him to do so.[63]

It is hard to believe that s.3(6) was intended to work in this way, partly because it is so obviously intended as a constructive notice provision and partly because this interpretation would render otiose the later words in the subsection which delay the date of knowledge so long as the expert advice has been sought. Conversely, to regard s.3(6) as simply a constructive notice provision along the same lines as the comparable parts of s.14A would be to ignore the difference in wording, an approach which appears to violate established canons of statutory construction. It is nevertheless submitted that should the point arise, a court will construe s.3(6)(b) as if it referred to facts ascertainable by the claimant rather than to facts ascertained by him; only in this way can the evident intention of this section be achieved. **6.032**

Effect of section 3

As mentioned above, when the conditions of applicability are satisfied, s.3(1) provides that a fresh cause of action in respect of the negligence **6.033**

---

[62] See para.8.015.
[63] See para.8.015.

137

causing the damage shall accrue to the person acquiring the interest on the date when he acquires it. This provision serves to circumvent the difficulty that a subsequent purchaser of an interest in the property might well be a person to whom no duty of care was owed under the ordinary principles of the law of tort. This right of action is subject to a number of constraints, which are considered in the following paragraphs.

Nature of cause of action

6.034 The cause of action which accrues to the acquirer of the interest is treated as being based on breach of a common law duty to take reasonable care, such duty being owed to the person to whom it accrues,[64] i.e. it is an action in tort for negligence.

Accrual of cause of action

6.035 The cause of action created by section 3 is treated for the purpose of s.14A of the 1980 Act as having accrued on the date on which the cause of action of the original owner of the property accrued.[65] This rule ensures that the limitation period does not automatically start afresh every time the property changes hands. It is nevertheless possible that the acquisition of the new interest will operate to extend time. This will occur where the date of knowledge of the acquirer is later than the date of the original owner.

Disability

6.036 Section 3(3) provides that s.28 of the 1980 Act shall not apply to the cause of action created by this section. This does not mean that the limitation period cannot be extended in cases of disability. The inapplicability of s.28 allows s.28A to apply,[66] and the effect of this is that the vital time for determining whether the claimant (in this context the subsequent acquirer of the interest) is under a disability, is the earliest date on which that person had both the necessary knowledge and the interest in the property which is necessary to support his right to bring an action in respect of the damage.

Persons excluded from section 3

6.037 Section 3(4) provides that the benefit of s.3 cannot be taken by any person who acquires an interest in the property, and in whom the original cause of action thereupon vests by operation of law (such as a trustee in bankruptcy), or any person in whom the interest in the property vests by virtue of a court order under s.538 of the Companies Act 1985 (the statute allowing the court to vest the property of a company in its liquidator). So

---

[64] LDA 1986, s.3(2).
[65] LDA 1986, s.3(2)(b).
[66] See paras 19.022–19.023.

far as the former of these categories is concerned, there is no need for the operation of s.3, since the trustee in bankruptcy acquires the original cause of action and does not require a statutory provision to vest a new cause of action in him. The position of the liquidator is more problematical; however, a court order under s.538 is sufficient to confer upon the liquidator the power to take all such actions as the company could otherwise have taken on its own behalf, so that s.3 is again unnecessary in this context.

Application to the Crown

The LDA 1986 binds the Crown, but, so far as liability in tort is concerned, is not to be construed as imposing any greater liability than exists already by virtue of the Crown Proceedings Act 1947. This is of importance only in the context of s.3, where it makes clear that any liability imposed on the Crown to a person subsequently acquiring an interest is to be treated as a liability in tort for the purposes of the 1947 Act.   6.038

Transitional provisions

Section 4 of the LDA 1986 contains transitional provisions.[67] Sections 1 and 2 of the Act do not operate to revive any cause of action which was barred at the time when the LDA came into force.[68] In addition, they do not apply to any action commenced before the enforcement date. They do, however, apply to causes of action which accrued before the Act came into force, but which were not barred, and in respect of which no action had been commenced at the enforcement date of the Act. Section 3 of the Act operates differently. There is no express provision that it cannot revive a cause of action which is already barred. The section applies only in cases where an interest in damaged property is acquired after the LDA 1986 came into force, and it is irrelevant for this purpose whether the original cause of action accrued before or after its enforcement. This rule is further qualified by s.4(4) of the LDA 1986. This applies where a person acquires an interest in damaged property after the Act came into force, and in such circumstances that a cause of action would otherwise accrue to him, but where the original action accrued before September 18, 1980 (i.e. six years before the Act came into force). In these circumstances the person acquiring the interest shall not acquire a cause of action under s.3(1) of the LDA 1986, unless s.32(1)(b) of the 1980 Act would apply to any action founded on the original cause of action. This provision has two consequences. First, an action which was already time-barred at September 18, 1986 could not be   6.039

---

[67] See also para.6.043.
[68] September 18, 1986.

revived under s.3.[69] Secondly, there might have been actions which were not barred at September 18, 1986, but where the subsequent acquirer of an interest in the property cannot obtain a cause of action under s.3. This will occur where the running of time has been postponed for any reason other than s.32(1)(b). Examples of this would be cases under s.32(1)(a) or (c) and cases where the time for the bringing of an action on the original right of action has been extended by acknowledgment. It is thought that the passage of time has now exhausted the effect of these transitional provisions, more than 15 years having expired since September 18, 1986.

The practical effect of the LDA 1986

6.040 As was explained above, the LDA 1986 was intended to alleviate some of the problems that arose as a result of the decision in *Pirelli General Cable Works v Oscar Faber and Partners*.[70] In surveying the law in the light of the Act a number of questions must be asked, as follows:

(1) Has the Act effectively overruled the decision in *Pirelli*?

(2) What is the status of Lord Fraser's reference in *Pirelli* to the possibility of a building being "doomed from the start"?

(3) How does the Act operate in other cases of latent damage?

(4) How does the Act affect the position where there are two occasions of damage?

(5) How does the Act relate to other limitation provisions?

1. The status of the decision in *Pirelli*[71]

6.041 The harshness of the decision in this case, that the action accrued when the damage occurred, even though it was not reasonably discoverable by the plaintiffs until later, was recognised by their Lordships, who nevertheless felt unable to do anything judicially to ameliorate the position. The LDA 1986 is clearly of immense significance in cases of this kind, but that is not to say that the result in *Pirelli* would now be different. There are two possible limitation periods—six years from the date of damage, or three years from the date of knowledge, i.e. the date on which the damage was reasonably discoverable. In *Pirelli* the first of these expired in 1976, but it is not wholly clear when the second would have expired. The Court found

---

[69] An action to which the 1980 Act s.32(1)(b) applies is not properly described as time-barred, since time will not have run, notwithstanding that six years will have expired since the accrual of the cause of action.

[70] [1983] 2 A.C. 1, HL. For the details of this case, see para.5.008.

[71] This discussion considers only the possible effect of the LDA on *Pirelli*.

that the damage was not discoverable before October 1972, but that was obviously chosen because it was exactly six years before the issue of the writ, and there was no decision to the effect that the damage was reasonably discoverable in October 1972. Unless the damage remained undiscoverable until October 1975—a point which will never now be resolved—the result in *Pirelli* would not be affected by the 1986 Act. Thus the Act is potentially important in cases of this kind, but care is needed not to exaggerate its importance. In particular, the three-year period running from the date of discoverability will be of no use to a claimant unless the starting date is at least three years after the date when the cause of the action accrues.

2. "Doomed from the start"

In *Pirelli* the House of Lords held that a cause of action in tort accrues when the claimant suffers damage as a result of the defendants' breach of duty. Lord Fraser of Tullybelton, giving the leading speech, observed that in the case of a negligently designed house this would normally be at the time when physical damage occurred to the house, although there might be cases where the defect was so gross that the building could be said to be "doomed from the start". In these cases the cause of action would accrue when the building was completed. A few months earlier, in *Junior Books v Veitchi Co. Ltd*,[72] the House of Lords had held that the owners of a building could recover expectation losses in tort for defective (but not dangerous) work carried out by nominated sub-contractors with whom they were not in a contractual relationship. Two major questions arise from these two decisions. First, what is the relationship between the *Junior Books* action and the notion that time runs only from the happening of physical damage? Secondly, what did Lord Fraser have in mind when he spoke of houses being "doomed from the start"? The first of these questions is considered at para.5.023. The second question is considered in detail at paras 5.015–5.017. It may be noted here, however, that there will be very few cases where it is appropriate for the defendant to rely on the concept that a product was doomed from the start.[73] Further, in the context of latent damage, the importance of the defence is reduced by the fact that the action can be brought up to three years from the starting date, even if the cause of action accrued much earlier.

6.042

3. Other cases of latent damage

Latent damage can also be a problem in cases of purely economic loss, as distinct from loss arising from physical damage. The most common examples of this in the reported cases arise from the giving of negligent

6.043

---

[72] [1983] A.C. 520; see Ch.5.
[73] The three cases where this defence has been accepted are examined at para.5.015.

professional advice, particularly by solicitors, and it is instructive to consider how some of these cases might be decided under the LDA 1986. In *Forster v Outred*,[74] where Mrs Forster's writ against the solicitors was held to be out of time, the effect of the LDA 1986 is unclear. The damage that was suffered in 1973 was apparently discoverable only by taking further expert advice, though on the facts of that particular case the court might be prepared to hold that since it was so obviously unwise to take out the mortgage, professional advice was unnecessary. It may be possible for the claimant to rely on what is now the proviso to s.14A(9)(b) of the 1980 Act, which provides:

"A person shall not be taken by virtue of this subsection to have knowledge of a fact ascertainable only with the help of expert advice so long as he has taken all reasonable steps to obtain . . . that advice."

6.044   The difficulty here is that Mrs Forster's unwise conduct was so apparent that professional advice hardly seems necessary.[75] A more appropriate basis for comparison would perhaps be *Ferrier v D.W. Moore & Co. Ltd*,[76] where the defendant solicitors had so negligently drafted a service contract that it was ineffective to prevent the employee from leaving the plaintiffs' business and setting up in competition with them. It was held that the cause of action accrued when the contract was signed rather than when the employee began to compete. Neill L.J. expressed the view that the case might well be decided differently under the LDA 1986,[77] but it is by no means clear that this is so.

This problem may be expressed in this way: if the claimant engages a solicitor, and that solicitor performs his duties negligently, when will it become reasonably possible for the claimant to discover the breach of duty? In practice the likelihood is that the breach will in fact be discovered only when the loss materialises, but it is possible for the solicitor to argue that the claimant should reasonably have realised the error at an earlier stage? An instinctive reaction might well be that the solicitor should not be allowed to plead this point, but reflection will show that the more flagrant the breach of duty, i.e. the more negligent the solicitor has been, the more likely it is that the breach will have been reasonably discoverable at an earlier stage. Generally, it obviously cannot be the law that a client is required to retain one solicitor to check on the work of another, so the

---

[74] [1982] 1 W.L.R. 86. For the details of this case, see paras 5.026–5.027.

[75] One difficulty with this argument is that it may lead to the conclusion that there was in truth no negligence on the part of the solicitors, since the risks involved should have been sufficiently obvious to their client. From this point of view it is regrettable that the substantive issue of negligence never came to be tried. Certainly, *Forster v Outred* needs to be treated with some caution in a limitation context.

[76] [1988] 1 W.L.R. 267, CA; (1998) 104 L.Q.R. 376.

[77] [1988] 1 All E.R. 400 at 405.

provision that a claimant's knowledge includes facts which he could have discovered with the help of expert advice that it was reasonable for him to seek (s.14A(10)) will be of no significance. However, the claimants in *Moore v Ferrier* may appear to be in a somewhat different position. They had no reason to be aware that they had suffered any damage, since this awareness would have required them to have the legal knowledge necessary to appreciate that the term "member" in relation to a company refers only to the shareholders. This may be a ground for suggesting that the LDA 1986 would have a decisive impact on this case. A comparison between these two cases illustrates the difficulties in this area of the law. The question of whether a solicitor's negligence should be regarded as immediately discoverable will depend upon the precise facts of each case, and it is virtually impossible to lay down any reliable general rule.

A more important general issue arising from these cases is whether the LDA 1986 does in fact apply to cases of pure economic loss. It has been argued[78] that the references in the Act to "damage" rather than "loss" show that the Act is properly applicable only in cases of damage to property. However, this is contrary to the weight of judicial dicta to date[79] and it is submitted that it is incorrect. Although the difference between "damage" and "loss" cannot be denied, it has been common in cases of solicitors' negligence, for example, to speak of the date on which the claimant suffers "damage" and it seems unlikely that the draftsman of the LDA 1986 was seeking to draw the suggested distinction. Equally, there is now authority that the Act is not limited to the activities of professionals in the "design team" in the construction industry.[80]

6.045

4. Two occasions of damage

The decision in *Forster v Outred* illustrates a fundamental problem of the law of limitation periods—it cannot cope adequately with the situation where the damage resulting from a particular breach of duty does not happen all at once. In this case, Mrs Forster had suffered loss on executing the mortgage, but the value of her interest in the house was not reduced to nil, since there was always the possibility that her son's business would prosper. It was only in 1977 that she suffered the remaining loss, and by holding that the cause of action accrued in 1977 the court made it impossible for Mrs Forster ever to recover the extra damage which she suffered in April 1977. It is clear that the provisions of the Latent Damage Act 1986 will have no effect on this problem, unless it can be shown that

6.046

---

[78] Terence Prime and Gary Scanlan, *The Modern Law of Limitation* (2001), p.155.
[79] In addition to the observations of Neill L.J. cited above, see *Bell v Peter Browne & Co.* [1990] 2 Q.B. 495 at 502, per Nicholls L.J. and Ralph Gibson L.J. in *Berg v Glentworth Bulb Co.* (September 30, 1988, Unreported).
[80] *Horbury v Craig Hall & Rutley* [1991] C.I.L.L. 692; [1991] E.G.C.S. 81, Judge Bowsher Q.C.

the damage which occurred on the first occasion was not then reasonably discoverable, and that the starting date did not arrive until, at the earliest, the second occasion of damage.

A further problem in this context arises from the operation of the long-stop. It will be recalled[81] that the longstop operates from the date of the last act of negligence. In cases involving two occasions of damage the position will usually be that there has only been one act of negligence. If the second occasion of damage happens long enough after the first the result may be that any action in respect of this is barred by the longstop, quite apart from the questions relating to the identification of the starting date discussed in the previous paragraph. It must be admitted, though, that this will be a somewhat uncommon problem, given the length of the longstop period.

5. Other limitation provisions

6.047   The LDA 1986 follows the common modern trend of superimposing its limitation periods on those already existing. Thus, the period of three years from the date of knowledge applies in addition to the six-year period from date of accrual provided for by s.2 of the 1980 Act, the applicable period in cases of conflict being the one more favourable to the claimant.

CONCLUSION

6.048   The Latent Damage Act 1986 is a significant statute, though its significance may now be less than was thought when it was enacted. This results from the trend of recent years towards restricting the scope of liability in tort for purely defective, as distinct from damaged, property.[82] One effect of this trend is that causes of action may accrue later than they would otherwise have done (assuming that they accrue at all) and may be more readily discoverable. Nevertheless, the effect of the LDA 1986 should not be underestimated. It will in some cases prevent the kind of injustice which inevitably resulted from the decision of the House of Lords in *Pirelli*, but this has been achieved at the price of increased uncertainty, made worse than it need have been by unhappy drafting. In addition, the passage of the statute shows all the worst tendencies of law reform in the present system: it is an ad hoc response to one small part of the difficulties in this area of the law; it makes no effort to deal with the subject as a whole, and little thought has apparently been given to the place of the new provisions within the law of limitation periods generally.

---

[81] See para.6.021.
[82] *D. & F. Estates v Church Commissioners for England* [1989] A.C. 177, HL; *Murphy v Brentwood CC* [1991] 1 A.C. 398, HL.

THE LAW COMMISSION'S PROPOSALS

The Law Commission Report Paper proposes adopting a general uniform **6.049** three-year limitation period, similar to that found in the Latent Damage Act 1986. However, this period would be as a replacement to the existing six-year period rather than as a complement to it. A further slight difference arises from the change in the definition of significance of loss. The hypothetical claimant would no longer be required to assume that the defendant has the means to satisfy a judgment, though the artificial assumption that liability will not be disputed is retained.

CHAPTER 7

The Consumer Protection Act 1987

The Consumer Protection Act 1987 (the CPA 1987) was enacted in order to comply with the requirements of the European Union with regard to manufacturers' liability for defective products.[1] Essentially, the effect of the Act is to impose something akin to strict liability on the producers of products for damage caused by defects in those products. Therefore, in a case such as *Donoghue v Stevenson*[2] the injured pursuer would now be able to proceed under the CPA 1987 as an alternative to bringing an action in tort. The Act deals principally with personal injury, though damage to property can also be recovered subject to certain conditions. To a limited extent (the exact ambit of which remains uncertain 15 years after the passage of the Act) it creates new causes of action not previously recognised by English law.[3] Schedule 1 to the Act adds a new s.11A to the Limitation Act 1980, creating special periods of limitation applicable only to actions under the CPA 1987. A number of consequential amendments to ss.14, 28, 32 and 33 of the 1980 Act are also made. As appears below, those periods are likely in many cases to expire sooner than the corresponding periods for actions in tort or contract founded on the same set of facts. Careful attention to the details of these periods is therefore essential.

7.001

THREE-YEAR PERIOD

The basic provision inserted by Sch.1 to the CPA 1987 is the new s.11A of the 1980 Act. Section 11A(4) provides that in the case of an action under Pt I of the CPA 1987 (dealing with liability for defective products) the rules in

7.002

---

[1] Directive 85/374.
[2] [1932] A.C. 562, HL.
[3] The intention of the CPA 1987 appears to be to spare the claimant the need to prove negligence. Unfortunately the combination of the definition of "defect" in CPA 1987, s.3 and the inclusion of the development-risks defence in s.4 may reduce the standard imposed by the Act to nothing higher than the existing negligence standard.

s.2 of the 1980 Act shall not apply. Instead, the period of limitation shall be three years.

COMMENCEMENT OF PERIOD

7.003 The three-year period will begin to run on the later of two dates. The first is the date when the cause of action accrues, whilst the second is the date on which the claimant knew or could with reasonable diligence have discovered the existence of his cause of action.

Accrual

7.004 The legislation contains no definition of the time at which the cause of action accrues but, since s.11A takes its place as a new section in the 1980 Act,[4] it is submitted that it should be construed in accordance with the principles of that Act. Since the gist of the action under the CPA 1987 is damage, it seems appropriate here to refer to the ordinary rules in tort cases, i.e. the cause of action accrues when the claimant has suffered any damage which is not minimal,[5] and it is irrelevant that he is unaware of this damage.

PERSONAL INJURY CAUSING DEATH

7.005 Where an action is brought for personal injury under the CPA 1987, and the injured person (who need not be the claimant)[6] dies before the expiry of the three-year period described in the preceding paragraphs, the three-year period runs from the later of the date of death and the date of the personal representative's knowledge, rather than from the date of accrual of the cause of action.[7] Knowledge for a personal representative has the same meaning as for the claimant. If there is more than one personal representative and their dates of knowledge are different, then the earliest date of knowledge of any personal representative is the decisive one.[8]

---

[4] Inserted by CPA 1987, Sch.1, para.1.
[5] *Pirelli General Cable Works v Oscar Faber & Partners* [1983] 2 A.C. 1, HL. See also Ch.5.
[6] 1980 Act s.11A(4) as added by CPA 1987, Sch.1.
[7] 1980 Act s.11A(6) as added by CPA 1987, Sch.1.
[8] 1980 Act s.11A(7) as added by CPA 1987, Sch.1.

Discoverability

Section 14(1A) of the 1980 Act, as added by Sch.1 to the CPA 1987, defines   **7.006**
the meaning of "discoverability" for the purposes of actions under the CPA
1987. That date occurs when the claimant first has knowledge of:

"(a) such facts about the damage caused by the defect as would lead a
reasonable person who had suffered such damage to consider it
sufficiently serious to justify his instituting proceedings for damages
against a defendant who did not dispute liability and was able to
satisfy a judgment;
(b) that the damage was wholly or partly attributable to the facts and
circumstances alleged to constitute the defect;
(c) the identity of the defendant."[9]

But there shall be disregarded any knowledge on the part of the claimant
of whether or not the facts or circumstances could as a matter of law
constitute a defect, and, in a case involving damage to property, any
knowledge which that person had on a date on which he had no right of
action under Pt I of the CPA 1987 in respect of the loss or damage. This
definition is discussed in the following paragraphs.

Paragraph (a) of the above definition is in similar terms to those used in   **7.007**
the test for discoverability in the case of an action for personal injuries[10]
and in the case of latent damage.[11] Cases involving damage caused by
medicines and by chemicals are likely to be especially problematic here.
These are cases where defective products cause damage, but where some
considerable time is likely to elapse either before the damage becomes
apparent or before the claimant appreciates what the cause of the damage
was. In such cases it is inevitable that reliance will be placed on the discoverability provisions. Another difficulty which is commonly felt with this
wording is that of establishing under what circumstances a claimant would
not think it worthwhile to sue a defendant who admitted liability and had
the funds to satisfy a judgment. A possible answer may be found in the case
where the claimant has suffered damage from the defendant's acts, but
expects to suffer further, significantly greater, damage at a later stage. If an
action is brought immediately, the claimant will recover only the damage
already suffered, plus, possibly, a further sum calculated on the contingency
that the future damage will materialise. Only by waiting for that further
damage can the claimant be sure of being compensated for it, and it is at

---

[9] CPA 1987, Sch.1, para.3.
[10] 1980 Act s.14.
[11] 1980 Act s.14A, as added by the Latent Damage Act 1986; see also Ch.6.

least arguable that in this situation a reasonable claimant would think the damage insufficient to warrant the bringing of an action.[12]

7.008 In considering paragraph (b) it is necessary to bear in mind the distinction between factual causation and legal causation. The wording is again similar to that used in the context of personal injuries[13] and latent damage,[14] and must be interpreted in the light of the proviso to the definition, which makes the claimant's knowledge of the legal, as distinct from the factual position irrelevant for this purpose. Although the provision has not yet been judicially construed in the context of the CPA 1987, analogies may helpfully be drawn with the interpretation placed on it in the personal injuries cases, where it has been held that knowledge, in a general sense, that the defendant has committed a breach of duty which has led to the damage is sufficient, it being unnecessary to show that the claimant could identify particular breaches of duty and their exact consequences.[15]

Paragraph (c) requires the claimant to know the identity of the defendant. This apparently self-evident requirement covers situations such as that where the defendant is a company and the claimant is unable until a late stage to identify accurately the name of the company.[16]

The proviso to the definition makes clear that it is only the claimant's knowledge of the facts which is relevant—his appreciation of the legal position is irrelevant. The equivalent provision in the context of personal injuries[17] was introduced to reverse the effect of a number of Court of Appeal decisions,[18] which had held that the claimant was not fixed with knowledge of his cause of action until he had taken legal advice on his position.

7.009 The concluding clause of the proviso has no equivalent in any previous legislation. It is limited to actions in respect of loss or damage to property, and its effect is twofold. First, the date of knowledge in respect of such an action cannot arise before the cause of action has accrued. Secondly, if, for any reason, the claimant can show that he no longer had the necessary knowledge by the time his cause of action accrues, then the running of time will be postponed until he regains the knowledge.

In certain cases the same incident may give rise to two separate periods of limitation under the CPA 1987. If the claimant wishes to sue for both personal injury and damage to property, then any knowledge which he had on a date prior to the accrual of these causes of action (assuming here that

---

[12] For a possible example of this, admittedly not in a consumer protection context, see *D. W. Moore Ltd v Ferrier* [1988] 1 W.L.R. 267, CA; 104 L.Q.R. 376 (see Chs 5 and 6).
[13] 1980 Act s.14.
[14] 1980 Act s.14A.
[15] *Wilkinson v Ancliff (B.L.T.) Ltd* [1986] 1 W.L.R. 1352, CA; see also paras 8.021 et seq. and the cases discussed there.
[16] *Simpson v Norwest Holst (Southern) Ltd* [1980] 1 W.L.R. 968, CA.
[17] 1980 Act s.14(2)(b).
[18] Perhaps the best known is *Pickles v National Coal Board* [1968] 1 W.L.R. 997, CA.

they accrued at the same time) will be disregarded for the purpose of the running of time in the action for property damage, but will not be disregarded when considering the running of time in the personal injuries action. In practice it must be likely that the claimant will want to sue for both forms of damage in the same action. The proviso does not make it entirely clear what will happen in such a case, but it is submitted that the claimant should not be able to obtain the benefit of the disregard of this knowledge in respect of the personal injuries action merely because he also sues for property damage. The wording is markedly different from that employed in the context of personal injuries.[19] Further, there is the opportunity for procedural abuse if any action for property damage also secures the disregard of the knowledge for personal injuries purposes— every claimant in an action under the CPA 1987 will simply ensure that some form of property damage is pleaded.

THE LONGSTOP

In addition to the extended period of limitation provided by s.11A, the new section also imposes a final time-limit on the bringing of any action under Pt I of the CPA 1987. This limit is 10 years from the date when the product in question is last supplied by someone to whom s.2(2) of the Act applies.

7.010

Section 2(2)

This provision applies to anyone who is the producer of the product in question, or who has held himself out as the producer by applying his own distinguishing mark to it or who has imported the product into the European Union from outside the European Union. Essentially this is the class of persons who may be liable under the Act for a defect in a product.

7.011

This timing provision is of critical importance in understanding the operation of the longstop under the CPA 1987, and it is necessary to examine each of its three limbs in turn.

Who is a producer?

The answer to this is supplied by s.1(2) of the Act. The term encompasses the manufacturer of a product, in the case of a mineral the person who has won or abstracted it, and in the case of a product that is neither manu-

7.012

---

[19] 1980 Act s.11(1).

factured nor won or abstracted, anyone who has applied to it any process to which any of its essential characteristics is attributable.

Applying a distinguishing mark

7.013 This element of the definition encompasses the case where a person (often, but not necessarily, the supplier of the product to the ultimate consumer) buys the product from a manufacturer or intermediate supplier and then markets it under his own brand name. In such a case the person applying his own brand name becomes potentially liable under the CPA 1987.

The importer

7.014 The CPA 1987 was passed in order to ensure the United Kingdom's compliance with the Product Liability Directive,[20] which is intended to ensure an EU-wide scheme of consumer protection. In order to complete the scheme of protection it is necessary to have some person who can be held responsible for products which are imported into the Union rather than produced within it. Section 1(2) of the CPA 1987 imposes liability in such a case on the person who had first imported the product into the Union. Where the product is later re-exported and then reimported, it appears that liability under this limb will rest with the person who first imported it. However, it will be important to identify the product in question. A raw material which is incorporated into another product between re-export and subsequent reimport does not, it is submitted, remain the same product when reimported.

The longstop will operate to prevent the bringing of an action even where the cause of action has not accrued when the period expires.[21] However, in a case of this kind the limitation period for an action in tort (whether for personal injuries or for damage to property) will not yet have begun to run.[22] Consequently, at least in a case involving negligence on the part of the defendant, the claimant will be able to recover by means of an action in tort notwithstanding the longstop. The longstop runs from the date on which the defendant acts as a producer in respect of the product. One consequence of this is that the 10-year period may expire at different times against different people in the chain of manufacture and distribution. Therefore, if A manufactures a product in 2006, B applies his distinguishing mark to it in 2007 and C sells it to a consumer in 2008, the longstop is reached for A in 2016, for B in 2017 and for C in 2018.

---

[20] Directive 85/374.
[21] 1980 Act s.11A(3).
[22] 1980 Act ss.2 and 11.

'Supply' and 'putting into circulation'

Section 4, s.2(2) of the CPA 1987 and s.11A of LA 1980, taken together,   **7.015**
appear to be the United Kingsom's attempt to implement Art.11 of the
Directive, which reads:

> "Member States shall provide in their legislation that the rights conferred
> upon the injured person pursuant to this Directive shall be extinguished
> upon the expiry of a period of 10 years from the date on which the
> producer put into circulation the actual product which caused the
> damage, unless the injured person has in the meantime instituted pro-
> ceedings against the producer."

It is to be noted, however, that the UK legislation does not mention the
concept of 'putting into circulation'. The meaning of these words was
considered in *O'Byrne v Sanofi Pasteur MSD Ltd*,[23] where the specific point
referred to the ECJ was whether a product was 'put into circulation' when
the manufacturer supplied it to a distributor which was its wholly owned
subsidiary, or whether the product was not put into circulation until it
passed out of the control of the manufacturer. The ECJ's answer was that
Art.11 of the Directive was to be interpreted as meaning that a product was
put into circulation when it was taken out of the manufacturing process
operated by the producer and entered a marketing process in the form in
which it was offered to the public in order to be used or consumed. This
marketing process might or might not be done by a subsidiary of the
manufacturer, but that was not the determining factor. On the facts of the
particular case it would seem likely that the English court will hold that the
product was put into circulation when supplied to the distributor.

Effect of longstop

Section 11A(3) provides that the expiry of the 10-year longstop shall
operate to extinguish the claimant's right of action. The effect of this   **7.016**
appears to be to create an exception to the general principle[24] (at least
outside the area of real property) that the expiry of the limitation period
bars the claimant's remedy but does not extinguish his right. It is unfortunate that the statutory provision refers to extinguishing a right of action,
a phrase which conflates the barring of a right of action with the extinguishing of the underlying right. Nevertheless, in view of the obvious legislative intention that upon the expiry of the longstop all claims should be

---

[23] (Case C-127/04) Court Of Justice Of The European Communities (First Chamber) [2006]
All ER (D) 117 (Feb).
[24] Discussed in Ch.2.

finally at an end, it is submitted that the expiry of the longstop period does indeed extinguish the claimant's rights.[25] If this is correct, then it will be unnecessary for the defendant to plead the longstop. In addition, the methods of indirect enforcement which are otherwise available in respect of a time-barred claim will not be available where the action is precluded by the longstop. Once the longstop has expired, the court's discretion under s.35 of the 1980 Act and CPR r.19.5 to add or substitute a party after the expiry of a relevant limitation period does not apply.[26]

CLAIMANT UNDER DISABILITY

7.017 Schedule 1, para.4 to the CPA 1987 modifies s.28 of the 1980 Act (which deals with the situation where the claimant is under a disability).[27] It provides, first, that s.28(1) does not apply to the longstop provided by s.11A(3) of the 1980 Act, i.e. the 10-year longstop cannot be extended by reason of the claimant's disability. Paragraph 4 provides, secondly, that s.28(1) otherwise has effect in relation to actions under the CPA 1987 by substituting "three years" for "six years". Therefore, the claimant's action must be brought within three years of the ending of the disability or of the claimant's death if he dies while still under a disability.

FRAUD, CONCEALMENT OR MISTAKE

7.018 Schedule 1, para.5 to the CPA 1987 deals with the relationship between actions under the CPA 1987 and the provisions of the 1980 Act relating to postponement of the running of time in cases of fraud, concealment or mistake.[28] It introduces a new s.32(4A), which provides that s.32 shall not operate to extend the period of limitation beyond the 10-year longstop imposed by s.11A(3). Therefore, as with disability, the provisions of s.32 are made subject to those of s.11A(3). However, the implication of this must be that s.32 can be used to extend the basic three-year period. In practice this is not likely to be of great significance, since this three-year period runs from the later of accrual of cause of action and date of knowledge and since the effect of s.32 could only be to postpone the running of time until the action was reasonably discoverable, this would appear to be the same as the date of knowledge.

---

[25] See also paras 15.003–15.005.
[26] *OB v Aventis Pasteur* [2010] UKSC 23, giving effect to the decision of the ECJ in *Aventis Pasteur v OB* Case C-358-08 on December 2, 2009.
[27] See also Ch.19.
[28] 1980 Act s.32; see also Ch.20.

Discretionary extension of time

Schedule 1, para.6 to the CPA 1987 concerns the application of s.33 of the 1980 Act (which deals with the discretionary extension of the time-limit in cases of personal injury).[29] It forbids the application of s.33 to an action for personal injuries under the CPA 1987 where the cause of action is barred by virtue of the longstop provision. It goes on to provide that no other provision of the 1980 Act shall be disapplied in an action under the CPA 1987 where the damages are confined to damages for loss of or damage to property. Thus, in personal injury cases s.33 may still be applied so long as the longstop period has not expired, but s.33 has no application to cases of damage to property under the CPA 1987. Indeed, it is hard to see why a specific provision to this effect was required. Section 33 by its terms applies only to cases of personal injury, and therefore could not possibly apply to actions brought solely in respect of property damage.   7.019

ACTION FOR NON-DISCLOSURE OF NAME

Section 2(3) of the CPA 1987 creates an additional right of action where a person injured by a defect in a product has requested the person who supplied it to him to identify any person who is liable for such defect under Pt I of the CPA 1987 and the supplier has failed to do so within a reasonable time. The supplier to the claimant then becomes liable for the damage. As this is itself an action under Pt I of the CPA 1987, it must follow that the special limitation rules discussed in this chapter apply to it as well. A point of some difficulty here concerns the application of the 10-year longstop to such cases. The longstop takes effect 10 years from the "relevant time" as defined in section 4 of the CPA 1987. Where the action is against a person to whom section 2(2) of the Act does not apply (this includes a supplier who is neither a producer nor an own-brander nor an importer) the relevant time is the date when the product was last supplied by someone to whom section 2(2) does apply. In cases where there is a lengthy chain of distribution this provision is capable of producing unsatisfactory results. Consider the following example: 7.020

A, a manufacturer, supplies the product to B, a wholesaler, in 1998. B supplies it to C, a distributor in 2000. C supplies it to D, a distributor in 2002. D supplies it to E, a retailer in 2004. E sells it to P, the consumer, in 2006, and P is injured by it in 2007. In 2009 E is asked for the name of his supplier, but is unable or unwilling to give it.

The last supplier to whom section 2(2) applied was A (assuming that there has been no own-branding in the interim) and the longstop for the

---

[29] See Ch.8.

7.021 action against A expires in 2008, 10 years after his supply. Therefore, P does not have three years from the date of injury in which to bring his action against A. What is unclear is whether the action against E for failure to disclose the name of his supplier is also barred. On one view it is not, since the gist of this action is not the damage originally suffered by P, but the further difficulty caused by E's failure to reveal the name of his supplier. On the other side, it has been argued[30] that this result is obviously unjust, especially to B in the above example, and is contrary to the intention of the legislation because it allows liability to extend beyond the longstop period. According to this view, the liability on the intermediate supplier was only intended to come into existence where the original producer could not be found. It is therefore excessive to impose liability on an intermediate supplier in circumstances where the producer can be identified but cannot be sued because of the longstop.

In truth this is not really a limitation question, since it depends upon what view is taken about the liability of the intermediate supplier in cases where he is, quite reasonably, unable to name his own supplier. It is hard to deny that the imposition of liability in such cases is harsh, but that is the result produced by a strict construction of the legislation, though probably not by a more teleological construction giving more emphasis to the purposes of the Directive on which the legislation is based.

---

[30] *Childs* (1996) 47 N.I.L.Q. 98 at 102–103.

CHAPTER 8

Personal Injuries and Defamation

These two apparently unrelated topics are joined in the same chapter   **8.001**
because, almost uniquely[1] in the law of limitations, both are the subject of a
judicial discretion to extend the primary limitation period on grounds of
equity.

Discoverability

Since 1963 the law of limitations in personal injury cases has included   **8.002**
provision that the date at which the claimant is first reasonably able to
discover the existence of his cause of action shall be relevant in determining
when time expires. The details of these provisions have been amended from
time to time. The present rules are contained in ss.11 and 14 of the Limitation Act 1980. The present rules in defamation cases are found in s.4A of
the Limitation Act 1980, as substituted by s.5 of the Defamation Act 1996.

Judicial discretion

Personal injury and defamation cases are almost unique in that the court   **8.003**
has a discretion to allow the bringing of an action even when the time
limited by ss.4A, 11 and 14 (often referred to as the primary limitation
period) has expired. This discretion, first introduced by the Limitation Act
1975 in the case of personal injury actions, is now contained in s.33 of the
1980 Act. For defamation actions the discretion originates in the Administration of Justice Act 1985, which reduced the limitation period for
defamation cases from six years to three.[2] Section 5 of the Defamation Act

---

[1] The Merchant Shipping Act 1995, considered in Ch.24, also confers such a discretion, as
  do some of the Carriage Statutes mentioned in Ch.26.
[2] Administration of Justice Act 1985 s.57.

1996 subsequently reduced it still further to one year. These provisions are considered in detail below.[3]

The Fatal Accident Acts

8.004 Section 12 of the 1980 Act provides special rules for situations where claims are brought under the Fatal Accidents Acts. These also are considered below.[4]

PERSONAL INJURIES[5]

The basic rule

8.005 In an action for damages which consist of, or include, damages for personal injury to the claimant or any other person[6] arising from negligence, nuisance or breach of duty, the period of limitation is three years.[7] This period runs from the later of the date on which the cause of action accrues and the date of knowledge of the person injured.[8] The concept of accrual is examined in Ch.5, since the principles are the same for any case based on negligence, whilst the notion of date of knowledge is considered below.[9]

Mixed actions

8.006 The three-year period applies where the damages include any claim for personal injuries.[10] Thus the inclusion of a personal injuries element, however slight, means that the three-year period applies to the whole action.[11] Where the personal injuries claim is a small part of the claimant's total loss it may therefore be thought more prudent to forego it. This is not problematic where the original claim omits the personal injuries. Where the original claim does include personal injuries, the claimant may subse-

---

[3] See paras 8.071–8.078.

[4] See paras 8.064–8.067.

[5] For a general critical account of the limitation rules relating to personal injuries law, see McGee (1990) 9 C.J.Q. 326.

[6] Including a child in utero where the damages are claimed by the mother: *Das v Ganju* (1998) 42 B.M.L.R. 28.

[7] 1980 Act s.11(4).

[8] 1980 Act.

[9] See paras 8.013–8.025.

[10] Except where the claim is brought under the Protection from Harassment Act 1997— Limitation Act 1980 s11(1A) as inserted by the Protection from Harassment Act 1997 s.6.

[11] See for example *Smith v Surrey Hampshire Borders NHS Trust* [2004] EWHC 2101 (QB), Judge Wilkie and *Azaz v Denton* [2009] EWHC 1759 QB Judge Seymour, where the point was considered at length.

quently seek to amend the particulars of claim by removing the personal injuries element if it becomes clear that there is a limitation problem with that part of the claim. In *Oates v Harte Reade & Co.*[12] Singer J. considered at length whether such an amendment constituted the addition or substitution of a new cause of action for the purposes of s.35(2)(a) of the Limitation Act 1980. He held that it did not have that effect, but went on to decide that the amendment sought should not be permitted as a matter of discretion because the defendant's solicitors in this case had a cast-iron limitation defence which the amendment sought would destroy. In *Shade v Compton Partnership (A Firm)*[13] the Court of Appeal regarded the reasoning of Singer J. as "less than fully satisfactory". Robert Walker L.J. went on:

"It may be arid to discuss whether the deletion of part of a pleading should be regarded as the substitution of one cause of action for another. It is possible to think of some cases in which that would, at least at first sight, be so, such as a case where the deletion of the single word 'fraudulently' might substitute a claim based on innocent misrepresentation for one based on deceit. Simply to delete some parts of the damages claimed to have been caused by a single breach of duty is not easily described as a substitution and it is clearly not an addition to a claim."

It is submitted that Robert Walker L.J. is right. Although the point is not expressly dealt with in the CPR, in most cases there will be no reason to refuse to allow such an amendment—a claimant ought to be allowed to abandon any part of his claim at any time, subject, of course, to any appropriate costs orders which might follow from that decision.

Where claimant dies

Section 11(5) of the 1980 Act governs the case where the claimant dies **8.007** before the expiry of the basic three-year period. In such a case the period applicable, as regards the cause of action surviving for the benefit of his estate, is three years from the later of the date of his death and the date when his personal representative first has knowledge of the facts relevant to the cause of action (as defined in s.14 of the Act).[14] This provision refers only to the estate's cause of action—it has no relevance to any action under the Fatal Accidents Acts, which would fall under s.12, as explained below.[15] Section 11(5) is further amplified by s.11(6) and (7). The term "personal representative" includes, by s.11(6), anyone who is or has been a personal representative of the deceased, including an executor who has not

---

[12] [1999] 1 F.L.R. 1221; [1999] Fam. Law 383.
[13] July 22, 1999, Unreported, CA.
[14] For s.14, see paras 8.013-8.030.
[15] See paras 8.064-8.067.

proved the will (whether or not he has renounced probate). The term, however, does not include anyone appointed only as a special personal representative in relation to settled land. Regard is to be had to any knowledge acquired by a person within this definition, even if that knowledge was acquired before he became a personal representative.

Two important points emerge from this subsection. The first is that a deceased person may have more than one personal representative for this purpose (and there may be different personal representatives at different times). Secondly, a personal representative cannot escape the three-year rule by pleading that he acquired relevant knowledge before becoming a personal representative. Conversely, though, it appears that the estate is not fixed with knowledge which a person acquires for the first time after ceasing to be a personal representative. Section 11(7) deals with some of the complications which may arise where there is more than one personal representative, and their dates of knowledge are different. In these circumstances references to the personal representatives' date of knowledge are references to the earliest date of knowledge of any of them.

Ambit of the section

8.008   Section 11(1) makes the special rules discussed in this chapter applicable to "any action for damages for negligence, nuisance or breach of duty" if the damages "consist of or include" damages in respect of personal injury.[16] Both elements of this definition have given rise to difficulty.

The phrase "negligence, nuisance or breach of duty" may be regarded as tautologous, since both negligence and nuisance might properly be described as examples of breach of duty. To this extent, there is repetition in the statute, but this does not render the phrase "breach of duty" irrelevant, since it can extend to a breach of contractual duty involving neither negligence nor nuisance.

A more difficult point in this area has been the application of s.11 to intentional torts and to those torts which can be committed without negligence. The problem has been considered in two cases in the context of trespass. This is a tort that can be committed either intentionally or negligently. In *Letang v Cooper*[17] the plaintiff was knocked down by a car driven by the defendant. He did not bring his action within the period applicable to a personal injuries case, and sought to avoid the effect of this by pleading the case in trespass as well as in negligence. The Court of Appeal, reversing the decision of Elwes J., held that in the case of an

---

[16] This must be read as subject to the Merchant Shipping Act 1995. In cases to which s.190 of that Act applies, the limitation period will be two years.
[17] [1964] 2 Q.B. 53, Elwes J.; [1965] 1 Q.B. 232, CA. On the general question of categorisation see also paras 4.002 et seq.

unintentional injury to the person, the only cause of action at the present day lies in negligence. In the alternative the Court held that the unintentional infliction of physical injury is classed as a breach of duty. On either basis the result must be that an action for unintentional trespass to the person falls within the special rules applicable to personal injury cases. This decision left open the question of the proper treatment of cases of intentional trespass, though obiter dicta in *Letang v Cooper* suggested that both forms of trespass should be treated in the same way for this purpose.

In *A v Hoare and other appeals*[18] the House of Lords has taken the opportunity to depart from its previous decision in *Stubbings v Webb*[19] and to reinstate the effect of the decision in *Letang v Cooper*[20]. The basis of this eminently sensible decision was that Parliament could not have intended to exclude from those who had been intentionally injured the benefit of the date of knowledge provisions in s.14 and of the court's general discretion to extend time under s.33. Thus, *Stubbings v Webb*, a decision much criticised can now be recognised for the regrettable aberration which it was, and the law is now settled on the basis that an action for intentional trespass is within s.11 of the 1980 Act, with the result that the s.33 discretion is available in relation to it. At a subsequent hearing[21] Coulson J. exercised the s.33 discretion in favour of the claimant   8.009

One consequence of the decision in *A v Hoare* is that there will be more s.33 applications by claimants based on events alleged to have happened many years previously. The courts will have to be careful in scrutinising such applications, not least because there will inevitable be cases where the lapse of time makes a fair trial impossible.[22]   8.010

PERSONAL INJURIES

In *Walkin v South Manchester HA*[23] it was held that a claimant who becomes pregnant after a failed sterilisation operation suffers personal injuries for the purposes of s.11. The definition of the term in s.38 of the 1980 Act extends to any bodily or mental impairment, and some bodily impairment is a normal and natural consequence of pregnancy. Similarly, a claimant who continues with a pregnancy after suffering rubella and being   8.011

---

[18] [2008] UKHL 6; [2008] 2 All ER 1; this renders irrelevant the well-made criticisms by Holland J. in *AB v Nugent Care Society (formerly Catholic Social Services (Liverpool))* [2006] EWHC 3031 (QB).

[19] [1993] 1 All E.R. 322 H.L.

[20] [1964] 2 All ER 929.

[21] [2008] EWHC 1573 (QB).

[22] *NXS v London Borough of Camden* [2009] EWHC 1786 (QB) at paras 187-195 per Swift J.

[23] [1995] 4 All E.R. 132.

advised of the possible dangers to the foetus suffers an ongoing personal injury.[24] A claim for damages for failure to advise the claimant of welfare benefits which he could obtain as a result of having suffered personal injuries is probably not a claim for damages for personal injury within s.11.[25] *Adams v Bracknell Forest BC*[26] established that the damage caused to a claimant who suffers dyslexia which is not diagnosed and treated by the local authority responsible for his education is a personal injury for the purposes of s.11. In so doing their Lordships considered *Phelps v Hillingdon London BC*[27] where Lord Slynn of Hadley said [2001] 2 AC 619, [2000] 4 All ER 504, 654 that psychological injury could constitute damage for the purposes of a claim in negligence and:

> "So . . . can a failure to diagnose a congenital condition and to take appropriate action as a result of which failure a child's level of achievement is reduced, which leads to loss of employment and wages."

And *Anderton v Clwyd CC,* heard together with *Phelps,* where it was held that a claim based on failure to diagnose dyslexia was a "claim in respect of personal injuries" within the meaning of s.33(2) of the Senior Courts Act 1981. Although that was obviously not a limitation court, the House of Lords in *Anderton* treated it as relevant by analogy, since the same considerations ought to apply in both contexts. In *Godfrey v Gloucestershire Royal Infirmary NHS Trust*[28], the claimant attended the defendant NHS trust for ante-natal care. A routine ultra-sound scan revealed abnormalities, and over the subsequent months the prognosis for her child and the question of termination were discussed. Shortly after the child was born, the claimant complained to the defendant that she had not been given appropriate or accurate information sufficient to make an informed decision about the question of termination of the pregnancy. It was held that claims for pre-natal pain and suffering and post-natal economic loss in relation to an unwanted pregnancy arose from the same cause of action, namely physical injury. Accordingly s.11 applied.

Accrual

8.012   There is no definition in the 1980 Act of the concept of accrual of cause of action, and an understanding of this term must be sought in the case law.

---

[24] *Das v Ganju* (1998) 42 BMLR 28, QBD, Garland J.
[25] *Gaud v Leeds HA, The Times,* May 14, 1999, CA.
[26] [2004] UKHL 29; see also *Robinson v St Helens MBC* [2002] All ER (D) 388 (Jul), [2002] EWCA Civ 1099, [2002] ELR 681.
[27] [1998] ELR 38 CA reversed [2001] 2 AC 619, [2000] 4 All ER 504.
[28] [2003] EWHC 549 (QB), [2003] All ER (D) 346 (Mar) Leveson J.

The two leading authorities are *Cartledge v E. Jopling & Sons Ltd*[29] and *Pirelli General Cable Works v Oscar Faber & Partners Ltd*.[30] The combined effect of these two cases, which are considered at greater length elsewhere,[31] is that the cause of action must be considered to have accrued as soon as the claimant has suffered any damage which is more than minimal, notwithstanding that he is unaware of the fact and could not reasonably have been aware of it. In personal injury cases the running of time may be postponed in these circumstances,[32] but the cause of action will nevertheless have accrued.

The date of knowledge

Section 11(4) of the 1980 Act provides that the period of limitation for a **8.013** personal injuries action is three years from the later of the date when the cause of action accrues and the date of knowledge (if later) of the person injured. The term "date of knowledge" is defined in s.14 of the Act as the date on which the claimant first had knowledge of the following facts:

"(a) that the injury in question was significant and
(b) that the injury was attributable in whole or in part to the act or omission which is alleged to constitute negligence, nuisance or breach of duty and
(c) the identity of the defendant and
(d) if it is alleged that the act or omission was that of a person other than the defendant, the identity of that person and the additional facts supporting the bringing of an action against the defendant and knowledge that any acts or omissions did or did not, as a matter of law, involve negligence, nuisance or breach of duty is irrelevant."[33]

Each of the elements of this definition requires careful consideration.

Injury

A claimant who has had an operation does not without more knowledge **8.014** that he has suffered an "injury". Until he knows this he cannot possibly appreciate its significance, so time cannot run.[34] However, the position is

---

[29] [1963] A.C. 758, HL; see also *Brazier v Ministry of Defence* [1956] 1 Lloyd's Rep. 26.
[30] [1983] 2 A.C. 1, HL.
[31] See paras 5.008 et seq.
[32] See paras 8.013–8.025.
[33] 1980 Act s.14(1).
[34] *James v E.Dorset HA, The Times*, December 7, 1999, CA; see also *Smith v W.Lancs HA* [1995] P.I.Q.R. 514.

different where the claimant has had a surgical amputation, since it is then obvious that there has been an injury.[35]

Knowledge

8.015   In *Driscoll-Varley v Parkside HA*[36] the plaintiff had been assaulted by her husband and had suffered quite serious injuries. This case arose out of the medical treatment which she received as a result of those injuries. The essence of the complaint was that the treatment had in some ways made the condition worse, but there had been a long course of treatment, and the plaintiff argued that only at a late stage had she realised that certain aspects of the treatment were aggravating her condition. Hidden J. held that "knowledge" in s.14 is a high standard, mere suspicion is not enough. Thus, the plaintiff needed to be more or less sure that her injuries were attributable to the defendants' negligence. Some difference of judicial view was found in *Adams v Bracknell Forest BC*[37], where the House of Lords considered at length the question of the objective and subjective elements within the definition of "knowledge" in s.14(3). Lord Hoffmann was inclined to favour a strongly objective approach to this question, paying little regard to the characteristics of the claimant, whereas Baroness Hale was more willing to allow some element of subjectivity, and Lord Walker was inclined to think that the answer might lie somewhere between these two positions. However, subsequent cases have opted firmly for a strictly objective approach, in particular *AB v Nugent Care*[38] and *KR v Bryn Alan Community (Holdings) Ltd*[39], and this point must be regarded as settled for the time being.

8.016   However, in all the sexual abuse cases it is necessary to focus clearly on what loss is the subject of the claim. In *Hodges v Northampton CC*[40] the claim was expressed as being for post traumatic stress disorder, and the Court of Appeal stressed the need in such cases to bear in mind that the symptoms of this might not manifest themselves for many years, with the result that the claimant may legitimately remain unaware of them for a long time.

8.017   **Agents to know**   In *O'Driscoll v Dudley HA*[41] the plaintiff suffered from cerebral palsy. She was not a patient, but had left the management of her affairs to her parents. The Court of Appeal held that the court should have

---

[35] *Forbes v Wandsworth HA* [1997] Q.B. 402; [1996] 4 All E.R. 881, CA.
[36] [1991] 2 Med.L.R. 346, Hidden J.
[37] [2004] UKHL 29; see also *Robinson v St Helens MBC* [2002] All ER (D) 388 (Jul), [2002] EWCA Civ 1099, [2002] ELR 681.
[38] [2009] EWCA Civ 827.
[39] [2003] EWCA Civ 85 [2003] QB 1441; see also *Albonetti v Wirral MBC* [2008] EWCA Civ 783.
[40] [2004] EWCA CIV 526, [2004] All ER (D) 315 (Apr).
[41] [1998] Lloyd's Rep. Med. 210, CA.

regard therefore simply to what the plaintiff knew herself not to what her parents knew. They were not to be treated as agents to know.

Section 14(3) of the 1980 Act contains further guidance as to when a person will and will not be deemed to have knowledge of a particular fact.

"A person's knowledge includes knowledge which he might reasonably have been expected to acquire from facts observable or ascertainable by him or from facts ascertainable by him with the help of medical or other appropriate expert advice which it is reasonable for him to seek."

In effect, this provision imposes a test of reasonable discoverability—a person is fixed with constructive knowledge of facts which he ought reasonably to have discovered, and cannot avoid the effect of the three-year limit by proving that he did not in fact know them. However, there may be a degree of subjectivity in this test—the question is whether seeking the medical advice was reasonable for him, not whether it would have been reasonable for the hypothetical reasonable man.[42] In *Smith v Leicester HA* Roch L.J. said:

"Whether it was reasonable for the [claimant] to seek such advice depends on the facts and circumstances of each case, but excluding the character traits of the individual [claimant]."[43]

On the other hand, in *Nash v Eli Lilly & Co.*[44] Purchas LJ said:

"The standard of reasonableness in connection with the observations and/or the effort to ascertain are therefore finally objective but must be qualified to take into consideration the position, and circumstances and character of the [claimant]."

There is thus some disagreement in the reported authorities. It is submitted that the *Forbes* approach is to be preferred as being in line with the wording of the statute and as producing a result which is sensitive to the differing characteristics of individual claimants. The rule is further mitigated by the proviso to s.14(3), which is that a person is not to be fixed under s.14(3) with knowledge of a fact ascertainable only with the help of expert advice so long as he has taken all reasonable steps to obtain and, where appropriate, to act on that advice. This proviso appears to be sig-

---

[42] *Newton v Cammell Laird & Co.* [1969] 1 W.L.R. 413, Park J. and *Nash v Eli Lilly & Co.* [1993] 1 W.L.R. 782, CA.

[43] [1998] Lloyd's Rep. Med. 77. See also *Forbes v Wandsworth HA* [1997] Q.B. 402; [1996] 4 All E.R. 881, CA.

[44] [1993] 4 All E.R. 383; [1993] 1 W.L.R. 782, CA; and see *Ali v Courtaulds Textiles Ltd* [1999] Lloyd's Rep. Med. 301, CA, though that decision does not cite *Forbes* or *Smith—Fenech v East London & City HA* [2000] Lloyd's Rep. Med. 35, CA.

nificant in three situations, which are considered in the following paragraphs.

8.018 **Advice not sought**   The first is where the claimant has not sought expert advice and must rely on persuading the court that this omission was reasonable. The difficulty arising from the wording is that he must seek such advice as it is "reasonable" for him to seek. Stuart Smith L.J. in *Forbes v Wandsworth HA*[45] said:

> "One of the problems with the language of s.14(3)(b) is that two alternative courses of action may be perfectly reasonable. Thus, it may be perfectly reasonable for a person who is not cured when he hoped to be to say, 'Oh well, it is just one of those things. I expect the doctors did their best.' Alternatively, the explanation for the lack of success may be due to want of care on the part of those in whose charge he was, in which case it would be perfectly reasonable to take a second opinion. And I do not think that the person who adopts the first alternative can necessarily be said to be acting unreasonably. But he is in effect making a choice, either consciously by deciding to do nothing, or unconsciously by in fact doing nothing. Can a person who has effectively made this choice, many years later, and without any alteration of circumstances, change his mind and then seek advice which reveals that all along he had a claim. I think not. . ."

Thus, in cases where either course of action is reasonable a claimant cannot escape the operation of the Act by saying that it was reasonable for him not to seek the advice. To put it another way, the words "which it is reasonable for him to seek" do not mean the same as "which it is unreasonable for him not to seek". In *Skingsley v Cape Asbestos Co. Ltd*[46] the plaintiff was forced to retire from work through disability, but only some time later, after hearing from former colleagues that others were taking action against the employer, did he seek expert advice on his own position. The Court of Appeal held that he could not reasonably have been expected to seek advice at an earlier stage, with the result that time did not start to run against him. On its particular facts the decision may perhaps be regarded as somewhat generous to the plaintiff, but the soundness of the principle which it lays down cannot be doubted.

8.019   An interesting example of this problem occurred in *Smith v Central Asbestos Co. Ltd.*[47] This was a workmen's compensation case in which the plaintiffs had received erroneous advice as to their legal position from the

---

[45] [1997] Q.B. 402; [1996] 4 All E.R. 881.
[46] [1968] 2 All E.R. 201, CA.
[47] [1972] 1 Q.B. 244, CA affirmed [1972] 2 All E.R. 1135, HL; but see also *Harper v National Coal Board* [1974] Q.B. 614.

defendants' works manager. It was held that they had acted reasonably in relying on this advice and not seeking an independent opinion, so that time did not run against them. The reasonableness of such reliance will depend heavily upon the character of the claimant and that of the adviser. In this case the plaintiffs were unskilled workmen, who were advised by their former superior, and therefore it was surely not unnatural that they should rely on him. The position would no doubt be different were the plaintiff a member of the professional classes, better able to appreciate the problems of conflict of interest which this situation poses. In *Carr v Cammell Laird*[48] it was said, obiter, that in any case where the claimant knows that he has suffered significant injury it is reasonable for him to seek medical advice. In *Nash v Eli Lilly & Co.*[49] the Court of Appeal held that a claimant who is virtually certain that his injury is attributable to the acts of the defendants will not immediately be fixed with knowledge if he reasonably decides to await expert confirmation of this before taking any legal steps.

In a series of recent cases[50] it has been held that a claimant who has suffered injury as a result of medical treatment may reasonably be allowed some time, varying according to the seriousness of the injury, to get over what has happened, before seeking expert advice as to possible claims.

Advice not yet received The second situation is where the claimant has sought expert advice on the point in issue but has not yet received it. Here, his date of knowledge cannot in general be earlier than the date on which that advice is rendered to him. Attention is drawn, however, to the decision of Lord Widgery C.J. in *Jones v Bennett*.[51] The plaintiff consulted a solicitor about her case, but no detailed advice was ever given, apparently because the plaintiff could not afford to pay for it. It was held that the plaintiff had constructive knowledge of the relevant facts as soon as it was reasonable for her to seek the advice. This is not strictly correct; a more accurate formulation of the law is that where the claimant seeks advice, time runs from the point when the advice is received, or from when the claimant abandons the attempt to obtain the advice, either by withdrawing the instructions or by taking some other step which ensures that the advice will not be given. 8.020

Information not disclosed The third situation is where the expert advice fails to disclose the information as, for example, where the plaintiff undergoes a medical examination that does not detect the occurrence of some injury. He is entitled to rely upon the medical opinion as a ground for 8.021

---

[48] July 30, 1990, Simon Brown J., Unreported.
[49] [1993] 1 W.L.R. 782, CA.
[50] *Forbes v Wandsworth HA* [1996] 4 All E.R. 481, CA; *Johnson v Busfield*, July 29, 1996, Nelson J., Unreported; *O'Driscoll v Dudley HA* [1998] Lloyd's Rep. Med. 210, CA.
[51] [1976] 1 Lloyd's Rep. 484.

being unaware of the injury. However, the claimant may be fixed with knowledge that he has an injury if his symptoms are severe enough, even though the medical advice is that no recognised condition can be found.[52] The position is the same if the medical advisers make a conscious decision to conceal the information from the plaintiff.[53] The scope of this principle is not limited to medical advisers, but extends to any form of expert advice.[54]

Who is an expert

8.022 There is no definition in the Act of who is an expert for the purposes of s.14. In most cases this will not give rise to any particular difficulty, but attention is drawn to *Farrell v National Coal Board*,[55] where it was held that a solicitor is not an expert for the purpose of discovering the identity of a further defendant. This decision emphasises the possibility that a person may be an expert for some purposes only, and it is therefore necessary to look at the exact matters on which he has been called upon to advise. Similarly, in *Henderson v Temple Pier Co. Ltd*,[56] a solicitor was held not to be an expert for the purposes of finding out who owned a particular ship, such information being readily available by a search in the appropriate register. A solicitor would no doubt count as an expert for the purposes of advising on matters of law, but these are, of course, irrelevant to knowledge under s.14.

Significance of injury

8.023 Section 14(2) provides that:

"an injury is significant if the person whose date of knowledge is in question would reasonably have considered it sufficiently serious to justify his instituting proceedings for damages against a defendant who did not dispute liability and was able to satisfy a judgment."

Two points arise from this curiously drafted provision. The first is that there is apparently some element of subjectivity built into the test; the question is not whether the hypothetical reasonable man would have thought the injury sufficiently serious, but whether the particular claimant would reasonably have done so. The form of wording suggests that the characteristics of the claimant himself can in some way be taken into account, but the exact extent of this is uncertain. Secondly, it is not immediately obvious why anyone would not think the institution of pro-

---

[52] *Joseph Sniezek v Bundy (Letchworth) Ltd*, July 7, 2000, Unreported, CA; however, such a case may well justify the exercise of the s.33 discretion.
[53] *Newton v Cammell Laird & Co.* [1969] 1 W.L.R. 415, Park J., CA.
[54] *Marston v British Railways Board* [1976] I.C.R. 124, Croom-Johnson J.
[55] *The Times*, May 28, 1986, CA.
[56] [1998] 3 All E.R. 324, CA.

ceedings justified if the defendant admitted liability and had the funds to satisfy a judgment. However, there may be rare cases in which this provision is of importance. As the action in respect of any cause of action can be brought only once, if the claimant believes (no doubt on the basis of competent medical advice) that the damage which he has so far suffered is only minor, but that much greater damage is likely to manifest itself later, then he may be justified in delaying the bringing of his action,[57] since by bringing it immediately he could obtain only a proportion of the possible damages if the later injury did materialise. However, in two reported cases in which this point has been considered, *McCafferty v Metropolitan Police Receiver*[58] and *Miller v London Electrical Manufacturing*,[59] the Court of Appeal held that the plaintiff must be considered to have known all the material facts when the original injury was diagnosed, so that the action could only be allowed if the facts were such as to justify the invoking of the s.33 discretion. However, this point might well be decided differently today, more recent cases[60] having drawn attention to the possible desirability of delaying the action.

The s.14(2) test of 'significance' has been further considered in a number of important authorities. In *Catholic Care (Diocese of Leeds) v Young*[61] the Court of Appeal reconsidered the decision in *KR v Bryn Alyn Community (Holdings) Ltd*[62] in the light of the subsequent House of Lords decision in *Adams v Bracknell Forest BC*.[63] In *Bryn Alyn* the Court of Appeal, relying on *McCafferty v Metropolitan Police District Receiver*,[64] held that the test of significance was partly subjective in that account could be taken of the particular character of the claimant. However, in *Adams* (which was a case on s.14(3) rather than s.14(2)) the House of Lords preferred a more objective test. The Court of Appeal was of the view that it would be inappropriate to have different tests for s.14(2) and s.14(3), and therefore held that the decision in *Bryn Alan* (at least as it relates to the subjective/objective question in s.14(2)) has not survived the decision in *Adams*. These authorities were further considered and synthesised by Neuberger L.J. in *McCoubrey v Ministry of Defence*.[65] He put forward three propositions in

8.024

---

[57] For a consideration of this point in the context of non-personal injury actions, see paras 5.023–5.024 and McGee (1998) 104 L.Q.R. 376.

[58] [1977] 1 W.L.R. 1073, CA.

[59] [1976] 2 Lloyd's Rep. 284, CA; see also *Young v GLC & Massey* [1987] C.L.Y. 2328, Owen J.

[60] *Forster v Outred & Co.* [1982] 1 W.L.R. 86, CA; *D.W. Moore & Co. Ltd v Ferrier* [1988] 1 W.L.R. 267, CA.

[61] [2006] EWCA Civ 1534.

[62] [2003] EWCA Civ 85, [2003] QB 1441, [2004] 2 All ER 716.

[63] 2004] UKHL 29, [2005] 1 AC 76, [2004] 3 All ER 897.

[64] [1977] 2 All ER 756, [1977] 1 WLR 1073, 1081 G-H, [1977] ICR 799 followed in *Nash v Eli Lilly & Co* [1993] 4 All ER 383, [1993] 1 WLR 782, 791, 14 BMLR 1):

[65] [2007] EWCA Civ 17; further considered and applied in *Khairule v North West Strategic HA* [2008] EWHC 1537 (QB) Cox J.

relation to s.14(2).[66] First, the decisions in the *Adams* and *Young* cases mean that the law as it had been previously understood and applied, at least in the *Bryn Alyn* case, purportedly following in particular the *McCafferty* case, has changed. The test under s.14(2) is substantially objective, and is not the mixture of subjective and objective in the way in which the analysis of Geoffrey Lane LJ in the *McCafferty* case was interpreted as indicating in a number of cases, culminating with the *Bryn Alyn* case. Second, the question of whether an injury is "significant" within s.14(1)(a), as expanded in s.14(2), must be decided by reference to the seriousness of the injury, and not by reference to its effect, let alone its subjectively perceived effect, on the claimant's private life or career. Thus, the scope of application of s.14(2) is somewhat narrower than had previously been thought. Third, the person contemplated by ss.14(2) and 14(3) is a person who is in the same position, in objective terms, as the claimant. The proper approach to the question raised by s.14(2) is to consider, on the hypothesis postulated by the section, the reaction to the injury (as opposed to its possible consequences) of a reasonable person in the objective circumstances of the actual claimant, while disregarding his actual personal attributes, such as intelligence, aspirations, aggressiveness and the like. *In Field v British Coal Corporation (Department for Business Enterprise and Regulatory Reform)*[67] the Court of Appeal summarised the position by saying that the material to which the test for what counted as a 'significant injury' applied is generally 'subjective' in the sense that it was applied to what the claimant knew of his injury, rather than the injury as it actually was. The test itself is an impersonal standard—it is not whether the claimant himself would have considered the injury sufficiently serious to justify proceedings, but whether he would 'reasonably' have done so.

Injury reasonably believed trivial

8.025 The cases discussed above must be contrasted with the situation where the claimant reasonably believes the injury to be too trivial to merit an action. In *Harding v PDSA*[68] the plaintiff suffered an injury at work. She had previously suffered a similar injury, which had cleared up fairly rapidly. She therefore assumed that the same would happen again and concluded that it was not worth suing. It was held that she did not know that the injury was "significant" until the later date when it became clear that the second injury was more serious than the first and would not clear up.

The question is whether the bringing of an action was objectively justified on the facts known to the claimant within the limitation period.[69] If so, the claimant's personal opinion is irrelevant. Where the claimant's medical

---

[66] Paras 37ff.
[67] [2008] EWCA Civ 912.
[68] February 14, 1994, CA, Unreported.
[69] *Goodchild v Greatness Timber Co. Ltd* [1968] 2 Q.B. 372, CA.

advisers conceal from him both diagnosis and prognosis the court may be more inclined to hold that the claimant did not have the necessary knowledge.[70]

Attributability

This part of s.14(1) must be read in conjunction with the proviso (para.8.027) about knowledge of the legal position. Consequently, it must be interpreted as referring exclusively to the question of factual causation. The paragraph does not make clear exactly how much knowledge the claimant must have. The leading modern authorities[71] on the point are *Nash v Eli Lilly*[72] and *Broadley v Guy Clapham & Co.*[73] The former was a case arising out of the use of the drug Opren. One of the questions here was how soon the various plaintiffs had known that their injuries were attributable to the use of Opren. There was evidence that media attention had focused on this possibility at a relatively early stage, though the defendants had always denied any causal link, and indeed continued to do so at the date of the trial, which was concerned only with the limitation issues. The Court of Appeal held that the plaintiff does not have the necessary knowledge until he knows the essence of the act to which the injury was attributable, but that the plaintiff need not know exactly how the defendant will be alleged to have committed a breach of duty. In *Spargo v North Essex District HA*[74] the issue was the date when the plaintiff knew that her sufferings were attributable to a misdiagnosis of organic brain damage. Brooke L.J. drew the following principles from a number of authorities, including *Nash v Eli Lilly & Co.*:

8.026

"(1) The knowledge required to satisfy s.14(1)(b) is a broad knowledge of the essence of the causally relevant act or omission to which the injury is attributable;
(2) 'Attributable' in this context means 'capable of being attributed to', in the sense of being a real possibility;
(3) A plaintiff has the requisite knowledge when she knows enough to make it reasonable for her to begin to investigate whether or not she has a case against the defendant. Another way of putting this is to say that she will have such knowledge if she so firmly believes that her condition is capable of being attributed to an act or omission which

---

[70] *Newton v Cammell Laird & Co.* [1969] 1 W.L.R. 415, Park J., CA.
[71] Earlier cases include *Wilkinson v Ancliff (B.L.T.) Ltd* [1986] 1 W.L.R. 1352, CA; *Guidera v NEI Projects (India)*, January 30, 1990, CA, Unreported. Followed in *Carr v Cammell Laird* (July 30, 1990, Brown J. Unreported), *Driscoll-Varley v Parkside HA*, see above, fn.26, and *Bentley v Bristol & Weston HA* [1991] 2 Med.L.R. 3.
[72] [1993] 1 W.L.R. 782.
[73] [1994] 4 All E.R. 439; 17 B.M.L.R. 56.
[74] [1997] P.I.Q.R. 235, CA.

she can identify (in broad terms) that she goes to a solicitor to seek advice about making a claim for compensation;

(4) On the other hand she will not have the requisite knowledge if she thinks she knows the acts or omissions she should investigate but in fact is barking up the wrong tree; or if her knowledge of what the defendant did or did not do is so vague or general that she cannot fairly be expected to know what she should investigate; or if her state of mind is such that she thinks her condition is capable of being attributed to the act or omission alleged to constitute negligence, but she is not sure about this, and would need to check with an expert before she could be properly said to know that it was."[75]

This statement should now be regarded as being an authoritative account of the principles applicable on this point.[76]

8.027   In *Furniss v Firth Brown Tools Ltd*[77] the Court of Appeal observed[78] that it cannot be said that, as soon as a man is aware of some minor inconvenience in respect of his hearing, he is to be fixed with the knowledge that he would acquire if he immediately took expert advice. In the same case the Court stressed the need for trial judges to make findings about all the elements of the s.14 test for the date of knowledge, in case the decision is appealed.

Identity of defendant

8.028   Perhaps the most common application of this provision will be to the case of the claimant injured by a hit-and-run driver. For the purposes of the action against that driver, time will not start to run unless and until his identity is known to the claimant. In this situation, the claimant has the alternative of suing the Motor Insurers' Bureau under the Uninsured Drivers' Agreement,[79] and for the purposes of this action the identity of the defendant is known as soon as the accident happens.[80] The same principle can be applied to the addition of a second defendant, even where that

---

[75] Where the claimant suspects that he may have a cause of action but realises that he needs medical advice to confirm the nature of the condition and its possible causes, he does not know that the injury is attributable to the alleged negligence until he receives the relevant medical advice; *Ali v Courtaulds Textiles Ltd, The Times*, May 28, 1999, CA; see also *Nash v Eli Lilly*, above.

[76] See also *O'Driscoll v Dudley HA* [1998] Lloyd's Rep. Med. 210, CA.

[77] [2008] EWCA Civ 182.

[78] At para.26.

[79] For detailed treatment of this Agreement, see A. McGee *The Modern Law of Insurance* 2nd edn (2006), Ch.37.

[80] However, in the case of an uninsured driver the action against the Motor Insurance Bureau is not competent until judgment has been obtained against the driver and has remained unsatisfied for seven days. It is uncertain whether this prevents time running for the purposes of that action, though it is clearly desirable that time should not run until such time as the action can be brought. See also the cases discussed at paras 5.059-5.062.

defendant has already become a third party, if the third party's name and address do not become known to the claimant until a late stage.[81] Another situation where this provision may be important was revealed in *Simpson v Norwest Holst Southern Ltd*.[82] This was an action by the plaintiff against his employer. The writ had been issued against the company named in the employee's written statement of terms and shown as the employer on the employee's payslips. It was held that the employee was entitled to assume that this company was in fact the employer, and time did not begin to run against him until he could reasonably have discovered that, strictly speaking, he was employed by another company in the same group.

Vicarious liability

Section 14(1)(d) relates to the situation where the claimant sues a person   8.029
who is vicariously liable for the acts of the original tortfeasor. In such cases the time for the purpose of the action against the person vicariously responsible does not run until the claimant could reasonably have discovered that person's identity and the facts (such as that the tortfeasor was acting in the course of employment) which entitle the claimant to bring the action. In such cases the claimant always has the alternative of suing the original tortfeasor and s.14(1)(d) does not operate to postpone the running of time in respect of this action.

Matters of law

Once the claimant knows the relevant facts, it is irrelevant that he does not   8.030
understand their legal significance.[83] Reliance on expert advice is limited to questions of fact. The most important consequence of this is that the claimant cannot rely on incorrect legal advice which he has received as a ground for postponing the date of knowledge. He must take the consequences of his adviser's errors,[84] and will be left to pursue his remedies against them in negligence. Similarly, it will not avail him to plead that he did not take legal advice until a late stage.[85] The ambit of an earlier equivalent of this provision was considered in *Drinkwater v Joseph Lucas (Electrical) Ltd*.[86] This was a workman's compensation case in which the plaintiff had sought advice from his trade union, and had been told (incorrectly) that his claim was out of time. The Court of Appeal held that the plaintiff had been in ignorance of a material fact, namely that there were facts establishing negligence or breach of duty on the part of the

---

[81] *Walford v Richards* [1976] 1 Lloyd's Rep. 526, CA.
[82] [1980] 1 W.L.R. 968.
[83] *Bull v Devon AHA*, April 9, 1987, Tucker J., unreported.
[84] *Farmer v National Coal Board*, *The Times*, April 27, 1985, CA.
[85] *Pickles v National Coal Board* [1968] 1 W.L.R. 997, CA, must therefore be regarded as no longer being good law.
[86] [1970] 3 All E.R. 769, CA.

defendant. This decision requires to be applied with caution. It is important to observe that the merits of the plaintiff's claim had apparently never been investigated, the trade union's advice being confined to the narrow issue of limitation. On these special facts it is submitted that the Court of Appeal was right to hold that the date of knowledge had not arrived. However, in the much more common case where the claimant is wrongly advised[87] that he has no case on the merits, it is clear that he cannot rely on this to postpone the date of knowledge. Moreover, *Rowe v Kingston upon Hull City Council*[88] considered the effect upon s.14 of a case where the claimant knows that he has suffered injury, but believes that on the state of the law at that time he cannot recover for that injury. The Court of Appeal held that a claimant in this situation nevertheless has enough knowledge to set time running.

Estoppel

8.031   A difficult case concerning matters of law occurred in *Smith v Central Asbestos Co. Ltd*,[89] where some of the plaintiffs were told by the defendants' works manager that as a matter of law they could not both claim a disability pension from the company and sue for damages. It was held that the plaintiffs' consequent misapprehension on this point amounted to ignorance of a material fact. The reasoning here cannot be supported under the wording of the 1980 Act[90]: the mistake which the plaintiffs made was clearly one of law. The real objection to allowing the defendants to plead limitation was that the plaintiffs' inactivity arose directly from the conduct of the defendants' servant. However, the decision should still be the same under the present law, on the ground that the defendants are estopped from pleading limitation by virtue of the conduct of the works manager.

Other advice

8.032   In *Howell v West Midlands Passenger Transport Executive*[91] the plaintiff had been contacted after her injury by a firm of assessors[92] who offered to take over her case for a proportion of the damages and then wrongly advised her that she had no case. In reliance on this she did not sue until after the three years had expired. The Court of Appeal granted ex parte leave to bring the action under s.33 of the 1980 Act,[93] but expressed the

---

[87] By someone other than his employer. See below, "Estoppel".

[88] [2003] All ER (D) 426 (Jul).

[89] [1972] 1 Q.B. 244, CA affirmed [1973] A.C. 518, HL; but see also *Harper v National Coal Board* [1974] Q.B. 614, where a two-man Court of Appeal declined to apply the House of Lords' reasoning on the grounds that it contained no discernible ratio decidendi.

[90] Though it may arguably have been correct under the 1963 Act.

[91] [1973] 1 Lloyd's Rep. 199, CA.

[92] Described by Lord Denning M.R. at ibid., 200 as "ambulance chasers", a phrase which at that time carried distinctly perjorative overtones.

[93] See paras 8.059-8.061.

view that it was impossible to predict what would happen at the trial if the defendants sought to have this leave set aside.

Burdens of proof

In general it is for the defendant to plead limitation, and then for the claimant to show that his action is in time.[94] However, there has been a conflict of authority in the context of provisions, such as those of s.14 of the 1980 Act, which may allow time to run from a date later than that when the cause of action accrues. In *Farrell v National Coal Board*,[95] it was held that in personal injury cases the initial burden is on the defendant to show that the cause of action did not accrue within three years, after which the burden shifts to the claimant to show that the date of knowledge is later than the date of accrual. If this is right, then the rule in personal injury cases is apparently more favourable to the claimant than is the rule in other forms of action, where the defendant can put the burden on to the claimant merely by pleading the statute. This decision is not fully reported and is in conflict with *Crocker v British Coal Corporation*,[96] where it was held that it is not for the defendants to prove that the claimant had the required knowledge more than three years before the commencement of the action. But in *Nash v Eli Lilly*[97] it was again said that it is for the defendant to establish that the claimant had the relevant knowledge soon enough for time to have run. It is submitted that the view taken in Crocker is to be preferred, since it accords with general principles of the burden of proof and avoids the creation of an unnecessary and unjustified anomaly.

8.033

Discretionary extension

Section 33 of the 1980 Act gives the court a discretion to allow a claimant to bring an action for personal injuries, notwithstanding that the time limited by ss.11 and 12 of the Act has expired, if it appears to the court that it would be equitable to do so having regard to the degree to which ss.11 or 12 of the Act prejudice the claimant, or any person whom he represents, and the degree to which any decision under this section would prejudice the defendant, or any person whom he represents. Applicants under s.33 must disclose all relevant circumstances at the hearing of the application, especially where this is made without notice.[98] Until recently it was thought that

8.034

---

[94] See generally para.8.033.
[95] *The Times*, May 28, 1986, CA, Unreported.
[96] (1995) 29 B.M.L.R. 159.
[97] [1993] 1 W.L.R. 782, CA; see also *William Augustine Lennon v Alvis Industries Plc*, July 27, 2000, Unreported, CA.
[98] *Long v Tolchard & Sons Ltd*, *The Times*, January 5, 2000.

s.33 could be invoked only where the claimant is prejudiced by the operation of ss.11 or 12. If the prejudice results from any other provision or rule of law, the discretion was not thought to be available (except perhaps in wholly exceptional circumstances[99]). This view was derived from the decision of the House of Lords in *Walkley v Precision Forgings*.[100] However, in a series of subsequent cases the courts sought to distinguish or refine the *Walkley* principle or to find ways of identifying the sort of exceptional circumstances which would allow them to ignore it. [101]

8.035   These attempts to undermine *Walkley* culminated in the decision of the House of Lords in *Horton v Sadler*,[102] where their Lordships expressly departed from *Walkley*, holding instead that the discretion under s.33 must remain unfettered, and that the decision in *Walkley* was unsound because it ignored the fact that in cases where there have been previous proceedings but the limitation period has now expired, the claimant is affected by s.11 in that this section will cause his second action to fail unless it is disapplied. It is submitted that this reasoning is somewhat unconvincing. The reality is that courts have to decide what weight to give to the existence of previous proceedings. In *Walkley* the House of Lords took the view that the previous proceedings could have been pursued to judgment, with the result that the real cause of the claimant's problem was the failure to prosecute the first action rather than the expiry of the limitation period. In *Horton* a later House of Lords has chosen to characterise the causation issues in the opposite way, focusing on the expiry of the limitation period as the effective cause. The decision in *Walkley* is the more logically attractive of the two approaches, but it has proved generally unpopular in a society which is increasingly claimant-oriented, and it has now been abandoned.

8.036   However, it does not follow that in all cases where there have been previous proceedings a s.33 application will now succeed. The effect of *Horton* is only that a s.33 application is now possible. In exercising its discretion the court must still take account of all relevant factors, including the existence of the previous proceedings. It is possible to exercise the s.33 discretion in the claimant's favour even where CPR 7.6 would have prevented the extension of the first claim form.[103]

---

[99] In *Forward v Hendricks* [1997] 2 All E.R. 395, CA, it was confirmed that the circumstances would have to be wholly exceptional, rather than merely slightly out of the ordinary, such as estoppel or misrepresentation. Reliance was also placed on *Whitfield v N. Durham HA* (1994) 24 B.M.L.R. 39, CA.

[100] [1979] 1 W.L.R. 606, HL; see also *Deerness v John R. Keeble & Son (Brantham) Ltd* [1983] 2 Lloyd's Rep. 260, HL; *Reynolds v Sponsal* (London) Ltd, March 13, 1989, CA, Unreported.

[101] Cases of this kind include *Rose v Express Welding Ltd* January 21, 1986, CA, Unreported; *White v Glass The Times*, February 18, 1989, CA; *Shapland v Palmer* [1999] 1 W.L.R. 2068; [1999] 3 All E.R. 50, CA; *McEvoy v AA Welding and Fabrication Ltd* [1998] PIQR P266 CA. Cases where the principle was followed include *Whitfield v North Durham HA* [1994] 24 B.M.L.R. 39, CA and *Young v Western Power* [2003] EWCA Civ 1034.

[102] *The Times*, June 19, 2006.

[103] *McKay v Hamlani* [2009] 2 All E.R. 579; [2009] 3 W.L.R. 551; for CPR 7.6 see Ch.22.

Disapplication of section 12

Section 33(2) provides that the court shall not disapply s.12(1), which is **8.037** examined in detail below, except where the reason why the person injured could no longer maintain an action was because of the three-year time-limit in s.11. The intention of this provision, as the example which it provides makes clear, is to preclude the disapplication of s.12 in a case which is subject to some other, shorter, time-limit such as the one year limit imposed by the Carriage by Air Act 1961.[104]

Discretion unfettered

Essentially s.33 requires the court to engage in a balancing exercise, **8.038** weighing the prejudice to the claimant if the time-limit is not extended against the prejudice to the defendant if it is extended. Section 33(3) requires a number of particular factors to be taken into account, but also states clearly that the court must have regard to all the circumstances.[105] This matter was considered by the Court of Appeal in *Conry v Simpson*,[106] and by the House of Lords in *Thompson v Brown Construction (Ebbw Vale) Ltd.*[107] Both cases confirm that the s.33 discretion is unfettered[108]. It is not proper to rely solely on one factor: rather, the various factors must be balanced against each other.[109] The six specific factors are examined below. It has been suggested that there is a conflict between the balancing exercise contemplated by s.33(1) and the requirement in s.33(3) that all the circumstances shall be taken into account. It is submitted that this confusion is entirely illusory. The circumstances mentioned in s.33(3) are the circumstances relevant to the balancing exercise required by s.33(1). Once s.33(3) is put into that context, it can be seen that it is merely supplementary to s.33(1). The fact that the claimant appears to have a strong case does not automatically entitle him to the exercise of the s.33 discretion.[110] In *Fletcher v Containerbase (Manchester) Ltd*[111] the Court of Appeal upheld an exercise of the s.33 discretion in favour of the claimant in a case where it was only after the expiry of the limitation period that he had obtained medical evidence that his condition was common to a number of his fellow employees and only then considered that his case was strong enough to

---

[104] For the Carriage by Air Act, see paras 26.023–26.030.
[105] *Taylor v Taylor, The Times*, April 14, 1984, CA.
[106] [1983] 3 All E.R. 369, CA.
[107] [1981] 2 All E.R. 296, HL. See also *Hartley v Birmingham CC* [1992] 1 W.L.R. 968, CA and *Ramsden v Lee* [1992] 2 All E.R. 204, CA.
[108] However, it is necessary to balance the respective prejudices of applying or not applying the strict time limit. The question is not simply whether the claimant has acted reasonably—*McGhie v British Telecommunications plc* [2005] EWCA Civ 48.
[109] *McDonnell v Walker* [2009] EWCA Civ 1257 at para.18.
[110] *Long v Tolchard & Son Ltd*, above.
[111] [2003] All ER (D) 516 (Oct) CA.

justify bringing proceedings. It was also relevant that the delay had not caused significant prejudice to the defendant.

8.039   More recently in *Various Claimants v Bryn Alyn Community (Holdings) Ltd (In Liquidation) and Royal* and *Sun Alliance plc* [112] (another sexual abuse case) the Court of Appeal gave further guidance as to the approach to be adopted in cases involving the s.33 discretion. Auld LJ said:

> "68 The discretion of a judge under s.33 is fettered only to the extent that it provides a non-exhaustive list of circumstances to which he should have regard. However, the matter is not determined simply by assessing comparative scales of hardship; *Long v Tolchard & Sons Ltd* [2001] PIQR PAT, CA. The overall question is one of equity, namely whether it would be 'equitable' to disapply the limitation provisions having regard to the balance of potential prejudice weighed with regard to all the circumstances of the case, including those specifically mentioned in s.33(3); *Nash v Eli Lilly & Co* [1993] 1 WLR 782, CA, and *Whitfield v North Durham HA* [1995] 6 Med LR 32, CA, per Waite LJ, at 39.
>
> 69 The width of the discretion is such that an appellate court should not intervene save where the judge was so plainly wrong that his decision exceeded the ambit within which reasonable disagreement is possible; *Coad v Cornwall and Isles of Scilly HA* [1997] 8 Med LR 154, CA, per Ward LJ at 159. That includes the exercise of wrong principles, taking account of irrelevant factors, ignoring relevant factors or the making of a decision that is 'palpably' or 'plainly' wrong. *Farthing v North East Essex HA* [1998] 2 Lloyds LR, Med 37, CA, and *Margolis v Imperial Tobacco Ltd* [2000] MLC 204, CA. If the Court intervenes on any of those grounds, it should treat the matter as at large and exercise its own discretion in accordance with s.33."

This emphasises the width of the discretion, and in *Burke v Ashe Construction Ltd*[113] the Court of Appeal relied upon it in upholding a judge's decision to disapply s.33 in a case of a simple workplace accident where proceedings were not issued until seven years after the accident, apparently as a result of various failures by a series of professional advisers engaged by the claimant.

In *Kamar v Nightingale*[114] Eady J. observed that it is not enough for a claimant to show that a defendant will not be prejudiced by the disapplication of the limitation period, or that, if he was, it was his own fault. It is necessary to consider the claimant's conduct. If that conduct is in some way culpable, then that is a factor which the judge should take into account when deciding whether it would be equitable to disapply the limitation

---

[112] [2003] EWCA Civ 85; [2003] 1 FCR 385.
[113] [2003] EWCA Civ 717.
[114] [2007] EWHC 2982 (QB Eady J.)

period under s.33. In *McHugh v Gray*[115] Beatson J. reiterated the important general principle that the s.33 discretion is very wide[116] and the decision of the trial judge can be altered only where he is shown to have been palpably wrong or to have exercised his discretion wholly unreasonably. So long as he takes account of all relevant factors, it is for him to decide what weight each factor should have.[117] It is not possible to set any tariff based on the period of delay in starting proceedings because that would cut down the breadth of the discretion in an unacceptable way.[118] In *Cain v Francis McKay*[119] the Court of Appeal ruled that the existence of a limitation defence is in principle a windfall for the defendant, with the result that the loss of it when the s.33 discretion is exercised in the claimant's favour is not to be regarded as a relevant prejudice arising from the exercise of that discretion and is thus not to be taken into account.

Appellate courts

Conry v Simpson[120] also confirms that the discretion under s.33 is essentially vested in the judge of first instance, with the consequence that an appellate court will not lightly interfere with his decision, and will certainly not do so where there was evidence upon which he could reasonably have made the decision he did make.[121] CPR Part 52 now makes it clear that permission is required for any appeal against the judge's decision in this regard. Given the highly discretionary nature of the decision, it appears that such permission is not easily obtained. In *Harrison v Allerdale District Council*[122] the Court of Appeal was invited to lay down general guidelines for the application of the s.33 discretion. On the facts of the case, this proved unnecessary, but Ralph Gibson L.J. also suggested that the idea was inappropriate anyway.   8.040

The relevant factors

The factors to be taken into account in s.33(3) are as follows.   8.041

Section 33(3)(a), length of and reasons for delay. The delay which is referred to here is the delay after the expiry of the primary limitation period, not the total delay from the time when the cause of action accrued.   8.042

---

[115] [2006] EWHC 1968 (QB).
[116] At para.19.
[117] At para.21.
[118] At para.22.
[119] [2008] EWCA Civ 1451.
[120] [1983] 3 All E.R. 369, CA.
[121] See also *Bradley v Hanseatic Shipping* [1986] 2 Lloyd's Rep. 34, CA and *Yellin v Levitt Bernstein Associates*, June 26, 1986, CA, Unreported.
[122] April 19, 1989, CA, Ralph Gibson L.J. as single judge, Unreported.

However, the court's duty to consider all relevant factors means that delay during the primary limitation is to be considered, though not strictly speaking as part of this paragraph.[123] There is no general principle that the claimant is automatically entitled to an extension of time where the delay has been very short,[124] though a delay of only one day will almost always lead to the granting of an extension.[125] Clearly, the longer the delay on the claimant's part, the more cogent the explanation will need to be. What is required is an explanation that will account for whatever delay has taken place. However, that delay does not have to be "reasonable" according to an objective test.[126] In *Buck v English Electric Co. Ltd*[127] Kilner Brown J., reasoning by analogy with the cases on want of prosecution, propounded two general principles. The first was that extreme delay does not by itself preclude the exercise of the s.33 discretion. Secondly, a delay of five years or more creates a rebuttable presumption that the delay has been excessive, though this is still liable to be rebutted if the claimant can provide an adequate explanation.

This second principle, if it has any validity at all, can be no more than a very rough guideline. It cannot be the case that leave will always be given when the writ is issued within five years of time starting to run, since that would rewrite s.11. Beyond the five-year period it must also be the case that the longer the period the more cogent the explanation will need to be. This case should therefore be treated with some caution. The fact that the claimant was unaware of having a legal right to sue the defendants can be taken into account under this paragraph, though it is, of course, irrelevant under s.14.[128]

8.043 **Section 33(3)(b), cogency of evidence.** The court must consider the extent to which the delay has rendered the available evidence less cogent than it would have been had the action been brought within the time-limit of s.11 or s.12, as the case may be. In personal injury cases this commonly takes the form of the defendants (or their insurers) destroying the file on the case after the lapse of some time, as happened in *Conry v Simpson*.[129] In that case the Court of Appeal was eventually able to hold that the destruction was reasonable, but that the defendant was not greatly prejudiced by it. More difficult problems will arise where either or both of these conditions is

---

[123] *Donovan v Gwentoys Ltd* [1990] 1 W.L.R. 472, HL.
[124] *Ramsden v Lee* [1992] 2 All E.R. 204, CA.
[125] *Hartley v Birmingham CC* [1992] 1 W.L.R. 968, CA; in *Grenville v Waltham Forest HA* (November 18, 1992, CA, Unreported), a similar view was taken about a delay of three days.
[126] *Coad v Cornwall and Isles of Scilly HA* [1997] 1 W.L.R. 189; (1997) 33 B.M.L.R. 168, CA.
[127] [1977] 1 W.L.R. 806, Kilner Brown J.
[128] *Halford v Brookes, The Independent*, November 27, 1990, CA. This has now been reversed by [1991] 1 W.L.R. 428; [1991] 3 All E.R. 559, CA.
[129] [1983] 3 All E.R. 369, CA.

absent. The point does not appear to have been considered in any reported case, but it may be surmised that the effect on the other party is likely to be a very important consideration. Where this is slight, little account will be taken of the destruction; where it is considerable, the destruction will surely point strongly in favour of giving leave, unless the defendant can convince the court that he has acted properly. The effect of the destruction of evidence may vary according to the nature of the case. Where the event is unique, it is more likely that destruction of records will seriously impede the chance of a fair hearing, but where it is a matter of investigating a system of working, more reliance can be placed on witnesses' memories.[130] In exceptional cases the lapse of time may bring progress in scientific research which adds to the cogency of the evidence available.[131] In a motor accident case, if the Motor Insurers' Bureau become involved, prejudice to them from the lapse of time can be taken into account under s.33.[132]

Section 33(3)(c), defendant's conduct.   The third factor which must be   8.044
considered is the defendant's conduct after the cause of action arose. This includes the extent to which he responded to requests reasonably made by the claimant for information or inspection for the purpose of ascertaining facts which were, or might be, relevant to the claimant's cause of action against the defendant. A particular point that may be of significance here is the conduct of the defendant who deliberately protracts negotiations aimed at achieving a settlement in the hope of causing the time-limit to expire without a writ having been issued. Conduct of this kind can legitimately be taken into account under this paragraph, although it will not prevent time from running for the purposes of s.11.[133] It has been held[134] that such negotiations may amount to an implied agreement to defer service of the writ where it has been issued,[135] and by analogy there may be an implied agreement not to plead limitation where negotiations before the writ are protracted.

The defendant's conduct was held to be relevant in *Marston v British Railways Board*,[136] a workman's compensation case in which the defendant had issued a hammer to the plaintiff, stating untruthfully that it was new. This claim was maintained for some time after the cause of action arose,

---

[130] *Brooks v J. & P. Coates (U.K.) Ltd* [1984] 1 All E.R. 702, Boreham J. and *Carr v Cammell Laird* (July 30, 1990, Simon Brown J. Unreported), where a distinction was drawn between those parts of the action which related to a system of working and those which depended on specific instances. The action was allowed to continue in respect of the former, but not of the latter.

[131] *Carr v Cammell Laird*, July 30, 1990, Simon Brown J., Unreported.

[132] *Davis v Soltenpur* (1983) 133 New L.J. 720, Hobhouse J.; an application for leave to appeal was dismissed by Sir John Donaldson M.R. on July 15, 1983.

[133] *Easy v Universal Anchorage Co.* [1974] 1 W.L.R. 899.

[134] *Hare v Personal Representatives of Mohammed Yunis Malik* (1980) 124 S.J. 328, CA.

[135] See paras 21.020–21.022.

[136] [1976] I.C.R. 124, Croom-Johnson J.

apparently through an honest mistake, and it was only on discovering the truth that the plaintiff appreciated the possibility of negligence on the part of the defendants. Croom-Johnson J. held that the giving of the incorrect information could justify the exercise of the discretion in the plaintiff's favour. It should also be noted that the obligations which this paragraph imposes on the defendant extend to his insurers and his solicitors in so far as the case may permit.[137] A more unusual application of this paragraph was seen in *Marshall v Martin*,[138] where the defendant had made an interim payment in respect of the plaintiff's claim. Mustill L.J. held that this was a fact about the defendant's conduct which could be taken into account as suggesting that it would be equitable to disapply the time-limit in s.11, since it pointed to the plaintiff having a strong claim.

8.045 **Section 33(3)(d), claimant's disability.** Account must be taken of the duration of any disability of the claimant arising after the date of accrual of the cause of action. The term "disability" as used in s.33(3)(d) is a term of art, being defined for the purposes of the 1980 Act by s.38(2) of the Act as referring to a person who is an infant or who is of unsound mind. This view is supported by *Dawson v Spain-Gower*,[139] where Glidewell L.J. observed that a claimant can be mentally ill for some purposes without thereby being incapable of managing his own affairs within the meaning of s.38 of the 1980 Act, and by *Yates v Thakeham Tiles Ltd*,[140] where it was also observed that incapacity falling short of disability can be taken into account as being another relevant factor in exercising the discretion, even though it does not fall under this paragraph. Any disability which arose before the date when the cause of action accrued and was still subsisting at that date would fall under s.28 of the 1980 Act[141] and would prevent time from running at all. The view of Eastham J. in *Matthew Pilmore v Northern Trawlers Ltd*,[142] that a plaintiff who had been incapacitated from pursing his action by intermittent attacks of dermatitis had suffered from a "disability" for the purposes of s.33, is clearly wholly incorrect, though of course the dermatitis could have been regarded as a relevant factor under the court's general discretion, had the judge seen fit to take that view.

8.046 **Section 33(3)(e), claimant's conduct.** The court must consider the extent to which the claimant acted promptly and reasonably once he knew whether or not the act or omission of the defendant, to which the injury was

---

[137] *Thompson v Brown Construction (Ebbw Vale) Ltd* [1981] 2 All E.R. 296, HL, per Lord Diplock.
[138] June 10, 1987, Mustill L.J. as single judge of the Court of Appeal, Unreported.
[139] October 18, 1988, Glidewell L.J. as single judge of the Court of Appeal, Unreported.
[140] *The Times*, May 19, 1994, CA; see also *Jones v City and Hackney HA* (December 21, 1993, Colman J., Unreported).
[141] See Ch.19.
[142] [1986] 1 Lloyd's Rep. 552, Eastham J.

attributable, might be capable at that time of giving rise to an action for damages. This refers to the date on which the claimant in fact appreciated the position, as distinct from the date on which he had the constructive knowledge of it which is sufficient to bring s.11 into operation.[143] In *McCafferty v Metropolitan Police Receiver*[144] the plaintiff had refrained from suing his employers at an earlier stage partly because he considered the injury too trivial (it later became more serious) and partly because he wished to preserve good relations with them. The Court of Appeal held that the former reason could not be a ground for exercising the s.33 discretion, but that the latter reason could be taken into account. The same approach was adopted in *Buck v English Electric Co. Ltd*,[145] where the plaintiff was in receipt of a disability pension and considered that it would have been "sponging" on his employers to sue them for damages as well. By contrast, in *Miller v London Electrical Manufacturing*[146] it was held that the plaintiff's reluctance to bring an action against his employers because he feared that he would lose his job if he did so was reasonable. The reference in this paragraph to conduct applies to both the claimant and his advisers.[147] Thus the conduct of the claimant's advisers can also be considered. In a case of medical negligence at the birth of a child[148] it has been held that it is not reasonable for the parents to delay bringing the action merely because time will not run against the child until majority.

Section 33(3)(f), expert advice. The final factor to be considered is the 8.047
steps, if any, taken by the claimant to obtain medical, legal or other expert advice and the nature of any such advice he may have received. It was shown above[149] that the claimant cannot escape the operation of s.11 by showing that he received defective legal advice. However, it appears that this fact may be a ground on which the court can exercise the s.33 discretion.[150] In addition to this, any failure on the part of the claimant to seek appropriate expert advice is likely to disincline the court to look sympathetically upon his argument that he did not in fact know of the existence of the cause of action.

By contrast, if medical or other advice is sought, but the facts are not revealed, the claimant is not fixed with constructive knowledge (s.14(3)). This apparent anomaly can be reconciled by saying that s.14(3) relates only

---

[143] *Eastman v London County Bus Services, The Times*, November 23, 1985, CA.
[144] [1977] 1 W.L.R. 1073, CA.
[145] [1977] 1 W.L.R. 806, Kilner Brown J.
[146] [1976] 2 Lloyd's Rep. 284, CA.
[147] *Thompson v Brown Construction (Ebbw Vale) Ltd* [1981] 2 All E.R. 296, HL, per Lord Diplock.
[148] *Obembe v City of Hackney HA*, June 9, 1989, Drake J., Unreported.
[149] See para.8.030.
[150] *Waghorn v Lewisham and North Southwark HA*, June 23, 1987, S.N. McKinnon Q.C. Unreported.

to the period between the seeking of the advice and its receipt. Chronologically, this paragraph should come before paragraph (e),[151] since it relates to what happens before the cause of action is discovered. It refers to the claimant's own conduct as well as to that of his advisers, but the effect is that, as long as the claimant himself acts promptly and reasonably, he is not to be prejudiced for the purposes of the s.33 application by the dilatoriness of his legal advisers.[152]

Where injured person dies

8.048   Section 33(4) amplifies these provisions in the case where the person injured has died at a time when he could no longer have maintained an action, i.e. after time had expired. In such cases the court is required to have regard especially to the length of and reasons for the delay on the part of the claimant. This provision is relevant in two situations. The first is where an action is brought on behalf of the estate, and the second is where an action is brought on behalf of the dependants under the Fatal Accidents Act 1976. Section 33(4) has two effects. It concentrates attention on the claimant's delay at the expense of the delay of his executors or his dependants. It also reduces the importance for s.33 purposes of the other factors mentioned in that section as being relevant considerations.

Alternative remedy

8.049   An argument sometimes put forward on behalf of defendants in s.33 applications is that the claimant will be able to sue his own professional advisers and is therefore not prejudiced by the refusal of leave under s.33. In *Conry v Simpson*[153] the argument was largely discounted on the basis that the claim would not by any means have been cast-iron, so that there would have been an element of uncertainty in leaving the claimant to this remedy.[154] The point was considered at length by the House of Lords in *Thompson v Brown Construction (Ebbw Vale) Ltd*,[155] where the trial judge had gone so far as to hold that he had no jurisdiction to apply s.33 because the plaintiff had a cast-iron case against his solicitors. The House of Lords held that this was the wrong approach. The s.33 discretion is unfettered, so there is always jurisdiction to extend the period. At the same time, the existence of an alternative remedy is naturally a weighty consideration.[156]

---

[151] *Thompson v Brown Construction (Ebbw Vale) Ltd* [1981] 2 All E.R. 296, HL, per Lord Diplock.
[152] *Thompson v Brown Construction (Ebbw Vale) Ltd* [1981].
[153] [1983] 3 All E.R. 369, CA.
[154] See also *Hartley v Birmingham CC* [1992] 1 W.L.R. 968, CA.
[155] [1981] 2 All E.R. 296.
[156] The case was accordingly remitted to the trial judge for further consideration. More recently a similar approach was taken by the Court of Appeal in *Ramsden v Lee* [1992] 2 All E.R. 204, CA and *Hartley v Birmingham City CC* [1992] 1 W.L.R. 968, CA.

However, it has also been said that where a claimant instructs solicitors promptly, their delay in instituting proceedings should not be held against him under s.33.[157]

A variant on this approach was seen in *Browes v Jones & Middleton*,[158] where the plaintiff sued his solicitors for not instituting proceedings in time, but wished to protect himself by joining the person responsible for his injuries as second defendant. To do this he required leave under s.33. The Court of Appeal refused this leave, holding that the balance of advantage clearly lay in leaving the plaintiff to sue his solicitor. Although the case is incompletely reported, it appears from the report that the Court of Appeal assumed that it had jurisdiction to allow the application, and that the only question was as to the application of the balance of convenience test. This problem has been further considered in *Harrison v Allerdale Council*[159] and *Reynolds v Sponsal (London) Ltd*.[160] In the former it was argued that the plaintiff might suffer prejudice if left to sue his solicitor, since the damages in that action, even assuming that it succeeded, would be less than those in the personal injuries action, since they would have to be reduced to take account of the chance that the personal injuries action might have failed. The point did not need to be resolved in that case, but in a more appropriate case it is a factor to which detailed consideration could properly be given. In the latter case the Court of Appeal made the point that in cases of very long delay, the action against the solicitor could itself be time-barred, without the possibility of any extension, since it would not be a personal injuries action. On such facts the balance of convenience would tilt back considerably in the direction of allowing the plaintiff's personal injuries action to proceed.

Negligent solicitors

Where it is sought to disapply the limitation period in order to allow a **8.050** negligent firm of solicitors to bring proceedings which it should have brought or pursued at an earlier date, the application is unlikely to be successful.[161] However, in *Richardson v Watson*[162] an action was brought against the defendant in a Road Traffic Act case without giving the timely notice to the Motor Insurance Bureau ("MIB") that was a condition precedent to the liability of the MIB to meet any liability established against the defendant. The claimant then discontinued that claim and commenced a fresh action against the defendant, giving, on this occasion, timely notice to

---

[157] *Corbin v Penfold Metallising Co. Ltd*, *The Times*, May 2, 2000, CA.; *Steeds v Peverel Management Services Ltd* [2001] EWCA Civ 419.
[158] (1979) 123 S.J. 123, CA.
[159] April 19, 1989, Ralph Gibson L.J. as single judge of the CA, Unreported.
[160] March 13, 1989, CA, Unreported.
[161] *Williams v Johnstone* Judge McKenna.
[162] [2006] EWCA Civ 1662.

the MIB. The action was, however, commenced outside the three year limitation period. By the time the matter came before the Court of Appeal the House of Lords had given judgment in *Horton v Sadler,* and the existence of the previous proceedings was no longer to be treated as an absolute bar to the second action. Further it was not an abuse of process to bring a second action in order to cure the defect in the first action. As a matter of general principle that is obviously right, and no difficulty need arise where the second action is brought within the limitation period. The problems seem to start when the second action is brought outside the primary limitation period, as in this case. In that event the Court of Appeal in *Richardson v Watson* took the view that the s.33 discretion still existed (as plainly it does) and that the fact of the earlier action was irrelevant. The discretion was to be exercised in the usual way. Viewed in this light the decision in *Richardson v Watson* does not contradict that in *Williams v Johnstone,* though the latter must be regarded as depending on its own facts in that the judge there held that in effect the only beneficiary of the second action would be the negligent solicitors.

Insurance

8.051 In *Kelly v Bastible (Executors of the Estate of Christopher Bastible—Deceased)*[163] the Court of Appeal considered the relevance in a s.33 context of the fact that the defendant is insured. It was argued, relying on *Hartley v Birmingham CC,*[164] that a fully insured defendant suffers no prejudice when the court exercises its discretion to allow an action to continue, since by definition the loss will not fall on the defendant personally. In *Kelly v Bastible* the Court of Appeal rejected this approach, declaring that it represented a misunderstanding of what had been said in *Hartley v Birmingham CC.* The correct approach is to regard the defendant and his insurer as a single composite unit. The prejudice to be taken into account is therefore that which results to both defendant and insurer from, for example, the fact that the claim is now very stale.

Just as the prospect of an alternative remedy for the claimant may be taken into account, so too may the fact that the defendant is insured and will therefore not personally suffer any great prejudice if he is ultimately found liable.

Legal aid

8.052 A well-known problem in all types of case where the claimant is publicly funded and the defendant is not is that the defendant, if successful, has little or no prospect of recovering anything by way of costs from the claimant.

---

[163] (1997) 141 S.J.L.B. 5; *The Independent,* December 10, 1996; *The Times,* November 1996, CA.
[164] [1992] 1 W.L.R. 968, CA.

This was the situation in *Lye v Marks & Spencer Plc*,[165] where the plaintiff sought leave under s.33 to bring the action out of time. The Court of Appeal held that the legal aid position could be a factor to be taken into account in deciding whether to exercise the s.33 discretion in the plaintiff's favour, but that it could not by itself be decisive.

Case law developments

A claimant may delay bringing an action because on the state of the authorities at the time he has no prospect of success. At a later date, when time has theoretically expired, a development in the case law may show that the action could, after all, have succeeded. There is no reported case on the question of whether this is a factor to be considered under s.33, but some assistance may possibly be derived from the decision of the Employment Appeal Tribunal in *Foster v South Glamorgan HA*.[166] This was a sex discrimination case in which the applicant sought leave to proceed out of time (the Sex Discrimination Act 1975 empowers the Tribunal to give such leave). The basis of the application was that the then recent decision of the European Court of Justice in *Marshall v Southampton & South-West Area HA*[167] had altered the law in a material way. The Employment Appeals Tribunal held that the decision of the European Court of Justice must be regarded as purely declaratory, so that there had not been a change in the law, but that as a matter of discretion it would be appropriate to give leave to proceed out of time. It may well be argued that the essential considerations are the same where the House of Lords delivers a decision that radically changes the profession's perception of the law, but the point has yet to be tested in the context of s.33. The question can, of course, be relevant only in those cases where there is discretion to extend time.

8.053

Strength of claimant's case

In *Beer v London Borough of Waltham Forest*[168] Hodgson J. held that the apparent strength of the plaintiff's case was a factor which could legitimately be taken into account in deciding whether to exercise the s.33 discretion, a very strong case being a factor pointing in the direction of allowing the action to be brought.[169]

8.054

---

[165] *The Times*, February 15, 1988, CA.
[166] [1988] I.C.R. 526.
[167] [1986] Q.B. 401.
[168] December 16, 1987, Hodgson J., Unreported.
[169] See also *Smith v Ministry of Defence* [2005] EWHC 682 (QB), [2005] All ER (D) 254 (Apr) Silber J.

Claimant's condition

8.055   In *Rule v Atlas Stone Co.*[170] the plaintiff's wife had been killed, allegedly through the negligence of the defendants. He sued in his own capacity and as executor of her estate. Although a letter before action was sent at an early stage, no writ was issued until after the limitation period had expired. It was held that the action should be allowed to proceed under s.33, as there had been no prejudice to the defendants and as the plaintiff's conduct could be adequately explained by the distress caused to him by the death of his wife.

Economic prejudice

8.056   In two medical negligence cases the argument has been put forward on behalf of defendant health authorities that the delay in bringing the action to trial has caused them prejudice because of a change in the arrangements between themselves and their liability insurer, the Medical Defence Union. The effect of this change has been to increase the proportion of any claim which individual health authorities must meet from their own resources; whether the old or the new arrangement applies to any given case depends upon the date of judgment. In *Antcliffe v Gloucester HA*[171] Schiemann J. held that this could not be a relevant factor, since it did not prejudice the defendants' case, but merely their position if they lost the case. In *Gascoigne v Haringey HA*[172] it was pointed out by Tudor-Evans J. that this suggestion involved too narrow a view of the discretion within s.33. By analogy, it may be noted that in relation to striking out for want of prosecution, damage to the defendant's commercial interests is a relevant factor.[173] Although the position under s.33 cannot yet be regarded as settled, it is suggested that the decision of Tudor-Evans J. is to be preferred to that of Schiemann J.

Group actions

8.057   The principles applicable under s.33 are not in any way modified in the case of group actions.[174]

---

[170] [1987] C.L.Y. para.2325.
[171] July 31, 1991, Schiemann J., Unreported.
[172] December 20, 1991, Tudor-Evans J., Unreported.
[173] *Dept. of Transport v Chris Smaller (Transport) Ltd* [1989] 1 All E.R. 897, HL.
[174] *Dept. of Transport v Chris Smaller (Transport) Ltd* [1989]. For group actions, generally see now CPR Pt 19.

Two Claim Forms

Problems arise where the plaintiff issues a claim form within the limitation **8.058** period, but fails to serve it within the four months allowed by CPR rule 7.5(2) and then issues a second writ outside the limitation period. There is a conflict of authority on the proper response of the court in such cases. In *Firman v Ellis*[175] the Court of Appeal suggested that the action in the second writ might be allowed to proceed, but the law on this point must be regarded as settled by the decision in *Chappell v Cooper*,[176] where the Court of Appeal held that the proper course is to set aside the second claim form, leaving the plaintiff to seek an extension of time for the first claim form under CPR rule 7.6.

Procedure under s.33

Section 33(1) allows the discretion to be exercised if it appears to the court **8.059** that it would be equitable to do so. Section 33(7) defines "the court" for this purpose as the court in which the action has been brought. The ambit of this definition was considered in *Firman v Ellis*,[177] where the Court of Appeal said that it is not limited to the particular court which tries the case, but extends to any judge of the High Court or the county court, as the case may be (including a judge in chambers or a judge hearing an application as a preliminary issue), but does not extend to a Master or a Registrar. Under the present regime it is clear that District Judges and Masters can and commonly do hear such applications. On this basis it would follow that there are a number of permissible ways of proceeding when the claimant wishes to seek the exercise of the s.33 discretion. The first is to make a preliminary without notice application before the claim form is issued. In *Re Clark v Forbes Stuart (Thames Street) Ltd*[178] application for an extension of time was made ex parte.[179] The Court of Appeal approved this as being a proper procedure, but pointed out that the leave could only be provisional, since it would be necessary to hear the other party before firm approval could be given. Consequently, it would be open to the defendant to raise the point again at the trial. This form of procedure was considered further in *Goodchild v Greatness Timber Co. Ltd*,[180] where it was said that the court should not be over ready to give leave on an ex parte application, since to do so risked the throwing away of costs in respect of a case which

---

[175] [1978] Q.B. 886, CA.
[176] [1980] 1 W.L.R. 958, CA.
[177] [1978] Q.B. 86, CA.
[178] [1964] 1 W.L.R. 836, CA.
[179] The grounds of the application were such as would now have prevented time from running at all—1980 Act s.14(2)(c)—but this does not affect the procedural point in the case.
[180] [1968] 2 Q.B. 372, CA.

would not survive scrutiny at trial. At the present day it is not usual to adopt this method of proceeding.

8.060   The second method of proceeding is to issue the claim form and then, after the close of pleadings, apply to have the s.33 question tried as a preliminary point of law. Clearly this risks incurring greater costs than the application made before the issue of the claim form. It is likely that this will be the method used if the claimant does not apply ex parte, since it is to be presumed that the defendant will plead limitation and will want to have the point determined at the earliest possible stage. Occasionally it may be necessary for the court to hear all the evidence in the case even under this procedure, for example where questions of causation are inextricably linked with those of limitation.[181] This is the method most commonly adopted at present. The third option is to leave the determination of the s.33 point until the trial itself. In costs terms this is the most expensive approach, and it appears that it is rarely adopted.

Defendant's procedure

8.061   In *Cozens v North Devon Hospital Management Committee*[182] the plaintiff had applied without notice for leave under s.33, which had been granted. The defendant then applied on notice to have this set aside. The Court of Appeal held that this was not the proper procedure. The defendant should wait until the trial of the action, when he will have the chance to argue that the original leave was improperly granted.

Contribution cases

8.062   The decision of the Court of Appeal in *Kennett v Brown*[183] illustrates a procedural difficulty which arises in personal injury cases where the defendant makes a claim for contribution. If that claim is made outside the limitation period, the defendant will need to seek the leave of the court under s.33, and the question is at what stage this should be done. In *Kennett v Brown* it was held that the application need not be made until the second defendant raises the limitation issue. This follows from the general principle that it is for the defendant to plead limitation and that the court will not take the point of its own motion.[184]

Evidence

8.063   In *Jones v G.D. Searle & Co. Ltd*[185] the plaintiff sought the exercise of the s.33 discretion, alleging that she had only just received favourable advice as

---

[181] *Fletcher v Sheffield HA*, May 25, 1993, CA, Unreported.
[182] [1966] 2 Q.B. 318, Thompson J.; [1966] 2 Q.B. 336, CA.
[183] [1988] 2 All E.R. 600.
[184] See paras 21.002–21.005.
[185] [1978] 3 All E.R. 654, CA.

to her prospects of success in the action. The defendant sought to administer interrogatories (the modern equivalent would be to make a Pt 18 request for further information) aimed at discovering the content of any previous legal advice given to the plaintiff on this point, but the plaintiff resisted this as being inconsistent with professional privilege. The Court of Appeal held that the provisions of the 1980 Act overrode professional privilege, so that the interrogatories must be allowed. This was an unnecessary decision: the burden is on the plaintiff to satisfy the court as to the desirability of exercising the discretion. It would therefore surely be sufficient to say that the interrogatories need not be answered, but that if they are not answered the court is likely to conclude that the plaintiff's case is not sufficiently made out. This case was considered in *Tatlock v G.P. Worsley & Co. Ltd.*[186] That case is not directly on the same point as *Jones v Searle*, for it also relates to production of documents. The Court of Appeal held that this is generally not required, though the plaintiff may have waived privilege by reproducing part or all of the document in his pleading. The waiver will apply only to those parts of the pleading which have in fact been so reproduced. The case does affirm *Jones v Searle* on the point that under s.33 the plaintiff may have to give brief details of the nature of the advice which he has received in order to enable the court to decide whether to grant the s.33 application.

The Fatal Accidents Act

Section 12 of the 1980 Act applies to actions under the Fatal Accidents Act 1976. These are actions brought by the dependants of a deceased person in respect of the loss caused to them by the death of the person who had supported them. Section 12(1) provides that such an action shall not be brought if the death occurred at a time when the person injured could no longer maintain an action and recover damages in respect of the injury, whether because of a time-limit in the 1980 Act or for any other reason. Further, in determining whether the injured person's action would have been barred under s.11, no account shall be taken of the possibility of that time-limit being overridden under s.33 of the Act.   **8.064**

Time-limit

In addition to the restriction of s.12(1), mentioned above, s.12(2) imposes a further limit, namely that an action under the Fatal Accidents Act 1976 shall not be brought more than three years after the later of the date of   **8.065**

---

[186] June 22, 1989, CA, Unreported.

death and the date of knowledge of the person for whose benefit the action is brought.[187] This is in substitution for any limit contained in any other section of the Act. Therefore, this is another date of knowledge provision, but in this instance the date of knowledge is defined by reference to the dependant for whose benefit the action is brought. It must be remembered that this limit is in addition to that provided by s.12(1). The process for determining whether the Fatal Accidents Act 1976 action is barred is therefore as follows. Ask whether the deceased's action was barred by s.11 (disregarding s.33) and, if so, the Fatal Accidents Act 1976 action is similarly barred. If not, ask whether both the three-year periods of s.12(2) have expired. If so, the action is barred, but otherwise it may still be brought. If the result of this process is that the action is barred, it is still possible to ask the court to exercise the s.33 discretion. If such a request is successful, the effect is to extend time in respect of the dependant's action only—there is no effect on any action on behalf of the deceased's estate.

More than one dependant

8.066   Section 13 of the 1980 Act governs the case where an action under the Fatal Accidents Act is brought for the benefit of more than one person. Section 13(1) provides that s.12(2)(b) is to be applied to each of them separately. Section 12(2)(b) is the provision that allows the running of time for the dependant's action to be postponed until the date of knowledge. The effect of this is that time is judged separately in respect of each possible claimant, and it may therefore happen that some dependants find their claim time-barred, whilst the claims of other dependants are still in time. This gives rise to further problems where an action is brought on behalf of a number of dependants, and it is alleged that the claim is time-barred as regards some, but not all, of them. Section 13(2) provides that in these circumstances the court shall direct that those persons whose claim is barred shall be excluded from those for whom the action is brought. Section 13(3) qualifies this by providing that no such direction shall be given in respect of a claimant where it is shown that the action would not be barred if brought solely for the benefit of that person, whether by reason of s.28 of the 1980 Act (which relates to persons under disability[188]) or an agreement between the parties not to raise the defence, or otherwise. Section 13(3) is apparently unnecessary, since in the cases with which it deals the requirements of s.13(2) would in any event not be satisfied. It should perhaps be regarded as having been included for the avoidance of doubt. It also serves the useful purpose of emphasising the possibility of contracting-out of the use of the limitation defence.[189]

---

[187] This is subject to s.39, so that any other shorter time-limit provided by this or any other Act will prevail over s.12.

[188] See Ch.19.

[189] See Ch.1.

Parts II and III of the 1980 Act

By s.12(3) the time-limits imposed by s.12 are subject to extension in the   8.067
case of disability (s.28) or in pursuance of the discretion of the court under
s.33. Further, the complex rules relating to the addition of new parties to
the action, as laid down in s.35, apply to these actions. However, the time-
limits cannot be extended by acknowledgment,[190] nor do fraud, concealment or mistake postpone the running of time.[191] Section 37, which applies
the provisions of the Act to cases involving the Crown, is also inapplicable
to s.12 actions. The remaining provisions of Pts II and III are by their nature
incapable of applying to s.12 actions, apart from s.39, which does apply.

Obsolete cause of action

In *Ward v Foss;*[192] the plaintiffs brought an action claiming damages on   8.068
behalf of the deceased. The cause of action had accrued at a time when it
was still possible in such actions to obtain damages for loss of earnings
accruing after the date of death, though by the time the writ was issued this
rule had been reversed by the Administration of Justice Act 1982. The
Court of Appeal nevertheless held that it would be equitable to allow the
action to continue under s.33, and effectively disregarded the anomalous
effect of allowing such an action to be brought at the present day.

Effect on damages where action partially barred

Where the claimant's injuries have accrued over a period of time it may   8.069
happen that the cause of action in respect of some of the damage (but not
all of it) is time-barred. In *Clarkson v Modern Foundries*[193] the plaintiff
sued his employers in respect of pneumoconiosis which he had contracted
in the course of his employment. It was established that the injuries had
begun to accrue in 1940, but had not been discovered until 1951.[194] It was
also accepted that events within the limitation period had materially contributed to the plaintiff's disability. This meant that some of the damage
was on the face of it time-barred, on the basis that a fresh cause of action
accrues every day.[195] Donovan J. held that the plaintiff was entitled to
recover in respect of all the damage he had suffered, since the defendant
was unable to discharge the burden of showing that all the injuries occurred

---

[190] 1980 Act ss.29–31; see Ch.18.
[191] 1980 Act s.32; see Ch.20.
[192] *The Times*, November 29, 1993, CA.
[193] [1957] 1 W.L.R. 1210, Donovan J.
[194] This case pre-dates the rules which delay the running of time in these circumstances; a modern equivalent would be where the damage was discoverable at an earlier stage, but was not in fact discovered until later.
[195] *Berry v Stone Manganese & Marine Ltd* [1972] 1 Lloyd's Rep. 182, Ashworth J.

out of time. The decision must, however, be regarded as open to serious question. Donovan J. relies on *Bonnington Castings v Wardlaw*.[196] That was a case in which the defendants had not been negligent in respect of all the injuries suffered by the plaintiff, and it was held that the burden lay on the defendants to show that all the injuries were attributable to the non-negligent conduct.

8.070   In the law of limitations it is well established that the burden shifts to the claimant as soon as the defendant pleads limitation.[197] In principle it would appear that the right result is to hold that no damages can be recovered for the injuries which accrued outside the limitation period. The correctness of the decision in *Clarkson* was questioned by the Court of Appeal in *Cartledge v Jopling*,[198] and in *Cartwright v G.K.N. Sankey Ltd*[199] Latey J. suggested that the damages should have been apportioned. The correct method of apportionment must in part depend upon the nature of the injuries suffered. A good example of this is *Berry v Stone Manganese & Marine Ltd*,[200] where the plaintiff gradually went deaf in consequence of being exposed to noise at work. The case is reported only on the preliminary point of when time began to run, but the facts illustrate a difficulty which may arise if damages are simply apportioned by time on the basis of how much deafness was caused within the limitation period. With deafness, and some other disabilities, the incremental effects are considerable. If the damage accrues over a period of 10 years, and the claimant is totally deaf at the end of that time, it is not appropriate to award 30 per cent of the damages given for total deafness, since it may well be that after seven of the 10 years the claimant was only 25 per cent deaf. It is necessary to inquire in each case how much extra damage was in fact caused within the limitation period.

DEFAMATION

Extension of time in defamation cases

8.071   An action for defamation or other malicious faleshood must be brought within one year of the date on which the cause of action accrues.[201] However, s.32A of the 1980 Act[202] confers on the court a limited discretion

---

[196] [1956] 1 A.C. 613.
[197] See para.21.010.
[198] [1962] 1 Q.B. 189.
[199] [1972] 2 Lloyd's Rep. 242.
[200] [1972] 1 Lloyd's Rep. 182, Ashworth J.
[201] 1980 Act s.4A, as inserted by the Defamation Act 1996 s.5; see para.8.002. There are also special rules in the case of disability; see para.19.030.
[202] As inserted by the Administration of Justice Act 1985 s.57.

to allow an action to be brought outside that one-year period. The court will be reluctant to allow claimants to avoid the effect of this rule by characterising what is in truth an action for malicious falsehood as an action for "unlawful interference with rights", a concept which is as yet far from fully developed in English law.[203]

The conditions of the extension

The conditions are similar to those in s.33 of the Act.   8.072

If it appears to the court that it would be equitable to allow an action to proceed having regard to the degree to which—the operation of s.4A prejudices the plaintiff or any person whom he represents, and any decision of the court under this subsection would prejudice the defendant or any person whom he represents, the court may direct that that section shall not apply to the action or shall not apply to any specified cause of action to which the action relates. In exercising this discretion the court must have regard to all the circumstances of the case and in particular to the length of, and the reasons for, the delay on the part of the plaintiff. Where the reason or one of the reasons for the delay was that all or any of the facts relevant to the cause of action did not become known to the plaintiff until after the end of the one-year period, the court takes into account the date on which any such facts did become known to him, and the extent to which he acted promptly and reasonably once he knew whether or not the facts in question might be capable of giving rise to an action; and the extent to which, having regard to the delay, relevant evidence is likely to be unavailable, or to be less cogent than if the action had been brought within the one-year period. In *Adelson v Associated Newspapers Ltd*[204] Eady J. made some observations on the exercise of the discretion in s.32A of the 1980 Act to extend time in defamation cases. He accepted that the insertion of s.32A into the 1980 Act[205] signified Parliament's intention to put in place a more flexible regime, in the sense that the much shorter period of limitation was to be balanced by a broader discretion on the court's part to extend the period, having regard to what was equitable in the circumstances of the case. Thus the discretion may be regarded as broader and more flexible than that under s.33. The conduct of the parties and the apparent strength or weakness of the Claimant's case can be taken into account. However, genuine libel claims still had to be pursued with vigour: that was the most important policy consideration underlying the legislative change.

The same judge added some further useful comments in *Buckley v Dal-*   8.073
ziel[206]. He pointed out that s.32A was considered by the Court of Appeal in

---

[203] *Cornwall Gardens Pte Ltd v R O Garrard & Co. Ltd*, May 9, 2001, Unreported, CA.
[204] [2008] EWHC 278 (QB).
[205] By the Defamation Act 1996.
[206] [2007] EWHC 1025 (QB).

Steedman v BBC,[207] where it was there suggested that the exercise of this discretion should be approached with some caution. While it was recognised, for example, that sometimes a claimant might reasonably delay the commencement of proceedings while awaiting the outcome of some other inquiry, such as a police or disciplinary investigation, it was also suggested that little sympathy might be expected where a claim came out of the blue following the expiry of the primary limitation period without any prior warning. In this case, no warning was given to Mrs Dalziel that she herself was on risk of defamation proceedings during the 12 month period. In particular, there was no letter before action to that effect. It is obviously not correct to suggest that the strict limitation period should be disapplied in every case where either the period of "incremental delay" is short or where little or no prejudice has been occasioned to the defendant's ability to advance his or her case. Ultimately the question is whether it would be "equitable" in the circumstances for the defendant to be deprived of the benefit of the short limitation period for some other reason.

8.074   Relevant facts are not defined in s.32A, but the phrase should and very probably will be construed in much the same way as the expression "material fact" has been construed for the purposes of determining whether the date of knowledge has arrived under ss.11 and 14 of the 1980 Act.[208] It has been suggested that the claimant will not know all the relevant facts until after the action has been commenced,[209] but it is clear that the term cannot possibly bear so wide a meaning in this context. In *C v Mirror Group Newspapers*[210] it was held that facts relevant to the claimant's cause of action do not include the availability or non-availability of defences. Thus, where P knew that the words complained of had been spoken but was under the misapprehension that they had been said in court and were thus absolutely privileged, she knew all the relevant facts so as to set time running.

8.075   In *Maccaba v Litchenstein*[211] the claimant issued proceedings alleging slander and harassment in respect of nine statements spoken by the defendant, all to much the same effect. Two of the statements were outside the primary limitation period for the purposes of the slander action under the terms of s.4A, but were still in time for the purposes of the harassment action. In view of the similarity of the statements and the existence of the harassment case, it was inevitable that the relevant two statements would have to go before the jury even if time-barred. The claimant argued that the court should exercise its discretion to disapply the one year limitation period, since the inclusion of the two statements would not cause the

---

[207] [2001] EWCA Civ 1534.
[208] See paras 8.012–8.024.
[209] Annotations to the Administration of Justice Act in Current Law Statutes Annotated 1985.
[210] [1996] 4 All E.R. 511, CA.
[211] [2003] All ER (D) 266 (Apr).

defendant undue prejudice; that the circumstances of the case were exceptional in so far as they concerned the multi-publication of similar statements; that the action would still proceed even if the statements were time-barred, and that to exclude them would create an artificial situation at trial since it would not be possible to excise reference to them. The defendant contended, inter alia, that the claimant had failed to explain the delay in issuing proceedings until after the expiry of the primary limitation period in respect of the two statements, and that it was not appropriate to disapply the time limit. The court held that the crucial question is whether it is equitable in the circumstances to take the exceptional course of dis-applying the one year limitation period. In the instant case, given that the action would proceed to trial in any case, and that the two statements would always be adjudicated upon in the harassment action, the prejudice that would be caused to the defendant by disapplying the limitation period was slight, and was outweighed by the prejudice that would be caused to the claimant if the primary limitation period was held to apply. While the lack of explanation for the delay in issuing proceedings militated against disapplying the limitation period, it was wrong to elevate that issue to a position where it became determinative. The limitation period would be disapplied.[212]

In *Heard v Kemp*[213] the Court of Appeal held that the apparent weakness **8.076** of a claim for libel was a legitimate consideration in refusing to extend time under s.4A.[214]

In *Hunter (trading as Connect Computers) v Rxworks.com Ltd*[215] the **8.077** defendants in an intellectual property action initially took a considered decision not to sue for defamation when they discovered the allegedly defamatory material. When they sought to sue outside the one-year period, Mann J. refused them permission to do so, observing that while there might have been commercial or tactical reasons to do so now, they were not exceptional and did not warrant the exercise of the court's discretion.

Applications for permission

Where a claimant applies for discretionary permission to bring a defama- **8.078** tion action out of time, the application must be made on notice.[216] To apply ex parte is an irregularity, and any leave obtained in this way is liable to be set aside.

---

[212] See also *Steedman v British Broadcasting Corporation* [2001] EWCA Civ 1534; [2001] All E.R. (D) 316 (Oct).
[213] [2002] EWCA Civ 1506.
[214] See also *Sarayiah v Suren* [2004] EWHC 1981 (QB) Tugendhat J.
[215] [2005] All ER (D) 162 (Jun) Mann J.
[216] *Oyston v Sir Peter Blaker* [1996] E.M.L.R. 125; *The Times*, November 15, 1995, CA.

The Law Commission's Proposals

8.079 The Consultation Paper proposed the removal of the judicial discretion to extend time. Sections 4A and 33 of the 1980 Act would thus have ceased to have effect. This would have been a fundamental change, but it did not survive to the Final Report, which proposes to retain this discretion. The change in the definition of "significance", noted in relation to Chapter 6, would again be important.

CHAPTER 9

Judicial Review and Other Crown Proceedings

This chapter deals with two categories of case. The first involves applica- **9.001** tions for judicial review. Although these are not covered at all by the Limitation Act 1980, they have their own statutory rules, including limitation periods. These periods are significantly shorter than those encountered elsewhere. The second category of case is that to which the Crown is a party. For historical reasons (which might by now legitimately be regarded as obsolete) there are special rules applying to such cases; again these rules include limitation periods.

JUDICIAL REVIEW

Where the applicant brings an action for judicial review, the Crown will be **9.002** the nominal claimant, notwithstanding that in many cases a Minister of the Crown will be the nominal defendant. It is for this reason that judicial review is considered here. The rules in relation to judicial review actions are now found in CPR Pt 54.[1] A two-stage process is involved, the first stage being that the applicant must obtain the permission of a single judge to apply for judicial review. If such permission is granted, then the application will subsequently be heard by a judge. CPR rule 54.5 provides that, subject to any statutory time-limit for the bringing of such actions,[2] the claim form must be filed promptly and in any event within three months of the date on which the grounds for the application arose unless the court considers that

---

[1] Replacing the former RSC Ord. 53. although there are differences of wording, the creation of CPR Pt 54 does not appear to have made any substantive changes in this area.
[2] As to which see below.

there is good reason for extending this period.[3] An application is not necessarily made promptly merely because it is made within the three-month period.[4]

It should be noted that, despite the wording of this rule, the three-month time-limit relates only to the initial application for leave—there is no rule that the hearing of the substantive application must take place within the three-month period.[5] At the same time the applicant is not entitled as of right to three months from the date when the grounds for the application arise; there is an overriding duty to act promptly, and what amounts to acting promptly may vary with the circumstances of each case. Leave may therefore be refused under this head even though the application is made within the three-month period.

When the grounds arise, CPR 54PD 4.1 provides that where the relief sought is in respect of any judgment, order, conviction or other proceedings, the date when the grounds for the application first arose shall be taken to be the date of that judgment, order, conviction or other proceedings. The ambit of the word "proceedings" in this sub-rule is unclear, but it is submitted that it must be construed ejusdem generis with the words which precede it, so that it is limited to judicial proceedings. This leaves open the question of when the grounds will arise in other cases.

9.003   This problem can best be approached by analogy with the concept of accrual of cause of action in private law. The grounds for the application must therefore be considered to have arisen as soon as the decision has been made of which the applicant will ultimately complain. It is irrelevant to this point that the decision has not yet been communicated to the appellant,[6] in the same way that the claimant's knowledge of the damage is irrelevant to the accrual of a cause of action in private law. It is submitted, however, that such ignorance, particularly when caused by a deliberate failure to communicate the decision to those affected by it, will be a strong factor in influencing the court to grant a discretionary extension of the three-month period.[7]

9.004   A point which arose in the case of *Hardy v Pembrokeshire CC*[8] was when permission could be refused on an application made within the three-month time limit. Keene LJ said[9], in relation to an earlier case:

---

[3] In *Cheong v Herts CC*, *The Times*, April 4, 1986, the Court of Appeal held that it would be proper to extend time where the instigation of proceedings had been delayed pending the outcome of a test case.

[4] *R. v Independent Television Commission, ex p. TV NI Ltd*, *The Times*, December 30, 1991.

[5] *R. v Stratford-on-Avon DC, ex p. Jackson* [1985] 1 W.L.R. 1319; [1985] 3 All E.R. 769.

[6] *R. v Department of Transport, ex p. Presvac Engineering Ltd*, *The Times*, July 10, 1991, CA.

[7] *R. v London Borough of Redbridge, ex p. G*, March 20, 1991, DC, Unreported. See also below.

[8] [2006] EWCA Civ 240.

[9] At para.10.

"The court there refused applications for judicial review because of a lack of promptness, even though the applications had been made within the three month period. The reasons for such an approach are clear from a large number of authorities. A public law decision by a public body in almost all cases affects the rights of parties other than the decision-maker and the Applicant seeking to challenge such a decision. It is important that those parties, and indeed the public generally, should be able to proceed on the basis that the decision is valid and can be relied on, and that they can plan their lives and make personal and business decisions accordingly. As it was put by Sir John Donaldson, MR, in *R v Monopolies and Mergers Commission, ex parte Argyll Group Plc* [1986] 1 WLR 763, at 774 H-775 B 'Good public administration requires decisiveness and finality, unless there are compelling reasons to the contrary.' "

This passage was further considered in *Crown Prosecution Service v City of London Magistrates' Court*[10], where Sedley L J set out[11] what he described as the court's rule of thumb, that is to use the three-month time limit as its primary test but to listen to any argument or, if necessary, to take the point itself, that a lack of promptness renders it unfair or wrong to let an application proceed or succeed, albeit brought within the three months.

Where an action for judicial review is brought purely on the grounds of a breach of ECHR, the relevant limitation period is one year under HRA s7(5) rather than three months.[12]   **9.005**

It is not appropriate to extend time under CPR 54.5 where the point in issue is already the subject of a ruling in the Crown Court.[13]   **9.006**

Discretionary extensions of time and the need to act promptly

The court is empowered to extend the three-month time-limit where it considers that there are good reasons for doing so. At the same time there is a duty on the applicant to act promptly. This duty may be regarded as arising from two separate provisions. The first is CPR r.3.1(2)(a), whilst the second is s.31 of the Senior Courts Act 1981. Section 31(6) provides that the High Court may refuse either leave to apply for judicial review or the substantive application for judicial review if there has been undue delay in   **9.007**

---

[10] [2007] EWHC 1924 (Admin).
[11] At para.21.
[12] *R (on the application of Playfoot) v Governing Body of Millais School* [2007] EWHC 1698 (Admin) Michael Supperstone Q.C.
[13] *R (on the application of Securiplan Plc and others) v Security Industry Authority* [2008] EWHC 1762 (Admin).

making the application for judicial review and the Court considers that the granting of the relief sought is likely to cause substantial hardship to or substantially prejudice the rights of any person or would be detrimental to good administration. Section 31(7) goes on to provide that s.31(6) is without prejudice to any enactment or rule of court limiting the time within which an application for judicial review must be made. At first sight there appears to be some confusion between these various provisions, and the difficulties in this area were authoritatively considered by the House of Lords in *R. v Dairy Produce Quota Tribunal for England and Wales, ex p. Caswell*,[14] where the applicants issued in 1987 proceedings to challenge a decision made in 1984, their excuse being that they were not originally aware that the decision was susceptible to judicial review. The speech of Lord Goff in that case has acquired such pre-eminence as a statement of the relevant principles that a lengthy extract from it is reproduced here[15]:

"First, when s.31(6) and (7) refers to 'an application for judicial review', those words must be read as referring, where appropriate, to an application for leave to apply for judicial review. Next, as I read r.4(1),[16] the effect of the rule is to limit the time within which an application for leave to apply for judicial review may be made in accordance with its terms, i.e. promptly and in any event within three months. The court has, however, power to grant leave to apply despite the fact that an application is late if it considers that there is good reason to exercise that power this is done by extending the period . . . Furthermore, the combined effect of s.31(7) and r.4(1) is that there is undue delay for the purposes of s.31(6) whenever the application for leave to apply is not made promptly and in any event within three months from the relevant date. It follows that when an application for leave to apply is not made promptly and in any event within three months the court may refuse leave on the grounds of delay unless it considers that there is good reason for extending the period but, even if it considers that there is such good reason, it may still refuse leave (or, where leave has been granted, substantive relief) if in its opinion the granting of the relief sought would be likely to produce hardship or prejudice (as specified in s.31(6)) or would be detrimental to good administration. I imagine that on an ex parte application for leave to apply before a single judge the question most likely to be considered by him, if there has been such delay, is whether there is good reason for extending the period under r.4(1). Questions of hardship or prejudice or detriment under s.31(6) are, I imagine, unlikely to arise on an ex parte

---

[14] [1990] 2 All E.R. 434.
[15] P. 439. Although this extract refers to the RSC provisions, there seems no reason to suppose that the discretion under the CPR will be exercised differently.
[16] The former RSC Ord. 53 r.4(1); now CPR r.3.1.

application, when the necessary material would in all probability not be available to the judge. Such questions could arise on a contested application for leave to apply, as indeed they did in ex p. Jackson,[17] but even then, as in that case, it may be thought better to grant leave where there is considered to be good reason to extend the period under r.4(1), leaving questions arising under s.31(6) to be explored in depth on the hearing of the substantive application. In this way, I believe, sensible effect can be given to these two provisions without doing violence to the language of either. Unlike the Court of Appeal I do not consider that r.4(3) and s.31(7) lead to a circulus inextricabilis, because s.31(6) does not limit 'the time within which an application for judicial review may be made' (the words used in r.4(3)). Section 31(6) simply contains particular grounds for refusing leave or substantive relief, not referred to in r.4(1), to which the court is bound to give effect, independently of any rule of court."

Exercising the discretion to extend time

Although the discretion to extend time is couched in the most general terms, it may be useful to refer to some of the cases where its exercise has been in issue. Where the applicant has available to him an alternative remedy, such as a statutory appeal in a planning matter, the court will be very reluctant to extend time.[18] Time will readily be extended where the applicant had no means of knowing about the decision which is challenged until relatively recently,[19] or where the delay results in part from the failure of the respondents to deal with the matter promptly.[20] A misapprehension of law apparently shared by all parties to the case until a late stage may be sufficient ground for an extension of time.[21]   9.008

Refusing relief on the grounds of delay

Where an extension of time has been granted, it is not open to the defendant at the substantive hearing to seek to reopen that decision.[22] However, even where time has been extended, relief may still be refused on the grounds of delay[23] if it appears that granting the relief would be likely to cause   9.009

---

[17] R. v Stratford-on-Avon DC, ex p. Jackson [1985] 1 W.L.R. 1319.
[18] R. v Elmbridge BC, ex p. Health Care Corp. Ltd [1991] 3 P.L.R. 63.
[19] R. v London Borough of Redbridge, ex p. G, March 20, 1991, DC, Unreported; R. v Sec. of State for Trade and Industry, ex p. Greenpeace Ltd [1998] Env. L.R. 415.
[20] R. v Dacorum BC, ex p. Brown (1989) 21 H.L.R. 405; [1989] C.O.D. 521, Farquharson J.
[21] R. v Minister of Agriculture Fisheries and Food, ex p. Bostock [1991] C.M.L.R. 681, CA.
[22] R. v Criminal Injuries Compensation Board, ex p. A [1999] 2 A.C. 330, HL.
[23] R. v Swale BC, ex p. RSPB [1990] C.O.D. 263, Simon Brown J.; R. v Lichfield DC [2001] E.W.C.A. Civ. 304.

substantial hardship to, or substantially prejudice the rights of, any person or would be detrimental to good administration.[24] It is not necessary to show any causal connection between the delay and the prejudice, hardship or detriment—the only question is whether granting the relief would cause prejudice, hardship or detriment.[25]

European Law

9.010   In *R. v Dairy Produce Quota Tribunal for England, ex p. Dent*[26] the applicant argued that the three-month time-limit in applying for judicial review was contrary to European law because it made the obtaining of the remedy effectively impossible in many cases. The argument was rejected as being inaccurate in fact, but it may be noted that a limitation period which did have that effect could not be allowed to stand.[27]

OTHER CROWN PROCEEDINGS

9.011   Traditionally the Crown has occupied a special place in English legal theory. Before 1947 private law actions against the Crown could be brought only by means of the cumbersome procedure of a Petition of Right. That rule was abolished by the Crown Proceedings Act 1947,[28] and the modern rules relating to actions of this kind are examined in this chapter.

Actions for judicial review, formerly prerogative writs and then prerogative orders, are now usually regarded as falling into public law rather than private law. The procedure for these is now governed by CPR Pt 54, and special short time-limits apply to actions of this kind. The normal rules relating to limitation periods are in a number of instances modified where the plaintiff is the Crown or is a spiritual or eleemosynary corporation sole (these are hereinafter collectively referred to as "privileged corporations"). This chapter collects together the special rules which apply to such bodies. There is a marked shortage of authority on these provisions.

---

[24] Senior Courts Act 1981, s.31(6).
[25] *R. v Secretary of State for Health, ex p. Furneaux* (July 1, 1993, CA), disapproving *R. v Woking BC, ex p. Dempsey* (November 20, 1992, Louis Blom-Cooper Q.C., Unreported).
[26] July 8, 1991, Simon Brown J., Unreported.
[27] For the relevant principles of European law, see Ch.27.
[28] For a surviving example of this doctrine, see para.9.026.

Eleemosynary corporations sole

This expression is one of the relics of the distant past still surviving in the **9.012** law of limitations. The phrase is not defined in the 1980 Act, but there is old authority[29] that in earlier statutes it did not extend to corporations aggregate. These bodies might be entirely spiritual (e.g. a dean and chapter) or quasi-spiritual (the Ecclesiastical Commissioners) or entirely lay. It appears that this restriction on the ambit of their privileged status is still good law at the present day. In *Hayward v Chaloner*[30] it was said, obiter, that the rector of a parish could be a corporation sole, so that adverse possession by one rector could be added to possession by his successor for the purpose of establishing squatter's title, even where there was an interval of time between one rector leaving and the next arriving.

Land

Schedule 1, Pt II to the Limitation Act 1980 makes special provision for **9.013** amended periods of limitation in respect of actions to recover land where the claimant is the Crown[31] or a Privileged Corporation. These periods are also examined in Ch.13,[32] but are summarised here for the sake of completeness.

Section 15(1)

Section 15(1) of the 1980 Act, which imposes a limit of 12 years on the **9.014** bringing of actions for the recovery of land (within the extended meaning given to that term by s.38(1)) shall apply in the case of actions by any privileged corporation as if the period were 30 years instead of 12.[33]

Section 15(2)

Section 15(2) of the 1980 Act deals with actions to recover future interests **9.015** in land. It imposes alternative limitation periods (the plaintiff being allowed to sue at any time until the expiry of whichever expires later). There are 12 years from the date on which the right of action accrued to the person entitled to the preceding estate or interest, and six years from the date on

---

[29] *Ecclesiastical Commissioners v Rowe* (1880) 5 App.Cas. 736 at 744, per Lord Selborne.
[30] [1968] 1 Q.B. 107, CA.
[31] For the exact ambit of this term in the present context see below, para.9.023.
[32] See paras 13.088 et seq.
[33] Sch.1, para.10.

which the cause of action accrued to the person entitled to the succeeding interest.[34] Where the plaintiff is a privileged corporation, these periods are amended to 30 years and 12 years respectively.[35]

9.016   Schedule 1 para.12 provides:

> "where in the case of any action brought by a person other than the Crown . . . the right of action first accrued to the Crown . . . through whom the person in question claims, the action may be brought at any time before the expiration of—(a) the period during which the action could have been brought by the Crown . . . or (b) 12 years from the date on which the right of action accrued to some person other than the Crown . . . whichever period first expires."

In *Hill v Transport for London*[36] it was held that 'first' in this provision only means 'previously'—it does not mean 'originally'. So long as title has been held by the Crown at some point, the holder of the paper title will have the benefit of whichever of the above periods expires first.

Foreshore

9.017   The Crown may bring an action to recover foreshore[37] at any time within 60 years of the accrual of the cause of action.[38] Where the land has ceased to be foreshore, but remains in the ownership of the Crown, and the right of action accrued while the land was still foreshore there are alternative limitation periods; the action must be brought before the expiry of the first of 60 years from the accrual of the cause of action and 30 years from the date when the land ceased to be foreshore.[39] This is an unusual provision, the normal practice in the case of alternative periods being to allow the plaintiff whichever of the two periods expires later.

Accrual to other person

9.018   Where an action is brought other than by a privileged corporation, but the plaintiff claims through a privileged corporation, to whom the right first accrued, the action must be brought within the shorter of two periods: the first is the period during which the action could have been brought by the corporation sole (which will be governed by para.11 of Sch.1) and the second is 12 years from the date on which the cause of action first accrued

---

[34] For a fuller account of these provisions, see para.13.005.
[35] Sch.1, para.13.
[36] [2005] EWHC 856 (Ch), [2005] Ch. 379 Rimer J.
[37] Defined as the shore and bed of the sea and of any tidal water below the line of the medium high tide between the spring tides and the neap tides; Sch.1, para.11(3).
[38] Sch.1, para.11(1). Sch.1, para.11(2).
[39] Sch.1, para.11(2).

to some person other than a privileged corporation.[40] Note that this is not necessarily the same as the date on which the right of action first accrued to the plaintiff. The second period starts to run as soon as the right accrues to anyone other than a privileged corporation.

Conveyance to Crown

No difficulty in the operation of these provisions is likely to arise where the land has belonged to the Crown at all material times. Where the land is conveyed to the Crown after the cause of action has accrued, time runs from the accrual of the cause of action rather than from the conveyance to the Crown. One of the consequences of this is that conveyance to the Crown cannot operate to revive a cause of action which is already barred. Therefore, if the cause of action under s.15(1) accrues to X in 1980, and he conveys the land to the Crown in 1985, the action will be barred in 2010. If he conveys in 2005, the action is already barred, and the conveyance is ineffective, since X no longer has any title to pass.

9.019

Leases

Paragraph 6 of Sch.1 to the 1980 Act governs the case where a person is in possession of land under a lease in writing by which a rent of not less than £10[41] a year is reserved and the rent is received by some other person wrongfully claiming to be entitled to the reversion. It provides that the right of action to recover the land of the person rightfully so entitled shall be deemed to accrue on the date when rent was first received by the person wrongfully claiming to be entitled to the reversion. The significance of this provision in the present context is that, by para.6(2), it is inapplicable to any lease granted by the Crown. Consequently, where the lease in question is granted by the Crown, the cause of action will be deemed to accrue on the date when the lease determines, since that is the date which would be applicable to other leases in the absence of para.6(1). Therefore, time does not run in favour of a tenant at will of Crown land (i.e. one who remains in possession without paying rent to the Crown) since the running of time in the tenant's favour is postponed until the tenancy ends, at which point ex hypothesi the tenant no longer has adverse possession. Similarly, the person wrongfully receiving the rent cannot in that way acquire good title, since time cannot run in his favour until the tenancy determines, and would then do so only if he went into possession at that point.

9.020

---

[40] Sch.1, para.12.
[41] Or £1 in the case of a lease granted before August 1, 1980: Sch.2, para.8.

Squatter's title

9.021 A corporation sole can acquire a squatter's title so as to bar the title of a rightful owner.[42]

Extinction of Crown's title

9.022 Subject to the modifications described above, s.15 does bind the Crown, as does s.17. Consequently, the Crown's title to land will be extinguished once the appropriate period of limitation has expired.

Ambit of Schedule 1, Part II and section 25[43]

9.023 Section 37(4) of the 1980 Act provides that for the purposes of the limitation provisions relating to the recovery of land and those relating to advowsons references to the Crown, shall include references to Her Majesty in right of the Duchy of Lancaster. Further, those provisions shall apply to lands and advowsons forming part of the possessions of the Duchy of Cornwall as if for the references to the Crown there were substituted references to the Duke of Cornwall as defined in the Duchy of Cornwall Management Act 1863.

Application to Crown

9.024 It should be observed that s.37 of the 1980 Act makes the provisions of that Act applicable in actions involving the Crown in the same way as they apply to actions between subjects. This principle is subject to specified exceptions. Section 37(2) disapplies the Act in the case of proceedings for any tax or duty[44] (or interest thereon), forfeiture proceedings under the Customs and Excise Acts[45] and proceedings for the forfeiture of a ship.[46] It is to be noted that the taxing statutes normally include their own time-limits.[47]

---

[42] *Hayward v Chaloner* [1968] 1 Q.B. 107.

[43] See also paras 17.010–17.012.

[44] The term includes any debt due to Her Majesty under s.16 of the Tithe Act 1936: 1980 Act s.37(2). For an example of the application of this section see *Ahmad v Commissioners Of Inland Revenue* [2004] EWHC 2292 (Ch); [2005] BPIR 541 Evans-Lombe J.

[45] As defined in the Customs and Excise Management Act 1979: 1980 Act, s.37(2)(b).

[46] Which includes every description of vessel used in navigation not propelled by oars: 1980 Act s.37(2).

[47] The principal statute is the Taxes Management Act 1970, and the usual limit on proceedings is six years, though this is subject to extension in the case of fraud. See further Ch.27.

Ambit of section 37

Section 37(3) provides that in this section the expression "The Crown" **9.025** includes Her Majesty in right of the Duchy of Lancaster,[48] any Government department or any officer of the Crown as such, or any person acting on behalf of the Crown[49] and the Duke of Cornwall.[50] However, the term does not for this purpose extend to the Privileged Corporations—for them the law of limitation is modified only in those cases mentioned in Sch.1, Pt II of the 1980 Act.[51]

Royal prerogative

Section 37(6) contains a further specialised saving in favour of the Crown. **9.026** It states that nothing in the 1980 Act shall affect the prerogative right of Her Majesty (whether in right of the Crown or of the Duchy of Lancaster) or of the Duke of Cornwall to any gold or silver mine. The practical effect of this is that no period of limitation applies to a claim by the Crown in respect of such rights. Where the Crown takes property of a subject in the exercise of the royal prerogative, the rule of constitutional law is that compensation must be paid to the subject.

The period of limitation applicable to a claim for such compensation was considered by the House of Lords in *Burmah Oil v Lord Advocate*.[52] The case concerned expropriation of property during the Second World War, at a time when the Public Authorities Protection Act 1893, which imposed a six-month time-limit in the case of actions against public authorities, was in force. The case for the Crown was that the claim had become barred under this Act many years before the issue of the writ. The House of Lords rejected this defence on the grounds that the 1893 Act applied only to cases where there had been wrongdoing by the public authority by definition, an act done in exercise of the royal prerogative is not wrongful, notwith-standing that it gives rise to a claim for compensation. The 1893 Act accordingly had no application to the case. The relevant provision of the 1893 Act was repealed by the Law Reform (Limitation of Actions, etc.) Act 1954, which came into force on June 4, 1954. It is nevertheless submitted that the approach adopted by the House of Lords in this case continues to be of great significance. If any of the periods of limitation prescribed by the 1980 Act is to apply to a claim of this kind, it is necessary to decide what is the basis of the action by the subject. It is clear that none of the causes of

---

[48] s.37(3)(a). The Sovereign is also the Duke of Lancaster.
[49] s.37(3)(b).
[50] s.37(3)(c): the heir to the throne is the Duke of Cornwall.
[51] See para.9.022.
[52] [1965] A.C. 75.

action specified by the 1980 Act meets the case—the action is clearly not contractual, nor can it be tortious, since that involves a breach of duty, which would amount to wrongdoing. The only possible conclusion is that reached by the House of Lords in *Burmah Oil*, namely that no period of limitation applies to an action of this kind.

Petitions of right

9.027　In general, petitions of right were abolished by the Crown Proceedings Act 1947, but s.40 of that Act contains limited savings for actions against the sovereign in a personal capacity and for an action against the Crown in respect of matters arising outside the United Kingdom. Section 37(5) provides that proceedings by way of petition of right shall be treated for limitation purposes as having been commenced on the date on which the petition is presented.[53]

Advowsons

9.028　The 1980 Act contained a provision (s.25) extending time-limits laid down by the Act in favour of the Crown where by reason of lapse the right to collate or present to any ecclesiastical benefice passes to the Crown. Section 25 has now been repealed by the Parsonage (Benefices) Measure 1986.[54] The new scheme for the registration of patronage, together with its attendant limitation rules, is considered at paragraphs 17.011–17.012.

Other enactments

9.029　Section 37 of the 1980 Act is expressed to be subject to s.39 of that Act,[55] and indeed the latter section refers expressly to the position of the Crown. If the Crown is a party to an action whose period of limitation is governed by some statute other than the 1980 Act, then the same period of limitation applies to this action as would apply if it were an action between subjects, i.e. for the purposes of any other statute with a limitation period, the Crown is in the same position as a subject. If no statutory provision governs the case, then time does not run against the Crown, any more than it would run against a subject in the same circumstances.

---

[53] See also *Franklin v Attorney-General* [1974] Q.B. 185.
[54] Parsonage (Benefices) Measure 1986, ss.1(2), 4(3).
[55] 1980 Act, s.37(1).

The Foreign Limitation Periods Act 1984

This statute, which is treated in detail in Chapter 25, applies the same rule   9.030
as does the Limitation Act 1980, namely that it applies to actions involving
the Crown in the same way as to actions between subjects.[56] The definition
of the Crown for these purposes is the same as that found in s.37 of the
1980 Act.[57]

The Latent Damage Act 1986

Section 3 of this statute provides that the statute[58] is to bind the Crown, but   9.031
that so far as liability in tort is concerned shall not bind the Crown to any
greater extent than the Crown is made liable in tort under the Crown
Proceedings Act 1947. The importance of this is that s.3 of the Act allows
for the accrual of a right of action in respect of damaged property to a
person other than the original owner of the property. When the liability
correlative to this cause of action falls on the Crown it is treated for the
purposes of the 1947 Act as being a liability in tort.

The Merchant Shipping Act 1995

This Act, which is fully considered in Ch.24, does bind the Crown, but the   9.032
obligation on the court under s.8 of the Act to extend time for the service of
proceedings where there has been no reasonable opportunity of service
within the basic two-year period, does not apply when the action is brought
against a vessel belonging to the Crown.[59]

---

[56] Foreign Limitation Periods Act 1984 s.6(1).
[57] Foreign Limitation Periods Act 1984 s.6(2).
[58] In so far as its provisions are not incorporated into the 1980 Act.
[59] Crown Proceedings Act 1947 s.30; see also paras 24.017 et seq.

CHAPTER 10

Accrual of Cause of Action in Contract

This chapter examines the problems surrounding the accrual of a cause of action in contract. The rules are the same whether the contract is simple or special, and these two types of contract are therefore considered together.[1] **10.001**

RIGHT ACCRUES ON BREACH

The basic rule in contract is that the right of action accrues as soon as there is a breach of contract, notwithstanding that at that time no damage (beyond the purely nominal) has been suffered by the claimant. In *Gibbs v Guild*[2] Field J. traced this rule back to the action of assumpsit, which was one of the historical predecessors of contract: **10.002**

"It was well settled that in actions on assumpsit the time ran from the breach of the contract, for that was the gist of the action, and the subsequent damage, though happening within six years next before the suit, did not prevent the application of the Statute."[3]

This principle is still good law with regard to contract actions, and it therefore follows that in an action based on contract time runs from the breach. Since the Latent Damage Act 1986 does not apply to actions founded on contract,[4] there is no general provision for delaying the running

---

[1] For the difference between a simple contract and a specialty, see Ch.4.
[2] (1881) 8 Q.B.D 296.
[3] (1881) 8 Q.B.D 296 at 302. See also *Battley v Faulkner* (1820) 3 B. & Ald. 288; *Lynn v Bamber* [1930] 2 K.B. 72.
[4] *Iron Trades Mutual Insurance v J.K. Buckenham* [1990] 1 All E.R. 808, K.S. Rokison Q.C.; *Islander Trucking Ltd v Hogg Robinson & Gardner Mountain (Marine) Ltd* [1990] 1 All E.R. 826, Evans J.; see paras 6.003–6.006.

time until the existence of the cause of action becomes reasonably discoverable, though of course the running of time may be postponed in cases of fraud, concealment or mistake under s.32 of the Limitation Act 1980.[5] The rule is potentially a considerable inconvenience for claimants, since it commonly happens that the breach of contract itself occasions relatively little damage: in the same way as in tort the damage may follow some time after the breach of duty, so in contract there may be an interval between the breach and the damage. Where that interval exceeds the appropriate limitation period it will be impossible to recover in full the damage suffered. The difficulty may be illustrated by reference to *Howell v Young*.[6] This was an action against a solicitor for negligently advising a client to enter into a mortgage, which subsequently proved an inadequate security for the loan granted. More than six years elapsed between the making of the mortgage and the discovery that the security was inadequate. It was held that the action against the solicitor was time-barred, having accrued when the mortgage was executed.[7] In *Northern & Shell v John Laing* [8] it was held that a warranty contained in a deed could by express term be made to operate retrospectively, so that time ran from a date earlier than the date of the deed. This illustrates the possibility of contracting out of the statutory limitation period by causing time to expire earlier as well as by postponing expiry.[9]

10.003   In a construction contract which provides for a third party (such as an engineer) to issue certificates for interim payments for work done followed by a final certificate at the end of the contract, the right of action in relation to work included in interim certificates accrues when the certificate is, or under the terms of the contract ought to be, issued, rather than when the work is done. However, a claim based on the final certificate is a different cause of action from that based on interim certificates because the interim certificates merely amount to a provisional estimate of the work done, whereas the final certificate is the engineer's definitive view of the value of the work.[10] The exact scope of this rule may be regarded as being open to doubt in the light of the decision in *Birse Construction Ltd v McCormick (UK) Ltd (formerly McCormick (UK) Plc)*[11] where it was held that the cause of action in relation to construction services accrued on the doing of the work. The answer appears to be that the date of accrual depends on the exact terms of the contract, though even on that basis it is not immediately

---

[5] See Ch.20.
[6] (1826) 5 B. & C. 259.
[7] It is unclear whether this was an action in contract or in tort. The law governing a solicitor's tortious liability to his client was less well established in 1826 than it is today. For a similar point in a modern context, see *Forster v Outred* [1982] 1 W.L.R. 86, CA (see Ch.5).
[8] [2002] EWHC 2258 (TCC), 85 Con LR 179 Judge Thornton Q.C.
[9] On extending time and estoppel generally in relation to limitation see Ch.21.
[10] *Henry Boot Construction Ltd v Alstom Combined Cycles Ltd* [2005] EWCA Civ 814, [2005] 3 All ER 932 C.A.
[11] [2004] EWHC 3053 (TCC); 99 Con LR 181 Judge Coulson Q.C.

apparent how the two cases can be reconciled, for in both cases there was provision for payment by instalment. One possible distinction is that the *Henry Boot* case involved interim payment certificates by a third party, whereas Birse Construction did not. A further point arising in Birse Construction was the argument that the defendant had had a duty to consider fairly the claimant's claims for payment, and that this was a separate duty with its own limitation period. Judge Coulson upheld that argument, though on the facts he also held that the claim for the alleged breach of this duty was statute-barred.

In recent years the significance of this rule has been somewhat diminished by these developments in the law which have led to the view that in many cases a claimant may have simultaneous rights of action in contract and in tort against the same defendant arising out of the same facts.[12] That view has been reaffirmed by the House of Lords in *Henderson v Merrett Syndicates Ltd*[13]; the possibility of concurrent actions clearly reduces somewhat the importance of the contractual rule, since a significant number of claimants will have the option of circumventing that rule by suing in tort instead. At the present day the principal difficulty that arises in contractual cases is to determine the date of breach, particularly in a number of specialised areas, which are dealt with in the remainder of this chapter. **10.004**

RESTITUTIONARY CLAIMS

Claims for the repayment of tax paid pursuant to an unlawful demand, which are essentially restituonary in nature, are governed by s.5 of the 1980 Act.[14] **10.005**

ANTICIPATORY BREACH

The case of *Hochster v de la Tour*[15] establishes the general principle of English law that a party may sue for breach of contract even though the due date for performance has not arrived if the other party has manifested an unequivocal intention not to perform his obligations under the contract. It is therefore necessary to ask when time begins to run in such a case. As a matter of principle the answer must be that time runs as soon as the claimant is able to sue, since that is when his cause of action accrues. Conse- **10.006**

---

[12] A development that can perhaps be traced to the decision of Oliver J. in *Midland Bank v Hett, Stubbs & Kemp* [1979] Ch. 384.

[13] [1994] 3 All E.R. 506.

[14] *Deutsche Morgan Grenfell Group Plc v Inland Revenue Commissioners and the Attorney General* [2005] EWCA Civ 78, [2005] 3 All ER 1025, [2005] STC 329 C.A.

[15] (1853) 2 E. & B. 678.

quently, time begins to run from the anticipatory breach. It should be noted in passing that the case of *Eaglehill v Needham*[16] is not properly to be regarded as an exception to this principle, since the essence of that case is that the action can only be brought when the notice of dishonour is received; in other words, that case decides that there is no breach until that time.

BREACH A QUESTION OF FACT

10.007 When the breach of contract occurs will normally be a question of fact, to be determined in the light of the surrounding circumstances. A good example of this principle is to be found in *Transoceanic Petroleum Carriers v Cook Industries Inc.: The "Mary Lou"*.[17] This was a charterparty case in which the charters were required to nominate a "safe port" of destination for the ship. The port which they chose unfortunately proved not to be safe, and the ship consequently suffered damage. The question was when the cause of action in respect of the failure to nominate a safe port arose. Mustill J. held that there is no absolute rule that the breach must happen as soon as the port is nominated. It may happen, for example, that the port is safe at that time, but ceases to be so at some later stage. In this event the breach will occur only when the port becomes unsafe. Indeed, it may happen at any time up to the occurrence of the damage. The principle illustrated by this case is of general application. *Byatt v Nash* [18] considered the date when a solicitor's cause of action against his client for unpaid fees accrues. There is a general presumption that a solicitor's retainer is an entire contract, so that he is not entitled to be paid until the matter is completed. Here, however, the proposed transaction was aborted, and it was held that the cause of action accrued once it became apparent that the transaction would not proceed.

ACCOUNTS

10.008 Where two parties deal with each other on the basis of an account it may be necessary to decide whether the creditor's right to demand payment from the debtor accrues as soon as there is any sum outstanding on the account or only when a formal demand for payment is made. The problem is related to, but distinct from, that discussed below of the position where a loan is expressed to be repayable on demand. It was suggested by Upjohn J. in

---

[16] [1973] A.C. 992, HL; see para.10.017.
[17] [1981] 2 Lloyd's Rep. 272.
[18] 28 June 2002 John Crowley Q.C.

Lloyds Bank v Margolis[19] that in the case of a current account there is no need for a formal demand, i.e. that the cause of action accrues (and time begins to run) as soon as there is any amount outstanding. However, the point was not directly before the court in that case, and these observations must be regarded as obiter dicta.[20]

Bank accounts

The previous paragraph dealt with the position under loan contracts of various kinds. There is authority which shows that special rules apply to accounts maintained with banks and building societies. In the case of a deposit account it has been settled since the decision in *Atkinson v Bradford Third Equitable Building Society*[21] that repayment is not due until a demand has been made. It was thought for a long time that a different rule applied to current bank accounts[22]; however, in *N. Joachimson v Swiss Bank Corporation*[23] the Court of Appeal held that the rule is the same for both current and deposit accounts, a demand being a prerequisite to the right of action in either case. It may be noted in passing that the same rule does not apply to the bank's right to sue on an overdraft.[24]   **10.009**

Wrongful debits

In *National Bank of Commerce v National Westminster Bank*[25] the plaintiffs alleged that the defendants had wrongfully debited the plaintiffs' bank account with the defendants on eight occasions by accepting as valid money transfer orders on which the signatures had in fact been forged. Demands for repayment/reimbursement of these sums had been made at various times, and ultimately proceedings were issued. It is important to note that the plaintiff made two separate claims: **10.010**

---

[19] [1954] 1 W.L.R. 644.

[20] A further difficulty in this area concerns running accounts for the supply of goods. If a number of items are outstanding, some of which may be or become statute-barred, and the debtor makes a payment on account without indicating to which items the payment is to be attributed, it may be necessary at a later date to determine which items are and are not paid for: see, e.g., *Re Footman Bower & Co. Ltd* [1961] Ch.443, Buckley J. However, this problem falls more naturally under the heading of acknowledgment and part payment, and is therefore treated in detail at para.18.037.

[21] (1890) 25 Q.B.D. 377.

[22] *Foley v Hill* (1844) 2 H.L.Cas. 28; *Poll v Clegg* (1847) 10 M. & W. 321. These cases appeared to establish that the customer's right of action on the account would be barred if there was no dealing with it for six years.

[23] [1921] 3 K.B. 110.

[24] *Parr's Banking Co. v Yates* [1898] 2 Q.B. 460.

[25] [1990] 2 Lloyd's Rep. 514, Webster J.

(1) for repayment of the sums wrongfully debited, together with the interest which would have been accrued to the plaintiffs on those sums had the wrongful debits not been made;

(2) for damages for the breach of the contract between the parties.

This action was the trial of a preliminary point of law, and it was unclear on the original pleadings whether the breach alleged was the original making of the debits or the failure to repay the debits when called upon to do so by the plaintiffs.

10.011   On the first of these claims *N. Joachimson v Swiss Bank* appears at first sight to show that no cause of action can accrue until the demand for repayment is made. However, the defendants argued that *Joachimson* does not apply to the situation where the customer does not demand repayment of all sums due on the account, but merely complains of the making of wrongful debits. In such cases, the defendants argued, the loss happens as soon as the debit is made, and the cause of action consequently accrues. In response to this the plaintiffs argued that the purported debits were ineffective as between the parties. Thus, the plaintiffs would still have been entitled to demand payment as if no debits had been made, and no new cause of action accrued when the debits were made. In this extreme form the argument was rejected—the making of the debits was, on the assumed facts, wrongful, and the plaintiff must have had an immediate right to at least nominal damages. However, there is authority that the plaintiffs would indeed have been entitled to demand payment as if the debits had not been made.[26]

10.012   These two findings would appear to be in contradiction, but Webster J. held that the latter should prevail. Thus, the cause of action in respect of the reimbursement for wrongful debits was held to accrue only when the demand for repayment was made. This is a convenient result, and may be justified on the ground that the action for damages is something different from the claim for reimbursement. The apparent anomaly results from the need in the context of ongoing bank accounts to depart from the general principle that the cause of action accrues as soon as the claimant is in a position to sue. The specific case of wrongful debits falls close to the borderline of this rule, but it is held here that the normal bank accounts rule does apply.

A related problem is whether the same rule would apply if the plaintiffs' account with the defendants had been in debit at any of the material times. The point does not arise directly in this case, but Webster J. considered it in passing. He suggested that the position might then be different. This in part depends upon certain dicta of Staughton J. in the *Limpgrange* case. It is not

---

[26] *Limpgrange v Bank of Credit and Commerce International SA* [1986] F.L.R. 36, Staughton J.

obvious why the position should be any different, however. Even if the account had been in debit, or had been placed in debit by means of the wrongful actions of the defendants, the position would surely still have been that the plaintiffs were entitled to have the account treated as if those actions had not taken place. There would have been an immediate right to sue for damages, and in this situation the damages might well have been more than nominal, since the debit position on the account could have led to interest (or increased interest) becoming payable. It is submitted that the position in regard to the action for reimbursement would have been the same.

On the claim for interest, Webster J. held that it was impossible to establish the position beyond doubt at this stage. The result depends upon the agreement between the parties as to the way in which such interest is to be treated. If it was to be treated as simply part of the debt owed by the defendants to the plaintiffs, then the cause of action again accrues only on demand, since the principles applicable will be the same as those already outlined. On the other hand, if it were to be paid separately, and instalments had therefore fallen due on specific dates, the result would be that a cause of action in respect of the shortfall of interest would accrue each time an instalment was due. **10.013**

With regard to the action for damages, Webster J. was again unable to come to a definite conclusion. This resulted from the uncertainty over the nature of the breach for which damages were being sought. As explained above, there were two possible breaches. As time runs from the breach, the date of expiry of time would have to depend upon which breach was being alleged. This point could not be resolved upon the trial of a preliminary point of law.

PAYMENT ON DEMAND

Where A lends money to B on terms that it is to be repayable on demand, the question has arisen whether the making of a formal demand is a necessary prerequisite to A's right of action, so that time will not start to run against him until such demand is made. The general rule appears to have been established as long ago as 1837 in *Norton v Ellam*[27], and to have been confirmed in a number of cases since, notably *Re Brown*[28] (though in that case it was held as a matter of construction time ran only from the making of the demand) and *Lloyds Bank v* Margolis[29]. That case concerned a mortgage of land, the mortgage moneys being repayable on demand. The **10.014**

---

[27] (1837) 2 M & W 461.
[28] [1893] 2 Ch.300.
[29] [1954] 1 WLR 644.

defendant mortgagor argued that in the case of advances which preceded the mortgage, time ran from the date of the mortgage, whilst in the case of subsequent advances, time ran from the making of the advances. Upjohn J. rejected this argument, holding that P could not recover the moneys without making a formal demand, with the result that his cause of action did not accrue until that demand was made. A further possibility can be illustrated by reference to *Reeves v Butcher*.[30] The plaintiff lent money to the defendant for two years, subject to an immediate right to reclaim the principal if any instalment of interest was overdue by 21 days. The Court of Appeal held that the right of action for the principal accrued immediately on the expiry of the 21 days, and could not be postponed to the expiry of the two years. This is an example of a case where the contract implicitly provides alternative dates for the accrual of the cause of action and it is necessary to look at the events which have happened in order to see which of those dates is the applicable one. Of course the contract may, expressly or by implication, make such demand necessary, and the provisions of the contract will then be decisive.[31] At the time of *Norton v Ellam* the rule could legitimately be regarded as being there for the protection of creditors in that it removed the need to make a formal demand before bringing proceedings. The limitation consequences of this rule appear to have been a more or less unintended consequence of the benefit to creditors. The most recent consideration of the issue is found in *Boot v Boot*,[32] which supported the *Norton v Ellam* rule, though it may be that this case should be regarded as dealing primarily with s.6 of the 1980 Act. Finally, in *Allendale Ltd v Moualem*[33] the Court of Appeal refused permission to appeal against a ruling that in a simple promissory note (i.e. one which involves no element of collateral security) time runs from the date of the note, even if it is expressed to be payable on demand. The Court rejected a submission that the rule derived from *Ellam v Norton*[34] and *Re Brown's Estate*[35] is now out of date and due for reconsideration.

10.015 The Privy Council case of *Lankshmijit v Sharani*[36] further emphasises the importance of looking carefully at the terms of the contract. This was a sale of land case, in which the contract provided that the purchase price was to be paid by instalments, and that in the event of default in paying any instalment the vendor could immediately give notice either to rescind the contract or to declare the whole of the outstanding purchase moneys due. The sale took place in 1948, and there were repeated defaults in payment,

---

[30] [1891] 2 Q.B. 509, CA.
[31] *Re Brown's Estate* [1893] 2 Ch. 300; *Sicklemore v Thistleton* (1817) 6 M. & S. 9; *Lankshmijit v Sherani* [1974] A.C. 605, PC.
[32] TLR 9 May 1996.
[33] 6 July 2004 Unreported C.A.
[34] 2 M & W 461.
[35] [1893] 2 Ch.300.
[36] [1974] A.C. 605, PC.

but it was only in 1967 that the vendor purported to exercise his right to rescind the contract. The Privy Council appear to have ignored any complications which might have arisen, at least under English law, from the fact that the vendor was seeking an equitable remedy,[37] and to have treated the case on the basis that the only question was when the vendor's rights under the contract first accrued. The majority of the Privy Council[38] held that the rights arose only when the vendor gave the notice contemplated under the contract either to rescind or to make all the purchase price payable immediately. Therefore, the cause of action accrued in 1967 and was not time-barred. The decision has been criticised[39] on the ground that the vendor could have sued as soon as there was default in making any payment, but the case serves to illustrate again the general principle that it is essential to construe the terms of the contract closely. Here the majority of the Privy Council attached overriding importance to the requirement of notice, making this an essential precondition of the cause of action.

More recently, in *Bank of Boroda v Panessar*,[40] an attempt was made to postpone still further the date of accrual of the cause of action in such cases. This case involved debentures which were expressed to be repayable on demand, and the question was whether the cause of action arose immediately the demand was made, or whether the debtor was entitled to a reasonable time to raise the money, so that the cause of action accrued only on the expiry of that period. Walton J. held that the debtor has no such right. He is entitled only to sufficient time to arrange the mechanics of payment, and what is a sufficient time is to be calculated upon the assumption that he has the necessary funds easily available to him; once this very limited time has elapsed he is in breach of his obligations and time is running in respect of the contractual action to enforce those obligations.

10.016

Bills of exchange

In *Eaglehill Ltd v J. Needham (Builders) Ltd*[41] the House of Lords had to consider the date of accrual of an action based on the dishonouring of bills of exchange. It was held that the vital date is that when the notice of dishonour is received, or (if earlier) the date when it would have been received in the ordinary course of business. It is irrelevant that both parties knew at an earlier stage that the dishonour was inevitable. As is explained above,[42] this case can be reconciled with the general principles of law relating to anticipatory breach. The necessary corollary of this is, of course,

10.017

---

[37] 1980 Act, s.36; see paras 3.015–3.018.
[38] Lord Diplock and Lord Cross of Chelsea: Viscount Dilhorne dissented.
[39] (1974) 90 L.Q.R. 2; for a discussion of the substantive points of criticism see para.3.018.
[40] [1987] Ch. 335.
[41] [1973] A.C. 992, HL.
[42] See para.10.006.

that no cause of action accrues until that date, and a bill of exchange can therefore be presented for the first time at any date.[43]

Sureties

10.018   Further difficult issues arise where the contractual obligation takes the form of a surety agreement. In *Re Brown's Estate*[44] the defendant became the surety on a mortgage. The principal sum was payable on demand, with interest to be paid "in the meantime". After the defendant's death a demand was made on his estate. The question was whether time ran from the granting of the surety or only from the making of the demand. Chitty J. held that time ran from the demand. The distinction that must be drawn here is that between a promise to pay collateral sum and a present debt.[45] The distinction is without doubt a difficult one, but is essential in this context. Clearly much will turn upon the construction of the document creating the obligation, but two factors in the present case which may be of general significance are: first, the fact that the defendant was merely a surety, rather than a principal obligor—this makes the court more likely to view the obligation as being one to pay a collateral sum; and, secondly, the reference in the mortgage deed to the obligation to pay interest in the meantime. This suggested that the obligation to pay the principal was not intended to arise immediately.

Co-sureties

10.019   It is well settled that a co-surety who has had to meet all or part of the debt is entitled to sue his co-surety for a rateable part of the amount which he had paid out. In a limitation context the problem is to know when that right of action accrues. In *Wolmershausen v Gullick*[46] Wright J. held that the accrual of the right is not necessarily delayed until the co-surety has actually made the payment, so long as it can be shown that the principal debtor is insolvent. The earliest possible date of accrual is when the amount of the liability is quantified. However, Wright J.'s remarks on this point were obiter dicta, since it was not strictly necessary for him to choose between the two dates for the purposes of the decision. It may also be observed that the cases on other forms of indemnity contract, considered at paragraphs 10.025–10.030, were not cited in this case. In principle the same rule ought to apply to all forms of indemnity contracts, so that the cause of action should not be considered as accruing until the co-surety has actually paid the creditor.

---

[43] *Glasscock v Balls* (1889) 24 Q.B.D. 13, CA.
[44] [1893] 2 Ch. 300, Chitty J.
[45] *Birks v Trippett* (1666) 2 Keb. 126; (1666) 1 Wms. Saund. 32.
[46] [1893] 2 Ch. 514, Wright J.

Principal debt barred

Where a surety for a debt is given some time after the original debt is incurred, it may happen that the principal debt becomes time-barred fewer than six years after the giving of the surety. This situation was considered in two nineteenth-century cases,[47] where it was held that the surety's liability was unaffected by the barring of the principal debt. This is in principle correct—the surety's obligation is different from that of the principal debtor, and there is no reason why the two must stand or fall together. At the same time the decision represents a potential pitfall for sureties, since there is little to stop the principal debtor from pleading limitation after the six years, in which event the creditor will presumably wish to proceed against the surety.

10.020

ASCERTAINMENT OF SUMS DUE

A common problem in relation to contracts arises where the contract provides that in specified events one party shall pay to the other a sum of money to be ascertained by the decision of some third party. Sometimes a clause of this kind will amount to an arbitration agreement, in which case the rules relating to arbitrations[48] will apply but in other cases the third party may be required to act as expert rather than as arbitrator, and in this event it may sometimes happen that the decision of the third party is a prerequisite to the accrual of the cause of action in respect of the sum awarded.[49]

10.021

CONTINUING OBLIGATIONS

Where the defendant omits to do something which he was under a contractual obligation to do, there may be difficulty in determining when the cause of action arises. The problem occurs where it is unclear what was the earliest or the latest time at which the obligation could properly have been performed. Two cases illustrate this principal. *Shaw v Shaw*[50] was a case of breach of promise of marriage.[51] The defendant went through a bigamous marriage with the plaintiff in 1938. The defendant's lawful wife died in

10.022

---

[47] *Carter v White* (1883) 25 Ch.D. 666; *Curwen v Milburn* (1889) 42 Ch.D. 424.
[48] See Ch.16.
[49] *Royal Norwegian Government v Constant & Constant* [1960] 2 Lloyd's Rep. 431.
[50] [1954] 2 Q.B. 429, CA.
[51] Although the action for breach of promise of marriage was abolished by the Family Law Reform Act 1969, the general principles laid down in this case are unaffected by that repeal.

1950 and the defendant died in 1952. Only then did the plaintiff discover the defendant's former marriage. She sued the defendant's estate for damages, and limitation was pleaded. The Court of Appeal held that the action in respect of breach of promise accrued only in 1950. This view apparently rests on the rule that a promise of marriage by a person already married was void as being contrary to public policy.[52] At the same time there was from 1938 onwards a continuing warranty by the defendant that he was free to marry. This warranty continued to be breached until 1950 (after which it became true), and the Court of Appeal assumed that time in respect of the action for the breach of this warranty ran only from 1950. A similar point arose in a different context in *Vai Industries (UK) Ltd v Bostock & Bramley and others*[53], which concerned a contractual warranty of fitness for purpose for a period of two years from delivery. The form of words used was: "The warranty period is for no longer than 24 months from FOB".

It appeared that the goods had never been fit for purpose, and the question was when time began to run for the purposes of the warranty claim. There were three possibilities:[54]

(i) that the warranty was a promissory warranty that each day the equipment would be free from defects in design and in conformity with the specification.

(ii) that the twenty-four month period simply defined the reasonable time after delivery that the equipment is to continue to be of proper quality.

(iii) that the two year period serves to limit the duration of the warranty (i.e. that complaints had to be made within that period).

The majority of the Court of Appeal[55] held that as a matter of construction the warranty fell into the second category (Ward LJ would have held that it fell into the first category). Newman J. also commented[56] that cases such as *Shaw v Shaw* and *Bell v Peter Browne &Co*:

"have a continuing quality and character giving rise to an 'exceptional' obligation and, in my judgment, are of no assistance when considering a commercial contract for the supply of goods."

---

[52] *Spiers v Hunt* [1908] 1 K.B. 720.
[53] [2003] EWCA Civ 1069, 23 July 2003.
[54] Per Ward LJ at para.28.
[55] Carnwath LJ and Newman J, Ward LJ dissenting.
[56] At para.56.

That observation of Newman J. is of interest in considering a number of other cases, which may otherwise appear to be in conflict with the decision in *Vai Industries Midland Bank Trust Co. v Hett, Stubbs & Kemp*[57] was a case of solicitor's negligence, in which the breach of duty consisted of the failure to register an option to purchase land as an estate contract. It was argued that the duty must have been to register the option within a reasonable time, and that this reasonable time had elapsed more than six years before the action was brought. Oliver J. held that the only duty on the solicitor was to effect a valid registration of the option. Consequently the breach occurred only at the moment when this became impossible. This could occur either when the land concerned was sold to a third party (so that the registration of the option would no longer be effective) or when the limitation period in respect of the option expired (so that it could no longer validly be exercised). This case may be contrasted with *Bell v Peter Browne & Co*.[58] The negligence in this case took the form of failure to cause the execution of a declaration of trust in respect of the matrimonial home on the plaintiff's divorce and/or failure to register a caution at the Land Registry against dealings with the property. As a result the plaintiff lost one-sixth interest in the proceeds of sale which had been agreed as part of the divorce settlement. The settlement happened in 1978, but the action was not commenced until 1987.[59] On the contract point it was held that the contract action accrued in 1978 as that was the date of the breach. It was not correct here (though it might be in some cases) to say that there was a continuing breach which accrued afresh each day.

10.023

This aspect of the case appears to cause some difficulty. The plaintiff naturally sought to draw an analogy with *Midland Bank v Hett, Stubbs & Kemp*. So far as the failure to obtain a declaration of trust is concerned, the case is obviously distinguishable, since that was something which had to be done at the time of the divorce if it was to be done at all. The failure to register the caution in the present case seems to be more directly comparable with the failure to register the option in the earlier case, and it is submitted that this aspect of the decision leaves the law in a state of undesirable confusion. The principle explained in *Bell v Peter Browne & Co*[60] was considered further in *Great North Eastern Railway Ltd v JLT Corporate Risks Ltd (formerly Jardine Insurance Services Ltd)*[61] in relation to the question of whether an insurance broker owed a continuing duty to his clients once the policy had been effected. Although the judge was able to avoid deciding the point, it should be noted that the examples of continuing duty which he considered were examples of duties to inform the insured

10.024

---

[57] [1979] Ch.384.
[58] [1990] 2 Q.B. 459, CA.
[59] For the tort aspects of the case, see para.5.030.
[60] [1990] 2 Q.B. 495.
[61] [2006] EWHC 1478 (QB), 2004/482, Queen's Bench Division (Commercial Court) Cresswell J.

about matters arising post-policy, such as the insured becoming uninsured through the collapse of the insurer. There appears to be no reported case where it has been held that a broker has a continuing duty to disclose that the policy he has effected was inadequate from the outset, whether because it was voidable or because it contained a term (such as an exclusion) which should not have been there.

10.025   The general point that may be extracted from these cases is that it is vital to establish exactly when the breach of contract occurs; this may also involve, as in *Shaw v Shaw*, describing carefully the content of the obligation. Where the obligation can be performed at any time during an extended period, the cause of action cannot accrue before the beginning of that period, and will accrue at the latest at the very end of that period. On the basis of Newman J.'s comment in *Vai Industries* it would seem that a judgment must be made in each as to whether there is the necessary "continuing" quality about the obligation. It does not appear possible to lay down any clear guideline for when that quality will and will not be present.

INDEMNITY CONTRACTS

10.026   A number of cases have considered the problem of accrual of cause of action under indemnity contracts. The question which commonly arises is whether the claimant's cause of action accrues when he incurs the loss (which may include a liability to a third party) or only when the extent of that liability is quantified, which may be achieved by a finding of liability by a court. This problem is different from that of claims for contribution between joint wrongdoers.[62] Those claims, which are governed by the Civil Liability (Contribution) Act 1978, arise only where both defendants have contributed to the claimant's loss, whereas the claims presently under consideration arise because one party, who has not contributed to the original loss, has agreed to indemnify another against loss. The cases in this area have drawn some fine distinctions, and may at first sight appear to be in conflict. They consequently require analysis.

In *Bosma v Larsen*[63] the charterers under a charterparty agreed to indemnify the owners of the vessel against "all consequences or liabilities" arising out of certain events. The owners incurred liabilities to a third party, which they duly discharged. The question before McNair J. was whether the owners' right to indemnity had accrued when they incurred the liability to the third party or when they discharged it. McNair J. resolved this question by careful attention to the words used. He held that the use of the

---

[62] These problems are considered in Ch.15.
[63] [1966] 1 Lloyd's Rep. 22.

word "liabilities" implied that it was the incurring of the liability rather than the discharge of it which gave rise to the cause of action.[64] This case serves to make the important point that the date of accrual of the cause of action will inevitably depend on construction of the terms of the indemnity. It should also be said that the case does not deal with the related point of whether it is necessary for the liability to be quantified before the right of action under the indemnity contract can accrue. *Heath Lambert v Sociedad de Corretaje de Seguros*[65] concerned an insurance broker's right to be indemnified by the policyholder for premiums which he was obliged to pay to the insurer.[66] It was held that the broker's cause of action arose on the inception of the policy, whether or not he had in fact paid the insurer at that point, and irrespective of any ongoing accounting arrangements between himself and the insurer.

Bosma v Larsen has had something of a chequered history. In *Jenner v County & District Properties*[67] Swanwick J. declined to follow it. He held that the cause of action accrues when the liability which is the basis of the indemnity contract is established. In Swanwick J.'s view, even this rule amounts to an equitable relaxation of the common law rule that the liability did not arise until the liability for which indemnity is claimed is actually discharged.[68]   **10.027**

The decision in *Jenner v County & District Properties* left an apparent contradiction of first-instance authorities on this point. The conflict has now been analysed, and a reconciliation suggested in what is now the leading authority in this area, *Telfair Shipping Corporation v Inersea Carriers SA: The Caroline P.*[69] This was a charterparty case, in which the charterparty required the master of the vessel to sign bills of lading "as presented". The bills of lading that were presented imposed on the owners obligations in respect of the cargo in excess of those provided for in the charterparty. The owners incurred liability under these obligations and sought indemnity from the charterers. The question was when the owners' right of indemnity arose. Neill J. analysed in detail the circumstances under which A, who has become liable to B, may be able to obtain redress from C. He held that these fell into three categories:

(a) Actions based on breach of contract. These cases fall within the usual principles applicable to contract cases, so that time runs from the breach of contract by C.

(b) Actions based on an express indemnity agreement. Here the date of

---

[64] See also *Collinge v Heywood* (1839) 9 Ad. & El. 633; *Spark v Heslop* (1859) 1 E. & E. 563.
[65] [2003] EWHC 2269 (Comm), [2003] All ER (D) 224 (Oct) Jonathan Hirst QC.
[66] Marine Insurance Act 1906 s.53.
[67] (1974) 230 E.G. 1589.
[68] See *Collinge v Heywood* (1839) 9 Ad. & El. 633.
[69] [1985] 1 W.L.R. 553.

accrual will depend upon the terms of the indemnity. If the indemnity is expressed as being against liability (as in *Bosma v Larsen*) then it is likely that the cause of action will accrue when the liability is incurred. In other cases, though, the cause of action will normally accrue when A's liability to B has been established and ascertained.[70]

(c) Actions based upon an implied indemnity. It will normally be assumed that this is an indemnity against the discharge of a liability rather than against the incurring of that liability, so that the cause of action will accrue only when the liability is established and quantified. It was accepted that before the Judicature Acts 1873–1875 equity might in some cases have required the defendant to set aside a fund to meet the liability in advance of its being ascertained.[71] However, even in equity the defendant would not have been compelled to pay over this fund in advance of the establishment of the liability, and the obligation to establish the fund would not be sufficient to cause the action to accrue for limitation purposes.

10.028   The judgment in *Telfair Shipping Corporation v Inersea Carriers SA* offers a detailed and convincing analysis of the problems of accrual of action in indemnity contracts.[72] Nevertheless, it leaves a number of potentially significant difficulties in this area unresolved. First, Neill J. carefully couches his judgment in terms of general propositions, leaving open the possibility that there may be exceptions to the general principles. It is therefore necessary to consider under what circumstances these exceptions might arise. So far as express indemnity is concerned it may be suggested that only clauses which speak of indemnity against "liability" will be construed as departing from the general rule, whilst in the case of implied indemnity it is even more unlikely that a court will be prepared to find a

---

[70] For a different approach, see *Wardley Australia Ltd v State of Western Australia* (1992) 109 A.L.R. 247, High Court of Australia, where Brennan J. said that no loss was suffered until it was reasonably ascertainable that, by bearing the burdens of a transaction in which there are benefits and burdens, the plaintiff was worse off than if he had not entered into the transaction. On the facts, this was held to be the time when an absolute liability to pay under the guarantee was established. The result is therefore the same as that contemplated by Neill J., though the reasoning is different, concentrating on weighing at any given time the relevant benefits and disbenefits. In the course of elaborating this approach the court cast doubt on cases such as *Forster v Outred* [1982] 2 All E.R. 753, CA, and adopted instead an approach similar to that employed in *Nykredit v Edward Erdman & Co.* [1997] 1 W.L.R. 1627, HL.

[71] For a detailed explanation of the history of this practice, see *Re Richardson* [1911] 2 K.B. 705, CA; at common law the plaintiff was always obliged to meet the liability in full before making any claim against the third party, but this strict rule was somewhat relaxed in equity.

[72] Neill J's approach has been approved by the Court of Appeal in *The Fanti* [1991] 2 A.C. 1 and *Padre Island* [1989] 1 Lloyd's Rep. 239, though without any detailed analysis of the issues involved. The subsequent reversal of these decisions by the House of Lords ([1990] 1 All E.R. 705) does not affect this point.

departure from the general principle. In effect *Bosma v Larsen*[73] has been confined to its own facts, though not overruled. The second outstanding point concerns the nature of the indemnity which is implied in these cases. Neill J. expressed the view that any indemnity, even if construed as an indemnity against the incurring of liability, would only cover actual, as distinct from potential, liability. In other words, where only part of the liability materialises immediately, the action for the indemnity nevertheless accrues, and, if the remainder of the liability does not materialise for more than six years, the result will apparently be that it cannot be reclaimed under the indemnity.

INSURANCE CONTRACTS

The most common example of a contract of indemnity is, of course, an   10.029
insurance contract. This is an example of an express indemnity, as described by Neill J. in the *Telfair Shipping* case.[74] A claim on an insurance policy is a claim for unliquidated damages. The breach arises as soon as the loss is suffered by the insured because the insurer has failed to hold the insured harmless against the relevant loss.[75] Consequently, the date when the cause of action accrues will depend upon the terms of the contract, but the usual rule may be illustrated by reference to *Chandris v Argo Insurance Co.*[76] This was a marine insurance case which involved general average losses and particular average losses under the Marine Insurance Act 1906. In accordance with the usual marine insurance practice, average adjusters were employed to determine the proportions in which the losses should be borne by the various cargo owners involved. Average adjustment can be a protracted process, as happened here, and the result was that the action, which was to recover sums specified in the adjusters' award, was brought more than six years after the losses happened, though fewer than six years after the making of the award.

It is the practice in marine insurance that underwriters do not pay on a   10.030
claim until the award of the average adjusters is published, and the plaintiff accordingly argued that the cause of action could not accrue until that time. Megaw J. rejected this argument, holding that the cause of action accrued when the loss was incurred—the insurers' refusal could not be a relevant factor in the decision. His Lordship relied particularly on *Central Electricity*

---

[73] [1966] 1 Lloyd's Rep. 22.
[74] See para.10.027.
[75] *Castle Insurance Co. Ltd v Hong Kong Islands Shipping Co. Ltd* [1984] 1 A.C. 226; [1983] 3 All E.R. 706, PC, in particular at 237–238 of the former report; *Firma C-Trade SA v Newcastle Protection and Indemnity Association: The "Fanti"* [1991] 2 A.C. 1; [1990] 2 All E.R. 705 per Lord Goff at 35 of the former report, and, most recently, the decision of Sir Peter Webster in *Callaghan v Dominion Insurance* [1997] 2 Lloyd's Rep. 541.
[76] [1963] 2 Lloyd's Rep. 65.

Generating Board v Halifax Corporation,[77] where it was held that a cause of action is to be treated as accruing, notwithstanding that P is unaware of the relevant facts or is unable to prove them. The principle stated in that case is, of course, of general application, and its correctness as a general principle is beyond doubt. The case may be treated as showing that in insurance contracts, the right of recovery against the insurer accrues on the happening of the loss rather than at any later stage. This principle is generally sound, but Megaw J.'s reasoning in applying to the facts of this particular case is unconvincing. Given the custom of the market that no payment is made until the award is published, it surely makes more sense to hold that the parties have agreed that the cause of action does not accrue until that time. To adopt the classification later developed by Neill J. in the *Telfair Shipping* case, this is a case of express indemnity, and the date of accrual depends on the terms of the indemnity. If one of those terms is that the indemnity is not payable until a date which will always be significantly later than the date of the loss, this must strongly suggest that it is only at the later time that the cause of action accrues. It is interesting to contrast *British Credit Trust Holdings v UK Insurance Ltd*.[78] That case concerned a policy of insurance to cover losses on hire purchase lending. The sum insured was the difference between the outstanding loan and the sum for which the vehicle was sold after repossession. It was held that the cause of action in relation to any particular loss did not arise until the vehicle was sold and the amount of the loss ascertained.

10.031   The principle was again illustrated, and this time correctly applied, in *Lefevre v White*.[79] The plaintiff brought a personal injuries action, which was successful. The defendant became bankrupt, so the plaintiff sought to sue the defendant's liability insurers under the 1930 Act. The writ against the insurers was issued more than three years after the injury was suffered. The plaintiff argued[80] that the cause of action against the insurers did not arise until the defendant became bankrupt, but it was held that the action against the insurers accrues at the same time as the plaintiff's original action against the defendant, notwithstanding that at that stage the plaintiff could not have sued the insurers. The case may perhaps be compared with *O'Connor v Isaacs*,[81] where a procedural bar to suing the defendant did not prevent the running of time. Although that case concerned an action in tort, it is thought that similar principles apply in this situation. The present decision is to be explained on the basis that the right which is transferred to the claimant under the 1930 Act is the defendant's right to sue his own liability insurers. Under an express contract of indemnity this, of course,

---

[77] [1963] A.C. 765, HL. Other aspects of this case are considered in Chs 4 and 11.
[78] [2003] EWHC 2404 (Comm), [2003] All ER (D) 412 (Oct).
[79] [1990] 1 Lloyd's Rep. 569, Popplewell J.
[80] For the other point in this case, see para.2.001.
[81] [1956] 2 Q.B. 288; see para.5.060.

accrues as soon as the loss occurs, notwithstanding that the quantum of loss has not at that time been established. Thus in *Universities Superannuation Scheme Ltd v Royal Insurance*[82] it was held that the insured's cause of action under a fidelity insurance policy arose as soon as a dishonest employee misappropriated money, even though the loss was not immediately discovered. Moreover, it made no difference that the policy contained a clause limiting cover to situations where the loss was in fact discovered within 24 months of its occurrence. That clause limited the scope of the cover, but the discovery of the loss was not a prerequisite to the right to claim on the policy. By contrast, in *Virk v Gan Life Holdings*[83] the plaintiff had a critical illness policy, under which he was to receive £22,000 if he suffered a stroke, provided that he was alive 30 days thereafter. It was held that his survival for the additional 30 days was a precondition to his right of action, which therefore did not accrue until the 30 days expired.

CONTRACTS OF GUARANTEE

Contracts of guarantee do not appear to present any special features from a limitation point of view. As usual, the vital question is the date at which the guarantee became enforceable, and this depends upon the construction of the terms of the guarantee. A point that has sometimes given rise to difficulty arises where a loan is guaranteed together with the attendant interest. If the interest, according to the terms of the loan, becomes due in instalments (as will commonly be the case) the liability for each instalment runs only from the date when it falls due. The effect of this may in some cases be that the guarantee in respect of the principal of the loan is timebarred, but that the guarantor can still be made liable for some or all of the interest.[84]   **10.032**

CONTRACTS OF LOAN

Section 6 of the 1980 Act contains special rules relating to certain loans. These rules vary the principle stated in s.5 that an action founded on simple contract is barred six years after the cause of action accrues. Section 6   **10.033**[85]

---

[82] [2000] 1 All E.R. (Comm.) 266, Langley J.
[83] (2000) 52 B.M.L.R. 207.
[84] *Parr's Banking Co. v Yates* [1898] 2 Q.B. 460.
[85] This paragraph was cited in *Hong Guet Eng v Wu Wai Hong (liquidator of Xiang Man Lou Food Court Pte Ltd)* [2006] SGHC 42 in a discussion of the merits of excluding family loans from the operation of the Limitation Act.

applies to contracts of loan which do not provide for repayment of the debt on or before a fixed or determinable date and do not make the obligation to repay conditional upon a demand for payment or upon anything else.[86] The section is satisfied where the terms provide only for payment on or after a specified date.[87] It is therefore unlikely that this section will be of much relevance when dealing with loans of a commercial character, since contracts for such loans will normally deal expressly with these matters.[88] Rather, the section will most commonly apply to loans of an informal character, and this is consistent with the history of the provision, which began as s.6 of the Limitation Amendment Act 1980, following a recommendation of the Law Reform Committee in 1977.[89] There is one other point of difficulty which arises in connection with what the Law Reform Committee called "family loans". There is authority that within family relationships, agreements are not normally to be construed as legally enforceable contracts, since there is a presumption that the parties do not intend to create legal relations.[90] It is therefore surely open to question whether such loans are properly described as "contracts of loan". In *Westminster Property Management Ltd*[91] it was suggested that s.6 of the 1980 Act might be inapplicable where a loan was made in breach of company law requirements and the company was therefore entitled to avoid the transaction. Ferris J rejected this argument. The agreement was rendered voidable by the breach of the Companies Acts, not void, and the company had no right of action unless and until it exercised its right to avoid the contract. Moreover, it is irrelevant that the Law Reform Committee apparently intended it to apply only to informal and family transactions. What matters is the wording of s.6, which contains no such restriction.

Collateral obligations

10.034 The general rule of s.6(1) is excluded by s.6(2) if in connection with taking the loan the debtor enters into any collateral obligation to pay any or all of

---

[86] At common law such loans would be repayable immediately, so that time would run from the date of the advance: *Norton v Ellam* (1837) 2 M. & W. 461; *Re J. Brown's Estate* [1893] 2 Ch. 300.

[87] *Von Goetz v Rogers* July 29, 1998, Unreported, CA.

[88] Derek Morgan suggests (Morgan, *Current Law Statutes Annotated* (1980), vol. II) that these requirements should have been alternative rather than cumulative. His argument on the issue of policy is persuasive, but it is submitted that the drafting of the provision is unambiguously to the opposite effect.

[89] Law Reform Committee, 21st Report, Final Report on Limitation of Actions, Cmnd. 6923. See also the discussion of this point by the Court of Appeal in *Boot v Boot* (1996) 73 P. & C.R. 137. *Re Westminster Property Management Ltd*, March 27, 2002, Unreported, Ferris J. held that the application of s.6 is not limited to family loans.

[90] *Balfour v Balfour* [1919] 2 K.B. 571, CA; *Jones v Padavatton* [1969] 1 W.L.R. 328, CA.

[91] [2002] EWHC 52, 27 March 2002 Ferris J.

the debt and the terms of that obligation would exclude the application of s.6(1) if they applied directly to the repayment of the debt. This will serve to exclude a number of cases of commercial loans which might otherwise fall within the ambit of s.6, though it could also apply to a "family loan" in which collateral security was offered. The drafting of the exception is somewhat inelegant, but the effect is that the terms of the collateral security must be read into the terms of the loan. If those terms are inconsistent with the application of the s.6 rule that time does not run immediately, then the case ceases to qualify for the application of s.6 and falls back into the general rule of s.5.[92]

The expression "in connection with" in this subsection is not further defined. It is submitted, however, that the entering into the obligation must be causally connected with the granting of the original loan; usually this will mean that the collateral obligation is part of the consideration which the debtor gives for the creditor's granting the loan. Clearly, then, the two things will normally happen more or less contemporaneously, and whilst it is no doubt correct to say that the subsection does not expressly require this, there can surely be very few cases where the collateral obligation is entered into years after the loan is made but is still "in connection with" the taking of the loan. Section 6(2) gives an example of a collateral obligation—the giving of a promissory note—and this example serves to make the point that the collateral obligation can arise between debtor and creditor as well as between debtor and third party. However, the example is not in any way conclusive, and it is clear that any form of collateral obligation will suffice. Where s.6 applies to a contract of loan, the effect is expressed to be that s.5 of the 1980 Act shall not bar the right of action on the loan. Effectively this means that time simply does not run against the creditor so long as the requirements of s.6(2) are met. This must, however, be understood subject to s.6(3). Section 6(3) deals with the situation where a formal demand for the repayment of a debt falling within s.6(1) is in fact made by or on behalf of any or all of the creditors. In this event the cause of action for the recovery of the debt is to be treated as having accrued upon the making of that formal demand, and the six-year period provided for by s.5 will therefore run from that date. **10.035**

THE LAW COMMISSION'S PROPOSALS

The abolition of the six-year period running from the date of accrual would clearly have fundamental effects on the law described in this chapter. The concepts of discoverability and the longstop would for the first time become **10.036**

---

[92] *Boot v Boot* (1996) 73 P. & C.R. 137, CA.

of general[93] relevance in contractual claims. Contract would cease to be a separate head of claim for limitation purposes, being instead simply subsumed within the general core regime. Although this would not remove the potential difference between the date of accrual in contract and that in tort, it apparently would in most cases remove the difference between the dates at which time would start to run in the tort action and the contract action, since it is to be assumed that both actions would become discoverable at the same time. A possible exception to this would arise where the contract action had accrued but the tort action had not. If the contract action was discoverable at that point, then presumably time would run in the contract action but not in the tort action. A possible answer to this would be that if the claimant could obtain only nominal damages in the contract action, then time would not run because the loss would not be significant, whereas if he could obtain substantial damages in the contract action, then there would presumably be significant loss for the purposes of the tort action as well.

---

[93] Discoverability is already relevant to contractual claims for damages for personal injuries.

CHAPTER 11

Actions to Recover Sums Due Under Statute

The problems of categorisation relating to actions to recover sums of money due under an enactment were discussed in Ch.4.[1] It may be noted here that this category of action did not exist as a separate class for limitation purposes before the Limitation Act 1939. Prior to that time, statutes were treated as a class of specialty, and the standard 20-year period applicable to specialties applied to them also.[2] Consequently all the cases dealing with what is now s.9 of the Limitation Act 1980 post-date the coming into force of the 1939 Act.

11.001

SECTION 9 OF THE 1980 ACT

Section 9 of the 1980 Act deals with actions to recover a sum of money due under an enactment. One of the most difficult problems in dealing with this section is to establish its scope. Section 8 of the 1980 Act deals with actions on a specialty,[3] and it is well known that Acts of Parliament are sealed. One way of resolving this apparent contradiction is to say that actions under statute are simply an exception to the principle that the limitation period for a specialty is 12 years.[4] However, the true position is more complex. Section 9 does not apply to all cases where an action is based upon a statute, but only to an action to recover a sum of money due under an enactment. This provision can be analysed into two parts. There must be:

11.002

---

[1] See paras 4.014–4.021.
[2] Civil Procedure Act 1833; *Cork & Bandon Railway Co. v Goode* (1853) 13 C.B. 827; *Talory v Jackson* (1638) Cro.Car. 513.
[3] i.e. a document under seal.
[4] Such exceptions are expressly contemplated by s.8(2).

(a) a sum of money recoverable and (b) a statute which makes that sum of money recoverable.[5]

SUM OF MONEY DUE

11.003 The difficulty under this heading turns upon the meaning of the phrase "sum of money". Six classes of statute may be identified:

(a) Those which impose a duty, but fail to specify the consequences of a breach of that duty. The Factories Acts 1902–1961 provide examples of this.

(b) Those which impose a duty, and state that a breach of that duty shall be actionable in damages, but leave the damages unliquidated (whether or not they specify on what basis the damages shall be calculated). Section 2 of the Misrepresentation Act 1967 is an example of this class.

(c) Statutes which imply obligations into contracts between persons, with the express or implied consequence that a breach of those obligations shall give rise to an action for damages. The best known example of this would, no doubt, be the Sale of Goods Act 1979.

(d) Those which provide that in given cases a person shall be entitled to recover a specified sum of money from another. A useful example here is provided by statutes allowing for compensation arising out of the transfer of areas of land between local authorities.[6]

(e) Statutes which confer upon a person a right of a non-monetary character. An illuminating example here is the Leasehold Reform Act 1967, which confers upon certain tenants the right to require their landlord to sell to them his freehold interest.

(f) Statutes which confer a right to compensation, subject to an option for the payer of the compensation to make good any damage caused. An example is provided by the Coal Mining Subsidence Act 1991,[7] which deals with subsidence caused by coal-mining activities. The British Coal Corporation is obliged to pay compensation for this damage, but may at its option choose instead to make good the damage.

---

[5] For a fuller exposition of the difficulties of categorisation, see Ch.4.
[6] *West Riding of Yorks CC v Huddersfield Corporation* [1957] 1 Q.B. 540, Lord Goddard C.J.
[7] Formerly the Coal Industry Act 1975 s.2.

Actions within category (a) are clearly not actions to recover a sum of money due under an enactment. If the enactment does not provide for the recovery of any sum, then it can only be by common law principles that the action is allowed. In the case of category (c) the correct approach is to apply the period applicable to contractual claims, since this is a case of an action founded on contract, albeit that the terms of the contract are partly determined by statute. In the case of category (e) there can be no doubt that the claim is not within s.9, since it does not relate to a sum of money. It is unclear whether any limitation period applies, but it may be that the 12-year period of s.8 is appropriate.[8] At the other extreme there can surely be no doubt that actions within category (d) are caught by s.9—they are the paradigm case of an enactment making a sum of money due, though it may also be observed that there are very few statutes falling within category (d). **11.004**

An exceptional example is provided by the case of *West Riding of Yorks CC v Huddersfield Corporation*.[9] In that case, land had been transferred from the jurisdiction of the plaintiff authority to that of the defendant authority. The statute which effected the transfer provided for the payment of compensation by the acquiring authority to the ceding authority in respect of any loss caused, the amount to be determined by arbitration in default of agreement. Lord Goddard C.J. held that this was a clear case of an action within s.9, since the statute provided for the payment of money and specified the basis of the calculation. By extension of this principle in *BP Oil v Kent CC*[10] a compulsory purchase order had been made by the defendant, which had entered into an agreement with the dispossessed owner as to the procedure for determining compensation. The Court of Appeal held that the right to compensation nevertheless arose under the statutory provisions rather than under the agreement, so that s.9 was the relevant section for determining the limitation period.

The major difficulty arises in connection with category (b). The difference between category (b) and category (d) is a fine one, but it might be argued that cases within the former category are not strictly speaking cases of sums due under an enactment, and therefore should not fall within s.9. The decision of the Court of Appeal in *Moore v Gadd*[11] rather undermines this argument by holding that an action against a company director in respect of wrongful trading under s.214 of the Insolvency Act 1986 is within s.9 and therefore has a six-year limitation period. In *Rowan Companies Inc. v Lambert Eggink Offshore Transport Consultants Vof*[12] Clarke J. dealt with the point expressly, holding that a claim for unliquidated damages under a statute does fall within s.9. **11.005**

---

[8] *Collin v Duke of Westminster* [1985] Q.B. 581, CA; see further para.4.018.
[9] [1957] 1 Q.B. 540, Lord Goddard C.J.
[10] [2003] EWCA Civ 798, [2003] RVR 276.
[11] (1997) 141 S.J.L.B. 45; *The Times*, February 17, 1997, CA; see also para.4.020.
[12] [1999] 2 Lloyd's Rep. 443.

Category (f) may be regarded as being a hybrid between categories (d) and (e). The obligation to pay compensation falls within category (d), whereas the option to make good appears to fall within category (e). In *British Coal Corporation v Ellistown Pipes Ltd (Hepworth Building Products)*[13] it was argued that the two obligations should be treated as being alternatives, each with its own limitation period—six years for the duty to compensate, 12 years for the duty to make good if that were chosen. The Court of Appeal rejected this argument, considering that an undesirable anomaly would be introduced into the law if it were decided that the same section could create two incompatible limitation periods. Instead, the section was interpreted as creating a primary duty to compensate, to which the six-year limitation period applied. The duty to make good was regarded as being merely an alternative, and the court emphasised that this duty could not arise unless the defendant specifically elected for it. Two questions were left open. First, whether time in relation to the duty to make good would run from the date of the defendant's election or from the date of the damage. Secondly, whether the limitation period would be six years or 12 if it could be said that the defendant had unambiguously opted to make good. The logic underlying the court's approach must be that in the latter event the period would still be six years.

11.006 It therefore appears that the six categories identified above may be capable of being reduced for practical purposes to four categories: (b) and (d) may be merged, despite their conceptual differences, whilst category (f) cases resolve themselves on examination into category (d) cases. There is no doubt that the underlying trend here is to categorise any action which may be regarded as based on a statutory provision (to use a deliberately neutral term) as falling within s.9 and thus having a six-year limitation period. The only major exception now is the category (e) case where it is clear that no sum of money can become payable under the statute. These cases have a 12-year limitation period.

DUE UNDER AN ENACTMENT

11.007 This is the form of wording adopted in the 1980 Act. The equivalent provision of the 1939 Act, which first introduced this category of action into the law of limitations,[14] spoke of sums recoverable "by virtue of any enactment", whilst the Civil Procedure Act 1833, which previously governed all claims involving specialties, referred to an action "upon a specialty". These expressions were considered in a number of the older cases. The effect of these decisions was that the Civil Procedure Act 1833 did not

---

[13] [1994] R.V.R. 81, CA.
[14] 1939 Act s.2(1)(d).

apply unless the action was upon the statute in the sense of being one which could not have been brought in the absence of the statute.[15] Before the Judicature Acts 1873–1875, this required also that the action be one properly pleaded in debt, rather than upon the case.[16] Thus, actions in respect of breach of statutory duty, which were actions upon the case,[17] did not fall within this provision. However, in the old law, the effect of this was that the six-year period applied.

The distinction drawn in these cases approximately corresponds to that drawn above between category (a) and category (c). As was shown in the discussion of those categories, the choice is now between a 12-year limit and a six-year limit. It has been suggested[18] that the effect of the 1939 Act was to abolish these distinctions and substitute a uniform six-year period. On the basis of the arguments adduced above, this is regrettably incorrect. Neither s.2(1)(d) of the 1939 Act, nor s.9 of the 1980 Act (which are apparently indistinguishable in effect, despite the slight difference in wording) has done away with the problem of deciding whether the sum of money is due "by virtue of" or "under" an enactment. This problem in turn is really only a reformulation of the earlier question of whether the action is "upon" the statute. Consequently, the principles of these earlier cases continue to be relevant at the present day. It is necessary also to refer to some of the cases decided on the 1939 provision.

In *Brueton v Woodward*[19] the action was to recover money due pursuant **11.008** to the Gaming Act 1835, and Singleton J. declined to decide whether this was an action upon specialty or an action within s.2(1)(d) of the 1939 Act (the claim was barred upon either assumption). In *Mountain v Bermondsey BC*[20] Hilberry J. apparently accepted that an action by a registration officer for expenses recoverable under the Representation of the People Act 1918 could be an action upon a specialty, though again the point was not strictly necessary to the decision.[21] These cases highlight very clearly the dilemma which still exists about the ambit of what is now s.9 of the 1980 Act. It is submitted that the obiter dicta of these two judges were entirely correct and that, whatever may have been Parliament's intention in enacting s.2(1)(d) of the 1939 Act and then s.9 of the 1980 Act, the problem of categorisation has not been removed, though it is true that its importance has been reduced, at least in those cases where the choice is between s.9 and either s.2 or s.5, since the limitation period is now the same in all three cases.

---

[15] *Shepherd v Hills* (1855) 11 Ex. 55; *Gutsell v Reeve* [1936] 1 K.B. 272; *Aylott v West Ham Corp.* [1927] 1 Ch. 30.

[16] *Pratt v Cook, Son & Co. (St Paul's) Ltd* [1940] A.C. 437. See also *Thomson v Lord Clanmorris* [1900] 1 Ch. 718; *Jarvis v Surrey County Council* [1925] 1 K.B. 554; *Tees Conservancy Commissioners v James* [1935] Ch. 544.

[17] See cases cited in previous note.

[18] C.H.S. Preston and G.N. Newsom *Limitation of Actions* (3rd edn, 1953), p.52.

[19] [1941] 1 K.B. 680.

[20] [1942] 1 K.B. 204.

[21] The other point in this case turns upon a provision now repealed.

The approach adopted in the preceding paragraphs makes it necessary to consider at some length the decision of the House of Lords in *Central Electricity Generating Board v Halifax Corporation*.[22] The CEGB was in possession of a sum of money to which the Halifax Corporation claimed to be entitled, and that claim turned on whether the Board held the money in its capacity as successor to the body which controlled the relevant part of the electricity industry before nationalisation; if so, then the nationalising statute, which came into force on April 1, 1948, conferred on the Corporation the right to the money. The statute also provided that in the event of dispute the matter of entitlement was to be resolved by the relevant Minister.[23] The first issue was whether the limitation period was six years or 12 years. The House of Lords held that the appropriate period was six years, since this was an action to recover a sum recoverable "by virtue of an enactment". In reaching this conclusion their Lordships also observed that the old distinction between suing on a statute and suing in respect of a cause of action given by a statute had been rendered obsolete by the 1939 Act.

11.009   Although the point is not wholly clear, it appears that this is another way of expressing the distinction discussed above between actions in debt and actions on the case. It must be pointed out that so wide a formulation of the effect of s.2(1)(d) of the 1939 Act goes beyond what was necessary for the decision in the case. Further, it is hard to see how this statement can be right if it suggests that the cases of, for example, action for breach of statutory duty, fall under what is now s.9. The real difficulty, though, concerns those cases which are listed as category (b) at para.11.003. The decision in this case seems directly to apply a six-year limitation period to these cases. The outcome of the case can be justified on the basis that this is a claim for a liquidated sum; as such, it is a case which properly falls within category (c), for which it is accepted that a six-year period is applicable. However, it is not clear from the report whether this is indeed an action for a liquidated sum. If it is not, then the above argument obviously collapses. In this event it is probably necessary to recognise that the courts are not willing to follow the train of reasoning advanced in this paragraph to its logical conclusion. It seems that there is a tendency on the part of the judges to assume that any action for a monetary amount which is in any way based on a statute will fall under s.9. Category (e) listed at para.11.003 consisted of those statutes which grant a right or impose a duty which does not take the form of the payment of a sum of money.

11.010   A good example of the problems that arise in these cases can be found in *Collin v Duke of Westminster*.[24] This was an application under the Leasehold Reform Act 1967, which gives tenants of leasehold property the right, in certain specified circumstances, to buy their landlord's interest. The

---

[22] [1963] A.C. 785, HL.
[23] For this point, see para.11.012.
[24] [1985] Q.B. 581, CA.

Court of Appeal was required to decide what limitation period applied to this claim. They held that the rights and duties of the parties arose from s.8(1) of the 1967 Act, so that this was an action on a specialty, for which the appropriate period of limitation was 12 years. This was sufficient to decide the case, but the court added, obiter, that there appeared to be an argument for saying that no period of limitation provided by the 1980 Act was appropriate to the case. Two points may be made. First, there is no good reason for such hesitancy about applying s.8 of the 1980 Act. The view that the 1967 Act governs the rights and duties of the parties is clearly correct. Secondly, the way in which the decision is phrased is liable to give rise to confusion. The first step is indeed to see that the cause of action depends upon the statutory provision. Given that this is so, it is then necessary to inquire whether the case is governed by s.8 or s.9 of the 1980 Act. If it is an action to recover a sum of money due under the enactment, then s.9 applies; otherwise s.8, with its 12-year period, is the appropriate provision. On this basis, the decision of the Court of Appeal in this case can be seen to be correct, but inadequately reasoned. A similar point arose in *Rahman v Sterling Credit Ltd*,[25] which concerned the reopening of extortionate credit bargains under the Consumer Credit Act 1974. The Court of Appeal rightly drew a distinction between an application to be released from making further payments under the agreement and an application for the return of sums already paid. The former is subject to the 12-year limitation period (since it is not a claim for money), whereas the latter is subject to the 6-year limitation period.

TORTIOUS ACTIONS

At this point attention must be drawn to the curious observations of the **11.011** House of Lords in *Sevcon Ltd v Lucas (CAV) Ltd*,[26] where it was assumed, apparently without argument, that an action for damages for patent infringement is an action in tort. It clearly is not, but as a claim for unliquidated damages given by statue it now clearly falls within s.9.[27]

ACCRUAL OF CAUSE OF ACTION

When s.11 applies, the rule is that the action may not be brought more than **11.012** six years after the date on which the cause of action accrues. On the face of

---

[25] [2001] 1 W.L.R. 496, CA.
[26] [1986] 1 W.L.R. 462, HL; (1986) 49 M.L.R. 650.
[27] *Rowan Companies Inc. v Lambert Eggink Offshore Transport Consultants Vof* [1999] 2 Lloyd's Rep. 443, Clarke J.

it this appears to mirror the rule in tort and contract, but the major difficulty here is to ascertain when the cause of action does accrue. The 1980 Act gives no guidance as to the date at which the cause of action under s.9 accrues. It is therefore necessary to determine the question by reference to general principles. The test laid down by the Court of Appeal in *Coburn v Colledge*[28] referred expressly to actions in tort, but it can equally well be applied here. That test was the existence of "every fact which is material to be proved to enable the plaintiff to succeed, every fact which the defendant would have a right to traverse". The major problem that arises in the context of actions under statute concerns the position where the right to a sum of money, usually some form of compensation, is dependent upon the decision of some other body, which in practice would normally be either an arbitrator or a Minister of the Crown, or upon agreement between the parties. An example of this occurred in *Central Electricity Generating Board v Halifax Corporation*.[29] The facts of this case are set out at para.11.008 above, where the question of the appropriate limitation period is considered. The other issue in the case was when the cause of action accrued. The difficulty was that nationalisation had taken place on April 1, 1948, but the reference of the dispute to the Minister was made only on January 3, 1957, and his decision was not given until September 18, 1958. The House of Lords held that the cause of action accrued in 1948. The basis for this apparently surprising decision was that the Minister's decision was only evidence of the facts upon which the claim could be based, and was not a precondition to the bringing of an action.

11.013   Two important points may usefully be made about this decision. The first is that it does not lay down a general principle that the decision of the third party in cases of this kind is irrelevant to the running of time. What it shows is that time will run once an action can be brought, even if that is before the third party has made a decision; but it will be necessary in each case to examine whether the action can in fact be brought before that decision is made. Secondly, the rule here appears to be different from that applicable to actions in tort, where there is authority to suggest that time may run even though some procedural[30] or even statutory[31] obstacle prevents the bringing of an action. More recently, in *Swansea City Council v Glass*,[32] the Court of Appeal had to consider s.10 of the Housing Act 1957, which allows councils to repair tenanted properties and then charge the work to the owner. The council in this case did this. The action was commenced more than six years after the work was done, but less than six years after the demand for payment was served. Section 10 expressly provides that where

---

[28] [1897] 1 Q.B. 702 at 706–707.
[29] [1963] A.C. 785, HL.
[30] *O'Connor v Isaacs* [1956] 2 W.L.R. 585, Diplock J.; [1956] Q.B. 288, CA.
[31] *Sevcon v Lucas* (CAV) Ltd [1986] 1 W.L.R. 462; (1986) 49 M.L.R. 650.
[32] [1992] 2 All E.R. 680, CA.

summary proceedings are brought time runs from the date of the demand, but there is nothing in the section to say expressly when time starts to run if proceedings by writ or summons are issued (as in this case). It was held, relying on *Coburn v Colledge, Sevcon v Lucas*, etc., that the cause of action was complete as soon as the work was done, the service of the demand being no more than a procedural element in the matter. Accordingly, this action was time-barred.

Where notice to treat was served under the Land Compensation Act 1961 and later withdrawn by agreement, it was held that the cause of action for compensation accrued on the date of the withdrawal.[33]

In relation to both Council Tax[34] and Child Maintenance[35] it has been held that the right of action to sue on an assessment of liability accrues on the date of the assessment, even where that assessment is in part retrospective. In both cases this appears to rest on the wording of the particular legislation, rather than on any more general principle.   **11.014**

"Compensation"

Where a statute provides that in specified circumstances compensation is to be paid to a person who has suffered loss, it may be necessary to decide whether the cause of action accrues when the damage is incurred or when the claimant has the expense of having it repaired.[36] The point arose directly in *Yorkshire Electricity Board v British Telecommunications*,[37] a claim under s.26(6) of the Public Utilities Street Works Act 1950. The Court of Appeal held that the action accrued when the damage was incurred, notwithstanding that it could not at that stage be quantified. Robert Goff L.J., delivering the judgment of the Court, placed great stress on the fact that the relevant statutory provision used the word "compensation" to describe what became payable. From the rather brief report of the case, it is not easy to understand why this should be so important, but the decision may perhaps be compared with that in *West Riding of Yorks CC v Huddersfield Corporation*,[38] where the same result was reached for similar reasons. Certainly this is a point which may well be of general importance, in view of the relatively large number of statutes that employ wording of this kind.   **11.015**

---

[33] *Williams v Blaenau Gwent County BC (No. 2)* Lands Tribunal [1999] 2 E.G.L.R. 195. See also *BP Oil UK Ltd v Kent CC*, June 28, 2002, Lands Tribunal, Unreported, where time ran from the date when the local authority entered the land.

[34] *Regentford v Thanet DC* [2004] EWHC 246 (Admin) Lightman J.

[35] *R (on the application of Sutherland) v Secretary of State for Work and Pensions* [2004] EWHC 800 (Admin Court) 25 March 2004 Collins J.

[36] This point arises also in the context of indemnity contracts; the relevant authorities are considered at paras 10.023–10.025.

[37] (1985) 129 S.J. 468, CA.

[38] [1957] 1 Q.B. 540, Lord Goddard C.J.; see para.11.004.

Interest on compensation

11.016 Two cases on the Compulsory Purchase Act 1965 have shown that there may be a difference in the date of accrual of the cause of action between a claim for statutory compensation and a claim for interest on that compensation, even where the right to interest is given by the statute. Section 11 of the Compulsory Purchase Act 1965 gives a right to compensation, with interest, in certain cases of compulsory purchase. In *Hillingdon LBC v ARC Ltd*[39] it was held that the cause of action in respect of a claim under the section arose at the date when the local authority entered on the land. It was irrelevant that the amount of compensation might not be determined by the Lands Tribunal or agreed between the parties until many years later. By contrast, in *Halstead v Manchester CC*[40] it was held that the cause of action in respect of the right to claim interest on sums due under the section does not accrue until the amount of the compensation on which interest is to be claimed has been determined or agreed.

11.017 In *Legal Services Commission v Rasool*[41] the Court of Appeal, following *Hillingdon London Borough Council v A.R.C. Ltd* [42], held that the LSC's cause of action to recover from the assisted person costs paid to the assisted person's opponent under a Legal Aid Certificate which had been revoked accrued on the date when the certificate was revoked, rather than on the later date when the bill of costs was assessed. The odd consequence of this is that the right to recover from the assisted party can accrue before the costs have in fact been paid to the opponent. In effect the process of assessment is treated here as a procedural bar, with *Sevcon Ltd v Lucas CAV Ltd*[43] being cited in support.

SUCCESSIVE CAUSES OF ACTION

11.018 In *Smith Stone & Knight Ltd v City of Birmingham DC*[44] a subsidence claim was made under the Public Health Acts (of which the major Act is the Public Health Act 1936), and it appeared that subsidence had occurred on more than one occasion. It was held that each occasion of subsidence represented a fresh cause of action with its own limitation period. The rule

---

[39] [1997] 3 All E.R. 506, Stanley Burnton Q.C. as Deputy High Court Judge. See also *The Executors of the Estate of the Right Honourable Herbert Robert Cayzer Baron Rotherwick v Oxfordshire County Council Lands Tribunal* (George Bartlett Q.C.), March 21, 2000.
[40] October 23, 1997, CA, Unreported.
[41] [2008] EWCA Civ 154.
[42] [1999] Ch. 139.
[43] [1986] 1 W.L.R. 462 H.L.; see para 4.025.
[44] March 30, 1988, Judge Bowsher, Unreported.

in this respect appears to follow that applying in cases of continuing nuisance.[45]

THE LAW COMMISSION'S PROPOSALS

This is another class of action that would disappear for limitation purposes **11.019** if the Law Commission's proposals were adopted. All actions dealt with in this chapter would be subject to the uniform three-year period. This would, of course, remove some of the difficulties of categorisation discussed in this chapter.

---

[45] *Darley Main Colliery Co. v Mitchell* (1886) 11 App.Cas. 127, HL.

CHAPTER 12

Personal Property

This chapter deals with a number of provisions that relate specifically to personal property. Sections 3 and 4 of the Limitation Act 1980 deal with problems arising from theft and conversion; much of s.20 (which deals also with mortgages of land[1]) is restricted to personal property, and certain aspects of s.29, relating to acknowledgments, also require separate consideration in their application to personal property, especially where that property is subject to mortgage. Section 3 and 4 of the 1980 Act lay down special rules to deal with the situation where property has been stolen and/or converted. These rules date from 1980, the rules contained in ss.3 and 4 of the 1939 Act having been somewhat amended at that time. The new rules have been criticised for the obscurity of their wording,[2] but have still attracted very little in the way of judicial attention.

12.001

The rules contained in ss.3 and 4 constitute a limited exception to the general principle[3] that in cases of tort the expiration of the limitation period bars the plaintiff's remedy against the defendant but does not extinguish his right. The exception applies in certain cases of conversion, as explained in the following paragraphs.[4]

CONVERSION

Conversion is now governed by the Torts (Interference with Goods) Act 1977.[5] The changes made by that Act, particularly s.2(2), which are con-

12.002

---

[1] On mortgages generally, see paras 13.073-13.081.
[2] Derek Morgan, *Current Law Statutes Annotated* (1980), vol. II.
[3] This is more fully explained in Ch.23.
[4] For these purposes an allegation of theft may be treated as including an allegation of conversion, since the greater wrong includes the lesser: *Union of India v Bumper Development Corp.*, February 17, 1988, Kennedy J., Unreported.
[5] "Goods" are defined by that Act (s.14(1)) as including all chattels personal other than things in action or money.

sequent upon the Act's abolition of the concept of detinue,[6] extend the right of action for conversion to those cases of detinue which did not previously give rise to an action in conversion. The action for conversion is an action in tort for the purposes of limitation, so that the period of limitation is prima facie six years from the date on which the cause of action accrues, as provided by s.2 of the 1980 Act. That date will normally be the date of the wrongful interference with the plaintiff's goods. Where the interference consists of a wrongful taking, the cause of action will accrue upon the taking.[7] Where the interference takes the form of a wrongful detention, time runs from the date when the defendant unequivocally refuses to deliver up the goods in the face of a lawful demand.[8] Only in exceptional cases will mere inaction amount to an unequivocal refusal.[9]

12.003   It is important to understand that at common law there are essentially two remedies for conversion. The first is to bring an action for the recovery of the thing itself against whoever is currently in possession of it; the second is to bring an action for damages against any person who has been guilty of converting the thing. The latter does not depend upon showing that the defendant is in possession of the thing, and is therefore in many cases more useful.

Effect of second conversion

12.004   Section 3 of the 1980 Act applies (subject to s.4, as to which see paras 12.004–12.006) where a cause of action in respect of the conversion of a chattel has accrued to any person and a further conversion takes place before the rightful owner has regained possession of the chattel. In these circumstances s.3 brings about two consequences. First, no action in respect of the second conversion can be brought more than six years after the accrual of the cause of action in respect of the first conversion,[10] i.e. the time-limit for suing on the second conversion expires at the same time as the time-limit for suing on the first conversion. In the great majority of cases this will be six years from the date of the first conversion. Secondly, on the expiry of a time-limit for suing in respect of a conversion (whether first or subsequent), the title to the goods of the rightful owner is extinguished, if he has not by then regained possession of the chattel.[11] However, the Act does not state that his right to damages for the conversion, as distinct from his remedy in respect of that right, is extinguished. It therefore appears to

---

[6] Torts (Interference with Goods) Act 1977 s.1(3).
[7] *Granger v George* (1826) 5 H. & C. 149.
[8] *Philpott v Kelley* (1835) 3 Ad. & El. 106; *Miller v Dell* [1891] 1 Q.B. 468.
[9] *Schwarzschild v Harrods Ltd* [2008] EWHC 521 (QB) Eady J. The leading authority on the old law was *Clayton v Le Roy* [1911] 2 KB 1031 CA.
[10] See s.3(1).
[11] See s.3(2).

follow that the plaintiff is entitled, within the usual limits,[12] to enforce his right to damages by non-judicial means.

If the second conversion takes place more than six years after the first, then the original owner can have no right to sue on it because s.3(2) extinguishes his right to the chattel, and there is thus no second conversion as against him.[13] The term "chattel" is not defined in the 1980 Act, and must be presumed to take its ordinary English meaning, since it is apparently not a term of art.

THEFT

Section 4 of the 1980 Act includes provisions which modify the effect of s.3   **12.005**
in cases where a chattel is stolen. It should be observed that for the purposes of this provision, theft includes any conduct outside England and Wales which would be theft if committed in England and Wales and any obtaining of property by deception within s.15(1)[14] of the Theft Act 1968 and any obtaining by blackmail within s.21 of that Act.[15] The right of the person from whom the chattel is stolen to bring an action in respect of the theft is not subject to the six-year time-limits in ss.2 and 3(1).[16] Therefore, in principle at least, time does not run in favour of a thief. However, s.4(1) further provides that if the plaintiff's title to the goods has been extinguished under s.3(2), then action can be brought only in respect of a theft preceding the loss of his title and only if that theft also preceded the conversion from which time began to run for the purposes of s.3(2). This is a convoluted provision, which requires careful explanation. The following paragraphs explore its difficulties.

Where title is not extinguished

So long as the rightful owner's title to the goods has not been extinguished   **12.006**
under s.3(2), i.e. within six years of the original theft, it is certain that an action can be brought in respect of the theft.

---

[12] See paras 2.015–2.024.
[13] Childs (1996) 47 N.I.L.Q. 98 at 104.
[14] Later cases on the relationship between these two sections include *Dobson v General Accident Fire and Life Assurance Corp.* [1990] 1 Q.B. 274, CA.
[15] The importance of the inclusion of blackmail is somewhat diminished by the fact that "goods" for the purposes of the Torts (Interference With Goods) Act 1977 do not include money: see s.2(2).
[16] 1980 Act s.4(1).

Title extinguished—thief still in possession

12.007　The position here is very unclear. Section 4(1) disapplies ss.2 and 3(1), but it also clearly contemplates that s.3(2) may apply, since it makes further provision for what happens in such a case. However, if s.3(2) can apply, it must follow that the owner's title can be extinguished even where the original thief remains in possession. On that basis, it is hard to see how the plaintiff can assert a proprietary claim to the goods against the thief—he cannot show that he has a better title than the thief. At the same time, s.4(1) expressly allows him to bring an action in respect of the theft. It is submitted that the only possible reconciliation of this conflict is that the plaintiff may bring an action for damages for conversion, but may not claim the return of the goods. It must be recognised that this result appears to conflict with the intention behind the introduction of these provisions at the time of the 1980 consolidation,[17] but the logic is clear.[18]

Theft from owner—subsequent conversion

12.008　Here the position depends upon whether the subsequent conversion is by way of a sale to a bona fide purchaser. If it is not, then it is disregarded for the purpose of applying ss.3(1) and 3(2)[19]; therefore the position is apparently the same as if the original thief were still in possession, except that, presumably, the action for damages can now be brought against the thief or against any person who has subsequently converted the goods. By contrast, where a person subsequently purchases the goods in good faith, neither that purchase, nor any subsequent dealing with the goods, is regarded as related to the original conversion. Consequently, time begins to run in favour of the innocent purchaser (and any subsequent purchaser). It must be observed, though, that it is only the purchase which is not related to the original conversion. It appears that the sale which corresponds to that purchase continues to be so related, so that the transaction does not set time running in favour of the person who sells to the innocent purchaser.

LIMITED INTERESTS IN GOODS

12.009　Section 3(2) speaks of a person's "title to the goods" being extinguished. The most natural application of this expression is to the case of the outright

---

[17] Limitation Amendment Act 1980 s.2.
[18] The position is to a limited effect altered by s.27A of the 1980 Act, inserted by Proceeds of Crime Act 2002 s.288. See para.27.034.
[19] 1980 Act s.4(3).

owner, but it is necessary to consider whether it extends also to persons with a limited interest in the goods, such as bailees, pawnees, pledgees and mortgagees. It may be said that strictly speaking none of these has title to the goods, but only a special property in them. However, the same pedantic approach might well lead to the conclusion that the outright owner does not have title to the goods but only title to the ownership of the goods. This would obviously leave s.3(2) without effect and clearly cannot be right. It is submitted that the matter can be satisfactorily resolved by holding that "title to the goods" means simply whatever title a particular person has. Thus, all the limited owners mentioned above are liable to have their limited title defeated in the circumstances mentioned in s.3(2) of the 1980 Act.

RELATIONSHIP WITH FRAUD

In *Eddis v Chichester Constable*[20] Goff J. had to consider the relationship **12.010** between the rules on conversion and the provisions in what is now s.32 of the 1980 Act, which operate to postpone the running of time in cases where, inter alia, the right of action is based on fraud or a material fact has been concealed by the defendant. Before 1939 the fraud of a person through whom the defendant claimed did not stop time from running in the defendant's favour in a case of conversion.[21] Nevertheless, Goff J. held that the changes in wording introduced by the 1939 Act reversed this rule, so that the plaintiff can rely on the fraud of a person through whom the defendant claims as well as on the fraud of the defendant himself. In this context, however, attention is drawn to the decision of Streatfield J. in *R.B. Policies at Lloyd's v Butler*,[22] which shows that in many cases of conversion no material fact will have been concealed from the plaintiff by the defendant, even where the plaintiff is unaware of a fact such as the whereabouts of the defendant.

RELATIONSHIP WITH ACKNOWLEDGMENT

Another problem with the rules on conversion concerns their relationship **12.011** with ss.29–31 of the 1980 Act,[23] which extend the limitation period in cases where the defendant makes some acknowledgment of the plaintiff's right of action. Examination of s.29 will show that there is no provision extending time in the case of an action to recover property which has been converted,

---

[20] [1969] 2 Ch. 345; see also para.20.036.
[21] [1969] 1 All E.R. 546 at 551.
[22] [1950] 1 K.B. 76. The case is more fully considered at para.20.009.
[23] These sections are fully considered in Ch.18.

and it must therefore follow that the right to recover converted property cannot be extended by acknowledgment. At the same time, s.29(5) allows the extension by acknowledgment of a right of action to recover any liquidated pecuniary claim. Consequently, where the value of converted property can be established with sufficient certainty to allow a liquidated claim, s.29 allows the right of action for damages to be extended, provided the acknowledgment complies with the requirements of s.30.

MORTGAGES OF PERSONAL PROPERTY

12.012 Section 20 of the 1980 Act contains provisions which apply to mortgages of personal property. Section 20(2) provides that no foreclosure action in respect of mortgaged personal property shall be brought more than 12 years after the accrual of the right to foreclose. This provision does not affect any other remedy which the mortgagee might have; in particular, any right to sue for the principal sum or any accrued interest thereon is governed by ss.20(5), (6) and (7) (see paras 13.063–13.066). However, it seems likely that the section applies only to actions by a mortgagee. Certainly, subss.(2) to (4) and (6) and (7), and possibly also (5) can by their terms only be relevant to an action by a mortgagee, and the more convincing interpretation seems to be that the section as a whole should be treated as being so limited[24]. Thus, where a mortgagor sues the mortgagee for failure to pay over the net proceeds of sale in full, s.20 cannot apply.

Accrual of right to foreclose

12.013 Section 20(2) goes on to provide that if the mortgagee is in possession of the mortgaged property at any time after the date on which the right to foreclose accrues, then the right to foreclose shall not be treated as accruing until that possession discontinues. In other words, the taking of possession by the mortgagee puts an end to the foreclosure action, and time starts to run afresh once the possession comes to an end. Further, s.20(3) provides that the right to foreclose on property subject to a mortgage shall not be deemed to accrue so long as the property in question comprises any future interest or life assurance policy which has not matured.

---

[24] *Brady v Natwest Bank* 24 February 2006, Unreported Recorder Males Q.C.

Ambit of section 20(2)

A conspicuous and curious point is that s.20(2) refers only to mortgaged **12.014** property—it makes no mention of property which is subject to any other form of charge. It is tempting to avoid the difficulties that this may pose by saying that the term "mortgaged property" means simply property which is subject to a charge. The obstacle in the way of this approach is that s.20(3) and (5) refer expressly to property subject to a mortgage "or other charge". In these circumstances it seems impossible to adopt the wide construction of "mortgaged property" in s.20(2). Therefore it appears that there is no time-limit provided by the Act for a foreclosure action in respect of personal property which is subject to any other form of charge than a mortgage. This is all the more peculiar in view of the fact that s.20(3) expressly postpones in certain circumstances[25] the accrual of the right to foreclose on property subject to a "mortgage or other charge". The interpretation suggested in this paragraph has the unfortunate effect of rendering the words "or other charge" in s.20(3) otiose, since on this view it is irrelevant when such a right accrues.

Other charges

It is submitted that for the purposes of s.20 other charges include liens, **12.015** pledges and charges arising from judgments and analogous statutory burdens.

ACTION FOR PRINCIPAL SUM

Section 20(1) provides that an action to recover any principal sum of money **12.016** secured by a mortgage or other charge shall not be brought after the expiry of 12 years from the date on which the right to receive the money accrued. The wording here is unusual in that the 1980 Act normally makes time run from the date on which the cause of action accrues. The difference of wording was considered by the Court of Appeal in *Doodes v Gotham*[26]. In that case a trustee in bankruptcy had obtained a charging order on the bankrupt's house. The question was whether the 12-year period ran from the date of the Order or from some later date when the trustee had a right to enforce the Order by sale. At first instance Lindsay J. had relied on *Hornsey Local Board v Monarch Investment Building Society*[27] as showing

---

[25] See para.13.076.
[26] [2006] EWCA Civ 1080 reversing Lindsay J. [2005] EWHC 2576 17 November 2005.
[27] (1889) 24 QBD 1 CA, 54 JP 391; see also para.14.034.

that there is a conceptual difference between "the date on which the cause of action accrued" and "the date on which the right to receive the sum of money accrued". The Court of Appeal distinguished *Hornsey* on the basis that in that case the only thing which prevented the Local Authority from having an immediate right to sue for the money was its own inaction in failing to apportion the sums due among the potential defendants. By contrast, in *Doodes v Gotham* there could be no right to receive the money until the sale took place, which depended on on order of the court.

12.017   In *Doodes v Gotham* the Court of Appeal also rejected arguments that a charge imposed under Insolvency Act 1986 s.313 was not a charge for the purposes of s.20(1) and that the trustee in bankruptcy's application for an order for sale was not an 'action' for the purposes of the Limitation Act 1980.

12.018   An action to recover the shortfall which remains after mortgaged property has been sold by the mortgagee remains an action to recover a sum of money due on a mortgage. English law classified the nature of the obligation for limitation purposes at the date when that obligation arises, and the claimant cannot change that classification by his own subsequent act.[28]

ACTION FOR ARREARS OF INTEREST

12.019   Section 20(5) provides that no action to recover arrears of interest payable in respect of any sum of money secured by a mortgage or other charge (or damages in respect of such arrears) shall be brought more than six years after the date on which the interest became due. This is so even where there is a covenant to pay interest, contained, for example, in a mortgage deed. Such a covenant would, of course, be a specialty, but s.20(5) must be regarded as a provision imposing a shorter period of limitation for the purposes of s.8(2) of the 1980 Act. The question of when such interest becomes due was considered by the Court of Appeal in *Barclays Bank v Walters*.[29] The defendants had obtained a secured business loan from the plaintiffs on terms requiring monthly repayments over five years. The loan agreement did not contain a clause making all outstanding sums payable in the event of failure to pay any instalment. The defendant was unable to keep up the instalment payments, and eventually the bank sued on the agreement. The question was whether the right to recover each instalment accrued immediately on the failure to pay (in which case some at least of the instalments would be time-barred) or only at the end of the five-year term (in which case all outstanding sums would still be recoverable). The Court of Appeal held that it was for the defendant to show that the loan agree-

---

[28] *West Bromwich Building Society v Wilkinson* [2005] UKHL 44; [2005] 4 All E.R. 97 HL.
[29] *The Times*, October 20, 1988, CA.

ment made the instalments recoverable immediately; the usual way of discharging this onus would be to point to a default clause in the contract. In the absence of such a clause it is unlikely that the defendant will be able to discharge the burden upon him, though the court appears to leave open the possibility of his doing so. In the present case that onus had not been discharged, and the plaintiffs were therefore able to recover all outstanding sums.

In principle the approach of the Court of Appeal in this case appears to be correct—the date of accrual of the right to receive the sums will depend upon the contract between the parties, though it is perhaps slightly odd that the burden of proof here was held to lie upon the defendant. The normal rule in limitations is surely that once the defendant pleads the statute it is for the plaintiff to show that the action is not barred.[30]

Bristol & West v Bartlett[31] resolved a longstanding question about the **12.020** limitation period in actions by mortgagees for the shortfall after a mortgaged property has been repossessed and sold. It was held that there is a six-year limitation period in respect of interest, but a 12-year limitation period for recovery of capital[32]. The time limit cannot be extended by arguing that there is an implied term that the whole sum outstanding becomes due to the mortgagee when the house is sold—there is a single obligation to repay, and time runs from the breach of the obligation, which will normally be the date of the last payment by the borrower (subject to any issues as to acknowledgement and part payment, as to which see Ch.20).[33]

Savings

Section 20(5) is subject to the further provision of s.20(6) and (7). Section **12.021** 20(6) deals with the situation where a prior mortgagee or incumbrancer (i.e. prior to the plaintiff in the action in question) has been in possession of the property charged. If the plaintiff brings an action within one year of the prior incumbrancer discontinuing possession, he may recover all the arrears which fell due during the prior incumbrancer's period of possession (or damages in respect of those arrears) even though the prior incumbrancer's period of possession exceeded six years. Section 20(7) applies where the property subject to the mortgage or charge comprises any future interest or life policy and it is a term of the mortgage that arrears of interest shall be treated as part of the principal sum of money secured by the mortgage or charge. In these circumstances interest shall not be treated for limitation

---

[30] See paras 21.010–21.013.
[31] [2002] 4 All ER 544 C.A.
[32] see also *Scottish Equitable v Thompson* [2003] EWCA Civ 211 [2003] HLR 48 C.A.
[33] *West Bromwich Building Society v Wilkinson and another* [2004] EWCA CIV 1063, [2004] All ER (D) 585 (Jul), CA.

purposes as becoming due before the right to recover the principal sum of money has accrued or is treated as having accrued.

Effect on redemption actions

12.022 Although the mortgagee cannot recover the arrears of interest once they are six years old, this is without prejudice to the rule that a mortgagor who wishes to redeem must pay all arrears of interest, including those which are statute-barred.[34]

EFFECT OF EXPIRY OF PERIOD

12.023 The 1980 Act speaks at various places (discussed in the preceding paragraphs) of precluding the bringing of certain actions to protect security interests after the lapse of specified periods of time. Two questions arise from this. The first is whether, in the case of rights to receive money, the expiry of the period extinguishes the right or merely bars the remedy. Secondly, whether the loss of the remedy for the security interest also puts an end to the security interest. So far as the former is concerned, there is no reason to depart from the general principle that expiry of time merely bars the remedy without extinguishing the right. Therefore, if the mortgagee can obtain the arrears of interest or the capital sum by some other means, he is entitled to retain them. Attention is also drawn to the rule, mentioned above,[35] that in the case of redemption, the mortgagee is entitled to all arrears, even those which are statute-barred. If this conclusion is right, there appears to be no reason to suggest that the expiry of the period will have any effect on the security interest, and it is submitted that this is in fact the position.

12.024 EU Directive 93/7 and the 1995 UNIDROIT Convention on the International Return of Stolen or Illegally Exported Cultural Objects make special provision in relation to objects of this type. Article 7 of the Directive provides a time-limit of 30 years after the object was unlawfully removed in which to bring proceedings, a period extended to 75 years in the case of objects forming part of public collections. The Directive, and in particular Art.7, has been given legislative force in this country in the Return of Cultural Objects Regulations 1994 (SI 1994/501), but it is to be noted that the Regulations apply only to cultural objects unlawfully removed from a territory of the Member State on or after January 1, 1993 (see reg.1(3)).

---

[34] *Edmunds v Waugh* (1866) L.R. 1 Eq. 418; *Holmes v Cowcher* [1970] 1 W.L.R. 834, Stamp J.; see paras 21.015 et seq., below.
[35] See para.12.015.

The UK did not give retrospective effect to the Regulations as it would have been entitled to do under Art.14(2) of the Directive.

THE LAW COMMISSION'S PROPOSALS

This difficult area receives special consideration in the Consultation Paper. **12.025** The Commission proposes that the core regime should apply to conversions not related to theft, and that the longstop should run from the date of the first conversion. In the case of conversions involving theft, the proposal is that, as at present, time should run only in favour of a bona fide purchaser, the limitation period being three years from the date of discoverability by the owner of the stolen property. The Commission raises as a further possibility the suggestion that discoverability in this specific context might be extended to include knowledge of the whereabouts of the property in addition to knowledge of the identity of the wrongdoer. This may be justified on the ground that without this knowledge the plaintiff might not know in which jurisdiction to bring proceedings against the defendant. It is further proposed that there should be no longstop in cases of theftuous conversion, and that where the plaintiff is seeking the recovery of stolen property the expiry of the limitation period should not extinguish the plaintiff's title.

CHAPTER 13

Real Property

This chapter covers the limitation problems that arise in relation to real **13.001** property. The relevant provisions are contained in ss.15–20 of the Limitation Act 1980, together with Sch.1 to the Act. These provisions differ from the majority of those considered in this work in that they provide that the expiry of the relevant limitation period shall extinguish the plaintiff's right rather than merely barring his remedy.[1] This is an illustration of the fundamental rule of the English law of real property that possession is the root of title to land. A person in possession is presumed to be the owner, unless someone else can show a better title. If the possession remains undisturbed for long enough, then it will become an absolute title, even if the possession was originally acquired wrongfully. A number of quite different topics are subsumed under this chapter, which covers both freehold and leasehold land, as well as the limitation rules relating to mortgages. For this reason the chapter is further subdivided into main headings.

LAND

Sections 15–18 of the 1980 Act set out a number of rules relating to periods **13.002** of limitation in different cases relating to land. These are considered below, but must be read subject to the effect of the Land Registration Act 2002.

The Land Registration Act 2002

This Act, which came into force on 13 October 2003 makes significant **13.003** changes to the limitation regime in relation to land. The underlying philosophy of the Act is to base all future land law and conveyancing practice around registered land. As part of that process, ss.96 and 97 of the Act will

---

[1] 1980 Act s.17; see further paras 2.024-2.025.

effectively replace ss.15 to 17 of the Limitation Act 1980.[2] By s.96, no period of limitation under s.15 shall run against any person, other than a chargee, in relation to an estate in land or rentcharge the title to which is registered. No period of limitation under s.16 shall run against any person in relation to such an estate in land or rentcharge and, consequently, s.17 shall not operate to extinguish the title of any person where, by virtue of s.96, a period of limitation does not run against him. Instead s.97 gives effect to the provisions of Sch.6 to the Act, which determine who may apply to be registered as an adverse possessor.

13.004   Schedule 6 provides that a person may apply to the registrar to be registered as the proprietor of a registered estate in land if he has been in adverse possession of the estate for the period of 10 years ending on the date of the application. A person may also apply to the registrar to be registered as the proprietor of a registered estate in land if he has in the period of six months ending on the date of the application ceased to be in adverse possession of the estate because of eviction by the registered proprietor, or a person claiming under the registered proprietor, on the day before his eviction he was entitled to make an application to be registered, and the eviction was not pursuant to a judgment for possession. However, a person may not make an application if he is a defendant in proceedings which involve asserting a right to possession of the land, or judgment for possession of the land has been given against him in the last two years. The remainder of Sch.6 contains further detailed provisions for the conduct of applications to be registered.

13.005   The new rules make significant changes in this area of the law. The limitation period is reduced to 10 years, but the expiry of that period does not bar the rights of the holder of the paper title; rather, it will merely give the squatter the right to apply to be registered. Until that registration is affected, the rights of the holder of the paper title will not be affected. However, the concepts of dispossession and discontinuance are not affected by the new legislation—it is only the length of the limitation period and the consequences of its expiry which change.

Definition

13.006   "Land" for the purposes of the Limitation Act is partly defined in s.38(1) of the 1980 Act, which provides that the term includes corporeal hereditaments, tithes and rent charges and any legal or equitable estate or interest therein, including an interest in the proceeds of sale of land held on trust for sale, but does not otherwise include any incorporeal hereditament.

---

[2] *See Overseas and Commericial Developments Ltd v Cox*, April 25, 2002, CA, Unreported.

Action to recover land

Section 15(1) provides that no action to recover land shall be brought after **13.007** the expiry of 12 years from the date on which the right of action accrued to the plaintiff, or, if the plaintiff claims through some other person, to that person. By s.38(7) of the Act, references to a right of action to recover land include references to a right to enter into possession of the land, or, in the case of rent charges and tithes, to distrain for arrears of rent or tithe, and references to the bringing of such an action shall include references to the making of such an entry or distress. Therefore, in those situations where the right to bring an action to recover land is said to be barred, the right to enter into possession or to distrain for arrears is similarly barred. An "action" for these purposes does not include an application to the Land Registry,[3] and an action to recover land does not include an action by which the claimant does not seek to recover land, but merely seeks, for example, to warn off cautions against the land.[4]

Future interests

Section 15(2) provides for a limitation period in certain cases relating to **13.008** future interests in land. Where the right of action to claim any future interest accrues on the date on which the estate or interest fell into possession by the determination of the preceding estate or interest and the person entitled to the preceding estate or interest (not being a term of years absolute) was not in possession of the land on that date, the limitation period expires on the later of two alternative dates. The first is 12 years from the date on which the right of action accrued to the person entitled to the preceding estate or interest, and the second is six years from the date on which the right of action accrued to the person entitled to the succeeding estate or interest.[5] Thus in the case of settled land (within the meaning of the Settled Land Act 1925) if the tenant for life is dispossessed of the land, the right of the remainderman to sue for possession becomes barred 12 years after the date on which the tenant for life is dispossessed or six years after the date on which the life interest comes to an end, whichever is the later. This provision does not apply to any estate or interest which falls into possession on the determination of an entailed interest, and which might have been barred by the person entitled to the entailed interest.[6]

[3] *JA Pye (Oxford) Ltd v Graham* [2000] 3 W.L.R. 242, Neuberger J.
[4] *JA Pye (Oxford) Ltd v Graham* [2000] 3 W.L.R. 242, Neuberger J.
[5] As to the date of accrual, see below, paras 13.011–13.013.
[6] 1980 Act s.15(3).

Assurances

13.009 Section 15(4) relates to actions to recover any interest or estate in land under an assurance. If the assurance takes effect after the right of action has accrued to the person making the assurance, or to some person through whom he claims, or to some person entitled to a preceding estate or interest, the action must be brought within the period that would have been applicable to an action brought by the person who made the assurance. Thus the making of the assurance cannot be used as a way of extending the limitation period. In dealing with assurances it is necessary to allude also to s.27 of the 1980 Act. This relates to defective disentailing assurances. Where a person entitled in remainder to an entailed interest in any land makes an assurance of his interest which fails to bar the entailed interest, or which purports to bar other interests, then, under the Fines and Recoveries Act 1833, the assurance is ineffective to pass any title to the person in whose favour it is made. Problems may then arise if that person enters into possession of the land pursuant to the assurance. Section 27 deals with this situation by providing that the assurance shall be treated as being and having always been effective to bar the entail and transfer the interest once the person in whose favour it was made has been in possession for a period of 12 years after the earliest time at which the maker of the assurance could validly have disposed of his interest in the land without the consent of any other person.[7] Generally, this date will arrive only when the maker of the assurance has an interest in possession in the land.

Double entitlement

13.010 Where a person is entitled to an interest or estate in land in possession, and is simultaneously entitled to a future interest in that land, s.15(5) applies. It provides that such a person (or someone claiming through him) shall not bring an action in respect of the future estate or interest unless in the meantime possession of the land has been recovered by a person entitled to an intermediate estate or interest. The limitation period applicable in the case of future interests, explained at paras 13.011–13.018, cannot be used here unless the plaintiff has been dispossessed in the interim period.

Date of accrual

13.011 The rule laid down by s.15(1) makes it vital to determine in any given case when the cause of action for the recovery of land accrues. Some guidance

---

[7] See s.27(3).

on this point is given by the provisions of Sch.1 to the Act. These provisions are considered in the following paragraphs.

Accrual in case of present interests

Paragraphs 1–3 of Sch.1 to the 1980 Act deal with present interests in land. Where the person bringing the action (or some person through whom he claims) has been in possession of the land and has, while entitled to the land, been dispossessed or has discontinued his possession, the right of action shall be treated as having accrued on the date of the dispossession or discontinuance.[8] This is much the most common case. The vital concepts of dispossession and discontinuance are examined below at paras 13.025–13.041. **13.012**

Where an action is brought to recover land of a deceased person and the deceased was at the date of his death in possession of the land or, in the case of a rentcharge created by will or taking effect upon his death, in possession of the land charged, and was the last person entitled to be in possession of it, the right of action shall be treated as having accrued on the date of his death.[9] **13.013**

Where an action is brought to recover land, in respect of an estate or interest in land assured to the plaintiff (or to some person through whom he claims) otherwise than by will, the cause of action is treated as having accrued on the date when the assurance took effect, so long as the following two conditions are satisfied. First, that the person making the assurance was on the date when the assurance took effect in possession of the land (or in the case of a rentcharge created by the assurance, in possession of the land charged). Secondly, that no person has been in possession of the land by virtue of the assurance.[10] Where these conditions are not satisfied it is necessary to have recourse to the other provisions of the Act. If the person making the assurance was not in possession, then the right of action will already have accrued, and time will run from that accrual. Once any person has been in possession by virtue of the assurance, any pre-existing claim to possession under the assurance will thereby have become extinguished. A subsequent dispossession or discontinuance will create a new right of action, in respect of which time will run from the date of the dispossession or discontinuance.

---

[8] Sch.1, para.1.
[9] Sch.1, para.2.
[10] Sch.1, para.3.

Accrual in case of future interests in land

13.014   Where the estate or interest claimed in an action to recover land is a future interest and no person has taken possession of the land by virtue of the estate or interest claimed, the cause of action is treated as having accrued on the date on which the estate or interest fell into possession by the determination of the preceding estate or interest.[11] Presumably, although the statute does not say so, if some person has taken possession by virtue of estate or interest in question, the cause of action accrues on the taking of that possession, if it was wrongful, and on its termination (whether by discontinuance or dispossession), if it was lawful.

Tenants and licensees

13.015   What is a lease? In *Long v Tower Hamlets London BC*[12] it was held that for the purposes of Sch.1, para.5(1) to the 1980 Act a "lease" must be a dispositive document. In other words it must create, in and of itself, a legal interest in the land. It is not sufficient that it merely evidences an existing lease. In the case in question the tenancy document was not executed as a deed, and could therefore create a legal estate in land only if it complied with s.54 of the Law of Property Act 1925. To do this it had to be a lease taking effect in possession for a period not exceeding three years. However, the lease in this case conferred no immediate right to possession, and was therefore not a lease "taking effect in possession". The document was therefore of no legal effect. However, as the tenant had entered possession and was paying rent, a common law periodic tenancy arose. The case illustrates the importance in a limitation context of identifying exactly the nature of the rights of the occupier of the land.

Tenancies from year to year

13.016   The basic rule here is that a tenancy from year to year or other period, without a lease in writing, shall be treated for limitation purposes as having determined at the end of the first year or other period.[13] There is an exception to this general rule where any rent has been received in respect of the tenancy after the expiry of that period. In such cases the cause of action is treated as having accrued on the date of the last receipt of rent. Therefore, if the tenancy continues for a number of periods after the expiry of the first period, a fresh cause of action will accrue (so that time will start to run afresh) every time a payment of rent is made. The statutory rules are clumsily worded, but the effect which they seek to achieve is reasonably clear. So long as the tenant goes on paying rent, time does not run in his

---

[11] Sch.1, para.4.
[12] [1996] 2 All E.R. 683, James Munby QC.
[13] Sch.1, para.5(1).

favour, but once payment ceases, time begins to run. It follows that if no payment is made for a period of 12 years, and the tenant continues in possession throughout that period, the effect will be to bar the freehold title.[14] This rule applies even where the occupier has ceased to pay rent with the permission of the landlord[15] and where the adverse possessor is under the mistaken impression that he is in fact paying rent.[16]

Tenancies at will

The principle stated in the previous paragraph applies also to the creation of tenancies at will. In *Hughes v Griffin*[17] the deceased had in 1951 conveyed his house to his nephew, the plaintiff, but had continued to live in it rent free with the nephew's consent. This consent was reiterated in conversations in 1959 and 1960. The deceased died in 1965, and the plaintiff sought an order for possession against his widow, who pleaded 12 years' adverse possession. The Court of Appeal rejected this defence, holding that the conversations in 1959 and 1960 had created new tenancies at will, so that a new period of adverse possession could not start until the expiry of one year from these conversations. A further point of some practical importance in this connection is illustrated by the decision of the Court of Appeal in *Foster v Robinson*,[18] where it was held that an agreement between landlord and tenant to vary the terms of a lease could (but did not necessarily) amount to a surrender of the lease by operation of law coupled with the grant of a new lease.

13.017

Licensees

The position is different in the case of a mere licensee, for time can never run in his favour.[19] It may therefore be essential to distinguish between a tenant at will and a mere licensee, as is shown by the case of *Palfrey v Palfrey*.[20] Prior to 1928 the defendant had held the house on a weekly tenancy. In 1928 the then owner made an oral gift of it to her, and thereafter she paid no rent. In 1930 the house was conveyed to the plaintiff, though neither the plaintiff nor the defendant was aware of this at the time, and the defendant continued in possession until 1968. The question was whether she had obtained good title, and this in turn depended upon whether the defendant had remained in possession under the tenancy or whether she had become a licensee upon the oral gift of the house to her.

13.018

---

[14] *Hayward v Chaloner* [1968] 1 Q.B. 107, CA.
[15] *Moses v Lovegrove* [1952] 2 Q.B. 533; *Price v Hartley (Deceased)*, May 1, 1995, CA, Unreported. See also *Williams v Jones*, July 10, 2002, CA, Unreported.
[16] *Lodge v Wakefield MDC* [1995] 38 E.G. 136, [1995] 2 E.G.L.R. 127, CA.
[17] [1969] 1 W.L.R. 23, CA; for the other points in this case see below, para.13.029.
[18] [1951] 1 K.B. 149.
[19] *Heslop v Burns* [1974] 1 W.L.R. 1241, CA.
[20] (1973) 229 E.G. 648, CA.

The Court of Appeal held that she had continued to be a tenant, apparently on the basis that it was impossible to imply a licence when she had been told that the house was hers. Consequently, she had been a person in whose favour time could run, and had acquired a good title.

13.019   The obvious difficulty with this reasoning is that the obstacle to finding that there was a licence appears to apply equally to finding that there was a tenancy—the parties clearly did not intend either relationship; they presumably intended that the defendant should have the fee simple, and the law is left to deal with the implications on these facts of the rule that oral conveyances of freehold interests are ineffective. It is nevertheless submitted that the decision is correct, though for slightly different reasons. The purported oral conveyance must surely take effect as a declaration of trust in respect of the freehold interest. The original lease must be regarded as having been surrendered by mutual agreement, and, in the absence of any intention to create a licence, the law will imply a tenancy at will. Admittedly, this too is not what the parties decided, but it does at least have the merit of producing the effect which they would have wished without departing from the conceptual framework of English law. It is necessarily a question of fact whether a licence has been granted, but as a general point may be observed that a court is more likely to be prepared to find the grant of an informal licence between members of the same family.[21]

Implied licence

13.020   Where a person takes possession of land and then offers to buy it, the question may arise whether their possession during a period of negotiation is with the owner's consent so as to prevent time from running. There are three cases in which this argument has been considered. *B.P. properties v Buckler* concerned an express licence, which was held to prevent time from running. In *Bath & North Somerset DC v Nicholson*[22] and again in *Colin Dawson Windows Ltd v Borough Council of King's Lynn & West Norfolk*[23] implied licences were held to have the same effect. In the last of these cases Rix LJ commented[24] that in order to establish an effective licence two conditions must be satisfied:

> "First there must have been some overt act by the landowner or some demonstrable circumstances from which the inference can be drawn that permission was in fact given. Secondly, that a reasonable person would

---

[21] *Straham v Doxey*, November 21, 1994, CA, Unreported.
[22] 22 February 2002, Unreported Kim Lewison QC.
[23] [2005] EWCA Civ 09, [2005] 2 P&CR 333.
[24] At para.34.

have appreciated that the user was with the permission of the landowner".

Possession under agreement for lease

In *Warren v Murray*[25] the defendants were in possession of land pursuant **13.021** to an agreement for a lease from the plaintiffs, who were the owners. No lease was ever executed, and it became necessary to decide whether the defendants were in adverse possession. The Court of Appeal held that they were not. They could at any time have obtained specific performance of the lease agreement. Consequently, their possession was lawful, and time could not run in their favour. Paragraph 6 of Sch.1 deals with the situation where rent is paid to a person other than the person entitled to it. If the rent reserved by the lease (which for the purposes of this paragraph must be in writing) is at least £10 a year, then the cause of action by the lessor for the recovery of the land is treated as accruing on the date when rent is first received by the person wrongfully claiming to be entitled to it. Paragraph 6 has no application to any lease granted by the Crown. In those cases of leases to which this paragraph does not apply, it appears that time will run from the date on which the lease is determined. The paragraph adds the further requirement that no rent be subsequently received by the person rightfully entitled to it. The effect of this is unclear. It may be that where rent is so received after a wrongful payment, the disapplication of the paragraph requires the cause of action to be treated as accruing on the date of the termination of the lease. Therefore, this would be the date of accrual for all actions in respect of wrongful payments which are followed by rightful payments. Only the final wrongful payment (i.e. that which was never followed by a rightful payment) would create a cause of action accruing on the date of the receipt of the wrongful payment.[26] In *Sandhu v Farooqui*[27] the defendant had been allowed into possession pending completion of a sale of the property to her. Within a few months it became apparent that the sale would not proceed, though there was no communication between the parties about this. Thereafter the defendant remained in possession and subsequently asserted a squatter's title on the basis that her licence to occupy had been implicitly terminated once it became apparent that the sale would not proceed. The Court of Appeal rejected this argument, holding that there must be at least some communication from which the termination of the licence could be deduced. It is submitted that this is somewhat formalistic. There might well be cases (though this was

---

[25] [1894] 2 Q.B. 648, CA.
[26] On payment of rent, see paras 13.082-13.083.
[27] [2003] EWCA Civ 531.

not necessarily one of them) where termination could properly be inferred without the need for formal communication.

Forfeiture and breach of condition

13.022 A right of action to recover land by virtue of a forfeiture or breach of condition is, in general, treated as accruing when the forfeiture is incurred or the condition broken.[28] The exception to this general rule occurs where the right has accrued to a person entitled in reversion or remainder and the land has not been recovered by virtue of that right. In such cases the right is not treated as accruing to that person until his estate or interest has fallen into possession, as if no such breach or forfeiture had occurred.[29] The words of the last clause are puzzling, since this provision would make perfect sense without them. Presumably the intention is to make abundantly clear that the forfeiture or breach is ignored until the interest falls into possession.

Relevance of adverse possession

13.023 Paragraph 8 of Sch.1 is a provision of extreme importance in this context. Paragraph 8(1) provides that the cause of action shall not be treated as accruing unless the land is in the possession of some person in whose favour the period of limitation can run (a state of affairs referred to in the statute as "adverse possession"). All the provisions of Sch.1 which have so far been discussed must be read subject to this rule, for, even if all the requirements for a cause of action have been satisfied, none can accrue until adverse possession is taken of the land.

Interruption of adverse possession

13.024 Where adverse possession is interrupted by the rightful owner[30] after having started, the cause of action for the recovery of the land is no longer treated as having accrued. Nor is it treated as having accrued again until there is again some person in adverse possession of the land.[31] In principle, the rightful owner or a subsequent squatter will need to show that the squatter has himself discontinued possession or has been dispossessed. For the purposes of this provision, possession subject to a rentcharge (other than by the person entitled to the rentcharge) without paying that rentcharge is adverse possession, as is receipt of rent under a lease by a person wrongly

---

[28] Sch.1, para.7.
[29] Sch.1, para.7(2).
[30] *Mount Carmel Investments Ltd v Peter Thurlow Ltd* [1988] 1 W.L.R. 1078, CA.
[31] Sch.1, para.8(2).

claiming to be entitled to the interest immediately expectant upon the determination of the lease.[32] In *Moses v Lovegrove*[33] it was held that adverse possession, which had begun in 1939 by nonpayment of rent on a de-controlled dwelling, was not interrupted by wartime legislation in 1939 which altered the status of the dwelling so that the rent became controlled. In *Mount Carmel Investments Ltd v Peter Thurlow Ltd*[34] the plaintiff's solicitors wrote a letter to the squatter requiring him to give up possession within 28 days. The Court of Appeal held that this by itself could not be sufficient to interrupt the wrongful possession. As the squatter did not give up possession, time continued to run in his favour. Similarly, in *Markfield Investments Ltd v Evans*[35] unsuccessful legal proceedings aimed at regaining possession of the land did not interrupt the squatter's possession.

Successive squatters

In *Mount Carmel Investments Ltd v Peter Thurlow Ltd*[36] the Court of Appeal had to consider the legal position where the rightful owner is dispossessed by one squatter, who in turn transfers possession to another squatter. The total period of wrongful possession in this case exceeded 12 years, and the second squatter claimed to have acquired a title by possession. The Court of Appeal upheld this claim. It may be of significance that here the first squatter had abandoned his claim to the land—he had voluntarily transferred his interest in it to the second squatter and had left the country. The position where the first squatter is involuntarily dispossessed by the second is less clear. It is submitted that the decision in *Mount Carmel* does not directly govern such a case; as against the first squatter, the second squatter is entitled to count only the period of his own possession, though as against the rightful owner the total period of that owner's dispossession may be counted.

13.025

Meaning of adverse possession

This is an area which has altered very significantly in recent years. It is the subject of a mass of authority, some of it conflicting. Paragraph 8 of Sch.1 to the 1980 Act also contains some limited guidance on particular difficult cases. Essentially, adverse possession can occur where either of two requirements is satisfied. One is that there shall have been dispossession; the

13.026

---

[32] Sch.1, para.8(3).
[33] [1952] 2 Q.B. 533, CA.
[34] [1988] 1 W.L.R. 1078, CA.
[35] [2001] 2 All E.R. 238, CA.
[36] [1988] 1 W.L.R. 1078, CA.

other is that there shall have been discontinuance of possession by the rightful owner. In *Buckinghamshire CC v Moran*[37] Slade L.J. said:

" . . . the difference between the dispossession and the discontinuance of possession might be expressed in this way—the one is where a person comes in and drives out the others from possession, the other case is where the person in possession goes out and is followed into possession by other persons."[38]

He went on to say:

"If the law is to attribute possession of land to a person who can establish no paper title to possession, he must be shown to have both factual possession and the requisite intention to possess (animus possidendi). A person claiming to have 'dispossessed' another must similarly fulfil both these requirements. However, a further requirement which the alleged dispossessor claiming the benefit of the Act of 1980 must satisfy is to show that his possession has been 'adverse' within the meaning of the Act."

13.027   The nature of these two statements requires further analysis, but three preliminary points should be made. The first is that there can be no adverse possession where a person is in possession of the land with the consent of the rightful owner.[39] To put this another way, time will not run unless the rightful owner could succeed in an action for possession against the person currently in possession.[40]

Secondly, there can be adverse possession, and therefore eventually the acquisition of title, even against an owner who has no power to alienate the land, such as a charity.[41] Thirdly, it is generally quite irrelevant that the rightful owner does not realise that he has been dispossessed. Therefore, in *Rains v Buxton*[42] the plaintiff had dispossessed the defendant of a cellar under the defendant's land, but the defendant did not immediately discover this. Fry J. held that in the absence of fraud, of which there was no evidence here, time ran from the dispossession, not from the discovery of the dispossession.

---

[37] [1990] 1 Ch. 623; [1989] 2 All E.R. 225.
[38] Quoting from Fry J. in *Rains v Buxton* [1880] 14 Ch.D. 537.
[39] *Hughes v Griffin* [1969] 1 W.L.R. 23, CA; see also para.13.014.
[40] *Smith v Lawson* (1998) 75 P. & C.R. 466, CA.
[41] *Midland Railway Co. v Wright* [1901] 1 Ch. 738, Byrne J.
[42] (1880) 14 Ch.D. 537, Fry J. See also *Wilson v Martin* [1993] 24 E.G. 119, CA.

Relevance of intention

In *Powell v McFarlane*[43] it was held that the concept of possession implies   **13.028**
both occupation and a certain animus possidendi. In a passage that has
come to be regarded as the foundation of the modern law in this area, Slade
L.J. said[44]:

> "Factual possession signifies an appropriate degree of physical control. It
> must be a single and conclusive[45] possession, though there can be a single
> possession exercised by or on behalf of several persons jointly. Thus an
> owner of land and a person intruding on that land without his consent
> cannot both be in possession of the land at the same time. The question
> what acts constitute a sufficient degree of exclusive physical control must
> depend on the circumstances, in particular the nature of the land and the
> manner in which land of that nature is commonly used or enjoyed . . .
> Whether or not acts of possession done on parts of an area establish title
> of the whole area must, however, be a matter of degree . . . Everything
> must depend on the particular circumstances, but broadly, I think what
> must be shown as constituting factual possession is that the alleged
> possessor has been dealing with the land in question as an occupying
> owner might have been expected to deal with it and that no one else has
> done so."

In the same case it was said that the necessary animus possidendi is the   **13.029**
intention to exclude the whole world so far as practicable.[46] In *Colchester
BC v Tillson*[47] it was held that animus possidendi involves only an intention
to possess. It is not necessary to show intention to own or to acquire
ownership. By extension, dispossession implies taking possession from
another, and doing so with the necessary intention. However, in *Hughes v
Cork*[48] the plaintiff and his predecessors in title had been in possession of
the disputed land for many years under the honest belief that they owned it.
It was argued for the holders of the paper title that there could be no
intention to dispossess on the part of a person who thought he already
owned the land. Beldam L.J. said:

> "The fallacy in [counsel's] argument lies in the failure to distinguish
> between an intention to possess, which is required, and an intention to
> dispossess, which is not."

---

[43] (1979) 38 P. & C.R. 462, Slade J.
[44] (1979) 38 P. & C.R. at 470.
[45] This is usually understood to be a misprint for "exclusive"—*Burns v Anthony*, July 15, 1997, CA, Unreported.
[46] See also *Wilson v Martin* [1993] 24 E.G. 1119, CA.; *Prudential Assurance Co. Ltd v Waterloo Real Estate Inc.* January 22, 1999, CA.
[47] [1991] 2 All E.R. 29, Ferris J. affirmed on a different ground [1992] Ch. 421, CA.
[48] February 14, 1994, CA (Civil Division), Unreported.

13.030   This observation can be reconciled with Colchester *BC v Tillson* on the basis that the necessary intention to is hold the land to the exclusion of others, but that it does not matter whether the plaintiff thinks that he holds it as a squatter or as the rightful owner. Thus, in *Lodge v Wakefield MCC*[49] it was held that the belief of the person in possession that he was there as a tenant and that he was in fact paying rent, though on the facts he had stopped paying rent, was not sufficient to negate the necessary intention to possess. But there is no absolute rule about this. In *J.A. Pye (Oxford) Ltd v Graham*[50] it was held that a squatter who orally communicated that he was prepared to take a licence or tenancy of the land he occupied acknowledged the ability of the owner to reclaim possession if he chose, but this was not inconsistent with the squatter being in actual possession or having the requisite intention to possess the land. A willingness to accept a licence may, depending on the circumstances, show that the squatter lacked the requisite intention to possess but was not conclusive. In *Rhondda Cynon Taff BC v Watkins*[51] it was held, obviously correctly, that a freeholder who dispossesses his tenant can begin to acquire a possessory title against that tenant since he is in possession wrongfully. In *Williams v Jones*[52] it was held that an ex-tenant who holds over after the end of the lease does not have to satisfy the *Powell v McFarlane* requirements as to adverse possession because the freeholder had allowed the tenant into possession, and he would normally continue in possession. In *Palfrey v Wilson*[53] the Court of Appeal commented that in deciding whether adverse possession is established in a particular case the judge's task was to consider the whole of the evidence and evaluate it with a view to deciding whether the defendants had satisfied the five conditions to establish adverse possession (namely (i) having possession (ii) which had to be exclusive (iii) and dispossessed the paper owner (iv) with the intention to possess (v) adversely in the sense of ss.15(1) and 17 of the Limitation Act 1980 and paras 1 and 8(1) of Sch.1 to the Act) a holistic approach is required. The judge is not required to fine-slice each and every event and assess its individual merit.

13.031   The *Powell v McFarlane* criteria were authoritatively reviewed by the House of Lords in *JA Pye (Oxford) Ltd v Graham*.[54] Their Lordships held that for the purposes of the 1980 Act the words "possession" and "dispossession" bore their ordinary meaning. Thus "possession" involves a sufficient degree of occupation or physical control coupled with an intention to possess and "dispossession" occurred where the squatter assumed "possession" as so understood; but that it is wrong to suggest that the

---

[49] [1995] 38 E.G. 136; [1995] 2 E.G.L.R. 127; see also Louise Tee, *Adverse Possession and the Intention to Possess* (2000) 64 Conv. 113.
[50] July 4, 2002, HL, Unreported.
[51] [2003] EWCA Civ 129.
[52] [2002] EWCA Civ 1097, [2002] 40 EG 169.
[53] [2007] EWCA Civ 94.
[54] [2002] UKHL 30, [2003] 1 AC 419.

squatter is required to oust or exclude the paper title owner as well as all others or to act inconsistently with his user or adversely towards him. "Adverse possession" for these purposes refers not to the nature of the possession but to the capacity of the squatter. A squatter establishes adverse possession by showing absence of the paper owner's consent, a single and exclusive possession and such acts as demonstrated that in the circumstances, in particular the nature of the land and the way it was commonly used, he had dealt with it as an occupying owner might normally be expected to do and that no other person had done so; that the requisite intention was, not to own or acquire ownership, but to possess and on one's own behalf in one's own name to exclude the world at large, including the paper title owner, so far as was reasonably possible, and that it was not, therefore, inconsistent for a squatter to be willing, if asked, to pay the paper title owner while being in possession in the meantime.[55]

In *JA Pye (Oxford) Ltd v United Kingdom*[56] the European Court of Human Rights considered a question of fundamental importance to the English law of limitation of actions, namely whether the rule that title to land can be lost after 12 years of adverse possession is compatible with the European Convention on Human Rights. The more general Human Rights implications of this question and of the decision of the Court are considered in Ch.28. This paragraph will deal with the specific land law issues. This was a case where in the domestic courts[57] the dispute had been about whether there had been the necessary animus possidendi to amount to dispossession of the paper title holder. The applicants before the ECHR were the paper title holders, who had lost before the House of Lords, and who argued that the taking away of ownership of their land because of 12 years' adverse possession upset the fair balance required by art.1 of the First Protocol to the Convention for the Protection of Human Rights and Fundamental Freedoms and was a disproportionate interference with their property rights. Thus they made a fundamental attack on the statutory regime by which title was extinguished at the end of the limitation period without compensation rather than the manner of execution of the law by the courts. The Chamber ((2005) 19 BHRC 705) held that there had been a violation of art.1 of the First Protocol and the application was therefore referred to the Grand Chamber, which, by a majority, held that an interference with the right to the peaceful enjoyment of possessions had to strike a 'fair balance' between the demands of the general interest of the community and the requirements of the protection of the individual's fundamental rights. In enforcing such laws as states deemed necessary to control the use of property in accordance with the general interest, there had also to

13.032

---

[55] *Disapproving R v Secretary of State for the Environment, Ex p Davies* (1990) 61 P & CR 487, CA.
[56] App No 4403/02 (2007) 23 BHRC 405.
[57] *Sub nom JA Pye (Oxford) Ltd v Graham.*

exist a reasonable relationship of proportionality between the means employed and the aim sought to be realised. In that respect, states enjoyed a wide margin of appreciation with regard both to choosing the means of enforcement and to ascertaining whether the consequences of enforcement were justified in the general interest for the purpose of achieving the object of the law in question. In spheres such as housing, the legislature's judgment as to what was in the general interest would be respected unless that judgment was manifestly without reasonable foundation. Even though the general position in English law was that the expiry of a limitation period barred the remedy but not the right, where an action for recovery of land was statute-barred, termination of the title of the paper owner did little more than regularise the respective positions, namely to confirm that the person who had acquired title by 12 years' adverse possession was the owner. Moreover, the law reflected the aim of the land registration legislation, which was to replicate the pre-registration law so far as practicable. Such a regime could not be considered as manifestly without reasonable foundation. The interference with the applicant companies' possessions was a control of use, rather than a deprivation of possessions. A requirement of compensation for the situation brought about by a party failing to observe a limitation period would sit uneasily alongside the very concept of limitation periods, whose aim was to further legal certainty by preventing a party from pursuing an action after a certain date. Furthermore, the applicant companies were not without procedural protection. While the limitation period was running, and if they failed to agree terms with Mr and Mrs G which put an end to the adverse possession, it was open to them to remedy the position by bringing a court action for re-possession of the land. Such an action would have stopped time running. After expiry of the period, it remained open to the applicant companies to argue before the domestic courts, as they did, that the occupiers of their land had not been in 'adverse possession' as defined by domestic law. In addition the registered land regime in the UK was a reflection of a long-established system in which a term of years' possession gave sufficient title to sell. Such arrangements fell within the state's margin of appreciation, unless they gave rise to results which were so anomalous as to render the legislation unacceptable. The acquisition of unassailable rights by the adverse possessor had to go hand in hand with a corresponding loss of property rights for the former owner. Any windfall for Mr and Mrs G did not affect the overall assessment of the proportionality of the legislation. As to the loss for the applicant companies, it was not disputed that the land lost by them would have been worth a substantial sum of money. However, limitation periods, if they were to fulfil their purpose, had to apply regardless of the size of the claim. The value of the land could not therefore be of any consequence to the outcome of the instant case. Accordingly the fair balance required by art.1 of the First Protocol to the Convention was not upset. It followed that there had been no violation of art.1 of the First Protocol. It is submitted that this is an eminently sensible resolution of the issues in this case. It is of course true that the taking away of the title of the paper title holder is a serious step—and of course in this regard ss.15 and 17 have a feature not found in other areas of limitation law, where the expiry of time generally does not extinguish rights, merely barring access to judicial remedies.

The effect of the decision of the ECHR in *Pye v United Kingdom*[58] was **13.033** considered in *Ofulue v Bossert*[59] where the Court held firstly that English courts should follow that decision. It is hard to see how any other conclusion could have been reached on that point. Section 2(1) of the Human Rights Act 1998 provides that:

"A court or tribunal determining a question which has arisen in connection with a Convention right must take into account any—

(a) judgment. . .of the [Strasbourg court]. . .

whenever made or given, so far as, in the opinion of the court or tribunal, it is relevant to the proceedings in which that question has arisen."

So, if a party asserts that a Convention right is engaged, the court must "take into account" Strasbourg jurisprudence. The House of Lords has held that, save in special circumstances "the duty of national courts under s.2 of the Human Rights Act 1998 is to keep pace with Strasbourg jurisprudence as it unfolds over time: no more but certainly no less."[60] The Court of Appeal court would therefore need very good reasons for departing from Strasbourg jurisprudence, for example if the domestic court was satisfied that the Strasbourg court had misunderstood the effect of domestic law. No such reasons existed here.

On the substantive point in the case it was held that a claim for title by adverse possession is not defeated by the fact that at one point the squatters had acknowledged the freehold title of the paper title holder. They had not, on the facts, admitted that the paper title holder was entitled to possession of property (because they had claimed to have a tenancy). Thus they were in possession with the intention to possess, as required by the decision in *Pye v Graham*.[61]

The tests laid down in *Powell* and in *Pye* (in the House of Lords) were **13.034** restated by the Court of Appeal in *Topplan Estates Ltd v Townley*[62]. The term "adverse" in the expression "adverse possession" refers not to the quality of the possession but to the capacity of the party claiming possessory title ("the squatter") as being a person in whose favour the period of

---

[58] Discussed at para.28.037.
[59] [2008] EWCA Civ 7; *The Times* 13 March 2009 H.L. [2009] UKHL 16.
[60] (per Lord Bingham in *R (Ullah) v Special Adjudicator* [2004] 2 AC 323, 350).
[61] [2003] 1 AC 419.
[62] [2004] EWCA Civ 1369, [2004] New Property Cases 158 per Parker L.J.; see also *Wretham v Ross* [2005] EWHC 1259 (Ch), David Richards J.

limitation can run. It does not connote any element of aggression, hostility or subterfuge nor does it throw any light on the question whether the squatter is in possession of the land (*ibid*.). The word "possession" in the expression "adverse possession" means no more than "ordinary possession of the land." In order to establish possession in this context, the squatter must prove (a) sufficient objective acts to constitute physical possession ("factual possession") coupled with (b) an intention to possess (animus possidendi). Occupation of the land alone is not enough, nor is an intention to occupy which is not put into effect by action. An intention to possess must be distinguished from an intention to own: it is only the former which is relevant in the context of adverse possession. An intention to possess may be, and frequently is, deduced from the objective acts of physical possession. However, where the acts relied on as objective acts of physical possession are equivocal, further evidence of intention may be required. An intention to possess means, in this context, "an intention to occupy and use the land as one's own". It is not necessary for the squatter to establish that he had a deliberate intention to exclude the true owner. It is enough that he intends to exclude the owner "as best he can". The intention to possess must be manifested to the true owner, but where the objective acts of physical possession are clear and unequivocal, those acts themselves will generally consititute a sufficient manifestation of the intention to possess. As to factual possession the question what acts constitute a sufficient degree of exclusive physical control must depend on the circumstances, in particular the nature of the land and the manner in which land of that nature is commonly used or enjoyed. In general, therefore, a squatter will establish factual possession if he can show that he used the land in the way one would expect him to use it if he were the true owner and in such a way that the owner is excluded

Presumption of possession

13.035   In the absence of evidence to the contrary, the person holding the paper title to land will be presumed to be in possession.[63] Anyone seeking to rebut this presumption will need to show that he has taken exclusive possession of the land, and has done so with the intention of excluding the rest of the world so far as practicable.[64] In *Littledale v Liverpool College*[65] the plaintiff had a right of way over the defendant's land and he erected a fence to preclude access to the land. It was held that this was not sufficient to set time running in his favour against the defendant, since it was equivocal in intention—it might have been done simply to prevent strangers from coming on to the land. Similarly, in *Wilson v Martin*[66] the plaintiff had walked the bound-

---

[63] *Powell v McFarlane* (1979) 38 P. & C.R. 452, Slade J.
[64] *Powell v McFarlane* (1979) 38 P. & C.R. 452, Slade J.
[65] [1900] 1 Ch. 19.
[66] [1993] 24 E.G. 1119, CA.

aries of the land, had cut timber from it and had repaired a fence on it, but the Court of Appeal held that none of these actions was sufficiently unequivocal to amount to adverse possession.

It is possible for the owner of a vessel that is moored in a particular place **13.036** on a tidal river to acquire title by adverse possession to a part of the river bed where the title to the river bed has not yet been registered and the vessel rests on the bed at low tide.[67] The judge went on to hold that the total area between the extreme points where the boat had had contact with the river bed over the years (including through her anchor) would be included in the area to which the owner of the boat had acquired title (together with the space above the bed through which water flows and the air column to a reasonable height above that). Although the question of whether any further part of the river bed beneath the outline of the boat's deck could also be said to have been in the boat owner's possession was not directly before the court, the judge suggested that it should be included. The case does not deal with the case of a vessel continuously moored for the necessary period away from the riverbank, or in a non-tidal river. This curious and interesting case clearly leaves a number of significant issues to be resolved in the future (including the position in such circumstances of the riparian owner).

It is not possible to acquire title to any part of a highway by adverse **13.037** possession[68]. Although the maxim 'once a highway always a highway'[69] may put matters too high, the rights of the public to use a highway cannot be lost by discontinuance or possession.[70]

Dispossession and discontinuance

This section considers the case law on the two important concepts of dis- **13.038** possession and discontinuance. It should be read subject to the general guidance on adverse possession given above, especially the observations of the Court of Appeal in *Buckinghamshire CC v Moran*.

Dispossession

In *Tecbild v Chamberlain*[71] it was held that dispossession requires some **13.039** degree of intention to use the land in a fashion adverse to the rightful owner. In *Wallis's Cayton Bay Holiday Camp Ltd v Shell-Mex and B.P. Ltd*[72] the defendants were holding land with a view to possible future

---

[67] *Port of London Authority v Ashmore* [2009] EWHC 954 (Ch) Stephen Smith Q.C.
[68] *R (on the application of Smith) v Land Registry* [2010] EWCA Civ 200.
[69] Apparently derived from the judgment of Byles J. in *Dawson v Hawkins* (1860) 29 LJCP 343.
[70] *Suffolk CC v Mason* [1979] A.C. 705 at 710; [1979] 2 All E.R. 369; 77 LGR 621 per Lord Diplock.
[71] (1969) 20 P. & C.R. 633, CA.
[72] [1975] Q.B. 94, CA.

development, but were not using it otherwise. The plaintiffs took possession of that land, and from 1961 to 1971 used it as agricultural land, either as pasture or for wheat. In 1971 they began to use it for the purposes of their holiday camp, but they did not put caravans on it. In October 1972 the defendants offered to sell the land to the plaintiffs, an offer which they repeated in December 1972 and April 1973. The plaintiffs failed to reply to these offers, but later claimed to have acquired a possessory title to the land in 1973. The Court of Appeal dismissed the plaintiffs' action. Dispossession requires the plaintiff to do something which is inconsistent with the defendant's use of the land for the purposes for which the defendant is holding that land. Here, the defendant was holding the land with the long-term objective of developing it. The plaintiff's activities, being of an essentially transitory nature, and capable of being discontinued at short notice, were not inconsistent with that objective, and there had therefore been no dispossession of the defendant. Later, in *Powell v McFarlane*,[73] this case was explained by Slade J. as being justified on the basis that the squatter is to be regarded as a licensee so long as his activities do not interfere with the rightful owner's use of the land. This explanation, whilst doubtless convenient, is logically unsound.

13.040   The law on this point was materially altered by the Limitation Amendment Act 1980, and the relevant provision is now Sch.1, para.8(4) to the Limitation Act 1980. This provides that it shall not be assumed by implication of law that a squatter is in possession with the consent of the rightful owner merely because his possession is not inconsistent with that of the rightful owner. It appears that these facts may nevertheless be evidence (albeit not conclusive evidence) that the possession is not adverse.

In *Bligh v Martin*[74] the same plot of land was accidentally conveyed at different times to both the plaintiff and the defendant, the defendant's conveyance being the earlier. However, both parties believed that the plaintiff was the rightful owner. Until 1960 the defendant worked on the land for the plaintiff as a seasonal contractor; thereafter he had a seasonal grazing tenancy of the land. Only in 1965 was the truth about the earlier conveyance to the defendant discovered. Plowman J. held that the plaintiff had acquired a good title to the land by adverse possession. The occasional occupation of the land by the defendant up to 1960 did not amount to dispossession of the plaintiff. After 1960 the plaintiff was in receipt of rent for the land. For the purposes of the Limitation Act 1939 he was therefore to be treated as being in possession of the land,[75] notwithstanding that the rent was being received from the true owner of the land. This case may be

---

[73] (1979) 38 P. & C.R. 452, Slade J.
[74] [1968] 1 W.L.R. 804, Plowman J.
[75] See now the 1980 Act s.38(8).

contrasted with *Chamber Colliery Co. v Hopwood*,[76] where both the owner and the squatter believed that the squatter was in possession as of right, and it was held that time did not run in the squatter's favour because his possession was not hostile to the true owner. In this case, however, there was no receipt of rent, and it is possible to reconcile the two cases on the basis that there is a statutory rule requiring that the receiver of rent be treated as in possession. However, this provision does not say that such possession must be treated as adverse, and it may therefore be argued that failure to advert to this distinction weakens the authority of the reasoning in *Bligh v Martin*, though the decision itself can no doubt be explained on the basis that it is a question of fact whether there has been dispossession.

Squatter must take possession

It is inherent in the notion of dispossession that the squatter must himself take possession of the land. Therefore acts which fall short of possession will not cause time to start running. It is a question of fact in each case what is necessary to amount to dispossession,[77] and this may well vary according to the character of the land.[78] Where a party used a small strip of land for temporary storage of materials in the course of transportation it was held that this did not amount to possession.[79] Similarly, in *Basildon DC v Manning*[80] the defendant had fenced off the land, and had used it, first to dump, burn and disperse poultry manure, then later to keep chickens. It was held that these acts were too trivial to amount to adverse possession.   **13.041**

These cases may be contrasted with *Treloar v Nute*.[81] The land in question was derelict, and there was no evidence that the rightful owner had any specific future use in mind for it. In 1961–1962 the defendant placed spoil in a gully running across it, with a view to levelling it for the erection of a building. In 1963 he erected a fence along the boundary of the land. The plaintiff protested, and removed the fence, but the defendant restored it. In 1966 the defendant rejected a protest from the plaintiff about dumping on the land by claiming to be the owner, and in 1974 he began to build a bungalow on it. The plaintiff sought a declaration that she was the rightful owner of the land. The Court of Appeal held that the defendant had taken possession in 1961–1962, and had therefore acquired title. Particular stress was laid on the placing of spoil, as being an act which would justify a finding that possession had been taken. It is irrelevant in this context that   **13.042**

---

[76] (1886) 32 Ch.D. 549, CA; see also *Earl de la Warr v Miles* (1881) 17 Ch.D. 535, Bacon V.-C.
[77] *Red House Farms (Thornden) Ltd v Catchpole* (1977) 244 E.G. 295, CA.
[78] *Marshall v Taylor* [1895] 1 Ch. 641, CA.
[79] *British Railways Board v G.J. Holdings Ltd* (1974) 230 E.G. 973, CA, relying on *Leigh v Jack* (1879) 5 Ex.D. 264 and *Williams Brothers Direct Supply Stores Ltd v Raftery* [1958] 1 Q.B. 159, CA.
[80] (1975) 237 E.G. 879, Foster J.
[81] [1977] 1 W.L.R. 1295, CA.

the squatter's actions do not inconvenience the rightful owner—if they amount to possession, then the latter is, in the absence of contrary evidence (such as anything to suggest shared possession)[82] to be treated as having been dispossessed.[83] Similarly, in *Williams v Usherwood*[84] it was held that fencing off land and later enclosing it by a wall were acts sufficient to justify a finding of adverse possession. Where a party incorporates land into the curtilage of his dwelling house, this is an act of possession sufficient to set time running.[85]

Perhaps the best summary of the position here is to say that much will depend upon the circumstances. If the squatter's acts are aimed at excluding other parties, and are to a large extent inconsistent with possession by others, then a finding of adverse possession is more likely. No dogmatic general rule can be laid down, however.

Parking of cars

13.043   Whether parking cars on land is sufficient to amount to adverse possession will depend upon the circumstances.[86] If the land in question is waste land, then parking cars will often be irrelevant, but the position is likely to be otherwise where, as in *Williams v Usherwood*, a party parks cars on the driveway to a house.[87]

Other acts

13.044   A variety of actions may sometimes be relied upon as amounting to adverse possession. This includes such things as filling in ditches, planting flowers, storing material, minor building and/or maintenance works, frequent but intermittent trespassing. Although it is always a question of fact, whether there has been adverse possession, the general trend of the case law may be summarised by saying that the courts are reluctant to recognise these relatively minor acts as amounting to possession, since few, if any, of them are sufficient to indicate an intention to exclude others from the land.[88]

Shared possession

13.045   A squatter cannot acquire a title by adverse possession if he is sharing possession of the land with the rightful owner, since this does not amount to dispossession.[89]

---

[82] See para.13.045.
[83] And see now the 1980 Act Sch.1, para.8(4).
[84] (1981) 45 P. & C.R. 235, CA.
[85] *Rudgwick Clay Works v Baker, The Times*, April 13, 1984.
[86] *Williams v Usherwood* (1981) 45 P. & C.R. 235, CA.
[87] It may be that in these cases it is more relevant to think of the acquisition of an easement by prescription.
[88] See e.g. *Tennant v Adamczyk* [2005] All ER (D) 29 (Oct) C.A.
[89] *Morris v Pinches* (1969) 212 E.G. 1141, Buckley J.

Joint tenants and tenants in common

A difficult question in this area concerns the effect on one joint owner of possession by other joint owners. In *Culley v Doe d. Taylerson*[90] the court had to consider whether time could run in favour of one joint owner who was in sole possession of the land, so as to bar the title of the other joint owners. It was held that at common law the one who was in possession would be presumed to be so on behalf of all, so that time could never run against the others. It is to be noted that the court treated joint tenants and tenants in common as being on the same footing for these purposes. In *Paradise Beach and Transportation Co. Ltd v Price-Robinson*[91] land was held on a tenancy in common; some of the tenants in common (the plaintiffs) were in possession, but others (the defendants) were not. The question was when time began to run against the defendants. The Privy Council held that the defendants' right of action accrued as soon as the plaintiffs went into possession, and that it was unnecessary to consider whether that possession was adverse.[92] This was a case from the Bahamas, and was decided on legislation similar to the English Real Property Limitation Acts of 1833 and 1874.

13.046

On the face of it the two cases are in conflict, but so far as the present position is concerned these cases need to be treated with some caution for a number of reasons. First, *Culley v Doe d. Taylerson* appears to say only that there is a presumption that one joint owner occupies for all. If the word presumption is accurately used here, the presumption must be rebuttable. Consequently, this case need not be seen as incompatible with the *Paradise Beach* case—each may be regarded as a correct application of a general principle to particular facts. The second point concerns the relevant statutory provisions. Section 12 of the Real Property Limitation Act 1833 disapplied the common law presumption of joint possession in any case where one joint owner had been in possession to the exclusion of the others. In *Culley v Doe d. Taylerson* the decision was that the possession of one joint owner had not been "to the exclusion" of the others. In *Paradise Beach* this point seems to have been treated as irrelevant, which must weaken the authority of the decision. Whether the defendants acquired an immediate right of action when the plaintiffs went into possession must surely depend upon whether that possession was with or without their permission. If the former, they would not acquire any right of action. This is merely another way of saying that the plaintiffs' possession would not have been adverse to them, and this therefore shows also that it cannot be correct to say that the adverse character of the possession is irrelevant.

13.047

---

[90] (1840) 11 Ad. & El. 1008, 113 E.R. 697.
[91] [1968] A.C. 1072, PC.
[92] *Nepean v Doe d. Knight* (1837) 2 M. & W. 894 at 911, per Lord Denman C.J.; *Re Manchester Gas Act, ex p. Hasell* (1839) 3 Y. & C. Ex. 617; *Doe d. Jones v Williams* (1836) 5 Ad. & El. 291.

13.048   Further, the leading English authorities in this area, such as *Leigh v Jack*,[93] were not considered. The most important point of all, though, is that s.12 of the Real Property Limitation Act 1833 is not reproduced anywhere in the current legislation. On ordinary principles of statutory interpretation the result of this would appear to be that the common law presumption is revived. This still leaves the issue of whether the presumption can be rebutted (and if so, how) in the case of joint owners. It is submitted that s.12 of the 1833 Act did no more than declare a principle which the common law would have applied anyway, namely that the presumption of joint possession could be rebutted by proper evidence that one joint owner had in fact taken possession to the exclusion of the others. Consequently, *Culley v Doe d. Taylerson* is still good law, but the reasoning in *Paradise Beach* cannot be supported to the extent that it regards the adverse character of the possession as irrelevant, though the case may well be correctly decided on its own facts.

Deemed possession

13.049   Section 38(8) of the 1980 Act provides that references to the possession of land shall in the case of tithes and rentcharges be construed as references to the receipt of the tithe or rent, and references to the date of dispossession or discontinuance of possession of land shall in the case of rentcharges be construed as references to the date of the last receipt of rent. Thus a landlord's title can be extinguished if the tenant remains in possession without paying rent for 12 years.[94] This rule is not displaced by a change in the character of the property, such as bringing it within the scope of rent controls.[95]

Revocable deeds

13.050   In *Hampersad Rambogan v Chaitlal Rambogan*[96] the land had originally been conveyed to the defendant under a revocable deed, and he remained in possession thereafter. Seventeen years later the deed was revoked and the land was conveyed to the plaintiff. The defendant argued, inter alia, that he had acquired title by adverse possession. The Privy Council held that under the revocable deed he was to be treated as having had only a tenancy, so that the result depended upon whether that tenancy had terminated by operation of law after one year so as to make him a trespasser. It is perhaps fortunate that the device of conveying land by means of a revocable deed is

---

[93] (1879) 5 Ex.D. 264.
[94] *Hayward v Chaloner* [1968] 1 Q.B. 107, CA; contra *Barrat v Richardson* [1930] 1 K.B. 686, Wright J. This case cannot be regarded as correct at the present day in view of the provisions of Sch.1 to the 1980 Act.
[95] *Moses v Lovegrove* [1952] 2 Q.B. 533, CA.
[96] November 9, 1989, PC, Unreported.

not commonly found in this country, for this case shows that it gives rise to serious problems of interpretation in a limitation context.

In general it seems that the ordinary English law rule of determining a **13.051** man's intention objectively by reference to his actions will prevail. In some cases, though, the acts of the putative adverse possessor are in themselves ambiguous as to whether they amount to adverse possession. In *George Wimpey & Co. Ltd v Sohn*[97] it was held that in such circumstances the court is entitled to take account of subjective intentions when deciding whether there is adverse possession. An offer by the alleged dispossessor to pay rent for the land will normally be inconsistent with the necessary animus possidendi.[98] Presumably, though, the burden of establishing such intention will rest upon the party alleging it, and it may be supposed that discharging this burden will not be easy.[99] A further point which arises from *Powell v McFarlane* is that compelling evidence will be required in order to establish the necessary animus possidendi where the squatter enters the land as a trespasser.[100]

Vendor and purchaser

Curious situations may arise where the squatter who claims title is a person **13.052** who is in the process of buying the land from the rightful owner. In *Hyde v Pearce*[101] the plaintiff bought a property at auction in 1958, and immediately went into possession with the vendor's consent. A dispute then arose, and the contract was never completed, the purchaser remaining in possession despite the vendor's request that he should leave. In 1972 the vendor conveyed the land to the defendant while the defendant was in prison, and the defendant took possession. The plaintiff sought to recover possession on the basis of his own squatter's title. The Court of Appeal held that the plaintiff had never acquired such title; initially his possession had not been adverse to the owner, since it was with the latter's permission. In respect of the period after the dispute arose, the plaintiff could not be heard to say that the possession was adverse, since in setting up his claim to the land he had relied on the contract, which was the basis of his permission from the owner to be there. Templeman L.J., giving the leading judgment of the Court of Appeal, implies that there is a further difficulty in that the plaintiff had in any event some sort of claim to possession, having been the equitable owner since contracts were exchanged. The reasoning is somewhat difficult to understand. First, the plaintiff had relied on the contract only to explain

---

[97] [1967] Ch. 487, CA.
[98] *R. v Secretary of State for the Environment, ex p. Davies, The Independent*, October 31, 1990, CA.
[99] See also *Thomas W. Ward Ltd v Alexander Bruce (Grays) Ltd* [1958] 2 Lloyd's Rep. 412, Vaisey J.
[100] See also *Buckinghamshire CC v Moran* [1990] Ch. 623, CA.
[101] [1982] 1 W.L.R. 560, CA.

how he came to be in possession—there was surely nothing inconsistent in his saying that he was originally in possession as a licensee, but that such possession became adverse when the owner asked him to leave. Secondly, the plaintiff's equitable title to the land would surely not prevent his possession from being adverse to that of the legal owner, whom he had quite clearly dispossessed.

Possession on behalf of another

13.053   There is a somewhat difficult line of authority which deals with the possibility of the tenant taking possession of land on behalf of his landlord. The principles of these authorities may be illustrated by reference to *Smirk v Lyndale Developments*.[102] The plaintiff occupied one of two adjoining houses under a service tenancy, the landlord being the British Railways Board (BRB). Behind each house was a strip of land, not included in the tenancy, which also belonged to the BRB. The plaintiff took over these two strips for gardening purposes. Later the defendant bought the houses and the adjoining strips from the BRB, but the plaintiff claimed to have acquired a good possessory title to the strips of land. Pennycuick V.-C. dismissed the plaintiff's claim, holding that when a tenant takes possession of land during a tenancy there is a presumption that he does so for the benefit of his landlord. The presumption applies even where the land taken is not adjacent to that demised, but can be rebutted if the tenant communicates to the landlord some disclaimer of the landlord's title.[103] The suggestion that the presumption applies even to non-adjacent land, which is an obiter dictum in the context of this case, must be regarded as open to question, not least since it gives rise to insoluble problems where the tenant holds different parcels of land simultaneously from two different landlords—in such a case, for which of the landlords is he deemed to acquire the land which he takes? In effect, the presumption must disappear in such cases, leaving the question to be decided on the facts.

Discontinuance

13.054   In *Tecbild Ltd v Chamberlain*[104] it was held that discontinuance does not arise merely because the owner ceases to use the land (presumably ceasing to use is different from ceasing to occupy). The same conclusion was

---

[102] [1975] Ch. 317, Pennycuick V.-C.; the decision of Pennycuick V.-C. was reversed by the CA (also reported at [1975] Ch. 317) on the grounds that a new tenancy on different terms had been created by the issue of a new rent book. This does not appear to affect the general principle laid down at first instance. See also *Tabor v Godfrey* (1895) 64 L.J.Q.B. 245, Charles J.

[103] *Kingsmill v Millard* (1855) 11 Exch. 313; *Whitmore v Humphries* (1871–72) L.R. 7, C.P. 1; *Tabor v Godfrey* (1895) 64 L.J.Q.B. 245; *Lord Hastings v Saddler* (1898) 79 L.T. 355.

[104] (1969) 20 P. & C.R. 633, CA.

reached by the Court of Appeal in *Wallis's Cayton Bay Holiday Camp Ltd v Shell-Mex and BP Ltd.*[105] In *Williams Brothers Direct Supply Stores Ltd v Raftery*[106] the concept of discontinuance was further considered. Between 1937 and 1957, when this action was brought, the plaintiffs had made very little use of the land, though they had put a gate in a fence between it and the roadway, had applied for planning permission in respect of it and had dumped rubbish on it. From 1940 to 1943 a third party had cultivated it, apparently with the plaintiff's permission, as part of the "Dig for Victory" campaign. From 1943 the defendant used it, without the plaintiff's permission, first as an allotment, then for a greyhound shed. The Court of Appeal held that the plaintiff had not discontinued possession, so that his claim for possession in 1957 was bound to succeed. In determining whether the plaintiff had discontinued possession it is necessary to take account of the nature of the property. The Court does not explain how this test is to be applied here, but it may be surmised that less in the way of active use will be required in the case of land which by reason of its size and/or location is not suitable for extensive use.

A further point that arises from *Williams Brother Direct Supply Stores Ltd v Raftery* is that the plaintiff may be considered not to have discontinued use of the land, even when some other person is using it. Further, as was shown above,[107] the use by another may not amount to dispossession, so that even in these circumstances it is possible that time will not run. **13.055**

In *Ellett-Brown v Tallishire Ltd*[108] going on the land to clip the hedge which bordered the land was alleged as discontinuance, but was held insufficient on the facts. There are two earlier cases about clipping of hedges in the context of adverse possession, but the court was able to distinguish these. In *Norton v LNWR Rly*[109] there was on the facts abandonment of the land by the Railway Company; in *Marshall v Taylor*[110] permission to go on to the land was sought, so that possession was never adverse. It is suggested that only very rarely will the clipping of a hedge be sufficient adverse possession. Even where it is, it is much more likely to be evidence of dispossession than of discontinuance.

Registered land

The overwhelming majority of the 1980 Act provisions relating to land are couched in terminology appropriate to unregistered land but not to registered land. The relationship between these provisions and those of the Land Registration Acts 1925–1988 has been considered in only a few reported **13.056**

---

[105] [1975] Q.B. 94. For the facts of this case, see para.13.039.
[106] [1958] 1 Q.B. 159, CA.
[107] See paras 13.045–13.046.
[108] March 29, 1990, CA, Unreported.
[109] (1879) 13 Ch.D. 268.
[110] [1895] 1 Ch. 641.

cases, but is bound to become a matter of ever-increasing importance, now that registration of title is mandatory on all transactions and registered land has become the normal expectation.

Effect of expiry of period

13.057   Section 17 of the 1980 Act provides that as a general rule at the expiration of the period provided by the Act for any person to bring an action to recover land (including a redemption action) the title of that person to the land shall be extinguished. It should be noted first that the phrase "action to recover land" is further defined by s.38(7), which was discussed above.[111] It can be seen from the earlier discussion that the ambit of the phrase extends considerably beyond the simple case of the fee simple owner seeking to recover possession of land from a squatter. Section 17 also imposes two qualifications on the general rule, namely the provisions of s.18 of the 1980 Act and those of s.75 of the Land Registration Act 1925.

Section 18

13.058   Section 18(2), (3) and (4), all of which are discussed below,[112] provide exceptions to the general rule of s.17, by extending the time in which an action may be brought to include the time allowed to some person other than the claimant.

Land Registration Act 1925, s.75

13.059   This section deals with the consequences of adverse possession in registered land. It provides that a person who has acquired title to registered land by adverse possession is entitled to be registered as proprietor of that land for the appropriate interest. Until such registration is effected the registered proprietor is declared by s.75(1) to hold the legal estate on trust for the adverse possessor. Consequently, the general statement in s.17 of the 1980 Act that title to land is extinguished after 12 years adverse possession does not apply to registered land. The exact nature of the trust imposed by s.75 is unclear. In *Fairweather v St Marylebone Co. Ltd*[113] Lord Reid questioned whether the trust could really be of the proprietor's existing title, on the ground that this title will not be transferred to the squatter: rather, a new title will be created for him. The conceptual difficulty is a genuine one, but it is impossible to escape the very clear words of s.75(1), and it must be concluded that the registered proprietor does hold his own title on trust for

---

[111] See para.13.007.
[112] See para.13.087.
[113] [1962] 1 Q.B. 498, CA, affirmed [1963] A.C. 510, HL.

the squatter. The consequences of this rule are explored further at paras 13.054–13.056.

Consequences of extinction of title

The simplest case is that of the fee simple owner, whose title becomes barred by a squatter's adverse possession. The owner ceases to have the legal title to the land, and the squatter becomes entitled to possession by virtue of the lapse of time. Much more difficult questions arise when land is subject to a lease, and in this context it is necessary to examine carefully the extremely important decision of the House of Lords in *Fairweather v St Marylebone Property Co. Ltd.*[114] In this case a shed had been built, on land which was originally in common ownership, but which was later sold off so that the shed stood partly on A's land, partly on B's land. The entrance was on A's land. The shed was regularly sub-let with A's land. A's lessee obtained a squatter's title in respect of the shed against B's lessee in 1932, though in 1959 the then tenant made an acknowledgment that he had no rights against B's lessee. The leases on both properties were due to expire in 1992, but the lease on B's property was surrendered early, and B sought to eject A's tenant from that part of the shed which stood on B's land. A's tenant pleaded limitation, but it was held by the Court of Appeal[115] that B was entitled to possession, and this decision was subsequently affirmed by the House of Lords.[116] In 1932 B's tenant's rights were extinguished, but this did not transfer those rights to A's tenant, nor did it extinguish B's rights; the freeholder's rights remained intact, and were deferred to the end of the lease. The vital time for the latter point is when the lease actually determines, not the point at which it was originally intended to determine. Further, the acknowledgment was irrelevant, since an acknowledgment given to the freeholder cannot deprive the tenant of any proprietary right previously acquired.[117] A number of points arising out of this decision require further examination.

13.060

Non-transfer of title

It is a general point of some importance that the extinction of a person's title to land does not operate as a "parliamentary conveyance" of the title to the person in whose favour time has run. That person acquires a pos-

13.061

---

[114] [1962] 1 Q.B. 498, CA, affirmed [1963] A.C. 510, HL. For earlier authorities in this area see *Taylor v Twinberrow* [1930] 2 K.B. 16, DC and *Walter v Yalden* [1902] 2 K.B. 304, DC.
[115] Holroyd Pearce and Pearson L.JJ., Willmer L.J. dissenting.
[116] Lord Radcliffe, Lord Denning, Lord Morris and Lord Guest.
[117] See further para.18.007.

sessory title,[118] which will be valid to the extent that there is no better claim. Where the interest to which he acquires title is leasehold, the expiry of time does not put him into privity of contract or estate with the free-holder.[119] Therefore, if the freeholder forfeits the lease and exercises a right of re-entry after the tenant's title has become barred in favour of a squatter, the squatter is not entitled to apply to court for relief from forfeiture under s.147 of the Law of Property Act 1925, since he is not the landlord's tenant.[120] If the squatter takes advantage of a clause in the lease he may become bound to observe its terms under the doctrine of benefit and burden.[121]

Freeholder's rights

13.062   As is made clear in Sch.1 to the 1980 Act,[122] the freeholder's rights against a squatter who has evicted his tenant do not accrue until the lease comes to an end. Clearly this may be much more than 12 years from the time when the squatter goes into possession.

Rights in different strata

13.063   In *Midland Railway Co. v Wright*[123] the plaintiffs built a railway tunnel under land which they owned. As a railway company incorporated by Act of Parliament they were not competent to dispose of this land unless it was surplus to their requirements, which it was not. Later the land was con-veyed to the defendants, who used it continuously for 30 years,[124] though during that time the plaintiffs continued to use the railway tunnel. The plaintiffs then sought to restrain the defendants from using the land as their own. Byrne J. dismissed this claim, holding that the defendants had acquired good title to the land by adverse possession despite the plaintiffs' lack of capacity to dispose of it. This title extended to the substrata and up to the skies. The rights in the substrata were subject to the plaintiffs' statutory right to use the tunnel, but the rights over the air above the land sufficed to entitle the defendants to an injunction to restrain the plaintiffs from erecting telegraph poles on the land.

---

[118] For the position in registered land see para.13.054.
[119] *Tichborne v Weir* (1892) 67 L.T. 375, CA; nevertheless it appears that a squatter is bound by restrictive covenants in the lease. Time does not run against the covenantee until the breach, and a squatter without notice is not in the same position as a purchaser without notice: *Re Nisbet & Pott's Contract* [1906] 1 Ch. 386.
[120] *Tickner v Buzzacott* [1965] 1 Ch. 426, Plowman J.
[121] *Tito v Waddell (No. 2)* [1977] Ch. 106.
[122] Sch.1, para.5.
[123] [1901] 1 Ch. 738, Byrne J.
[124] This was then the relevant limitation period under the Real Property Limitation Act 1833.

One point which is not resolved by this decision concerns the position where the owner of the tunnel has no statutory right to use it; it is unclear whether in these circumstances the adverse title would preclude the use of the tunnel. In *Williams v Usherwood*[125] the Court of Appeal held that the law can recognise the existence of different rights in different strata of land, but this time in the context of the retention of rights over the surface. Thus, where a squatter has acquired good title by adverse possession, there may still be easements or quasi-easements over the surface of the land, where the implication of these can be justified according to the rules generally applicable to easements.

Registered land

The decision in *Fairweather v St Marylebone*[126] is a decision on the prin-   **13.064**
ciples applicable to unregistered land. In dealing with registered land, it is necessary to take into account the provisions of the Land Registration Act 1925 (the LRA 1925). The problems which arise in this context were considered by Browne-Wilkinson J. in *Spectrum Investment Co. v Holmes*.[127] The defendant had acquired squatter's title to a registered leasehold interest, and had been registered as proprietor, pursuant to s.75 of the LRA 1925. The plaintiff was the owner of the freehold interest, and he and the former registered lessee executed a document purporting to surrender the former leasehold title, for which the Register had by then been closed. The plaintiff then claimed to hold the freehold unencumbered by the defendant's leasehold interest; in the alternative the former registered lessee claimed rectification of the Register by the deletion of the defendant's registered leasehold title. Browne-Wilkinson J. held that both applications must fail. As to the plaintiff's application, s.69(1) of the LRA 1925 vests the legal term of the lease in the squatter on registration. Consequently, the former lessee had no title at the date of the purported surrender, and, by ss.18 and 21 of the LRA 1925, only the registered proprietor of an interest can dispose of it. The purported surrender was therefore invalid. With regard to the former lessee's application for rectification, it was held that the registration of the defendant as proprietor had been perfectly proper, since the latter had obtained the legal title by 12 years' adverse possession. It is important to observe that there is here a fundamental distinction between the position in registered land and that in unregistered land. As was shown above,[128] in unregistered land the title of a person who has acquired squatter's title to a leasehold interest can be defeated by a sur-

---

[125] (1981) 45 P. & C.R. 235, CA.
[126] [1963] A.C. 288, HL; see paras. 13.059-13.060.
[127] [1981] 1 W.L.R. 221.
[128] See para.13.060.

render of the original leasehold interest. In registered land this consequence is prevented by the principle of the LRA 1925 that the Register is conclusive evidence of title.[129]

Registration of squatter's title

13.065   It is not entirely clear with what class of title a squatter should be registered on an application under s.75 of the LRA 1925. Section 75(3) states that the squatter shall be registered with absolute, qualified, possessory or good leasehold title, as may be appropriate. However, it is difficult to see how it can ever be appropriate to register a squatter initially with anything better than possessory title. Although he will have been in possession for 12 years, this is not by itself conclusive of his title, for a previous proprietor may be able to avoid the operation of the 1980 Act by alleging fraud, for example. In view of this it can only be very rarely that the Registrar will be satisfied that it is appropriate to award an absolute title.[130] A possessory title may subsequently be upgraded to absolute title on application to the Registrar after it has been registered for 12 years in the case of freehold land and 10 years in the case of leasehold land.[131]

An unresolved question after the decision in *Spectrum Investment Co. v Holmes* concerns the position after the squatter has been in adverse possession for 12 years of unregistered leasehold land which is subject to registration on transfer, but has not yet been registered, for example because the lease was created at a time when the land was not in an area of compulsory registration. The difficulty arises if S has acquired squatter's title to the leasehold interest, but in the interval before registration T, the lessee, disposes of his interest. Unregistered land principles govern this situation. T's interest is therefore extinguished when S's squatter's title is complete, and this is a case of a purported disposition by a non-owner, which as such is wholly ineffective. A quite different result is reached where title is already registered and P, the registered proprietor of the lease, makes a transfer after S has acquired squatter's title. This is a case of a disposition by a trustee of the legal interest in the land. It would appear to be a breach of trust by P, for which he may be liable to S in damages. The further question is whether S's beneficial interest in the lease is overreached to the proceeds of sale. It is submitted that this is determined according to the normal principle that the overreaching of a beneficial interest depends upon the purchase money having been paid to two trustees. If this requirement is not met, then S can enforce his title against the transferee of P's registered leasehold title.

---

[129] Subject only to overriding interests, which are not in point here: LRA 1925 s.70.

[130] This suggestion is also supported by Ruoff, *Land Registration Forms* (3rd edn, 1983) and it may be noted that possessory title was granted in *Spectrum Investment v Holmes* [1981] 1 W.L.R. 221.

[131] LRA 1925 s.77, as amended by LRA 1986 s.1(1).

The principle that the Register is conclusive evidence of title should not **13.066** be taken too far. However, *Bridges v Mees*[132] illustrates the way in which the possibility of rectification of the Register can interact with the rules on limitation. The plaintiff had bought land, which was already subject to compulsory registration, from a company in 1936 and had immediately gone into possession, though no conveyance in the plaintiff's favour was ever executed. In 1955 the company, which was by then in liquidation, contracted (by its liquidator) to sell the same land to the defendant, who was duly registered as proprietor. The plaintiff claimed rectification of the Register on the basis that he had been in possession since 1936 and had therefore acquired a good title against the company. Harman J. held that the defendant had an interest in fee simple in the land by virtue of the Register and the plaintiff could therefore not be the registered proprietor. However, the defendant held that interest as a trustee for the plaintiff. The company had become a bare trustee for the plaintiff in 1937, when the last instalment of the purchase price was paid consequently, it was only that bare legal title which the company could pass to the defendant. The plaintiff could break that bare trust by calling for a transfer of the legal estate. Alternatively, the same result could be reached on the basis that the plaintiff had become entitled to the legal estate as against the trustee by 12 years' adverse possession. Since the 1939 Act (but not before) time can run in favour of a cestui que trust who is in possession adversely to his trustee.[133]

Registered land and sub-tenants

The interaction between the principles of registered land and the limitation **13.067** rules is further complicated where there are sub-tenancies. In *Jessamine Investment Co. v Schwartz*[134] the defendant held a weekly sub-tenancy of the property from 1937. In 1939 the head tenancy became a statutory tenancy by operation of law. The defendant paid no rent after 1945, and in 1973 made an unsuccessful application to be registered with possessory title. In the same year the original contractual lease expired, and the plaintiff, the freeholder, sought possession. The first point was that the tenant's right of action against the sub-tenant had accrued in 1945 on the non-payment of rent,[135] so that the tenant's rights became barred in 1957. The question which followed from that was whether this put the sub-tenant in the position of having a squatter's title against both the tenant and the freeholder. It was held that it did not—as against the tenant there was a good possessory title, but as against the plaintiff the defendant must be treated as being in possession by virtue of the statutory tenancy. This gave

---

[132] [1957] Ch. 475, Harman J.
[133] This follows from the repeal of a proviso to s.7 of the Real Property Limitation Act 1833.
[134] [1978] Q.B. 264, CA.
[135] 1980 Act, Sch.1, para.5. Also see paras 13.009–13.012.

the defendant statutory security of tenure, so that the plaintiff's claim for possession was bound to fail.

13.068   It should be noted that the position here apparently differs from that applicable where there is only one tenant. It was shown above[136] that in such a case the squatter acquires good possessory title against the freeholder, and is therefore able to succeed to the position of the person whom he has displaced. In a sense the same principle may be said to operate here, since the sub-tenant acquires possessory title against his immediate superior in the chain of ownership. The result is likely to differ, though, because that title does not extend any further up the chain. In *Central London Commercial Estates Ltd v Kato Kagaku Co. Ltd (Axa Equity and Law Life Assurance Society plc, Third Party)*[137] a lease of land was granted for 94 years from June 24, 1934. In 1935 all but the last 10 days of the leasehold term were sub-let to the Crown and the sub-demise included buildings below ground level but not the surface of the courtyard to the property. In 1942 the leasehold interest passed to the third party and in 1989 the freehold interest passed to the plaintiff. Both the freehold and leasehold estates had at all material times been registered, the plaintiff's with title absolute and the third party's with good leasehold title. In 1996 the third party by deed surrendered the headlease to the plaintiff and, rather than replace the third party with the plaintiff as the registered proprietor of the leasehold interest, the Land Registry closed the title to the headlease and reregistered the freehold title subject only to the under-lease. For more than 12 years prior to the date of surrender the part of the courtyard which had been demised to the third party had been in continuous adverse possession of the first defendant. When the plaintiff sought to recover possession of the courtyard from the first defendant, the question arose whether, by virtue of s.75 of the Land Registration Act 1925, the surrender of the headlease had had the effect of defeating the first defendant's squatter's rights. It was held that it did not. In the case of registered land, such a surrender lifts the extinguishing effect of the 1980 Act and substitutes, from the moment of extinction, a trust of the leasehold interest preserving the squatter's statutory right under s.75(2) to be substituted by registration for the leaseholder.

Proceeds of sale

13.069   An action to recover the proceeds of sale of land is governed by s.20 of the 1980 Act. That section also relates to matters concerning mortgages,[138] and the ambit of the reference in s.20 to action to recover the proceeds of sale is unclear, not least since the proceeds of sale are within the definition of

---

[136] See para.13.064.
[137] [1998] 4 All E.R. 948; [1998] 46 E.G. 185; [1998] 3 E.G.L.R. 55.
[138] See paras 13.074–13.082.

"land" in s.38(1), so that it may appear that s.15(1) governs such an action, rendering this part of s.20 otiose. It is submitted that such a view is incorrect. In s.38 it is only the proceeds of land held on trust for sale which are treated as land. In cases where there is no such trust, as where an unpaid vendor seeks to enforce his lien, or where trust property has wrongly been sold, s.20 can apply. Where s.20 does apply, the limitation period is 12 years from the date on which the right to receive the money accrued. It has been suggested[139] that the terminus a quo differs from that applicable when the statute refers to time running from the accrual of the cause of action. This must be regarded as doubtful, unless there is any case where the right of action has accrued but cannot be enforced for some procedural reason.[140]

Effect of judgment

In *BP Properties v Buckler*[141] the facts were that the landlords had obtained a possession order in 1955, followed by another in 1962 in the same terms. Only in 1974 did they obtain leave to enforce that order. Before that leave could become effective, the landlords granted the defendant's mother a licence to occupy the property for life, rent free. On the death of the defendant's mother the landlords sought possession. The defendant pleaded that his mother had obtained a good title, the limitation period having expired before 1974, so that the purported grant of the licence was ineffective. The Court of Appeal rejected this argument. The proceedings of 1962 were commenced within the 12-year limitation period, and the commencement of proceedings stops the running of time. The landlords were then entitled to 12 years from 1962 (the date of the possession order) in which to enforce it, since time must be considered as starting to run again. This period had not expired when the licence was granted, and the grant was therefore effective. The defendant's mother thereupon became a lawful occupier of the premises, and it is, of course, axiomatic that time cannot run in favour of a lawful occupier.[142] The landlords' action therefore succeeded.

13.070

---

[139] See Derek Morgan, *Current Law Statutes Annotated* (1980).
[140] Compare, in other contexts, *O'Connor v Isaacs* [1956] 2 Q.B. 288, Diplock J.; [1956] 2 All E.R. 417, CA; and *Sevcon v Lucas (CAV) Ltd* [1986] 1 W.L.R. 462, HL.
[141] (1988) 55 P. & C.R. 337, CA.
[142] *Chamber Colliery Co. v Hopwood* (1886) 32 Ch.D. 549, CA, where time was held not to run when both parties mistakenly believed that the possession was as of right.

Expiry of time and actions for damages

13.071 A person who wrongfully dispossesses another of land commits trespass, a tort which is in principle actionable in damages. In *Mount Carmel Investments Ltd v Peter Thurlow Ltd*[143] an action for such damages was brought after the limitation period for an action to recover the land had expired. The Court of Appeal held that no damages could be awarded, even in respect of the period before title was extinguished. This decision is as unfortunate as it is surprising. It is based upon the old rule that there could be no account of mesne profits once time had expired,[144] but there is surely no satisfactory reason why the expiry of time should operate in this retrospective fashion.

The School Sites Act 1841

13.072 This obscure statute has generated some authority in a limitation context. The material provisions of the Act state that where land is held on trust for the educational purposes specified in the Act, the trustees shall receive a determinable fee simple. When the Act was passed, this was a legal estate in the land, but one of the effects of the 1925 property legislation was to reduce the number of legal interests which could subsist in land, and a determinable fee simple cannot now exist at law. The point in *Re Rowhook Mission Hall, Horsham*[145] was to determine the effect of the land ceasing to be held upon the trusts specified in the Act. The choice was between a reversion to the grantor, and the trustees holding on trust for the grantor, rather than for the purposes mentioned in the Act. If the former solution were adopted, then for limitation purposes time could run against the revertee—the trustees being in adverse possession. Adopting the latter solution would mean that time would not run in favour of the trustees, since time does not run in favour of trustees who are in possession of their beneficiaries' land.[146] Nourse J. ruled in favour of the former interpretation, relying on the wording of s.7(1) of the Law of Property Act 1925 (LPA 1925), notwithstanding that the effect of this construction is to render s.3(3) of the LPA 1925 largely otiose. In so doing Nourse J. approved the decision in *Re Ingleton Charity*[147] but refused to follow, and indeed trenchantly criticised, the decision in *Re Clayton's Deed Poll*.[148] A consequence

---

[143] [1988] 1 W.L.R. 1078, CA.
[144] *Re Jolly, Gathercole v Norfolk* [1900] 2 Ch. 616.
[145] [1985] Ch. 62, Nourse J.; see also *The Bath & Wells Diocesan Board of Finance v Hector*, July 31, 2000, Evans-Lombe J.
[146] 1980 Act s.21(1); *Re Landi* [1939] Ch. 828.
[147] [1956] Ch. 585, Danckwerts J.
[148] [1980] Ch. 99.

of this choice was seen in *Fraser v Canterbury Diocesan Board of Finance*[149] where land had been conveyed under the School Sites Act 1841 for the purpose of creating a Church of England "voluntary" school, but a change in the organisation of the school in 1874 meant that it became a non-denominational "provided" school. As a result of that change, the school was no longer being used for the purpose for which it had been devoted, and so reverted back to the settlor under s.2 of that Act. Consequently, proceedings commenced in 1998 to recover the site were statute-barred.

The Reverter of Sites Act 1987 now materially affects the status of these decisions. This Act provides that in cases where the purpose of the trust fails there is to be a trust for sale of the land with the revertee of the land as the beneficiary. This has the convenient effect of allowing the making of a scheme under the cy-près doctrine when the revertee cannot be found. This effectively approves the solution adopted by Nourse J., but goes further; it deals with the problem of the otiose words in s.3(3) of the LPA 1925 by repealing the words in question. From a limitation point of view the result appears to be that time can run in favour of the trustees in these cases. Section 1(4) of the Reverter of Sites Act provides that no cause of action barred at the coming into force of the Act is to be revived thereby. **13.073**

MORTGAGES

In the context of mortgages a number of remedies are available in various circumstances, either to the mortgagor or, more commonly, to the mortgagee. These various remedies are dealt with in the following paragraphs. **13.074**

Redemption actions

Section 16 of the 1980 Act deals with redemption actions where the mortgagee is in possession of any of the mortgaged land. It provides that the mortgagor (and any person claiming through him) loses the right to bring a redemption action in respect of the mortgaged land of which the mortgagee is in possession once that possession[150] has lasted for 12 years. Therefore, the right to bring a redemption action may be extinguished at different times for different parts of the mortgaged land if the mortgagee's possession dates from different times. No period of limitation is provided by the statute where the mortgagee is not in possession of any of the mortgaged **13.075**

---

[149] November 24, 2000, Unreported, CA.
[150] For the meaning of "possession", see paras 13.026–13.041.

land.[151] Further, it is a general principle of the law of mortgages that a mortgagor is always entitled to redeem the mortgage upon fully discharging the loan for which the mortgage was security, together with any accrued interest and costs.[152]

Mortgagee's remedies

13.076 Section 20 of the 1980 Act deals with the rights of the mortgagee, and the ways in which they can be affected by lapse of time. Subsection (1) imposes a limit of 12 years on the bringing of an action to recover any principal sum (but not interest)[153] secured by a mortgage or other charge on property, or to recover the proceeds of the sale of the land in question. Time runs from the date on which the cause of action accrued.[154] It is to be observed that this section applies also to mortgages of personal property.[155] However, it is not expressed to apply to foreclosure actions, which are dealt with below.

Foreclosure actions

13.077 The right to foreclose on a mortgage arises on the legal date for the redemption of that mortgage, notwithstanding any power of the court to give relief against foreclosure.[156] Thus in *Purnell v Roche*[157] it was held to be irrelevant that interest had been paid for some five years after the arrival of the legal date for redemption. Such actions fall within s.15, not s.20, since they are actions to recover possession of land.[158]

Mortgage interest

13.078 The time-limit for an action to recover arrears of interest on a mortgage is six years.[159] However, *Holmes v Cowcher*[160] illustrates an important point about the relationship between redemption actions and arrears of interest. The mortgagor in this case brought a redemption action at a time when interest was more than six years in arrears. The mortgagee claimed to be entitled to retain the statute-barred interest out of the proceeds of sale. Stamp J. found for the mortgagee. S.20 of the 1980 Act does not apply since

---

[151] Section 36 of the Act, which deals with equitable remedies generally, is not expressed as applying to any time-limit under s.16.
[152] *Noakes v Rice* [1902] A.C. 24.
[153] For the position with regard to interest, see "Mortgage interest", below.
[154] For the date of accrual, see paras 13.009–13.011.
[155] As to such mortgages, see paras 12.011–12.013.
[156] *Williams v Morgan* [1906] 1 Ch.D. 804.
[157] [1927] 2 Ch.142, Romer J.
[158] *Kensington & Chelsea RBC v Amanullah Khan*, June 8, 2001, Unreported, Lawrence Collins J.
[159] 1980 Act s.20.
[160] [1970] 1 W.L.R. 834, Stamp J.

this is not an action to recover interest, and the case must be decided by reference to the general principles governing redemption actions. The most important of these for present purposes is that redemption is an equitable remedy, the granting of which has always been conditional on the repayment of all arrears, even if technically statute barred.[161] This rule applies equally whether the mortgagor or the mortgagee is in possession of the proceeds of sale.[162]

Section 20(2) and (3) deal with foreclosure actions in respect of personal property,[163] but s.20(4) provides that foreclosure actions in respect of mortgaged land are treated as actions to recover land, and as such are subject to the regime of s.15.[164]

Successive mortgages

Very complex problems can arise where land is subject to more than one mortgage. The difficulties can helpfully be illustrated by reference to *Cotterell v Price*.[165] Both the mortgages in this case were made in 1930, and the mortgagor (the third defendant in the case) became bankrupt in 1938. The first mortgage was vested in the first and second defendants, whilst the second was vested in the plaintiff. In 1958 the plaintiff sought to prove in the bankruptcy for his security. It was accepted that his rights against the mortgagor were barred—no interest on the mortgage had ever been paid, and the legal date for redemption had been in 1930, so that right action had become barred in 1942. He nevertheless contended that he was entitled as against the first two defendants to redeem the first mortgage, and that he had a statutory title to the property under the Bankruptcy Act 1914, having duly served a notice on the trustee in bankruptcy, requiring him to elect whether or not to redeem the security, and having received no reply within the specified time.[166] Buckley J. held that these ingenious arguments failed. All enforcement rights under the second mortgage were lost in 1942, as the plaintiff had admitted, and the right to redeem the first mortgage disappeared at the same time, since the right to redeem an earlier mortgage is incidental to the status of mortgagee. Further, the service of the statutory notice was out of time. Although there is a doctrine that time ceases to run once a receiving order is made, this applies only for the purposes of the

13.079

---

[161] *Dingle v Coppen* [1899] 1 Ch. 726; *Edmunds v Waugh* (1866) L.R. 1 Eq. 418; *Lloyd v Lloyd* [1903] 1 Ch. 385; *Marshfield v Hutchfield* (1887) 34 Ch.D. 721.
[162] *Lloyd v Lloyd* [1903] 1 Ch. 385, CA.
[163] See further para.13.009.
[164] Examined at paras 13.004–13.008.
[165] [1960] 1 W.L.R. 1097, Buckley J.
[166] As to the special rules which apply in bankruptcy/insolvency, see paras 17.021–17.041.

13.080   bankruptcy itself, and has no effect on the position of secured creditors.[167]
A related problem arose in *Young v Clarey*.[168] Again there were two mortgages: the first mortgage was a legal charge made in 1923, whilst the second mortgage was a puisne mortgage made in 1926. The first mortgagee took possession of the land in 1933; there being neither payment of interest nor acknowledgment, the titles of the mortgagor and the second mortgagee were extinguished in 1945. In 1946 the second mortgagee agreed to sell the land "as mortgagee" and this sale was completed in 1947. The issue in the case concerned the proper destination of the proceeds of sale, the second mortgagee claiming to be entitled to any surplus after the first mortgage had been discharged (the mortgagor took no part in the action). The first mortgagee sold the land in exercise of the statutory power of sale conferred by s.101 of the Law of Property Act 1925, and by s.105 held the proceeds on trust for the person entitled to the property or authorised to give a receipt for those proceeds. On the facts this meant himself, since the effect of what are now ss.15 and 17 of the 1980 Act is to extinguish all other titles and rights in the property.

Shortfall claims

13.081   When a mortgagee has foreclosed and sold the mortgaged land, there may still be a shortfall on the debt secured by the mortgage. The balance remains outstanding and recoverable by the mortgagee. For present purposes the question is what limitation period applies to an action to recover the shortfall. Section 20 forbids an action in the cases to which it relates, namely actions to recover a sum secured by a mortgage. However, in a shortfall action it is highly arguable that the sum claimed is no longer secured by a mortgage, because the mortgage has gone. It is necessary to ask whether the words mean "which is at the date of the claim form secured by a mortgage" or whether they only mean "which was at some time so secured". On the face of it the former might seem more likely, but it is then necessary to ask what is the basis of the undoubted liability to pay the shortfall? The answer is not that at the date of the claim it is secured by the mortgage. This is arguably somewhat similar to s.395 of the Companies Act 1985, where a charge is void for non-registration. The charge falls, but the debt does not, because they are separate, though obviously related. Thus there must be an independent obligation to repay the debt, even where the mortgage contains a personal covenant on the part of the borrower to repay. This analysis clearly tends in the direction of saying that the shortfall is not secured by the mortgage, which points to six years; but that must run from the date of breach. The obligation to pay the shortfall, if independent,

---

[167] Then Bankruptcy Act 1914 s.7(2): see now Insolvency Act 1986 s.285(4). On the position if the plaintiff had been an unsecured creditor, see paras 17.021–17.023.
[168] [1948] Ch. 191, Harman J.

does not arise until the sale of the security, and the breach presumably follows shortly thereafter, at least in most cases. These issues were discussed, but not decided, in *Global Financial Recoveries Ltd v Jones*,[169] where it was said to be at least arguable that the applicable period was six years. In *Scottish Equitable plc v Thompson*[170] it was held that where a legal charge contains no express covenant on the part of the borrower to repay the principal sum, which was intended to be paid from the proceeds of an insurance policy, the limitation period for recovery of that sum was six years from the date of demand for repayment. This is, of course, not the usual case, since there is normally a covenant for repayment: its absence in this case was due to the special circumstance that the parties expected that a maturing insurance policy would provide the necessary funds.

Extinction of Mortgages

Ashe v National Westminster Bank plc[171] decides that in relation to a   **13.082** mortgage time runs against the mortgagee from the earliest date when he could have taken proceedings for possession of the land. As a general rule[172] a mortgagee has a right to possession from the date of the mortgage.[173] Where the mortgage provides that the mortgagee is not entitled to possession until the mortgagor defaults, however, time for claiming possession does not run until there is a default: *Wilkinson v Hall*.[174] In the light of this rule time runs even though the mortgagor's possession cannot be viewed as being adverse to the mortgagee. Para 8 of Sch.1 Pt 1 to the 1980 Act, which imposes the requirement for adverse possession is not expressed to apply, and does not apply, to actions by a mortgagee who has never been in possession. The logic of this view is hard to fault, but the potential consequences appear to be somewhat unfortunate. In a mortgage which does not exclude the common law rule that the mortgagee is entitled to immediate possession, time must run from the date of the mortgage, even though there has been no default. In the case of a dwelling-house, this consequence is presumably mitigated by the rule that the mortgagee cannot take possession without a court order[175] but in other cases it could have unfortunate results. The court gave a declaration that the mortgage had been extinguished, but without considering the cases cited in the main text, which would suggest that the redemption of the mortgage is an equitable

[169] February 23, 2000, Unreported, Robert Englehart Q.C.
[170] April 10, 2002, Unreported, Central London County Court.
[171] [2007] EWHC 494 (Ch), Richard Arnold Q.C.
[172] Para.34 of the judgment.
[173] *Four-Maids Ltd v Dudley Marshall (Properties) Ltd* [1957] Ch 317, 320, [1957] 2 All ER 35, [1957] 2 WLR 931.
[174] (1837) 3 Bing NC 508, 6 LJCP 82, 3 Hodg 56.
[175] AJA 1970 s.35.

remedy which depends on payment of all arrears even if statute-barred. It is not clear how this principle applies in registered land, where the remedy which the mortgagor seeks is not the redemption of the mortgage but its removal from the Register.

RENT

13.083   Section 19 of the 1980 Act deals with actions to recover rent. It provides that no action shall be brought, or distress made, to recover arrears of rent, or damages in respect of arrears of rent, after the expiration of six years from the date on which the arrears became due.

Definition

13.084   "Rent" is partially defined for the purposes of the Limitation Act in s.38(1) of the 1980 Act, which provides that the term includes a rentcharge and a rentservice. "Rentcharge" is defined in the same subsection as meaning any annuity or periodical sum of money charged upon or payable out of land, other than a rentservice or interest on a mortgage of land.

Section 19 applies whether the attempt to recover the arrears is made by way of action or by way of distress, though distress is in any case a remedy only rarely resorted to. Although the section does not refer to the position of a surety, in *Romain v Scuba TV Ltd*[176] it was held to apply also to actions against any guarantor of the lessee's obligation to pay rent in the same way as it applies to an action against the lessor. It was pointed out that if this were not the case, the reference in s.19 to an action for damages for non-payment of rent would have no clear meaning.

It appears that s.19 merely bars the remedy, rather than extinguishing the plaintiff's right to the arrears of rent. It should also be noted that the effect of the section cannot be circumvented by the device of bringing an action for damages for non-payment, since this also is caught by s.19. Leases commonly contain a covenant on the part of the lessee to pay the rent. Although this is a specialty, it apparently does not serve to extend the period of limitation to 12 years, presumably on the basis that this is an action for which a specific period of limitation is provided by the Act, so that s.8(2) applies.[177]

---

[176] [1996] 2 All E.R. 377, CA.
[177] See further para.4.013.

Leasehold Reform Act 1967

A number of troublesome points about rent have arisen in cases under the **13.085** Leasehold Reform Act 1967,[178] which allows tenants in certain circumstances compulsorily to acquire their landlord's interest in a property. In *Re Howell's Application*[179] the tenant sought enfranchisement on the ground that the landlord could not be found.[180] Section 27 of the Act provides that when an application is made under this head the tenant must pay into court "the amount remaining unpaid of any pecuniary rent payable" up to the date of conveyance. No rent had been paid for a period in excess of six years, the tenant being unable to find the landlord. Pennycuick V.-C. held that arrears which were statute-barred were nevertheless "payable" for the purposes of s.27 of the Leasehold Reform Act 1967. The decision is presented as simply a matter of putting a reasonable construction on s.27, but it may be noted that it accords with the policy adopted in other cases[181] of regarding the expiry of time in a rent action as barring only the remedy.

LAND HELD ON TRUST[182]

Section 18 of the 1980 Act applies here. The general rule, set out in s.18(1), **13.086** is that the provisions of the 1980 Act apply to equitable interests in land (including interests in the proceeds of sale of land held on trust for sale) as they apply to legal interests in land.[183] Therefore, a person entitled in possession to an equitable interest is treated for limitation purposes as if his right of action accrued on the same day as it would have accrued had it been a legal estate in the land.[184]

Land held on trust for sale

Similar provisions[185] to the above exist in the case of land held on trust for **13.087** sale. In this case the interest whose extinction is delayed is that of the trustee rather than that of the tenant for life. Their interest is extinguished,

---

[178] Other points arising under this Act are considered at paras 4.017–4.020.
[179] [1972] Ch.509.
[180] Under s.4 of the Leasehold Reform Act.
[181] *Barratt v Richardson & Cresswell* [1930] 1 K.B. 686; *Re General Rolling Stock Co.* (1872) 7 Ch.App. 646; *Re River Steamer Co.* (1871) 6 Ch.App. 822; *Re Lorillard* [1922] 2 Ch. 638.
[182] See also paras 14.024–14.025.
[183] This is to some extent a derogation from the principle, stated in s.36 of the Act, that limitation periods do not apply to equitable remedies: see para.3.002.
[184] 1980 Act s.18(1).
[185] 1980 Act s.18(3).

not when their right of action to recover the land becomes time-barred, but when the right of recovery of all those entitled to a beneficial interest in the land or the proceeds of sale has become time-barred.[186]

Actions on behalf of beneficiaries

13.088   Section 18(4) provides that the tenant for life or trustees, as the case may be, may bring an action on behalf of any person entitled to a beneficial interest in the land or the proceeds of sale, notwithstanding that the right of action of the tenant for life or trustees has itself become time-barred. This provision is possibly not strictly necessary, since in such cases the true plaintiffs will be the beneficiaries, whose right of action is by definition not time-barred; the subsection should perhaps be regarded as being included ex majore cautela. Attention is drawn also to Sch.1, para.9 to the 1980 Act. This provides that where any settled land or land held on trust for sale is in the possession of a person entitled to a beneficial interest in it or in the proceeds of sale (other than a person absolutely entitled to the land or the proceeds), no right of action to recover the land shall be treated for limitation purposes as accruing to the tenant for life, statutory owner or trustee (as the case may be) or to any other person entitled to a beneficial interest in the land or in the proceeds of sale. The effect of this is that time never runs in favour of a beneficiary in possession of the land, either against the trustee or against any other beneficiary. Thus one of a number of joint tenants who is in possession to the exclusion of the other joint tenants can never by his exclusive occupation acquire a title against them.[187] This rule does not apply to land held under any other form of trust.[188]

SPECIAL RULES FOR THE CROWN, ETC.

13.089   Part II of Schedule 1 to the 1980 Act lays down certain rules which apply only to actions brought by the Crown or by any spiritual or eleemosynary corporation. Paragraph 10 provides that the usual 12-year time-limit in the case of actions to recover land shall be replaced by a period of 30 years for these special classes of plaintiff. Given that the Crown is claimant, it is irrelevant that it may derive its title via a third party.[189] This is, however, subject to para.11, which applies to actions to recover foreshore. For such actions the period of limitation is 60 years, unless the land has, since the

---

[186] 1980 Act s.18(3).
[187] *Earnshaw v Hartley* [2000] Ch. 155, CA.
[188] *Bridges v Mees* [1957] Ch. 475, Harman J.
[189] *Secretary of State for Foreign and Commonwealth Affairs v Tomlin The Times*, 4 December 1990; Court of Appeal (Civil Division) Transcript No 1091 of 1990.

accrual of the case of action, ceased to be foreshore (while remaining vested in the Crown). In such cases time expires on the earlier of: (a) 60 years from the date when the cause of action accrued or (b) 30 years from the date when the land ceased to be foreshore.[190]

"Foreshore" is defined for these purposes as the shore and bed of the sea and of any tidal water, below the line of the medium high tide between the spring tides and the neap tides. It should also be observed that in the case of foreshore not all acts of encroachment will destroy exclusive possession.[191] Temporary encroachments which are not inconsistent with the continuing rights of the Crown will not have this effect. The question in *Roberts v Crown Estate Commissioners*[192] was whether it is open to the Crown to acquire title by adverse possession. After an interesting and wide-ranging of review of authorities going back as far as Magna Carta, the Court of Appeal held that the Crown can acquire title in this way. So far as the modern law is concerned, the matter might be thought to be settled by s.37(1) of the 1980 Act, which reads:

"Except as otherwise expressly provided in this Act, and without pre-judice to section 39, this Act shall apply to proceedings by or against the Crown in like manner as it applies to proceedings between subjects."

There is no relevant exception in the 1980 Act which could affect the present question.

If the action is brought by a person other than the Crown or one of the privileged corporations, but first accrued to such a person (so that the plaintiff claims through such a person) then Sch.1, para.12 provides that the period of limitation expires on the earlier of: (a) the period during which the privileged body could have brought the action or (b) 12 years from the date on which the cause of action first accrued to some person other than a privileged corporation. In *Hill v Transport for London*[193] it was held that para.12 contains a complete code for claims brought by persons claiming through the Crown. This paragraph provides:

13.090

"This code applies whether the right of action accrued originally to the Crown or only so accrued earlier, and "first" meant "earlier" or "pre-viously" rather than "originally". In effect the interposition of the Crown as freeholder at any point has the effect of allowing the paper title-holder the benefit of whichever of the two limitation periods referred to in paragraph 12 expires first Section 15(2) of the 1980 Act (which deals

---

[190] 1980 Act, Sch.1, para.11(2).
[191] *Fowley Marine (Emsorth) Ltd v Gafford* [1967] 2 Q.B. 808, Megaw J.; [1968] 2 Q.B. 818, CA.
[192] [2008] EWCA Civ 98.
[193] [2005] EWHC 856 (Ch), [2005] Ch 379 Rimer J.

with actions in respect of future interests) is also modified in favour of these claimants. Where that section imposes a 12-year limit, these plaintiffs have 30 years in which to bring the action. Where that section imposes a six-year limit, it is modified to 12 years.[194]"

Landlord and Tenant Act 1954

13.091   This statute appears to be almost unique[195] in English law in imposing a minimum time-limit for the bringing of certain actions as well as a maximum time-limit. This peculiarity has given rise to some litigation. In *Kammins Ballroom Company Ltd v Zenith Investments (Torquay) Ltd*[196] the tenant's application for a new tenancy was made before the expiry of two months from the service of the notice to quit, in breach of the procedural requirements of the Act. The House of Lords held that it is possible for a landlord to waive this aspect of the Act's requirements, but, by a bare majority, that there had been no such waiver in this case since the landlord (who had not originally noticed the error) had taken no step inconsistent with the subsequent assertion of his rights. ·

Two points remain unresolved after this decision. The first is whether the landlords would have been precluded from relying on their strict legal rights had they noticed it earlier and merely kept silent about it. The second is what would have been necessary to constitute a valid waiver of those rights. Perhaps if the landlords had made proposals for the terms of a new tenancy, the court would have held that this amounted to waiver.

13.092   This case may be compared with *Shelley v United Artists Corporation Ltd*,[197] which deals with the situation where the notice is served after the expiry of the four-month time-limit. A notice to terminate the tenancy was served on the plaintiffs by their immediate landlords. Shortly thereafter these landlords sold their interest in the property to their own immediate landlords (the eventual defendants). Under the 1954 Act this prevented them from being the competent landlords, i.e. the parties upon whom the plaintiffs were required to serve a notice requesting a new tenancy. In ignorance of the sale the plaintiffs nevertheless served the notice on these landlords. By the time the error was discovered and the plaintiffs were able to serve a new notice on the defendants, who had become the competent landlords on agreeing to buy the property, the four-month limit had expired, and the defendants took this point. Realising that they were too late to commence new proceedings against the defendants, the plaintiffs sought leave to join the defendants to the action against the original

---

[194] Sch.1, para.13.
[195] See also the Matrimonial Causes Act 1973; see para.27.010.
[196] [1970] 1 Q.B. 573, CA, affirmed [1971] A.C. 850, HL.
[197] (1989) 58 P. & C.R. 34, Mervyn Davies J.

landlords as additional defendants. This appears to infringe the principle laid down in CPR r.17.4 that no additional party should be joined when to do so would have the effect of defeating an accrued limitation defence. The plaintiffs naturally argued that this was a case where the court should exercise its discretion to permit the joinder notwithstanding the limitation defence, since the plaintiff was innocent of any wrongdoing. However, Mervyn Davies J. held that the ordinary principles should apply, so that joinder should not be permitted.

This seems a harsh decision, but it is submitted that it follows inevitably **13.093** from the provisions of CPR r.17.4. That rule does provide for certain situations in which joinder may be permitted, notwithstanding the expiry of the limitation period. These situations are dealt with at paras 23.019–23.024. The only one that could possibly apply is that the limitation period was current when the action was started and the addition of the new party is necessary to the determination of the action. The former requirement is satisfied in this case, but as to the latter requirement it is necessary to look at CPR r.17.4, which lists the cases where such addition will be deemed necessary. Unfortunately, none of these is capable of applying to the present situation. The inevitable, if regrettable, consequence is that the time-limit cannot be circumvented.

A question which may be raised here concerns the conduct of the defendants. In some cases (though not this one) it might be shown that the sale to another party was simply a device to prevent the tenant from exercising his rights under the Landlord and Tenant Act 1954. In such a case it may be suggested that the court would be slow to allow the defendant to rely upon the limitation defence. It is, of course, established that a defendant may be estopped from pleading limitation[198] and it is possible that a court would be prepared to find an estoppel in a case of this kind.

The Law Commission's proposals

Land has always been treated as a distinct category for limitation purposes, **13.094** and it is therefore perhaps not surprising that the Consultation Paper does not propose to apply the core regime in its full vigour to cases involving land. The Commission proposes that the core regime's three-year limitation period should not apply. Instead, the longstop of 10 or 15 years should apply and should be the only applicable period for cases involving the recovery of land. The same should apply to actions to recover principal or interest secured by a mortgage. However, the three-year period should apply to actions to recover arrears of rent.

The Commission justify the proposal to exempt actions for the recovery

---

[198] *Colchester BC v Tillson* [1991] 2 All E.R. 29, affirmed [1992] Ch.421, CA.

of land from the core regime on the basis that the consequences of the expiry of time in such cases are more serious than those in non-land cases, in that the expiry of time extinguishes the owner's title to the land. This argument, although factually correct, seems unconvincing. If the priority is to encourage the prompt institution of proceedings, and if time runs from discoverability rather than from accrual, it is suggested that no injustice would be done by applying the core regime to all cases.

Commonhold and Leasehold Reform Act 2002

13.095 This Act creates a new system of landholding known as commonhold. Section 37 of the Act allows actions to be brought to enforce rights and duties arising under the Act. Such an action shall not be brought after the expiration of six years from the date on which the cause of action accrued.[199]

---

[199] Limitation Act 1980 s.19A, inserted by the Commonhold and Leasehold Reform Act 2002 s.68 and Sch.

CHAPTER 14

Trustees and Personal Representatives

Section 21 of the Limitation Act 1980 deals with the position of trustees, though, as appears below,[1] the rules relating to trusts of interests in land are slightly different. Section 22 relates to claims against the estates of deceased persons. The two sections are connected in that s.22 is expressly made subject to s.21(1) and (2). This is reinforced by the interpretation section (s.38) of the 1980 Act which provides that "trust" and "trustee" are to have the same meanings as in the Trustee Act 1925. Section 68(17) of that Act states that "trustee", where the context admits, shall include a personal representative. It is for these reasons that trusts and estates of deceased persons are dealt with together.

14.001

WHEN DOES A TRUST EXIST?

The importance of this question in a limitation context was stressed by Diplock J. in *Royal Norwegian Government v Constant & Constant*.[2] Unfortunately, there is no one definition of the conditions that are necessary and sufficient for the existence of a trust. For a detailed consideration of these matters, refer to the specialist works on trusts, but there will generally be a trust in any case where the legal and beneficial title to property of any kind are in different hands. In addition, there may be statutory trusts even where these conditions are not satisfied. Two very important examples of this are settlements under the Settled Land Act 1925, and the trust for sale imposed by the Law of Property Act 1925 in any case where property is jointly owned.

14.002

---

[1] See paras 14.024–14.026.
[2] [1960] 2 Lloyd's Rep. 431.

The purpose of s.21 is to protect beneficiaries whose trustees have wrongfully appropriated property. However, the section distinguishes at various points between trustees who have acted fraudulently and those who have merely been negligent. Section 21(1) provides that a period of limitation shall neither apply to an action in respect of any fraud or fraudulent breach of trust to which the trustee was party or privy, nor to any action to recover from the trustee trust property or the proceeds of trust property in the possession of the trustee, or previously received by the trustee and converted to his use. Section 21(3) goes on to provide that any other action by a beneficiary to recover trust property or in respect of any breach of trust, shall be subject to a limitation period of six years, time running from the accrual of the cause of action.

BREACH OF TRUST

14.003 The meaning of the expression "breach of trust" was considered at some length (though entirely obiter) by Megarry V.-C. in *Tito v Waddell (No. 2)*.[3] Curiously, there does not appear to be any prior authority directly in point, and the definition of the phrase is one which has divided writers on this topic. Megarry V.-C. referred to the opinions of two leading American writers, Pomerey[4] and Scott.[5] The former states "every omission or violation by a trustee of a duty which equity lays on him . . . is a breach of trust", whilst the latter states "a trustee commits a breach of trust if he violates any duty which he owes as trustee to the beneficiaries". Ultimately Megarry V.-C. was not prepared to decide on the meaning of the phrase "breach of trust", but his observations on the narrower point which he was considering are instructive in this context. The issue which had been raised was whether breaches of the self-dealing rule[6] and/or the fair-dealing rule[7] by a trustee amounted to a breach of trust for the purpose of the Limitation Acts. His Lordship held that these were not breaches of trust. These rules are properly to be dealt with under the heading of "disabilities of trustees", and those books which treat them under "duties of trustees" are wrong.[8]

---

[3] [1977] 3 All E.R. 129 at 246–248.
[4] *Equity Jurisprudence* (3rd edn, 1955), vol. III, p.2086.
[5] *Scott on Trusts* (3rd edn, 1967), vol.III, p.1605.
[6] i.e. the rule that a trustee must not sell trust property to himself.
[7] i.e. the rule that a trustee must deal fairly with the trust property and must not prejudice the interests of the beneficiaries.
[8] [1977] 3 All E.R. 129 at 250.

Fraud or fraudulent breach of trust

The previous paragraph dealt with the question of whether there is a breach **14.004** of trust at all. For the purposes of s.21(1)(a), it is necessary to consider also whether there has been fraud or whether any breach of trust has been fraudulent. These expressions are not defined in the Act. The concept of fraud is also relevant to s.32 of the Act, though, as is explained below, the provisions of s.32 have no direct relevance to cases within s.21(1). It may nevertheless be that the authorities on the meaning of fraud in that section can be used by way of analogy here. Essentially, those cases say that an action is based on fraud when a plea of fraud is an essential element in the cause of action.[9] Therefore, an action for conversion is not an action based on fraud, since conversion can be committed without fraud. In *Armitage v Nurse*[10] the Court of Appeal held that, for the purposes of this provision, fraud means "actual fraud" i.e. dishonesty which:

> "connotes at the minimum an intention on the part of the trustee to pursue a particular course of action, either knowing that it is contrary to the interests of the beneficiaries or being recklessly indifferent whether it is contrary to their interests or not."[11]

In *Newgate Stud Company v Penfold*[12] David Richards J. added that this would include a deliberate concealment of a material interest which the trustee knew should be disclosed However, the extended concept of equitable fraud does not apply in this context. In addition, the fraud of which the beneficiary complains must be in connection with the trust.[13] An action against a director in relation to a deliberate non-disclosure of an interest forming part of a dishonest breach of trust is caught by s.21.[14]

Actions against third parties

The provisions of s.21(1)(a) are not by their terms limited to actions against **14.005** trustees,[15] though that will no doubt be the situation where they are most

---

[9] *Beaman v A.R.T.S. Ltd* [1949] 1 K.B. 550, Denning J.; reversed [1949] 1 All E.R. 465, CA. For a similar point in a bankruptcy context see *Woodland-Ferrari v UCL Group Retirement Scheme*, July 5, 2002, Ferris J., Unreported. For more on the meaning of fraud, see paras 20.008–20.009.

[10] *The Independent*, April 11, 1997, CA.

[11] *Armitage v Nurse* [1998] Ch 241, [1997] 2 All ER 705, at 251, 260 per Millett LJ and see *Gwembe Valley Development Co Ltd v Koshy* [2003] EWCA Civ 1048, [2004] 1 BCLC 131 at 170 (para.131).

[12] [2004] EWHC 2993 (Ch).

[13] *UCB Home Loans Corporation v Carr*, April 19, 2000, Unreported, Crane J.

[14] *DEG Deutsche Investitions v Koshy*, December 10, 2001, Rimer J., Unreported.

[15] In this respect it is useful to contrast s.21(1)(b), which is expressly limited to actions to recover property from the trustee.

commonly invoked. Once it is established that there has been fraud or a fraudulent breach of trust, the action may be brought against a third party who is now in possession of trust property. This was the situation in *G.L. Baker Ltd v Medway Building and Supplies Ltd*,[16] where T, a director of the defendant company and the accountant of the plaintiff company, unlawfully transferred £6,000 from the latter to the former.[17] The action was brought more than six years later, and the plaintiffs relied on what is now s.21(1)(a) of the 1980 Act. Danckwerts J. held that as this provision did apply it is unnecessary that the action should be brought against the trustee, so long as it is "in respect of" the trustees' fraud, and this requirement will be satisfied where the fraud is the basis of the cause of action.

The possible difficulty with this approach arises from s.32 of the 1980 Act, which deals expressly with cases where the action is based on fraud. In such cases the running of time is postponed until the existence of the cause of action is or could with reasonable diligence have been discovered by the claimant; there is also an express saving in s.32(3) for bona fide purchasers of property. This appears to conflict with the rule in s.21.[18] The apparent conflict can, however, be resolved. Section 32 is expressly to apply "in the case of any action for which a period of limitation is prescribed by this Act",[19] but the whole point of s.21(1) is that where it applies no period of limitation is prescribed by the Act. Consequently, s.32 has no application to such cases, and the action can be brought without limit of time and without any protection for innocent third-party purchasers. The application of s.21(1) to accessories to the fraudulent breaches of trust of others with the result that no period of limitation is applicable to claims against them was confirmed in *Statek Corporation v Alford*[20]. The decision of the House of Lords in *Dubai Aluminium Co Ltd v Salaam*[21] is not authority to the contrary. In coming to this conclusion Evans-Lombe J. followed the decision of Dankwerts J in *G L Baker Ltd v Medway Building and Supplies Ltd*[22] and the obiter dicta of Lord Esher and Bowen LJ in *Soar v Ashwell* [1893] 2 QB 390 and disapproved the decision of Richard Sheldon QC in *Cattley v Pollard*.[23]

---

[16] [1958] 1 W.L.R. 1216, Danckwerts J.; reversed [1958] 3 All E.R. 532, but on a point which does not affect the limitation issues.

[17] The case falls within the rules on breach of trust because directors are treated as trustees of the company's money, see *Thorne v Heard* [1894] 1 Ch. 599 at 610.

[18] See Derek Morgan, *Current Law Statutes Annotated* (1980), vol.II.

[19] See s.32(1).

[20] *Statek Corporation v Alford* [2008] EWHC 32 (Ch) Evans-Lombe J.

[21] [2002] UKHL 48, [2003] 2 AC 366, [2003] 1 All ER 97.

[22] [1958] 3 All ER 540, [1958] 1 WLR 1216.

[23] [2006] EWHC 3130 (Ch), [2007] 2 All ER 1086, [2007] 3 WLR 317.

To which the trustee was party or privy

This expression also dates from the Trustee Act 1888. It was considered in **14.006** *Thorne v Heard*,[24] where the defendants, first mortgagees of land, had employed a solicitor to sell the land for them. He then wrongfully retained the balance of the proceeds of sale and converted them to his own use, instead of paying them over to the plaintiffs, who were the second mortgagees. Among the issues that arose[25] was whether the defendants had been party or privy to the fraud committed by the solicitor. It was held that they had not: the solicitor had not acted as their agent or with their approval when retaining the proceeds of sale; indeed, they had been unaware of his actions. Kay L.J. suggested[26] that the expression "party or privy" must indicate some degree of moral complicity in the wrongdoing.

Section 21(1)(b)

It is to be observed that para.21(1)(b) applies only to actions to recover **14.007** against the trustee, in which respect it may be contrasted with s.21(1)(a). At the same time it encompasses two slightly different actions. The first is an action to recover trust property which is still in the trustee's possession, whereas the second is an action to recover the proceeds of trust property which the trustee has previously received and converted to his use. This provision was considered by Millett LJ in *Paragon Finance Plc v D B Thakerar & Co*[27] who distinguished between cases of constructive trust arising where the defendant, although not expressly appointed as trustee, has assumed the duties of trustee by a lawful transaction[28] which was independent of and preceded the breach of trust, and cases where the trust obligation arose as the direct consequence of the unlawful transaction which was impeached by the plaintiff. The second kind of case arises where, if the defendant received trust property at all, it is adversely to the plaintiff by an unlawful transaction and the constructive trust is a remedial constructive trust. Millett L.J. doubted whether s.21 applied at all to the position of a constructive trustee of the second kind, but in *James v Williams*[29] the Court of Appeal assumed that it did so apply.[30] However, in *Halton International Inc v Guernroy Ltd*[31] a different composition of the

---

[24] [1894] 1 Ch. 599, CA.
[25] For other issues in the case, see the next paragraph.
[26] [1894] 1 Ch. 599 at 608.
[27] [1999] 1 All ER 400 at 407f et seq.
[28] see e.g *Pallant v Morgan* [1953] Ch 43, [1952] 2 All ER 951.
[29] [1999] 3 All ER 309, [1999] 3 WLR 451.
[30] See also *Martin v Myers* [2004] EWHC 1947 (Ch) Nicholas Strauss QC, where *James v Williams* was followed.
[31] [2006] EWCA Civ 801, [2006] All ER (D) 302 (Jun).

Court of Appeal, without citing *James v Williams*, held that Millett LJ had been right and that s.21 does not apply to remedial constructive trusts. This appears to be the preferable view, though it is surely desirable that the Court of Appeal should now take the first opportunity to review the matter and the authorities at rather more length.

Trust property or the proceeds of trust property

14.008 For the most part the expression "trust property" requires no special consideration, it being merely a matter of construction to determine whether the property in question was subject to a trust of which the defendant was a trustee. A particular point in this area arose in *Re Howlett (Dec'd)*.[32] The defendant had taken possession of land in Kent under the pre-1926 custom of "gavelkind". After his remarriage he lost the right to occupy it, but remained in occupation to the exclusion of his son who was entitled to the occupation. His son later sued him for the rents and profits which should have been received during that time. The defendant pleaded that s.21(1)(b) had no application because he had not in fact received anything. Danckwerts J. rejected this argument, holding that a defendant who has been in possession of land as bailiff for the claimant (as was held to be the case here) could not be heard to say that he had not received rents and profits.

The case provides a remarkable example of applying this provision to proceeds which should have been received, but in fact were not received. A number of other cases have explored the limits of this expression.[33] In *Re Sharp*[34] trustees were held liable to pay the tax which should have been deducted on annuities that they paid to themselves gross.

14.009 In *Wassell v Leggatt*[35] the section was held to apply to a husband who took and wrongfully retained property which had been separately devised to his wife. In *Re Clark*[36] the provision was applied where a trustee procured trust property to be leased for his own personal benefit at an undervalue. A remarkable decision in this area is that of Whitford J. in *Attorney-General v Manchester City Council*.[37] This was an action for a declaration that certain property was held on charitable trusts. The learned judge held that this was an action to recover trust property within the

---

[32] [1949] Ch. 767, Danckwerts J.
[33] In addition to the cases mentioned in the text, *Re Eyre-Williams* [1923] 2 Ch. 533; *Mitchinson v Spencer* (1902) 86 L.T. 618; *Re National Bank of Wales* [1899] 2 Ch. 629; *Moore v Knight* [1891] 1 Ch. 547; see Morgan, *Current Law Statutes Annotated* (1980), vol.II.
[34] [1906] 1 Ch. 793.
[35] [1896] 1 Ch. 554.
[36] (1920) 150 L.T. 94.
[37] March 7, 1983, Unreported.

meaning of this provision, since the recovery of such property would be a natural consequence of granting the declaration. It is submitted that this cannot be right. No one in this case was seeking to recover anything, and to hold that this action falls within s.21 is to do violence to the ordinary meaning of the words used.

"In the possession of the trustee . . ."

In addition to showing that the action is to recover trust property or the proceeds thereof, the claimant must also show that the property is in the trustee's possession or was previously received and converted by him. The case of *Re Howlett (Dec'd)*,[38] discussed in para.14.008, is again relevant, since it deems the trustee to have received and converted notional property, which it then treats as trust property. It is also appropriate to mention here the decision of the Court of Appeal in *Thorne v Heard*.[39] In that case the defendant had never received the mortgage money which the plaintiff was seeking to recover, it having been wrongfully retained by the defendants' solicitor, who had apparently spent it. The case was decided under the 1888 Act, the relevant provision of which referred to property "still retained" by the trustee. This is no different in effect from the present wording, which speaks of property "in the possession of" the trustee. The argument for the plaintiff was that the defendants were entitled to call on the solicitor to hand over the money, and that it was therefore to be treated as "still retained" by them. This argument was rejected by the Court of Appeal, which held that the phrase "still retained" covered cases where the defendant had the money or could readily get possession of it, but did not extend to cases where the money had been lost, so that the defendant could not get it. If, as suggested above, the principles are the same under the present s.21, this case would appear to be good authority that a trustee will not be treated as being in possession of trust property where he neither has it nor is in a position to get it. If he has never received it, then, subject to the principle laid down in *Re Howlett (Dec'd)*, s.21(1)(b) will not apply to him, and he will be able to rely on the ordinary six-year limitation period. **14.010**

Section 21(2) did not appear in the 1939 Act. It was introduced by s.5(1) of the Limitation Amendment Act 1980. It concerns the position of a trustee who is also a beneficiary under the trust. If he receives or retains trust property or its proceeds as his share on a distribution of trust property under the trust, his liability in any action brought under s.21(1)(b) (recovery from trustee of trust property in his possession or formerly converted to his use) is limited to the excess of the amount received or retained over his proper share. Thus, if he is aware of four beneficiaries, and dis- **14.011**

---

[38] [1949] Ch.767, Danckwerts J.
[39] [1894] 1 Ch. 599; see also para.14.006.

tributes the fund to them equally, each will receive 25 per cent. If another beneficiary appears on the scene after the end of the limitation period of six years laid down by s.21(3),[40] the trustee is liable only to pay to him the difference between the 20 per cent which he should have received and the 25 per cent which he should have received. Previously he would have been liable to make good the full 25 per cent without limit of time. However, this relieving provision applies only if the trustee acted honestly and reasonably in making the distribution. Therefore, the gist of this subsection is that a trustee who distributes trust property to himself in excess of the amount to which he is entitled may, after the expiry of six years, keep that part to which he was entitled, so long as the mistake which he made was both honest and reasonable.

Section 21(3)

14.012   In all cases of actions by a beneficiary in respect of fraud or fraudulent breach of trust, or to recover trust property, other than those to which s.21(1) applies and those for which some other provision of the 1980 Act provides a period of limitation, s.21(3) applies a limitation period of six years, running from the date on which the cause of action accrued. The form of this provision makes it necessary to decide when a beneficiary's cause of action in respect of a breach of trust accrues. The general answer to this, as established in *Thorne v Heard*,[41] is that it accrues as soon as the breach of trust has been committed,[42] and not, if different, at the date when the beneficiary suffers loss.

However, close examination of *Thorne v Heard* reveals some ambiguity in this analysis. The material facts of that case were that the defendants' solicitor properly received money raised by exercising a mortgagee's power of sale. He then wrongfully converted it to his own use instead of paying it to the plaintiff second mortgagees. The Court of Appeal held that the cause of action accrued as soon as the solicitor received the money. The difficulty with this is that the solicitor had surely not committed any breach of trust at that stage—his obligation was to pay the money to the plaintiffs within a reasonable time, and the breach of trust occurred only when he failed to do so. If taken literally, the observations of the Court of Appeal would suggest that the cause of action against the trustee accrues as soon as he receives the trust property, and this clearly cannot be correct. It may be noted, however, that in *Thorne v Heard* the Court of Appeal was not required to choose between the date of receipt and the expiry of a reasonable time thereafter,

---

[40] Section 21(2) has no relevance to an action brought within this period; in such a case, the old rule still applies.
[41] [1894] 1 Ch.599, CA.
[42] See also *Swain v Bringeman* [1891] 3 Ch. 233; *Somerset v Earl Poulett* [1894] 1 Ch. 231.

since on either assumption the action would have been barred. The court's observations on this point therefore can and should be regarded as obiter dicta.

IDENTIFYING THE BASIS OF THE ACTION

This point is of great importance, since the correct classification of the action will determine whether the claim is subject to the six-year limitation period of s.21(3) or whether it is free from any limitation period under s.21(1).

14.013

FIDUCIARY DUTIES

This point was first considered by Laddie J. in *Nelson v Rye*.[43] The defendant had been the plaintiff's agent, handling money on his behalf and retaining out of that money an agreed commission. When the plaintiff brought an action alleging impropriety in the handling of this money, questions of limitation arose. The defendant had clearly been in a fiduciary position, and it was argued for the plaintiff that time never runs in favour of fiduciaries, since no section of the Limitation Act 1980 applies to them. Laddie J. accepted that actions for breach of fiduciary duty simpliciter fall outside the Act, but went on to hold that the position is different where the fiduciary duty also gives rise to a trust, as in the present case. If there is a trust, then it is necessary to look at s.21 of the Limitation Act 1980 to see what period of limitation, if any, applies to the case. Whether a trust arises must, of course, be a question of fact depending on the circumstances of each case.[44] The point has been considered in a number of further cases, where attempts have been made to extend the relevant limitation period by invoking s.21 in relation to claims against persons in fiduciary positions, notably solicitors. For present purposes it is sufficient to say that the attempt to characterise all breaches of fiduciary duty as breaches of trust has now been decisively rejected. In *Bristol and West Building Society v Mothew (t/a Stapley & Co.)*[45] Millett L.J observed:

14.014

"Despite the warning given by Fletcher Moulton L.J. in *Re Coomber; Coomber v Coomber* [1911] 1 Ch. 723, 728, this branch of the law has been bedevilled by unthinking resort to verbal formulae. It is therefore necessary to begin by defining one's terms. The expression 'fiduciary

---

[43] [1996] 2 All E.R. 186.
[44] See also para.4.001.
[45] [1998] Ch.1 at 16; [1996] 4 All E.R. 698 at 710, CA.

duty' is properly confined to those duties which are peculiar to fiduciaries and the breach of which attracts legal consequences differing from those consequent upon the breach of other duties. Unless the expression is so limited it is lacking in practical utility. In this sense it is obvious that not every breach of duty by a fiduciary is a breach of fiduciary duty. I would endorse the observations of Southin J. in *Girardet v Crease & Co.* (1987) 11 B.C.L.R. (2d) 361, 362:

> 'The word "fiduciary" is flung around now as if it applied to all breaches of duty by solicitors, directors of companies and so forth . . . That a lawyer can commit a breach of the special duty [of a fiduciary] . . . by entering into a contract with the client without full disclosure . . . and so forth is clear. But to say that simple carelessness in giving advice is such a breach is a perversion of words.' "[46]

14.015　　It is similarly inappropriate to apply the expression to the obligation of a trustee or other fiduciary to use proper skill and care in the discharge of his duties. If it is confined to cases where the fiduciary nature of the duty has special legal consequences, then the fact that the source of the duty is to be found in equity rather than the common law does not make it a fiduciary duty. The common law and equity each developed the duty of care, but they did so independently of each other and the standard of care required is not always the same.[47] However, *Gwembe Valley v Koshy*[48] was a claim against a company director for damages for breach of fiduciary duty. The remedy claimed was an account, and the action was brought more than six years after the original breach. The Court of Appeal had to consider which section of the Limitation Act applied, and it was held that the matter was governed by s.21, being in substance a matter of breach of fiduciary duty, rather than s.23, which deals with account more generally, The point is of practical importance, because it allowed the court to apply s.21(1), excluding the operation of any limitation period in cases where the fiduciary is party to a fraud. As Rimer J.[49] had held the defendant to have acted dishonestly, this subsection applied to the case.

---

[46] A view reiterated more recently in *Halton International Inc (Holdings) SARL v Guernroy Ltd* [2005] EWHC 1968 (Ch); [2006] 1 BCLC 78 Patten J.

[47] At 16–17 of the former report. See also *Henderson v Merrett Syndicates* [1995] 2 A.C. 145 at 205, per Lord Browne-Wilkinson; *Lac Minerals Ltd v International Corona Resources Ltd* (1989) 61 D.L.R. (4th) 14 at 28, per LaForest J.; *Permanent Building Society v Wheeler* (1994) 14 A.C.S.R. 109 at 157, per Ipp J.; and see Millett J's analysis in *Paragon Finance Plc v D.B. Thakerar & Co. (A Firm)* [1999] 1 All E.R. 400; *Coulthard v Disco Mix Club Ltd* [1999] 2 All E.R. 457; [2000] 1 W.L.R. 707; [1999] F.S.R. 900; [1999] E.M.L.R. 434, per Jules Sher Q.C.

[48] see also *JJ Harrison v Harrison* [2002] BCLC 162.

[49] sub nom *Deg-Deutsche Investitions Und Entwicklungsgesellschaft mbH v Koshy* [2001] All ER (D) 389 (Oct).

FUTURE INTERESTS

Section 21(3) contains a proviso to the effect that the right of action under **14.016** that subsection shall not be treated as having accrued to any beneficiary entitled to a future interest in the property until the interest falls into possession. This provision was considered in *Re Paulings Settlement Trusts, Younghusband v Coutt's & Co.*[50] The trustees in this case had made an advance of capital which was invalid because it was in breach of trust. It was held that this did not cause the interest to fall into possession for the purposes of the proviso. There are only two ways in which a future interest can fall into possession, namely a release of the prior interest (here a life interest) and a valid advance out of the capital.

Trustee Act 1925, section 61

This section is not directly relevant to limitation issues, but may be men- **14.017** tioned here in passing. It empowers the court to grant a trustee relief against the consequences of any breach of trust to which he has been party if it appears just to do so. It is therefore an alternative basis upon which a trustee may escape liability when s.21(1) prevents him from pleading limitation.

CHARITABLE TRUSTS

Section 21(3) refers to actions by beneficiaries, and this makes it necessary **14.018** to decide who is a beneficiary. A particular problem arises in connection with charitable trusts, which must normally be for the public, or a section thereof.[51] The trustees' obligations under such a trust cannot be enforced by any of the discretionary beneficiaries—the proper claimant in such an action is the Attorney-General.[52] A case of this kind is *Attorney-General v Cocke*,[53] where the claim was for injunctions[54] restraining the trustees from certain actions and for an order for an account in respect of past profits. Harman J. held that this was not an action by a beneficiary. The Attorney-General himself was obviously not a beneficiary, and the judge held that he did not act as agent for the beneficiaries, but as the protector of the public

---

[50] [1962] 1 W.L.R. 86, Wilberforce J.; affirmed [1964] Ch.303 CA.
[51] *Verge v Somerville* [1924] A.C. 496, HL; the rule does not apply to trusts for the relief of poverty—*Dingle v Turner* [1972] A.C. 601, HL.
[52] *Wallis v S.-G. for New Zealand* [1903] A.C. 173, PC; *Hauxwell v Barton-upon-Humber UDC* [1974] Ch. 432.
[53] [1988] Ch. 414, Harman J.
[54] As the claim was for an equitable remedy, this must be treated as a case where the statute is applied by analogy: see paras 3.006–3.010.

interest. Consequently, s.21(3) has no application to such a case. Where, as here, there is no attempt to recover trust property, the result must be that no provision of the 1980 Act applies, and the action is consequently not subject to any period of limitation.[55]

Other actions by the Attorney-General

14.019   As part of his responsibility to protect beneficiaries of charities, the Attorney-General may also take action to set aside certain transactions entered into by charities. The limitation periods applicable to such actions were considered in a number of nineteenth-century cases. In *Governors of Magdalen College, Oxford v Attorney-General*[56] the college had granted a perpetual lease of charity land. It was held that proceedings to impeach this grant must be brought within 20[57] years of the grant. In *Attorney-General v Davey*[58] it was held that the same rule applied to a lease of charity land for 500 years where this was granted in breach of trust, and the principle was further extended in *Attorney-General v Payne*[59] to the case of a lease improvidently granted by a charitable corporation. Finally, in *Magdalen College Hospital v Knotts*[60] it was held that time ran from the date when the lease was granted, rather than from the time when the decision to set aside the lease was taken by the charity, since the action of ejectment could be brought at any time after the earlier date.

EXPRESS AND CONSTRUCTIVE TRUSTEES

14.020   The question of a possible distinction for limitation purposes between express and constructive trustees has been the subject of judicial consideration. In *Tintin Exploration Syndicate Ltd v Sandys*[61] the defendant was a company director who had received an ultra vires payment from the company. Clearly he was liable to repay it, but he pleaded limitation, and the question was whether he was within what is now the 1980 Act, s.21(1)(b). On his behalf it was contended that he was not caught by this provision, being only a constructive trustee. Roxburgh J. rejected this argument, holding on the basis of *Soar v Ashwell*[62] that he was an express trustee. The interesting point for present purposes is the assumption made

---

[55] See also *Magdalen College Oxford v Attorney-General* (1857) 6 H.L.Cas. 189.
[56] (1857) 6 H.L.Cas. 189.
[57] This was the period applicable under Real Property Limitation Act 1833 at the present day the period would be 12 years (1980 Act s.15).
[58] (1861) 4 De G. & J. 136.
[59] (1857) 27 Beav. 168.
[60] (1878) 8 Ch.D. 709, Fry J., CA; affirmed (1879) 4 App.Cas. 324, HL.
[61] (1947) 177 L.T. 412, Roxburgh J.
[62] Relying on *Soar v Ashwell* [1893] 2 Q.B. 390; (1893) 69 L.T. 585, CA.

in the case that s.21 applies only to express trustees. The assumption is profoundly puzzling in the light of the definitions of "trust" and "trustee". The Limitation Act 1980, like the Limitation Act 1939, incorporates the definition given in s.68(17) of the Trustee Act 1925:

> " 'Trust' does not include the duties incident to an estate conveyed by way of mortgage, but with this exception the expressions 'trust' and 'trustee' extend to implied and constructive trusts, and to cases where the trustee has a beneficial interest in the trust property, and to the duties incident to the office of a personal representative, and 'trustee,' where the context admits, includes a personal representative."

Halton International Inc v Guernroy Ltd[63] considered further the distinction drawn by Millett L.J. in *Paragon Finance plc v DB Thakerar & Co*[64] between two classes of constructive trust:

14.021

> ". . . the expressions 'constructive trust' and 'constructive trustee' have been used by equity lawyers to describe two entirely different situations. The first covers those cases . . . where the Defendant, though not expressly appointed as trustee, has assumed the duties of a trustee by a lawful transaction which was independent of and preceded the breach of trust and is not impeached by the Plaintiff. The second covers those cases where the trust obligation arises as a direct consequence of the unlawful transaction which is impeached by the Plaintiff."

Breach of duty by the first category of trustee is treated as falling within s.21(1)(a) of the Limitation Act 1980, so that no period of limitation applies, but breach by the second category of trustee is not so treated, and the ordinary six-year limitation period applies. The Court of Appeal in Halton contrasted two earlier Court of Appeal decisions, which were held to fall either side of the line. These were *JJ Harrison (Properties) Ltd v Harrison*[65], and *Gwembe Valley Development Co Ltd v Koshy.*[66] In *Harrison* the claimant was a family property company, of which the defendant was a director. In 1985 a property owned by the company was valued at £8,400, but in a side letter the valuer said that it "may have some development potential" and that the valuation did not take this into account. The side letter was not disclosed to the company, but the director was aware of it. In 1986 he bought the property from the company without disclosing the side letter, or the fact that he had himself made an application for planning permission. He later sold it for a very substantial profit. More

---

[63] [2006] EWCA Civ 801.
[64] [1999] 1 All ER 400, 408.
[65] [2001] EWCA Civ 1467, [2002] 1 BCLC 162.
[66] [2003] EWCA Civ 1048, [2004] 1 BCLC 131.

than six years later the company sued him for an account of the proceeds of sale of the land. His limitation defence failed because the claim was within class 1. By contrast, in *Gwembe Valley*, the defendant was managing director of the claimant company, GVDC, and a shareholder in it. He also owned a majority of the shares in and controlled another company, Lasco, which lent money to GVDC. He arranged the loans. As a result of the loans GVDC acknowledged a debt to Lasco of U$5.8m. This was on the basis that the sum advanced 56.4m kwacha (Zambian currency) was equivalent to U$5.8m at the official exchange rate. However, the kwacha advanced to GVDC by Lasco had been obtained for only about U$1m by the defendant. The case against the defendant was that he did not disclose to the board of GVDC his interest in Lasco, or the profit that Lasco made on the loans to GVDC. It was held that, apart from fraud, the claim would have been time-barred, because his liability to account for the secret profit was not within class 1, and therefore the exception provided by s.21(1)(b) did not apply. The difference between the two cases was that while in the former the director had a pre-existing "trustee-like responsibility" in relation to the particular property which was the subject of the action, in the latter he did not. The comparison between the two cases is interesting because both involved a company director who to some extent misused his position. The decisions differ because it is necessary to consider closely the nature of the duty which has been breached.

14.022 A similar point was considered in *Soar v Ashwell* where both Bowen L.J. and Kay L.J. observed that a constructive trustee had always been treated differently from an express trustee for the purposes of limitation. However, it is submitted that reliance on that case was inappropriate in 1947 and is equally inappropriate now. There are two reasons for this. The first is that *Soar v Ashwell* predates the Trustee Act 1925, so that there was no relevant statutory definition of the term "trustee". The second, possibly more important, reason is that there was then no limitation enactment dealing with the position of trustees. The court in *Soar v Ashwell* was seeking to apply the notion of limitation in an equitable context by analogy with the statute in the same way that s.36 of the 1980 Act now requires the court to do in a number of cases, of which s.21 is not one. Thus, the court was able to consider the matter from the point of view of general principle without being constrained by specific statutory provisions. Section 68(17) of the Trustee Act 1925 has at least partly abrogated the general distinction between express and constructive trustees, and the combination of that section with s.21 of the 1980 Act appears effectively to overrule *Soar v Ashwell*. It is therefore submitted that the approach adopted in *Tintin v Sandys* was entirely misplaced, though of course the decision in the case is correct.[67]

---

[67] On this point see also *Lee v Sankey* (1873) L.R. 15 Eq. 204; *Re Eyre-Williams* [1923] 2 Ch. 533.

Two problems remain in this area. Section 68(17) of the Trustee Act does not mention trustees holding on a resulting trust. By application of the maxim expressio unius, exclusio alterius, it might be argued that s.21 has no application to such trustees. Also, it was held under the 1888 Act that a trustee in bankruptcy was not a trustee,[68] and the definition in the 1925 Act is no wider that that in s.1 of the 1888 Act; the same point appears to apply to a receiver appointed by the court.[69]

Section 21(4)

This subsection deals with the situation where one beneficiary's action has become time-barred, but that of another beneficiary has not. This can only arise in connection with future interests, where the provisions of s.21(3)[70] may preserve the right of action of the holder of a future interest (such as a remainderman) whilst barring the action of the holder of a present interest (such as a life tenant). In such situations s.21(4) provides that the life tenant shall obtain no greater benefit from the remainderman's action than he would have done had he himself brought the action and been met with a plea of the statute. The intention clearly is to prevent the life tenant from taking the benefit of any later action by the remainderman. The effect appears to be that no order for restitution of property misappropriated can be made in favour of the life tenant once the six years have expired. If the life tenant is entitled to the income of the trust, this will mean that the trustees become entitled to it once the six years have expired, though of course they do not become entitled to the underlying capital.

EQUITABLE INTERESTS IN LAND

In this area there is an obvious potential for conflict between different provisions of the 1980 Act. On the face of it both the provisions on trusts and the provisions on interests in land could apply. Section 18 resolves this overlap. Section 18(1) provides that, subject to s.21(1) and (2), the rules on legal estates in land apply equally to equitable estates in land.[71] Thus, the time of accrual of a cause of action to recover an equitable interest in land (which is here expressed to include an interest in the proceeds of sale of land held on trust for sale) is determined in accordance with Sch.1 to the 1980 Act. The separate question of what period of limitation (if any) applies to

14.023

14.024

---

[68] *Re Cornish* [1896] 1 Q.B. 99, CA.
[69] *Re Gallard* [1897] 2 Q.B. 8.
[70] See para.14.015.
[71] For the rules on interests in land generally, see Ch.13.

that action is determined according to the rules set out in s.21 of the 1980 Act and examined at length above.[72]

14.025   The remainder of s.18 contains provisions to deal with the situation where the tenant for life, statutory owner or trustee can no longer bring an action. In such cases it may be necessary to protect the position of other persons beneficially interested in the land. The accrual of their right of action (and consequently the date, if any, at which their action becomes barred) will be decided in accordance with the previous paragraph, but their interests would be liable to be defeated if the title of the tenant for life, statutory owner or trustee could be extinguished when his action became barred. Section 18(2)–(4) prevents this consequence by providing that the legal estate of such person shall not be treated as extinguished so long as there is some other person who is entitled to a beneficial interest in the land and whose right of action in respect of that interest either has not accrued or has not become barred by lapse of time. Clearly this provision does not preserve the right of action of the tenant for life, statutory owner or trustee rather, it merely varies the normal rule in land cases that upon the expiry of the limitation period the title is extinguished. Only those with subsequent equitable interests can benefit from this variation.

Section 18(4) enacts a further useful procedural rule. Generally, trustees or statutory owners may bring an action on behalf of their beneficiaries to enforce the latters' right under the trust. Section 18(4) preserves the power to bring this action even where the trustees' right to bring an action in respect of their own legal estate has become barred by lapse of time. Although s.18(4) does not expressly say so, it is clear that this rule can only apply where the interest of the beneficiary is not similarly barred.

Pleading the statute

14.026   The court will not take limitation points of its own motion: a defendant who wishes to rely on limitation must plead it expressly.[73] There is there-fore a choice as to whether or not to plead limitation. In *Thomson v Bruty*[74] it was suggested that trustees are under a duty to plead limitation if it is available to them, except where the action is one by a cestui que trust. It is submitted that this suggestion is correct. Trustees, unlike most other liti-gants, act for the benefit of others, and the duties imposed on them by their fiduciary capacity are onerous. It is entirely consistent with this that they should be required to take advantage of any rule of law properly applicable to their case in order to protect the interests of the beneficiaries. In *Attorney General v Trustees of the British Museum (Commission for Looted Art in*

---

[72] See paras 14.001–14.017.
[73] CPR 16PD 14.1.
[74] [1920] 1 Ch. 508, Eve J.

Europe intervening)[75] it was held that the Trustees of the British Museum were under a duty to take a limitation defence, but that was in the context of a statute—the British Museums Act 1963—which severely restricted the power of the trustees to dispose of or relinquish objects within the Museums's collection. It was held that a deliberate failure to raise a limitation defence which was available to them, with the result that an object might be lost, was to be viewed in the same way as a deliberate disposal. Clearly the logic of requiring the trustees to take a strict line does not extend to the case where they are sued by a beneficiary. It might be suggested that their duty to the beneficiary here is to refrain from pleading limitation, but such a suggestion is unsound. When they are sued by persons outside the trust they act for the benefit of the beneficiaries, but when they are sued by beneficiaries it is their own personal liability which is in issue. It cannot be correct to preclude them from relying on a right given to them by an Act of Parliament.

LACHES

In the case of a trust created by a gift to trustees on trust for beneficiaries, where the beneficiaries are not generally expected to do anything except receive the benefits provided for under the trust, it is unlikely that the doctrine of laches will apply in relation to any claim which they bring against the trustees. But this rule does not apply where the trust is of a more commercial character.[76] The doctrine of laches is in principle available even in a claim to which no limitation period applies, such as s.21.[77] That section provides that no period of limitation 'prescribed by this Act' applies. That is not the same thing as saying that no period of limitation or other equitable time limit applies.

14.027

ESTATES OF DECEASED PERSONS

Section 22 of the 1980 Act deals with actions in respect of the estates of deceased persons. That section is expressly made subject to s.21(1) and (2) (but not to s.21(3) and (4)). The section creates two different periods of limitation. Section 22(a) relates to claims to the personal estate of a deceased person or to any share or interest in any such estate. It applies whether the claim arises by will or on the intestacy of the deceased. It imposes a limitation period of 12 years from the date on which the right to

14.028

---

[75] [2005] EWHC 1089 (Ch), [2005] Ch 397 Sir Andrew Morritt V-C.
[76] *Patel v Shah* [2005] EWCA 157 per Mummery LJ at para.33.
[77] *Re Loftus* (below).

receive the share or interest accrued. Section 22(b) applies to actions to recover arrears of interest in respect of any legacy or damages in respect of such arrears. Here the limitation period is six years, and time runs from the date on which the interest becomes due.

14.029   Section 22(a) does not apply to an application to remove a person as administrator of an estate, because this is not 'a action in respect of any claim to the personal estate'—whatever claims there might be to the personal estate are quite unaffected by the identity of the administrator[78] . The same case also shows[79] that actions against an administrator for an account and payment are within s.21(1)(b) of the 1980 Act—either directly or indirectly, by reason of s.23 of that Act. Because they fall within s.21, they cannot fall within s.22.

Interaction with section 21

14.030   The effect of making s.22 subject to s.21(1) and (2) is to draw a distinction between cases where the action is brought against the personal representatives in that capacity, and cases where it is brought against them as trustees. In the former case s.22 will apply, whilst in the latter case s.21 will be the relevant provision.[80] In addition, time will not run in favour of a personal representative in any case whose facts fall within s.21(1) or (2), and it should be remembered that for this purpose the word "trustee" in s.21 includes personal representatives.[81] It is to be observed that there is here an important difference between the position of trustees and that of personal representatives: for the former the normal limitation period is six years, whereas for the latter it is 12 years. It might therefore be thought beneficial for personal representatives to execute vesting assents to property in favour of themselves as trustees at the earliest possible date in order to set time running in their favour. It should be remembered, however, that if this is done for reasons involving fraud, the case will fall under s.21(1) and time will never run in their favour. A further point is that where the claim is for the recovery of an interest in land, s.18 will apply[82] and the relevant period of limitation will be 12 years against both trustee and personal representative. However, a beneficiary under an intestacy who knows that he is not solely entitled to property, but takes possession of the property as if he owned it, instead of taking out letters of administration, is an executor de son tort. Although he is not an express trustee, he is under an equitable duty to hold the property for his siblings and will be deemed to be a constructive trustee. In that situation an application to recover an interest in the prop-

---

[78] *Re Loftus* (deceased); *Green v Gaul* [2006] EWCA Civ 1124.
[79] Para.32.
[80] *Re Oliver* [1927] 2 Ch. 323.
[81] 1980 Act s.38(1), incorporating Trustee Act 1925 s.68(17).
[82] See paras 14.024–14.025.

erty by a sibling will not be statute-barred because under s.21(1) there is no limitation period.[83]

It is also necessary to refer to Sch.1 to the 1980 Act. Part I of this **14.031** Schedule deals with the dates of accrual of causes of action to recover land, and para.2 relates specifically to actions to recover the land of a deceased person. The cause of action will be deemed to have accrued on the death of the deceased if certain conditions are met. The conditions are: that the deceased was at the date of his death in possession of the land (or in the case of a rentcharge created by will or taking effect upon his death in possession of the land charged) and that the deceased was the last person entitled to the land to be in possession of it. If these conditions are not satisfied, then the provisions of this Schedule do not help in determining when the cause of action accrues. It is submitted that in such cases the proper approach is to consider the general principle that there is no cause of action until there is both a claimant who can sue and a defendant who can be sued.

Meaning of "in respect of any claim to the personal estate"[84]

In *Re Diplock's Estate*[85] the Court of Appeal and House of Lords had to **14.032** consider the ambit of what is now s.22. The specific issue was whether the section applied to action against recipients of the estate other than the personal representatives. The facts were that the deceased's personal representatives had distributed the estate in accordance with the provisions of the will. Subsequently that will was held to be void for uncertainty. This action was brought by those entitled on the deceased's intestacy, and the defendants were both the personal representatives, and those who had wrongly received the estate on the distribution. The argument centred on the question of whether the provisions of s.22 applied to the case, it having been held in *Re Johnson, Sly and Blake*[86] that the earlier provision in s.8 of the Real Property Limitation Act 1833 applied only to actions against personal representatives so that before 1940 no period of limitation applied to these actions. It was held that the new provisions did extend to actions against beneficiaries for the recovery of the estate.

Re Loftus[87] is also a useful reminder of a point sometimes overlooked, **14.033** namely that s.22(a) has no application to a claim to the real estate of a deceased person. That apparent anomaly appears to stem from the fact that at the time of the predecessor of s.22(a) real estate did not in any event devolve upon a personal representative. The section is derived from s.40 of

---

[83] *James v Williams* [2000] Ch.1, CA.
[84] See the 1980 Act s.22(a).
[85] [1948] Ch.465, CA, affirmed [1951] A.C. 251, HL, sub nom. *Ministry of Health v Simpson*.
[86] (1885) 29 Ch.D. 964.
[87] above.

the Real Property Limitation Act 1833 (3&4 William IV Cap 27) and s.13 of the Law of Property Amendment Act 1860 (23&24 Victoria Cap 38). The section had no application to a claim to remove a personal representative and to appoint another in his or her place because prior to the Judicial Trustees Act 1896, the Court had no power to make such an order.

When does time begin to run?

14.034 Under s.22(a) time runs from the date on which the right to receive the share or interest accrues. This wording differs from that normally employed in limitation provisions, which most commonly make time run from the date of accrual of the cause of action.[88] It is unclear whether this difference in wording gives rise to any difference of substance. In the case of a will the difficulty arises from the rule that the executor is entitled to the "Executor's Year" before being obliged to distribute the assets.[89] Consequently, the beneficiary is not entitled to bring an action within this time. It has nevertheless been said that the right to receive the share accrues on death,[90] the reasoning being that the right to receive the share is not the same thing as the right to enforce payment of the share.[91] However, this rule must be limited to the case of an immediate legacy. Therefore, where the legacy is to be paid out of a reversionary fund, time cannot start to run until the reversion falls in.[92] The point was carefully considered in *Re Loftus (deceased); Green v Gaul*[93], where the point was made that *Re Diplock's Estate*[94] did not need to decide the question of when time begins to run under this provision. Lawrence Collins J. held that time ran from the later of the end of the executor's year and the date when the relevant interest fell into possession. He pointed out that this avoids the undesirable result that if the date from which time ran were the completion of the administration the limitation period might never begin. This conclusion, which appears eminently sensible is incompatible with *Evans v Westcombe*[95], and it is suggested that the latter decision is now unlikely to be followed.

---

[88] Though similar wording is to be found in s.20(1) of the Limitation Act 1980; see para.12.015.

[89] Administration of Estates Act 1925 s.44.

[90] *Re Diplock's Estate* [1948] Ch. 465, CA, though the point did not directly arise there. A better analogy, though in a different context, is offered by *Hornsey Local Board v Monarch Investment Building Society* (1889) 24 Q.B.D. 1.

[91] This apparently odd distinction is mirrored in a quite different context by the decision of the House of Lords in *Sevcon Ltd v Lucas CAV Ltd* [1986] 1 W.L.R. 462.

[92] *Earle v Bellingham* (No. 2) (1857) 24 Beav. 448; *Re Ludlum: Ludlum v Ludlum* (1890) 563 L.T. 330.

[93] [2005] EWHC 406 (Ch), [2005] 2 All ER 700 Lawrence Collins J. in which an earlier version of this paragraph was referred to.

[94] [1948] Ch. 465, CA; see above, para.14.029.

[95] [1999] 2 All E.R. 777, Richard McCombe Q.C.

Re Loftus also suggests[96] that the period under s.22(a) of the 1980 Act **14.035** will not begin to run until the administrator has paid the costs, funeral and testamentary and administration expenses, debts and other liabilities properly payable out of the assets in his hands, and provided for the payment of any pecuniary legacies. It is not until then that he is in a position to distribute the residuary estate to those entitled under s.46 of the Administration of Estates Act 1925; because it is not until then that "the residuary estate of the intestate" can be identified—s.33(4) of that Act. This is an interpretation rather more generous to beneficiaries than the application of the "Executor's Year" suggested in the main text, and the Court of Appeal suggests, albeit obiter, that that rule cannot be strictly applied.

Claims by creditors

In addition to the claims of beneficiaries, the estate of the deceased must **14.036** satisfy valid claims by creditors of the deceased. Claims subsisting at the moment of death survive death and can be enforced against the estate.[97] These actions do not call for further consideration here: the limitation period applicable to them depends upon their character and is unaffected by the death. There is, however, a further possibility here of an action against the personal representatives. This will arise where they have paid away the estate of the deceased to the beneficiaries without making proper efforts to find and pay the creditors. This failure of duty is known as devastavit. It is important to understand that actions for devastavit do not fall within s.21 or s.22. Which section does apply to them is a matter of some doubt, since it is unclear whether an action in respect of devastavit is founded on contract or on tort. The point is of importance because of s.6 of the 1980 Act (which originally entered English law as s.1 of the Limitation Amendment Act 1980). This section, which is fully considered at paras 10.030–10.032, postpones the running of time in respect of certain contracts of loan until the creditor makes a formal demand. The section operates only in cases which are in principle within s.5 of the 1980 Act, i.e. actions founded on simple contract.

In the present context two questions therefore arise: first, whether an **14.037** action for devastavit is founded on simple contract and, secondly, whether the action against the personal representative is properly described as being on a contract of loan, when the creditor seeks repayment of a loan owed by the deceased. It is submitted that the action is properly regarded as an action in tort. This is not a matter of the personal representative being sued

---

[96] Paras 28-30.
[97] Law Reform (Miscellaneous Provisions) Act 1934 s.1; Proceedings Against Estates Act 1970 s.1.

as a representative of the deceased; rather, the action is brought against the personal representative for his own wrongdoing, and it is very difficult to see how there can be any contract between the parties on this point. Certainly there is no express contract, and it is submitted that it is neither necessary nor proper to imply one.[98] If this view is correct, then the second question clearly does not arise. If it is incorrect, the suggestion has been made that the action is still not within s.6 since it is in respect of the personal representative's own wrongdoing and is therefore not "on a contract of loan".[99] It is true that there is a distinction between deeming a contract between the creditor and the personal representative and deeming that contract to be a contract of loan. However, the resolution of this issue will depend upon whether the deemed contract is to be based upon the contract between creditor and deceased. If so, the logic must presumably be that it will be a contract of loan. It is submitted, nevertheless, that any deemed contract between creditor and personal representative cannot realistically be based upon the contract between the creditor and the deceased, so that the provisions of s.6 can never be relevant in any action for devastavit.

When time starts to run

14.038   In an action of this kind time runs from the date of the wrongful distribution[100] rather than from the date of death. In *Lacons v Warmoll*[101] the Court of Appeal held that the date of the wrongful distribution was the appropriate date even where the liability against which the personal representatives had failed to guard was a purely contingent liability, which did not in fact materialise until some years after the death. There can be no doubt that the breach of duty occurred on the making of the distribution, but it is a more difficult matter to determine when the loss occurred. The case may be seen as raising issues very similar to those involved in cases such as *Forster v Outred*,[102] and the result reached is entirely consistent with that in the more modern cases.[103]

---

[98]   This view also corresponds with the approach of Chitty J. in *Re Hyatt* (1883) 38 Ch.D. 609 at 616, though it would be dangerous to place great reliance on this case, since the question of categorisation was not strictly an issue there.

[99]   Derek Morgan, *Current Law Statutes Annotated* (1980), vol. II.

[100]   Re Gale (1883) 22 Ch.D. 820; Re Blow [1914] 1 Ch. 233.

[101]   [1907] 2 K.B. 350, CA; (1908) 24 L.Q.R. 4.

[102]   [1982] 1 W.L.R. 86, CA.

[103]   The decision has been criticised for failing to distinguish properly *Thorne v Kerr* (1855) 2 K. & J. 63 and *Re Gale*, above. At the present day the analogy with *Forster v Outred* seems more illuminating. For a detailed discussion of the merits of *Forster v Outred*, see paras 5.026–5.032.

Trust for repayment

The above observations about the nature of the action for devastavit will   **14.039**
not be relevant if the deceased's will contains an express trust of funds to be
used for repayment of debts. In these circumstances the case is within s.21,
and the principles set out at paragraphs 13.045–13.056 will apply.[104] The
position in the absence of any express trust does not appear to be covered
by authority, but it is submitted that in such cases the rules in s.22 should
apply.

Dual capacity

The limitation problems become more acute where the administration of   **14.040**
the estate is taken over by a person who is either a creditor or a debtor of
the estate. In *Bowring-Hanbury's Trustee v Bowring-Hanbury*[105] the Court
of Appeal held that time does not cease to run where a creditor becomes
executor, though the position may be different where the creditor becomes
administrator.

OTHER PERSONS TREATED AS TRUSTEES

Persons who occupy a fiduciary position may be treated for the purpose of   **14.041**
limitation as trustees, so that time never runs in their favour.[106] Therefore,
the rule has been applied to a solicitor holding client money,[107] to persons
who have received money from others for the purposes of investment[108] and
to those entrusted with the general management of the affairs of others.[109]
It should be observed, however, that in all these cases the fiduciary relationship predated the receipt of the money by the fiduciary. The trusts rules
do not apply where the fiduciary relationship is created by the receipt of the
very money which the claimant seeks to recover.[110]

Perhaps the most important category of fiduciary relationships here is
that which subsists between partners. So long as the partnership subsists,
time can never run in respect of an action between the partners based on
their fiduciary obligations towards each other.[111] It will start to run on the

---

[104] *Re Oliver* [1927] 2 Ch. 323, Tomlin J.
[105] [1943] Ch. 104, Bennett J.; [1943] 1 All E.R. 48, CA; (1942) 58 L.Q.R. 461; (1943) 59
L.Q.R. 117.
[106] For the limits of this principle, see para.14.014, above.
[107] *Burdick v Garrick* (1870) L.R. 5 Ch. 233.
[108] *North American Land and Timber Co. v Watkins* [1904] 1 Ch. 242.
[109] *Hardwicke v Vernon* (1808) 14 Ves. 504.
[110] *Clarkson v Davies* [1923] A.C. 100.
[111] *Miller v Miller* (1869) L.R. 8, Eq. 499.

dissolution of the partnership, even where this happens by operation of law, as, for example, on the death of a partner,[112] though this will apply only to claims involving the deceased partner, at least where the survivors continue in a de facto partnership.[113] Such claims between partners must be brought by way of an account, and are statute-barred six years after the dissolution of the partnership.[114]

THE LAW COMMISSION'S PROPOSALS

14.042 Section 21(1) of the 1980 Act is an exceptional provision in that it expressly provides that no period of limitation is to apply to certain cases. So far as trust law is concerned the most important effect of the Law Commission's proposals would be to remove this exception. The Commission rightly makes the point that the core regime, with time running from discoverability and an in-built extension of time in cases of fraud and deliberate concealment, should remove any need for this exception. It is therefore proposed to apply the core regime, without exception, to cases of breach of trust. This seems an eminently sensible approach.

---

[112] *Knox v Gye* (1872) L.R. 5, H.L. 656.
[113] *Betjemann v Betjemann* [1895] 2 Ch. 474.
[114] *Marshall v Bullock* [2000] 1 E.G.L.R. 92, CA.

CHAPTER 15

Contribution

The right of one wrongdoer to claim contribution from another person who   15.001
has participated in the same wrong is now governed by the Civil Liability
(Contribution) Act 1978 (the CL(C)A 1978). This replaced the provisions
contained in the Law Reform (Married Women and Tortfeasors) Act 1935,
in the light of the recommendations contained in the Law Commission's
1977 Report[1] on the subject of contribution. Proceedings are now brought
under CPR Pt 20, but the introduction of the new Rules does not appear to
have made any substantive changes. In order to understand the limitation
position, a short summary of the substantive law on contribution is
necessary.

The CL(C)A 1978[2] does not affect the rights of claimants against joint
wrongdoers, and the old rule that the claimant may choose which to sue
(and may sue more than one, subject only to not being able to recover twice
for the same loss) is still good law. The major change in the law introduced
by the Act is the widening of the situations in which contribution may be
claimed. Under s.6 of the Law Reform (Married Women and Tortfeasors)
Act 1935, which was previously the relevant provision, contribution was
available only between joint tortfeasors. Section 1(1) of the CL(C)A 1978
provides that any person liable in respect of any damage suffered by
another person may recover contribution from any other person liable in
respect of the same damage (whether jointly with him or otherwise). Section 6(1) of the CL(C)A 1978 amplifies this by providing that for the
purposes of the Act a person is liable in respect of any damage if the person
who suffered it (or anyone representing his estate or dependants) is entitled
to recover compensation from him in respect of that damage (whatever the
basis of his legal liability, whether tort, breach of contract, breach of trust
or otherwise). Where one defendant seeks contribution from another, the

---

[1] Law Commission No. 79, Law of Contract, Report on Contribution.
[2] The Act took effect on January 1, 1979. Any subsisting claim for damage which occurred
earlier than that will still be subject to the rules in the 1935 Act, though these provisions are
now surely spent.

law now is that he must prove two things. First, that he was himself legally liable to the claimant who he has compensated. By s.1(2) of the CL(C)A 1978 the time for judging this liability is immediately before the compensation was agreed or ordered.[3] The second matter to be proved is that the claimant could successfully have sued the third party in respect of the loss.[4]

THE SAME DAMAGE

15.002   The meaning of the term "the same damage" in s.1(1) has been considered in a number of cases in the past few years. The first was *Friends' Provident Life Office v Hillier Parker May & Rowden (A Firm) (Estates and General plc, Third Parties).*[5] The arguments there concerned the form of remedy sought. The plaintiff had funded part of the cost of a property development in expectation of a share of the profits. The defendants were surveyors engaged to advise the plaintiff and to check and authorise payment of the developers' claims for the plaintiff's share of the cost. Payments of such claims were by the contract between the plaintiff and the developers, expressed to be "non-refundable" to the other party. The plaintiff sued the defendants in negligence and breach of contract for allegedly authorising overpayments, having abandoned an earlier action against the developers for repayment. The defendants joined the developers as third parties, claiming contribution under the 1978 Act on the grounds (among others) that (i) the overpayments, if established, were made under a mistake of fact or for no consideration, and so repayable by the developers, or (ii) the developers were trustees of any money overpaid and liable to compensate the plaintiff for breach of trust. Auld L.J. said[6]:

> "In my judgment, despite the distinction between a claim for restitution and one for damages, each may be a claim for compensation for damage under ss. 1(1) and 6(1) of the 1978 Act. The difference between asking for a particular sum of money back or for an equivalent sum of money for the damage suffered because of the withholding of it is immaterial in this statutory context, which is concerned with 'compensation' for damage . . . It is difficult to imagine a broader formulation of an entitlement to contribution. It clearly spans a variety of causes of action, forms of damage in the sense of loss of some sort, and remedies, the last of which are gathered together under the umbrella of compensation."

---

[3] Thus it is irrelevant that the action has become time-barred by the time the contribution action is brought.

[4] CL(C)A s.1(6).

[5] [1995] 4 All E.R. 260; [1997] Q.B. 85; the decision is criticised by Goff and Jones, *The Law of Restitution* (5th edn, 1998), p.396.

[6] [1995] 4 All E.R. 260 at 272; [1997] Q.B. 85 at 102–103.

Thus, more or less any claim is capable of falling within the Act, and arguments about the legal basis of the claim or about the nature of the remedy sought are unlikely to be in point. That is, however, a separate question from the issue whether the contribution is sought in respect of the same damage as that for which the defendant may become liable.

In *Birse Construction Ltd v Haiste Ltd (Watson, Third Parties)*[7] the plaintiff contractor had settled a claim by the employer, arising out of the construction of a reservoir, and then sued the defendant, its consultant engineer. The defendant joined as third party the employer's certifying engineer, claiming contribution under the 1978 Act. The Court of Appeal held that the relevant claims were not in respect of the "same damage" within s.1(1) of the Act, one of their reasons being that it was not suffered by the same claimant.

In *Jameson (Executors of Jameson, dec'd) v Central Electricity Generating Board (Babcock Energy Ltd, Third Party)*,[8] the Court of Appeal held that a claim by a deceased workman against his former employer for negligence and breach of statutory duty was a claim in respect of the "same damage", for the purposes of the 1978 Act, as one by his executors under s.1 of the Fatal Accidents Act 1976 for loss of dependency, since the relevant damage was the wrong that caused both the injury and the death.

All these cases were examined in some detail by Judge Hicks in *Royal Brompton Hospital NHT v Hammond (No. 3)*.[9] This case arose out of building works at the Royal Brompton Hospital. The contractor made claims against the employer for some £22 million for variations, delay, disruption and other matters. The employer paid some £5.2 million and in due course the contractor commenced arbitration proceedings in which it claimed some £15 million and the employer counterclaimed for some £6.6 million. The arbitration was settled on terms that the employer paid the contractor £6.2 million. The employer then sought to bring Pt 20 proceedings against various of the sub-contractors on the basis that their conduct had contributed to the need for the employer to pay this sum. The question was whether the damage suffered by the employer—the need to make payments to the contractor and/or the loss of the right to deduct sums from those due to the contractor—was the "same damage" as that which it claimed in the Pt 20 proceedings. Judge Hicks held that the proper characterisation of the loss which the employer was claiming was:

"the weakening or impairment of its prospects of success, or the increase of its prospects of defeat, as against [the contractor] in arbitration or negotiation, or as a reduction in the value of its chance of success or an increase in the value of its chance of defeat",

15.003

15.004

---

[7] [1996] 2 All E.R. 1; [1996] 1 W.L.R. 675.
[8] [1997] 4 All E.R. 38, [1998] Q.B. 323.
[9] (2000) 69 Con. L.R. 145.

and that this was not the same loss as that claimed by the contractor against the employer. He added:

> "They are no more the same than the personal injury suffered by the victim of a road accident is the same damage as the economic loss which he suffers if his solicitors' negligence results in the dismissal of his claim for damages against the negligent driver who caused the accident.[10] The analogy is even closer if the client is himself a driver against whom there is a plea of contributory negligence and a counterclaim, and if the primary action is not dismissed but so negligently conducted that the client accepts a less advantageous settlement than he could have obtained had it been competently handled. No analogy is exact, and that one is complicated by the incidence of insurance in the road accident example, but the principle is clear. The distinction can be characterised more abstractly as that between primary and secondary claims, secondary claims being for this purpose those arising from the loss or devaluation of primary claims."

15.005   The decision of Judge Hicks was subsequently upheld by the Court of Appeal[11] and the House of Lords.[12] In the latter court Lord Bingham analysed the history of the law of contribution and showed that the notion of common liability between the defendant and the Pt 20 defendant lay at the root of contribution. However, Lord Steyn observed that for the purposes of the CL(C)A1978 the crucial question is whether the parties are liable in respect of the "same damage"; it is not sufficient that they be liable in respect of "similar damage" or damage which is "materially the same". The statutory words cannot be glossed in this way. Clearly the various cases adopt somewhat different approaches, and the decision of the House of Lords, whilst offering a welcome reminder of the need to attend to the words of the Act, does not entirely resolve the issues about what is meant by "the same damage". It is submitted that apparent inconsistencies between the earlier cases result from a confusion about the word "damage" in s.1 of the Act. In the simplest case the defendants will be joint wrongdoers or jointly liable, as for example under a contract which provides for joint liability. These cases obviously fall within s.1. In other cases, however, the defendant will bring Pt 20 proceedings against someone who is alleged to have contributed to the damage, but by doing something different from

---

[10] A comparable analogy would be that suggested by *Ackbar v C.F. Green & Co.* [1975] Q.B. 582 where a motorist had to pay damages to a person injured by his negligent driving. He was uninsured because of an error by his brokers. Although the damages which he paid were damages for personal injuries, it was held that his claim against the brokers to recover these sums was not a claim for personal injuries within the meaning of s.11 of the Act. See also Ch.4 of questions of characterisation.

[11] [2000] Lloyd's Rep. PN 643.

[12] *The Times*, April 26, 2002.

what the defendant did. It cannot be fatal to the Pt 20 claim that the two parties did different things. Section 1 does not refer to the same "breach of duty". Equally, as is clear from the *Friends Provident* case, it is not necessary that the same remedy be claimed in both actions.[13] What is necessary is to identify the damage suffered, first by the original claimant and secondly by the defendant/Pt 20 claimant. Only if these are the same can there be a contribution claim within the meaning of the Act. What the *Royal Brompton* case emphasises is that a defendant who seeks to pass on all or part of a liability by means of Pt 20 proceedings is in danger of finding that his loss is not characterised in the same way as the loss for which he was sued by the claimant, so that the Act does not apply. It may be added that from this point of view the decision in *Jameson* seems somewhat curious, since it appears to focus on the breach of duty rather than on the resulting damage. It also appears to ignore the point made in *Birse Construction* that the "same damage" has to be at issue in both actions and the same damage must mean damage suffered by the same person. A concise summary might be that if the Pt 20 claim is truly in respect of damage suffered by the original claimant ("primary damage" in Judge Hicks's terminology), then it falls within the Act. If it is truly for the loss suffered by the defendant/Pt 20 claimant as a result of the claimant's loss ("secondary damage" in Judge Hicks's terminology) then it is not within the Act.

15.006   The fact that the damage is not within the Act is not necessarily fatal to the defendant's attempt to pass on all or part of it, but it will mean that he will need to show that the Pt 20 defendant owed him an independent duty not to cause that loss. From a limitation point of view there is also an important consequence. A true contribution claim within the meaning of the Act attracts the two-year limitation period of s.10, whereas a free-standing claim not under the CL(C)A 1978 does not.

15.007   Where a company liquidator commenced proceedings against the company's former directors under ss.212 (misfeasance), 214 (wrongful trading), 238 and 239 (preferences) of the Insolvency Act 1986, and the directors sought to bring a Pt 20 claim against the insolvency practitioners who had advised the directors and the company, it was held that (with the possible exception of the s.212 claim, depending on how it was draftred) the Pt 20 claim was not in respect of the same damage as the original claim, with the result that the 1978 Act did not apply.[14] The decision is plainly correct, since the claim against the directors is for breaches of duties under statute, causing loss to creditors whereas the Pt 20 claim is for negligence at common law, causing loss to the company.

---

[13] Though Lord Steyn in the *Royal Brompton Hospital* case indicates that the *Friends Provident* decision is probably no longer to be regarded as good law.
[14] *Re International Championship Management Ltd; Cohen v Davis* [2006] EWHC 768 (CH), [2006] All ER (D) 84 (Apr).

DEFENDANT'S LEGAL LIABILITY TO CLAIMANT

15.008   It is sufficient that D would have been legally liable to C immediately before the compensation was agreed or ordered. Therefore, it is irrelevant that by the time the contribution action is brought C's action against D would have been time-barred, so long as it was not already time-barred when D's liability was established. A further point is that D must show that he was indeed legally liable—a payment which is ex gratia will not found a right to contribution, though s.10(4) of the Limitation Act 1980 clearly contemplates that the right to contribution is not excluded merely because there is no formal admission of liability. Therefore in *Harper v Gray & Walker*[15] C had settled his action against D1 and D2 on terms involving no statement as to the presence or absence of liability. It was held that this settlement did not preclude D3 from recovering contribution from D1 and D2.[16]

THIRD PARTY'S LIABILITY TO THE CLAIMANT

15.009   Once again, the vital time for determining the third party's liability to C is immediately before D's liability to C was established. A major problem which arises here concerns the effect of expiry of time for a hypothetical action between C and the third party. If that time had not expired when D's liability to C was established then there can be no objection to a contribution action by D. The position is more difficult where that time had already expired. In these circumstances s.1(3) of the CL(C)A 1978 applies. It provides that:

> "a person shall be liable to make contribution . . . notwithstanding that he has ceased to be liable in respect of the damage in question since the time when the damage occurred, unless he ceased to be liable by virtue of the expiry of a period of limitation or prescription which extinguished the right on which the claim against him in respect of the damage was based."[17]

Therefore, if the limitation period which has expired is one which merely bars the claimant's remedy, then the third party continues to be vulnerable to a contribution action. By contrast, if the limitation period had the effect of extinguishing the claimant's right, the third party ceases to be exposed to

---

[15] [1985] 1 W.L.R. 1196, Judge Newey Q.C.
[16] See also CL(C)A 1978 s.1(4).
[17] The purpose of this amendment to the law was to reverse the effect of the decision in *Littlewood v George Wimpey & Co. Ltd* [1953] 1 W.L.R. 426, Parker J.

a contribution action. At the time when the section was enacted, the only general limitation period in English law which was accepted as having this effect was the 12-year period in relation to actions for the recovery of land.[18] At the present day, more difficulty is caused by the two longstop periods in ss.11A and 14B of the 1980 Act. The obvious difficulty on looking at the statutory words is that they simultaneously speak of "barring", which is the term normally used in relation to the effect of the expiry of a limitation period on the remedy, and refer to the "right", which is the term normally used in relation to limitation periods which have extinctive effect.

First, it has been pointed out that s.14B(1), like ss.2 and 5 of the 1980 Act, uses the form of words "an action . . . shall not be brought". It is well known that in ss.2 and 5 this merely has the effect of barring the remedy. Indeed, it is commonly observed that the form of words is fundamentally misleading, since these sections do not prevent the bringing of an action— they merely offer the defendant a defence of which he may or may not choose to avail himself. The difficulty with this argument is that exactly the same form of words is found in s.15(1) of the 1980 Act, dealing with actions for the recovery of land, yet it is clear that in this context the effect of the expiry of time is to extinguish the claimant's title. This is expressly provided by s.17. The only possible conclusion is that the words "no action shall be brought" may be presumed merely to bar the remedy, but that this presumption can be rebutted by further provisions elsewhere in the Act. That throws the debate back to the effect of s.14B(2) and to the question whether that provision does rebut the presumption. **15.010**

Secondly, it has been said that it would be contrary to what might be called the "classical doctrine" of limitation in English law to say that a limitation period (outside the area of real property) has the effect of extinguishing the claimant's rights. This argument may be regarded as being an extension of the first argument, above. The contention is no doubt true as far as it goes, but the classical doctrine did not have to accommodate longstops, which appeared in English law for the first time in 1986. The longstop is a new creature, and its effects cannot be judged simply by reference to the effects of more "traditional" limitation periods.

In the end, all of this simply returns the debate to the question of how the longstop in s.14B should be viewed as a matter of construction. Attempting a literal interpretation of the words is not going to help, because the words are capable of either interpretation. A purposive interpretation of the statute is perhaps a more appropriate approach. In this context attention is drawn to the purposes for which the longstop was introduced. It will be recalled that the Latent Damage Act 1986, which introduced s.14B, was passed as a result of the recommendation of the Law Reform Committee, **15.011**

---

[18] Now contained in s.15(1) of the 1980 Act.

which had considered the question of latent damage in the light of the decision in *Pirelli General Cable Works v Oscar Faber & Partners Ltd.*[19] That Committee recommended the introduction of a test of discoverability in cases of latent damage, but wanted that balanced with a longstop in order to provide defendants with finality after a reasonable period of time. The importance attached to finality in this context is emphasised when one considers that part of s.14B(2) which makes it clear that the longstop operates even though the cause of action has not yet accrued or the starting date has not yet arrived. These are provisions which can clearly operate very harshly from the point of view of claimants, since it is possible to have cases where the action is barred even though the claimant has never been in a position to sue.

15.012   Although the Law Reform Committee does not appear particularly to have had the issue of contribution claims in mind, it seems quite contrary to the spirit of its recommendations to say that a defendant who is otherwise protected by a longstop may have that protection defeated by a contribution claim, and it is submitted that a court ought to hold that the effect of the expiry of the longstop is to extinguish the claimant's right, rather than merely barring his remedy. It also appears that the problem of contribution claims is the only situation where the distinction is likely to be of practical significance, and in this context the purposive arguments mentioned above point quite strongly to the extinction of the right. It is reasonably clear that in all other cases the expiry of the limitation period merely bars the remedy.

A further problem arising from the distinction between limitation periods which extinguish the right and those which merely bar the remedy occurs where the longstop expires before the action between P and D1 has been concluded. As the longstop approaches, D1 may be tempted to issue a third party notice in order to protect his position. However, if D1's own liability to P has still not been established, then it appears that his right of action against D2 has not accrued, so that the issue of proceedings is premature. The point is not important if the expiry of the longstop merely bars the remedy, because in that event s.1(3) of the CL(C)A 1978, quoted above, preserves the right to bring a contribution action. However, if the expiry of the period extinguishes the right, then the right to claim contribution may be lost before it has accrued. Although this is obviously capable of working injustice, two observations are called for. First, it will be only very rarely that the longstop date arrives before the action between P and D1 is concluded, so that the injustice will arise in only a very few cases. Secondly, limitation law is by its nature prone to this kind of injustice, a risk that is exacerbated by the introduction of longstops of any kind.

---

[19] [1983] 2 A.C. 1.

TIMING

Claims for contribution may be made at a number of different stages in any **15.013** proceedings between P and D. The 1980 Act, by making time run from the date when the liability is quantified, encourages one to think in terms of the action being brought only after that time. In practice such actions are frequently commenced before D's liability has been established. This is done by means of Third Party Proceedings within the CPR, Pt 20. The detailed rules as to the joinder of new parties to an action are considered at length in Ch.22, but a number of difficulties require to be considered here. In *Harper v Gray & Walker*[20] P sued D1, D2 and D3. The actions against D1 and D2 were settled out of court, and D3 thereupon (and before P had given notice of discontinuance against D1 and D2) issued a contribution notice against D1 and D2. Judge Newey held that the notice was valid, since D1 and D2 remained parties to the action until the notice of discontinuance was served. He went on to say that the contribution notice would have been valid even after that time because the notice of discontinuance could not prejudice the action of D3 against D1 and D2, which remained alive. This conclusion, whilst doubtless convenient, seems unconvincing. Before the settlement there had never been an action of D3 against D1 and D2, and it ought therefore to follow that, had the contribution notice not been served before the discontinuance, Ord.16 would have required D3 to obtain leave (though on the facts this would doubtless have been granted).

The 1980 Act introduced new provisions to deal with the problem of **15.014** limitation in respect of contribution claims. Under the old law a series of cases[21] had dealt with the question of whether the limitation period ran from the time when a defendant incurred liability to the plaintiff or from the time when that liability was ascertained and quantified. The relevant authority under the modern law is s.10 of the 1980 Act. However, an important distinction is to be drawn between cases of contribution on the one hand and cases of indemnity on the other. The rules in s.10 apply to the former, but the latter are subject to their own line of authority on the question of when the cause of action accrues. These cases are dealt with at paragraphs 10.023–10.028.

Section 10(1) lays down the basic period of limitation. This is two years, and runs from the date on which the defendant's liability to the plaintiff is quantified. Problems arise because the liability is not necessarily quantified in judicial proceedings, and additional provisions are required to specify when time begins to run in cases where liability is quantified by some other

---

[20] [1985] 1 W.L.R. 1196, Judge Newey Q.C.
[21] *Merlihan v A.C. Pope (Pagnello Third Party)* [1946] K.B. 166, Birkett J.; *Hordern-Richmond v Duncan* [1947] 1 K.B. 545, Cassels J.; *Littlewood v George Wimpey & Co.* [1953] 1 W.L.R. 426, Parker J.

means. Sections 10(3) and 10(4) define when time starts to run for the purposes of s.10. Section 10(3) deals with those cases where a person is held liable either by a judgment in civil proceedings or by an award made on any arbitration. In the former event time starts to run on the date on which the judgment is given. If quantum is decided at a later date than liability (as may happen where there is a split trial, or where a disposal hearing is ordered) then the relevant date is when quantum is determined.[22] In the latter event it runs from the date of the award (which is presumably the date which the award bears on its face). Section 10(3) further provides that for the purposes of this subsection no account is to be taken of any judgment or award given or made on appeal in so far as it varies the amount of damages awarded against the person in question.

15.015   It is submitted that this proviso requires careful interpretation. It is clear that if D1 is found liable at first instance (which expression here includes both a court and an arbitration) then time runs against him immediately for the purposes of his contribution claim, and it is irrelevant that on appeal the proportion of his liability (either against the plaintiff or against another defendant) is varied; but the problem is surely more difficult where D1 is found not liable at first instance, but this decision is reversed by an appellate court. In this situation it is submitted that time cannot begin to run for the purposes of the contribution claim until the decision of the appellate court is given. Partly this is a matter of common sense, but it also accords with the words of the statute, which refer to time running from the date of "that judgment", where the judgment in question is one by which D is held liable. A decision which finds wholly in D's favour is not a decision by which he is held liable, and therefore cannot bring s.10(3) into operation. Once D has been found liable by a court (even in the smallest of proportions) time begins to run for the purposes of his contribution claim, and any subsequent variation in the proportion of his liability is irrelevant. Clearly this rule can have unfortunate consequences, especially bearing in mind the length of time which a case can take between trial and appellate level (or, for that matter, between the Court of Appeal and the House of Lords).

15.016   A defendant may find that the proportion of his liability is significantly varied after his claim for contribution has become barred. This may not matter if a contribution claim has been begun—it may be possible to argue that this is simply a matter which affects the quantum of damage recoverable in the action, since s.10(3) provides that the appellate decision is to be disregarded for the purpose of the running of time, but says nothing about disregarding it when calculating the damages recoverable. By contrast, a defendant who has decided that a contribution claim is not worthwhile because, for example, the trial court has assessed the plaintiff's contributory negligence at 80 per cent will find himself in an awkward

---

[22] *AER Lingus Plc v Gildacroft Ltd* [2006] EWCA Civ 4, [2006] All ER (D) 71 (Jan) CA.

position if three years later the Court of Appeal decides that the contributory negligence should have been assessed at only 20 per cent.

The payment contemplated by s.10(3) may be a payment in kind, at least **15.017** where that is capable of valuation in monetary terms. An example would be the doing of remedial work as a response to a claim in contract. In this event the value paid by the party doing the work is the value of the work.[23]

WHAT MUST BE AGREED?

Section 10(4) governs the case where the defendant's liability to the plaintiff **15.018** is established by some means other than those specified in s.10(3). Essentially this refers to out-of-court settlements, and indeed the subsection speaks of the defendant making or agreeing to make any payment to one or more persons in respect of the damage. In these circumstances time runs from the earliest date on which the amount to be paid is agreed between the defendant and the person (or each of the persons, as the case may be) to whom the payment is made. This subsection creates a number of problems of construction which are explored in the following paragraphs

Section 10(4) states quite clearly that time runs from the date on which **15.019** the amount of compensation is agreed. In out-of-court settlements there may well be a number of other matters requiring to be agreed, such as date of payment, possibility of instalments and method of payment, but none of these has any relevance. Agreement on them will not set time running, but absence of agreement on them will not prevent it from running—it is only the amount of compensation that must be agreed. *Knight v Rochdale Healthcare NHS Trust*[24] deals with the relationship between s.10(3) and s.10(4). In a case where an agreement to pay compensation had been made and then embodied in a consent order it was held that time ran from the making of the agreement and not from the later date when the consent order was made. Thus there is no overlap between s.10(3) and s.10(4). Although it would have been possible for Parliament to provide that the making of the consent order reset the clock, it had not in fact done so.[25] However, it is likely that the court will want to see evidence of a finalised agreement rather than merely a preliminary agreement.[26]

---

[23] *Baker & Davies plc v Leslie Wilks Associates (a firm)* [2005] EWHC 1179 (TCC), [2005] 3 All ER 603, 101 ConLR 82 Judge Havery Q.C.

[24] [2003] EWHC 1831 (QB), [2003] 4 All ER 416 Crane J.

[25] See also *Hamiltons v Stafford* 17 January 2003 Judge Marshall Evans.

[26] *Baker & Davies plc v Leslie Wilks Associates (a firm)* [2005] EWHC 1179 (TCC), [2005]. 3 All ER 603, 101 ConLR 82.

ADMISSION OF LIABILITY IRRELEVANT

15.020   Section 10(4) by its express terms applies irrespective of whether the defendant makes any admission of liability—even a payment which is expressed to be ex gratia will set time running if it is in respect of the damage in question.

PAYMENTS INTO COURT

15.021   Where a settlement is effected by means of the acceptance of a payment into court, it may be necessary to decide when the agreement to pay is made for the purposes of setting time running under s.10. It is submitted that the mere fact of payment in cannot be sufficient for the purposes of s.10(4)—this is at most an offer, and does not by itself constitute an agreement. Once the plaintiff gives notice of acceptance of the payment in, it is submitted that s.10(4) is satisfied, and time begins to run. At that stage there is a concluded contract of compromise between the parties, and the amount to be paid is therefore settled. It is not necessary that the money in court shall actually have been paid out.

MULTIPLE CLAIMANTS

15.022   Where there is more than one claimant in the same action, careful attention to the wording of s.10(4) is necessary. This provision states that the relevant date is the earliest date on which the amount of compensation is agreed between D and each of the persons to whom the payment is to be made. This suggests that time does not run for the contribution action until D's liability to each and every one of the claimants has been settled. However, this is not the only possible interpretation. An alternative view is that there may be separate periods of limitation in respect of each settlement. Thus, if A, B and C all sue D, and D settles with A in 1988, B in 1989 and C in 1990, then for the purposes of any contribution claim brought by D and against D2 time expires in 1990 in respect of the sum paid to A, 1991 in respect of the sum paid to B and 1992 in respect of sum paid to C. Equally, more than one claimant may be included in a particular settlement, and time then starts to run at the date of the settlement in respect of all sums to be paid under that settlement. This approach is undeniably more convenient, and, if adopted, will avoid the problems considered in the next paragraph. Unfortunately, it is by no means clear that it is correct as a matter of statutory construction.

15.023   If the more convenient of the approaches considered in the previous paragraph is ultimately held to be unsustainable as a matter of statutory construction, it will become necessary to consider the position where a number of claimants bring a consolidated action against the same defendant, and some of these actions are settled out of court, whilst others proceed to trial. So far as the settled claims are concerned, it is clear that time under s.10 cannot begin to run until the last settlement is reached, at the earliest.

Two problems remain. First, it may not immediately be obvious that no other claims are to be settled, so that D may not know that time is running. Secondly, does time in fact start to run before the outcome of the trial is known? It is submitted that it does; s.10(4) applies only to cases which are not decided at trial, so in this example those cases which proceed to trial are not within s.10(4) at all. The result of this is that time for a contribution action for the settled claims runs from the date of the last settlement, whilst time for a contribution action for the contested claims runs from the date of the judgment or award, as provided in s.10(3).

Acknowledgments

Section 10(5) provides that ss.29–31 of the 1980 Act (which deal with **15.024** acknowledgments) do not apply for the purposes of s.10. Therefore the two-year period provided by s.10(1) is not liable to extension by virtue of any acknowledgment of liability given by the party against whom contribution is claimed.

Personal injury cases

Section 10(5) provides that s.33 of the 1980 Act does not apply for the **15.025** purposes of s.10. Therefore, even in a personal injuries case, the court has no discretion to extend the period of limitation for a contribution action. It may be observed in passing that s.33 is in any case probably incapable of applying to a contribution claim. That provision gives the court discretion only where the hardship to the plaintiff results from the time-limits in ss.11 or 12, whereas in a contribution action any hardship would presumably result from the time-limit in s.10. At this point it is necessary to consider the potentially confusing decision of the Court of Appeal in *Kennet v Brown*,[27] where the Court considered the application of s.33 to an action by one defendant against another. It is essential to understand that there were in this case two claims by D1: the first was a claim for contribution in respect of the injuries which D1 had caused to the plaintiff, whilst the second was a

---

[27] [1988] 1 W.L.R. 582.

claim against D2 for D1's own injuries. It was only in the context of the second claim that the Court of Appeal considered the s.33 discretion. It would indeed have been entirely wrong to consider it in connection with the contribution claim.

Section 35

15.026 Section 10(5) provides that s.35 of the 1980 Act applies for the purposes of s.10. The very complex provisions of s.35 are dealt with at length in Ch.23. In the present context it may be observed that the provisions as to set-off and counterclaim contained in that section will apply to actions for contribution. *Holland v Yates Building Co. Ltd*[28] is a reminder that s.35 applies where a new claim, as defined, is made in the original proceedings, but s.10 applies where the original defendant brings contribution proceedings after his own liability has been established (whether by judgment or by out-of-court settlement). This means that, in those cases where a contribution action is available (and not all s.35 cases fall within this category) the original defendant has a choice whether to bring in the proposed contributory as a new party in the original action or to bring a separate contribution action. Questions of cost may appear to point in the direction of the former choice, but the operation of s.35 may mandate the latter. The former choice is subject to s.35, and may therefore be impossible if the claimant's limitation period against the new party has expired. This will, of course, depend upon the capacity in which the new party is to be added. Addition as a third-party will count as a third-party claim, which cannot be backdated, but addition as a second defendant falls into the category of cases where backdating (and thus addition outside the limitation period) may be allowed if the various requirements of s.35 are satisfied).

By contrast, the effect of s.10 is apparently that the defendant acquires a new right of action against the contributory when his own liability is established. Thus, in some cases a contribution action will be possible even though the addition of the contributory under s.35 would not. The only qualification on this is that found in s.1(3) of the Civil Liability (Contribution) Act 1978. This prohibits a contribution action if the proposed contributory has ceased to be liable to the original claimant by virtue of the expiry of a limitation period which extinguished his right to damages.

---

[28] *The Times*, December 5, 1989, CA.

Equitable remedies

Section 10(5) disapplies s.36 of the 1980 Act for the purposes of s.10. **15.027**
Section 36, which is examined more fully in Ch.3, is the section that stipulates that the statutory limitation periods do not apply to claims for
equitable remedies. There, in the relatively rare case of a contribution claim
which is a claim for equitable damages, the two-year period of s.10 will
continue to apply.

Disability

The two-year period of s.10 is subject to extension in accordance with s.28 **15.028**
of the 1980 Act where the claimant is under a disability at the time when
the cause of action accrues, as defined by s.10(2).[29] In such cases the limitation period expires two years[30] after the claimant ceases to be under
disability, or dies, whichever occurs first.

Fraud, mistake and concealment

The two-year period for a contribution claim is subject to extension where **15.029**
the action is based on fraud, where a material fact has been concealed from
the claimant by the defendant or where the action is for relief from the
consequences of a mistake.[31] In such cases time will not start to run until
the claimant is aware of the facts relating to the cause of action, or could
have become aware of them had he acted with reasonable diligence, but the
applicable period remains two years—s.32 does not operate to allow a
period of six years from the date of discoverability.

Effect on the Crown

The provisions of s.10 are binding on the Crown to the extent and with the **15.030**
limitations specified in s.37 of the Act.[32]

---

[29] 1980 Act s.10(5); for the rules on disability, see Ch.19.
[30] 1980 Act s.28(5).
[31] 1980 Act s.10(5). Fraud, mistake and concealment are dealt with in Ch.20.
[32] 1980 Act; for the special position of the Crown, see Ch.9.

Representative actions

15.031 Where an action is brought against defendants in a representative capacity, CPR 19.6.4 makes the resulting judgment binding on all those whom the defendants represent and enforceable with the permission of the court. This, however, does not entitle a representative defendant to claim contributions from another defendant after the expiry of the two-year time-limit.[33]

THE LAW COMMISSION'S PROPOSALS

15.032 The Commission proposes that all contribution actions arising out of the same facts should be subject to a single initial limitation period, with time running from the date of judgment in the original action (or, presumably, the date of settlement). This proposal appears to give rise to some practical difficulties. It is not clear why the settlement of an action as against one or more defendants, but not as against all defendants, should cause time to start running for the purposes of a contribution action by those defendants who continue to defend the claim. The Commission invites comments on whether the limitation period in these cases should stay at the present two years or whether it should be increased to three years in line with the core regime.

It is also proposed that the longstop should apply to contribution actions, the period running from the date of judgment or settlement.

---

[33] *Choudhury v Hussain, The Times*, October 10, 1989, CA; (1989) 139 New L.J. 1416.

CHAPTER 16

Arbitration

Section 34 of the Limitation Act 1980 dealt with arbitrations,[1] but was **16.001** repealed by Sch.4 to the Arbitration Act 1996, and it is the provisions of the latter Act which must be considered in relation to limitation issues arising in arbitrations commenced after January 31, 1997. Consequently, the old provisions are now more or less spent for practical purposes. The time-limit for commencing proceedings in an arbitration is the same as would be applicable if the proceedings were commenced by way of action in the High Court. However, a number of other problems can arise in the context of arbitrations, and these are explored in this chapter.

STATUTORY AND CONTRACTUAL TIME-LIMITS

Arbitrations are necessarily conducted pursuant either to statute or, more **16.002** commonly, to an arbitration agreement between the parties. In many cases an arbitration agreement will contain a time-limit of its own for the institution of proceedings. In general these time-limits will be enforced by the courts,[2] and they require to be considered in conjunction with the statutory time-limits. It should be noted, however, that contractual time-limits for arbitration proceedings are likely to be disapplied where the parties agree to forego arbitration and to proceed direct to litigation instead.[3]

---

[1] A good account of the procedural problems which arise in arbitrations from the operation of time-limits can be found in M. Mustill and A. Boyd, *Commercial Arbitration* (4th edn, 2000), Ch.16.
[2] See paras 16.020–16.026.
[3] *Indian Oil Corporation v Vanol Inc.* [1992] 2 Lloyd's Rep. 563, CA.

MEANING OF "DISPUTE UNDER THE AGREEMENT"

16.003 The standard forms of arbitration agreement commonly used in the course of international trade often provide that any "dispute under the agreement" shall be referred to arbitration. In *Alma Shipping Corporation v Union of India*[4] Roskill J. held that the word "dispute" in the Austrowheat Form extended to cover a claim for general average contribution, notwithstanding that the rules of law relating to general average contribution were not expressly incorporated into the charterparty. A dispute can arise "under" an agreement if it relates to the events which the agreement was intended to govern, even where the relevant rules are to be found in the general law.

ACCRUAL OF CAUSE OF ACTION

16.004 Any attempt by the parties to the arbitration to provide by prior agreement that no cause of action shall accrue until the making of the arbitrator's award is void, and the cause of action accrues when it would have done in the absence of the agreement.[5] Although it is impossible to delay the accrual of the cause of action until the arbitrator's award is made, the question when the cause of action accrues can still be an important one. It has given rise to a number of difficult cases. The first point to be made is that the phrase "cause of action" must be read in the present context as "cause of arbitration". Secondly, the cause of arbitration has to be classified in the same way as is a cause of action, i.e. being based on tort or contract or statute or as the case may be. This is important in order to establish what limitation period applies to the commencement of the arbitration. The problem cases in this area have generally arisen where the arbitration is provided for by statute.

16.005 In *Pegler v Railway Executive*[6] the plaintiff was employed by a railway company which was taken over by the defendants. The consequent reorganisation of the business caused the plaintiff to lose some seniority, and his promotion was delayed. The statute which authorised the takeover provided for persons in the plaintiff's position to receive compensation for any loss of wages caused by the takeover, the quantum to be determined by arbitration. The takeover was completed in 1924; the plaintiff would in the absence of the takeover have been promoted in 1933 but was in fact promoted in 1936. He commenced the arbitration proceedings in 1942. The

---

[4] [1971] 2 Lloyd's Rep. 494.
[5] See s.34(2): this overrules the decision of the House of Lords in *Board of Trade v Cayzer, Irvine & Co.* [1927] A.C. 610.
[6] [1946] W.N. 132, Atkinson J.; [1947] 1 All E.R. 355, CA; [1948] A.C. 332, HL; *sub nom. Pegler v Great Western Railway.*

rules on arbitrations apply to an arbitration under an Act of Parliament as they do to an arbitration agreement,[7] except that the court's discretion to extend the time for commencing proceedings is not applicable to a statutory arbitration.[8] All the courts in *Pegler v Railway Executive* held that the plaintiff's cause of arbitration had accrued in 1924, because it was then certain that he would be adversely affected. The point may be explained by analogy with the rules on accrual of a cause of action: once the plaintiff can sue, the cause of action has accrued. Similarly, once the plaintiff is in a position to commence arbitration proceedings, the cause of arbitration has accrued.

In *Christian Salvesen (Properties) Ltd v Central Electricity Generating Board*[9] this approach may have been taken rather too far. The CEGB had lawfully erected a pylon on land, and the case was a claim under s.22 of the Electric Lighting Act 1882 for compensation because the presence of the pylon had caused the plaintiff to be refused planning permission. The limitation point did not ultimately fall to be decided, but the court said that the cause of arbitration accrued when the pylon was erected rather than when the planning permission was refused. Given that there can at that stage have been no certainty that the permission would be refused, this appears to be an excessive application of the principle that the cause of arbitration accrues as soon as there is more than minimal damage. It must surely be the case that no arbitration could have been commenced upon the purely hypothetical possibility that planning permission would be refused. It is submitted that the obiter dicta on this point are wrong, and that the cause of arbitration accrued only when planning permission was refused.[10]

16.006

RUNNING OF TIME

Where the time-limit is expressed to run from the date of an event which should have happened but did not happen, the court may have to decide when that event would have happened in the ordinary course of things, so as to decide when time starts to run. In *Bulk Transport Corporation v Stinnes Interoil AG*[11] time was expressed to run from the date when the cargo was discharged, but the dispute arose from the fact that it had never even been loaded. It was held that the defendant bore the burden of establishing that the relevant date should have been long enough ago to make the claim time-barred.

16.007

---

[7] 1980 Act s.34(6).
[8] Arbitration Act 1996 s.12 (formerly Arbitration Act 1950 s.27); see further paras 16.015–16.027.
[9] (1985) 48 P. & C.R. 465, Lands Tribunal.
[10] See also *Vincent v Thames Conservancy* (1953) 4 P. & C.R. 66, Lands Tribunal.
[11] February 27, 1992, QBD, Unreported.

COMMENCEMENT OF THE ARBITRATION

16.008 The next matter to be considered is what steps have to be taken to commence proceedings and stop time running. In the case of proceedings in the High Court or county court there is substantial authority on what amounts to commencing proceedings.[12] The following paragraphs examine the comparable authorities in the context of arbitration.

Commencement of arbitration

16.009 Section 14 of the Arbitration Act 1996 allows the parties to agree in advance when arbitral proceedings are to be regarded as commenced for limitation purposes,[13] but goes on to lay down rules which apply in the absence of agreement. Where the arbitrator is named or designated in the arbitration agreement, arbitral proceedings are commenced in respect of a matter when one party serves on the other party or parties notice in writing requiring him or them to submit that matter to the person so named or designated. Where the arbitrator or arbitrators are to be appointed by the parties, arbitral proceedings are commenced in respect of a matter when one party serves on the other party or parties notice in writing requiring him or them to appoint an arbitrator or to agree to the appointment of an arbitrator in respect of that matter. There has been some dispute over whether it is essential to require the appointment of an arbitrator or whether it is sufficient merely to state that the matter is being referred to arbitration. In an early case[14] it was held that requiring appointment of an arbitrator was essential, but the opposite view was taken in *Allianz Versicherungs Aktiengesellschaft v Fortuna Co. Inc. (The "Baltic Universal")*,[15] where a notice was served one day before time expired, clearly for the purpose of protecting the position. Moore-Bick J. held that in these circumstances the notice was obviously intended to be the commencement of an arbitration and should be so treated. A similar view was taken by Rix J. in *Ocean Laser Shipping Ltd; George Roussos Sons SA; Ocean Laser Shipping Ltd v Charles M. Willie & Co. (Shipping) Ltd (The "Smaro")*[16], by Moore-Bick J. in *Atlanska Plovidba and another v Consignaciones Asturianas S.A.. (the "Lapad")*[17] and by Judge Mackie in *Bulk and Metal*

---

[12] See para.2.003.

[13] 1996 Act s.14(1).

[14] *Vosnoc Ltd v Transglobal Projects Ltd* [1998] 2 All E.R. 990; [1998] 1 W.L.R. 101, Judge Jack (as High Court Judge).

[15] [1999] 1 Lloyd's Rep. 497, Moore-Bick J., who did not follow *Vosnoc Ltd v Transglobal Projects Ltd* [1998] 2 All E.R. 990.

[16] [1999] 1 Lloyd's Rep. 225, Rix J. See also *Seabridge Shipping AB v AC Orssleff's Eftf's A/S* [1999] 2 Lloyd's Rep. 685, Thomas J.

[17] [2004] EWHC 1273 (Comm), (2004) 2 Lloyd's Rep 109.

Transport (UK) LLP v Voc Bulk Ultra Handymax Pool LLC; The Voc Gallant.[18] It is submitted that the view adopted in the latter cases is to be preferred. Section 14 should be regarded as providing a non-exhaustive list of ways in which an arbitration can be commenced. The alternative approach is excessively technical and likely to lead to injustice.

Where the arbitrator or arbitrators are to be appointed by a person other than a party to the proceedings, arbitral proceedings are commenced in respect of a matter when one party gives notice in writing to that person requesting him to make the appointment in respect of that matter. An agreement regulating when an arbitration is deemed to commence does not need to refer expressly to limitation, but it must be a clear agreement as to deemed commencement—an agreement which merely specifies how proceedings are to be commenced is unlikely to meet that requirement.[19]

It was observed in *Vosnoc Ltd v Transglobal Projects Ltd*[20] that:　　**16.010**

"Section 14 is evidently intended to be a complete code covering all situations. Unless the meaning of 'a person designated' in an agreement is in some way to be stretched to cover persons to be appointed by a designated person, sections 27(3) and 34(3) would not cover those numerous cases where the arbitrator is to be appointed by, for example, the president of a professional body. Section 14 also avoids the use of 'deemed' and 'treated as', which occur in its predecessors."

Admirably logical though the new scheme is, it is not at all clear that it will by itself avoid the difficulties which used to arise in relation to s.34(4), discussed below. This is because these difficulties center around identifying what constitutes the giving of notice, which remains an essential requirement in the new scheme.

Notice of claim

Arbitration clauses sometimes specify that the step which the claimant must　　**16.011** take in order to stop time from running is the giving of notice of a claim. In such cases the clause must give a sufficiently definite indication that a claim is being made—a mere indication that a claim might be made in the future is insufficient.[21] It is also necessary that the notice should give sufficient details of the claim in order to enable the defendant to identify accurately the case which he has to meet.[22]

---

[18] [2009] EWHC 288 (Comm).
[19] *Taylor Woodrow Construction v RMD Kwikform Ltd* [2008] EWHC 825 (TCC), Ramsey J.
[20] Above.
[21] *A/S Rendal v Acros Ltd* (1937) 58 Lloyd's Rep. 287.
[22] *A/S Rendal v Acros Ltd.*

Method of service

16.012 Section 76 of the Arbitration Act makes provisions relating to the manner of serving notices in arbitrations. It provides:

> "(1) The parties are free to agree on the manner of service of any notice or other document required or authorised to be given or served in pursuance of the arbitration agreement or for the purposes of the arbitral proceedings.
>
> (2) If or to the extent that there is no such agreement the following provisions apply.
>
> (3) A notice or other document may be served on a person by any effective means.
>
> (4) If a notice or other document is addressed, pre-paid and delivered by post—
>
> (a) to the addressee's last known principal residence or, if he is or has been carrying on a trade, profession or business, his last known principal business address, or
>
> (b) where the addressee is a body corporate, to the body's registered or principal office, it shall be treated as effectively served.
>
> (5) This section does not apply to the service of documents for the purposes of legal proceedings, for which provision is made by rules of court.
>
> (6) References in this Part to a notice or other document include any form of communication in writing and references to giving or serving a notice or other document shall be construed accordingly."

Section 76(3) is a very broad provision, which should serve to eliminate many of the former disputes about what constituted effective service.

Section 76(4) must be regarded as a deeming provision which confirms that the methods there specified are always effective. Note, though, that it requires the notice to be delivered. It is therefore not sufficient merely to prove posting. Section 76(5) must be read in the light of the Arbitration Practice Direction, which deals with applications to court in relation to arbitration proceedings.

16.013 Section 77 goes on to confer further powers on the court in relation to the service of documents.

> "(1) This section applies where service of a document on a person in the manner agreed by the parties, or in accordance with provisions of section 76 having effect in default of agreement, is not reasonably practicable.
>
> (2) Unless otherwise agreed by the parties, the court may make such order as it thinks fit—

(a) for service in such manner as the court may direct, or

(b) dispensing with service of the document.

(3) Any party to the arbitration agreement may apply for an order, but only after exhausting any available arbitral process for resolving the matter."

Non-existent party

Where the legal advisers responsible for the claim mistakenly issue the proceedings in the name of a party which does not exist (perhaps because it has been merged into another company) the proceedings are a nullity. This is not a mere procedural irregularity which can later be corrected.[23]   **16.014**

A point of considerable practical importance is that many of the arbitrations which give rise to difficulties arise in an international trade context. The Carriage of Goods by Sea Act 1971 incorporates into English law the Hague-Visby Rules; consequently, arbitrations in this area are usually conducted under those rules, which provide a time-limit of one year from the time when the vessel arrives (or should have arrived) in port. For this reason a good knowledge of the rules relating to international carriage of goods by sea is advantageous in this context.[24]

EXTENDING THE TIME-LIMITS

Section 12 of the Arbitration Act 1996 allows the court to extend the time-limit for the commencement of an arbitration if it thinks it just to do so. The following paragraphs examine the exercise of this discretion. It is important to observe that the s.12 discretion is cast in different and more restrictive[25] terms than that in the former s.27 of the Arbitration Act 1950. Case law on the earlier provision is therefore to be treated with great care in relation to the exercise of the s.12 discretion.   **16.015**

Exercising the section 12 discretion

Section 12 provides: **16.016**

"(3) The court shall make an order only if satisfied—

---

[23] *Carneli & Co. SrL v Neotank Carriers Ltd*, April 1, 1992, QBD, Unreported.

[24] The limitation aspects of these rules are considered in detail at paras 26.001–26.021.

[25] *Fox & Widley v Guram*, [1998] 03 E.G. 142, QBD; *Harbour and General Works Ltd v The Environment Agency* [2000] 1 All E.R. 50; [2000] 1 W.L.R. 950; [2000] 1 Lloyd's Rep. 65; (2000) 68 Con. L.R. 1, CA, per Tuckey L.J.

(a) that the circumstances are such as were outside the reasonable contemplation of the parties when they agreed the provision in question, and that it would be just to extend the time, or

(b) that the conduct of one party makes it unjust to hold the other party to the strict terms of the provision in question.

(4) The court may extend the time for such period and on such terms as it thinks fit, and may do so whether or not the time previously fixed (by agreement or by a previous order) has expired.

(5) An order under this section does not affect the operation of the Limitation Acts (see section 13)."

The requirement that the circumstances must be outside the reasonable contemplation of the parties was not present in the 1950 Act, and clearly restricts the range of cases in which the discretion will be available.[26]

The requirement that the extension of time would be just mirrors the 1950 provision. Section 12(3)(b) is entirely new.

Section 12(5) is new, but does no more than make express what was always implicit. The former s.34(5) of the 1980 Act has been replaced by s.13 of the 1996 Act, considered at para.16.027, below.

16.017   The conditions for the exercise of the s.12 discretion have now been considered in a number of cases.

Section 12(3)(a) was considered in *Harbour and General Works Ltd v The Environment Agency*,[27] where Tuckey L.J. said:

"The subsection is concerned with party autonomy. Its aim seems to me to be to allow the Court to consider an extension in relation to circumstances where the parties would not reasonably have contemplated them as being ones where the time bar would apply, or to put it the other way round the section is concerned not to allow the court to interfere with a contractual bargain unless the circumstances are such that if they had been drawn to the attention of the parties when they agreed the provision, the parties would at the very least have contemplated that the time bar might not apply; it then being for the court finally to rule whether justice required an extension of time to be given."

In *Cathiship SA v Allanasons Ltd (The "Catherine Helen")*[28] Judge Lloyd held that for the purposes of s.12(3) the "circumstances" are all those placed before the court, and the court had to consider those circumstances as a whole and focus on those which appeared particularly relevant.

The relevant time to consider when deciding what was in the con-

---

[26] *Harbour and General Works Ltd v Environment Agency* [1999] B.L.R. 143, Colman J.
[27] [2000] 1 All E.R. 50; [2000] 1 W.L.R. 950; [2000] 1 Lloyd's Rep. 65; (2000) 68 Con. L.R. 1, CA.
[28] [1998] 3 All E.R. 714; [1998] 2 Lloyd's Rep. 511, Judge Humphrey Lloyd Q.C.

templation of the parties is the time when the parties agreed the arbitration clause and not some later time, such as when or after the dispute arose; and the persons whose reasonable contemplation is relevant are both parties and not merely one party. The court is not concerned only with what the parties actually contemplated at that time, but what they reasonably would have contemplated. In deciding this question the court must consider the relevant transaction, ordinary practices within that type of transaction and the reasonable expectation of parties involved in such a transaction.

The failure of the claimant to read the provisions of the contract relating to time-limits for commencing the arbitration is not a factor which gives the court discretion to extend time.[29]

Under the old law there was a substantial body of authority on the exercise of the discretion under s.27. The more restrictive form of s.12 means that not all of this will still be relevant. It may be helpful here to review the older cases and consider to what extent they are still of value. A number of factors were commonly of importance.[30]   **16.018**

(a) The length of the delay. Clearly, the longer the delay, the more reluctant the court will be to allow the application. In *McLaughlin & Harvey Plc v P & O Developments Ltd*[31] the contractual time-limit was 14 days, and the court allowed an application to extend this to 23 days. Relevant now to the "justice" criterion in s.12(3)(a), but only where the circumstances have been held to be outside the reasonable contemplation of the parties.

(b) The amount at stake. In *Peel Securities Ltd v Patel*[32] the fact that the disputed element of the rent was about 30 per cent of the total rent was treated as showing that the amount was substantial, and therefore as pointing in favour of allowing an extension of time. Relevant now to the "justice" criterion in s.12(3)(a), but only where the circumstances have been held to be outside the reasonable contemplation of the parties.

(c) Whether the delay was due to the fault of the applicant or to circumstances outside his control.[33] In *The Jocelyne*[34] the plaintiff had

---

[29] *Harbour and General Works Ltd v The Environment Agency* [2000] 1 All E.R. 50; [2000] 1 W.L.R. 950; [2000] 1 Lloyd's Rep. 65; (2000) 68 Con. L.R. 1, CA.

[30] *Pittalis v Sherrefettin* [1986] 1 Q.B. 868 at 890, per Neill L.J., approving the judgment of Brandon L.J. in *Libra Shipping and Trading Corporation Ltd v Northern Sales* [1981] 1 Lloyd's Rep. 273 at 279.

[31] (1997) 55 Build.L.R. 101.

[32] [1992] 30 E.G. 88.

[33] A factor which will tell strongly against the granting of such an extension is that the claimant's disregard of the time-limit was deliberate, rather than merely inadvertent—*First Steamship Co. Ltd v CTS Commodity Transport Shipping Schiffahrtsgesellschaft ("The Ever Splendor")* [1988] 1 Lloyd's Rep. 245, Phillips J.

[34] [1977] 2 Lloyd's Rep. 121, Brandon J.

been guilty of undue delay in commencing the arbitration proceedings. Brandon J. held that in view of this there should be no extension of time. In *Vosnoc Ltd v Transglobal Projects Ltd*[35] the uncertainty over whether the claimants' chosen method of commencing the arbitration was effective (it was held that it was not) was regarded as a relevant factor in considering an application for extention of time. Relevant under s.12(3)(b).

(d) If it was due to the fault of the applicant, the extent of that fault. In *Phoenix Shipping (Pty) Ltd v General Feeds Inc.*[36] Moore-Bick J. took the view that the missing of the time-bar by the plaintiff's solicitors was not of itself a very grave fault, since such mistakes inevitably happen, even in the best-regulated offices. The fault of the applicant would seem now to be a more or less complete bar to the application, at least under s.12(3)(b). It would also be very relevant to "justice" under s.12(3)(a).

In this context the possibility that the applicant might be able to sue his legal advisers for negligence in failing to comply with the time-limit is a factor to which some, relatively modest, weight should be given.[37]

(e) The conduct of the other party. In *Consolidated Investment and Contracting Co. v Sapanoria Shipping Co. Ltd*[38] an extension of time was given when it appeared that the defendants had taken no step in the action, apparently in the hope that time would run out. Very relevant under s.12(3)(b). Potentially of some relevance also under s.12(3)(a).

(f) Whether the other party has been prejudiced by the delay and, if so, to what extent. In *Peel Securities Ltd v Patel*[39] an extension of time was granted in order to enable the tenant to initiate arbitration under a rent review clause, but on terms that the disputed amount of rent should be placed in an interest-bearing account pending the outcome of the arbitration. In this way it was possible to prevent the landlord from suffering any prejudice from the delay. Primarily relevant under s.12(3)(a).

---

[35] [1998] 2 All E.R. 990; [1998] 1 W.L.R. 101, Judge Jack as High Court Judge.
[36] May 10, 1996, Moore-Bick J., Unreported.
[37] *Unitramp SA v Jenson & Nicholson PTE Ltd ("The Baiona")* [1992] 1 W.L.R. 862; [1992] 1 All E.R. 346. *Phoenix Shipping (Pty) v General Feeds Inc.*, above.
[38] [1978] 1 W.L.R. 986.
[39] [1992] 30 E.G. 88.

Procedure

The Arbitration Practice Direction, made under CPR Pt 49, allows appli- **16.019**
cations to be made to court to determine matters arising in an arbitration.
Under the former RSC, Ord.73 there was express provision to the effect
that an application for a declaration that the commencement of an arbitration was in time might be combined with an application for an extension
of time under s.12.[40] The Practice Direction does not expressly state that
the same position still prevails, but Pt I of the Practice Direction, dealing
with applications under the 1996 Act, lists applications that may be made,
including applications to extend time, without suggesting that there is any
limitation on combining applications in the same proceedings. It is therefore to be assumed that the former practice remains valid.

Need for express clause

The court's jurisdiction under s.12 is available only where the time-bar **16.020**
clause is expressly included in the charterparty.[41] Mere incorporation by
reference is not sufficient.[42] This rule is highly unsatisfactory, introducing a
wholly artificial distinction into this branch of the law. It is submitted that
the decision of Kerr J. to this effect is wrong and should not be followed.

Section 12 incorporated by reference

In *Consolidated Investment v Saponaria* (which is discussed above) Ormrod **16.021**
L.J. suggested that the incorporation into a charterparty of art.III, r.6 of the
Hague-Visby Rules (the rule creating the one year time-limit) also incor-
porates by reference the provisions of s.12 of the Arbitration Act 1996.[43]

There is no justification for imputing any such intention to the parties,
nor for implying such a term as a matter of law. It is sufficient to hold that
s.12 should be construed as applying to such cases. The point may at
present be important because of the change in the terms of the section in
1996. An incorporation of the section by reference would presumably have
to be an incorporation of the section as it stood at the time of the formation
of the contract, rather than of any subsequent form.

---

[40] RSC, Ord.73, r.12. See also *Grimaldi Compagnia di Navigazione SpA v Sekihyo Line Ltd*
[1998] 3 All E.R. 943; [1999] 1 W.L.R. 708; [1998] 2 Lloyd's Rep. 638, Mance J.
[41] S.12(1).
[42] *Ch. E. Rolimpex Ltd v Avra Shipping Co. Ltd ("The Angeliki")* [1973] 2 Lloyd's Rep. 226,
Kerr J.
[43] At that time s.27 of the 1950 Act.

Section 12 and the Hague-Visby Rules

16.022　In *Aries Tanker Corporation v Total Transport Ltd*[44] the House of Lords held that where time has expired in respect of a claim under the Hague-Visby Rules the effect is to extinguish the claimant's right rather than simply to bar his remedy. The relationship between this principle and the power to extend time was also considered by the Court of Appeal in *Consolidated Investment and Contracting Co. v Saponaria Shipping Co. Ltd.*[45] The Court unanimously held that the jurisdiction to extend time was nevertheless available, that section covering the extinguishing of the plaintiff's right as well as the barring of his remedy. This decision can be explained on the basis that the effect of extending time is to delay (retro-spectively if necessary) the arrival of the point at which the time-bar operates, rather than to disregard a purely procedural bar to the judicial enforcement of the claimant's rights. Either interpretation is possible, and it was surely somewhat disingenuous of Lord Denning M.R. to suggest in his judgment in that case that the result could be achieved by a straightforward piece of statutory construction. The Court of Appeal took a policy decision that the power to extend time should apply in these cases.

ARBITRATORS' DISCRETION

16.023　Some of the standard forms in common use in international trade set out time-limits, but also contain an overriding provision that any of these limits may be waived by the arbitrators if they see fit. That was the position in *Compagnie Européenne de Cereales SA v Tradax Export SA*,[46] where the arbitrators had purported to disapply the provisions of the Limitation Act 1980. Hobhouse J. held that the clause did not give them this power, since it referred only to the provisions of the agreement itself, and the 1980 Act rules did not derive their force from the agreement. The point is important because an exercise of discretion under such a clause by arbitrators is vir-tually impossible to challenge, whereas the decision in this case restored the judge's power to decide whether this was an appropriate case to apply the extension provisions of the Arbitration Act.

16.024　A related problem to that explored in the preceding paragraph arises where the agreement provides that on the expiry of the time-limit the claimant's claim is to be barred unless the arbitrators shall in their discre-tion decide otherwise. In this instance it is clear that the arbitrators do have

---

[44] [1977] 1 W.L.R. 185, HL; see also paras 26.003–26.004.

[45] [1978] 1 W.L.R. 986; for a further example along the same lines, see *Metalfer Corporation v Pan Ocean Shipping Co Ltd* [1998] 2 Lloyd's Rep. 632, QBD.

[46] [1986] 2 Lloyd's Rep. 301, Hobhouse J.; the arbitration was conducted under the GAFTA 125 Form.

power to disapply the time-limits, and that, on appropriate wording, this power can extend to disapplying the Limitation Act as well as any other contractual time-limit. The question is whether the court can in these circumstances use the statutory discretion to extend time after the arbitrators have declined to do so. The point was obliquely considered in *The Cunard Carrier*[47] and in *Ets Soules et Cie v International Trade Development Co. Ltd,*[48] in both of which it was assumed that the court would have such discretion. The first direct consideration of the question came in *Timmerman's Graan-en Maalhandel en Maalderij BV v Sachs,*[49] where Parker J. held that the court had no jurisdiction to grant an extension of time in these circumstances. Leggatt J. then took the opposite view in *European Grain & Shipping Ltd v Dansk Land Grovvareslskab.*[50]

All these cases were extensively reviewed by the House of Lords in *Comdel Commodities Ltd v Siporex Trade SA (No. 2).*[51] In this case the agreement provided for an initial decision on the point by the arbitrators, followed if necessary by an appeal to a further tribunal, although the existence of this additional layer does not appear to affect the result of the case. The House of Lords affirmed the decision of the Court of Appeal that the discretion is general and universal. Thus, the court retains the discretion to extend time irrespective of what is in the arbitration agreement. In reaching this conclusion the House of Lords offered some observations about the nature and exercise of the discretion.

The claimant will be able to come to court only after exhausting the **16.025** procedures available to him under the arbitration agreement. The court must weigh the conflicting arguments as to whether to extend time. Where the arbitrators have given reasons for their decision, the court will give those reasons as much weight as seems proper. Where no reasons have been given, the court should decide the matter without taking any account of the arbitrators' decision.

EXPIRY OF TIME IN OTHER CONTRACTUAL CASES

The discussion above has concentrated on the Hague-Visby Rules; some **16.026** other contractual time-limits in arbitrations follow the same principles, but there are also some which do not. A distinction must be made between time-limits which extinguish the claim and those which merely bar the right to arbitration. Where the claim is extinguished, the principles of the Hague-Visby cases are applicable. By contrast, a curious result is produced where

---

[47] [1977] 2 Lloyd's Rep. 261 at 265.
[48] [1979] 2 Lloyd's Rep. 122 at 138.
[49] [1980] 1 Lloyd's Rep. 194.
[50] [1986] 1 Lloyd's Rep. 163.
[51] [1991] 1 A.C. 148, HL.

only the right to arbitration is barred. Here, the claim subsists and may be pursued through the ordinary court system. All that is lost is the right to go to arbitration. Determining the category into which a clause falls is obviously a matter of construction, but as a general principle it may be said that the court will lean in the direction of holding that a clause extinguishes the claim—it is hard to see why the parties should want the passage of time to force the matter to be litigated in the High Court rather than before an arbitrator, but rather easier to see why the parties might wish the claim to be extinguished entirely.

SUING ON AN AWARD

16.027 Section 7 of the 1980 Act imposes a time-limit of six years for bringing an action on an award where the submission is not under seal. Although this is an enforcement of an award, no analogy can be drawn with s.24 of the 1980 Act, and s.7 applies in the same was as did s.26 of its predecessor, the Arbitration Act 1950.[52]

"Award" in this section means an award pursuant to an arbitration,[53] and time runs from the date on which the cause of action accrues. The identification of this date was at issue in *Agromet Motoimport Ltd v Maulden Engineering Co. (Beds.) Ltd.*[54] This was a breach of contract case which had gone to arbitration, resulting in an award in favour of the claimant; the latter now sued on the award, and Otton J. held that any arbitration clause includes an implied promise to perform any validly made award under it. An action on the award is an action for the breach of that promise, and time consequently runs from the date of that breach. It follows from this that, for s.7 purposes, time runs neither from the date of the original breach of contract which gives rise to the arbitration nor from the date of the arbitration award, but from an indeterminate later date when the promise to perform the award is broken. In identifying this time it will presumably be necessary to show that one of the following things has happened:

(a) the time (if any) provided in the contract for performing the award has expired;

(b) (where (a) does not apply) the time (if any) stipulated in the award for its performance has expired;

---

[52] *National Ability SA v Tinna Oils and Chemicals Ltd* [2009] EWCA Civ 1330 [2010] 2 All E.R. 899.

[53] S.14 of the Arbitration Act 1950 allows an arbitration award to be enforced in the same manner as a judgment of the High Court.

[54] [1985] 1 W.L.R. 762, Otton J.

(c) (where neither (a) nor (b) applies) a reasonable time for performance has elapsed since the making of the award;

(d) (in any case) the defendant has manifested a clear and unequivocal intention not to be bound by the award.[55]

No cause of action before award

An arbitration agreement may provide that there is to be no cause of action before the award is made. As was explained at paras 16.007–16.008 above, s.34(2) of the 1980 Act avoids such agreements, and the cause of action accrues when it would have done in the absence of such agreement.   16.028

POSTPONEMENT OF RUNNING OF TIME

The former s.34(5) of the 1980 Act has been replaced by s.13 of the 1996 Act, which provides: 16.029

"(1) The Limitation Acts apply to arbitral proceedings as they apply to legal proceedings.

(2) The court may order that in computing the time prescribed by the Limitation Acts for the commencement of proceedings (including arbitral proceedings) in respect of a dispute which was the subject matter—

(a) of an award which the court orders to be set aside or declares to be of no effect, or

(b) of the affected part of an award which the court orders to be set aside in part, or declares to be in part of no effect, the period between the commencement of the arbitration and the date of the order referred to in paragraph (a) or (b) shall be excluded.

(3) In determining for the purposes of the Limitation Acts when a cause of action accrued, any provision that an award is a condition precedent to the bringing of legal proceedings in respect of a matter to which an arbitration agreement applies shall be disregarded.

(4) In this Part "the Limitation Acts" means—

(a) in England and Wales, the Limitation Act 1980, the Foreign Limitation Periods Act 1984 and any other enactment (when-ever passed) relating to the limitation of actions;

(b) in Northern Ireland, the Limitation (Northern Ireland) Order

---

[55] By analogy with cases of anticipatory breach such as *Hochster v de la Tour* (1853) 2 E. & B. 678.

1989, the Foreign Limitation Periods (Northern Ireland) Order 1985 and any other enactment (whenever passed) relating to the limitation of actions."

This provision appears to be the same effect as the former s.34(5), despite minor changes of wording. It applies where the High Court orders that an award shall be set aside or that an arbitration agreement shall cease to have effect with respect to the dispute referred under it. In these circumstances the court has a discretion to order in addition that the time elapsing between the commencement of the arbitration and the date of the order shall be excluded in calculating the expiry of time under the 1980 Act or any other limitation enactment. The effect of such an order is to restore the claimant to the position in which he found himself immediately before commencing the arbitration, and with the same amount of time available for commencing new proceedings as he then had. One point of difficulty in this subsection concerns the reference to other limitation enactments. This may be contrasted with the reference in s.39 of the 1980 Act to "any other enactment". In relation to the former provision it was suggested[56] that the phrase "other limitation enactments" was confined to statutes which deal primarily with limitation, but it is by no means clear that this was correct. If anything, the new provision appears to cast the net more widely, and it must be regarded as strongly arguable that any individual provision which deals with limitation periods is a limitation enactment for this purpose, notwithstanding that such an interpretation may seem to be unacceptably wide.[57]

ARBITRATIONS AND SECTION 35 OF THE LIMITATION ACT 1980

16.030 Section 35 of the 1980 Act, which is dealt with in detail in Ch.23, makes detailed provision for counterclaims and set-offs. In particular, it enables counterclaims, in specified circumstances, to be treated as having been made at the date when the original action was commenced rather than at the date when the counterclaim was first raised; this rule can sometimes be used to save a counterclaim which would otherwise be out of time. In *Casillo Grani v Napier Shipping Co. ("The World Ares")*[58] an attempt was made to use s.35 as a way of avoiding the expiry of a time-limit under the Hague-Visby Rules. Neill J. held that s.35 has no application to a case where the effect of the expiry of time is to extinguish the claimant's right

---

[56] Mustill and Boyd, *Commercial Arbitration* (2nd edn, 1989).
[57] See para.1.001
[58] [1984] 2 Lloyd's Rep. 481, Neill J.

rather than merely to bar his remedy. In reaching this conclusion Neill J. relied on the following observations of Lord Wilberforce in *Aries Tanker Corporation v Total Transport Ltd*[59]:

> "The charterers' claim, after May 1974 and before the date of the writ, had not merely become unenforceable by action, it had simply ceased to exist, and I fail to understand how a claim which has ceased to exist can be introduced for any purpose into legal proceedings, whether by defence or (if this is different) as a means of reducing the owners' claim, or as a set-off, or in any way whatsoever."

A more extreme view was taken by Steyn J. in *Kenya Railways v Antares Co. Pte. Ltd ("The Antares") (No. 2)*.[60] His Lordship held that the provisions of s.35 of the 1980 Act, as well as the provisions of RSC, Ord.20, r.5, which deals with amendments to pleadings, had no application to arbitrations. This rule applies whatever the effect of the expiry of time, and its effect is apparently that the commencement of a counterclaim or other new claim cannot be backdated to the date when the original claim was made, nor has the arbitrator any discretion to allow amendments of the pleadings so as to add a new cause of action once the limitation period has expired.[61] This decision, which may at first sight seem slightly surprising, was based mainly upon the absence of any express indication in s.35 that it was intended to apply to arbitrations. It is submitted that this reasoning is misplaced. Section 34 of the Act states that the Act applies to arbitrations as it applies to High Court actions, and there is no doubt that s.35 applies to the latter. A more difficult point raised by Steyn J. is that logic would seem to require the s.35 discretion to be vested in the arbitrator, whereas there is no express provision giving him any of the powers which exist under s.35. This is a more awkward obstacle, but it is submitted that the s.35 discretion remains vested in the court rather than in the arbitrator, notwithstanding the practical difficulties to which this may occasionally give rise. 16.031

DELAY IN THE CONDUCT OF THE ARBITRATION

Where the conduct of an arbitration is unreasonably delayed, the question may arise as to what powers the court has to take action against a party who has been dilatory. In *Gulf Shipping Lines Ltd v Jadranska Slobodna Plovidba*[62] Neill J., relying on the Court of Appeal decision in *Bremer* 16.032

---

[59] [1977] 1 All E.R. 398 at 402.
[60] [1986] 2 Lloyd's Rep. 633.
[61] See para.22.033-22.036 for the comparable CPR provisions.
[62] [1981] 1 Lloyd's Rep. 31.

Vulkan Schiffbau und Maschinenfabrik v South India Shipping Corpora-tion,[63] held that the effect of delay could be to frustrate the arbitration agreement, and that in determining whether the delay which had happened was sufficient to achieve that effect, the court should apply the principles laid down by the House of Lords in *Birkett v James*[64] for deciding whether an action should be dismissed for want of prosecution.[65] However, when the *Bremer Vulkan* case reached the House of Lords[66] it was held that there is no jurisdiction in the arbitrator to treat the agreement as frustrated or to dismiss the claim for want of prosecution. In ordinary High Court actions the principle is that the defendant need do nothing, and can then seek the dismissal of the action after sufficient time has elapsed; but in an arbitration both parties have an obligation to proceed with due despatch.

THE ARBITRATOR'S POWERS IN CASES OF DELAY

16.033   Section 41(3) of the Arbitration Act 1996 gives arbitrators express power to dismiss arbitration proceedings on the ground of inordinate and inexcusable delay on the part of the claimant, where the delay gives rise to a substantial risk that it will not be possible to have a fair trial of the claim or has caused or is likely to cause serious prejudice to the respondent. The question of the approach to be taken by arbitrators in dealing with applications to strike out for want of prosecution was considered in *James Lazenby and Co. v McNicholas Construction Co. Ltd.*[67] Rix J. held that the same principles applied to the power to dismiss a claim for want of prosecution in arbitration as in litigation.[68] The test is similar to that laid down by the House of Lords in *Birkett v James*[69] for dismissal for want of prosecution in actions before the court. Section 13A does not give arbitrators power to strike out claims which had not yet become time-barred.

It would therefore be wrong for an arbitrator to dismiss a claim within its limitation period, barring exceptional circumstances. Delay, at any rate prior to the expiry of the limitation period, cannot be properly regarded as "inordinate".

---

[63] [1981] A.C. 909.
[64] [1977] A.C. 297.
[65] These principles are considered at length in Ch.22.
[66] [1981] A.C. 909.
[67] [1995] 3 All E.R. 820; [1995] 2 Lloyd's Rep. 30, Rix J.
[68] *Acme Metal Works v Shun Shing Construction and Engineering Co. Ltd* [1990] H.K.L.R 474.
[69] [1978] A.C. 297, HL.

THE COURT'S POWERS IN CASES OF DELAY

Arbitrations are always subject to the supervision of the High Court, and in **16.034** cases of extreme delay the Court may hold that the agreement has been frustrated. In *Stockport MBC v O'Reilly*[70] Neill J. held that this principle cannot be invoked within the time allowed by the arbitration agreement for going to arbitration. In other words, the rule in arbitrations is similar to that applicable to ordinary actions in the High Court: an arbitration will not be treated as frustrated if the claimant would still be within the permitted time to institute new proceedings under the same agreement in respect of the same dispute.[71]

---

[70] [1983] 2 Lloyd's Rep. 70.

[71] For a thorough review of the considerations applying in cases of delay (including the non-Limitation Act points) see the judgment of Potter J. in *Thai-Europe Tapioca Service Ltd v Seine Navigation Co. Inc.*, May 4, 1989, Unreported.

CHAPTER 17

Miscellaneous Cases

This chapter deals with a number of miscellaneous cases within the law of limitations, which are not covered elsewhere in this work.   **17.001**

ACTIONS FOR ACCOUNT

Section 23 of the Limitation Act 1980 imposes a time-limit in the case of   **17.002**
actions for an account. The principal difficulty to be addressed here is that
the action for an account was available, before the Judicature Acts 1873–
1875, in both the common law courts and the courts of equity. This led to
some discussion of the possibility that different rules applied to the two
forms of action, it being accepted that the Limitation Act 1980 does not
generally apply to claims for equitable relief,[1] which are governed instead
by the doctrine of laches.[2] An idea for reconciling this apparent oddity was
suggested by Megarry V.-C. in *Tito v Waddell (No. 2)*.[3] Although the Act
does not apply directly to claims for equitable relief, s.36(2) of the 1980 Act
allows the court to apply the common law periods of limitation to such
claims in those cases where they would have been applied by analogy before
1939. It may be that the action for an account is such a case. The problem is
greatly simplified by s.23 of the 1980 Act. This provides that the action for
an account shall not be brought after the expiry of any time-limit relating to
the action which is the basis of the claim for an account. This has the
practical advantage of treating claims for account as merely parasitic on
some other independent cause of action (since account is properly regarded
as merely a mechanism), and relating the time-limit to the independent

---

[1] See now the 1980 Act, s.36.
[2] *Re Pauling's Settlement Trusts* [1961] 3 All E.R. 713, Wilberforce J.; affirmed without
reference to this point [1963] 3 All E.R. 1, CA See also para.3.012.
[3] [1977] 3 All E.R. 129 at 250.

cause of action.[4] Where the account is sought as a consequence of the obtaining of a judgment, the Limitation Act does not apply, since no action is brought, but the court may require an explanation for any undue delay in proceeding and may deal with such delay by making an appropriate order for costs or by directing that any party to the action or the Official Solicitor take over the conduct of the proceedings.[5]

ACTIONS ON JUDGMENTS

17.003 Section 24 of the 1980 Act provides that no action shall be brought upon a judgment more than six years after the date on which it became enforceable. The practice of bringing an action on a judgment was common in the days when the common law presumption was that a judgment was satisfied after a year and a day if no execution had been issued. In such cases the only way to "enforce" the judgment was by an action of debt upon it.[6] The right to bring the second action has been said to depend upon an implied contract to honour the first judgment,[7] though that might be thought to be something of a fiction. Even today bringing a second action in this way is a matter of right,[8] although the court may decline to give judgment in the second action if it regards it as an abuse of process. In determining whether it is an abuse of process, the availability of execution is a relevant factor.[9] In *Kuwait Oil Tanker Co SAK and another v Al Bader and others*[10] Teare J. accepted that potential problems in enforcing abroad a judgment more than six years old amounted to good reason for bringing a second action, which was therefore not an abuse of process.

17.004 In *Bank of Scotland v Bennett*[11] the bank had obtained judgment against the defendants, but did not enforce it within six years. One day before the expiry of that six-year period it started a second action against the defendants based on the first judgment. The defendants submitted that the second action was an abuse of process as the bank had already obtained the first judgment. The Court of Appeal held that it could not be an abuse of process per se to commence a second action. Section 24(1) permitted a party with

---

[4] Consequently an action between former partners for an account is barred six years after the dissolution of the partnership, even where the later claim is for an asset not included in the original account—*Marshall v Bullock*, March 27, 1998, Unreported, CA.

[5] CPR 40PD 6.2.

[6] *E.D. & F. Man (Sugar) Ltd v Haryanto*, *The Times*, August 9, 1996, CA.

[7] *Kuwait Oil Tanker Co SAK v Al Bader* [2008] EWHC 2432 (Comm) Teare J.

[8] *Williams v Jones* (1845) 13 M. & W. 628, approved in *E.D. & F. Man (Sugar) Ltd v Haryanto*, above.

[9] *E.D. & F. Man (Sugar) Ltd v Haryanto*, above.

[10] Above.

[11] [2004] EWCA CIV 988, [2004] All ER (D) 417.

the benefit of an earlier judgment to commence proceedings on that judgment any time within six years of the judgment being obtained.

Ridgeway Motors Isleworth[12] establishes that a winding-up petition based on a judgment debt is not an action on the judgment within the meaning of s.24 of the 1980 Act. The same point was made in relation to a statutory demand in bankruptcy in *Bailey v Hill*.[13]

Patel v Singh[14] concerned the court's discretion to allow execution of a judgment more than six years after the date of the judgment. The matter is of course not governed by the Limitation Act 1980, but by RSC Ord.46 (now one of the few surviving provisions of the old RSC). Peter Gibson L.J. referred to *Duer v Frazer*[15] and added:

"[19] To my mind, it is obvious that the court must start from the position that there has been the six-year passage of time which is now equal to the applicable limitation period if the judgment were sought to be enforced by a fresh action. The policy underlying s.24 must be that the judgment creditor has to get on with enforcing his judgment. Similarly there can be no issue of a writ of execution pursuant to Ord 46 r 2(1)(a) after six years without the court's permission.

[20] I accept, as the *Lowsley* case dictates, that whether a writ of execution will be allowed to be issued is a procedural matter and that the intention was that the court should have a discretion. But it seems to me to be impossible to ignore the fact that, whereas in the six-year period the judgment creditor was entirely free to issue execution on his judgment in any way he chose, that freedom has been removed after the expiry of the period and it is left to the court to decide whether to allow the judgment creditor to proceed with one form of execution, the issuing of a writ of execution.

[21] The policy of the rule seems to me to be that ordinarily after six years permission will not be given and that is underlined by the provisions of Ord 46 r 4(2), requiring the judgment creditor to explain his delay. In contrast there is no rule that the judgment debtor is to file evidence to state what prejudice, if any, he has suffered by the delay. In my judgment, therefore, consistently with what this court said in Powney, the court must start from the position that the lapse of six years may, and will ordinarily, in itself justify refusing the judgment creditor permission to issue the writ of execution, unless the judgment creditor can justify the granting of permission by showing that the circumstances of

---

[12] [2004] All ER (D) 320 (May) Judge Rich QC.

[13] [2003] EWHC 2646 (Ch) Peter Leaver QC; it therefore appears that the earlier decision of Judge Baker Q.C. in *Re A Debtor* (No 50A of 1995) [1997] Ch. 310, [1997] 2 WLR 57, [1996] BPIR 565, [1997] 2 All ER 789, ChD can no longer be considered good law, though it has not been expressly overruled.

[14] [2002] EWCA Civ 1938 13 December 2002.

[15] [2001] 1 All ER 249 Evans-Lombe J.

his or her case takes it out of the ordinary. That may be done by showing the presence of something in relation to the judgment creditor's own position, or, as Sir Anthony Evans suggested in the course of the argument, in relation to the judgment debtor's position. Thus the judgment creditor might be able to point, for example, to the fact that for many years the judgment debtor was thought to have no money and so was not worth powder and shot but that, on the judgment creditor winning the lottery or having some other change of financial fortune, it has become worthwhile for the judgment creditor to seek to pursue the judgment debtor."

Patel v Singh was itself referred to with approval in *Good Challenger Naveganet*[16], and it may now be treated as settled that permission to issue execution more than six years after the judgment will be given only in exceptional cases.

CHARGING ORDERS

17.005 Where the claimant obtains a judgment debt and then executes that by obtaining a charging order, an attempt to enforce the charging order is not an action on the original judgment for these purposes, since the charging order has a life of its own independent of the original judgment.[17] However, the charging order does not confer a present right to receive a sum of money for the purposes of s.20(1) of the Limitation Act 1980.[18]

Difference between enforcing and suing

17.006 It is essential to understand that this section applies only to the process of bringing an action upon a judgment. It does not extend to seeking execution of a judgment: the latter is a purely procedural step, and is not an "action" within the meaning of the 1980 Act.[19] The provision is of only very limited importance at the present day, since the bringing of an action upon a judgment is rare[20] : the most common example at the present day is where a foreign judgment is not registrable because there are no reciprocal

---

[16] [2003] EWCA Civ 1668, [2003] All ER (D) 320 (Nov).
[17] *Ezekiel v Orakpo* [1997] 1 W.L.R 340, CA.
[18] *Doodes v Gotham* [2006] EWCA Civ 1080. And see para.12.016.
[19] *National Westminster Bank v Powney* [1991] Ch. 339, CA approving *W.T. Lamb & Sons v Rider* [1948] 2 K.B. 331, CA, and disapproving *Lougher v Donovan* [1948] 2 All E.R. 11, CA.
[20] It was held as long ago as 1899 in *Pritchett v English and Colonial Syndicate* [1899] 2 Q.B. 428 that the bringing of such an action could be an abuse of process if some more appropriate way of proceeding were open to the claimant.

arrangements between England and the jurisdiction where the judgment was given.[21] In *Lowsley v Forbes (t/a L.E. Design Services)*[22] the plaintiffs in 1981 obtained a judgment against the defendant in the sum of £70,000. In 1992 the plaintiffs obtained leave from the master to enforce the judgment under RSC Ord.46 r.2(1)(a),[23] and also a charging order nisi on the defendant's share of the matrimonial home, and a garnishee order nisi over his bank account. The House of Lords held that the word "action" in s.24(1) of the 1980 Act meant a fresh action, and did not include proceedings by way of execution. Accordingly, the section did not bar execution of a judgment after six years, but only barred the bringing of a fresh action on the judgment.[24] In *Edwards v Edwards*[25] the Court of Appeal held that an application by the Law Society to enforce its statutory charge over property recovered by a legally aided claimant is not within s.24, since it is the taking of a further step in an existing action rather than the commencement of a new action. In *Times Newspapers Ltd v Jaghit Singh Chohan*; sub nom in the *Matter of Jaghit Singh Chohan*[26] it was held that for the purposes of s.24 time does not run from the date when an order for the payment of costs "to be taxed" is made, but from the date when the amount of the costs in question is certified after taxation.

Interest on judgments

Section 24(2) provides that no arrears of interest in respect of any judgment debt shall be recovered more than six years after the date on which the interest became due. Thus, there are separate rules for the principal sum and for the interest on the principal sum. The point is of some importance, since the result may be that interest can be recovered although the action for the principal sum is barred. Therefore, an action for the interest will not become entirely barred until six years after the debt itself becomes barred. This rule appears to represent an exception to the general principle that an action for interest becomes barred once the action for the principal sum is barred.[27]

17.007

---

[21] For example, judgments given in any state of the United States of America fall into this category.

[22] [1998] 3 All E.R. 897; [1998] 3 W.L.R. 501; *The Times*, August 24, 1998.

[23] This rule remains in force despite the recent addition to the CPR of Pts 70–73, which deal with some aspects of the enforcement of judgments. In *Duer v Frazer*, April 19, 2000, Unreported, Evans-Lombe J., it was suggested that there is a presumption against allowing enforcement once the six years have expired, but it clearly remains a matter for the discretion of the court.

[24] For earlier case, see note 19, above.

[25] July 7, 1989, CA Unreported.

[26] [2001] 1 W.L.R. 1859, CA.

[27] *Elder v Northcott* [1930] 2 Ch. 422.

Section 24(2) presents another problem of interpretation. As drafted it appears to refer to any means of recovering interest on a judgment, including doing so by the ordinary processes of execution. However, this would mean that whilst s.24(1) does not apply to execution, s.24(2) does. It may be observed that the side-note to s.24 refers to "actions on judgments", and although this is not strictly admissible as an aid to construction, it would seem sensible to interpret both parts of the section as applying in the same way. In *Lowsley v Forbes*,[28] it was held that s.24(2) does apply to execution, so that only the last six years' worth of interest can be recovered by execution.

Setting aside a judgment

17.008   The CPR allow application to be made to set aside certain judgments, especially those entered in default of appearance or of the serving of a defence.[29] There is no provision of the 1980 Act which deals with such application, and it therefore appears that no statutory period of limitation applies to them. However, it is a general principle of the relevant rules of court[30] that an action of this kind must be brought promptly once the defendant becomes aware of the existence of the judgment against him. In practice, therefore, it seems likely that the period available for bringing an action of this kind will be significantly shorter than any laid down by the 1980 Act.

AWARDS

17.009   Section 7 of the 1980 Act provides that an action to enforce an award, where the submission is not by an instrument under seal, shall not be brought after the expiration of six years from the date on which the cause of action accrued. "Award" in this section refers to an award under an arbitration.[31] Where the submission is by an instrument under seal, this section does not apply.[32] Instead, this will be a case of an action on a specialty, to which s.8 of the Act applies a limitation period of 12 years.

---

[28] Above, fn.22.
[29] CPR Pt 13.
[30] CPR 13.3(2) makes this a relevant factor on a set-aside application.
[31] Arbitrations are dealt with in s.34 of the Act; see Ch.16.
[32] *Bremer Oeltransport GmbH v Drewry* [1933] 1 K.B. 753.

Accrual of cause of action

The action under s.7 is an action on the agreement to refer to arbitration, **17.010** rather than on the award itself.[33] Nevertheless, the cause of action accrues only when the award is made, since there can be no breach of the agreement until that date. Since the obligation to pay is based upon an implied promise to honour the award, the cause of action will normally accrue no later than that date. However, where the action is expressed as being for damages for failure to honour the implied promise, it may be possible to add a further short period, three months at most, to the date at which the cause of action accrues.[34] This period cannot be further extended by the actions of the parties during that period, nor is it correct to say that the action for damages does not accrue until the defendants have unequivocally refused to pay.[35]

It is uncertain whether this rule applies equally to the case of compensation awarded under a statute, to which s.9 of the 1980 Act applies.[36]

ADVOWSONS

An advowson is the right to present to a benefice (or living) in the Church of **17.011** England. The former s.25 of the 1980 Act has been repealed and replaced by the Patronage (Benefices) Measure 1986 (No.3). The administrative details relating to the change are dealt with in two statutory instruments, the Patronage (Benefice) Rules 1987,[37] which came into force on October 1, 1987, and the Patronage (Appeals) Rules 1988,[38] which came into force on January 1, 1989. The Measure effects a fundamental change in the system for enforcing patronage. The Registrar of each diocese is obliged to maintain a Register indicating in relation to every benefice in the diocese the person who is the patron of that benefice.[39]

The Register has a similar function in relation to patronage as the Land **17.012** Register has in relation to land; that is to say that it is intended to be a definitive record of patronage within the Church of England. To this end s.1(2) of the Measure provides that after the expiry of 15 months from the date on which the Measure comes into force (that 15-month period being referred to as "the registration period") no person shall have the right to

---

[33] *Bremer Oeltransport GmbH v Drewry* [1933] 1 K.B. 753.
[34] *IBSSL v Minerals and Metals Trading Corp. of India* [1996] 1 All E.R. 1017, CA.
[35] *IBSSL v Minerals and Metals Trading Corp. of India* [1996] 1 All E.R. 1017, CA.
[36] *West Riding CC v Huddersfield Corporation* [1957] 1 All E.R. 669, Lord Goddard C.J.: see para.11.004.
[37] SI 1987/773.
[38] SI 1988/1980.
[39] Patronage (Benefices) Measure 1986 (No. 3) s.1.

present to any benefice unless he is registered as the patron of that benefice. Section 1(4) provides that the registration of a person as a patron of a benefice shall be conclusive evidence of the matters registered. However, this conclusive character of the Register is subject to a jurisdiction to rectify the Register where it appears that incorrect particulars have been entered in it. It will be appreciated that under the new regime, obtaining the rectification of the Register is the only way in which a person who has been deprived of the right of presentation can regain that right, and s.4 of the Measure deals with the limitation implications of this change. By s.4(2), where an entry in the Register has been adverse to the claims of any person for a period of more than 30 years or (where the period of 30 years from the need of the registration period has not yet expired) the benefice has been held adversely to the claim of any person for more than 30 years, then no rectification of the Register in favour of the person deprived of the right of presentation may be made unless all persons interested agree to that rectification. There is no definition of "persons interested", but the phrase must include the person who is registered as the patron. There is, though, no reason why it should include the present clerk, since he is not liable to be deprived even if the Register is rectified. A further necessary consequence of this new regime, to which effect is given by s.4(3) of the Measure, is that s.25 of the 1980 Act ceased to have effect at the end of the registration period.

Practical significance

17.013   In 1977 the Law Reform Committee expressed the view that the rules on advowsons would in all likelihood shortly become obsolete.[40] However, the form in which the 1986 Measure has finally been enacted suggests an assumption by those responsible for it that the question of patronage is not entirely dead. From a limitation point of view it is instructive to note that there is apparently no reported case within the past 200 years which has had occasion to consider the question of the time-barring of the right to present to a benefice. It may be predicted with a fair degree of confidence that these new provisions will not open the floodgates of litigation.

COMPANY, INSOLVENCY AND BANKRUPTCY LAW

17.014   These areas of the law include a number of provisions which give rise to limitation issues. These are considered below.

---

[40] Law Reform Committee 21st Report, Final Report on Limitation of Actions, Cmnd. 6923.

Company Directors Disqualification Act 1986

Under the Company Directors Disqualification Act 1986 ("the CDDA **17.015**
1986") application may be made to court for the disqualification of a
director from acting as a director. Section 7 requires that an application for
the disqualification of a director be brought within two years of the date on
which the company of which the respondent is or has been a director
became insolvent. However, the section also gives the court a discretion to
authorise the bringing of proceedings out of time. No further guidance is
given in the statute as to the principles on which the discretion is to be
exercised or as to any consequential limitation questions which might arise
from the existence of the time-limit. There is, however, a body of case law
dealing with these issues.

When period expires

The period expires two years after the date when the last company in **17.016**
relation to which the director's conduct is challenged became insolvent.[41]
Where that period expires on a day when the court office is not open, the
expiry of the period is postponed to the next day on which it is open.[42]

Exercise of discretion

Where application is made to bring proceedings out of time the relevant **17.017**
factors for the court to take into account are the following[43]:

(1) In considering an application for leave to commence disqualification
    proceedings out of time, the applicant should show a good reason for
    the extension and the court should take into account:

    (a) the length of the delay;
    (b) the reasons for the delay;
    (c) the strength of the case (i.e. the gravity of the charges) against the
        director; and
    (d) the degree of prejudice caused to the director by the delay.

(2) The adequacy of the explanation for delay was a matter to be con-
    sidered together with all other relevant circumstances. There was no
    justification for treating the adequacy of the explanation as a free-
    standing or threshold test which had to be satisfied before other
    considerations could be taken into account.

---

[41] CDDA 1986 s.7(2).
[42] *Secretary of State v Lion*, March 7, 1994, CA, Unreported, applying *Pritam Kaur v s.Russell
    & Sons Ltd* [1973] Q.B. 336, Willis J. and CA.
[43] *Re Blackspur Group Plc* [1997] B.C.C. 235, CA; see also *Re Probe Data Systems Ltd (No.
    3)* [1992] B.C.L.C. 405; *Re Tasbian (No. 3)* [1993] B.C.L.C. 297.

(3) Apart from a deliberate decision to disregard the rules or to take an unfair advantage of the other side, there was no such thing as a reason for delay which was "good" or "bad" in itself regardless of the circumstances, or which was inherently acceptable or unacceptable in all the circumstances. There was only a reason for delay which could reasonably be accepted as sufficient to justify an extension of time in all the circumstances of the particular case.

(4) The Secretary of State had to show a good reason for being granted the extension of time which he sought, but that was not the same as having to show a good reason for the delay. The Secretary of State had to explain the delay: the better the explanation, the easier it would be for him to obtain leave.

(5) Section 7(2) simply requires an applicant to apply to the court for leave. The court's discretion is unfettered and there is no statutory threshold for the exercise of the discretion to grant leave. It was not a limitation period or time-bar such as was found in the Limitation Acts. The expiry of the two-year period creates no vested right in the director.

Applying for leave to proceed out of time

17.018 It is necessary to make an application for leave before issuing proceedings. It is not open to the court to ratify proceedings which have already been commenced out of time.[44]

Amendments after the period has expired[45]

17.019 In *Official Receiver v Pafundo*[46] proceedings had been started in the name of the Official Receiver in the county court after the company concerned had been wound up. The correct procedure in these circumstances is to start proceedings in the name of the Secretary of State in the High Court. The Court of Appeal held that the resulting proceedings were irregular but not a nullity. The next question was whether the irregularity could be corrected by substituting the name of the Secretary of State for the name of the Official Receiver. Harman J. had held that RSC Ord.15 r.6(2) and Ord.20 r.5(3) did not entitle him to substitute the Secretary of State for the Official Receiver as sought. The Court of Appeal pointed out that the severe restriction in that rule on joining new parties after the expiry of any relevant period of limitation had no application to the present case, since

---

[44] *Secretary of State v Cleland*, November 21, 1996, Lloyd J., Unreported, following the decision of Harman J. in *Re Crestjoy Products Ltd* [1990] B.C.L.C. 677; [1990] B.C.C. 23, in preference to the decision of Millett J. in *Re Probe Data Systems Ltd (No. 2)* [1990] B.C.L.C. 574; [1990] B.C.C. 21.

[45] For the general principles applicable to this topic, see paras 22.033–22.035.

[46] [2000] B.C.C. 164, CA.

"relevant period of limitation" was defined in Ord.15 r.6 as a period of limitation under the Limitation Act 1980, and the period under consideration here does not arise under that statute.[47] Consequently, there is jurisdiction to add a new party in these circumstances. It is then a matter for the court's discretion whether to do so, and the Court of Appeal treated this as in substance a question of balancing the interests of the parties and considering the justice of the case. On the facts the order for joinder was made.

Dismissal for want of prosecution

The ordinary principles for deciding whether to dismiss a case for want of **17.020** prosecution established by the House of Lords in *Birkett v James*[48] apply to cases under the CDDA 1986, subject to the modification that there is a public interest in obtaining the disqualification of an unfit director, whereas no such public interest generally exists in pure private law cases. This was established in *Re Manlon Trading Ltd*,[49] where it was said that the first crucial question in applications to dismiss disqualification proceedings for want of prosecution is whether a fair trial is still possible. If not, the proceedings should be dismissed. If a fair trial is still possible, then the proceedings should not normally be dismissed. The exception to this is where the prejudice caused to the respondent by the delay exceeds the public interest in obtaining a disqualification order. It must be remembered that this public interest does not diminish with the passage of time.

Bankruptcy and insolvency

A number of specialised limitation problems can arise where an individual **17.021** becomes bankrupt or a company becomes the subject of an administration order,[50] or goes into receivership or insolvent liquidation. Some of these problems have been dealt with elsewhere in this work, notably under acknowledgment (Ch.18) or land (Ch.13), but this section seeks to summarise the more important rules.

Administration orders

In *Re Maxwell Fleet and Facilities Management Ltd (In Administration)*[51] **17.022** the company went into administration in February 1992. The joint administrators retained 12 employees. The business of the company was

---

[47] See also *Re Blackspur Ltd* [1997] B.C.C. 235, CA.
[48] [1978] A.C. 297.
[49] [1995] 4 All E.R. 14, CA.
[50] Insolvency Act 1986 Pt II.
[51] [1999] 2 B.C.L.C. 721.

sold in April 1992 and the 12 employees were then dismissed. The employees had not issued proceedings, but the administrators applied to the court for directions as to whether the 12 employees' claims against the company were time-barred. It was held that the granting of an administration order does not stop time running for limitation purposes. It was further held that the employees' contractual claims accrued in April 1992 when they were dismissed. If the administrators did not pay those claims in the course of the administration, s.19(5) of the IA 1986 imposed a statutory obligation to pay them and a charge as security for that obligation at the end of the administration. Accordingly the claims could not be statute-barred because the property out of which they were statutorily payable had not been ascertained and the occasion for their enforcement had not arisen. So far as enforcement of the charge was concerned, s.20 of the Limitation Act 1980 applied, and the limitation period would be 12 years from the end of the administration period. Even if the date was the date when the underlying contractual obligation accrued, the 12 employees were within the 12-year period. The cause of action flowing from the statutory obligation to pay contained in s.19(5) was subject to the limitation period of six years laid down in s.9(1) of the Limitation Act 1980. Even if the claims were statute-barred, the statutory charge to secure such a debt created by s.19(5) would be perfectly capable of enforcement. Accordingly, the Limitation Act 1980 did not prevent the 12 employees from having a valid claim in relation to the company and/or the joint administrators.

Proving debts

17.023   In *Re General Rolling Stock Company*[52] the company was wound up in February 1865. In March 1871 the plaintiff sought to prove for debts owed to it by the company, subject to not disturbing any dividends already paid to creditors. Limitation was pleaded but the Court of Appeal rejected the defence. In cases of this kind time does not run from the making of the winding-up order. Rather, so long as there are assets of the company unadministered, any creditor is at liberty to prove his debt, so long as prior dividends are not disturbed. Although the point was not directly in issue, the Court of Appeal indicated that the same rule applies in bankruptcy. The logic of this decision appears to be that time could run only when the assets were finally administered; in fact, once that stage is reached there is no point in bringing an action, since by definition there are no assets against which the creditor can claim.

---

[52] (1872) 7 Ch.App.Cas. 646, CA.

Petitioning on statute-barred debts

In *Re Karnos Property Co. Ltd*[53] Mervyn Davies J. was faced with a **17.024** petition for the winding-up of a company. The petitioning creditor was the local authority, and the petition was based on arrears of rates. The difficulty in the case was that the arrears dated back some 15 years. To make matters more difficult, the company had paid off those arrears that had accrued within six years of the presentation of the petition. Consequently the petition had to be based entirely on arrears which were, on the face of it, statute-barred. It was accepted that the local authority could not as a general rule sue for arrears which were more than six years old, in consequence of s.9 of the Limitation Act 1980, which precludes the bringing of an action to recover any sum due by virtue of an enactment after the lapse of that period. In respect of certain of the arrears, however, distress warrants had been issued some years earlier, and the main argument for the local authority was that these warrants remained available for execution at any time, and that this fact preserved their status as a "creditor" of the company with the right to petition for a winding-up. The judge rejected this approach. Even if the warrants remained available without limit of time, which must be considered doubtful, since the warrants by their terms called to be executed "forthwith", it did not follow that the local authority was still a creditor for these purposes. There is nothing in the 1980 Act which suggests that the running of time is in any way affected by the availability of some form of execution, and it was therefore to be concluded that the action had become time-barred in the ordinary way.

The conclusion reached in this case seems unexceptionable, but the **17.025** reasoning is less than satisfactory. As a matter of strict law the only question was whether the local authority was a "creditor" of the company. The legislation does not define this term, and it is suggested that there are two possible approaches. First, to say that a creditor of the company is a person (legal or natural) to whom the company owes money, and, secondly, to say that a creditor is a person who is in a position to enforce a debt which the company owes to him. If the first approach is adopted, then it must be remembered that the expiry of the limitation period in cases of debt does not extinguish the creditor's right, but merely precludes him from obtaining a judicial remedy for the violation of that right. Consequently, on this approach the local authority was a creditor of the company, albeit a time-barred creditor. If the second approach is adopted, then the availability of the distress warrants must surely be a relevant consideration. Enforcement of a judgment or warrant is not the bringing of an "action" for the purposes of the 1980 Act[54] and the provisions of that statute do not affect this process. Of course it may be correct to say that the warrants were no longer

---

[53] (1989) 5 B.C.C. 14; see (1989) 10 Co. Law 234.
[54] *W.T. Lamb & Sons v Rider* [1948] 2 K.B. 331, CA.

available, but it is submitted that this point did arise for decision and should have been properly considered.

The vital point to be borne in mind here is that the Limitation Act issue is not necessarily determinative of the local authority's status. To hold otherwise, as did Mervyn Davies J., is to assume that "creditor" for these purposes is limited to a person who is owed a debt which can be recovered by bringing action before the court. It is submitted that there is no good reason for adopting this restrictive interpretation of the expression.

Suing a company in liquidation

17.026 Once a company goes into liquidation, s.231 of the Companies Act 1985 requires that a claimant wishing to sue it obtain leave first. In two cases[55] it has been held that a writ issued in defiance of this requirement is a nullity, which cannot be saved by the subsequent actions of the parties.

The position after dissolution

17.027 Once a company has ceased to exist, no action can be brought against it, since there is no defendant in existence to be sued. However, two provisions of the Companies Act 1985, ss.651 and 653, contemplate that in certain circumstances a company may be restored to the Register.

Section 651

17.028 Under s.651, where a company has been dissolved, any person interested may apply within two years of the date of dissolution for an order declaring the dissolution to have been void, or 20 years where the purpose of the application is to allow the bringing of an action for damages for personal injury or an action under the Fatal Accidents Act 1976. Such order may be granted on such terms as the court thinks fit, and, if the order is made, s.651(2) provides that thereupon such proceedings may be taken as could have been taken if the company had never been dissolved. The different rule for personal injuries cases may be justified on the ground that these are the cases which offer the greatest risk of the action remaining undiscoverable for a lengthy period.

The restoration of the company to the Register is a matter for the court's discretion, but a particular problem may arise in personal injury cases. To an extent this issue is important in any case of an application to restore, since it may appear to the court that the action which it is proposed to bring against the company will be time-barred. The extra dimension in personal injury cases and cases under the Fatal Accidents Act is that the Limitation Act 1980 makes time run from the date when the cause of action becomes

---

[55] *Rose v Express Welding Ltd*, January 21, 1986, CA, Unreported, and *Wilson v Banner Scaffolding Ltd*, The Times, June 26, 1982, Milmo J.

discoverable rather than from the date when the cause of action accrues, and gives the court a discretion to override the primary limitation period if it thinks it just to do so. These two factors make it unusually difficult to tell in advance of a proper exploration of the facts whether the action can be defeated by a plea of the Limitation Act. This in turn adds to the difficulty faced by the court in exercising its discretion on an application under s.651. The new s.651(5) and (6) attempt to deal with this aspect of the matter, but their drafting is less than clear. Section 651(5) prohibits the making of an order for restoration to the Register if it appears to the court that the proceedings would fail by virtue of any enactment as to the time within which proceedings must be brought.

This provision was considered in *Re Workvale Ltd*,[56] where the Court of Appeal held that the enactments referred to here include all aspects of the Limitation Act 1980 which are relevant to the case and especially s.33, which is the provision giving the court discretion to extend the limitation period. This is a necessary conclusion. If s.33 is ignored, then no order will ever be made once the period of three years from discoverability has expired, since in the absence of s.33 the action will be bound to fail. The logic of this is that where the three-year period has expired the court will have to consider whether there is an arguable case for granting leave under s.33,[57] and the hearing of the application will to some extent turn into a discussion of the merits of the s.33 application. That is not the end of the matter, however. Applications under s.651 will normally be made without notice, since at that stage the company is not in existence. Even if it is concluded that the s.33 application has a good chance of success, so that a s.651 order is appropriate, it will still be necessary, once the company has been restored to the Register, to make the s.33 application. These, too, are sometimes made ex parte, but an ex parte s.33 order is liable to be challenged at trial and may be set aside if on the inter partes hearing it appears that the order was wrongly made. | 17.029

There is another possibility in connection with s.651 applications which requires consideration. Section 651(6) provides that nothing in s.651(5) affects the power of the court when making a s.651 order to direct that the period between the dissolution of the company and the making of the order shall not count for the purposes of any limitation enactment. In *Re Workvale Ltd (In Dissolution)*,[58] the Court of Appeal said that this power could and in appropriate cases should be used in cases where the s.33 application appeared likely to succeed as an alternative and quicker method of dealing with the problem. An order to this effect may remove the need | 17.030

---

[56] sub nom. *Re Workvale (No. 2)* [1992] 1 W.L.R. 416, CA.

[57] *Re Workvale (In Dissolution)*, disapproving the suggestion at first instance that the order under s.651 should always be made unless there was a very high probability that a s.33 order would eventually be refused.

[58] Above.

for a s.33 application by bringing the action back within the three-year period under s.11. Of course, this will work only where there has been relatively little delay while the company was still on the Register. Where it is not clear that a s.33 application will succeed, it is likely to be more appropriate to restore the company to the Register but to refuse to make a direction suspending time. A separate s.33 application can then be made.[59]

An order for restoration under s.651 cannot have the effect of retrospectively continuing an action which was on foot when the company was dissolved.[60] Thus, the only way to resurrect such an action is to ask for an order under s.651 that the time between dissolution and restoration be ignored for limitation purposes and, if this is granted, to start a new action, assuming of course that this action is in time once the effect of the order has been taken into account.

Section 653

17.031 This applies where the Registrar of Companies has exercised his power under s.652 to strike from the Register a defunct company. In such cases the company or a member or creditor thereof may apply within 20 years of the striking-off for an order restoring the company to the Register. Such an order may give such directions and make such provisions as may be necessary for placing the company and other persons in the same position, as nearly as may be, as if the company's name had not been struck off.

Clearly these two sections give rise to some problems in a limitation context. In cases where they are invoked there will inevitably have been a period during which the company did not exist and therefore could neither sue nor be sued. If the company is subsequently restored to the Register, the question will arise whether that period of time is to be counted for limitation purposes. In *Re Donald Kenyon Ltd*[61] Roxburgh J. approved the inclusion in an order under s.653 of a provision to the effect that the time during which the company was off the Register should not count as against creditors whose claims were not time-barred at the date of striking-off. This has subsequently become a common form of order in cases of this kind. It may be noted, however, that it is open to argument whether this is really what the statute contemplates. An order in these terms puts the parties back into the position in which they were before the striking-off, rather than putting them into the position in which they would have been if the company had not been struck off. Indeed, there would be little point in merely putting the parties in the position as if the company had not been struck off, for no order other than the restoration of the company to the Register would be needed for that purpose. It is no doubt for that reason that the

---

[59] *Smith v White Knight Laundry Ltd* [2001] E.W.C.A. 660; [2002] 1 W.L.R. 616.
[60] *Re Philip Powis Ltd* [1998] B.C.C. 756, CA.
[61] [1956] 1 W.L.R. 1397; see also *Tyman's Ltd v Craven* [1952] 2 Q.B. 100, CA.

Donald Kenyon order is often referred to as an "as-you-were" order. Consequently, the decision of Laddie J. in *Re Priceland Ltd*[62] to the effect that he had no power to include in a s.653 order a provision protecting the position of a third party must be open to serious question. In *Regent Leisuretime v Natwest Bank Plc*[63] the Court of Appeal affirmed the principle that a direction under s.653 restoring a company to the Register can properly include an order that the time for which the company is off the Register is not to count for limitation purposes. Such a direction inevitably operates to give back to the company an opportunity which it might otherwise have lost. Although it is true that had there been no dissolution, time would have continued to run against the company, it does not follow that there is no jurisdiction to make a limitation direction in the company's favour: it is the position at the date of dissolution rather than at the date of restoration which has to be considered.

Re Advance Insulation Ltd[64] was a case that raised the question of the relationship between s.653 and s.33 of the 1980 Act. The usual reason for doing this is to allow an action to be brought against the company, and this was the case here. The order was in the standard form, but the difficulty in this case was that the claim which was to be made was a claim for personal injuries, and therefore in principle subject to the discretion of the court to extend time under s.33 of the 1980 Act. At the time of the decision in *Re Donald Kenyon Ltd* there was no provision in the English law of limitations which gave the court any discretion to extend a basic limitation period. Such provision was first introduced for personal injury by the Limitation Act 1975, and the relevant rules are now consolidated in s.33 of the 1980 Act. In the present case the material facts were that the company was struck off in 1968. The plaintiff had worked for the company in 1956, and was forced to give up work in 1979 through industrial illness. In 1986 his solicitors discovered that the company had had an employers' liability policy, and they sought the company's restoration to the Register so as to claim against it. An order for restoration was made in 1987, including the usual provision mentioned above. A writ was issued in August 1987 and served the following month with a statement of claim. After the action had been set down for trial the company's insurers appealed against the order restoring the company to the Register, on the ground that this was a way of circumventing the requirement under s.33 of the 1980 Act for the leave of the court to be obtained before commencing a personal injuries action out of time. Hoffmann J. was able to dismiss this appeal as having been made too late—it was out of time, and leave to appeal was therefore needed. This leave was refused on the basis that there would be undue prejudice to the plaintiff. The judge admitted that in taking this view he was avoiding

17.031

---

[62] [1997] B.C.C. 207; see also *Re Lindsay Bowman Ltd* [1969] 1 W.L.R. 1443, Megarry J.
[63] [2003] EWCA Civ 391.
[64] (1989) 5 B.C.C. 55; see also (1989) 10 Co. Law 235.

making a decision on the general issue of the relationship between s.653 and s.33.

17.033 The problem is that the usual proviso to a s.653 order means that time will not have run against creditors who were not time-barred at the date of dissolution, and this may expose the company to the risk of very stale actions. On the other hand, to omit the proviso risks going too far in the opposite direction. It must be remembered that only in personal injury cases does the court have any discretion to extend time—in all other cases the omission of the proviso is likely to mean that the relevant actions are irretrievably time-barred. What is apparently required is to provide that time shall run in the case of personal injury actions, but not in the case of any other actions. It is unclear, however, whether a s.653 order can be finely tuned to this extent. It might also be argued that even this would not be sufficient, since it would be unduly favourable to those holding non-personal injury claims against the company. The position would be much simpler if there were a general judicial discretion to extend the time-limits, or even if there were a discretion limited to cases under s.653. At the present time neither of these discretions exists. To some extent the problem can be circumvented if the Registrar dealing with a s.653 application is prepared to consider whether any pending claim ought to be allowed to continue. Even then, there is a problem if more than one claim is likely—if the company is restored, the restoration takes effect for all purposes and cannot be limited to allowing the bringing of certain specific claims.

17.034 Further problems arise in connection with this decision. The first is that the Donald Kenyon order prevents the running of time only for creditors whose claims are not statute-barred at the time of striking-off. The point is important only in cases where the court has a discretion to extend time, but in these cases it is relevant to know whether the period of absence from the Register is to be taken into account when considering the exercise of the discretion in respect of a claim which was already outside the primary limitation period at the date of striking-off. The Donald Kenyon order does not deal with this point, though it may be that it is more appropriately considered under s.33 of the 1980 Act which gives the court an unfettered discretion in these matters.[65]

The second point in this area is that the Donald Kenyon form of order says nothing about any claims by the company. In general these will have been pursued by the liquidator, and there should not normally be any such claims outstanding, but it is not impossible that claims may come to light at a later stage. Both s.651 and s.653 give the court a very wide discretion, which would extend to including a suitable form of words in the order,[66]

---

[65] See para.8.034.

[66] *Regent Leisuretime Ltd v County Natwest Ltd*, May 8, 2002, Unreported, Judge Overend. Affirmed by the Court of Appeal [2003] EWCA Civ 391; See also *Whitbread (Hotels) Ltd v Walkmore (95) Ltd*, January 4, 2002 CS(OH), Unreported.

notwithstanding the observation of the Court of Appeal in *City of Westminster Assurance Co. Ltd v Registrar of Companies*[67] to the effect that s.653 is intended to provide a remedy for a person who has a claim, whether against the company or a third party, which can be enforced only if the company is restored to the Register. In that case the Court was contrasting the wish to bring a claim against the company with the wish to bring a claim against a guarantor—it did not mean to say that the company can never be restored in order to enable it to bring an action. However, as a matter of the exercise of the court's discretion, the claims of creditors, who were not in control of the company and had no chance to prevent it from being struck off, are worthy of more consideration than the claims of the company, which could have prevented the problem from arising in the first place.[68] It may be noted in passing that the problem of making a claim against the company can sometimes be circumvented where, as in *Re Advance Insulation Ltd*, the company will need to make a claim on its liability insurers. Such a claim may normally be pursued directly against the insurers by virtue of the Third Parties (Rights Against Insurers) Act 1930, provided that the liability of the company to the third party had been established and quantified by the date of liquidation,[69] and that the insurers would not have had any other defence available to them against the company.[70]

Other company law rules

The Companies Act 1985 contains a number of other limitation periods relating to specific matters. Attention is drawn to two of these. Under s.92 an action by a shareholder, aggrieved by a breach of the pre-emption rights conferred by s.89 of the Act, must be brought within two years of the date on which the return of allotment relating to the shares in question is filed with the Register of Companies. Article 108 of Table A imposes a 12-year limitation period on the bringing by any shareholder of an action to recover dividends which have been declared by the company but which have not been paid.

17.035

Bankruptcy

The making of a bankruptcy order does not suspend the running of time in relation to those of the bankrupt's debts which are not included within the

17.036

---

[67] [1997] B.C.C. 960.
[68] [1997] B.C.C. 960.
[69] *Post Office v Norwich Union* [1967] 1 All E.R. 577.
[70] *The Padre Island* [1990] 2 All E.R. 705, HL.

bankruptcy,[71] even though no action can be brought during the period of bankruptcy.[72] By contrast, where there has been a composition between a debtor and his creditors, it is a matter of construction of the agreement whether the debtor can rely on limitation once the agreement has come to an end.[73]

17.037   Where a bankruptcy is annulled under s.282 of the Insolvency Act 1986, it is as if there never had been a bankruptcy and time runs throughout the period between the bankruptcy order and the annulment, notwithstanding that no action could have been brought during that period.[74]

Other applications under the Insolvency Act 1986

17.038   The Insolvency Act 1986 contains a number of provisions that allow a liquidator or a trustee in bankruptcy to seek to set aside transactions entered into by the company or the bankrupt, or to recover property transferred by them. None of these provisions contains a specific limitation period. In *Re Priory Garage (Walthamstow) Ltd*[75] it was held that applications to set aside transactions are normally actions on a specialty (the statute) and subject to a 12-year limitation period. However, where the application involves seeking to recover a sum of money, that will be subject to s.9 of the Limitation Act 1980 as a claim to recover money due under a statute, and the limitation period will be six years. In *Re Yates (A Bankrupt)*[76] Charles J. expressed some doubt as to whether to set-aside applications under IA 339 and 423 were specialties under s.8(1), but in *Hill v Spread Trustee Company Ltd*[77], the Court of Appeal upheld the decision of Charles J. that they are. The Court considered two important questions about s.423 claims, namely whether any limitation period applies to them, and, if so, when time starts to run. As to the first of these questions, it is scarcely surprising that the Court of Appeal reached the conclusion that such claims are subject to a period of limitation. It would be an extraordinary state of affairs if such claims could be brought without limit of time. Moreover, it seems clear that where a sum of money is claimed, this is an action to recover a sum of money due under an enactment, so that s.9 of the 1980 Act applies, and the limitation period is six years. Where a non-

---

[71] *Anglo-Manx Group Ltd v Aitken* [2002] B.P.I.R. 215, John Jarvis Q.C.; see also *Re Benzon* [1914] 2 Ch.68, CA.

[72] *Re General Rolling Stock Company* (1872) L.R. 7 Ch.App. 646.

[73] *O'Brien v Osborne* (1852) 10 Hare 91; 68 E.R. 852; *Re Stock* (1896) 4 Mans 324; *Seagram v Knight* (1867) L.R. 2 Ch.App. 628.

[74] *More v More* [1962] 1 Ch. 424; *Re Dennis, ex p. Dennis* [1895] 2 Q.B. 630.

[75] [2001] B.P.I.R. 202, John Randall Q.C.

[76] [2005] BPIR 476.

[77] [2006] EWCA Civ 542, [2007] 1 All ER 1106, [2007] 1 BCLC 450.

monetary remedy is sought, the claim is an action on a specialty (the statute) and the period is twelve years.

The question of when time starts to run is perhaps more problematic. The choice would seem to be between the date of the transaction and the date of the bankruptcy order, but both options give rise to some problems.

The argument that it begins on the appointment of the trustee (at least in those cases where an application is made by a trustee in bankruptcy under s.424(1)(a)) is that that section prevents any application being made under s.423 except by the persons mentioned in s.424(1). Thus the requirements for making an application cannot be satisfied in the case of a trustee in bankruptcy until he has been appointed. However, the difficulty is that this appears inconsistent with the normal principles for determining when a limitation period starts to run. The general principle is of course set out in *Coburn v Colledge*[78]—a period of limitation runs from the date on which the ingredients of the cause of action are complete. A cause of action is complete when all the facts which it would be necessary to prove, if traversed, in support of the right to a judgment of the court, can be pleaded. Where the application is made by the trustee, his appointment is an essential element of the cause of action, and his right of action cannot begin until he is appointed.

If the alternative theory is accepted, namely that for the purposes of limitation time begins to run from the date of the transaction, there may be no person at all at the start of the period. It would be odd if Parliament enacted a provision for victims where time started to run before the person who wanted to enforce his rights as a victim had become a victim. The answer to this conundrum is that in relation to claimants other then the trustee time runs once the transaction has taken place and there is a victim. There may thus be different limitation periods in respect to different claimants.

Actions arising from transactions at undervalue within Insolvency Act 1986 s.423 are claims which involve a 'breach of duty' within the meaning of s.32(2) of the 1980 Act[79]. Consequently, s.32 is, on appropriate facts, available to extend the limitation period in such cases. **17.039**

The decision in *Hill v Spread Trustee* was distinguished in *Goldfarb (liquidator of Eurocruit Europe Ltd) v Poppleton*,[80] a case on Insolvency Act 1986 s.212 (action for misfeasance by company director). Blackburne J. held that s.212, unlike s.423, is purely procedural in nature, providing a method by which claims may be made against delinquent company directors. Consequently, the right of action must be the right of action derived **17.040**

---

[78] [1897] 1 QB 702, 706, [1895-9] All ER Rep 539 (see also *Letang v Cooper* [1965] 1 QB 232, [1964] 2 All ER 929, [1964] 3 WLR 573 at 242 to 243.
[79] *Giles v Rhind* [2008] EWCA Civ 118.
[80] [2007] EWHC 1433 (Ch).

from the original wrongdoing, and time runs from that date, even if it precedes the appointment of the liquidator by more than six years.[81]

17.041   Where the payment of debts is suspended under an Individual Voluntary Arrangement, time will not run against the creditors in relation to their claims, because the IVA will be treated as incorproating an agreement by the debtor to forego the benefit of the statute in respect of these debts as long as the IVA is in place.[82]

THE LAW COMMISSION'S PROPOSALS

17.042   Given the somewhat miscellaneous nature of the cases considered in this chapter, it is not surprising that the Law Commission say little that relates specifically to them. The law on actions on judgments is accurately restated in the Consultation Paper, but it does not figure expressly in the discussion of reform (presumably, therefore, such actions would fall into the core regime). So far as the other matters dealt with in this chapter are concerned, attention may be drawn to the Commission's proposal that a new Limitation Act should include a sweeping-up provision to provide that the core regime is to apply to all causes of action, unless the Act or some other enactment expressly provides the contrary. This seems a sensible provision, but will not, of course, change the law in those cases where a different limitation regime already exists.

---

[81] See also in *Re Farmizer (Products) Ltd* [1997] 1 BCLC 589, [1997] BCC 655.and, on an earlier version of s.212 *Re Lands Allotment Company* [1894] 1 Ch. 616, 63 LJ Ch. 291, 1 Mans 107.

[82] *Tanner v Everitt* [2004] EWHC 1130 (Ch), [2004] BPIR 1026 Mann J.

CHAPTER 18

Acknowledgment and Part-payment

Acknowledgment and part-payment are dealt with by ss.29–31 of the **18.001** Limitation Act 1980. The concept of acknowledgment was developed by the courts before 1939 (when there was no statutory provision equivalent to ss.29–31) as a way of mitigating the effects of the Limitation Act 1623.[1] The doctrine was originally based upon the notion of an implied promise to pay, but this does not appear in the present legislation. The basic provision is s.29, and it is convenient to consider the operation of this section in relation to three different classes of person, as follows:

(a) person to whom a right of action to recover land has accrued (including a mortgagee);

(b) mortgagee of personal property to whom a right to bring a fore-closure action in respect of the property has accrued;

(c) person to whom a right of action has accrued to recover any debt or other liquidated claim or any claim to any share or interest in the estate of a deceased person.

LAND

A right of action to recover the land can only accrue where some other **18.002** person is wrongfully in possession of it.[2] If the person in possession of the land acknowledgcs the title of the person entitled to recover it, then the right of action for the recovery of the land is treated as having accrued on the date of the acknowledgment and not at any earlier time.[3] A further provision is necessary to deal with the case of a person whose right to

---

[1] The history of this area of law is well summarised by Kerr J. in *Surrendra Overseas Ltd v Government of Sri Lanka* [1977] 1 W.L.R. 565.

[2] 1980 Act Sch.1, para.8.

[3] See s.29(2)(a).

recover has arisen on the determination of an entailed interest in land. Section 27 makes special provision in the case of disentailing assurances,[4] and it is possible under that section for time to run against the person so entitled. Section 29(2)(b) provides that where an acknowledgment is made in such a case, s.27 shall cease to apply to the land in question.

Mortgagees of land

18.003 Special problems can arise where the mortgagee of land is in possession of the land. These are dealt with in s.29(4). Where a mortgagee in possession of the land receives a payment in respect of the mortgage (whether of capital or of interest) or where he acknowledges either the title of the mortgagor or the mortgagor's equity of redemption, the mortgagor is entitled to bring an action for the redemption of the land at any time within 12 years of the making of the payment or the acknowledgment.

MORTGAGES—GENERAL

18.004 Section 29(3) applies to any action (whether for foreclosure or otherwise) by a mortgagee of personal property or of land. If the person in possession of the property, or the person liable for the mortgage debt, makes any payment in respect of the mortgage, whether of capital or of interest, the mortgagee's right of action is treated as having accrued on the date of the payment and not at any earlier time. Therefore, where the mortgagor has been dispossessed by a stranger, it appears that he can prevent time from running in favour of that stranger and against the mortgagee (but not against himself) by making a payment in respect of the mortgage debt.

DEBTS, ETC.

18.005 Section 29(5) and (6) deal with acknowledgments in respect of other liquidated claims. The provisions of the statute on acknowledgment and part-payment have no application to unliquidated claims, and it therefore follows that these provisions will rarely be of significance outside the area of contract. Section 29(5) provides that where the person liable for the debt or claim acknowledges it, it is to be treated as accruing on the date of the acknowledgment and not at any earlier time. Section 29(6) is a difficult provision. It qualifies s.29(5) by providing that where a payment is made of

---

[4] S.27 is fully considered in Ch.13.

part of any rent or interest then due, this does not extend the time for claiming the remainder of that rent or interest. However, a payment of interest does operate as an effective acknowledgment in respect of the principal debt. Therefore time continues to run from the original date in respect of the remainder of the rent or interest, but begins to run afresh in respect of the principal debt when interest is paid. One consequence of this subsection is that, in a case where both interest and principal are due, it may be essential to determine to what extent a particular payment represents interest and to what extent it represents capital.[5]

Meaning of "liquidated claim"

This is a matter which has received a modest amount of judicial attention. In *Amantilla v Telefusion*[6] the claim was for a quantum meruit, and it became necessary to decide whether this was a liquidated claim. It was held that it was, the claim having a sufficiently certain contractual description for the amount to be ascertainable by the court. This should not be regarded as a decision that all quantum meruit claims are liquidated claims for this purpose. Rather, it is a question of fact in each case whether the particular claim is sufficiently certain. In *BP Oil Ltd v Kent CC*[7] the Court of Appeal rightly cast doubt on the suggestion that a claim for compensation for compulsory purchase which had yet to be determined by the Lands Tribunal could properly be regarded as 'liquidated' for the purposes of an effective acknowledgement. Most recently in *Dwr Cymru v Marthenshire CC*[8] it was argued that a claim in tort could be liquidated claim. Jackson J. gave four compelling reasons for rejecting this argument:[9]

18.006

1. In all legislation prior to 1939 the doctrine of acknowledgment applied only to claims in contract. If Parliament had intended to extend this doctrine to tortious claims it would have done so expressly. There is no express reference to tort in the subsection.

2. The phrase "liquidated claim" connotes a claim for a specific sum or, alternatively, for a sum which can be readily and precisely ascertained. . . A claim for damages in tort is by definition not a liquidated claim. The assessment of damages in tort involves the application of a set of common law rules to the particular circumstances of the case. The application of those rules may be relatively

---

[5] See paras 18.037.
[6] (1987) 9 Con.L.R. 139, Judge Davies Q.C.
[7] [2003] EWCA Civ 798, [2003] RVR 276 C.A.
[8] [2004] EWHC 2991 (TCC), HT0455, Jackson J.
[9] At para.49.

straightforward in some instances, but that does not make the claim a liquidated one.

3. The global phrase "any debt or other liquidated pecuniary claim" suggests a sum which is due to be paid pursuant to some contractual or similar obligation. The words on their natural meaning do not connote damages or compensation which the law requires to be paid by someone who has acted in breach of an obligation or duty.

4. In none of the cases cited by counsel or uncovered by my own researches has a claim in tort ever been revived by reason of an acknowledgment.

The point may properly be regarded as decisively settled.

18.007   In *Mehra v Shah* [10] acknowledgement was put forward in response to a limitation defence to an action for an account. The judge doubted whether acknowledgement could apply in such a case, and it is submitted that she was plainly right to do so. An action for an account cannot possibly be a liquidated claim.

Byatt v Nash[11] holds that a solicitor's claim against his client for a quantum meruit for fees on an aborted transaction is a liquidated claim for the purposes of s.29 of the Limitation Act 1980.[12]

Express disapplication

18.008   In some cases the 1980 Act expressly declares that particular rights of action shall not be liable to extension by acknowledgment; this is done by providing that ss.29–31 shall not apply to these claims. Therefore, the right of action in respect of a claim under the Fatal Accidents Act 1976 can never be extended by acknowledgment, even in the unlikely event that such a claim were for liquidated damages.[13] The same is true of claims for contribution between joint wrongdoers under the Civil Liability (Contribution) Act 1978.[14]

REPEATED EXTENSIONS

18.009   Section 29(7) provides that the period of limitation in respect of a cause of action may be repeatedly extended by acknowledgments which comply

[10] [2003] All ER (D) 15 (Aug) Sonia Proudman QC.
[11] 28 June 2002 John Crowley QC.
[12] Relying on *Amantilla v Telefusion* [1987] 9 Con. LR 139.
[13] See also paras 8.064–8.067.
[14] 1980 Act s.10(5); see paras 15.017–15.019.

with the requirements of the Act.[15] This is subject to the overriding rule, also contained in s.29(7), that once the cause of action becomes barred it cannot be revived by any subsequent acknowledgment or payment. Therefore, successive acknowledgments can be effective, so long as made within the limitation period, as extended by any previous acknowledgment, but not otherwise.

FORMAL PROVISIONS

Section 30 of the Act requires an acknowledgment to be in writing and signed by the person making it if it is to be effective for the purposes of s.29.[16] Section 30(2) qualifies this by adding that an effective acknowledgment can be given by the agent of the obligor, and this inevitably raises the question of authority to give an acknowledgment.   **18.010**

AUTHORITY TO ACKNOWLEDGE

Section 30(2)(a) of the 1980 Act provides that an acknowledgment may be given by a duly authorised agent of the obligor. The authority may be actual or apparent, as where solicitors acting for a mortgagor write a letter to the mortgagee which effectively acknowledges the latter's title. It is irrelevant whether or not the client has given them authority to do so.[17] Difficulties have arisen concerning the extent of authority to acknowledge. In *Re Transplanters (Holding Company) Ltd*[18] Wynn-Parry J. held that a company's auditors are not generally its agents for the purpose of acknowledging its indebtedness. Thus, the signature of the auditors on the company's balance sheet could not be a sufficient acknowledgment of any debts referred to therein. By contrast, in *Wright v Pepin*[19] a mortgagor's solicitor wrote a letter to the mortgagee containing words that were held to amount to an acknowledgment,[20] and the question which remained to be decided was whether the solicitor had the authority to give a valid acknowledgment. Harman J. held that there is no absolute rule requiring an agent to be expressly authorised to give an acknowledgment. Implied authority is sufficient, and his Lordship found that there was such authority on the particular facts of the case.   **18.011**

---

[15] *Busch v Stevens* [1963] 1 Q.B. 1, Lawton J.
[16] See s.30(1).
[17] *Agricultural Mortgage Corporation Plc v Williams*, May 15, 1995, CA, Unreported.
[18] [1958] 1 W.L.R. 822, Wynn-Parry J.
[19] [1954] 1 W.L.R. 635, Harman J.
[20] As to the sufficiency of acknowledgment, see paras 18.019–18.024.

18.012   In *Re Beavan*[21] a person became of unsound mind, and a trustee was appointed to manage his affairs. The trustee acknowledged various of the patient's debts during his lifetime. It was held that these acknowledgments did not operate to take the case out of the statute, since the trustee had no authority to give acknowledgments. This is a very puzzling decision: given that the trustee had been appointed to manage the patient's affairs, it is hard to see why he should not be able to do anything which the patient could properly have done on his own behalf. Perhaps the decision can be explained as an example of the lengths to which English law goes to protect those of unsound mind. At the present day this decision needs to be understood subject to the Enduring Powers of Attorney Act 1985. This Act allows for the creation of powers of attorney whose validity will survive the subsequent mental incapacity of the attornor. So long as the power is appropriately drafted and the registration and notice provisions of that Act are complied with, a power of attorney such as that in *Re Beavan* will, it is submitted, continue to be valid even where the attornor subsequently becomes a patient. If these requirements are not met, then the decision in *Re Beavan* will continue to apply.

An acknowledgment must be given to the person (or the agent of the person) whose title or claim is being acknowledged, or to whom the payment is being made.[22] Thus, in *Bowring-Hanbury's Trustee v Bowring-Hanbury*[23] it was held that the admission of a debt contained in an affidavit sworn for probate purposes could not be a sufficient acknowledgment, since it was not made to the creditor.

POSITION OF THIRD PARTIES

18.013   Section 31 of the 1980 Act contains a number of detailed provisions for particular cases of acknowledgment and/or part-payment where third and subsequent parties may be affected. The section is dealt with in the following paragraphs. As a general point, it is to be noted that the effect of a payment is often wider in this context than the effect of an acknowledgment.

An acknowledgment of title to any land or mortgaged personalty is binding on all the world throughout the ensuing period of limitation.[24] Therefore, if X has been in possession of P's land for (say) eight years and then acknowledges title, P has a further 12 years to bring an action for the recovery of the land. If, during those 12 years, X is dispossessed by D, this

---

[21] [1912] 1 Ch. 196, Neville J.
[22] s.30(2)(b); *Re Compania de Electricidad de la Provincia de Buenos Aires Ltd* [1980] Ch. 146.
[23] [1942] 1 All E.R. 516, Bennett J.; [1943] 1 All E.R. 48, CA.
[24] See s.31(1).

change in possession will have no effect on the running of time; P's right of action will be barred 12 years after X's acknowledgment.

Section 31(2) applies where a payment is made in respect of a mortgage debt. So far as the right of the mortgagee to recover the mortgaged property is concerned, such payment will be binding on all persons in possession of the property during the ensuing limitation period. For the effect as regards the recoverability of the debt, see para.18.017.

Two mortgagees

Section 31(3) and (4) deal with the situation where two or more mortgages are by virtue of the mortgage in possession of the mortgaged land. Section 31(3) provides that an acknowledgment of the mortgagor's title by one of the mortgagees is binding only on him and his successors, and not on the other mortgagee and his successors. "Successor" is defined[25] as a personal representative or any other person on whom the rights or liabilities under the mortgage may devolve.

Section 31(4) applies where the mortgagee by whom the acknowledgment is given is entitled to a part of the mortgaged land and not to any ascertained part of the mortgage debt. In such a case the mortgagor is entitled to redeem that part of the mortgaged land on payment (with interest) of the proportion of the mortgage debt which the value of that part of the land bears to the value of the whole land. This provision appears to be of limited application, since it will only rarely happen that the mortgagee is entitled to a specific part of the land rather than to the whole of it. Indeed this situation seems to arise only where there are two or more mortgagees, each of which affects only part of the land.

18.014

Two mortgagors

Where there are two mortgagors of the same land, s.31(5) provides that an acknowledgment of the title or equity of redemption made to any one of them shall be treated as having been made to all. The most common example of this will no doubt occur where joint tenants mortgage a property, but the subsection applies also where the mortgages are in respect of different interests in the land.

18.015

---

[25] See s.31(9); semble the term does not include a partner.

Liquidated pecuniary claims

18.016 Section 31(6) and (7) cover debts and other liquidated pecuniary claims. An acknowledgment in respect of such claims binds the acknowledger and his successors,[26] but no one else.[27] By contrast, a payment in respect of such a claim binds all those liable in respect of the debt.[28]

Personal representatives

18.017 An acknowledgment or a payment by a personal representative in respect of any claim against the estate of the deceased (including a claim to a share of the estate) is binding on the estate.[29]

18.018 The case law on acknowledgments and part-payments has dealt principally with two questions. First, what is a sufficient acknowledgment? Secondly, when must the acknowledgment be given? The following paragraphs deal with these questions, as well as with some subsidiary issues.

SUFFICIENT ACKNOWLEDGMENT

18.019 An acknowledgment must contain a sufficiently clear admission of the title or claim being acknowledged.[30] This requirement is not affected by the change in the law in 1939, which removed the rule that an acknowledgment must include at least an implied promise to pay.[31] A document referring to a claim advanced against the defendant, but which is expressly said to be without admission of liability, cannot be a good acknowledgement.[32] Therefore, the words "the question of outstanding rent can be settled in a separate account" have been held not to be a sufficient acknowledgment of arrears of rent.[33] In the same case it was further held that an acknowledgment must show the amount of the debt or at least provide some means

---

[26] See para.18.001.
[27] See s.31(6).
[28] See s.31(7).
[29] See s.31(8).
[30] *Kamouh v Associated Electrical Industries International Ltd* [1980] Q.B. 199, Parker J.
[31] *Surrendra Overseas Ltd v Government of Sri Lanka* [1977] 1 W.L.R. 565, Kerr J. The judgment contains a most interesting account of the pre-1939 law. The more important of the older cases are *Swann v Sowell* (1819) 2 B. & Ald. 759; *Cottam v Partridge* (1824) 4 Man. & G. 271; *Moodie v Bannister* (1859) 4 Drew 432 (which held that this requirement did not exist in cases under the Real Property Limitation Act 1833); Re Oliver [1927] 2 Ch. 323; *Spencer v Hemmerde* [1922] 2 A.C. 507, HL, which reviewed the old law at great length.
[32] *Commissioners for Her Majesty's Revenue and Customs v Benchdollar Ltd* [2009] EWHC 1310 (Ch), Briggs J.
[33] *Good v Parry* [1963] 2 Q.B. 418, CA.

by which that amount can be calculated. This is a very strict interpretation of the concept of acknowledgment, and it is submitted that it is incorrect. In *Dungate v Dungate*[34] the debtor wrote a letter to the plaintiff, which contained the words "keep a check on totals and amounts I owe you, and we will have account now and then". Both at first instance and in the Court of Appeal it was held that this was a sufficient acknowledgment.[35] The Court of Appeal distinguished *Good v Parry* on the basis that there had in that case been no acknowledgment of any indebtedness at all. This is a somewhat restrictive view of *Good v Parry*, which ignores the view adopted in that case[36] that the acknowledgment must also state the amount of the indebtedness. Perhaps this part of *Good v Parry* should be regarded as obiter, thus allowing the two decisions to be reconciled, as well as removing an unnecessary complication from this branch of the law.[37] More recently, in *Agricultural Mortgage Corporation Plc v Williams*,[38] solicitors acting for a mortgagor wrote a letter which was regarded by the court as making sense only on the assumption that the title of the mortgagees was valid. Although there was no reference to the amounts outstanding on the mortgage, it was held that this was a sufficient acknowledgment. In *Lia Oil SA v ERG Petroli SPA*[39] it was held that the handing over of a document at a without prejudice meeting cannot be a sufficient acknowledgement because it is not an 'open statement' of the defendant's position. In *Rehman v Benfield*[40] the Court of Appeal held that the putative tenant's signature on a purported lease of a property could be a sufficient acknowledgement of the Landlord's title, even when the tenant knew that the landlord had never agreed to the lease (indeed knew nothing of it) and had not executed the counterpart. In *Ashe v National Westminster Bank Plc*[41] it was held that the test for sufficiency of acknowledgement under s.29(2) is the same as that under s.29(5)—viewed as a whole, the statement in question must be an admission of the title of the person having the right of action. In *Allen v Matthews*[42] a purported acknowledgement of title to land was given by solicitors who claimed to be acting on behalf of a company which at the time of the acknowledgement was dissolved (and thus could not be in occupation of the land). The Court of Appeal held that this was not a sufficient

---

[34] [1965] 1 W.L.R. 1447, Edmund Davies J., CA.; approved by the House of Lords in *Bradford & Bingley Plc v Rashid*, *The Times* 13 July, 2006.

[35] This may be compared with *Langrish v Watts* [1903] 1 K.B. 636, CA, where the defendant disputed the amount of the debt but wrote to the plaintiff proposing the taking of an account. It was held that this was a sufficient acknowledgment in respect of whatever sum the account revealed as being due. Similary in *Ross v McGrath* [2004] EWCA Civ 1054, CA a letter promising to pay sums due, without quantifying them, was held sufficient.

[36] [1963] 2 Q.B. 418 at 422.

[37] (1966) 82 L.Q.R. 17.

[38] May 15, 1995, CA, Unreported.

[39] [2007] EWHC 505 (Comm) Julian Flaux QC.

[40] [2006] EWCA Civ 1392.

[41] [2007] EWHC 494 (Ch) Richard Arnold Q.C.

[42] [2007] EWCA Civ 216.

acknowledgement. Both the writer of the letter and the recipient understood it to be a letter on behalf of the company, and that was simply the wrong party—indeed a 'party' which could not do anything at the time. In coming to this conclusion the Court distinguished *London Borough of Lambeth v Bigden*[43] where letters apparently containing acknowledgements were written on behalf of the Oval Housing Co-operative (OHC) at a time when OHC had not been incorporated. Mummery LJ said (para.48) that at that time OHC was still an unincorporated association of individuals, and that it could be argued that the letters were acknowledgments of title by the individual members acting through an agent. The crucial difference is that in *Bigden* the letters were written on behalf of the Housing Co-operative representing the individual occupiers and the Council understood that. It was a pure technicality that it had not been incorporated. Moreover, the individuals who were to be members of OHC did exist, whereas the in *Allen v Matthews* the company did not.

18.020   The acknowledgement does not have to be given directly to the creditor. In *Re Compania de Electricidad*[44] Slade J. said:

"In my judgment, though no authority has been cited to me which either confirms or rejects such proposition, a written acknowledgment cannot be said to be made to a creditor or his agent, within the meaning of s.24(2) . . . [as that section then was] . . . unless either

(a) it is delivered to the creditor or his agent by or with the authority of the debtor or his agent or

(b) it is expressly or implicitly addressed to and is actually received by the creditor or his agent."

This principle was apparently applied in *London Borough of Wandsworth v Birchwood*,[45] where a judgment debtor gave an acknowledgement in the course of an oral examination. Although no representative of the judgment creditor was in court to hear this acknowledgement, it was held that this was a sufficient acknowledgement for the purposes of the statute.[46] In *The Good Challenger Navegante*[47] it was held that a typed signature on a telex or a fax is capable of amounting to a signature for the purposes of s.30 of the Limitation Act 1980, which requires an acknowledged to be 'signed' by the debtor. It is submitted that this is a good decision. Modern business depends extensively on such communications, and it would be highly unsatisfactory if the absence of a manuscript signature were held to be fatal. Disputes about whether the document was genuinely approved by the debtor are a separate matter and can be resolved by evidence of fact. It

---

[43] [2000] EWCA Civ 302, (2001) 33 HLR 43.
[44] [1980] Ch. 146 at 192F; [1978] 3 All E.R. 668, Slade J.
[45] June 16, 2000, Unreported, CA.
[46] Though it is hard to see how a purely oral acknowledgement could ever be effective.
[47] [2003] EWCA Civ 1668, [2003] All ER (D) 320 (Nov).

may be added that the arguments which apply to faxes (and telexes before them) appear to apply with equal force to e-mails.

A document referring to the claim but denying its validity cannot be a **18.021** good acknowledgment.[48] At first instance in *Dungate v Dungate*[49] it was held that tax-deduction certificates in respect of interest paid on a loan could amount to a sufficient acknowledgment. The Court of Appeal[50] chose to affirm the decision of Edmund Davies J. on a different ground. They were right to avoid approving the view of the trial judge on this point. The certificates were apparently not given to the plaintiff, thereby contravening the requirement in what is now s.30 of the 1980 Act. Further, it is not obvious why these documents should be treated as an admission that there is any sum of money outstanding.

In *Re Flynn (Dec'd) (No. 2)*[51] the acknowledgment on which the plaintiff sought to rely was a defence filed in proceedings in the state of New York. The defence had denied liability, but had been expressly rejected in judicial proceedings in that state. The plaintiff argued that this rejection could convert the denial into an effective acknowledgment, but Buckley J. held that it was not possible to construe an acknowledgment out of an explicit denial. In *Horner v Cartwright*[52] the same result was reached, but it was said, obiter, that an acknowledgment could be contained in a pleading if the pleading were an admission of the claim. It was further suggested that such an acknowledgment would not accrue from day to day after the service of the pleading, but would be effective only at the date of service. It is submitted that this is correct.

Company accounts

A number of cases have considered the sufficiency as an acknowledgment of **18.022** debt of a company's accounts in which the balance sheet shows the debt, often in the form of a composite item for creditors without distinguishing the particular debt owed to the plaintiff.[53] In *Jones v Bellgrove Properties*[54] it was held that such an acknowledgment could be sufficient, if the court was satisfied that the plaintiff's debt was among those alluded to in the balance sheet.

A further problem in the company accounts cases has been to decide

---

[48] *Horner v Cartwright*, July 11, 1989, CA, Unreported.
[49] [1965] 1 W.L.R. 1447, Edmund Davies J.
[50] [1965] 1 W.L.R. 1447, Edmund Davies J.
[51] [1969] 2 Ch. 403, Buckley J.
[52] July 11, 1989, CA, Unreported. cited with approval in *Ofulue v Bossert* [2008] EWCA Civ 7. See also below, para.18.030.
[53] The early cases include *Spencer v Hemmerde* [1922] 2 A.C. 501; *Green v Humphreys* (1884) 26 Ch.D. 474; *Re Beavan* [1912] 1 Ch. 196; *Re Coliseum (Barrow) Ltd* [1930] 2 Ch. 44.
[54] [1949] 1 All E.R. 498, Birkett J.; (1949) 65 L.Q.R. 430.

whether the acknowledgment is effectively given to the plaintiff, as is required by s.30(2)(b) of the 1980 Act. In most of these cases the plaintiff has been a shareholder of the company, and it has been in that capacity that he has received a copy of the accounts. In *Jones v Bellgrove Properties*[55] it was held that an acknowledgment was effective although it was given to the plaintiff in his capacity as shareholder rather than as creditor. There must, however, be evidence that the acknowledgment has been given to the plaintiff. Therefore a balance sheet is not a sufficient acknowledgment where it has never been received by the plaintiff.[56]

18.023   Alternatively the acknowledgment may be contained in the notes to the accounts, rather than in the balance sheet. This was the position in *Ledingham v Bermejo Estancia*,[57] where it was held that such an acknowledgment could, subject to its exact terms, be sufficient for the purposes of the Limitation Act 1980.[58]

However, a person may not give a sufficient acknowledgment of a debt owed to himself. In *Re Transplanters (Holding Company) Ltd*[59] the plaintiff was a director of the company. The acknowledgment of the debt was contained in the company's balance sheet, which had been signed by the plaintiff and another director, as well as by the auditors. Wynn-Parry J. held that this was insufficient. The balance sheet must be signed by two directors,[60] but the plaintiff himself is not allowed to be counted as one of them since he could then contribute to acknowledging his own debt. The position would presumably be otherwise if the balance sheet were signed by two directors other than the plaintiff. The signature of the auditors is also inadequate for limitation purposes. The auditors merely express a view on whether the accounts comply with the statutory requirements—they are not the agents of the company for the purpose of acknowledging debts.

18.024   The decision in *Re Transplanters (Holding Company) Ltd*[61] must now be read subject to that of Brightman J. in *Re Gee & Co. (Woolwich) Ltd*.[62] In that case the balance sheet containing an acknowledgment of indebtedness to the plaintiff was signed by the directors, who were also the plaintiff's executors. The acknowledgment of the debt was later ratified by a general meeting of the company attended only by the two directors. All the shares in the company were held either by the two directors or by one of the directors jointly with another person. Brightman J. held that the acknowledgment was effective. *Re Transplanters* accurately states the

---

[55] [1949] 1 All E.R. 498, Birkett J.; (1949) 65 L.Q.R. 430.
[56] *Re Compania de Electricidad de la Provincia de Buenos Aires Ltd* [1980] Ch. 146, Slade J.
[57] [1947] 1 All E.R. 749, Atkinson J.
[58] Companies Act 1985 Sch.4, para.35 provides that, at least in an accounting context, notes to the accounts are to be treated as forming part of the accounts.
[59] [1958] 1 W.L.R. 822, Wynn-Parry J.
[60] Companies Act 1985 s.238, as substituted by Companies Act 1989 s.4. The 1989 Act changes only the section number: the substance of the obligation is unaffected.
[61] See above, n. 59.
[62] [1975] Ch.52.

general rule that a director cannot acknowledge a debt in favour of himself or of a person whose personal representative he is, since it would be a breach of his fiduciary duty to the company to do so. But there is no breach of that duty where the acknowledgment is ratified by a general meeting of the company attended by persons representing all the shares in the company. That requirement was satisfied here, since the third shareholder held shares jointly with one of the directors. This example of a very technical application of the doctrine of incorporation may in many small companies provide a notable exception to the principle stated in Re Transplanters.[63]

Set-off

It sometimes happens that the defendant accepts the existence of a debt to the plaintiff, but claims that he has a set-off against that debt. In *Swann v Sowell*[64] the defendant wrote a letter admitting the debt, but adding "You owe me more money. I have a set-off against it." It was held that this was not a sufficient acknowledgment. *Re River Steamer Company*[65] is another case to a similar effect, though there it was held that as a matter of construction the defendant's claim was for a deduction from the contract price rather than a set-off. Two points are important about these cases. The first is that they predate the 1939 Act, and are therefore decided on the equitable doctrine of acknowledgment, which rested on the notion of an implied promise to pay. As explained above,[66] this doctrine does not exist under the present legislation. The second point is that in both cases the alleged set-off exceeded the amount of the debt which the plaintiff claimed, so that, quite apart from the difficulty of finding an implied promise, there is great difficulty in construing the letters as admissions of any net liability. It is therefore submitted that at the present day an acknowledgment of a debt coupled with an admission of a smaller set-off or counterclaim is capable of being an acknowledgment of the net amount of the debt, but that both the cases discussed in this paragraph are still good law on the ground of the absence of any net acknowledgment.   **18.025**

Joint obligors

It has been held that an acknowledgment by one of a number of joint and several debtors is binding on all.[67] It is submitted that this rule has no   **18.026**

---

[63] On the question of authority, see paras 18.011–18.012.
[64] (1819) 2 B. & Ald. 759; 106 E.R. 543.
[65] (1871) 6 Ch.App. 822, CA.
[66] See paras 18.011–18.012.
[67] *Whitcomb v Whiting* (1781) 2 Doug. K.B. 652; 99 E.R. 413.

application where the liability is merely several, since there is then no ground for imputing the acts of one debtor to the others. In *Read v Price*[68] it was argued that this principle should be limited to payments of interest on a loan, since these clearly enure to the benefit of all debtors, whereas a mere acknowledgment does not. The Court of Appeal held that earlier authorities[69] establish that this distinction is unmaintainable. In fact, examination of those cases shows that they merely decide the position with regard to payments of interest, so that the reasoning of the Court of Appeal is entirely unsatisfactory on this point. Nevertheless, it is apparently established at the present day that the position is the same for part-payments as for acknowledgments.

Relative title

18.027 In the case of land, an acknowledgment may be sufficient even though it does not indicate that the title which is acknowledged is flawless. In *Edgington v Clark*[70] the plaintiff was a squatter on the defendant's land. He did not know the identity of the owner, but wrote to a person whom he knew to be the owner's agent,[71] offering to buy the land. It was held that this was a sufficient acknowledgment—although the plaintiff had not admitted that the defendant had a perfect title, he had implicitly admitted that the defendant's title was better than his own (since an offer to buy would otherwise have been otiose). This was a sufficient acknowledgment of the defendant's title. The general principle was laid down as being[72]:

(1) All that is required to constitute an acknowledgement is that, as between himself and the paper-title owner, the person in possession acknowledges that the paper-title owner has the better title to the land.

(2) Whether or not a particular writing amounts to an acknowledgement depends on the true construction of the document in all the surrounding circumstances. It is not possible to lay down any more general rule than that.

---

[68] [1909] 2 K.B. 724, CA.
[69] *Roddan v Morley* (1857) 1 De G. & J. 1; *Re Lacey* [1907] 1 Ch. 350.
[70] [1964] 1 Q.B. 367, CA.
[71] See now the 1980 Act s.30(2)(b).
[72] And see *London Borough of Lambeth v Bigden*, December 1, 2000, Unreported, CA.

TIMING OF ACKNOWLEDGMENT

In *Consolidated Agencies Ltd v Bertram Ltd*[73] the alleged acknowledgment **18.028** was contained in a company's balance sheet. At the balance-sheet date the debt was not statute-barred, but it had become so by the rather later date at which the balance sheet was signed. The Privy Council[74] held that an effective acknowledgment must be of a debt which is not barred at the time of acknowledgment[75]; as the debt was barred at the date of acknowledgment, it followed that the acknowledgment could not be effective. However, in *Re Gee & Co. (Woolwich) Ltd*[76] Brightman J. refused to follow this decision, holding that it was inconsistent with English authority.[77] Consequently, His Lordship held that the directors' signatures on a balance sheet could be effective to create a new cause of action at the balance-sheet date. Unfortunately, this way of expressing the position gives rise to some confusion. The correct position must surely be that the signatures are a valid acknowledgment of an existing debt. The distinction between the two formulations is not mere semantics—if the debt were already barred at the balance-sheet date, the signature on the accounts would be ineffective to revive the debt.

This problem of terminology is secondary to the real issue in the case, which is whether the signatures should be treated as relating back to the balance-sheet date at all. The view taken in *Consolidated Agencies v Bertram*[78] is both logical and consistent with the statute, since it preserves the principle that a debt cannot be revived by acknowledgment once it has become barred; furthermore, it is notable that the case referred to by Brightman J. in *Re Gee & Co. (Woolwich) Ltd*[79] does not in truth establish the principle which that judge claims to uphold. These cases are inconclusive on the vital question of timing. Consequently, the reasoning of this case, as well as the decision in it, must be regarded as open to serious question. At the present time, however, English law has apparently chosen to say that the signatures do relate back to the balance-sheet date.

In *Ofulue v Bossert* the Court of Appeal also had to consider whether an **18.029** acknowledgment in a counterpart lease had been sufficiently communicated by the tenant to the landlord or his agent, as required by s.30(2) of the 1980 Act. The tenant's solicitors sent the signed counterpart to the solicitors who purported to act for the landlord. That firm was not the landlord's agent,

---

[73] [1965] A.C. 470, PC; (1966) 81 L.Q.R. 167.
[74] The case was decided under s.19 of the Indian Limitation Act 1908, whose provisions are in all material respects identical to those of the 1980 Act.
[75] See now the 1980 Act s.29(7).
[76] [1975] Ch. 52, Brightman J.
[77] *Howcutt v Bonser* (1849) 3 Exch. 491.
[78] [1965] A.C. 470, PC.
[79] [1975] Ch. 52.

although it thought it was. However, subsequently the signed counterpart did in fact come into the possession of another firm of solicitors instructed by the landlord. It was held that although the tenant had not sent the lease to the landlord, the acknowledgement, having come into the landlord's possession, was 'made to' the landlord, though the majority of the court expressly declined to address the question of whether it was 'made' on the date of signing or on the date when it was received by the landlord's solicitors (on the facts of the case both dates were within twelve years of the commencement of the proceedings). It is submitted that the date of delivery to the landlord ought to be the effective date—until then there is no valid acknowledgement. It is the fact of delivery which is the 'making' of the acknowledgement 'to' the landlord.

PLEADING

18.030 An admission in a pleading that a debt formerly existed is effective on the day when it is communicated to the other party, but does not enure from day to day so long as the action is in being.[80] *Busch v Stevens*[81] illustrates an important point about pleading acknowledgment. The plaintiff brought an action on a statute-barred debt. When the defendant pleaded limitation, the plaintiff put in a reply alleging acknowledgment. Lawton J. expressed disapproval of this form of procedure. The proper course would have been to plead the acknowledgment in the statement of claim, rather than leaving it to the reply. His Lordship indicated that a failure to observe this rule is liable to be penalised in costs.

INTERROGATORIES/REQUESTS FOR FURTHER INFORMATION

18.031 In *Lovell v Lovell*[82] the plaintiff sought leave to administer interrogatories to the defendant (the best modern equivaleny would be a Pt 18 Request for Further Information, though of course the analogy is not exact). The interrogatories fell into two classes: the first was designed to elicit from the defendant an admission that the debt in issue was due, whilst the second was designed to elicit an admission that a document written on a previous occasion was an acknowledgment of the debt. It was held that the latter class of interrogatories could be permitted, but the former could not. By definition the latter class did not seek to deprive the defendant of any

---

[80] *Horner v Cartwright*, July 11, 1989, CA, Unreported.
[81] [1963] 1 Q.B. 1, Lawton J.
[82] [1970] 1 W.L.R. 1451, CA.

accrued right under the Limitation Act—if the document were in truth an acknowledgment, then it followed that the right to plead limitation had never accrued. By contrast, the former class could have led to the plaintiff acquiring a new cause of action, on which he could have sued by issuing a fresh writ. There is serious confusion here: if the plaintiff's claim were already barred, an acknowledgment of it would not revive it. If it were not already barred, the acknowledgment would not have been relevant. In addition, answers to interrogatories are for the purposes of the present action only, and cannot be relied upon if a further action in respect of the same claim is brought.[83]

ACKNOWLEDGMENT AND ESTOPPEL

In *Colchester BC v Tillson*,[84] a case involving real property, there could be no valid acknowledgment, because the 12 years had expired, but the court was able to circumvent this by the use of estoppel. This is a somewhat surprising decision, and it may be noted that Ferris J. is unable to find any authority supporting this notion. The form of estoppel relied upon is estoppel by convention, in that, subsequent to the expiry of the 12-year limitation period, the parties executed a document under which D purported to take a lease of the property from P. Such document was clearly meaningless except on the basis that D was not the freeholder. It is submitted, however, that the correct course would have been to hold that the purported lease was void, either for common mistake or for simple impossibility. This decision seems to give rise to an undesirable method of circumventing the rule that the expiry of the 12-year period in relation to land extinguishes the paper-title holder's rights.

18.032

PART-PAYMENT

Problems arising from part-payment of a debt have been considered only rarely in the decided cases. One of the few instances is *Surrendra Overseas Ltd v Government of Sri Lanka*,[85] a shipping case, in which a claim had been partly admitted and partly disputed. A payment had been made in respect of that part which was admitted, and the plaintiff argued that this was effective to extend the limitation period in respect of the whole debt. Kerr J. rejected this argument. The law is that the payment must be "in

18.033

---

[83] There is also the possibility that a further action could be treated as an abuse of process, and struck out under CPR 3.4.
[84] [1991] Ch. 448, Ferris J.
[85] [1977] 1 W.L.R. 565, Kerr J.

respect of" the debt on which the plaintiff sues.[86] Where the defendant makes it clear that the payment is in respect of a different and severable part of the debt this requirement is not satisfied, and the payment does not extend time in respect of the remainder of the debt. In any event it is necessary to look at the intention of the defendant in making the payment. Where the defendant intends to pay part of a debt which is subsequently held to be void for illegality, the plaintiff cannot retrospectively appropriate the payment to another valid debt.[87]

SUFFICIENCY OF PAYMENT

18.034 The question of what can be counted as a payment for the purposes of the provisions on part-payment was considered in the difficult case of *Maber v Maber*.[88] The defendant was the widow and executrix of the plaintiff's son. The plaintiff had lent his son £80 at interest. For some years no payment of interest or capital was made, the son being abroad. Within the limitation period the son and his wife returned to England and the son, at a meeting with his father, offered to pay the outstanding interest, and put his hand into his pocket as if to produce the money. The plaintiff stopped him, and, turning to the defendant, who was also present, indicated that he would make her a present of the interest. The son's promissory note was then indorsed to this effect. The Court of Exchequer Chamber held, by a majority, that this was a sufficient payment to take the case out of the statute. The difference of opinion in the Court is about the possibility of a "deemed" payment. The majority[89] relied on the purported assignment of the interest to the defendant as showing that the money must be treated as having been paid to the plaintiff—without this he could not assign it. Bramwell B. dissented, taking the view that the legal position of the parties had not been altered. He asked how the events which happened differed from the hypothetical situation in which the plaintiff tells the defendant to keep the interest for himself.

18.035 There is some force in the arguments on both sides of this case, and it is very difficult to lay down general principles for this kind of case: what is required is a close examination of the facts. In some cases there will be an adequate acknowledgment; in *Maber v Maber*[90] itself the obstacles to this were that the son had made no written acknowledgment, whilst the indorsement of the promissory note was performed by the plaintiff, who clearly cannot be allowed to write his own acknowledgment. So far as the

---

[86] 1980 Act s.29.
[87] *Kleinwort Benson v s.Tyneside MBC* [1994] 4 All E.R. 972, Hobhouse J.
[88] (1867) L.R. 2 Exch. 153.
[89] Martin, Channell and Piggott BB.
[90] (1867) L.R. 2 Exch. 153.

payment is concerned, there must be at least a tender of the money by the defendant. A mere assignment by the plaintiff is not sufficient, since the law of assignment now allows this to be done without any payment being made. In the more difficult case where the plaintiff invites the defendant to keep the money himself, a distinction must be drawn between cases where the sum due is to be left outstanding and cases where it is to be written off. In the latter case there is no difficulty in holding that the legal position of the parties has been altered, whereas in the former case there is no proper answer to Bramwell B.'s objection on this point. Even in these cases, though, there must be a tender of payment by the defendant. To relax this requirement would allow the plaintiff to extend time by his own act of voluntarily writing off any small part of the outstanding sum.

UCB Corporate Services Ltd v Kohli[91] establishes two important points **18.036** about the effectiveness of part payments. First, a payment by one debtor binds all other debtors, even where they are not liable under the same instrument.[92] Second, it is only a payment in respect of the debt which is effective for limitation purposes. Thus, where the debtor had become a mortgagee in possession of the creditor's property and made a payment by way of accounting to the creditor for mesne profits, this was not to be treated as resetting the clock in relation to a separate debt. The vital point is to establish the character of the payment.

APPROPRIATION OF PAYMENTS

Where A owes B a number of separate (or severable debts) or where A and **18.037** B have a running account (which may be a bank account[93] or an account in respect of goods or services) it may happen that some but not all of the outstanding items of account become time-barred. If A then pays money to B it becomes essential to decide to which of the debts the money should be allocated. The legal rules governing this question may be summarised as follows:

(a) Where there are separate debts: The initial choice in appropriating the payment lies with the debtor.[94] If he indicates that it is to be applied to a particular debt, then it is treated as being so applied. If the debtor does not exercise this option, then the creditor may choose

---

[91] [2004] EWHC 1126 (CH), [2004] All ER (D) 205 (May), Richard Sheldon QC. See also *Harlock v Ashberry* (1881) 19 Ch D 539 and Re Lord Clifden, *Annaly v Agar-Ellis* [1900] 1 Ch 774.

[92] The position is of course different in the case of an acknowledgement, which binds only the acknowledgor and his 'successors'.

[93] See para.10.007.

[94] *Re Footman Bower & Co. Ltd* [1961] Ch. 443.

which debt is repaid.[95] If neither party expresses any choice, the law will assume that unbarred debts are paid before debts which have become barred.[96]

(b) Where there is a running account: In *Re Footman Bower & Co. Ltd*[97] the company was in liquidation, and the liquidator sought the advice of the court as to whether certain debts should be admitted. A running account had been maintained with a supplier of goods to the company. The company made periodic payments on account. Some of the items had been supplied more than six years before the creditor lodged his proof in the winding-up, but the last payment on account had been made within six years before that time. Buckley J. held that the liquidator should admit all the outstanding debt to proof. It is incorrect in such cases to apportion the debt among the various items which make up the balance: rather, there is one single balance. Consequently, when a payment is made on the account, it must be treated as being made "in respect of" the entire balance, and time is consequently extended for the whole of the debt.

Evidence of payment

18.038   Occasionally the defendant may admit a debt, but claim that it has been paid. On the face of it this appears to be a denial that any debt currently exists, and therefore incapable of being a sufficient acknowledgment. The plaintiff, however, may wish to bring evidence rebutting the plea of payment, so as to show that the debt still exists. In *Beale v Nind*[98] it was held that such rebuttal evidence was admissible only where the defendant gave such precise details of the payment he claimed to have made that negating them amounted to showing that the debt had not been paid at all.

There is apparently no modern authority on this point, and *Beale v Nind* calls for careful examination. First, it is not clear why the rebuttal evidence was acceptable at all. Even if the claim of payment was disproved, the fact remains that the defendant made that denial, when the vital matter was to prove that he acknowledged liability. The answer to this must lie in saying that a claim to have paid the debt which is admitted to have existed in the past is only a conditional denial of the debt, i.e. once the claim of payment is destroyed, what is left is an admission of the debt. This is a somewhat strained, though not wholly impossible, interpretation of the defendant's letter. Secondly, refuting a simple allegation of payment is extremely difficult—it is an example of trying to prove a negative. It appears that the

---

[95] *Mills v Fowkes* (1839) 5 Bing. (N.C.) 455.
[96] *Nash v Hodgson* (1855) 6 De G.M. & G. 474.
[97] [1961] Ch. 443, Buckley J.
[98] (1821) 4 B. & Ald. 568; 106 E.R. 1044.

court was effectively saying that the only way to refute adequately the plea of payment was to bring such evidence as would establish beyond doubt that no payment had been made, and that this is likely to be possible only where the defendant has given precise details of the alleged payment. Viewed in these terms, this otherwise puzzling decision appears perfectly sensible.

THE LAW COMMISSION'S PROPOSALS

The Commission recommend that acknowledgments and part-payments should start time running again for all classes of action, rather than just in liquidated claims, as at present. This is an entirely sensible suggestion, since there is no logical justification for the present distinction. The Commission recommend no change in the present rule that acknowledgments and part-payments cannot revive a cause of action once time has expired in relation to it, on the basis that a major objective of limitation statutes is to allow a defendant to be free from claims after a reasonable time, and that the present rule promotes that objective. The reasoning is not altogether convincing, since a defendant who wished to remain free of a claim could simply refuse to acknowledge or to pay. Alternatively, if he wished to make a part-payment, it could be expressed to be ex gratia so as to avoid reviving the claim. The truth appears to be that in this case each of the possible solutions is largely arbitrary, and that there is little to choose between them. **18.039**

It is also recommended that (except in relation to mortgages and actions for possession of land) acknowledgments and part-payments should bind only the acknowledger or payer (or their successor).

CHAPTER 19

Disability

Equity has always been vigilant to protect the interests of those unable to look after themselves, and this concern is reflected in the case of limitation periods by the rules in ss.28 and 28A[1] of the 1980 Act.

19.001

MEANING OF DISABILITY

In the law of limitations there are two classes of disability: infancy and unsound mind.[2]

19.002

Infancy

A person is under a disability for the purposes of the law when under the age of 18, that being the age of majority in English law.[3] Infancy causes relatively few problems in the law of limitations, perhaps because it is a disability which lasts for a finite period and can never recur once it has ended.

19.003

Unsound mind

The 1980 Act[4] gives an elaborate definition of this alternative ground of disability, and it is necessary to examine this definition with care. Section 38(3) provides that a person is of unsound mind for limitation purposes if he is a person who, by reason of mental disorder within the Mental Health

19.004

---

[1] As added by the Latent Damage Act 1986 s.2.
[2] 1980 Act s.38(2).
[3] Family Law Reform Act 1969 s.1.
[4] As amended by the Mental Health Act 1983.

Act 1983,[5] is incapable of managing and administering his property and affairs. Section 38(4) supplements this by providing that a person shall be conclusively presumed to be of unsound mind if he fulfils either of two conditions:

(a) while he is liable to be detained or subject to guardianship under the Mental Health Act 1959 and

(b) while he is receiving treatment as an in-patient in any hospital or mental nursing home within the meaning of that Act, without being liable to be detained under that Act, being treatment which follows without any interval a period during which he was liable to be detained or subject to guardianship under that Act or by virtue of any enactment repealed or excluded by that Act.

19.005   The effect of this is that the conclusive presumption will come into effect when the patient becomes liable to detention, or subject to guardianship, and will continue until he is neither so liable or subject, nor receiving treatment as an in-patient. Once the circumstances giving rise to the conclusive presumption cease, the presumption does not come back into operation until he is again liable to detention or subject to guardianship—a return to voluntary in-patient status will not have this effect. It should be noted also that s.38(5) deals only with cases of conclusive presumption. In every other case it must be a question of fact whether the claimant is at any given time incapable of managing and administering his property and affairs. In practical terms this is likely to be one of the most difficult problems arising in this area, particularly where it is alleged that the claimant has at all times been disabled over a considerable period of time.[6] Any cessation of that disability, however brief, will cause time to start running, and the burden is on the claimant to show that he has been disabled at all material times. Great reliance will be placed for this purpose on contemporary medical records,[7] and there is no rule that the concept of disability should be interpreted liberally so as to assist the claimant[8]—it must be remembered that an approach which is generous to claimants is likely at the same time to be harsh on defendants. The circumstances in which the Mental Health Act 1983 allows for such detention or guardianship are highly complex, and it is not possible here to give more than a brief account.

---

[5] Excluding ss.35 and 89 thereof.
[6] *Kirby v Leather* [1965] 2 Q.B. 367, per Winn L.J.
[7] *Penrose v Mansfield* (1971) S.J. 309, CA.
[8] *Penrose v Mansfield* (1971) S.J. 309, CA.

Guardianship

Guardianship is an arrangement whereby the administration of a person's **19.006** property and affairs is entrusted to another, known as the guardian, but that person is not committed to any form of institution. Any person who has reached the age of 16 may be received into guardianship. An order of the court is required; any person may apply for such an order, and the application must be supported by a statement from two registered medical practitioners to the effect that the patient is suffering from such mental illness or impairment as warrants a guardianship order and that such order is necessary for the protection of the patient or of other persons.[9] Guardianship orders last for a maximum of six months, but can be renewed upon the making of further application to the court.[10] From the limitation point of view the important matter here is that once the guardianship has been allowed to lapse, time will begin to run, and a subsequent renewal of the guardianship will not suspend the running of time.

In-patient treatment

The admission of a patient for treatment is governed by ss.2 and 3 of the **19.007** Mental Health Act 1983. The procedure for such admission under s.3 is very similar to that for the making of a guardianship order, except that the statement by the two medical practitioners must also declare that it is impossible to provide satisfactory treatment for the patient unless he is detained under this section. The provisions for ending detention are the same as those for ending guardianship. Section 2 relates to admission for assessment with a view to considering what treatment would be appropriate. Again, a statement by two medical practitioners is required, but orders under s.2 last only 28 days and cannot be renewed—the patient must then be released unless he has subsequently become liable to be detained under some other provision of the Mental Health Act 1983. A final point to note is that s.28 of the 1980 Act does not apply to a patient who is detained in hospital either because he had been remanded there after being convicted of a criminal offence (under s.35 of the Mental Health Act 1983) or because he has been apprehended after absconding from a mental hospital in the Isle of Man or the Channel Islands and is detained pending his return there (under s.89 of the Act). The above is not an exhaustive account of the possibilities or detention under the Act, but it covers the more important points. For other cases the reader is referred to the specialist texts on the Mental Health Act.

---

[9] These rules are to be found in s.7 of the Mental Health Act 1983.
[10] Mental Health Act 1983 s.20.

Other incapacities

19.008   The list of disabilities given in s.38 should be regarded as conclusive. Other incapacitating events which may make it more difficult for the claimant to pursue his action do not count as disabilities for limitation purposes. The point has arisen especially in relation to s.33 of the 1980 Act, where one of the factors required to be taken into account is any disability of the claimant arising after the cause of action accrued. It is now clear, after some earlier doubts, that "disability" in this context has the same limited meaning as is given by s.38 of the Act.[11] In *Chagos Islanders v AG*[12] a bold attempt was made to broaden the notion of disability by contending that the definition in s.38(2) of the 1980 Act is not exhaustive and that "disability" could include being outside the jurisdiction of the High Court as a result of the defendants' acts, and being impoverished, ignorant and illiterate and physically separated from those Courts as a result of their acts. The former had historically been a disability; he referred to the 1623 Limitation Act. Ouseley J. rightly rejected this somewhat desperate argument. The definition is not a deeming provision leaving other disabilities to be allowed for by judicial improvisation, or by reference to the repealed legislation of 1623. It is unwise to construe the 1980 Act as if it incorporated provisions from earlier repealed Acts without any express provision to that effect. Section 38(2) is clearly a definition section[13], and it relates to legal not to physical disability.

19.009   *Masterman-Lister v Brutton & Co; Masterman-Lister v Jewell and another*[14] was not a limitation case, but a case about re-opening a settlement achieved on behalf of a person who was allegedly a patient. It did therefore consider the meaning of the term patient within the meaning of the Mental Health Act 1983, and its observations are of interest in a limitation context.

The claimant was born in 1963. In 1980, he was involved in a serious road traffic accident and suffered severe brain damage. An action was commenced on his behalf, but later compromised, and it was this compromise which he sought to re-open on the basis that he had been a patient at the time and the approval of the court had not been obtained as required by RSC Ord.80, r.10, now CPR 21.1(2)(b).

At first instance the judge ruled that the court should only take over the individual's function of decision making when it was shown on the balance

---

[11] See *Dawson v Spain-Gower* (October 18, 1988, Glidewell L.J. as single judge of the CA, Unreported); *Yates v Thakeham Tiles Ltd, The Times*, May 19, 1994, CA; *Jones v City and Hackney HA* (December 21, 1993, Colman J. Unreported). The earlier decision of Eastham J. in *Matthew Pilmore v Northern Trawlers Ltd* [1986] 1 Lloyd's Rep. 552 should be regarded as no longer good law. See also para.8.038.
[12] [2003] EWHC 2222 (QB), [2003] All ER (D) 166 (Oct) Ouseley J.
[13] *Yates v Thakeham Tiles Ltd* [1995] PIQR 135 CA.
[14] [2002] EWCA Civ 1889, [2003] 3 All ER 162.

of probabilities that the individual did not have the capacity sufficiently to understand, absorb and retain information, including advice, relevant to the matters in question sufficiently to enable him or her to make decisions based upon such information. On that basis he concluded that the claimant had not been a patient at the relevant time. The Court of Appeal considered the general issues arising and held that the burden of proof rested on those asserting incapacity. The Human Rights Act 1998 was also relevant, because a finding that a person is a patient has the effect of depriving him of the right to conduct his own legal affairs. Consequently, the court should always, as a matter of practice, at the first convenient opportunity, investigate the question of capacity whenever there was any reason to suspect that it might be absent. A medical report might often be required for this purpose.

The test to be applied to determine whether a person is capable of managing his own affairs is issue-specific. What had to be considered was whether the party to legal proceedings was capable of understanding, with the assistance of such proper explanation from legal advisers and experts in other disciplines as the case might require, the issues on which his consent or decision was likely to be necessary in the course of those proceedings. If the party had capacity to understand that which he needed to understand in order to pursue or defend a claim there was no reason why the law, whether substantive or procedural, should require the interposition of a next friend or litigation friend. Moreover, a person should not be held unable to understand the information relevant to a decision if he could understand an explanation of that information in broad terms and simple language. Furthermore, he should not be regarded as unable to make a rational decision merely because the decision which he did, in fact, make was a decision which would not be made by a person of ordinary prudence[15] . On the facts the Court of Appeal upheld the decision that the claimant had not been a patient at the relevant time.[16]

It might well be said that in a limitation context the issues are somewhat different, since in limitation it is normally a benefit to a claimant to be classed as a patient because it prevents time from running against him. However, two points may be made. The first is that the definition of 'patient' in limitation is the same as the definition which was being considered here, and it is hard to see how there can be different definitions of that term in different contexts. The second is that the privileged category of patient is one which should not be conferred lightly, because of the prejudice which defendants may suffer from the fact that time never runs in

---

[15] See also *White v Fell* 12 November 1987, Unreported.

[16] For a further case reiterating the issue-specific nature of the test of capacity set out in *Masterman-Lister v Brutton & Co (Nos 1 & 2)* and *Sheffield CC v E* [2004] EWHC 2808 (Fam), [2005] Fam 326, [2005] 2 WLR 953 see *Marsh v Sofaer; Sofaer v Judkins (a firm)* [2006] EWHC 1217 (Ch), David Richards J.

their favour where the claimant is a patient. Consequently, it is submitted that the test in this case must now be regarded as the appropriate one to apply in a limitation context.[17]

THE EFFECT OF DISABILITY

19.010 Disability has a number of significant procedural consequences, some, but not all, of which are relevant to limitation issues. A person under disability is not allowed to bring or defend an action on his own behalf.[18] This does not mean that no action can be taken to protect his legal rights; however, the action must be instituted by another person on his behalf, and that person is known to the law as the litigation friend.[19] In the case of an infant this will commonly be his parent or guardian, though there is no requirement that this should be so.[20] The possibility of bringing an action in this way should be borne in mind when considering the problems discussed in this chapter. A person under disability may also be the defendant in a civil action. Again, it will be necessary to appoint a litigation friend,[21] a role which in the case of an infant will often, but not always, be filled by his parent or guardian.[22] Disability confers no immunity from suit.

THE RUNNING OF TIME

19.011 Where the claimant is under disability at the time when the cause of action accrues, s.28(1) provides that, notwithstanding the usual rules on the running of time, the time within which the action may be brought is to be measured from the earlier of the date on which the disability ceased and the date on which the claimant died. The period of limitation, as so measured, will be six years, except in two cases. First, where the action is for personal injuries (whether by the injured person or on behalf of the dependants of a deceased under the Fatal Accidents Acts[23]) the period is three years, and secondly, in the case of a contribution action under s.10 of the Act, it is two years.[24] Generally this means that the period is the one which would have

---

[17] A similar approach was adopted in *Morley v Hunt & Co (a firm)* [2005] All ER (D) 41 (Jan) Judge Reid QC.

[18] CPR, Pt 21.

[19] Formerly "next friend". See now CPR Pt 21.

[20] The rules relating to the appointment of the litigation friend are to be found in CPR Pt 21. Note that the parent or guardian cannot act if he/she has an interest in the case contrary to that of the child.

[21] Formerly "guardian ad litem".

[22] See CPR Pt 21.

[23] 1980 Act s.28(6).

[24] 1980 Act s.28(5).

been applicable to the action in the absence of disability, but measured from a different starting date. However, this principle does not extend to those cases for which the limitation period is normally 12 years.[25]

Alternative periods

The phrasing of s.28(1) can create alternative periods of limitation in a **19.012** number of cases. If the period which would have been applicable to the action in the absence of any disability is 12 years, as, for example, with specialty debts or actions to recover land, it is possible that the six-year period from the ending of the disability provided by s.28(1) will expire before the 12-year period from the accrual of the cause of action. In such circumstances the effect of s.28(1) is that the action may still be brought at any time within the 12-year period; i.e. in cases of this kind, s.28(1) can extend the limitation period, but can never abbreviate it.

INTERMITTENT DISABILITY

Intermittent disability, which must by definition be in the form of **19.013** unsoundness of mind, causes particular difficulties. It has been seen[26] that time does not immediately begin to run against a claimant who is under a disability when the cause of action accrues. However, it was held as long ago as 1661 in *Prideaux v Webber*[27] that once time has begun to run, nothing can interrupt it. The case was strong, since the impossibility of bringing the action resulted from the suspension of the King's Courts and their law during the period of the Commonwealth. It was held that the defendant was nevertheless entitled to plead limitation. This rule is obviously capable of producing injustice in a good many cases, but the only statutory qualifications on it at the present day are to be found in s.33(3)(d) and s.34(5) of the 1980 Act. Similarly, where the claimant is not under a disability when the cause of action accrues, the running of time will not be suspended where he later falls under a disability.[28]

---

[25] See also paras 19.024–19.030 for the position in relation to the Latent Damage Act 1986 and the Consumer Protection Act 1987.
[26] See para.19.010.
[27] (1661) 1 Lev. 31.
[28] *Purnell v Roche* [1927] 2 Ch. 142, Romer J.

THE POSITION IN PERSONAL INJURY CASES

19.014 Where the claimant's claim includes a claim for damages for personal injuries,[29] or a claim under Pt I of the Consumer Protection Act 1987,[30] the court has discretion to allow the bringing of an action, notwithstanding that the three-year limitation period has expired. One of the factors which the court is required to consider when contemplating the exercise of that discretion is the duration of any disability of the claimant which arose after the date on which the cause of action accrued. This is the one situation in English law where supervening disability can be relevant, and even here it is only one of the factors to be taken into account considering the exercise of the s.33 discretion. Clearly, the longer the disability, the more likely it is that the court will lean in the direction of allowing the action to be brought out of time.

SUCCESSIVE ACCRUALS

19.015 Where the person under a disability claims through some person not under a disability to whom the right of action first accrued, s.28 has no application. The concept of claiming through another is explained in s.38(5): a person claims through another if he became entitled by, through, under or by the act of that other person to the right claimed. There is some ambiguity about the ambit of this provision. It is clear enough that if the right first accrues to a person not under a disability, no person claiming through that person can take the benefit of s.28. If the right has passed through a number of hands, however, it may happen that some intermediate person in the chain was under a disability, though the person to whom the right first accrued was not. It is necessary to decide whether a person is treated as claiming through everyone above him in the chain, or only through the person from whom he directly acquired the right.

This question has not been considered in the context of s.28, but there is Court of Appeal authority in the context of s.32[31] that a person is treated as claiming through all those above him in the chain. If this authority does not apply to s.28, the problem is greatly simplified. It is only necessary to consider the position as between the claimant and the person from whom he acquired his right. If that person was never under a disability, then s.28 has no application, but if that person was under a disability from the time the cause of action accrued until the time the right passed to the claimant,

---

[29] 1980 Act s.33.
[30] 1980 Act s.11A, as added by the Consumer Protection Act 1987 Sch.1.
[31] *Eddis v Chichester Constable* [1969] 2 All E.R. 912, per Lord Denning M.R.; the conclusion was not reached without some hesitation. See also para.20.036.

the case is governed by s.28(3) (which is considered below[32]) if the right passes on the death of the first holder of the right. If the passes otherwise than on death, or if the previous holder of the right was not under a disability at all material times, then the position is extremely obscure.

Numerous possibilities may be identified:

19.016

(a) The previous holder of the right (P1) was under a disability when the right accrued, but later ceased to be so, and is not under a disability when the right passes to P2.

(b) P1 was not under a disability when the right first accrued, but later became so, and is under a disability when the right passes to P2.

(c) P1 was under a disability when the right accrued, but has subsequently recovered and relapsed, and so is under a disability when the right passes to P2.

(d) P1 was under a disability when the right accrued, has undergone recoveries and relapses, but is not under a disability when the right passes to P2.

(e) P1 was not under a disability when the right accrued, has subsequently suffered a disability, but has recovered by the time the right passes.

An important question in resolving these various situations appears to be whether the wording of s.28(2) requires that P1 be under a disability when the right of action first accrued to him. This is the natural interpretation of the words of the section; it also has the advantage of according with the interpretation which the courts gave to similar provisions in earlier statutes.[33] It would follow from this that s.28(2) has no application to situations (b) and (e) in the above list. It has been suggested[34] that s.28(2) is merely an instance of the general principle that the running of time cannot be halted once it has begun, which would mean that s.28 could not apply to any of the above five situations but the subsection clearly does not say this. It is submitted that s.28(2) has no application to situations (a), (c) or (d) above. Consequently, if the requirements of s.28(1) are satisfied in these cases, time will be extended. It is true that this appears to be contrary to the general principle laid down in *Prideaux v Webber*,[35] but it follows the words of the statute.

The problems discussed in the previous paragraph become even more intractable if it is assumed that a claimant is treated as claiming through

19.017

---

[32] See para.19.016.
[33] See especially *Goodall v Skerratt* (1855) 3 Drew. 216.
[34] Derek Morgan, *Current Law Statutes Annotated* (1980), vol.II.
[35] (1661) 1 Lev. 31.

every one above him in the chain of title. On this assumption, the odd position is reached that only the condition of the person to whom the right of action first accrued is relevant. That person must therefore be regarded as P1 in the examples given above, the condition of all those intervening between P1 and the claimant in question being irrelevant, except in the limited class of case dealt with by s.28(3). This is, no doubt, a cogent argument for adopting the more restrictive view of the phrase "claiming through" in s.28(2), but this point must be regarded as unsettled.

Accrual on death

19.018　Section 28(3) governs the situation where a right of action accrues to a person under a disability, and he dies while still under a disability, and the right thereupon vests in another person also under a disability. The subsection provides that in these circumstances no further extension of time can be allowed by reason of the disability of the second person. The effect of this is that time runs for the purposes of the action from the death of the first person (the period of limitation is determined in accordance with s.28(1), (5) or (6) as the case may be[36]). This provision will be of relevance where the person dying has been under a disability constantly since the cause of action accrued. If the disability ever ceases, time will start to run quite independently of this provision. There is, however, a possible conflict between this and the interpretation given above to s.28(2), since it was assumed there that the running of time could be suspended if a cause of action later accrued to a person under a disability, even though time had begun to run against the original holder of the right. This conflict can be resolved by regarding s.28(3) as a qualification to the general principle stated in s.28(2).

RELATIONSHIP BETWEEN DISABILITY AND WANT OF PROSECUTION

19.019　Where the claimant is under a disability when the cause of action accrues, time does not begin to run until that disability ends. It is nevertheless permissible for the claimant (or rather his litigation friend[37]) to commence an action on his behalf. If such an action is commenced, but then not proceeded with, the defendant may seek to have it dismissed for want of prosecution. The proper response of the court in this situation was con-

---

[36] See para.19.006.
[37] See para.19.009.

sidered by the House of Lords in *Tolley v Morris*.[38] The problem in this case was rendered more acute by the fact that the plaintiff was at the time of the accident only two years old, and would therefore remain under a disability until nearly 16 years after the accident. The House of Lords by a bare majority refused to dismiss the action for want of prosecution, holding that it would be useless to do so, since a new action could have been commenced immediately, the limitation period not having expired. The consequence of this decision is that a claimant under a disability is in some respects in a more favourable position than other claimants not under a disability. The ordinary rules relating to dismissal for want of prosecution[39] operate more leniently for such a claimant, who can get the best of both worlds by commencing an action immediately, but then not pursuing it if that seems tactically the more prudent course; a second action can be started at a later date without any difficulty, so long as this is done within the extended period of limitation provided by s.28. *Tolley v Morris* was decided under the 1939 Act, but the law is still the same at the present day, an attempt to amend the 1980 Act during its passage through Parliament to deal with this problem having failed.[40] Subsequently, in *Hogg v Hamilton*,[41] a plaintiff in a similar position had allowed a first writ to expire unserved and then, after several years' delay, had issued a second writ. The Court of Appeal struck out the second writ as an abuse of the process of the court.[42] Such a step will certainly happen only in exceptional cases, but this decision does indicate that a second writ is vulnerable to striking out.

DISABILITY AND ABUSE OF PROCESS

On the face of it the effect of s.28 is to give the claimant an extended **19.020** limitation period, and in accordance with general principles it might be thought that no procedural remedy would be available against a claimant who issued proceedings within the limitation period, even though the proceedings were not issued until very many years after the cause of action arises. The decision in *Tolley v Morris*, discussed above, is based on this assumption, and other later cases reiterate the principle. In *Turner v WH Malcolm Ltd*[43] Glidewell L.J., with whom the other members of the Court agreed, said:

"In sections 28 and 38 of the 1980 Act Parliament has in effect provided

---

[38] [1979] 1 W.L.R. 592.
[39] These are considered at length in Ch.22.
[40] Hansard, HL, Vol.400, col. 1223; Vol.401, col.1147.
[41] April 1, 1992, CA, Unreported.
[42] As to this see further para.1.037.
[43] *Times Law Reports*, August 24, 1992.

that there is no limitation period for a plaintiff who is under a permanent disability if he, or his solicitor, did not proceed with his action expeditiously. That meant that the maxim that it was in the public interest that there should be an end to litigation had little or no application to an action by such a plaintiff."

In *Bull v Devon AHA*[44] Mustill L.J. said:

"since the unfortunate plaintiff has been under a double disability for almost all of the time since the asserted cause of action arose those who have the charge of his interests are entitled under statute to delay the institution of proceedings beyond the point at which, as the Judge has rightly said, it would have been unfair to allow his mother to persist. Parliament must therefore have decided that the public interest in requiring factual disputes to be litigated promptly is outweighed, in cases such as this, by the public interest in giving the disadvantaged a long time within which to sue. By making this choice the legislature has imposed heavy burdens on the parties and also on the trial Judge. Heavy as they are, the law requires them to be assumed. And, after all, medical negligence cases are not unique amongst those in which claims are allowed to be brought long after the facts have faded from recollection."

However, in recent years it has become clear that rigid adherence to this rule can have undesirable consequences. Where the claimant in a personal injuries action is a patient as a result of the injuries, such as in those cases where the claimant suffers serious brain damage and has no prospect of ever recovering, the effect of s.28 is that time will never run during the claimant's lifetime, since the disability will end only on the claimant's death. Defendants may therefore be confronted with writs issues decades after the event, even though the nature and extent of the injuries were known to the claimant's advisers and carers at a much earlier stage.

19.021   A significant change in judicial attitude was seen in *Hogg v Hamilton*, discussed above, though that was concerned with a second writ. In *Headford v Bristol DHA*[45] the principle was for the first time extended to the issue of a first writ in such circumstances. The judge reviewed the earlier authorities and held that the terms of s.28 are permissive—they do not bestow an absolute right on a claimant under a disability to institute proceedings in all circumstances. The provision is subject to the inherent jurisdiction of the court to strike out a proceeding that is an abuse of the process.[46] He went on to hold that the delay in the case (28 years) should be

---

[44] [1993] 4 Med.L.Rev. 23.
[45] June 17, 1994, A. Tyrell Q.C. sitting as a Deputy Judge of the Queen's Bench Division, Unreported.
[46] *Hogg v Hamilton* [1992] P.I.Q.R. 387, above.

regarded as making the issue of the writ an abuse of process. It is, of course, a question of fact in every case whether the delay is so great as to make the issue of the writ an abuse of process. In *Headford* no good reasons for the delay were advanced, and the judge expressly used this fact to distinguish the case from other similar cases, such as *Atkinson v Oxford HA*,[47] where a defence under the Limitation Act based on a delay of 22 years failed on the ground that the plaintiff had not acted unreasonably. In that case the plaintiff and his mother had been attempting to obtain information from the defendant over many years, without success, and had instructed a succession of firms of solicitors to take the case. In *Alexander Linsey v National Health Service Litigation Authority*[48] it was held that an action brought 23 years after the date of accrual and based on the same facts as an earlier discontinued action was not an abuse of process, though it is submitted that this must be regarded as a decision on its own facts.

The position in relation to the use of the abuse of process defence must be regarded as unclear. *Headford* appears to be the only case where it has succeeded in relation to a first writ, *Hogg v Hamilton* being the only case where it has succeeded in relation to a second writ. *Headford* is only a first-instance decision, though *Hogg v Hamilton* has Court of Appeal status. Both decisions, however, are inconsistent with the reasoning underlying earlier authority of the Court of Appeal and, in *Tolley v Morris*, the House of Lords. It is easy to sympathise with those judges who regard the issue of a writ a quarter of a century after the cause of action has accrued as an abuse of process, but it is extremely difficult to resist the logic of *Tolley v Morris*, *Turner v Malcolm* and *Bull v Devon HA*. The fact surely is that Parliament has allowed a very extended limitation period in these cases; changing that state of affairs will require Parliamentary intervention.

Negative declarations

As appears from the preceding paragraphs, potential defendants to claims brought by those under disability may be unhappy at the prospect of having the action hanging over them for many years. One possible response is to seek a negative declaration i.e. a declaration that the potential defendant is not liable to the potential claimant. This approach was adopted in *Torpador v D*.[49] The potential claimant in that case was 10 years old at the time of the accident, so time had not yet begun to run against him when the defendant sought the negative declaration. There is no doubt that the court has a general power to grant declarations, including negative declarations.[50]

19.022

---

[47] [1993] Med.L.Rev. 18, Simon Tuckey Q.C.
[48] December 21, 2000, Unreported, N. Wilkinson Q.C.
[49] [2010] LRIR 358 Christopher Clarke J.; Patten (2010) 29 CJQ 284.
[50] CPR 40.20.

Christopher Clarke J. rejected an argument that the seeking of a negative declaration in cases involving child claimants is inappropriate because in effect it circumvents the protection which the law gives them. However, he refused the declaration on the facts and commented that the seeking of such a declaration will rarely be appropriate in personal injury cases.

19.023   It is submitted that this approach rather understates the difficulties involved in this case. As has been seen above, the law is quite clear that a claimant who is under disability has an extended limitation period. It is for him (or his litigation friend) to decide whether to bring a claim at any point within that period. The decision taken may be to delay the bringing of proceedings. To allow a defendant to force the issue by seeking a negative declaration surely undermines that rule. The point is by no means unimportant. There are many child victims of road accidents, and it does not seem unreasonable to suppose that defendants (in reality their insurers) might often be attracted by the idea of seeking a negative declaration. This is an issue which requires consideration at appellate level, and, if this practice becomes commonplace, it will no doubt receive such consideration before too long.

ACTIONS TO RECOVER LAND

19.024   Section 28(4) imposes an additional restriction in the case of actions to recover land (within the extended definition given by s.38(7)[51]). Although the disability rules of s.28 apply to such actions, they cannot be used to enable an action to be brought after the expiry of 30 years from the date when cause of action accrued.

RELATIONSHIP WITH OTHER GROUNDS OF EXTENSION

19.025   Section 28 is not the only ground on which the limitation period may be extended. It is necessary to consider here also extension by acknowledgment under ss.29 to 31 of the 1980 Act and extension in cases of fraud, concealment or mistake under s.32 of the same Act.[52] Essentially the position is that these three methods of postponing the running of time operate independently from each other. In effect each creates its own limitation period, running from the time when the suspensory factor ceases to operate. The action may be brought at any time before the end of the last of

---

[51] See paras 13.002–13.004.
[52] The relationship between s.28 and s.33 is considered at paras 19.011–19.013.

these periods to expire. Usually this will also be the last period to start running, but it should be remembered that the period granted by s.28 cannot extend for more than six years from the end of the disability, whilst the periods extended by ss.29 and 32 may be 12 years. The expiry dates of all periods which apply in a given case should therefore be calculated.

THE LATENT DAMAGE ACT 1986

Section 2 of the Latent Damage Act 1986 (LDA 1986) adds to the 1980 Act **19.026** a new section, s.28A, which governs the relationship between disability and the periods of limitation introduced by the 1986 Act.

Conditions of applicability

Section 28A applies to any action to which s.14A of the 1980 Act[53] applies **19.027** (essentially this means cases of latent damage to property) where three further conditions are also satisfied:

(a) the period applicable under s.14A(4) is that mentioned in s.14A(4)(b);

(b) on the starting date within s.14A the person then having the right to sue was under a disability;

(c) s.28 of the 1980 Act does not apply to the action.

These three conditions need to be considered in turn.

Section 14A(4)(b)

The very convoluted reference to this provision can readily be rendered into **19.028** simple English. The requirement is that the cause of action in respect of the damage not be discoverable with reasonable diligence on the part of the claimant until some time after it has accrued.

Disability at starting date

The second of the three conditions is that the person in whom the cause of **19.029** action was vested when it first became reasonably discoverable (the "starting date" as defined by s.14A(5) of the LDA 1986) should have been under a disability at that date. The point of this is that s.28 refers only to

---

[53] As added by s.1 of the LDA 1986: for the details, see Ch.6.

the date when the cause of action accrues, and in the cases where s.28A is concerned this will be a date different from the starting date.

Section 28 inapplicable

19.030   This requirement imposes severe limits on the ambit of s.28A. There is no provision for the purposes of that section generally. The only provision in the LDA 1986 which expressly disapplies s.28 is s.3(3), which relates to the case where property changes hands before the starting date. It is therefore submitted that s.28A does not apply to the case of the original owner of property who is under a disability at the starting date but not at the date when the cause of action accrued; that situation is governed by s.28, so that the only relevant date is the date of accrual. If the claimant was under a disability then, the running of time is postponed until he ceases to be under a disability, without regard to the position at the starting date. This is a very surprising conclusion, and it is hard to believe that it was what was intended by the draftsman. In the absence of any provision disapplying s.28 for the purposes of s.14A, it must, however, be correct. The result is that s.28A applies only to those cases where the property has changed hands before the starting date and the action is brought by the subsequent owner. Where the action is brought by the original owner, he will always have the alternative periods provided by s.14A(4). Where he was under a disability at the date when the cause of action accrued, he will also have the period provided by s.28, namely six years from the disability or the date when he died. In some cases this will be the last of the three periods to expire, and it may therefore be of considerable importance.

Effect of section 28A

19.031   In those very limited situations to which s.28A does apply, the result is that the action may be brought at any time within three years of the disability ceasing or the person under a disability dying, notwithstanding that the period provided by s.14A has expired. What this means is that the subsequent purchaser must have been under a disability at the starting date; his time for bringing an action is then extended as described above.

Relationship with longstop

19.032   Section 28A(2) goes on to consider the relationship between the extension of time provided for by s.28A(1) and the rule in s.14B of the 1980 Act[54] that in no circumstances may an action be brought more than 15 years after the date of the last act of negligence which the claimant alleges. The rule here is that the longstop provision prevails—the extension of time in

---

[54] As added by s.1 of the LDA 1986.

s.28A(1) cannot be used to bring an action after the expiry of the longstop period.

THE CONSUMER PROTECTION ACT 1987

Schedule 1 to this Act contains provisions amending the 1980 Act to deal with the new causes of action which the CPA 1987 creates.[55] The relevant provision for present purposes is para.4 of that Schedule, which adds a new s.28(7) to the 1980 Act. Section 28(7) has two effects—first, in relation to actions under the CPA 1987 the effect of a disability is to allow an action to be brought within three years (rather than six) of the end of the disability. Secondly, a disability cannot be used as a ground for bringing an action after the expiry of the 10-year longstop period provided for by s.11A(3) of the 1980 Act (as added by Sch.1 to the CPA 1987).

19.033

DISABILITY AND DEFAMATION

Section 57 of the Administration of Justice Act 1985 added new ss.4A and 32A to the Limitation Act 1980.[56] These impose a special one-year time-limit in the case of defamation actions. A new s.28(4A) was also added. This provides that in the case of actions to which s.4A applies (i.e. actions for libel or slander) if the person to whom the cause of action accrues is under a disability at the date of accrual, the action may be brought by him at any time before the expiration of three years from the date on which he ceased to be under a disability. This change is effected by s.57(3) of the Administration of Justice Act 1985; despite the convoluted wording of that subsection the effect is simply to apply to cases of libel and slander the general rules that time does not begin until the claimant ceases to be under a disability and that the period which then commences is as long as the period applicable to a claimant who was not under a disability when the cause of action accrued.

19.034

THE LAW COMMISSION'S PROPOSALS

The Commission proposes to retain the present rule that disability is a factor that prevents time from starting to run, but to add to that rule a new provision under which supervening disability would automatically suspend

19.035

---

[55] The CPA 1987 is dealt with in detail in Ch.7.
[56] These are dealt with at paras 8.002–8.003 and 8.071–8.078 respectively.

the running of time. A new definition of "lack of capacity" is proposed, in an attempt to deal with the problems presently surrounding the notion of unsoundness of mind. This definition is adapted from that proposed by the Law Commission in its review of mental incapacity.[57] It emphasises the inability of the claimant to make a decision in relation to his claim or to communicate that decision, where this inability is caused by a disability or disorder of the mind or brain, whether permanent or temporary, which results in an impairment or disturbance of mental functioning. As a separate, but related, question, the Commission asks whether the definition of lack of capacity in a limitation context should make special provision for the problems of victims of childhood sexual abuse.

The Commission also raises the difficult question of whether disability should prevent time from running even where the person under disability has a representative who could bring the action. Some of the cases discussed in this chapter have canvassed the possibility that wilful failure to bring an action in these circumstances might amount to abuse of process.

The Commission's proposals elsewhere for the introduction of a general longstop make it necessary to consider the relationship between disability and the longstop. If disability overrides the longstop, then the law may be considered to be over-protecting minors, but if the opposite view is taken, then minors may be unfairly prejudiced, especially if the longstop is set at 10 years—a three-year-old child who suffers a personal injury would find that action barred at the age of 13, even if there had never been a representative able to bring an action. In an effort to reconcile these two opposing problems, the Commission suggests a special limitation period for minors, to expire on the date when it would have expired if the claimant had not been a minor at the date of accrual, or on the claimant's 21st birthday, whichever is later.

---

[57] Law Com. No. 231 (1995).

CHAPTER 20

Fraud, Concealment and Mistake

These three topics are dealt with in s.32 of the 1980 Act. Within the limits **20.001** of that section the effect of each of them is to postpone the running of time until the fraud, concealment or mistake, as the case may be, is discovered, or could with reasonable diligence have been discovered, by the claimant.[1]

HISTORY

Section 32 was formerly s.26 of the 1939 Act, subject to a difference in **20.002** wording which is discussed at para.20.008. Before 1940 there were no statutory provisions for extending the limitation period in these cases, but the principle that equity will not allow a statute to be used as an engine of fraud had led to the development of case-law principles, which were codified in the 1939 Act.[2]

AMBIT OF SECTION

Section 32(1) provides that references in it to the actions of the defendant **20.003** include the actions of any person through whom the defendant claims. Therefore, where the action relates to property which has changed hands subsequent to the alleged wrongdoing, the later owner is liable to be fixed with the effects of the actions of an earlier owner. However, this rule is significantly modified by subss.(3) and (4), which are examined at length below.[3]

---

[1] 1980 Act s.32(a).
[2] For a more detailed account, see *G.L. Baker Ltd v Medway Building and Supplies Ltd* [1958] 2 All E.R. 532. Pre-1940 cases on this rule include *Lynn v Bamber* [1930] 2 K.B. 72 and *Lawrance v Lord Norreys* (1890) 15 App.Cas. 210, HL.
[3] See paras 20.027–20.032.

MEANING OF DILIGENCE

20.004   In those cases covered by s.32, time does not start to run until the claimant discovers the fraud, mistake or concealment, or could with reasonable diligence have done so.[4] The question what amounts to reasonable diligence was considered by Webster J. in *Peco Arts Inc. v Hazlitt Gallery Ltd.*[5] His Lordship held that the claimant is not required to do everything possible, but only to do what an ordinary prudent person would do having regard to all the circumstances.[6] Although this case concerned s.32(1)(c), there is no reason to doubt that the principle stated in it applies to any case in which s.32 is in point.

What must the claimant do?

20.005   A good illustration of the difficulties that arise in deciding whether the existence of the cause of action was reasonably discoverable is provided by the line of cases which has examined the date of accrual of the cause of action in cases of solicitor's negligence. Although s.32 does not appear to have been argued in any of these cases, they are relevant to this issue. The question whether there is deliberate concealment at all is considered later in this chapter.[7] For present purposes it is assumed that there is such concealment, and that the problem is to determine when the cause of action becomes reasonably discoverable. This aspect of the matter does not appear to have been considered in any reported case. The vital point here must surely be that the client is in principle entitled to assume that the work has been competently done and is not required to obtain a second professional opinion as to the quality of the work done by the first solicitor. However, there will inevitably come a point when the client becomes aware of the problem. Frequently this will occur only when the unfortunate consequences of the problem manifest themselves, though it is no doubt possible that the date might be earlier. In *Collins v Brebner*[8] Tuckey L.J. observed that a claimant could not be considered to have discovered a fact

---

[4] The observation in *Foreman v O'Driscoll & Partners (A Firm)* [2000] 1 Lloyd's Rep. 720 that constructive knowledge on the part of the claimant is not sufficient must be wrong, having regard to this part of s.32.

[5] [1983] 1 W.L.R. 1315.

[6] *Lawrance v Lord Norreys* (1890) 15 App.Cas. 210; *Chetham v Hoare* (1870) L.R. 9 Eq. 571; *Betjeman v Betjeman* [1895] 2 Ch. 474; *Baker v Courage & Co.* [1910] 1 K.B. 56; *Ecclesiastical Commissioners v N.E. Railway Co.* (1877) 4 Ch.D. 845; *Dean v Richards* (1863) 2 Moo.P.C.C.N.S. 1.

[7] See para.20.021.

[8] July 26, 2000, Unreported, CA.

so long as the defendant was telling him the opposite of that fact[9] and he had no compelling documentary evidence to suggest that the defendant was lying. The real difficulty here is found in those cases where the negligence is either so gross or of such a character as to be obvious even to a non-lawyer. It is arguable, for example, that *Forster v Outred*[10] falls into the latter category. The risks inherent in the transaction should have been obvious even to Mrs Forster, and it may therefore be that her cause of action was discoverable as soon as it accrued. An argument of this kind was described by Chadwick L.J. in *Haque v Bank of Credit and Commerce International SA*[11] as 'unattractive' but at the same time it was accepted that it could be legally valid. The position is perhaps different in cases such as *D.W. Moore & Co. Ltd v Ferrier*,[12] where expert legal knowledge would have been required to understand that in company law the term "member" applies only to shareholders.

Ezekiel v Lehrer[13] gives the Court of Appeal's authority to the (perhaps obvious) proposition that a claimant cannot rely on s.32 where he has been aware of a relevant fact but has subsequently forgotten it, even if the defendant subsequently does an act which might be regarded as deliberate concealment of it.   **20.006**

Burden of proof

The authoritative statement on the burden of proof in s.32 cases is that of Millett L.J. in *Paragon Finance plc v D.B. Thakarar & Co. (A Firm)*[14]:   **20.007**

"The first plaintiffs submit that they acted reasonably throughout. They cannot be criticised for their decision to concentrate on the repossession actions in the first instance, nor for their delay in instructing their present solicitors until October 1991. There was no need for urgency; they had almost six years in which to bring proceedings. In my judgment this reasoning is misconceived. The question is not whether the plaintiffs should have discovered the fraud sooner; but whether they could with reasonable diligence have done so. The burden of proof is on them. They must establish that they could not have discovered the fraud without exceptional measures which they could not reasonably have been expected to take. In this context the length of the applicable period of

---

[9] An oddity of this case is that the claimant relied on s.32(1)(a) and the Court of Appeal apparently overlooked the effect of *Beaman v ARTS Ltd* (below).

[10] [1982] 1 W.L.R. 86, CA.

[11] November 24, 1999, Unreported, CA.

[12] [1988] 1 W.L.R. 267, CA.

[13] [2002] EWCA Civ 16, [2002] Lloyd's Law Rep PN 260.

[14] [1999] 1 All E.R. 400 at 418. And see *Birmingham Midshires Building Society v Infields (A Firm)* (1999) 66 Con. L.R. 20, Judge Bowsher Q.C.

limitation is irrelevant. In the course of argument May L.J. observed that reasonable diligence must be measured against some standard, but that the six-year limitation period did not provide the relevant standard. He suggested that the test was how a person carrying on a business of the relevant kind would act if he had adequate but not unlimited staff and resources and was motivated by a reasonable but not excessive sense of urgency. I respectfully agree."

FRAUD

20.008 The meaning of this expression was considered in *Beaman v ARTS Ltd*.[15] The plaintiff entrusted property to the defendants to look after. During the Second World War the defendants, believing that the plaintiff could not be traced, and being fearful for the safety of the goods during the Blitz, gave the property away. After the War the plaintiff reappeared and demanded the return of her goods. She sued the defendants in conversion when they were unable to comply with this demand. They pleaded that the cause of action arose in 1940 when they disposed of the goods (on which assumption the action was out of time) but the plaintiff argued that the disposal of the goods was "fraud" within what is now s.32(1)(a) so that time did not start to run until she discovered the loss in 1946. Both Denning J. and the Court of Appeal held that the action was not based on fraud,[16] but their approaches to the definition of fraud in this context were different. Denning J. held that there was no fraud where the defendant honestly believed that the owner had consented to the disposal or that he would have done so had it been possible to contact him and seek his approval. The Court of Appeal laid down a more general test applicable to any case in which s.32(1)(a) is pleaded. An action is "based on fraud" for this purpose when (and only when) fraud is an essential element of the plaintiff's claim.[17] This requirement was not satisfied here, since the action was pleaded in conversion, a tort which can be committed without any fraud (though of course it may involve fraud).

By contrast, in *G.L. Baker Ltd v Medway Building and Supplies Ltd*[18] Danckwerts J. held that this provision did apply. A director of the defendant company, who was also the accountant of the plaintiff company, had fraudulently transferred money from the plaintiff to the defendant.[19] Since fraud was an essential ingredient of the plaintiff's claim, it followed that

---

[15] [1949] 1 K.B. 550, Denning J.; [1949] 1 All E.R. 465, CA.
[16] Though the Court of Appeal found for the plaintiff on a different ground: see para.20.011.
[17] *Phillips-Higgins v Harper* [1954] 1 K.B. 550, Pearson J.
[18] [1958] 1 W.L.R. 1216.
[19] For the application to this case of s.32(1)(b), see para.20.016

s.32(1)(a) applied. In *Regent Leisuretime v Natwest Bank Plc*[20] the Court of Appeal held that a claim for fraudulent misrepresentation is an action based on fraud for limitation purposes.

In *Chagos Islanders v AG* another ground on which the claimant sought to escape from the operation of the Limitation Act 1980 was that the action was based on fraud, not just because an action in deceit was a case based on fraud, but rather because "fraud" in this context meant unconscionable behaviour, falling short of "fraud" or even of moral turpitude. What was required was behaviour which made it unconscionable for a defendant to rely on the lapse of time as a bar to the claim.

In support of this proposition the claimant relied on a number of earlier authorities, including *Applegate v Moss*[21], *Clark v Woor*[22] and *Kitchen v RAF Association*[23]. However, all these cases are about the meaning of 'fraudulent concealment', a concept found in the Limitation Act 1939, but not repeated in the 1980 Act, which speaks instead of 'deliberate concealment'. They considered the predecessor provision of s.32, which was s.26 of the Limitation Act 1939. The Court rightly rejected this bold attempt to extend the meaning of fraud in this context, which should be confined to the narrow class of cases where it has already been held to apply.

For the purposes of s.32(1)(a) the necessary knowledge is knowledge of the fraud which is alleged to have been perpetrated. It is not sufficient that the claimant knows that there has been some unspecified deception.[24]

Untraced defendants

Section 32(1)(a) applies where the fraud on which the action is based is not immediately discoverable. It does not apply where the fraud is discoverable, even though the identity and/or whereabouts of the defendant may be unknown. In *R.B. Motor Policies at Lloyd's v Butler*[25] a car had been stolen from the insured of the plaintiff insurers, who were exercising rights of subrogation against an innocent third party to whom the vehicle had eventually been traced. The action was brought some 12 years after the original theft, the tracing of the vehicle having taken several years. Streatfield J. rejected the insurers' claim to rely on the undiscoverability of the

20.009

---

[20] [2003] EWCA Civ 391, [2003] All ER (D) 385 (Mar).
[21] [1971] 1QB 406 CA at p413, Lord Denning M.R.
[22] [1965] 1 WLR 650.
[23] [1958] 1 WLR 563.
[24] *Barnstaple Boat Co Ltd v Jones* [2007] EWCA Civ 727.
[25] [1950] 1 K.B. 76.

whereabouts of the car. Section 32 was the only limitation provision under which discoverability was then relevant,[26] and that section had no application where the damage was immediately discoverable.

CONCEALMENT

20.010   Section 32(1)(b) extends the limitation period where "any fact relevant to the plaintiff's cause of action has been deliberately concealed from him by the defendant". This form of words dates from 1980, the 1939 Act having required that the cause of action be fraudulently concealed. This wording, on which many of the cases considered here were decided, was very broadly interpreted. Indeed, it was said that the interpretation had become so liberal that fraudulent concealment required neither concealment nor fraud.[27] Some confusion is also caused in pre-1980 cases by references to this provision as the "concealed fraud" rule. The wording introduced by the 1980 Act appears to reflect the interpretation which the courts had put upon s.26 of the 1939 Act, and it is for this reason that the pre-1980 cases are still a useful guide in this area. Indeed, the present state of the law is perhaps best understood by an examination of the cases on the 1939 provision.

Wide meaning of fraud

20.011   In *Re McCallum*,[28] which was a case decided under the pre-1940 equitable jurisdiction to extend time in cases of fraudulent concealment, a mother executed a conveyance of her house in favour of her daughter, but omitted to notify the latter of the fact. The Court of Appeal held that this amounted to fraudulent concealment of the daughter's rights over the house so as to postpone the running of time against the daughter in respect of adverse possession. Whilst there is no doubt that the daughter's right of action had been concealed, it is hard to see how that concealment can properly be described as fraudulent, and the case must be regarded as an early example of the extreme breadth of the notion of fraudulent concealment. In *Beaman v ARTS Ltd*[29] the defendant bailees had wrongfully disposed of goods belonging to the plaintiff. As was explained at para.20.006 the Court of Appeal held that the plaintiff's action in conversion was not "based on fraud" within s.32(1)(a) since it was unnecessary for her to allege fraud in

---

[26] The law on this point is now radically different—see the 1980 Act, ss.11 and 14 (personal injuries) and the Latent Damage Act 1986 (other forms of latent damage). However, these changes do not affect the result in cases such as that presently under consideration.

[27] *Tito v Waddell (No. 2)* [1977] 3 All E.R. 129 at 244, per Megarry V.-C.

[28] [1901] 1 Ch.143, CA.

[29] [1948] 1 W.L.R. 563, Denning J.; [1949] 1 K.B. 550, CA.

order to succeed. They went on to hold that the plaintiff's right of action had been fraudulently concealed within s.32(1)(b). The defendants here had taken no positive step to hide the existence of the cause of the action from the plaintiff, but the Court of Appeal held that this did not matter. The notion of fraud in this paragraph extends to any case where the defendant may be said to have acted dishonestly or unconscionably, and this can include the situation where the wrongful act is committed surreptitiously. So far as the last of these points is concerned, attention is drawn to s.32(2) of the 1980 Act, which provides that deliberate commission of a wrong in circumstances in which it is unlikely to be discovered for some time amounts to deliberate concealment of the facts involved in that breach of duty.[30]

The broad test laid down by the Court of Appeal for fraudulent con-   **20.012**
cealment shows that the provision is of wide ambit, and it appears to have been widened still further in subsequent cases. In *Kitchen v Royal Air Force Association*[31] the plaintiff was injured through the breach of duty of the first defendants. She instructed the second defendants, a firm of solicitors, to pursue her claim in respect of this injury, but their negligent failure to do so caused her right of action to become time-barred. The second defendants persuaded the first defendants to agree to an ex gratia payment, on terms that the plaintiff was not to be told of its origin. The plaintiff was unwilling to accept this, and began to sue the second defendants for negligence. By this time the limitation period in respect of this action had also expired, and the second defendants pleaded the statute. The plaintiff relied on s.32(1)(b), and the Court of Appeal found in her favour. The wide test of "equitable fraud" laid down in the earlier cases was upheld, and the Court took the view that there was just sufficient in the way of concealment here to bring the provision into operation. It should be observed that the concealment here was only of the origin of the payment which the first defendants were to make, and, though the reasoning of the Court of Appeal is far from clear, it seems that the offer of this payment must be treated as being a fact relevant to the plaintiff's cause of action against the second defendants. It is hard to see how this can be correct, given that the payment was to be made strictly on an ex gratia basis. It is unlikely that the fact of the offer could have been used as evidence in the action against the second defendants.

---

[30] For s.32(2) generally, see para.20.023.
[31] [1958] 2 All E.R. 241, CA.

"Relevant to the plaintiff's right of action"

20.013   In *Johnson v Chief Constable of Surrey*[32] it was held that the phrase "fact relevant to the plaintiff's right of action" meant a fact without which the cause of action would be incomplete. It is not relevant that the defendant has concealed a fact which, if known, would merely strengthen an existing case. This is sometimes referred to as the "statement of claim test". In other words, one has to ask whether the claimant already knows (actually or constructively) facts which, by themselves, would enable him to produce an adequate statement of case. If so, then time runs against him, even if there are other facts which would helps his case and of which he is unaware[33] This rule was re-affirmed in *Services (UK) Ltd "The Kriti Palm"*.[34]

Mistaken concealment

20.014   In *Phillips-Higgins v Harper*,[35] which is considered more fully below,[36] Pearson J. held that a merely mistaken concealment of the cause of action cannot fall within s.32(1)(b). A similar approach was taken in *Foreman v O'Driscoll & Partners (A Firm)*.[37] However, as will be apparent from the cases considered in the preceding paragraphs, the courts have been very ready to hold that a particular concealment is fraudulent even where the defendant appears to have done little more than keep silent.

Misrepresentation

20.015   In *Lynn v Bamber*[38] the defendant sold plum trees to the plaintiff, falsely stating that they were of a high-quality variety. McCardie J. held that, assuming fraud to be proved, the plaintiff could have relied upon either simple fraud or fraudulent concealment.[39] The former proposition is uncontentious, but this appears to be the only case in which it has been held that s.32(1)(b) is applicable in cases of straightforward misrepresentation.

---

[32] *The Times*, November 23, 1992, CA; see also *Cottrell v Lock* (t/a Tilbrook Hunt & Lock (A Firm)), June 4, 1997, CA, Unreported and *Biggs v Sotnicks (A Firm)*, January 24, 2002, CA, Unreported; *Ezekiel v Lehrer*, January 30, 2002, CA, Unreported.

[33] See also *AIC Ltd v ITS Testing Services (UK) Ltd* [2005] EWHC 2122 (Comm) [2006] 1 Lloyd's Rep 1 Cresswell J. at para.310.

[34] [2006] EWCA Civ 1601.

[35] [1954] 1 All E.R. 116.

[36] See para.20.030.

[37] [2000] 1 Lloyd's Rep. 720, N. Baker Q.C.

[38] [1930] 2 K.B. 72.

[39] Although this case predates the 1939 Act, it is clear from the judgment that the principles applicable are those which were codified by the 1939 Act.

Concealment by agent

Section 32(1) is expressed as applying equally to the actions of the defendant, of the defendant's agent and of any person through whom the defendant claims and his agent. In *G.L. Baker Ltd v Medway Building and Supplies Ltd*[40] Danckwerts J. said, obiter, that s.32(1)(b) could apply to a case where a company's accountant defrauded it of money which he paid over to the defendant company, of which he was a director. It is hard to see how this can be right. There was no evidence of any concealment by the defendant company, even allowing for the wide meaning given to concealment in this context. The only possible concealment was by the delinquent director, and it is submitted that he was not the agent of the defendant company either in misappropriating the money or in paying it over to the defendant company.

20.016

As a general point, attention to the rules of agency is necessary in order to determine whether a person has acted as the defendant's agent on a particular occasion. Two examples of the problems in this area are to be found in the cases on defective buildings, which are considered below.[41] In *Archer v Moss*[42] the defendant was the developer of the land, whilst the use of inferior material which the Court of Appeal held to amount to fraudulent concealment was perpetrated by the builder. The Court nevertheless held that the developer was liable, since the builder was to be regarded as his agent for this purpose. In any other context the builder clearly would not be regarded as the developer's agent—there can, for example, be no doubt that purchasers made their contract with the builder rather than with the developer. The Court of Appeal was aware of the difficulty which this point posed, and resolved it by holding that "agent" for the purposes of s.32 has a somewhat wider meaning than simply a person who does not stand in the relationship of independent contractor to the alleged principal. Although the case is authority for the proposition that a builder can in some circumstances be the agent of the developer, at least for limitation purposes, the Court of Appeal unfortunately failed to indicate with any degree of exactitude how much wider is the concept of agency in s.32.

20.017

Agent's personal liability

In the subsequent case of *King v Victor Parsons & Co.*[43] the Court of Appeal, two members of which[44] had also participated in *Archer v Moss*,

20.018

---

[40] [1958] 1 W.L.R. 1216.
[41] See para.20.019.
[42] [1971] 1 All E.R. 747, CA.
[43] [1973] 1 All E.R. 206, CA.
[44] Lord Denning M.R. and Megaw L.J.

was concerned with a case in which houses had been built on the site of an old filled-in chalk pit. The defendants here were the estate agents who had acted for the builders. It was held that they were themselves liable to the plaintiffs, who had purchased houses on the site. At first instance[45]it was held, somewhat hesitantly, that s.32(1)(b) could apply to the estate agents in respect of their failure to disclose the existence of the old chalk pit, even if the plaintiff could establish only that the defendants had constructive knowledge of the relevant facts. In the Court of Appeal it was held that this view was, at least as a general proposition, too broad. However, their Lordships were able to avoid the necessity to re-cast it into a more acceptable form by their reinterpretation of the evidence below, which in their view justified a finding that the defendants did have actual knowledge of the existence of the chalk pit.

Two related questions are therefore apparently left open. The first is whether a person can be subject to s.32(1)(b) when he has only constructive knowledge of the facts alleged to have been concealed. The second, which did not arise for decision in this particular case, is whether a person can be liable for a concealment by his agent, when that agent has only constructive knowledge of the relevant facts. This question is made more complicated still by the possibility that the defendant himself may have actual knowledge of the facts, but may not be guilty of any concealment of them.

Actions against builders

20.019 A number of cases over a period of years explored the question of the application of s.32(1)(b) to actions against builders in respect of the defective construction of houses. The situations involved might at the present day be at least partially resolved by the provisions of the Latent Damage Act 1986,[46] though even under that statute the running of time for the purposes of s.2 of the 1980 Act can still be an important factor. In addition, these cases shed important light of the more general question of the ambit of s.32(1)(b).

In *Clark v Woor*[47] the plaintiff engaged the defendant to build a house for him. In breach of contract the defendant used inferior materials, but this did not become apparent until a later stage. Lawton J. held that s.32(1)(b) applied so as to postpone the running of time until the plaintiff could reasonably have discovered that inferior materials had been used. In reaching this conclusion his Lordship relied on the dictum of Lord Evershed M.R. in *Kitchen v RAF Association*[48] that "fraud" in this paragraph has the

---

[45] [1972] 1 All E.R. 626, Thesiger J.
[46] For a detailed examination of this statute, see Ch.6.
[47] [1965] 1 W.L.R. 650.
[48] See para.20.010.

extended meaning attributed to equitable fraud. A similar point arose in *Archer v Moss*,[49] though here the defect was in the foundations of the houses, which were thereby rendered virtually unsaleable. The Court of Appeal held that s.32(1)(b) applied, since the defendant had covered up the defective work when building on the foundations.[50] Two points may be noted. First, this case is different from *Clark v Worr* since in the latter the defective work had not been covered up, though it was not immediately obvious to the purchaser. Secondly, this appears to be the first reported case where the notion of "concealment" in this provision has been treated so literally. It was later followed by the Court of Appeal in *Dutton v Bognor Regis UDC*.[51] A similar approach was adopted in *Kijowski v New Capital Properties*.[52] In the event it was held that the writ was issued within the six-year limitation period, but there is an obiter dictum in that case that s.32 of the Limitation Act 1980 would have applied to the case anyway because:

"The builder has knowingly done bad work which was not of a trivial kind which had been covered up so that it was not likely to be discovered by the purchaser or his successors."

Mere silence as concealment

In *King v Victor Parsons & Co.*[53] doubts were expressed, both at first   20.020
instance and in the Court of Appeal, as to whether mere silence on the part of the defendant could amount to concealment for the purposes of this provision. However, the case law discussed in the earlier paragraphs of this chapter appears to establish, at least to the level of the Court of Appeal, that silence can amount to concealment. Reference may also be made to the earlier case of *Shaw v Shaw*,[54] where the Court of Appeal applied s.32 to an action for breach of promise of marriage by a woman whose purported husband had failed to tell her that he had a lawful wife living at the time of the marriage ceremony. More recent authority, however, casts some doubt on this. In *Ayles v LAH Ayles Ltd*[55] the defendant built a house for the plaintiff's predecessors in title. Defects appeared in the balconies. Under the NHBC Agreement there were remedies, but the plaintiff wanted to claim for inconvenience suffered. Originally the claim was pleaded in tort, but during the case the decision in *D. & F. Estates* made clear that the plaintiff could not hope to succeed in tort. Application was made to amend to plead in

---

[49] [1971] 1 All E.R. 747, CA.
[50] For the other point in this case, see para.20.018.
[51] [1972] 1 Q.B. 373.
[52] (1990) 15 Con. L.R. 1, Judge Esyr Lewis Q.C.
[53] [1972] 1 All E.R. 626, Thesiger J.; [1973] 1 All E.R. 206, CA.
[54] [1954] 2 Q.B. 429.
[55] February 8, 1990, Lloyd L.J. as single judge of CA.

contract. Questions of privity arose, but Lloyd L.J. relied instead on the limitation point. The house was built in 1973, the application to amend was dated 1989. Apparently the contract claim was hopelessly out of time, but the plaintiff relied on s.32(1)(b). The plaintiff argued that the defendants had been in possession of a letter from the architects in 1975, admitting design errors, and had not disclosed it to the plaintiff, and that the defects in the balconies had been physically covered up. It was held that the defendants were under no obligation to disclose the content of the letter, so that there had been no fraudulent concealment here (this relates to 1975, when the test was fraudulent, rather than deliberate concealment) and that nothing had been physically covered up, so that this could not amount to concealment.

This case appears to take a more sensible approach to the question of concealment, which ought, it is submitted, to be regarded as requiring something more than mere silence. That approach has been reinforced more recently in *Foreman v O'Driscoll & Partners*,[56] where it was said that:

"Initial negligence by a solicitor, followed by further negligence in not informing his client of that negligence, whether by act or omission initially, does not suffice to constitute deliberate concealment."

Williams v Fanshaw Porter & Hazelhurst (a firm)[57] raises again the difficult question of whether there can be deliberate concealment where a professional adviser fails to tell his client of a breach of duty which he has committed. The Court of Appeal appears to suggest that where the defendant is in fact aware of the breach, his failure to disclose it to his client may amount to deliberate concealment. It is suggested that this must be treated with some caution. A mere failure to disclose should not be treated as concealment; however, there will be cases, of which this is one, where the defendant is forced to resort to actual misstatement in order to avoid disclosing the breach. It is the misstatement which amounts to concealment, not the failure to disclose.

Professional negligence cases

20.021 In recent years much controversy has centred on a number of negligence cases involving advice given by solicitors. The cases[58] have been argued on the question of whether the cause of action accrues as soon as the advice is acted upon, or only at the (usually later) date when the resulting loss can be

---

[56] [2000] 1 Lloyd's Rep. 720, N. Baker Q.C.
[57] [2004] EWCA Civ 157, [2004] 2 All ER 616.
[58] Some of the best known are *Forster v Outred* [1982] 1 W.L.R. 86, CA; *Ferrier v D.W. Moore & Co. Ltd* [1988] 1 W.L.R. 267; *Baker v Ollard & Bentley* (1982) 126 S.J. 593, CA. The question of the date at which the cause of action accrues is dealt with in Ch.5

quantified. A question which has rarely been explored in these cases[59] is whether the provisions of s.32 might come to the aid of a claimant. In most such cases the origin of the difficulty lies in the failure of the solicitor to explain to the client some aspect of the consequences of the advice given. The usual reason for this is that the solicitor has not himself appreciated that consequence, but if it is said that he is negligent in not appreciating it, it must follow that he has at least constructive knowledge of it. However, it may be said that the defendant has not "deliberately" concealed the fact because that requires him to have some consciousness of it.

As a matter of principle it must be right that a client is not required to retain one solicitor to check on the work of another, but is entitled to assume without more that the first solicitor's work has been competently done.[60] There appears to be only one case where the question of fraud has been pleaded[61]; there, the defendant solicitor had inserted a rent review clause into the counterpart of a lease after its execution. Hirst J. held that the defendant had not acted unconscionably, having honestly believed that the omission was a genuine error, and that in making the alteration he was acting in accordance with the wishes of both parties, so that s.32 did not apply. The matter was considered at more length in the unreported decision of the Court of Appeal, which upheld the decision of Hirst J. on the ground (at least as to this point) that the defendant could not be said deliberately to have concealed the plaintiff's right of action, since he was by definition unaware that the plaintiff had any right of action. The logic of this approach is difficult to refute, though the result is regrettable. If this decision is applied in subsequent cases, it seems that the result will be to deprive the claimant of the opportunity to plead s.32, except perhaps in the case where he can show that at some later point the solicitor became aware of the possibility that he had been negligent. In such circumstances solicitors in particular may face a difficult dilemma. They need to alert the client to the wisdom of seeking alternative advice, but they need to do it without admitting negligence.[62] In *Khan v National Union of Rail, Maritime and Transport Workers*[63] the Court of Appeal thought it arguable that a letter from a firm of solicitors which advised the claimant to go elsewhere because her trade union had withdrawn its support, but which contained no reference to any question of negligence, might amount to a concealment under s.32(1)(b). This decision is perhaps somewhat generous to the claimant, but could possibly be justified on the very narrow basis that the letter

20.022

---

[59] With the exception of the unreported Court of Appeal decision in *Costa v Georghiou*, which is discussed later in this paragraph, and see fn.49.

[60] See further McGee (1988) 104 L.Q.R. 367.

[61] *Costa v Georghiou* (1984) 134 New L.J. 82, Hirst J.; the decision of the Court of Appeal is Unreported.

[62] Because such an admission may have an adverse effect on their professional indemnity cover.

[63] January 17, 2000, Unreported, CA.

said nothing at all about any other issue. It is more usual in such circumstances for the solicitor to write a letter alluding to the facts which might amount to negligence[64] and to suggest that the client seeks alternative advice. It is submitted that such a letter could not amount to a concealment.

Section 32(2)

20.023   This provides that deliberate commission of a breach of duty in circumstances where it is unlikely to be discovered for some time is to be treated as deliberate concealment of the facts involved in that breach of duty. In recent years this obscure provision has been interpreted by the courts in a way which for some time threw the law on deliberate concealment into a state of turmoil, from which it has only very recently been rescued. There are three decisions which require to be considered: *Brocklesby v Armitage & Guest*,[65] *Cave v Robinson, Jarvis and Rolf*[66] and *Liverpool R.C. Archdiocesen Trustees v Goldberg*.[67] In these cases it was initally held that a breach of duty is committed "deliberately" in any case where the defendant is aware that he is doing the act in question. It is not necessary for him to be aware that what he is doing is a breach of duty. This very broad construction of the word "deliberate" brought a vastly increased range of cases within s.32(1)(b), for the consequence would have been that virtually all negligent acts would have been regarded as deliberate for these purposes. Fortunately *Cave v Robinson, Jarvis and Rolf* was taken to the House of Lords, which decided in April 2002[68] that the scope of s.32(2) should be narrowed. Lord Millett, with whom the other members of the Appellate Committee agreed, said:

> "In my opinion, section 32 deprives a defendant of a limitation defence in two situations: (i) where he takes active steps to conceal his own breach of duty after he has become aware of it; and (ii) where he is guilty of deliberate wrongdoing and conceals or fails to disclose it in circumstances where it is unlikely to be discovered for some time. But it does not deprive a defendant of a limitation defence where he is charged with negligence if, being unaware of his error or that he has failed to take proper care, there has been nothing for him to disclose."

This dictum draws an appropriate and welcome line under an unfortunate series of decisions which are best consigned to legal history.

---

[64] Here, the missing of a limitation period.
[65] [2001] 1 All E.R. 172 C.A.
[66] [2001] E.W.C.A. Civ. 245; [2001] L.R.P.N. 290, CA.
[67] [2001] 1 All E.R. 182.
[68] [2002] 1 W.L.R. 581 HL.

In *Giles v Rhind*[69] the Court of Appeal considered the meaning of the   **20.024**
phrase "breach of duty" in s.32(2) of the 1980 Act. The immediate context
was a claim under Insolvency Act 1986 s.423 (transactions at undervalue)
but the Court made some general comments on the term "breach of duty".
The expression:

"does not extend to any legal wrongdoing whatsoever, there had to be a
legal wrongdoing of the kind that could properly be raised in an action to
which s 32 applied, which could be termed the 'wider reading' of 'breach
of duty'. Thus it would not cover legal wrongs which were not justici-
able. Nevertheless, it does include a claim under s 423 of the 1986 Act.
The right to relief under s 423 did not depend on showing the victim was
a person to whom some duty in contract or tort or some fiduciary duty
was owed. Furthermore, the expression 'concealed' in s 32(1)(b) has to
bear its normal meaning, which is that something is actually hidden from
view. This last point appears somewhat problematic, because, as is
pointed out in the main text, concealment can be both literal—the physical hiding of an object—or figurative—the 'concealing' of a fact by, for
example, destroying evidence relating to it, or simply telling an untruth
about it.

The word 'duty' is an ordinary English word, meaning obligation or
constraint and could mean simply a breach of legal obligation or constraint. Therefore, the wider meaning to be given to it was a legitimate
meaning of breach of duty. Secondly, having regard to the mischief to
which s 32(2) was directed, it is unnecessary to show, where a person
knowingly committed a wrong, his active steps to conceal his wrongdoing. The general structure of the 1980 Act shows s 32(2) is consistent
with the wider meaning. Further, the fact that the expression 'breach of
duty' was used in another part of the statute in a different context did not
necessarily restrict the meaning of breach of duty in s 32(2). S 32 does not
require the phrase to be given a narrower meaning, namely a breach of
duty in a tortious or contractual sense or in the sense of a breach of an
equitable or fiduciary duty since that narrower meaning did not promote
any part of the statutory purpose of s 32. A transaction under s 423 was a
type of transaction of which there was likely to be concealment and thus
there would be a heightened policy reason for the applicant of s 32(2) to
claims under that section. If Parliament had created a cause of action
which applied over a long period of time and to a large variety of
transactions, it would be wrong for the Court of Appeal to impose an
indirect restriction on s 423 by excluding it from s 32(2) if that provision
would otherwise on its natural meaning apply to it. Consequently, the
court expressed the view that for s 32(2) to apply, (i) there must be

---

[69] [2008] EWCA Civ 118.

deliberate commission of an act; (ii) that act must amount to a breach of duty; and (iii) that breach of duty must occur in circumstances in which it is unlikely to be discovered for some time. If those ingredients are satisfied, then the next step is to go back to s 32(1)(b) and to identify the facts that are involved in the relevant breach of duty. After that, those facts can be tested against the right of action relied on in the proceedings. There is no need on an ordinary reading of s 32(1)(b) to show that the right of action was for breach of duty. All that it is necessary to show is that the relevant facts involved a breach of duty."

20.025   *Brown v Bird & Lovibond*[70] was a rare consideration of the meaning of the phrase "unlikely to be discovered for some time" in s.32(2). It was observed that the test is objective in that it does not matter whether the defendant thinks that the breach of duty is unlikely to be discovered for some time. The case also lends support to the idea that a solicitor's client can legitimately rely on the solicitor and is not required to check on the completeness or appropriateness of the solicitor's advice in order to be able to take advantage of s.32(1)(b).

Subsequent concealment

20.026   All the cases discussed so far in this section assume that the concealment will predate the accrual of the cause of action. The wording of s.32(1)(b) reflects that assumption. However, in *Sheldon v Outhwaite*[71] the House of Lords was confronted with a case where it was alleged that there had been deliberate concealment after the cause of action arose. The question was whether in these circumstances s.32(1)(b) operated to postpone the running of time. The obvious difficulty is that on the face of it time began to run when the cause of action accrued, there being at that point no relevant concealment. If s.32 was to have any operation, it could only be by suspending the running of time pending the concealment or by resetting the clock to zero. The former of these is inconsistent with general principles of the English law of limitations; moreover, neither possibility appears to accord with the words of s.32, which says that time "shall not start to run" in specified circumstances. The problem does not, of course, arise in relation to s.32(1)(a) or (c), where the necessary elements will always be in place no later than the date when the cause of action accrues. It is therefore not surprising that the Court of Appeal[72] should have taken the view that s.32(1)(b) had no operation in these circumstances. However, this decision was reversed by the House of Lords, which held, by a bare majority, that in

---

[70] [2002] EWHC 719 (QB) Robert Moxon-Browne Q.C.
[71] [1995] 2 All E.R. 558, HL.
[72] [1994] 4 All E.R. 481.

these circumstances time does not start to run until the concealment is reasonably discoverable.

It has been pointed out[73] that this formulation of the rule, which is the one chosen by the majority of the House of Lords, makes little sense; between the date when the cause of action accrues and the date of the concealment, time must run. Thus, the decision of the House of Lords really means that a subsequent concealment resets the clock to zero. It is not at all clear what the position would be if the concealment happened when the action was already barred. A strict application of the logic of the decision in *Sheldon v Outhwaite* would suggest that the clock was still reset, but it may be doubted whether a court would be prepared to go quite this far. One answer to the point is that there will be few cases where the concealment happens at so late a date, but the real answer is that the majority's approach to the interpretation of s.32(1)(b) is deeply unconvincing. *Sheldon v Outhwaite* reveals a defect in the drafting of s.32 which had never previously come to light, and the proper response would have been to say that the section does not cover the facts of that case. Admittedly, this might seem to work injustice in the particular case, but the unsustainable reasoning adopted by the majority causes more problems than it solves.

20.027

A further problem arises where the claimant is already aware of the relevant facts and the defendant then perpetrates some form of concealment. Common sense would dictate that the clock is not reset to zero in these circumstances, but *Sheldon v Outhwaite* is silent on the point. Some support for the obvious solution is provided by the decision of the Court of Appeal in *Biggs v Sotnicks (A Firm)*,[74] where claimants in a solicitors' negligence action had known all the relevant facts in 1991, although they had not received the solicitors' file until 1997. It was held that time ran from 1991. Peter Smith J. followed the same approach in *Bocardo SA v Star Energy UK Onshore Ltd*.[75]

20.028

Section 32 is available to extend time in the case of an application under s.246 of POCA (to which s.27A of the Limitation Act 1980 applies).[76] Although in that case Mitting J. at first instance held that s.32 was not applicable to claims under s.27A, it is hard to see how that could possibly have been right. As Waller LJ points out[77], s.32 applies to all claims for which a period of limitation is provided by pt I of the 1980 Act, and s.27A has been placed in Pt I.

20.029

More difficult and interesting questions arise on the question of how s.32 applies to an application by the Assets Recovery Agency. It appears that s.32(1)(a) will rarely be relevant because few applications will be based on

---

[73] McGee (1995) 111 L.Q.R 562.
[74] January 24, 2002, Unreported.
[75] [2008] EWHC 1756 (Ch).
[76] *Director of the Assets Recovery Agency v Szepietowski* [2007] EWCA Civ 766; for s.27A see para.27.034.
[77] At para.82.

fraud in the sense that fraud, as distinct from some form of dishonest conduct, is an essential element in the cause of action. Moreover, it may well be suggested that s.32(1)(a) deals only with the case where the action is based on a fraud committed against the claimant. Where the ARA is a claimant, it will usually be proceeding on the basis that the defendant has committed dishonest conduct, possibly involving fraud, against someone else.

The application of s.32(1)(b) also raises questions. There will again be the question of whether concealment from persons other than the ARA (for example, concealment from lenders in the context of mortgage fraud) can be within s.32(1)(b). This is essentially the same as the question raised above in relation to s.32(1)(a). There is also the question of concealment from the ARA once an investigation has started. This is more obviously within s.32(1)(b) but this concealment may happen after the limitation period has on the face of it expired. The answer to this point, in the present state of the law, appears to be that given in *Sheldon v Outhwaite*,[78] namely that in the event of concealment after the expiry of time (and assuming that the claimant has not in fact become aware of the relevant facts) time has never run. Wall L.J. acknowledges[79] that this is a surprising conclusion, but it is impossible to deny that this is what *Sheldon v Outhwaite* appears to decide.

There is a further point. If it is to be assumed (as s.316(3) of the Act requires) that Pt 5 of the Act (which creates the ARA) was in force at times prior to commencement for the purpose of deciding whether or not property was recoverable, that must assume the existence of the ARA with a cause of action to which prima facie the limitation would apply. If that is so, deliberate acts to conceal participation in any unlawful conduct must also be assumed to be acts of concealment from the ARA, as Waller L.J. points out[80]. That arguably extends the period to 12 years from the date of discovery or the date when with reasonable diligence the concealment could have been discovered.

These problems appear to arise from a combination of three factors—the retrospective nature of POCA, the failure to think through the consequences of this for limitation periods and the odd decision in *Sheldon v Outhwaite*.

---

[78] [1995] 2 All E.R. 558 H.L.
[79] At para.51.
[80] At para.59.

MISTAKE

Section 32(1)(c) extends the limitation period where the claimant's action is **20.030** for relief from the consequences of a mistake. This provision, which again dates from 1939, has received relatively little judicial attention since then,[81] though the equitable discretion to extend time in these cases, which the 1939 Act codified for the first time, was considered in *Baker v Courage & Co.*[82] Hamilton J. held that it is necessary to distinguish between cases where both parties are mistaken and cases where only one party is mistaken. In the former class of case, time will begin to run as soon as the mistake takes effect, for example on the payment of the money under a mistake. In the latter case, time will not start to run until the party seeking to set the transaction aside has knowledge of the mistake. It is necessary to consider whether this formulation of the law remains good under the 1980 Act. It is submitted that it does not.

Section 32 draws no distinction for these purposes between different classes of mistake—the only question is whether the claimant has discovered or could with reasonable diligence have discovered the mistake. Only when this condition is satisfied will time begin to run. In *Phillips-Higgins v Harper*[83] the plaintiff was employed as an assistant solicitor to the defendant, but was entitled to a share in the net profits. In 1951 disputes arose between the parties as to the amounts payable under this agreement for the years back to 1938. The plaintiff brought an action for an account, and, in order to circumvent the Limitation Act, pleaded s.32(1)(c). Pearson J. held that the provision was inapplicable, being restricted to cases where mistake is an essential ingredient of the cause of action, such as claims for the recovery back of money paid under a mistake or where a contract is alleged to be void for mistake. In the present case it was irrelevant whether the alleged underpayment had arisen from mistake or otherwise. His Lordship observed, obiter, that there is no provision in s.32 to deal with the case of mistaken (as distinct from fraudulent—now deliberate) concealment of facts relevant to the cause of action. *Deutsche Morgan Grenfell Group Plc v Inland Revenue Commissioners and the Attorney General*[84] concerned a claim by a taxpayer to recover payments of tax made under a mistake as to an aspect of revenue law. Park J. held that such an action could lie, as a consequence of the decision of the House of Lords in *Kleinwort Benson v Lincoln CC*[85] and that it was an action for relief from

---

[81] The most recent case is *West Sussex Properties Ltd v Chichester DC*, June 28, 2000, CA, where the mistake in question was the inclusion in a lease of a clause which failed to reflect accurately the intentions of the parties.

[82] [1910] 1 K.B. 56, Hamilton J.

[83] [1954] 1 Q.B. 411; [1954] 1 All E.R. 116.

[84] [2003] EWHC 1779 (Ch); [2003] 4 All E.R. 645; [2003] STC 1017 Park J.

[85] [1999] 2 A.C. 349 HL.

the consequences of a mistake within s.32(1)(c) of the 1980 Act. In the House of Lords Lord Walker[86] accepted, with some reservations the view of Pearson J. that s.32(1)(c) applies only where mistake is an essential ingredient of the cause of action.

20.031   Finance Act 2004 s.320 excludes the operation of s.32(1)(c) in relation to a mistake of law relating to a taxation matter under the care and management of the Commissioners of Inland Revenue.[87] This new rule applies to actions brought on or after September 8, 2003. In actions brought before that date, any part of the claim which would have been saved by s.32(1)(c) is treated as having been discontinued on the coming into force of the Finance Act 2004.[88] This provision was introduced to alter the consequences (at least from a limitation point of view) of the decision of the House of Lords in *Deutsche Morgan Grenfell Group plc v Her Majesty's Commissioners of Inland Revenue and another*,[89] where it was held that English law did recognise a claim in restitution to recover taxes paid under mistake of law.[90]

20.032   The requirement that mistake be an essential ingredient of the cause of action was considered again in *Singer v Harrison Clark (A Firm)*,[91] where the defendant solicitors had caused their clients to lose the benefit of an option to renew a lease through their failure to register it in time. The plaintiffs' attempt to rely on s.32(1)(c) was rejected, since it was irrelevant to the cause of action whether the omission had been deliberate or inadvertent. As the judge pointed out, it would be odd if the plaintiff were in a better position where the error is merely inadvertent than where it is deliberate. The most detailed judicial consideration of the ambit of this provision is to be found in the decision of Webster J. in *Peco Arts Inc. v Hazlitt Gallery*.[92] In 1970 the plaintiff bought a painting from the defendant, the attribution of the work being an express term of the contract. The work was examined in 1976 and again in 1981. Only on the latter occasion was it discovered to be a reproduction rather than an original. The plaintiff sought rescission of the contract of sale on the ground of mistake, and the defendant pleaded limitation.[93] The case turned mostly on whether the plaintiff could have discovered the mistake before 1981,[94] but Webster J.

---

[86] [200] UKHL 49 [2007] 1 AC 558 at paras 146-7.

[87] s.320(1).

[88] S.320(3).

[89] [2006] UKHL 49.

[90] Academic writing on the limitation aspects of this problems includes Hedley, "*Tax Wrongly Paid—Basis of Recovery—Limitation*" [2005] CLJ F296, Edelman, "*Limitation Periods and the Theory of Unjust Enrichment*" (2005) 68 MLR 848.

[91] April 15, 1987, Julian Jeffs Q.C., sitting as a Deputy Judge of the Chancery Division, Unreported.

[92] [1983] 3 All E.R. 193.

[93] The plea of the statute in response to a claim for an equitable remedy was probably inappropriate anyway—1980 Act s.36, and see per Webster J. at 199.

[94] See above, para.20.004.

also suggested, obiter, that s.32 might not apply to a mistaken bona fide attribution forming a term of the contract, nor to a case where only the seller is mistaken as to the attribution. The latter of these suggestions may readily be accepted—it may be said that the money is not paid in consequence of the mistake when the buyer has not made the mistake—but the former suggestion is more difficult. It is true that in such a case there is a remedy for breach of contract, but that is no reason why s.32 should not apply.

Unreasonable mistake

In *West Sussex Properties Ltd v Chichester DC*[95] the question arose whe- **20.033** ther the allegedly unreasonable character of the claimant's mistake could affect the availability of s.32(1)(c). Morritt L.J. said:

"No doubt the mistake precedes and is different from a failure to exercise reasonable diligence after it has been made. But there may well be cases in which there is a claim for relief from the consequences of a mistake which was honestly but very stupidly made. I see no reason why the continuation of the facts which gave rise to the mistake on the part of the claimant in the first place should not also support a finding of failure to exercise reasonable diligence immediately after the mistake occurred."

Wilful delay

In *Ridyard v Hoath*[96] one of the grounds on which the plaintiff sought to **20.034** have time extended in his favour was that the defendant had induced him to delay the commencement of proceedings by, inter alia, making representations that he was willing to negotiate an out-of-court settlement. The plaintiff argued that this brought the case within s.32, but Lloyd L.J. correctly pointed out that this section does not deal with cases of wilful delay and procrastination on the part of the defendant.

RELATIONSHIP WITH CONVERSION

In *Eddis v Chichester Constable*[97] Goff J. had to determine the limitation **20.035** consequences where the existence of an action for conversion is concealed

---

[95] June 28, 2000, Unreported, CA.
[96] June 23, 1987, Lloyd L.J. as single judge of the Court of Appeal, Unreported.
[97] [1969] 1 W.L.R. 385.

by the fraud of the defendant. The difficulty was that actions in respect of conversion are expressed by s.3 of the 1980 Act to become barred six years after the original conversion, and it was therefore argued that s.32 could have no application to such an action. It was accepted that before the 1939 Act (which first put the rules as to fraudulent concealment on a statutory footing) time would have run despite the fraudulent concealment. However, Goff J. held, with some hesitation, that the position is altered by the 1939 Act, so that s.32 can be used by the claimant in a case of conversion. The Court of Appeal[98] affirmed this decision,[99] whilst pointing to some defects in the drafting of the legislation as it then stood. The changes necessary to deal with these criticisms were enacted in s.32(3) and (4) of the 1980 Act, the provisions of which are considered below.[100]

POSITION OF THIRD PARTIES

20.036 Section 32(3) and (4) deals with the situation where an innocent third party has purchased property that is the subject of an action. For this purpose s.32(4) defines "innocent third party" as a purchaser who, in a case falling under s.32(1)(a) or (b), was not a party to the fraud (or the fraudulent concealment) and who at the time of the purchase had neither actual nor constructive knowledge of the fraud or the concealment. In the case of an action falling under s.32(1)(c), an innocent third party is a purchaser who at the time of the purchase had neither actual nor constructive knowledge of the mistake. Section 32(3) provides that s.32 shall not operate so as to allow the bringing of any action to recover any property (or the value of such property) or to enforce any charge, or set aside any transaction affecting any property, against the purchaser of any property where an innocent third party has acquired that property for valuable consideration since the transaction involving the fraud, concealment or mistake, as the case may be.

Recovery of property or its value

20.037 Once an innocent third party has intervened in the chain of ownership, the original owner can sue neither for the return of the property nor for damages for its conversion. The uncertainty about the possibility of an action for conversion was the point which exercised the Court of Appeal in *Eddis v Chichester Constable*,[101] and the 1980 Act clarified the law in the

---

[98] Lord Denning M.R., Winn and Fenton Atkinson L.JJ.
[99] [1969] 2 Ch. 345.
[100] See paras 20.036–20.038.
[101] [1969] 2 Ch. 345.

way which the Court had advocated, by providing expressly that the action for damages is also barred.[102]

Enforcing charges

Where, for example, a vendor has supplied goods to a company under a reservation of title clause, this may amount to a charge on those goods.[103] The right to enforce such a charge will not be protected by s.32 where the goods have at some subsequent stage come into the hands of an innocent third-party purchaser.

20.038

Setting aside transactions

A sale induced by fraud is likely to be voidable at the option of the party deceived, as may some transactions induced by mistake.[104] The effect of these words in s.32(3) is that the existence of the fraud, concealment or mistake will not prevent time from running in respect of an action to set aside such a transaction once an innocent third-party purchaser has intervened. One puzzling point here is to know what limitation period is being extended in these cases. The action to set aside a contract is apparently not an action founded on simple contract within s.5, since the whole basis of the claim is that no full valid contract was ever formed. If it were such an action, then the six-year time-limit could be applied only by analogy, since s.36 makes this one of the time-limits which do not generally apply in actions for equitable relief. It may therefore appear that no limit contained in the 1980 Act applies to the case, in which event the reliance on s.32 is inappropriate. This would have the odd consequence of rendering the reference in s.32 to actions for relief from the consequences of a mistake largely irrelevant. It therefore appears that these actions must be treated as contractual or quasi-contractual for these purposes, so that the provisions of s.32 are being applied by analogy. This is a convenient solution, though it is submitted that it is conceptually unsound.

20.039

---

[102] The confusion under the old law had turned on the now obsolete distinction between conversion and detinue.

[103] *Borden (U.K.) Ltd v Scottish Timber Products* [1981] Ch. 25; *Re Bond Worth Ltd* [1980] Ch. 228.

[104] *Solle v Butcher* [1950] 1 K.B. 650, CA.

Who is protected?

20.040 It is important to observe that the right of action protected by s.32 is permanently lost once the property in question has been acquired for valuable consideration by an innocent third party. This is so even if the person in whom the property is presently vested is not an innocent third party within the meaning of s.32(4).

Claiming through another

20.041 The protection of s.32(3) extends to any innocent third-party purchaser, or anyone "claiming through" such a purchaser. This expression is defined by s.38(5) of the 1980 Act, which provides that A is treated as claiming through B if he became entitled by, through, or under, the act of B. The difficulty is to know whether a purchaser is treated as "claiming through" all previous owners, or only through his own immediate vendor. Danckwerts J. in *G.L. Baker Ltd v Medway Building and Supplies Ltd*[105] supported the former interpretation, and this was approved, obiter, and with some hesitation, by Lord Denning M.R. and Winn L.J. in *Eddis v Chichester Constable*.[106] There is no reported authority on the point since the 1980 Act, but it is submitted that the above dicta are correct, so that the intervention of an innocent third-party purchaser anywhere in the chain deprives the original owner of the benefit of s.32.

THE LATENT DAMAGE ACT 1986

20.042 Section 2 of the Latent Damage Act 1986 adds s.32(5) to the Limitation Act 1980. This provides that ss.14A and 14B of the 1980 Act (as added by the LDA 1986) do not apply to any case falling within s.32(1)(b), i.e. cases where any fact relevant to the claimant's action has been deliberately concealed from him by the defendant. It is to be noted that the exclusion of these two sections does not extend to cases within s.32(1)(a) or (c). Accordingly, s.2 of the 1980 Act is the appropriate section for determining the applicable limitation period in such a case. Therefore the claimant will have six years from the earliest date when the cause of action was reasonably discoverable, rather than the three allowed by s.14A. In addition the 15-year longstop period applicable under s.14A[107] will have no relevance in these cases.

---

[105] [1958] 1 W.L.R. 1216.
[106] [1969] 2 Ch. 345, CA.
[107] See Ch.6.

THE CONSUMER PROTECTION ACT 1987

The Consumer Protection Act 1987, which is dealt with extensively in **20.043**
Ch.7, creates a new right of action, with its own limitation periods. One of
these periods is a 10-year longstop, measured from the date on which the
product in question is put into circulation. The Act also inserts s.32(4A)
into the 1980 Act. This provision deals with the relationship between
extension of time under s.32 and the longstop provision. Its effect is that the
extension of time under s.32 can never be used to allow an action to be
brought after the expiry of the longstop. Thus the longstop overrides s.32.

THE LAW COMMISSION'S PROPOSALS

It is readily apparent that the adoption of a general discoverability test **20.044**
would radically reduce the significance of s.32 of the 1980 Act, since most
cases falling within that section could be dealt with on the basis that the
date of discoverability did not arrive until the claimant knew the material
facts. The difficult question remaining in this area concerns the relationship
between fraud, deliberate concealment and mistake on the one hand and
the proposed new longstop on the other. The question arises in the existing
law in relation to latent damage and actions under the CPA 1987, both of
which have a longstop. The Commission's proposal is that deliberate
concealment of material facts by the defendant should override the longstop, but that the longstop should not be overridden merely because the
action is based on fraud or is for relief from the consequences of a mistake.
This proposal may be considered to be justified on the basis that under the
new regime disapplication of the longstop will be a wholly exceptional
event, warranted only where the defendant has been guilty of unconscionable conduct specifically aimed at making it difficult for the claimant
to bring the action in good time.

CHAPTER 21

Pleading Questions

This chapter examines some of the issues which arise with regard to the **21.001**
pleading of a limitation point. The first point that must be made is that
limitation is a defence which must be pleaded specifically[1]—the court will
not of its own motion take the point that the plaintiff's claim is out of time.
This point was established very soon after the passing of the first Limitation
Act in *Thursby v Warren*[2] and *Stile v Finch*.[3]

HOW TO PLEAD

The plea of the Limitation Act should be raised expressly and unambigu- **21.002**
ously.[4] However, it is sufficient to state the fact of raising the plea—the
burden of proof on this point will then normally be transferred to the
claimant to show that the action is not time-barred.[5]

WHEN TO PLEAD

On receiving a statement of case which presents a claim to which he wishes **21.003**
to plead limitation, the defendant has a number of options available to him.
First, he may apply under CPR to have the pleading struck out as disclosing
no cause of action. Secondly, he may deliver a defence and then seek,
normally at case-management stage, to have the limitation point tried as a
preliminary issue with a view to obtaining summary judgment under CPR
Pt 24. Thirdly, he may allow the action to take its ordinary course, reser-

---

[1] *Ronex Properties Ltd v John Laing Construction Ltd* [1983] 1 Q.B. 393 at 404; CPR
16PD14.1.
[2] (1628) Cro.Car.159.
[3] (1634) Cro.Car.384.
[4] CPR 16PD para.13.1.
[5] See below, para.21.010.

ving the limitation defence to the full trial. As appears below, it is not normally proper to leave the matter until the closing speeches of the trial. The following paragraphs explore the tactical implications of these options, as well as the ways in which the exercise of them is restricted by the practice of the courts.

CPR 3.4

21.004   CPR 3.4 provides:

> "(2) The court may strike out a statement of case if it appears to the court—
>
> (a) that the statement of case discloses no reasonable grounds for bringing or defending the claim;
> (b) that the statement of case is an abuse of the court's process or is otherwise likely to obstruct the just disposal of the proceedings; or
> (c) that there has been a failure to comply with a rule, practice direction or court order."

There is extensive authority on the general use of the predecessor of these provisions, RSC, Ord.18, r.19,[6] but the wording is not identical and, as so often, it is dangerous to assume that the former practice has survived unchanged. The court may made an order under (a) or (b) of its own motion, though it is suggested that in a limitation context it is most unlikely to do so, save perhaps where the claim is on its face time-barred and the claimant makes no attempt to address the limitation issues. Under the old rules it was suggested in *Newell v Therm-A-Stor*,[7] that an application of this kind by a defendant should not normally be made until the pleadings have closed, since it is necessary to be clear about what is and is not in the pleadings.

21.005   Certainly, it can only be in the most blatant cases that an application under this paragraph is appropriate to a limitation defence. The test is to be found in the speech of Lord Bridge of Harwich in *Lonrho Plc v Fayed*.[8] The defendant must show that the claimant's claim is obviously doomed to fail. It may be said that the only such cases will be those where it appears from the terms of the statement of claim that the action is time-barred, and the claimant has not adduced any argument to show why the apparent barring

---

[6] Discussed in previous editions of this book.
[7] January 17, 1990, CA, Unreported.
[8] [1992] 1 A.C. 448 at 470. See also *Sion v Hampstead HA*, *The Times*, June 10, 1994, CA.

of the action should not prevent him from bringing it.[9] This view was adopted by the Court of Appeal in *Ronex Properties Ltd v John Laing Construction Ltd,*[10] where the point was made that a statement of claim which pleads only an action which is time-barred does normally disclose a cause of action, at least in those cases where the expiry of the limitation period serves only to bar the plaintiff's remedy rather than to extinguish his right. Another interesting case in this connection is *F. v Wirral Metropolitan BC and Liverpool City Council.*[11] This was an action for interference with parental rights. The Court of Appeal eventually held that no such tort existed, but there were incidental limitation questions. The Court of Appeal criticised the use of an Ord.18, r.19 application in this context. Although the same points are apparently valid under the CPR, it may be noted that the use of this provision would appear to be appropriate in cases where it is to be argued that the law simply does not recognise the claimant's cause of action. An unusual example of an action which was held to be abusive for limitation reasons occurred in *Pickthall v Hill Dickinson LLP,*[12] where the claimant had issued proceedings although the cause of action was at the time vested in his trustee in bankruptcy. This was done because the end of the limitation period was rapidly approaching. Although he had every intention of acquiring the right of action, the Court of Appeal nevertheless held that the action was an abuse of process.

The alternative procedure under CPR r.3.4(2) is to allege that the bringing of the action is an abuse of the process of the court. However, this will not normally succeed where the only basis for the application is that the claim is time-barred—it is not as a general proposition an abuse to bring an action on a time-barred claim, since there is always the possibility that the defendant will choose not to plead the statute. Consequently, an application on this ground will succeed only if the defendant is able to show something more, such as that a previous action on the same facts has been dismissed for disobedience to a peremptory order of the court[13]—mere dismissal for want of prosecution is insufficient.[14] The inevitable conclusion is that reliance on CPR r.3.4(2) will very rarely be appropriate,[15] and the judicial reluctance to use this provision will become virtually insurmountable if the plaintiff evinces an intention to rely on fraud under s.32 of the

21.006

---

[9] See, e.g., *Dawson v Spain-Gower* (October 18, 1988, CA, Unreported); *Cromlech Property Co. Ltd v Costain Construction Co. Ltd* (1986) 10 Con.L.R. 110, Judge Esyr Lewis; and *Newell v Therm-A-Stor* (January 17, 1990, CA, Unreported).

[10] [1983] Q.B. 398; see also *Dawkins v Penrhyn (Lord)* (1878) 4 App.Cas. 51, HL; *Dismore v Milton* [1938] 3 All E.R. 762, CA.

[11] *F v Wirral Metropolitan Borough Council and Liverpool City Council* [1991] 2 W.L.R. 1132, CA.

[12] [2009] EWCA Civ 543.

[13] *Janov v Morris* [1981] 1 W.L.R. 1389, CA; *Palmer v Brown* (1986) 83 L.S.Gaz. 125

[14] cf. *Birkett v James* [1978] A.C. 297, HL.

[15] For a rare example see *National Graphical Association v Thimbleby* (1984) 25 Build.L.R.91.

1980 Act.[16] It therefore seems that at least in relation to limitation CPR r.3.4(2) is a fairly good match for the old RSC, Ord.18, r.19.

Preliminary issues

21.007 This is perhaps the most common way of treating a limitation point, but the introduction of the CPR has made at least one significant change in the form of the provision in CPR Pt 24 that a defendant may apply for summary judgment. Preliminary points as to limitation are not always intended to lead to summary judgment, for they may relate to only part of the claim. Moreover, a decision in favour of the claimant may mean only that one obstacle to the claim has been overcome. However, there are certainly cases where the limitation defence, if it succeeds, is a knockout blow, and in such cases an application for summary judgment based on limitation may well be appropriate. Summary judgment applications cannot be made until the defence or an acknowledgement of service has been filed unless the court gives permission.[17] The framing of a preliminary issue may be proposed at a case-management conference, or the defendant may simply issue an application for summary judgment. The test is that set out in CPR r.24.2:

> The court may give summary judgment against a claimant or defendant on the whole of a claim or on a particular issue if—
>
> (a) it considers that—
>
> > (i) that claimant has no real prospect of succeeding on the claim or issue; or
> > (ii) that defendant has no real prospect of successfully defending the claim or issue; and
>
> (b) there is no other compelling reason why the case or issue should be disposed of at a trial.

The test of "no real prospect" is a difficult one for a defendant to surmount, for in effect he has to show that the claimant is bound to fail on the case as pleaded and set out in the witness statements—oral evidence is not normally received on a summary judgment application. In addition, it must be recognised that there are difficult tactical issues here. A defendant who has a limitation defence of uncertain strength may well prefer to preserve it in being as a bargaining counter, and may therefore be opposed to a preliminary issue. Conversely, a defendant who regards the limitation point as

---

[16] *Cromlech Property Co. Ltd v Costain Construction Co. Ltd* (1986) 10 Con.L.R. 110, Judge Esyr Lewis.
[17] CPR 24.4.

a strong one is likely to favour a preliminary issue. Naturally, the plaintiff's interests are the exact opposite of this. The granting of the application is a matter for the court's discretion, and a preliminary issue will not be ordered unless it appears that this is a convenient way to proceed, having regard to the facts and circumstances of the case.[18] The problems are well illustrated by *National Bank of Commerce v National Westminster Bank*,[19] where Webster J. observed that in all likelihood the trial of a preliminary point of law had not helped the speedy or just resolution of the case. The difficulty which Webster J. faced was that there was insufficient evidence before him to allow an answer to the questions. The evidence could not be supplemented because on the trial of a preliminary point it is necessary to proceed only upon the facts as pleaded in the case.

The full trial

The final possibility is to reserve consideration of the limitation point for the full trial. This is most likely to happen where the limitation point is not particularly strong or where it relates only to a part of the claimant's claim, since there is then less advantage in having the limitation issue resolved at the outset. At the same time the postponing of the issue in this way is liable to have costs implications, and the parties should therefore consider the position carefully before choosing this solution.   **21.008**

Closing arguments

In *Lewis v Hackney LBC*[20] the defendants did not initially plead limitation, but sought to rely on it in closing arguments. The judge declined to let them do so. The Court of Appeal held that this was a matter for the judge's discretion, and declined to interfere. The case illustrates the importance of making a timely decision to plead limitation if it is desired to do so. There can be no guarantee that a late plea will be allowed, and the case shows that there is very little prospect of a successful appeal against the trial judge's refusal of leave. Presumably the Court of Appeal would interfere if satisfied that the judge had exercised the discretion wholly unreasonably, but not otherwise. This rule is perhaps even stronger under the CPR than it was under the former rules because of 16PD 14.1 which explicitly mentions limitation as a matter which must be pleaded, whereas formerly this requirement was assumed to derive from RSC Ord.18, r.8, which merely   **21.009**

---

[18] *Chelmsford DC v Evers* (1986) 4 Con.L.R. 98, Judge Newey.
[19] [1990] 2 Lloyd's Rep. 514, Webster J.
[20] April 9, 1990, CA, Unreported.

required the pleading of anything which might take the other side by surprise.

BURDEN OF PROOF

21.010 The question of the onus may be important in cases involving the Limitation Act; there may be considerable difficulty in establishing exactly when a cause of action accrued,[21] and the fate of a limitation defence may then depend on the court's view as to the onus of proof. The rules as to burden of proof in this context are curiously obscure. It is commonly said that the rule of English law is that he who alleges must prove,[22] but this does not resolve the point, for it is then necessary to decide who is alleging. The question of limitation will almost invariably be raised by the defendant, and it might therefore be thought that he bears the burden of proving that the action is out of time.

There is, however, authority that once the defendant raises limitation as a defence it is for the plaintiff to show that the action is not barred.[23] In the early case of *Hurst v Parker*[24] it was held that the burden of proof lay on the plaintiff, whilst in *Wilby v Henman*[25] the decision was that the burden shifted to the plaintiff once the defendant raised the question of limitation. More recently, in *Ketteman v Hansel Properties Ltd*,[26] Lawton L.J. expressed the view that it was for the claimant to prove that the action accrued within the statutory time-limit. However, there have been occasional suggestions to the opposite effect. In *Barclays Bank v Walters*[27] it was held that a defendant who wished to rely on limitation must show that the claimant's right of action had accrued more than six years previously. It is submitted that the resolution of this point lies in understanding the nature of the burden which each party bears. It must be correct to say that the burden is initially on the defendant to plead limitation, but thereafter it is for the claimant to show when time began to run, either by reference to the date when the cause of action accrued, or, if appropriate, by reference to a disability of his or to fraud, concealment or mistake. As a practical and

---

[21] Good examples of the difficulties may be found in some of the leading cases on damage to buildings, such as *Pirelli General Cable Works Ltd v Oscar Faber & Partners* [1983] 2 A.C. 1, HL, and *London Congregational Union v Harriss & Harriss* [1988] 1 All E.R. 15, CA, where the question of burden of proof ultimately proved decisive.

[22] See, e.g. Rupert Cross and Colin Tapper, *Cross & Tapper on Evidence* (11th edn 2007), pp.110–130.

[23] Most recently *MAC Hotels Ltd v Rider Levett Bucknall UK Ltd* [2010] EWHC 767 (TCC), where Judge Havelock-Allen cited this paragraph with approval.

[24] (1817) 1 B. & Ald. 759; 106 E.R. 34.

[25] (1834) 2 Cr. & M. 658; 149 E.R. 924.

[26] [1985] 1 All E.R. 352, CA; the later decision of the House of Lords, reported at [1988] 1 All E.R. 38, does not touch on this point.

[27] *The Times*, October 20, 1988, CA.

tactical point, if the claimant is able to bring evidence establishing prima facie that the limitation period has not yet expired, then it will be necessary for the defendant to rebut this if he is to succeed on the limitation point, but the correct formulation is nevertheless to say that the burden of proof remains on the claimant. Indeed this is well illustrated by the decision of the Court of Appeal in *London Congregational Union v Harriss & Harriss*, where it was ultimately impossible to establish clearly when the cause of action accrued, and the defendants succeeded on that ground.[28] In *MAC Hotels Ltd v Rider Levett Bicknall Ltd*[29] Judge Havelock-Allan approved the view expressed here that it is for the claimant to prove that he has a cause of action which is not statute-barred[30]

It appears that the question of the burden of proof may be different as **21.011** between different limitation provisions. Therefore, in *Beer v London Borough of Waltham Forest*[31] Hodgson J. assumed that on an application under s.33 of the 1980 Act for the disapplication of a time-limit under s.11 or s.12 the burden of proof lies on the claimant. This assumption is clearly correct, since this is a situation where the plaintiff is seeking the exercise of a discretion in his favour, but this argument equally clearly does not apply to other limitation cases. In *Holland v Yates Building Co. Ltd*[32] it was held, following *Kennett v Brown*,[33] that in personal injury cases involving a second defendant, where the first defendant claims contribution from the second defendant, it is not appropriate to attempt to determine the limitation issue until the defendant raises it. The point here is that the first defendant may need the court to exercise its discretion under s.33 of the Limitation Act 1980 if the second defendant chooses to plead the statute. It might therefore be thought that the first defendant should, in formulating his claim, deal with the limitation point and make an immediate s.33 application. However, the Court of Appeal held that this is not so, since there is no absolute bar on bringing a statute-barred action. In the present case the principles set out in *Kennett v Brown* were held to apply equally to cases not involving personal injuries. Consequently, there is no need at the outset for the claimant to seek to show that the action is not time-barred. It will be sufficient for him to deal with this point if and when the defendant raises it. By contrast in *Driscoll-Varley v Parkside HA*,[34] Hidden J. held

---

[28] This decision must also be regarded as disapproving the approach adopted at first instances in *EDAC v William Moss Group* (1985) 2 Con.L.R. 1 and *Perry v Tendring DC* (1985) 3 Con.L.R. 74.

[29] [2010] EWHC 767 TCC.

[30] At para.42.

[31] December 16, 1987, Hodgson J., Unreported.

[32] *The Times*, December 5, 1989, CA.

[33] [1988] 2 All E.R. 600; although some aspects of this decision were overruled in *Redpath Dorman Long v Welsh Development Agency* [1994] 4 All E.R. 10, this point appears unaffected.

[34] January 15, 1990, Hidden J.

that it is initially for the plaintiff to show accrual within three years, after which the defendant must disprove this. Where it is obvious that limitation is an issue it may be sensible to plead this at the outset, since this is likely to further the overriding objective by clarifying the issues between the parties at the earliest possible date. In *Society of Lloyd's v Laws*[35] it was held in relation to the 15-year longstop under the Latent Damage Act 1986[36] that the burden is on the claimant once the defendant raises the issue.

21.012   The apparent confusion between the various cases rests, it is submitted, largely upon misapprehensions about what is involved in discharging the burden of proof and a failure to understand the difference between steps which need to be taken to discharge that burden and steps which it is practically convenient to take. Consideration of the burden of proof must begin with the proposition that it is for the claimant in a civil action to establish his case on the balance of probabilities. In order to do this he must convince the court of all the necessary elements of his cause of action. However, in those cases where the expiry of time does not extinguish the claimant's rights it is not an essential element at the outset to show that the action is not time-barred. This will only become essential if the defendant chooses to plead the statute. Thus, it is submitted that it is not strictly necessary for the claimant in such cases to begin by establishing the date of accrual. The position is probably different where the expiry of the limitation period extinguishes the claimant's rights, since it appears that in such cases the court must take the limitation point of its own motion (though CPR 16PD 14.1 still requires that the statute be pleaded in such cases). Once the defendant does plead the statute, it will probably become necessary for the claimant to rebut this plea. If there is a reply to the defence, then the plea of the statute can be expressly traversed, but this is probably not necessary, since failure to traverse the contents of the Defence is not treated as equivalent to admitting them: it would be sufficient to bring evidence to rebut the plea at trial.

21.013   This line of reasoning appears to explain *Holland v Yates*. Nevertheless, it is submitted that the court in *Driscoll-Varley* gave sensible advice, not as to the legal position, but as to the prudent way to proceed: where it is obvious that the action is on its face time-barred, and that a plea of the statute is reasonably to be expected, it is desirable, from the point of view of clarifying the issues between the parties at an early stage, that the statement of claim should deal with the limitation argument, pleading those facts which are to be relied upon to show that the action is not in reality time-barred. The distinction between that which is legally necessary and that which is prudent may be illustrated in this way: suppose a case where the action is apparently out of time. The claimant neglects to deal with the limitation point in the particulars of claim, but, contrary to reasonable

---

[35] [2004] EWHC 71 Cooke J.
[36] As to which see generally Ch.6.

462

expectations, the defendant does not plead the statute. The court will not dismiss the claim on limitation grounds, for the claimant has not neglected to do anything which was legally required. By contrast, if the defendant does plead the statute, then the claimant will need to rebut this plea.

Procedural delays and the burden of proof

The two preceding paragraphs have dealt with the burden of proof in **21.014** substantive limitation defences, but the problem can also arise where the defendant seeks to have an action dismissed for want of prosecution. There are two possible issues here. The first is as to the burden of proof for securing the exercise of the court's discretion to dismiss the action, whilst the second is as to the burden of proof in deciding whether time has in fact expired, since it is well settled that different principles apply to applications for dismissal after the expiry of the limitation period.[37] Neither of these issues appears to have received express consideration in any reported case, but the law appears to be as follows. So far as the exercise of discretion is concerned, it must be for the defendant, who is by definition the party seeking the exercise of that discretion, to satisfy the court that the necessary conditions are satisfied. Clearly, this task will become easier as the delay involved grows longer. As regards establishing whether the primary limitation period has expired, the position is less clear. The burden will initially fall on the defendant again, since it will be he who wishes to show that time has expired. As a matter of practice, however, there will inevitably be cases where at first sight time seems to have expired or where the defendant is able to advance a strong argument to that effect. In such cases the tactical burden will necessarily shift to the claimant, who will need to rebut the initial appearance if he is to avoid the consequences of the court finding that time has expired.

FOREGOING THE STATUTE

It is generally assumed that on the expiry of the limitation period the **21.015** defendant has an absolute right to plead the statute.[38] However, there is some authority which suggests that in certain circumstances this right may

---

[37] *Department of Transport v Chris Smaller (Transport) Ltd* [1989] 1 All E.R. 897, HL.
[38] Perhaps the most explicit examples of this assumption are to be found in the cases on amending the pleadings out of time: see paras 22.033-22.034

be lost.[39] Three specific matters require to be considered, the effect of prior admissions, the possibility of contracting out of the statute and estoppel.

The effect of prior admissions

21.016 This point has been considered in two reported cases. In *Wright v John Bagnall & Sons Ltd*[40] the plaintiff sued his employers under the Workmen's Compensation Acts. The defendants admitted liability, but each party reserved the right to go to court to have the quantum of damages assessed. This latter process of course necessitated the issue of a writ, and the employers pleaded that the action was out of time. The Court of Appeal held that the unambiguous admission of liability precluded the employers from relying on the statute. This decision was approved and followed in *Rendall v Hill's Dry Docks and Engineering Co.*[41] It is not entirely clear from these decisions whether the fact of admission is to be treated as amounting to a contract not to plead the statute, or whether it precludes the plea on more general equitable grounds. The former possibility is considered in the next paragraph. More recently, in *Cotterell (Executrix of Reece Deceased) v Leeds Day (A Firm)*[42] doubt was cast on the proposition that a mere admission could preclude reliance on the expiry of the limitation period. It is probably fair to say that in the earlier cases the factual context justified a finding that the admission was coupled with an agreement or an estoppel.

Contracting out of the statute

21.017 In *Lubovsky v Snelling*[43] the plaintiff's husband was killed in a road accident caused by the defendant's negligence, and she wished to proceed under the Fatal Accidents Acts. The defendant's solicitors, acting on the instructions of the defendant's insurers, wrote a letter to the plaintiff in which they promised that liability would not be contested, but reserving the question of quantum. A writ was later issued within the limitation period, but this was defective as the plaintiff had not at that stage taken out letters of administration to her husband's estate. By the time this error had been corrected, and a new writ issued, time had expired, and the insurers sought to plead the statute. The Court of Appeal held that they were unable to do so

---

[39] It is assumed here that time has genuinely expired. Therefore this section does not deal with matters such as fraud or acknowledgment, which have the effect of extending the limitation period.
[40] [1900] 2 Q.B. 240, CA.
[41] [1900] 2 Q.B. 245, CA.
[42] December 21, 1999, Jonathan Parker J., Unreported.
[43] [1944] K.B. 44.

the statute. The Court of Appeal held that they were unable to do so because of the promise in their earlier letter that they would not contest liability. Although it was clear that a writ would have to be issued in order to resolve the dispute over quantum, the date of this writ was immaterial because of the insurers' promise. The reasoning on this last point is perhaps not entirely convincing. There had been no promise to meet the claim in full, merely a promise not to contest liability. It might therefore have been thought that the need to issue a writ in time remained. The difficulty with this approach is that it would then allow the insurers to deny liability. The promise in their letter would be construed as meaning that liability would not be denied so long as a writ was issued in time, whereas the decision in the case did not prevent them from disputing the quantum, but did prevent them from denying liability entirely. It is helpful to contrast that case with *Cotterell (Executrix of Reece Deceased) v Leeds Day (A Firm)*,[44] where there was an admission of liability, but it was held that there had been no agreement not to plead limitation, despite the defendant's assurance that the claimant would not suffer loss financially because the defendant was insured. In effect Jonathan Parker J. held that this assurance meant only that the claimant would not suffer loss provided that proceedings were issued within the limitation period. It may fairly be said that claimants need to be very wary about relying on apparent assurances from defendants. In the absence of clear words it seems unlikely that an estoppel will be found. In *Clewley v Blake Lapthorn*[45] the claimant sued his former solicitors for professional negligence. Shortly before the limitation period was due to expire he wrote to them indicating that he was prepared to see the case dealt with in accordance with the professional negligence pre-action protocol, so long as they would agree not to take limitation points if proceedings were subsequently issued out of time. They never confirmed their agreement to this proposal, but the protocol was in fact followed. They subsequently pleaded limitation, and the court rejected the claimant's argument that they were estopped from doing so, holding that there had never been an unequivocal representation that they would not rely on limitation. The case illustrates again how difficult it is to succeed in establishing an estoppel of this kind. The same result followed in *Seechurn v Ace Insurance Sa-Nv*[46], where proceedings were issued over ten years after the accrual of the cause of action in contract. Although the Court of Appeal accepted that the defendant had written letters implying a possible willingness to consider further claims, it did not consider that there was a sufficiently clear, unequivocal and unconditional representation of an intention to forego the right to plead limitation.

---

[44] December 21, 1999, Jonathan Parker J., Unreported.
[45] [2003] All ER (D) 178 (Jun).
[46] [2002] EWCA Civ 67, [2002] 2 Lloyd's Rep 390.

These cases were further considered in *Law Society v Sephton*[47], where the need for a clear statement was again emphasised, and it was suggested that this might be a higher test than that suggested in *Lubovsky v Snelling*[48]; it is submitted that there is no real conflict in any of these cases. It is always a question of fact what the defendant has agreed to do or has represented that he will do, and the various cases are to be explained as turning on their own facts. What is now clear is that it matters little or nothing whether the claimant argues his case on the basis of a contract not to plead limitation or on the basis of an estoppel. The court will always be reluctant to conclude that limitation is not available and will require clear evidence to that effect[49].

21.018   Other cases on this point have concerned provisions in other statutes. In *The Sauria*[50] the plaintiffs applied for an extension of the two-year time-limit imposed by the Maritime Conventions Act 1911, pursuant to the discretion which that statute confers on the court. One of the grounds of the application was that there had been an agreement between the parties not to plead limitation. On the facts it was held that the alleged agreement never existed, but the Court of Appeal assumed that such agreement could amount to a good reason for the exercise of the discretion. Clearly, this case needs to be treated with care when considering the question of contracting out under the Limitation Act. Subject to a few exceptions, that Act does not give the court any discretion to extend time, so that the argument used in *The Sauria* could not be generally used. In *Co-operative Wholesale Society v Chester-le-Street DC*[51] it was held that s.10(3) of the Compulsory Purchase (Vesting Declarations) Act 1981, which establishes a six-year limitation period for compensation claims where an interest in land is vested in an acquiring authority pursuant to a general vesting declaration, is capable of being waived by agreement of the parties. Again, this decision relates to a particular statutory provision and should not necessarily be treated as authority for a more general doctrine of contracting out of the statute.

21.019   Another difficulty is that in *The Sauria* reference was made to *Lubovsky v Snelling* and to *Wright v John Bagnall & Sons Ltd* and *Rendall v Hill's Dry Docks and Engineering Co.*, and the Court of Appeal appeared to treat all four cases as belonging to the same line of authority. This makes it somewhat difficult to know whether admissions and contracting out are alternative ways of avoiding the effect of the statute or merely different ways of saying the same thing. It is submitted that they are conceptually different, but likely to overlap considerably in practice. There may, for example, be

---

[47] [2004] EWHC 544 (Ch) Michael Briggs Q.C.

[48] [1944] K.B. 44 C.A. see para.21.017.

[49] See also *Workman v Pannone & Partners (a firm)*[2002] EWHC 2366 (QB), [2002] All ER (D) 245 (Nov) and *Bridgestart Properties Limited v London Underground Limited* [2004] EWCA Civ 793.

[50] [1957] 1 Lloyd's Rep. 396, CA.

[51] 73 P. & C.R. 111; [1996] R.V.R. 185, Lands Tribunal.

an agreement not to plead the statute even though there is nothing in the nature of an admission of liability. For such agreement to be legally effective, it is submitted that it must genuinely amount to a contract, i.e. the plaintiff must give some consideration for the promise. Most commonly this consideration will be in the form of an agreement to delay the commencement of proceedings.[52] Where there is merely an admission of liability, by contrast, it now appears from the decision in *Cotterell (Executrix of Reece Deceased) v Leeds Day (A Firm)*[53] that the court is unlikely to find any sufficient ground for an estoppel.[54]

ESTOPPEL

In *Forward v Hendricks*[55] it was suggested that a defendant might be estopped from relying on limitation where a second writ had been issued out of time, the first not having been served as a result of any improper conduct on the defendant's part. However, these observations were obiter dicta, since on the facts it was held that there had been no improper conduct. In recent years a series of cases before the Lands Tribunal have raised the question of estoppel in circumstances where the parties have for some time negotiated on the assumption (more or less shared) that no limitation period applied to the claim in question. When this assumption was shown to be unfounded, it became necessary to decide whether defendants were as a result of the negotiations estopped from relying on limitation. Inevitably, this was a question of fact in every case, but it may be noted that very few pleas of estoppel have succeeded. In *Co-operative Wholesale Society v Chester-le-Street DC*,[56] a case concerning a specific statutory provision rather than the Limitation Act 1980, the plea failed. The possibility of relying on estoppel (or waiver) was also recognized in *Bytheway v British Steel Corporation Plc*.[57] In that case the defendants' insurers had dealt with over 8,000 industrial deafness cases on the terms of an understanding with the plaintiff's solicitors. This understanding included an agreement not to

21.020

---

[52] It is perhaps relevant to compare the cases under the Merchant Shipping Act 1995 (formerly the Maritime Conventions Act 1911) where the defendant has induced the plaintiff to delay commencing proceedings by holding out the prospect of an out-of-court settlement, and the plaintiff has consequently failed to commence proceedings within the two-year time-limit. On these facts the court has been prepared to exercise its discretion to extend the time-limit; the relevant cases are discussed at paras 24.005–24.016.

[53] December 21, 1999, Jonathan Parker J., Unreported.

[54] cf. *Stevens & Cutting Ltd v Anderson* (July 19, 1989, CA, Unreported), which appears to treat waiver and estoppel as identical, though the point was not directly in issue in that case. This confusion of the two concepts is to be deprecated, and it is unlikely that this case would be followed today.

[55] [1997] 2 All E.R. 395, CA.

[56] 73 P. & C.R. 111; [1996] R.V.R. 185, Lands Tribunal. On appeal [1998] E.G.C.S. 76.

[57] June 26, 1997, CA, Unreported.

take limitation points in return for, among other things, an agreement to settle for damages on an agreed scale. When the insurers lawfully terminated the scheme, the question arose as to whether plaintiffs whose claims were in the pipeline at the date of termination could continue to rely on the agreement to the extent of avoiding any limitation defences. It was held that they could not, largely because it was clear that the termination of the scheme allowed them to revert to suing for damages at common law, but the Court of Appeal treated it as obvious that while the scheme was in place the insurers would have been precluded from relying on limitation. It is submitted that this assumption is correct. As a matter of principle it is submitted that estoppel ought to be recognised as a possible response to a limitation defence, though of course it would be necessary in each case to show why the defendant's conduct (and presumably the plaintiff's response to it) made it inequitable for the defendant to be allowed to plead limitation. On the other side of the line is *Hillingdon London BC v Arc Ltd (No.2)*,[58] where the defendants had negotiated with the claimant in relation to a compensation claim following a compulsory purchase order. It was held that these negotiations did not preclude the defendant from subsequently pleading limitation. It is a question of fact whether there has been an agreement, or conduct, sufficient to amount to estoppel or waiver. That case also contains a thorough account of the conditions required to establish the various types of estoppel. It is clear from the judgment that establishing estoppel in relation to the Limitation Act is likely to be a formidable task and one which can be accomplished only in the most exceptional cases.[59] Such a case, however, is *Williams v Blaenau Gwent County BC (No.2)*,[60] where the Lands Tribunal was prepared to find that the parties had proceeded on the necessary shared assumption as to the validity of the claim and that on the facts it would be inequitable to deprive the claimant of the benefit of this assumption.

21.021   Where an estoppel by convention can be established, it is apparently possible for the defendant to give notice that it will take the limitation point if proceedings are not commenced promptly. Thereafter the claimant must commence proceedings within a reasonable time. In *The Executors of the Estate of the Right Honourable Herbert Robert Cayzer Baron Rotherwick v Oxfordshire CC*[61] it was held that a reasonable time was two months after the giving of the notice by the defendant.

---

[58] [2000] R.V.R. 283; see also *Rowan Companies Inc. v Lambert Eggink Offshore Transport Consultants VOF* [1999] 2 Lloyd's Rep. 443, Clarke J., where negotiations were held insufficient to found a plea of estoppel.

[59] This observation was expressly approved by HH Judge Coulson Q.C. in *Holding and Management (Solitaire) Ltd v Ideal Homes North West Ltd and others* [2004] EWHC 2408 (TCC), 96 ConLR 114. Another unsuccessful attempt to plead estoppel can be found in *Ace Insurance SA-NV v Seechurn* [2002] E.W.C.A. Civ. 67, CA.

[60] [1999] 2 E.G.L.R. 195, Lands Tribunal.

[61] March 21, 2000, Lands Tribunal, Unreported.

It is for the defendant initially to raise limitation, but it is then for the claimant to show, on the balance of probabilities, that his action is not time-barred. Where the defendant by his pleadings raises a specific point of argument for showing that the claim is time-barred it may be sufficient for the claimant to rebut this point. By contrast, where the defendant merely pleads the statute generally, the claimant will need to be ready to meet any point under the Limitation Act, though of course this can be narrowed down by requesting further information of the defence.[62] A further consequence of this is that where there is no evidence to show when the cause of action accrued the claimant will necessarily fail if the defendant pleads limitation.

21.022

PRE-ACTION DISCOVERY

Section 33(2) of the Senior Courts Act 1981 allows a potential claimant in a personal injuries action to apply before the commencement of the action for an order requiring a potential defendant to make discovery of documents in his possession which are relevant to the contemplated action. As a general rule, application for pre-action discovery will be rejected where the proposed action is based on "ill-founded, irresponsible and speculative allegations".[63] The application of this principle in a limitation context was considered by the Court of Appeal in *Harris v Newcastle HA*.[64] The principle to be applied is that a limitation defence should be used as a ground for rejecting an application under s.33(2) only where the application is clearly ill founded. In that case the cause of action was over 20 years old, but the Court of Appeal held that the application should be allowed since facts relevant to the exercise of discretion under s.33 of the 1980 Act might emerge on discovery. In the light of this it might almost be suggested that no application can ever be refused; pre-action discovery applies only to personal injuries actions, and there must nearly always be the possibility that relevant facts will emerge on discovery.

21.023

SECTION 33 AND APPEALS

When the claimant applies for the exercise of discretion under s.33 of the 1980 Act, and the trial judge either refuses or grants this application, the question of an appeal may arise. Such an appeal would now require per-

21.024

---

[62] CPR Pt 18.
[63] *Shaw v Vauxhall Motors Ltd* [1974] 1 W.L.R. 1035 *Dunning v Board of Governors of the United Liverpool Hospitals* [1973] 1 W.L.R. 586.
[64] November 2, 1988, Unreported.

mission, either from the trial judge or from the appellate court, pursuant to CPR Pt 52. Given the reluctance of appellate courts to interefere with the trial judge's discretion in such matters,[65] it is suggested that permission to appeal will only rarely be granted.

CONSOLIDATION

21.025   In *Arab Monetary Fund v Hashim (No. 4)*[66] the question arose whether orders consolidating actions against different defendants and granting consequential leave to serve process out of the jurisdiction under CPR 6.20 can properly be made where the effect of so doing would be to deprive the defendant of an accrued limitation defence in respect of one of the claims. The problem with doing this is that if leave is refused, the claimant will have to seek to join the second defendant to the main action, and this will not normally be allowed where an accrued limitation defence would thereby be overridden.[67] The Court of Appeal held that it is nevertheless within the discretion of the trial judge to allow such consolidation. It is submitted that this case should be treated with some caution, since the point was not even argued at first instance, and appears to have received only very brief consideration in the Court of Appeal. There are obvious dangers inherent in this decision, and it would seem desirable that the point should be more fully considered before the law is regarded as settled.

RATIFICATION

21.026   Where solicitors commence an action in the name of one of their clients without that client's authority, it is normally possible for the client subsequently to ratify those proceedings, provided that he does so at a time when he himself could have started the proceedings.[68] The ratification will be retrospective to the date when the proceedings were commenced. In *Presentaciones Musicales v Secunda*,[69] the Court of Appeal held that this doctrine extended to cases where the action was time-barred at the date of ratification. This decision appears to be correct, since the expiry of the limitation period does not prevent a plaintiff from bringing an action, but merely gives the defendant an effective defence if he chooses to plead it.

---

[65] *Conry v Simpson* [1983] 3 All E.R. 369, CA.
[66] [1992] 1 W.L.R. 1176, CA.
[67] See Ch.23.
[68] *Bird v Brown* (1850) 4 Exch. 786.
[69] *The Times*, November 29, 1993, CA.

THE LAW COMMISSION'S PROPOSALS

The Commission proposes to retain the present rule[70] that a limitation **21.027** period may be extended or reduced by agreement. It seeks the views of consultees on whether the same should apply to the longstop. In principle it would seem desirable to have the same rule for the longstop as for the basic limitation period, though, as the Commission recognises, there is a public-interest argument against allowing unlimited extensions of time.

---

[70] The Consultation Paper suggests that this issue is unresolved in the present law, but it is submitted that the cases discussed earlier in this chapter provide sufficient authority for the view that it is possible to do this.

CHAPTER 22

Procedural Delays

This chapter, together with Ch.23, deals with the more important of the **22.001** problems which can arise under the CPR where time expires after the issue of the claim form but before the termination of the action. Often, but not invariably, this situation will arise through some delay on the part of the claimant in prosecuting the action. The difficulties arising where the claim form is not issued before the end of the limitation period are considered in Ch.8, since it is only in the context of personal injuries and defamation that the time for issue of the writ can be extended. This chapter concentrates on problems of two kinds. The first arises where a party wishes to amend the claim form and/or pleadings in the action after time has expired for the bringing of the action. The second arises where there is a long delay in the prosecution of the action, and the defendant seeks to have the action dismissed on this ground.

This chapter is confined to problems arising as between the original parties to the action. The further issues involved where it is desired to join new parties to the action are considered in Ch.23. The rules relating to joinder, contained in s.35 of the 1980 Act and CPR Pts 17 and 19 are therefore spread across these two chapters.

AMENDING THE CLAIM FORM BEFORE SERVICE

This is not strictly speaking a limitation question, for the action cannot be **22.002** out of time so long as the claim form was issued in time and the relevant time-limit for serving it has not yet expired.[1] It is necessary, however, to consider the rules applicable here in order to understand the problems which have arisen in cases where the amendment is sought to be made at a later stage.

---

[1] CPR r.7.5. For the problems where the writ is not served within this period, see paras 22.003–22.015.

Amendment of the claim form is governed by CPR Pt 17. CPR r.17.1 allows the claim form to be amended without the permission of the court, at any time before it has been served. After service, CPR r.17.4 governs the amendment[2] of any statement of case. This rule is dealt with at paragraphs 22.021–22.023.

UNSERVED CLAIM FORMS

22.003   In *The Gniezno*[3] Brandon J. held that it is possible for a defendant to enter a voluntary appearance to an unserved claim form, whether or not the time for service of that claim form has expired.[4] The basis of the decision is that the rules requiring service of the claim form and limiting the time within which that service may be effected are enacted for the defendant's benefit, and it is therefore possible for him to waive them.[5] In *Re Kerley Son & Verden*[6] it was held that a solicitor's undertaking to enter an appearance to a claim form could be enforced even after the claim form had expired.[7] The somewhat exceptional situations considered in these two cases must be regarded as qualifications on the discussion that follows on the effect of failure to serve a claim form within the time allowed for doing so.

FAILURE TO SERVE THE CLAIM FORM IN TIME

22.004   A claim form is valid for four months from the date of issue (six months if endorsed for service out of the jurisdiction)[8] and may be served at any time during that period. However, CPR r.7.6 goes on to provide that the court may in its discretion extend the validity of a claim form beyond that period upon the application of the claimant. This discretion is available whether the application is made before or after the validity of the claim form has expired. Moreover, a claimant may apply for permission to serve out of the jurisdiction a claim form originally issued as being only for service within the jurisdiction, and may make this application more than four months

---

[2]   Though it may be possible to delete a time-barred cause of action from a writ without leave before the writ has been served.

[3]   [1967] 3 W.L.R. 705.

[4]   *Pike v Michael Nairn & Co. Ltd* [1960] Ch. 553; *Re Kerly, Son and Verden* [1901] 1 Ch. 467; *Bildt v Foy* (1892) 9 T.L.R. 34; (1892) 9 T.L.R. 83; *The Saxicava* [1924] P. 131; *Re General Railway Syndicate* [1900] 1 Ch. 365; *The Fairplay XIV* [1939] P. 57.

[5]   But this principle does not allow the defendant to make a counterclaim on an unserved writ.

[6]   [1901] 1 Ch. 467, Farwell J., CA.

[7]   This case may perhaps be explained on the basis that the exercise of the court's inherent jurisdiction over solicitors is not governed by the Limitation Act—see now *Bray v Stuart A. West & Co.* (1989) 139 New L.J. 753, Warner J.

[8]   CPR r.7.5.

after the issue of the claim form.[9] Applications to extend time (whether made before or after the expiry of the relevant period) are normally made without notice. Where the application is granted, the claimant must serve on the defendant a copy of the application notice, the evidence in support and the order.[10] The defendant then has seven days in which to apply to set aside the order extending the validity of the claim form.[11]

THE OLD AUTHORITIES

CPR r.7.6 is a development of the former RSC, Ord.6, r.8, but it is not quite in the same form, and it is therefore unwise to rely too closely on authorities decided under the former provision. CPR r.7.6 provides that as a general rule an application to extend the time for service must be made within the period for serving the claim form specified by r.7.5 or where an order has been made under this rule, within the period for service specified by that order. If the claimant applies for an order to extend the time for service of the claim form after the end of the period specified by r.7.5 or by an order made under this rule, the court may make such an order only where the court has been unable to serve the claim form or the claimant has taken all reasonable steps to serve the claim form but has been unable to do so and, in either case, the claimant has acted promptly in making the application. Where the claimant does not satisfy the requirements of CPR r.7.6(3) he cannot rescue himself by invoking the more general provisions as to relief from sanctions under CPR rs 3.9 and 3.10.[12]

22.005

Successive extensions

CPR r.7.6 clearly contemplates that there may be more than one extension of the validity of the claim form. Each such extension requires a further application and a further exercise of discretion.

22.006

The exercise of the discretion under RSC, Ord.6, r.8 has been the subject of extensive judicial consideration, but two decisions of the House of Lords authoritatively clarified many of the outstanding questions in this area. In *Kleinwort Benson Ltd v Barbrak Ltd ("The Myrto") (No. 3)*[13] the plaintiff bank had brought proceedings in rem against a ship in order to enforce a mortgage on that ship, and had arrested it. The bank attempted to negotiate

22.007

---

[9] *ST Shipping & Transport Inc v Vyzantio Shipping Ltd; 'The Byzantio' [2004] All ER (D) 219 (Dec), Judge Havelock-Allan.*
[10] CPR r.23.9.
[11] CPR r.23.10; and see *The Hai Hing* [2000] 1 Lloyd's Rep. 300, Rix J.
[12] *Satwimder Kaul v CTP Coil Ltd*, July 9, 2000, Unreported, CA.
[13] [1987] A.C. 597, HL.

a settlement with regard to expenses with the 141 owners of cargo laden on board the ship, and began test proceedings against the largest cargo owner. In due course an omnibus writ was also issued against all the cargo owners together with, where appropriate, their insurers or guarantors as a means of protecting the bank's position. In order to save costs the writ was not immediately served, and an extension of time for a further 12 months was granted on a without-notice application. After judgment had been given in favour of the bank in the action against the largest cargo owner, a further three-month extension of the writ was granted to give the bank time to calculate the amounts due from each of the defendants in the omnibus writ. Eventually (and within the time granted by the second extension) the bank served the writ. Four of the cargo owners applied to have the extensions of the writ set aside. The Court of Appeal set aside the service of the writ on the ground that no extension of a writ could be granted where there was no difficulty in serving it. In reversing this decision the House of Lords considered at length the principles to be applied where there is an application under Ord.6, r.8 for an extension of the validity of a writ. It has subsequently been held that the principles laid down in that case apply to third-party notices in the same way as they apply to claim forms.[14]

Discretion is a general one

22.008 The first issue was whether the discretion is one which can be exercised only in exceptional circumstances, or whether it is more generally available. The House of Lords held that it is unnecessary to show that there are exceptional circumstances; rather, there is discretion to grant the extension if it is shown that there is "good cause" or "good reason" for doing so.[15] It is then necessary to balance the hardship caused to the defendant if the extension is granted against the hardship caused to the claimant if it is refused. This principle is derived from the observation of Sachs L.J. in *Jones v Jones*[16] that in exercising the discretion the overriding consideration must be "the balance of justice between the parties". It is important to be aware that balance of hardship is not an independent ground for granting an extension; it is only when some other good reason has been shown that the task of weighing the balance of hardship falls to be performed.[17] By its very nature

---

[14] *Pecka v Pecka*, March 22, 1994, CA, Unreported.

[15] *Battersby v Anglo-American Oil Co. Ltd* [1945] K.B. 23, CA; *Heaven v Road and Rail Wagons Ltd* [1965] 2 Q.B. 355, Megaw J.; *Baker v Bowketts Cakes Ltd* [1966] 1 W.L.R. 86, CA; *Stevens v Services Window and General Cleaning Co. Ltd* [1967] 1 Q.B. 359, Chapman J.; *Jones v Jones* [1970] 2 Q.B. 576; *Osborne v Distillers Co. Ltd* (1967) 112 S.J. 50; *Austin Rover Group Ltd v Crouch Butler Savage Associates* [1986] 1 W.L.R. 1102, CA.

[16] [1970] 2 Q.B. 576 at 584 cited by Sheen J. at first instance in *The Myrto* [1985] 2 Lloyd's Rep. 565 at 571–572.

[17] *Waddon v Whitecroft-Scovill Ltd* [1988] 1 W.L.R. 309, HL. This case is considered extensively at paras 22.010–22.015.

the weighing of this balance is one as to which no general rules can be laid down—the judge is simply required to decide which of the two possible solutions will cause the lesser hardship of the particular facts of the case before him.

THE THREE CLASSES OF CASE

Although the discretion to extend the validity of a claim form is a general one, the speech of Lord Brandon in *The Myrto (No. 3)* makes clear that the ease with which such extension can be obtained will depend heavily upon the circumstances of the case. His Lordship distinguished three types of case[18]:   **22.009**

(a) where the application for extension is made at a time when the claim form is still valid and before the relevant period of limitation has expired;

(b) where the application for extension is made at a time when the claim form is still valid but after the relevant period of limitation has expired;

(c) where the application is made at a time when the claim form has ceased to be valid and after the relevant period of limitation has expired.[19]

A hypothetical fourth category of case, namely that where the validity of the claim form has expired but the relevant period of limitation has not, gives rise to no practical difficulty since in these cases there is nothing to prevent the claimant from issuing and serving a further claim form if he wishes to do so. Lord Brandon also draws a distinction between categories (a) and (b) on the one hand and category (c) on the other. In both category (a) and category (b) it is still possible for the claimant to serve the claim form if he wishes to do so, whereas in category (c) this option is no longer open to him. In addition, in category (a) (but not category (b)) it is open to the defendant to issue a fresh claim form,[20] which would remain valid for 12 months from the date of issue. Consequently, in both category (a) and category (b) it cannot be said that the defendant has any accrued right to plead limitation as a defence to the action, whereas in category (c) such a right obviously has arisen. It is noticeable that all but one of the cases relied

---

[18] [1987] A.C. 597 at 602.

[19] It is in relation to this category of cases that the CPR rules may be somewhat different from the RSC rules.

[20] Doubtless this explains why none of the cases cited in argument here was a category (a) case.

upon in *The Myrto (No. 3)* fall into category (c),[21] and this may help to explain the somewhat restrictive attitude to extension of validity which some of them appear to adopt. Lord Brandon lays down in *The Myrto (No. 3)* a general principle that in both category (b) and category (c) cases good reason is needed in order to justify the granting of an extension of time.[22] In particular, it is not correct to say that the claimant must show that he has had difficulties in effecting service of the claim form. In category (c) cases, however, the claimant faces the additional hurdle of explaining to the satisfaction of the court why he failed to seek an extension of the claim form during the period of its validity.[23] Therefore, the test is effectively more stringent in category (c) cases.

22.010   This point was further developed in the decision of the House of Lords in *Waddon v Whitecroft-Scovill Ltd*,[24] where the leading speech was again delivered by Lord Brandon. In that case it was argued for the plaintiff that the fact of having sought the extension before the claim form expired was to be counted in his favour. Lord Brandon rejected this idea, saying that the effect of the decision in *The Myrto (No. 3)* was only that failure to seek an extension before the claim form expired placed another hurdle in the claimant's way: the timely seeking of an extension did not create any form of presumption in the claimant's favour.

    The question of the proper approach to be adopted in category (a) cases has been further considered in *Rogers v Messrs Trethowans*,[25] where difficulties with the legal aid fund were considered just sufficient to warrant an extension of time. The Court of Appeal said that a more lenient approach should be taken in category (a) cases. This can be expressed either by saying that it is easier in these cases to show good reason for an extension or by saying that the possibility of the claimant issuing a fresh claim form can be taken into account in weighing the balance of hardship. The court appears to treat these two approaches as producing the same result, but this will not always be the result. The weighing of the balance of hardship is the second stage of the process, and is to be carried out only once the court is satisfied that there is good reason for extending the claim form. If the fact that the case falls into category (a) cannot be considered until the second stage, then there may be cases where that second stage is never reached, there being no other reason to extend the claim form. It is nevertheless submitted that this is the correct approach—there may well be cases in category (a) where the approach course is to strike out the first claim form and leave the claimant

---

[21] The one exception is *Stevens v Services Window & General Cleaning Co. Ltd* [1967] 1 All E.R. 984, Chapman J.

[22] [1987] 2 All E.R. 289 at 300.

[23] It is in any case a general rule that any delay beyond that allowed by the RSC must be satisfactorily explained—*Smith v Secretary of State for the Environment, The Times*, July 6, 1987, CA.

[24] [1988] 1 W.L.R. 309.

[25] February 23, 1989, CA, Unreported.

to reissue. Further, the fact that the case falls into category (a) is never by itself good reason for an extension, since it can never be a sufficient explanation for the initial failure to serve in time. *Robert v Momentum Services Ltd*[26] laid down the principles to be applied in an application to extend time made before the expiry of time for service. The correct approach is to concentrate on the prejudice that has been caused, or will be caused, to the defendant by the failure to serve the particulars of claim on time. The strength or weakness of the claim will rarely be relevant. Although the case does not say so (because the point did not arise) it is suggested that the fact that the limitation period has expired by the date of the application must be a highly relevant factor. It must be borne in mind that this case is concerned with service of the particulars of claim, not with service of the claim form.

CPR 6.9

A number of recent cases have considered the possibility of using CPR 6.9 **22.011** (which allows the court to dispense with service) as an alternative to seeking an extension of time for service under CPR 7.6. In *Nussberger v Phillips*[27] the particular question before the court was whether CPR 6.9 could be invoked as a way of retrospectively validating service in a case subject to the Lugano Convention, the effect of whose provisions is that as between the courts of two different Convention countries jurisdiction will fall to the court whose proceedings have been effectively served first. In *Nussberger* it was clear that the defendant had in fact received notice of the proceedings, though the attempt to serve was defective for technical reasons. The Court of Appeal held that in these circumstances it would not be right to validate the service retrospectively because to do so would undermine the basis on which the provisions of the Convention had been agreed to, namely that proper service was required in order to give the courts of a particular country jurisdiction and that 'queue-jumping' should not be allowed. However, the Court was of the view that in appropriate cases lacking such a foreign element it might well be appropriate to use CPR 6.9 for this purpose.[28]

Such a case has since arisen. In *Olafsson v Gissurarson*[29] the claimant **22.012** argued that the power in r.6.8 can be invoked in exceptional circumstances, which particularly could include an unsuccessful or ineffective attempt to serve the proceedings in a method that was prescribed, where that unsuccessful attempt has succeeded to the extent of putting the proceedings in the

---

[26] [2003] EWCA Civ 299, [2003] 2 All ER 74, [2003] WLR 1577.
[27] [2006] EWCA Civ 654.
[28] At para.66.
[29] [2006] EWHC 3214 (QB), HQ04X02463.

hands of the proposed defendant. The claimant sought to rely on the principles set out in earlier cases such as *Anderton v Clwyd CC*[30] where Mummery L.J. distinguished two different kinds of case. The first was an application by a claimant who had not even attempted to serve a claim form within time by one of the methods permitted by the rules. In that type of case the earlier case of *Godwin v Swindon BC* [2001] EWCA Civ 1478, [2001] 4 All ER 641, [2002] 1 WLR 997 was authority to the effect that such an attempt to "circumvent the limitations in r 7.6(3) on the grant of extensions of time for service of the claim form" would not be made. The second category was considered in para.58, namely an application by a claimant who had already made an ineffective attempt, in time, to serve a claim form by one of the methods allowed by r.6.2 in circumstances where the defendant or his legal advisor had in fact received and had his attention drawn to the claim form. Dealing with an application from such a claimant Mummery LJ said at para.58:

> "The basis of his application to dispense with service is that there is no point in requiring him to go through the motions of a second attempt to complete in law what he has already achieved in fact. The Defendant accepts that he has received the claim form before the end of the period for service of the claim form. Apart from losing the opportunity to take advantage of the point that service was not in time in accordance with the rules, the Defendant would not usually suffer prejudice as a result of the court dispensing with the formality of service of a document which has already come into his hands before the end of the period of service. The Claimant on the other hand will be prejudiced by the refusal of an order dispensing with service as, if he is still required to serve the claim form, he will be unable to do so because he cannot obtain an extension of time for service under rule 7.6(3)."

22.013   In *Cranfield v Bridgegrove Ltd*[31] the facts were that the claimant's solicitors had been told by the defendant, which was a limited company, that its solicitors would accept service. Despite that, the claimant's solicitors attempted to effect service at the defendant company's registered office. Although the Court of Appeal ultimately held that the service was good, it also acknowledged with approval the Anderton criteria and said that though the facts did not precisely fit those criteria that in the "very unusual" circumstances of the case they were considering, had it been necessary to do so they would have decided it was right to dispense with service under r.6.9. The defendant in *Olafsson* argued that this was an impermissible attempt to save proceedings which were otherwise statute barred. The Court inevitably accepted that this was the purpose of using CPR 6.9 here,

---

[30] [2002] EWCA Civ 933, [2002] 3 All ER 813, [2002] 1 WLR 3174.
[31] [2003] EWCA Civ 656, [2003] 3 All ER 129, [2003] 1 WLR 2441.

but did not accept that this made it impermissible. The failure to achieve valid service was for want of a mere technicality, in circumstances where the fact of service was accepted.

These cases, taken together, show that CPR 6.9 can be used to circumvent a failure of service, but not in a case where obligations under international Conventions would thereby be breached. Further, the use of CPR 6.9 will be appropriate only where the defendant has in fact had prompt notice of the proceedings and where the defect of service can properly be regarded as resulting only from a minor technicality.

Cranfield v Bridegrove[32] concerned the meaning of the words "unable to serve" in CPR 7.6(3)(a) in cases where the proceedings were to be served by the court. This is one of the criteria for allowing an extension of time to serve. The Court of Appeal held that these words included cases where the court had failed to serve, including mere oversight on its part. In most cases, where the real cause of the failure to serve in time was court neglect, it would be appropriate to grant an extension of time if the claimant had acted promptly in making the application under CPR 7.6(3)(c). However, where the true cause of the failure to serve was some error by the claimant, it was much less likely that an extension of time would be granted.

22.014

WHICH FACTORS ARE RELEVANT

The problems surrounding extensions of validity arose again in *Waddon v Whitecroft-Scovill Ltd.*[33] This was a personal injuries case in which a without-notice extension of validity had been granted, largely as a result of the plaintiff's difficulties in obtaining the removal of limitations on his legal aid certificate. The House of Lords upheld the decision of all the lower courts to set aside the extension as having been granted without sufficient reason. When the case reached the House of Lords no fewer than seven grounds of appeal were presented. One, namely that the trial judge had misapplied the "good cause" test propounded in *The Myrto (No. 3)*, raises no issue of general importance, and does not call for further examination here, whilst the grounds relating to the time when the application for extension was made and the weighing of the balance of hardship between the parties have been considered above.[34] The other four are considered seriatim below.

22.015

---

[32] [2003] EWCA Civ 656, [2003] All ER (D) 178 (May).
[33] [1988] 1 W.L.R. 309, HL.
[34] See para.22.006.

Claimant's solicitors not blameworthy

22.016 It was argued that the plaintiff's solicitors had not been at fault in failing to serve the claim form within its original period of validity, and that this was a factor pointing in the direction of exercising the discretion in the plaintiff's favour. Evidence was given to the effect that in the district registry concerned, extensions of time were given more or less automatically even in cases where limitation might be a factor. The House of Lords took the view that any such practice would be entirely contrary to law, and that the appellant's solicitors could not possibly have been justified in relying upon it. On the other hand in *Thurston v Coates Albutt Edmondson & Taylor*[35] the plaintiff's solicitors had allowed time to expire on the faith of an erroneous representation by court officials that their application for an extension of time had been considered and granted. Although it was arguable that they had been negligent in not serving the claim form earlier, the Court of Appeal held that the mistake by the court officials was an exceptional circumstance sufficient to justify an extension of time. However, absence of fault on the part of the plaintiff's solicitors cannot by itself amount to sufficient reason for granting an extension of validity. It may possibly be relevant when weighing the balance of hardship as between the parties, but even here it can have only a very small role to play.

Failure to serve and extension of validity

22.017 The next ground of appeal considered in *Waddon v Whitecroft-Scovill Ltd* was that the trial judge had addressed himself to the wrong question by asking whether there was any good reason for the failure to serve the writ in time, rather than whether there was a good reason for granting the extension of time. Lord Brandon observed that, at least in the great majority of cases, it will be impossible to establish the second of these without establishing the first. In most cases, including this one, the two matters are inextricably linked.[36]

Different rules for personal injury cases

22.018 It was also argued in *Waddon v Whitecroft-Scovill Ltd* that a different approach should be adopted when considering applications to extend the claim form in personal injury cases. The basis of this argument was that statute has provided a different scheme for personal injury rules in relation

---

[35] June 19,1997, CA, Unreported.
[36] cf., in an Admiralty context, *The Prins Bernhard* [1964] P. 117, Hewson J.

to extensions of the primary limitation period,[37] and that the policy of the legislation required the adoption of this scheme also in relation to extensions of the validity of the claim form in such cases. Lord Brandon accepted that the sorts of reasons which may justify an extension of the primary limitation period under s.33 might well also justify an extension of the validity of the claim form under RSC, Ord.6, r.8. It was held though, that it would be wrong to lay down any general rule to this effect. What is "good cause" must depend upon all the facts of the case, and there cannot be any distinct set of rules for personal injury cases. The position in this regard appears to be identical under CPR r.7.6.

Relevance of public funding

One of the problems faced by the plaintiff in this case was difficulty in securing the removal of limitations on his legal aid certificate. Michael Davies J. at first instance had concluded that he was bound by authority[38] to disregard the effect of any such difficulties. Before the House of Lords the plaintiff sought to challenge the correctness of those decisions. Lord Brandon suggested that the observations of Lord Denning in *Baker v Bowketts Cakes Ltd*[39] and of Chapman J. in *Stevens v Services Window and General Cleaning Co. Ltd*[40] might perhaps be regarded as being correct on the facts of those particular cases. He stressed, however, that there is no general rule that delays caused by the operation of the legal aid system are to be ignored[41]—such a rule would be unrealistic. On the basis of this view of the law it might have been expected that the House of Lords would have decided the case in favour of the plaintiff. Instead, Lord Brandon analysed carefully the role played in the history of the case by the legal aid restrictions. He concluded that it would have been possible for the appellant's solicitors to obtain the removal of the restrictions had they acted sufficiently promptly. Consequently, it could not truly be said that the legal aid system had caused the failure to serve the claim form in time.

    This is a point of some general importance in public-funding cases. Apparently, it will be necessary to show both that there were public-funding restrictions, and that they could not reasonably have been removed in time to allow the service of the claim form within its primary period of

22.019

---

[37] 1980 Act s.33; see Ch.8.
[38] *Baker v Bowketts Cakes Ltd* [1966] 2 All E.R. 290, CA; *Stevens v Services Window and General Cleaning Co. Ltd* [1967] 1 All E.R. 984, Chapman J.
[39] [1966] 2 All E.R. 290 at 292.
[40] [1967] 1 All E.R. 984 at 988.
[41] See also *Rogers v Trethowans* (February 23, 1989, CA, Unreported), where an extension of time was allowed because the plaintiffs had been denied access to important documents which had been lodged for taxation of costs.

validity. Difficulties in transferring a public-funding certificate from one firm of solicitors to another may also be taken into account.[42]

Delay caused by claimant's injuries

22.020   In *Martin v Turner*[43] it appeared that the delays in serving the writ arose from the plaintiff's failure to co-operate with his own solicitors. There was some evidence that the plaintiff's conduct was caused by the head injuries which were the subject of the action. The Court of Appeal refused to extend time for the service of the writ. It is unclear from the report whether the Court did not accept the evidence that the plaintiff's injuries were responsible for the failure or whether they treated it as irrelevant. It is submitted that facts of this character, if established to the satisfaction of the court, should incline the court strongly in the direction of granting an extension of time.

WHERE THE CLAIM FORM IS SERVED OUT OF TIME

What is 'Service' and when does it take place?

22.021   *Anderton v Clwyd CC*[44] establishes that the provisions in the CPR dealing with deemed dates of service are not, as had commonly been supposed, mere presumptions. They are rules of law as to when proceedings are deemed to have been served, and evidence that the defendant received the proceedings earlier is inadmissible.[45]

22.022   So far it has been assumed that after the expiry of the writ the claimant will seek an extension of time before serving it. In *Leal v Dunlop Bio-Processes International Ltd*[46] the plaintiff proceeded with service of the writ, notwithstanding that its validity had expired. The matter came before the Court of Appeal in the form of an application for a retrospective extension of time for service. The Court held that there was jurisdiction to make such an amendment, since the improper service fell to be treated as a mere irregularity, and was therefore capable of correction. However, the granting of such leave would not be appropriate in the absence of special circumstances, which did not exist in the present case. A claimant who seeks leave in such circumstances will need to explain why the claim form

---

[42] *Perkins v Smith, Morton & Long*, August 16, 1989, CA, Unreported.
[43] [1970] 1 W.L.R. 82, CA.
[44] [2002] 3 All ER 813.
[45] See also *Godwin v Swindon BC* [2001] EWCA Civ 1478, [2001] 4 All ER 641, [2002] 1 WLR 997.
[46] [1984] 2 W.L.R. 874, CA.

was not served in time, why no application for extension was made before the claim form expired and why he took the extraordinary step of serving the claim form without even seeking leave. Only if all these points can be satisfactorily answered will the court pass to the second stage, namely weighing the balance of hardship between the parties in accordance with the decision in *The Myrto (No. 3)*.[47] Again, it is suggested that the position would be no different under the CPR. The requirement in CPR r.23.9 that the claimant must serve on the defendant the application notice, evidence in support and order may give rise to further problems. It is not unknown for a claimant to serve a claim form which has been extended without complying with CPR r.23.9. In such a case the defendant's time for applying to set aside the extension of the claim form will not have started to run. It is submitted that the proper procedure for the court is to refuse to let the action proceed until CPR r.23.9 has been complied with and any resulting challenge to the order extending time has been resolved.

TIMING OF APPLICATION

In *Singh v Duport Harper Foundries Ltd*[48] it was held that an application **22.023** for renewal of the claim form must be made not later than four months from the date on which the original claim form expired. CPR r.7.6 contains no such provision, though CPR r.7.6(3) requires the court to take account of how promptly the claimant has acted in making the application, where it is made after the claim form has expired.

FOUR-MONTH CLAIM FORMS AND SIX-MONTH CLAIM FORMS

A claim form endorsed for service out of the jurisdiction is valid for six **22.024** months rather than four. This disparity can give rise to problems where a claim form is issued not for service out of the jurisdiction and it subsequently becomes apparent that it will need to be served out of the jurisdiction because, for example, it is discovered that the defendant has left the country.

The usual practice in such cases is to issue a concurrent claim form and seek permission (where required[49]) to serve that out of the jurisdiction. If

---

[47] [1987] A.C. 597, HL.
[48] [1994] 2 All E.R. 889, CA.
[49] The rules as to service out of the jurisdiction are at CPR rs 6.30 et seq. Although CPR Pt 6 was greatly amended in 2008, these amendments do not appear to affect the issues discussed here.

both the four-month period of validity of the original claim form and the limitation period in respect of the cause of action have expired, there is a question whether it is appropriate to give leave to serve the claim form out of the jurisdiction, since this apparently deprives the defendant of an accrued right to plead limitation. To put it another way, it may be asked whether the concurrent claim form should be valid for four months (running from the date of issue of the original claim form) or for six months. Although permission to serve out of the jurisdiction can be granted retrospectively, this should not be done where the effect is to deprive a defendant of a limitation defence (because the cause of action is time-barred and limitation would be available as a defence to a fresh action).[50]

22.025   The former provision in Ord.6, r.8(1)(A) read:

"A concurrent writ is valid in the first instance for the period of validity of the original writ which is unexpired at the date of issue of the concurrent writ."

This has no direct CPR equivalent, and it is not clear what rules apply at the present day. The old authorities, considered below, may offer some limited guidance, but it essential to bear in mind that they were decided in the context of Ord.6, r.8(1)(a).

22.026   In *Dong Wha Enterprise Co. Ltd v Crownson Shipping Ltd*[51] Mance J. held that the concurrent claim form was valid for six months. In *Saris v Westminster Transports SA and Kestrel Marine Ltd*[52] Colman J. held that such a claim form was valid for only four months. In *Caribbean Gold Ltd v Alga Shipping Ltd ("The Nova Scotia")*[53] Potter J. suggested that the way out of this dilemma was to seek leave to have the restriction on service out of the jurisdiction removed from the original claim form. All these authorities were reviewed at length by Waller J. in *Arab Business Consortium v Banque Franco-Tunisienne*.[54] At first sight the former provision might appear to support the view of Colman J., but Mance J. in *Dong Wha* was understandably concerned about the injustice which such a conclusion appears to produce. Waller J. held that where a claim form had been issued not for service outside the jurisdiction it is a material matter in considering whether leave to serve out a concurrent claim form should be given that the limitation period has expired, and it is particularly material if the four-month period of validity of the claim form has expired prior to the making of that application. The effect of this appears to be that the concurrent claim form is in the first instance valid for only four months. Thus an

---

[50] *ED & F Man Sugar Ltd v Lendoudis* [2007] EWHC 2268 (Comm) Christopher Clarke J.
[51] [1995] 1 Lloyd's Rep. 113.
[52] [1994] 1 Lloyd's Rep. 115.
[53] [1993] 1 Lloyd's Rep. 154.
[54] December 13, 1995, Unreported.

application for leave to serve out made after the expiry of the four months is in terms of the classification in *The Myrto* a category (c) case. It follows that leave can be given in such cases, subject to the principles applicable in category (c) cases. It also follows that the expiry of the limitation period is a material matter where an extension of the validity of the claim form beyond six months is sought and good reason must be shown for an extension of the claim form. In *Pirelli v United Thai Shipping Corporation*[55] it was held that even under the CPR applications to extend the validity of pre-CPR writs must be decided under the old rules.

22.027 The rules on extending the validity of a claim form received some interesting analysis in *Hoddinott v Persimmon Homes (Wessex) Ltd*[56]. Previous cases in this area, cited in the main text, have—understandably—focussed on CPR 7.6 and the somewhat restrictive conditions which it imposes for extending the validity of the claim form. In *Hoddinott* the Court of Appeal also referred to CPR 11, which deals with disputing the court's jurisdiction and in particular with the procedure for arguing that the court should not exercise its jurisdiction. CPR 11(4) and (5) deal with making an application that the court should not exercise its jurisdiction. They read:

(4) An application under this rule must

    (a) be made within 14 days after filing an acknowledgement of service; and

    (b) be supported by evidence.

(5) If the defendant (a) files an acknowledgement of service; and (b) does not make such an application within the period specified in paragraph (4), he is to be treated as having accepted that the court has jurisdiction to try the claim.

In this case a claim form was issued, which would have expired on 22 September 2006. On 13 September, without notice to the defendant, C made an application pursuant to CPR 7.6(2) to extend the time for service of the claim form. The application was supported by a witness statement purporting to set out the reasons which justified the application. The district judge made a without notice order extending time for service to 22 November. The following day, a copy of the claim form was sent to the defendant, who issued an application to set aside the order of 13 September. The claimants contended that in the light of CPR 11(5) and the terms of the acknowledgment of service, it was not open to the defendant to apply to set aside the order granting an extension of time for service; the claim form and particulars of claim were served on the defendant on 21

[55] April 5, 2000, Langley J., Unreported.
[56] [2007] EWCA Civ 1203.

November. On the application to set aside the extension of time the judge held that CPR 11 was relevant, but that the reasons put forward for extending the time for service of the claim form were inadequate. It was argued that the extension ought not to be set aside because the order extending time had given the claimants a false sense of security, but the answer to that was that a claimant who made an application without notice ran the risk that the order might subsequently be set aside. The order extending time was set aside, and the claimants appealed.

The Court of Appeal held that CPR 11 was relevant. In CPR 11(1) the word "jurisdiction" does not denote territorial jurisdiction; rather it is a reference to the court's power or authority to try a claim. Service of a claim form out of time does not by itself deprive the court of its jurisdiction, but that is not the point. Where a defendant asks the court not to hear a case because the claim form has been served out of time, that is an application that the court should not exercise its jurisdiction, and the procedure in CPR 11(4) and (5) must be followed. If the relevant application is not made, then the defendant is treated as not raising any plea to the jurisdiction, even if the acknowledgment of service indicates an intention to do so. The application to set aside the order extending time is not an application under CPR 11, and it appears that in cases such as this both applications must be made. The Court of Appeal accepted that this was somewhat surprising conclusion, but held that it was an inevitable consequence of the drafting of CPR 11.[57]

22.028   However, the claimants' argument about the giving of a false sense of security was a bad one. The judge had been right to hold that if a claimant applied for and obtained an extension of time for service of the claim form without giving notice to the defendant, he did so at his own peril, and should know that an order obtained in such circumstances might be set aside. Then the Court of Appeal went on to say that there was no good reason for the claimants' failure to serve within the four months' period. However, it was relevant to the exercise of judicial discretion that a copy of the claim form had been sent to the defendant on 14 September. The failure to take account of this was a material omission, meaning that the court had to exercise the discretion afresh. In the light of the unusual combination of the fact that the claim was not time-barred, and that a copy of the claim form had been sent to the defendant within the four months' period, the order should not have been set aside. The latter point is largely fact-specific, and in any event it may be regarded as not strictly necessary to the decision because the Court had already held that there was in procedural terms no challenge to the jurisdiction before the court.

The logic of the decision is difficult to fault, but it is hard to avoid feeling

---

[57] However, this rule does not apply where service has been effected and acknowledged and the defendant then wants to plead limitation—*Dunn v Parole Board* [2008] EWCA Civ 374. See para.28.036.

that it reveals a flaw in the rules, probably caused by a failure to think through the relationship between CPR 11 and CPR 7.6. It would not be surprising to see an amendment to the rules in the near future.

Agreements to extend time

CPR 2.11 reads   22.029

2.11 Unless these Rules or a practice direction provide otherwise or the court orders otherwise, the time specified by a rule or by the court for a person to do any act may be varied by the written agreement of the parties.

In *Thomas v Home Office*[58] it was held that this rule did operate to allow parties to agree to extend time for the service of a claim form[59] but that care is needed in analysing whether particular pieces of writing meet the requirements of the rule. There is no reason why an exchange of letters between the two solicitors concerned, in which the extension of time is agreed, would not constitute a "written agreement[60]". Further, an oral agreement which is then confirmed in writing by both sides is also within the concept of a "written agreement"[61]. Matters are more difficult where the parties, having orally agreed a variation, each subsequently refer to what has been agreed in correspondence passing between them.[62] Although it must always be a question of fact and degree whether there is a written agreement, mere references to what has been agreed, especially passing references in correspondence which is mainly about some other aspect of the case, are unlikely to be viewed as amounting to a written agreement. As the Court of Appeal observed, there is no good reason why any oral agreement should not be promptly confirmed in writing or by e-mail. That being so, the Court will not be keen to cobble together a written agreement from passing references. The Court also held that it is not possible to argue that one party's reliance on an oral agreement creates an estoppel preventing the other side from denying the agreement. The rules require a written agreement, and that requirement, put there for good reason, should not be undermined in this way.

---

[58] [2006] EWCA Civ 1355.
[59] But not, of course, for the *issue* of a claim form; for agreements and estoppels in that regard see para.23.010.
[60] Para.25.
[61] Para.26.
[62] Para.27.

ISSUING A SECOND CLAIM FORM

22.030 In *Horton v Sadler and another*[63] the House of Lords departed from its own previous decision in *Walkley v Precision Forgings Ltd*[64] to the effect that court may not exercise its power to disapply the ordinary time limit in a personal injuries action under what is now s.33 of the Limitation Act 1980 where a claimant had issued proceedings in respect of those injuries before the ordinary time limit expired and has brought a second action (in which the application under s.33 is made) after expiry of the ordinary time limit. There is no doubt that since the decision in Walkely lower courts have often felt uncomfortable with it and have varied between applying it with no expression of disapproval,[65] applying it with express reluctance,[66] and distinguishing it.[67] In *Horton v Sadler*, the leading speech was that of Lord Bingham, who focussed on the illogicality of giving more unfavourable treatment to claimants who had issued proceedings than to claimants who had not issued proceedings. Lord Bingham also attacked what he regarded as the illogicality of saying, as the House of Lords had said in *Walkley* that claimants who has issued proceedings in time but not proceeded with the action were prejudiced not by s.11 but by their own subsequent inaction. It is clear that for the foreseeable future the decision in *Horton v Sadler* represents the law, but it may be observed that claimants who have issued proceedings in time thereby demonstrate beyond doubt that they are aware of their cause of action and are in a position to pursue it. It is as a general rule hard to see why such claimants deserve the exercise of the court's discretion in their favour if they subsequently do not proceed properly with the action. Of course that is an argument going to discretion not to jurisdiction, but it might be supposed that even after *Horton v Sadler* there will be very few cases of this type where it will be appropriate to exercise the s.33 discretion in the claimant's favour.

22.031 If the first claim form has expired, but the limitation period has not, then it will clearly be permissible to issue a second claim form and proceed with that. Where time has expired, the issue of a second claim form will be useless, except possibly in cases of personal injury, where s.33 of the 1980

---

[63] [2006] UKHL 27.

[64] [1979] 2 All ER 548, [1979] 1 WLR 606.

[65] E.g. *Whitfield v North Durham HA* [1995] PIQR 361, *Forward v Hendricks* [1997] 2 All ER 395 and *Young, decd v Western Power Distribution (South West) Plc* [2003] EWCA Civ 1034, [2003] 1 WLR 2868.

[66] E.g *Chappell v Cooper* [1980] 2 All ER 463, [1980] 1 WLR 958, 967-8, per Ormrod LJ.

[67] E.g. *Rose v Express Welding Ltd* (21 January 1986, Unreported, Court of Appeal (Civil Division) Transcript No 31 of 1986), *White v Glass*, The Times, 18 February 1989, Court of Appeal (Civil Division) Transcript No 140 of 1989, *Re Workvale Ltd* [1992] 1 WLR 416, [1991] BCLC 528, [1992] BCC 349, *McEvoy v AA Welding and Fabrication Ltd* [1998] PIQR 266, *Shapland v Palmer* [1999] 3 All ER 50, [1999] 1 WLR 2068, *Piggott v Aulton, decd* [2003] EWCA Civ 24, [2003] RTR 540, and *Adams v Ali* [2006] EWCA Civ 91, [2006] 1 WLR 1330.

Act will apply. It is therefore possible in such cases for the claimant to seek the court's leave to continue the action out of time. Recent authorities have confirmed that the court does have discretion to allow the action to continue under s.33 even if CPR 7.6 would have precluded an extension of time for the service of the first claim form[68]

AMENDMENT OF THE CLAIM FORM/PLEADINGS

Once the claim form has been validly served, the most important question which arises in a limitation context concerns the possibility of amendment, either to the claim form or to subsequent pleadings (including the statement of claim in the case of a generally indorsed claim form). Such amendments may be required before time has expired for commencing the action as well as after it, though obviously in the former event no limitation point arises. It is therefore necessary to explain briefly the rules applicable to any application to amend in order to show the operation of the special rules for cases where time has expired. **22.032**

CPR PART 17

CPR Pt 17 deals with amendment of pleadings. CPR r.17.1(1) allows the claim form to be amended at any time without permission before it is served. Apparently this liberty may be exercised to make more than one amendment. After service the permission of the court will be required. CPR Pt 17 confers on the court a wide discretion to permit amendments, and the general rule is that amendments will be allowed wherever this is necessary in order to do justice between the parties by allowing the true issues in the case to be raised by the pleadings,[69] at least where the other party can be sufficiently compensated by the imposition of appropriate terms as to costs.[70] CPR r.17.4 deals specifically with the case where amendments are sought to be made after the expiry of any relevant limitation period. **22.033**

---

[68] *McKay v Hamlami* [2009] 2 All E.R. 579 [2009] 3 WLR 551.
[69] *G.L. Baker Ltd v Medway Building & Supplies Ltd* [1958] 3 All E.R. 540 at 546, per Jenkins L.J.
[70] *Cropper v Smith* (1893) 36 Ch.D. 700 at 710–711, per Bowen L.J.

CPR PARTS 17 AND 19 AND SECTION 35 OF THE 1980 ACT

22.034 The provisions of CPR Pts 17 and 19 have to be considered in the light of s.35 of the 1980 Act. This section deals with the addition of new parties[71] and with the addition of new claims. Section 35(2) deals with "new claims", which s.35 defines as including the addition of any new cause of action. Once time has expired the addition of such claims is forbidden by s.35, except in cases of personal injury (to which s.33 of the 1980 Act applies[72]) or as permitted by rules of court. Section 35 restricts the permitted ambit of these rules of court, and it is for this reason that the relevant CPR provisions are narrowly drafted. Although, as appears below, some pre-CPR provisions may still be relevant, care is needed in applying these because there are some subtle differences in the current form of wording.

AMENDMENT BY DEFENDANT

22.035 Although most of the problems under CPR Pt 17 have arisen because the claimant has sought to amend, it can sometimes happen that the defendant wishes to amend. If that amendment is consequent upon an amendment which the claimant has been allowed to make, then no further leave of the court is necessary. In other cases CPR Pt 17 will apply. In *Tersons Ltd v E. Alec Colman Investments Ltd*[73] the defendant sought to amend the defence by adding a set-off and counterclaim out of time. The Court of Appeal allowed the set-off, but not the counterclaim, observing that it would be unfair to allow an amendment which could result in the claimant paying damages to the defendant. The provisions of s.35 of the 1980 Act, which is considered in detail in Ch.23, would affect the decision in this case, but the basic principle of applying the discretion so as to do justice between the parties is still valid.

DEFECTIVE CLAIM FORMS

22.036 In *Brady v Barrow Steelworks*[74] the writ failed to assign the action to any of the Divisions of the High Court. Payne J. held that this was a mere irre-

---

[71] For the addition of new parties see Ch.23.
[72] See Ch.8.
[73] (1973) 225 E.G. 2300, CA.
[74] [1965] 2 Q.B. 182, Payne J.

gularity, which could be corrected although time had expired. The same result was reached in *Hill v Luton Corporation*,[75] where the endorsement on the writ was bad for insufficient particularity, but the writ was accompanied by a statement of claim which cured the defect. Devlin J. held that the action must be considered to have been commenced in time, since the error in the writ was a mere irregularity. As such it was capable of correction under RSC, Ord.2 (now CPR r.3.1(2)), and was corrected by the service of the statement of claim. An even stronger case on the same point is *Pontin v Wood*,[76] where the writ was again defective for want of particularity. By the time of the application to amend, time had expired, so that a refusal of the amendment would have left the plaintiff without a remedy. The Court of Appeal held that the amendment should be allowed.

Correcting name of party

The pre-CPR authorities in this area must now be regarded as obsolete. **22.037** CPR r.17.4(3) provides:

> "The court may allow an amendment to correct a mistake as to the name of a party, but only where the mistake was genuine and not one that would cause reasonable doubt as to the identity of the party in question."

It will no doubt be a question of fact in every case whether these requirements are satisfied, and it is to be noted that even where they are satisfied the granting of permission for the amendment remains a matter for the court's discretion. In *Gregson v Channel Four Television*[77] the Court of Appeal considered the relationship between CPR rr.17.4 and 19.5, which deals with the addition of new parties, and held that CPR r.19.5 is relevant only where the claimant seeks to add a party who was not intended to be named in the original claim form. CPR r.19.5 is relevant to questions under s.35 of the Limitation Act 1980.[78] In *Ramsey v Leonard Curtis (A Firm)*[79] the claimant attempted to bring proceedings against administrative receivers who were partners in a firm of accountants. The proceedings should have been brought against the receivers personally, but in error they were served on the firm, and were accordingly deemed to have been served on each partner as a partner. The Court of Appeal held that this mistake was not one that could be corrected once time had expired.

---

[75] [1951] 2 K.B. 387, Devlin J.
[76] [1962] 1 Q.B. 594, CA.
[77] *The Times*, August 11, 2000, CA; see also *International Distillers & Vintners Limited (t/a Percy Fox & Company) v J.F. Hillebrand (UK) Ltd*, *The Times*, January 25, 2000, David Foskett Q.C.
[78] See Ch.23.
[79] July 28, 1999, Unreported, CA.

ADDING A NEW CAUSE OF ACTION

22.038   This is the element of amendment which has given rise to the greatest difficulties. The rules in this area must be understood in the context of s.35(5) of the 1980 Act. This restricts the cases in which rules of court may allow for the addition of a new cause of action out of time to cases where the new cause of action arises out of the same facts or substantially the same facts as are already in issue in any claim previously made in the original action.[80] The rules are to be found in CPR r.17.4. The court may allow an amendment whose effect will be to add or substitute a new claim, but only if the new claim arises out of the same facts or substantially the same facts as a claim in respect of which the party applying for permission has already claimed a remedy in the proceedings.[81] This form of wording reproduces in part the former RSC, Ord.20, r.5, so earlier authorities may still be of relevance in this area. However, the new rule contains no specific reference to showing that it would be "just" to allow the amendment. It is nevertheless submitted that such a requirement must inevitably be implied where a judicial discretion is being exercised. There is a fine distinction between amendments which merely seek to clarify the existing issues between the parties, which do not fall within the scope of this rule, and amendments which seek to add a distinct cause of action. An amendment which merely adds a new particular to an existing cause of action will be allowed even though time has expired.[82] A good example of the difficulties in this area is to be found in *Dornan v J.W. Ellis & Co. Ltd.*[83] The plaintiff was blinded in an accident at work, and sued his employers under the Factories Acts 1897–1925. After time had expired he sought to amend the writ by pleading the negligence of a fellow employee, for whose acts the employers were clearly vicariously liable. He did not seek to have the fellow employee added as a second defendant. The Court of Appeal held that this amendment could be allowed on the basis that it did not amount to the addition of a new cause of action, but was merely an extension of the original claim. The Court openly accepted that this was a borderline decision. It is obviously true that the accident in question is the same one, but it is open to question whether the cause of action is really the same. Originally the plaintiff relied on a breach by the employers of their duties under the Factories Acts 1897–1925; by the amendment he sought to rely on a breach of duty by the fellow employee.

22.039   The case of *Hall v Meyrick*[84] provides an instructive contrast. The two plaintiffs sued their solicitor, but some confusion arose in the pleadings

---

[80] 1980 Act s.35(5)(a).
[81] For detailed analysis of this provision, see para.23.010.
[82] *Collins v Herts C.C.* [1947] 1 All E.R. 633, Hallett J.
[83] [1962] 1 Q.B. 583, CA.
[84] [1957] 2 Q.B. 455, CA.

over whether the solicitor had been retained on a joint or several basis. The plaintiffs therefore sought leave out of time to amend the pleadings so as to clarify this point. The Court of Appeal held that such leave should not be granted, since the effect of the amendment would be to allow the plaintiffs to rely on a different contract (and therefore a different cause of action) from that which they had previously alleged. In *Robinson v Unicos Property Corporation Ltd*[85] the claim was that P1 had made a contract on behalf of himself and P2 and P3 (his partners). Later the plaintiffs wished to amend so as to allege that P1 had made the contract on his own behalf, and that the right of action has subsequently become vested in P2 and P3 by assignment. The Court of Appeal upheld the decision of Glyn-Jones J. to allow the amendment, taking the view that the plaintiffs were essentially relying on the same contract and had merely changed the account of the origin of their title to sue on it.[86] It is by no means easy to reconcile all these cases, and it may be more prudent to accept that determining whether a proposed amendment seeks to introduce a new cause of action is ultimately a matter of impression, and it is dangerous to rely too heavily on precedent. More recently, in *Paragon Finance plc v D.B. Thakerar & Co. (A Firm); Paragon Finance Plc v Thimbleby & Co. (A Firm)*[87] it was held, in a solicitors' negligence case, that an amendment which sought to make a new allegation of intentional wrongdoing where previously no intentional wrongdoing had been alleged constituted the introduction of a new cause of action, since intentional and unintentional wrongdoing gave rise to distinct causes of action. At the same time, a claim based on allegations of fraud and dishonesty did not involve substantially the same facts as a claim based on allegations of negligence. Under CPR Pt 17 it would follow that leave to amend in this way outside the limitation period could not be granted.

It is only when the court determines that the amendment sought does **22.040** amount to a new cause of action that the discretion under CPR r.17.4(2) is required. This discretion reverses the earlier rule that no amendment would be allowed if its effect were to deprive a party of an accrued limitation defence.[88] Consequently, the defendant's "right" to plead limitation exists only to the extent that the court declines to exercise its discretion under this rule. In exercising the discretion it appears that a fairly lenient attitude has in the past been adopted, at least where the claimant wishes to amend so as to allege breach of duty at a different stage of the defendant's conduct from that on which he has previously relied.[89] The laying down of general

[85] [1962] 1 W.L.R. 520, CA.
[86] For other examples of the distinction see *Graff Brothers Estates Ltd v Rimrose Brook Joint Sewerage Board* [1953] 2 Q.B. 318, CA; *Pathak v James Nourse Ltd* [1962] 2 Lloyd's Rep. 467, CA.
[87] [1999] 1 All E.R. 400, CA.
[88] *Stanhope Steamship Co. v British Phosphate Commissioners* [1956] 2 Lloyd's Rep. 337, CA.
[89] [1965] 1 W.L.R. 948, CA.

principles is similarly difficult in connection with the second of these two questions. In *Weait v Jayanbee Joinery Ltd*[90] the plaintiff sued his employers after an injury at work. Only at a late stage did the defendants discover evidence suggesting that the plaintiff's condition might have been exacerbated by negligent medical treatment. The Court of Appeal gave leave for an amendment of the pleadings out of time so as to include this allegation; the vital point was held to be that the defendants had not been negligent in not discovering the information at an earlier stage. In *Turner v Ford Motor Company*,[91] another employers' liability case, the plaintiff was working for his employers at the defendants' premises when he was injured. He began by suing the defendants, and at a late stage they sought to amend their defence by alleging negligence on the part of the plaintiff. By this time the plaintiff was out of time for an action against his own employers, but the Court of Appeal nevertheless allowed the defendants' amendment, since the plaintiff could quite easily have commenced an action against his employers at an earlier stage had he wished to do so.

Taken together, these cases suggested that the exercise of the discretion depends upon balancing the hardship involved in allowing or disallowing the amendment, taking due account of the conduct of the parties in relation to the action.

ADDING A LATER CAUSE OF ACTION

22.041 As a general rule no amendment of the claim form will be allowed which involves adding a cause of action which has accrued since the date on which the claim form was issued.[92] In *P v D1 and D2: The C and J*[93] Neill J. held that this principle extended to claims for instalments of hire which had accrued due since the date of the writ.

AMENDMENTS AND RELATION BACK

22.042 An issue which has caused a great deal of difficulty in this area is the so-called "relation back" theory.[94] Controversy arose over the effect of allowing an amendment to the pleadings. One view was that such amendment took effect only from the date on which it was made. The alternative theory was that the amendment was retrospective, and related

---

[90] [1968] 1 Q.B. 239, CA.
[91] [1965] 1 W.L.R. 948, CA.
[92] *Eshelby v Federated European Bank Ltd* [1932] 1 K.B. 254; *Halliard Property Co. v Jack Segal Ltd* [1978] 1 W.L.R. 377.
[93] [1984] 2 Lloyd's Rep. 601.
[94] For the operation of this theory in relation to a joinder of parties, see paras 23.036–23.037.

back to the date which the pleading bore on its face.[95] In *Ketteman v Hansel Properties*[96] the House of Lords decided that the former of these views was the correct one.[97] However, that case was decided under the Limitation Act 1939, and s.35 of the 1980 Act differs in important ways from s.28 of the 1939 Act. Specifically, it provides that where a new claim is brought other than by way of third-party proceedings, that claim is treated for limitation purposes as a separate action and is deemed to have begun on the date on which the original action commenced. Therefore, in actions governed by the 1980 Act the *Ketteman* rule is no longer valid, though in actions governed by the 1939 Act, which must by the present date already be very rare, the *Ketteman* rule is still good law.

DISMISSAL FOR WANT OF PROSECUTION

This is a subject which had a lengthy history prior to the CPR when courts were inclined to take a relatively relaxed view of the progress of actions, at least in the High Court. The adoption of active case management techniques under the CPR has had the effect that the subject has more or less disappeared—cases simply do not suffer from the sorts of delay which led to applications to dismiss for want of prosecution. The consideration of the earlier authorities has therefore been excised from the text. **22.043**

LIMITATION AND ABUSE OF PROCESS

CPR r.3.4(2) allows the court, on the application of a party or on its own motion: **22.044**

"to strike out any claim form or pleading, in whole or in part, on any of the following grounds:

(a) that the statement of case discloses no reasonable grounds for bringing or defending the claim;

(b) that the statement of case is an abuse of the court's process or is otherwise likely to obstruct the just disposal of the proceedings; or

---

[95] *London Electricity Board v London Borough of Redbridge* (1985) 84 L.G.R. 146, Stocker J.

[96] [1987] A.C. 189, HL.

[97] This case arose in connection with the joinder of parties rather than of causes of action (a matter which is more fully dealt with in Ch.23). In either case the governing provisions are the 1980 Act s.35 and CPR Pts 17 and 19. It is therefore submitted that the principle applies equally to joinder of parties and joinder of actions.

"(c) that there has been a failure to comply with a rule, practice direction or court order."

This is the successor, with some amendment, to the former RSC, Ord.18, r.19. The similarities between the two rules are sufficient to justify continuing consideration of the old authorities. In *Dismore v Milton*[98] the Court of Appeal declined to allow the earlier equivalent of Ord.18, r.19 to be used in such a case, but in *Riches v DPP*,[99] an action for malicious prosecution, the defendant pleaded limitation, and sought to have the action dismissed under Ord.18, r.19[100]. The plaintiff did not allege that the case was governed by any of the provisions of the Limitation Acts which can serve to extend time, but argued that the use of r.19 was not appropriate in a limitation case. The Court of Appeal rejected this argument, holding that as a matter of convenience the use of this provision was the most sensible way to deal with a case of this kind. A further point to consider here is that on an application under r.19(1)(a) no evidence could be received.[101] Therefore, such applications are to be considered solely on the pleadings. For this reason it was often inappropriate to use this ground in a limitation case. At the present day it seems likely that an obvious limitation defence is likely to be used as the basis for a defendant's application for summary judgment under CPR Pt 24, which had no counterpart under the RSC. Even under CPR Pt 24, two problems arise. First, an action which is time-barred does generally disclose a reasonable cause of action—limitation must be specifically pleaded,[102] and the court will not take the point until it has been pleaded. Also, at least outside the area of real property, the expiry of the limitation period does not normally take away the plaintiff's right, but merely bars his remedy. Secondly, even an action which is time-barred on its face may be saved if the plaintiff can appeal to one of the provisions of Pt II of the 1980 Act, such as fraud[103] or disability. The investigation of all these points commonly requires oral evidence, however, and that is not normally permitted under CPR Pt 24. It is therefore better to seek to have the claim struck out as an abuse of process. However, this will be done only in a very clear case, of which *Riches v DPP*, discussed in the previous paragraph, may be seen as an example.

---

[98] [1938] 3 All E.R. 762, CA.

[99] [1973] 2 All E.R. 935, CA.

[100] The modern equivalent is CPR 3.4.

[101] RSC, Ord.18, r.19(2); the modern practice is identical in this regard.

[102] CPR 16PD—13.1. See also *Dawkins v Penrhyn* (1878) 4 App.Cas. 51, HL; *Dismore v Milton* [1938] 3 All E.R. 762, CA; *Ronex Properties Ltd v John Laing Construction Ltd* [1983] 3 Q.B. 398, CA.

[103] See, e.g., *London Borough of Lewisham v Leslie & Co. Ltd* (1978) 250 E.G. 1289, where the Court of Appeal refused to strike out a builders' negligence case based on concealed fraud, even though the plaintiffs had themselves been under a duty to inspect the building works.

THE LAW COMMISSION'S PROPOSALS

The Report gives relatively little attention to procedural issues of the kind **22.045** discussed in this chapter, being more concerned with the length of the limitation period and when time should start to run. However, the Commission does recommend the retention of the present rule that the event which stops time from running should be the issue of proceedings, rather than service. It will be recalled that the Courts and Legal Services Bill 1990 contained a proposal to change this rule so that time ran until service, but the proposal was dropped, and the matter does not seem to have received serious attention since. Certainly there is no evidence that the present system produces injustice, though there is no doubt that adoption of the date of service as the crucial date would greatly simplify the law by removing entirely the class of case concerned with renewal of the claim form after the expiry of time.[104]

The incidence of cases involving striking out for want of prosecution continues to decline, no doubt as a result of the more proactive case management techniques now employed.

---

[104] Indeed, it might well be that it would no longer be necessary to limit the validity of a claim form, since it would have no effect until served.

CHAPTER 23

Section 35

GENERAL

This chapter should be read in conjunction with those parts of Ch.22 which **23.001** deal with amendments of the writ and/or pleadings that seek to add new causes of action to those already in issue. Together, these chapters present a complete account of the limitation problems which arise in connection with joinder.[1]

Once an action has been begun, it may be desired to add additional parties. These new parties may occupy one (occasionally more than one) of three capacities, and the relationship between their addition and the rules on limitation periods depends upon which capacity they occupy. First, an additional claimant may be added, as where it is desired to consolidate actions by more than one person against the same defendant[2]; alternatively, where a group of companies is involved, it may be found necessary, for reasons relating to the doctrine of corporate personality, to add another company from the group as a co-claimant. Secondly, a party may be added as an additional defendant. This will often result from the discovery of facts not known to the claimant at the outset of the litigation and which suggest that responsibility for any alleged wrongs may be shared by more than one person. Thirdly, a person may be added as a third (or subsequent) party. This will arise where the defendant (or a third or subsequent party) wishes to claim that any liability which he might incur should be passed on, in whole or in part, to someone else who has allegedly committed a breach of duty as against the defendant or as against the claimant. In such a case the claimant is not concerned with the issues between the defendant and the third party. However, it commonly happens that the addition by the defendant of a third party is shortly followed by the claimant seeking to add that third party as second defendant. The tactical reason for this is that

---

[1] CPR Pt 19; for the non-limitation aspects of these matters, see Civil Procedure.
[2] The rules governing this are to be found in CPR Pt 19.

it allows the claimant to recover from the third party/second defendant if it is found that he, rather than the defendant, is responsible for the claimant's loss. CPR r.19.4 and 5 now provides a complete code for dealing with the addition of new parties.[3]

23.002 In some cases a party who has been added as a defendant or a third party may wish to be removed from the action on the ground that the action which is sought to be brought against him is time-barred. The rules relating to such applications are considered below.[4]

Alternatively, it may become desirable to introduce a new cause of action to the case. This may happen, for example, where facts come to light for the first time which suggest that the claimant may have a cause of action that was not previously thought to be available to him. A related, but separate, problem arises where the claimant now wishes to sue in a different capacity from that in which he began the action, as where a widow suing under the Fatal Accidents Acts in respect of her husband's death becomes his executrix and wishes to amend her claim so as to sue on behalf of his estate as well. These problems are dealt with at length in Ch.22.

It should be noted that this chapter does not deal with problems arising from lapse of time as between the original parties to the action. These are examined in detail in Ch.22.

In this area of the law there is a considerable overlap between the provisions of s.35 of the Limitation Act 1980 and various Rules of the Supreme Court. Section 35 allows for the making of rules of court relating to various matters, as explained below,[5] and these rules are contained in the parts of CPR Pts 17 and 19, which are discussed in this Chapter.

AMBIT OF SECTION 35

23.003 Section 35 of the Limitation Act. 1980, which replaced s.28 of the Limitation Act 1939, is without doubt one of the most convoluted provisions in the entire law of limitations.[6] It is therefore convenient to begin with a simplified summary of the workings of this section. The remainder of this chapter will then be devoted to examining the details of these principles. Essentially, s.35 provides that a defendant may always make one counterclaim against the claimant, even if the limitation period for the making of that claim has expired. This does not require leave, though it is subject to

---

[3] *Secured Residential Funding Plc v Hamptons Group Ltd*, December 7, 1999, Unreported, Master Bowles.
[4] See paras 23.048–23.049.
[5] See paras 23.006–23.009.
[6] Cited with approval by Lord Collins in *Roberts v Gill* [2010] UKSC 22 at para.3; that judgment also contains a detailed history of s.35 and its predecessors.

the general power of the court to strike out a pleading as an abuse of process.[7] By contrast, the making of any further counterclaim (by any party) or the institution of third-party proceedings does require leave if the limitation period for bringing an original action in respect of that claim has expired. Further, s.35 and the rules of court made under it significantly restrict the circumstances in which that leave can be given. Even in cases where the CPR do not apply, as under s.37(5) of the Patents Act 1977, there is a longstanding rule of practice that a new claim should not normally be allowed once time for the making of the original claim has expired. If it is uncertain whether time has expired, the proper course is to refuse permission for the amendment and leave the claimant to test the limitation position in a fresh action.[8]

The basic rule is expressed in s.35(1), which provides that for limitation purposes any new claim is treated as a separate claim and as having been commenced on one of two alternative dates. If it is a new claim made in or by way of third-party proceedings, it is treated as having been begun on the date on which it was in fact begun; if it is any other new claim, it is treated as having been begun on the date on which the original action was begun. This subsection necessitates the definition of a number of important terms which it uses, and the subsequent subsections of s.35 provide many of these definitions.

Meaning of "new claim"

Section 35(2) provides that a new claim in this context is any claim by way   **23.004**
of set-off or counterclaim, and any claim involving either the addition or substitution of a new cause of action[9] or the addition or substitution of a new party. Therefore, any form of joinder which would be subject to CPR r.17.4 will be a new claim for these purposes. Where the original statement of claim narrates a fact but does not make a claim under it, an amendment to claim under it involves a new cause of action.[10] By contrast, an amendment which claims a new remedy based on the same facts may not involve a new cause of action.[11] Further, the withdrawal of a previously made admission, thus reviving a claim which was contained in the original

---

[7] CPR 3.4; see *Ernst & Young v Butte Mining Plc* [1997] 2 All E.R. 471, CA.

[8] *Rhone-Poulenc Rorer International Holdings Inc v Yeda Research and Development Co Ltd* [2006] EWHC 160 (Ch), [2006] All ER (D) 223 (Feb) Lewison J. Affirmed by the Court of Appeal [2006] EWCA Civ 1094 [2006] All ER (D) 464 (Jul).

[9] Though the section does not define 'cause of action'—*Harland & Wolff Pension Trustees v Aon Consulting Financial Services Ltd* [2009] EWHC 1557 (Ch) Warren J.

[10] *Balfour Beatty Construction Ltd v Parsons Brown and Newton Ltd* (1990) 7 C.L.J. 205, CA; on the meaning of cause of action generally, see para.5.xxx; see also *Alliance & Leicester Plc v Pellys*, July 9, 1999, Unreported, Park J.

[11] *Lloyds Bank Plc v Rogers* [1999] 38 E.G. 187; [1999] 3 E.G.L.R. 83, CA.

statement of claim, does not amount to a new claim.[12] Nor is there a new claim where a party who has succeeded to the rights and liabilities of another seeks to be substituted for that other in existing proceedings without in any way changing the facts relied upon or the relief sought.[13] In *Anthony Stephen De Silva Farmer v Wood and Kingsford Dorman (A Firm)*[14] the Court of Appeal held that no new cause of action was involved when the claimant amended his claim to plead that a claim formerly vested in himself and his wife was now, by assignment, vested solely in him.

23.005   *Latreefers Incorporated v Hobson*[15] establishes that where a claimant seeks to amend by pleading that the action is governed by a different system of law from that first alleged, this will be a new cause of action. However, it may still arise out of the same or substantially the same facts as the original claim. Although the details of a foreign law are treated by the English court as questions of fact in the sense that they require evidence, this does not make them relevant 'facts' for the purposes of the s.35 discretion.

23.006   *Evans v CIG Mon Cymru Ltd*[16] involves an unusual set of circumstances where the claim form in a personal injuries case misdescribed the cause of action, but the accompanying particulars of claim gave the correct description. By the time the claimant applied to amend the claim form the limitation period had expired, but the Court of Appeal held that the amendment could nevertheless be allowed because it did not add a new cause of action; rather, it simply corrected an administrative error, as was obvious if the claim form and particulars of claim were read together. It appears that the result might have been different if the same error had occurred also on the particulars of claim, though even then it might presumably be argued that the error was purely administrative.

23.007   Where separate particulars of claim are served against different defendants, the later particulars of claim do not necessarily introduce a new cause of action[17]. This point does not appear to have arisen directly in any previous case, perhaps because it would have been assumed that the serving of different particulars of claim on different defendants was not permitted.

Meaning of "third-party proceedings"

23.008   Section 35(2) defines this phrase as meaning any proceedings brought in the course of the action by any party to the action against a person not previously party to the action, other than proceedings brought by joining any such person as defendant to any claim already made in the original action

---

[12] *Burton v MBC (Builders-Ashington) Ltd, The Times*, February 1, 1994, CA.
[13] *Yorkshire RHA v Fairclough Building Ltd* [1996] 1 All E.R. 519, CA.
[14] July 7, 2000, Unreported, CA.
[15] [2002] EWHC 1586 (Ch), (Transcript).
[16] [2008] EWCA Civ 390.
[17] *Tetrapak Ltd v Biddle and Co* [2010] EWHC 54 (Ch) Warren J.

by the party bringing the proceedings. Therefore there are two elements to third-party proceedings. First, the person proceeded against must not previously have been a party to the action. Secondly, the proceedings must not take the form of adding that person as a defendant to any claim made by the original claimant. Therefore the distinction between adding a person as third party and adding him as second defendant, alluded to at paragraph 23.001, is preserved.

Which new claims are allowed?

Section 35(3) imposes restrictions on the bringing of new claims. Subject to **23.009** s.33 (which deals with the court's discretion to override the three-year time-limit in the case of personal injury claims[18]) and any provision in the Rules of the Supreme Court,[19] neither the High Court nor the county court shall allow a new claim (other than one made by way of third-party proceedings) other than an original set-off or counterclaim to be made after the expiry of any time-limit which would affect a new action to enforce that claim.

Where expiry of time extinguishes rights

Section 35 cannot be used to allow amendments to pleadings in those cases **23.010** where the expiry of time extinguishes the claimant's claim entirely, such as claims under the Hague-Visby Rules.[20]

Meaning of "original set-off or counterclaim"

Section 35(3) goes on to define this term as meaning a claim made by way **23.011** of set-off or counterclaim by a party who has not previously made any claim in the action. Therefore, in any action a party may make only one original counterclaim or set-off. As soon as this is done, he becomes a party who has previously made a claim in the action (a set-off clearly counts as a claim for these purposes). The effect of s.35(3), therefore, is that, subject to the exceptions it mentions, a party is always entitled to make one claim by way of set-off or counterclaim, even if a new action to enforce that claim would be out of time. Thereafter, any further claim is subject to s.35(3).[21] The term "set-off" is limited to a legal set-off, i.e. it does not extend to an

---

[18] See Ch.8.
[19] CPR r.19.2; see paras 23.026–23.031.
[20] *Payabi v Armstel* [1992] 2 W.L.R. 898, Hobhouse J. For the Hague-Visby Rules see Ch.26.
[21] *Idyll Ltd v Dinerman Davison & Hillman* (1985) 4 Const.L.J. 294; *Crown Estate Commissioners v Whitfield Partners* (March 30, 1990, CA) which is further considered below, and *Leicester Wholesale Fruit Market Ltd v Grundy (No. 2)* (1996) 53 B.L.R. 6, CA.

equitable set-off.[22] In a claim under the Consumer Protection Act 1987 the court has no power to allow the substitution of a new defendant after the expiry of the ten-year longstop[23]. A 'counterclaim' for these purposes may be made by a party against whom no claim has yet been made. All that matters is that all the parties requisite to assert the cause of action are on one side of the record and one of the persons against whom the cause of action may be asserted is on the other side of the record.[24]

Restrictions on rules of court

23.012 Although s.35(3) allows rules of court to extend the category of cases in which new claims other than third-party proceedings may be brought after the expiry of the time-limit for bringing a new action in respect of them, s.35(4) and (5) qualifies that permission by providing that such rules may not apply unless at least two conditions are satisfied, and CPR r.17.4 closely follows the wording of these requirements.

"The same or substantially the same facts"

23.013 The first requirement is that, in the case of a claim involving a new cause of action, that cause of action must arise out of the same or substantially the same facts as are already in issue on any claim previously made in the original action. This has been held to be a mixed question of law and fact. The leading authority on the application of this test is *Steamship Mutual v Trollope & Colls*,[25] where May L.J. said:

> "In the light of the definitions of a cause of action already referred to, I do not think one can look only to the duty on a party, but one must look also to the nature and extent of the breach relied upon, as well as to the nature and extent of the damage complained of in deciding whether, as a matter of degree, a new cause of action is sought to be relied upon. The mere fact that one is considering what are, as it is said, after all only different defects to the same building, does not necessarily mean in any way that they are constituents of one and the same cause of action."

---

[22] *Westdeutsche Landesbank Girozentrale v Islington London BC, Kleinwort Benson Ltd v Sandwell BC* [1994] 4 All E.R. 890, Hobhouse J.; *Philip Collins Ltd v Davis* [2000] 3 All E.R. 808, Jonathan Parker J.
[23] *OB v Aventis Pasteur* [2010] UKSC 23, giving effect to the decision of the ECJ in *Aventis Pasteur v OB* Case C-358-08 on 2 December 2009; and see para.7.016.
[24] *Law Society of England and Wales v Wemyss* [2008] EWHC 2515 (Ch) Norris J., citing *Hodson v Mochi* (1878) 8 Ch D 569, 47 LJ Ch 604, 26 WR 590.
[25] (1986) 6 Con.L.R. 11; (1986) 33 Build.L.R. 77.

In the same case it was said that a useful way to test the position is to ask whether a new action brought on the proposed amended pleading after the conclusion of the case already in existence would be met with a successful plea of res judicata. If so, this is strong evidence that the facts arise out of the same cause of action.[26]

However, in *Stock v London Underground Ltd*[27] Pill L.J. said:

"I do not consider *Steamship* to be authority for the proposition that where there are heads of damage which are very different in size and nature that in itself establishes that there is more than one cause of action."

It is submitted that both May L.J. and Pill L.J. were correct. Taken together, their observations emphasise that there can be no blanket rule in this area. The question is always one of fact and impression.

In *Darlington Building Society v O'Rourke James Scourfield and McCarthy (sued as a firm)*[28] Sir Iain Glidewell, giving the judgment of the Court of Appeal, put the matter in slightly different terms when he said:

"In my view where an amendment pleads a duty which differs from that pleaded in the original Statement of Claim it will, or certainly will usually, raise a new cause of action. If there is no allegation of a different duty but different facts are alleged to constitute a breach of the duty it is more difficult to decide whether a new cause of action is pleaded."[29]

However, it is submitted that the difference is merely a matter of emphasis.

The application of the test has been considered in a number of cases. The first was *Fannon v Backhouse*,[30] whose complicated facts require to be narrated at some length. The defendant and his father had been in partnership, and a contractual dispute arose between the partnership and the plaintiff. By the time the plaintiff issued his writ the father had died, and the writ was issued against the defendant alone. While the action was pending the defendant was convicted of murder and sentenced to life imprisonment. The plaintiff then sought to have the executors of the father's estate added as additional defendants, since the defendant was now destitute. The limitation period had by now expired, and the question therefore was whether

23.014

---

[26] See also *Murray Film Finances v Film Finance Ltd*, May 19, 1994, CA, Unreported.

[27] *The Times*, August 13, 1999, CA.

[28] *The Times*, November 20, 1998, CA; issues of confidentiality as between clients and solicitors arose in that case, and this led Park J. in *Alliance & Leicester v Pellys* (July 9, 1999, Unreported) to describe the facts of the case as "rather special".

[29] Examples of the latter include *Brickfield Properties Ltd v Newton* [1971] 3 All E.R. 328; [1971] 1 W.L.R. 862; *Steamship Mutual v Trollope & Colls* (1986) 6 Con. L.R. 11; *Hamlin v Edwin Evans* [1996] 47 E.G. 141; (1999) 52 Con. L.R. 116.

[30] July 30, 1987, CA, Unreported.

the cause of action against the father's estate arose out of the same facts as the action against the defendant. The application was resisted on the ground that the plaintiff, in order to succeed against these defendants, would have to show that the father had died and that the executors had been duly appointed. Neither of these facts had any relevance to the action against the defendant personally, and it was therefore argued that the two actions did not arise out of the same facts. For the plaintiff the argument was that "same facts" in s.35(5)(a) meant "same disputed facts" and the additional facts here were not in dispute. The Court of Appeal decided the case in favour of the defendant, rejecting this narrower construction of "same facts".

23.015   This decision is potentially of general significance, since it is likely to restrict considerably the cases in which a new party can be joined after the expiry of the limitation period. *Sagar v Kingston & Esher AHA*[31] was a medical negligence case arising out of the delivery by Caesarean section of a baby who was allegedly damaged by the conduct of the delivery. After the expiry of the limitation period the plaintiff sought to amend the statement of claim to allege different acts of negligence by the defendant's employees, though the course of events which was pleaded was still the same. The Court of Appeal held that the new cause of action arose out of substantially the same facts as that originally pleaded, so that there was jurisdiction to permit the amendments. In *Sorata Ltd v Gardex Ltd*[32] the plaintiff sought to amend the statement of claim in a patent action by adding particulars of further infringements by the defendants. Falconer J. held that this amounted to adding a new cause of action,[33] which clearly did not arise out of the same set of facts as that originally pleaded, and therefore the court had no jurisdiction to allow the amendments. In *Crown Estate Commissioners v Whitfield Partners*[34] the original action was about defective air conditioning in a building. The new matter related to the level of lighting, which was also alleged to be inadequate. The Court of Appeal held that this was not a new cause of action, merely an amendment of the original pleading. It is in every case a mixed question of fact and law to decide on which side of the line a case falls. It is suggested that the latter case must fall very close to the dividing line. When determining whether two causes of action arise out of the same set of facts for the purposes of s.35 the question must be considered at a reasonable level of abstraction, but not necessarily at the very highest level of abstraction—it is not correct to approach the task by identifying only the bare minimum of facts which the claimant would need to plead.[35]

[31]   March 9, 1989, CA, Unreported.
[32]   [1984] R.P.C. 317, Falconer J.
[33]   cf. The *C. and J.* [1984] 2 Lloyd's Rep. 601.
[34]   March 30, 1990, CA, Unreported.
[35]   *Finlan v Eyton Morris Winfield (a firm)* [2007] EWHC 914 (Ch), Blackburne J. commenting on *Smith v Henniker-Major & Co (a firm)* [2002] EWCA Civ 762, [2003] Ch 182, [2002] 2 BCLC 655.

In *Dickinson v Lowery*[36] the plaintiff sought to set aside the conveyance **23.016** of her house to the defendant, as well as claiming damages from the solicitor who had originally been instructed to act for the vendor, but who, it was alleged, had wrongfully allowed himself to act for both parties. The basis of the action was that the defendant had exerted undue influence to procure the original conveyance. The defendant subsequently sought to bring third-party proceedings against her solicitor in respect of his involvement in the transaction. It is to be remembered that, although these are third-party proceedings, they do not fall within the definition of third-party proceedings contained in s.35 of the Limitation Act 1980, since the solicitor was already a party to the main action. For this reason the judge was correct to treat the application under s.35(1)(b), where the action, if permitted, is backdated to the date when the original action commenced, but is only to be permitted if the specified criteria are met. The solicitor argued that this was not a matter arising out of the same facts as the plaintiff's action against the defendant, since it related to the contract between the defendant and her solicitor, and the matters which would have to be proved in order to succeed in the action differed significantly from those relevant in the action between the plaintiff and the defendant. Auld J. rejected this argument. The question is not whether the facts to be proved are the same but whether the two matters arise out of the same facts. Here, both claims clearly related to the circumstances in which the plaintiff had come to convey her house to the defendant at a considerable undervalue. Accordingly, it would be appropriate to allow the solicitor to be joined as a third party.

The case is also to be noted for the observation of the judge that the provisions of s.35 are commonly treated as equivalent to rules of court. The point is important because s.35 itself provides that the addition of new parties is subject to rules of court, and no rules of court relating to this matter have been made.

In *Benzie v Happy Eater Ltd*[37] the parties owned adjoining plots of land. **23.017** Because of earlier excavations the plaintiff's land relied on the defendants' land for support. The defendants, who operated a restaurant on the site, wished to extend the car park, and for this purpose begin to dig up their own land, thereby threatening to undermine the plaintiff's land. The plaintiff began an action for nuisance, but at a later stage discovered that the defendants' land was subject to a restrictive covenant in favour of the plaintiff's land. This covenant prohibited use of the defendants' land for any purpose other than residential. The plaintiff wished to amend his statement of claim to include the breach of the restrictive covenant. As time had now expired, it was necessary to rely upon s.35. The judge held that the amendment should not be allowed, as the new claim represented a new

---

[36] March 23, 1990, Auld J., Unreported.
[37] May 18, 1990, Mr Recorder Mauleverer Q.C., Unreported.

cause of action rather than merely an addition to the existing cause of action. In this case the facts which had to be proved in order to succeed in the new claim were substantially different from those relevant under the original claim, and it would therefore not be correct to say that both claims arose out of the same set of facts.

23.018   In *Trade Development Bank v Deutsche Lufthansa AG*,[38] a case under the Warsaw Convention,[39] the plaintiffs wished to amend their statement of claim to allege that the loss was caused by the servants or agents of the defendants. This amendment would have allowed them to escape the limitation on liability otherwise imposed by art.22 of the Convention. The Court of Appeal held that an amendment made solely for this limited purpose was not to be construed as adding a new cause of action.

23.019   Other examples of the application of the doctrine include *Hoechst UK Ltd v Inland Revenue Commissioners*[40], which concerned an application for repayment of overpaid Corporation Tax. The claim as originally pleaded covered the years 1989-94. When it was sought to amend by pleading a claim for 1995 Park J. held that this was a new claim not arising out of the same facts as the original claim—since each year's events were different, with the result that there was no jurisdiction to allow the amendment. In *Maridive & Oil Services (Sae) v Cna Insurance Co (Europe) Ltd*[41] there were two separate demands on the same bond. The Court of Appeal held that claims following from the second demand did not arise from the same or substantially the same facts as claims under the first demand, since in relation to claims on the second demand the second demand was a fundamental element of the cause of action.

23.020   These cases together illustrate the difficulties of laying down any general rule in this area. Section 35 refers to actions on "the same or substantially the same facts"; although this has been held to be a mixed question of fact and law, it is also mostly a matter of impression for the judge.[42] This makes prediction of the result in any case difficult, as well as making appeals from the trial judge's decision nearly impossible.

23.021   In *Goode v Martin*[43] the Court of Appeal decided that in order for CPR 17.4(2) to be compliant with s.3(1) of the Human Rights Act 1998 and art.6 of the Human Rights Convention (entitlement to a fair hearing) the Rule should be interpreted as if it read:

"the court may allow an amendment whose effect will be to add . . . a new cause of action but only if the claim arises out of the same facts or

---

[38] December 3, 1990, CA, Unreported.
[39] For the Warsaw Convention, see Ch.26.
[40] [2003] All ER (D) 198 (Apr) Park J.
[41] [2002] EWCA Civ 369, [2002] 2 Lloyd's Rep 9.
[42] *Welsh Development Agency v Redpath Dorman Long Ltd* [1994] 4 All E.R. 10, CA; *Mortgage Corporation v Pratomo*, July 2, 1999, Unreported, CA.
[43] [2002] 1 All ER 620.

substantially the same facts *as are already in issue* on a claim in respect of which the party applying for permission has already claimed a remedy in the proceedings";

In that case the claimant sought to amend the claim so as to rely on facts raised in the defence but which had not been stated in the original claim. Colman J. reluctantly refused such leave on the basis that the statutory wording did not permit it,[44] but this decision was reversed by the Court of Appeal,[45] which held that the narrower construction would involve an unjustified restriction on the claimant's right of access to a court contrary to art.6. In effect the decision in *Goode v Martin* will allow the use of s.35 in a wider range of cases because it will allow claimants to rely on facts which they have not pleaded but which the defendant has pleaded. However, it will presumably be a relatively rare case in which the claimant is able to adopt the defendant's pleading as the basis of a further claim. By contrast, in *Compagnie Noga D'importation et D'Exportation SA v Australia and New Zealand Banking Group Ltd*[46] the proposed amendments sought to refute matters raised in the defence rather than adopting them. Langley J. held that this was a good reason for distinguishing *Goode v Martin*, since the Claimant was in substance not adopting facts which the defendant had pleaded.

The effects of *Goode v Martin* were further considered by Jackson J. in **23.022** *Charles Church Developments Ltd v Stent Foundations Ltd*.[47] The specific question in that case was formulated by Jackson J. as follows:[48]

"Suppose that there are two Defendants to an action. Let the Claimant be called "C" and the two Defendants be called "D1" and "D2". If one of the Defendants pleads facts by way of defence to C's claim, can C adopt those facts as the basis of a new claim against the other Defendant after expiry of the limitation period?"

Jackson J. held that this question should be answered in the affirmative. He gave five principal reasons for this conclusion[49]:

"(i) This interpretation follows naturally from the words of the expanded rule, as formulated by the Court of Appeal. It is not open to me as a first instance judge to put a gloss on the Court of Appeal's formulation, or to insert words which will narrow its effect.

(ii) Section 35(5)(a) of the 1980 provides an exception to the limitation

---

[44] *Goode v Martin* [2001] 3 All E.R. 652, Colman J.
[45] [2001] E.W.C.A. Civ. 1899; (1989) 152 N.L.J. 109.
[46] [2005] EWHC 225 (Comm).
[47] [2006] EWHC 3158.
[48] At para.36.
[49] At para.40.

principle. The rationale of this exception is that once particular facts have been put in issue in litigation, and therefore fall to be investigated, the Claimant should be entitled to claim any appropriate remedy upon the basis of those facts. This policy justification is equally valid irrespective of whether those facts have been put in issue by D1 or by D2 or by both Defendants.

(iii) The three policy considerations identified by the Defendant apply with much less force to new claims based upon facts which the court is bound to investigate in any event.

(iv) This interpretation of the expanded rule is in line with the reasoning and the general approach of the Court of Appeal in *Lloyds Bank v Rogers, Goode v Martin* and *Hemmingway v Smith Roddam*.

(v) Section 35(5) of the 1980, CPR r.17.4(2) and the expanded rule merely give the court a discretionary power to allow the pleading of new claims after expiry of the limitation period, if the threshold condition is met. Whether the court will in fact allow such amendments after expiry of the limitation period must depend upon the circumstances of each case. The court can and will protect a Defendant against injustice by refusing permission to amend."

"Necessary for the determination of the original action"

23.023   The second requirement is that, in the case of a claim involving a new party, the addition or substitution of the new party must be necessary for the determination of the original action. Necessity in this context is determined by reference to s.35(6), which provides that the addition or substitution of a new party shall not be regarded as necessary for the determination of the original action unless either the new party is substituted for a party whose name was given in any claim made in the original action in mistake for the new party's name or any claim made in the original action cannot be maintained by or against any original party without joining or substituting the new party as plaintiff or defendant in that action. In a case where a company had begun proceedings under s.212 Insolvency Act 1986 against a director while in administration and had then gone into liquidation, it was held that the substitution of the liquidator as claimant was necessary within the meaning of this rule because otherwise the action could not be carried on.[50] In *Reed Publishing Holdings Ltd v Kings Reach Investments Ltd*[51] P1 was suing D1 and D2, whilst P2 was suing only D1. When P2 sought leave out of time to proceed against D2, the Court of Appeal held that this amounted to the addition of a new party for the purposes of s.35.

---

[50] *Parkinson Engineering Services Plc v Swan and Yeldon* [2009] EWCA Civ 1366.
[51] May 25, 1983, CA, Unreported.

The exercise of the discretion

Even where both requirements are satisfied it lies in the discretion of the **23.024** court whether or not to permit the amendments. The leading authority on the exercise of the discretion is *Welsh Development Agency Ltd v Redpath Dorman Long Ltd*,[52] where it was held that leave should not be given unless the claimant could show that the defendant did not have even a reasonably arguable case on limitation which would be defeated by allowing the new claim. In *Hancock Shipping Co. Ltd v Kawasaki Heavy Industries Ltd ("The Casper Trader")*,[53] the Court of Appeal held that the exercise of the discretion (presumably in the absence of any arguable case for the defendant to argue limitation) involved balancing the relative hardship to the parties of either allowing or disallowing the amendments. However, the discretion is not to be exercised for disciplinary purposes, but for the purpose of doing justice between the parties. Once the two requirements are met, it is therefore very relevant to consider whether the prejudice to the defendant resulting from allowing the amendment can be adequately compensated for by an order for costs.[54] The burden is on the claimant to show that the amendments should be allowed.[55]

No title at commencement of action

Section 35(7) allows rules of court to be made permitting a party to claim **23.025** relief in a new capacity in respect of a new cause of action notwithstanding that he had no title to make that claim at the date when the action commenced. It has been suggested[56] that this amendment was inserted to deal with two particular problems which had arisen in the previous law. The first arose under the Proceedings Against Estates Act 1970, where the plaintiff sued the deceased, not realising that a grant of probate or administration had been taken out. There seems, however, to be some confusion on this point. It is unclear why the plaintiff would then be suing in a different capacity, unless the grant were in his name, but this surely could not happen without his knowledge. The second problem was that RSC, Ord.20, r.5 allowed a post-limitation amendment to change the capacity of a person who sued as executor (the executor's title, when granted, is retrospective to the date of death), but this did not apply to a person who sued as administrator, the general principle being that the administrator's title is not retrospective. Section 35(7) allows rules to be

---

[52] [1994] 4 All E.R. 10, CA.
[53] [1992] 1 W.L.R. 102, CA.
[54] *Trade Development Bank v Deutsche Lufthansa AG*, December 3, 1990, CA, Unreported.
[55] *The Casper Trader*, above, fn.53.
[56] Derek Morgan, *Current Law Statutes Annotated* (1980), vol.II.

made which will permit a retrospective change of capacity for the benefit of an administrator. However, these rules are subject to the same restrictions as are imposed for the purposes of s.35(3) by s.35(4) (5) and (6). It should be noted that s.35(7) is expressed not to apply to the rather different situation where a party wishes to claim relief in a new capacity without adding a new cause of action.[57] Section 35 also permits the addition of a Fatal Accidents Act claim to an existing personal injuries action by a living claimant, notwithstanding that the Fatal Accidents Act claim would obviously not have been valid at the date of the original writ.[58]

CPR PART 19

23.026   This provision deals with the joinder of causes of action and of parties. In this context joinder means the addition of new parties or causes of action to an action which has already begun. The rules on joinder generally are set out and thoroughly annotated in Civil Procedure. This work will concentrate on the aspects of those rules which are important in a limitation context. So far as joinder of parties is concerned, the relevant provision is CPR r.19.5. This provides that as a general rule no person shall be added or substituted as a party after the expiry of a relevant[59] period of limitation. It is to be noted that the rules of joinder of parties apply to the bringing of third-party proceedings, but not to the making of new claims as between the original parties—these are governed by the rules in CPR Pt 17 mentioned above.[60] In order to escape the operation of the general prohibition it is necessary to show that the relevant period was current when proceedings were commenced[61] and that the addition or substitution of the new party is necessary for the determination of the action. CPR r.19.5(3) provides further guidance as to when the addition or substitution of the new party shall be treated as necessary.[62]

23.027   *Ultra Furniture Ltd and another v KPMG Audit Plc* [63] was a claim for alleged negligent auditing. The claim was for negligence over a number of years and was originally brought solely against the defendant. When it was pointed out that in the earlier years the audit had been carried out by

---

[57] CPR 17.4(4).

[58] *Booker v Associated British Ports*, April 26, 1995, CA, Unreported.

[59] "Relevant period of limitation" is defined for this purpose as meaning any time-limit which applies to the action under the 1980 Act, or any foreign time-limit which applies to the action by virtue of the Foreign Limitation Periods Act 1984.

[60] See paras 22.023–22.025.

[61] Except in cases under s.11 or s.12 of the 1980 Act, as to which see below.

[62] But note that this paragraph applies only to actions governed by the 1980 Act; it does not apply to actions governed (as to limitation) by the law of another country under the Foreign Limitation Periods Act 1984.

[63] [2003] All ER (D) 302 (May) Judge Dean as High Court Judge.

KPMG as a partnership, application was made to add the partnership as an additional defendant. Although this did not involve dismissing the first defendant from that action, it was held that it was still a 'substitution' of the partnership, at least in respect of the earlier years, so that CPR 19.5 applied.

Morgan Est (Scotland) Ltd v Hanson Concrete Products Ltd[64] takes these points a stage further and contains a welcome attempt to bring some sense to the many confusing cases of mistakes as to the name of a party. As the judge there observes, in a sense every claim is intended to be brought in the name of the right claimant and against the right defendant, and this is not affected by whether a named party exists or not, nor by the reasons for the mistake. The real question is whether, on the facts of the particular case, there is real doubt about which party was intended to be claimant or defendant, as the case may be. If there is no real doubt, then the court should be inclined to allow the amendment fairly freely. **23.028**

In order to satisfy this condition the party seeking the joinder must show one of the following three things[65]: **23.029**

"(a) that the new party is to be substituted for a party who was named in the claim form in mistake for the new party;"

This provision is to be contrasted with CPR r.17.4.[66] It applies where the wrong party has been named in the sense that the person naming a party was under a genuine mistake as to whom to sue. CPR r.17.4 applies where the correct party was always known, but there was a mistake as to that party's name.[67] Rule 19.5(3)(a) was considered by the Court of Appeal in *Morgan Est (Scotland) Ltd v Hanson Concrete Products Ltd*[68] , where reference was made to the pre-CPR authorities which had established the rule that that if it were a case of right description/wrong name there could be amendment, but not if it were a case of wrong description/wrong name. The Court of Appeal held that the right approach was to apply the words of CPR 19.5, without regard to the right description/wrong name test, but with regard to the overriding objective of the CPR, bearing in mind that the limit of CPR 19.5 was the limit set by s.35 of the 1980 Act. Under CPR 19.5(3)(a), the court has to be satisfied that the new party was to be substituted for a party who had been named in the claim form in mistake for the new party, but 'in mistake' was not to be construed restrictively. The question is which claimant had been intended to be named, and in many cases the mistake could be put right without any prejudice to the

---

[64] [2004] EWHC 1778 (TCC) Richard Harvey QC.
[65] Attention is drawn to the fact that this list is different from that which appeared in the former RSC, Ord. r.6(6). The old rules were dealt with in previous editions of this book.
[66] See Ch.22.
[67] *Gregson v Channel Four Television*, July 11, 2000, Unreported, CA.
[68] [2005] EWCA Civ 134, [2005] 3 All ER 135.

defendants.[69] However, there is no requirement that the mistake must not be such as to cause any reasonable doubt as to the party intending to sue or be sued (though this may be relevant to the exercise of the court's discretion.[70]

23.030   In *ABB Asea Brown Boveri Ltd v Hiscox Dedicated Corporate Member Ltd; ABB Asea Brown Boveri Ltd v Jardine Lloyd Thompson Ltd*[71] Christopher Clarke J gave guidance on the correct approach to be adopted when it is sought, outside the limitation period, to amend a statement of case by substituting one party for another which is said to have been named by mistake within the meaning of CPR19.5(3)(a), a rule made pursuant to s.35(6)(a) of the 1980 Act. It is also necessary to consider CPR 17.4(3), which talks about amending a statement of case after the expiry of the limitation period and which lays down a slightly different test, namely that "the mistake was genuine and not one which would cause reasonable doubt as to the identity of the party in question."

As the judge points out, the courts have had some difficulty with the question—when is a mistake a mistake as to the *name* of a party and not one that would cause reasonable doubt as to the *identity* of the party intended to sue or be sued? In *"The Sardinia Sulcis"* [1991] 1 Lloyd's Rep 201 the Court of Appeal considered the meaning of the former RSC Ord.20 r.5(3). The rule was said to be that where it was possible to identify the intended plaintiff or defendant by a description which was more or less specific to the particular case, and the party seeking to amend had got that description right there was unlikely to be any doubt about the intended plaintiff or defendant[72]. On the other side of the line are cases where the promoter of the action intends to pursue a claim on behalf of or against a legal person whom he describes and names correctly, but who is not the right person to sue or be sued. In such cases the mistake is said to be one of identity. However, some of the cases appear to show the court taking a surprisingly liberal approach; thus the name may be corrected even though there is no similarity between the name pleaded and the name to be substituted (e.g. *Evans v Charrington*), and even where the proceedings had been commenced in the name of the original owner of a ship which had

---

[69] See also *The Sardinia Sulcis and Al Tawwab* [1991] 1 Lloyd's Rep 201. However, the Court of Appeal disapproved the decisions in *Horne-Roberts v SmithKline Beecham* (2001) 65 BMLR 79, *Parsons v George* [2004] 3 All ER 633 and *Kesslar v Moore & Tibbits (a firm)* [2004] All ER (D) 53 (Nov) as being based on *The Sardinia Sulcis and Al Tawwab* [1991] 1 Lloyd's Rep 201, in which the Court had proceeded on the basis of the old RSC O20 r.5, which should not be regarded as the proper starting point under the CPR.

[70] *SP Manweb Plc v Bechtel Water Technology Ltd* [2008] EWHC 2270 (TCC) Judge Raynor Q.C.

[71] [2007] EWHC 1150 (Commercial).

[72] See for example *Mitchell v Harris Engineering Co Ltd* [1967] 2 QB 703, [1967] 2 All ER 682, [1967] 3 WLR 447) *Evans Construction Co Ltd v Charrington & Co Ltd* [1983] QB 810, [1983] 1 All ER 310, [1983] 2 WLR 117 *Gregson v Channel Four Television Corporation* [2000] CP Rep 60 *Kesslar v Moore & Tibbits* [2004] EWCA Civ 1551.

ceased to exist and been merged with another company, whose name was substituted *"The Sardinia Sulcis"*. A complete stranger to the litigation with no connection with the existing parties can find himself added under this rule.[73] However, the *"identity of the person intending to sue"* is not an easy concept to grasp. In one sense a claimant always intends that the correct claimant should sue and intends to sue the person who is liable for the wrong that he has suffered; but the test cannot be as wide as that. The point was reiterated by the Court of Appeal in *Morgan Est (Scotland) Ltd v Hanson Concrete Products Ltd*.[74] In practice the answer to many of these interesting conceptual points may be that CPR 17.4 only applies *"where the mistake was genuine and not one which would cause reasonable doubt as to the identity of the party in question"*. If that identity is beyond reasonable doubt there is likely to be little room for a dispute as to whether the mistake is one of identity or name. It is also to be noted that CPR 19.5 applies a more lenient test because it requires only that the mistake be "genuine".

In *Broadhurst v Broadhurst*[75] it was held that CPR 19.5(3)(a) is limited, **23.031** as its words suggest, to the substitution of one party for another, and cannot therefore be sued where it is desired simply to add an additional party but without removing an existing party. This point had been left open in *Morgan Est*.[76] The judge also suggested that the approach to CPR 19.5 in *Weston v Gribben* was perhaps more restrictive than that in *Morgan Est*.[77] In *Weston* Lloyd LJ indicated that both r.17.4(3) and 19.5 required that there should have been a mistake as to the party to the claim (paras 25 and 26). However, only s.35(6)(a) and r.19.5(3)(a) (not 19.5(3)(b)) expressly use the words "in mistake". The judge accepted that in the present state of authority some "mistake" is required in 19.5(3)(b) as well. However, *Weston* has not survived further consideration by the Court of Appeal in *Adelson v Associated Newspapers Ltd*[78], where it was disapproved. That was a libel action where it appeared that the wrong companies had originally been named as claimants. When applications were made to substitute what were said to be the right companies, the judge pointed out that in libel each potential claimant has its own cause of action, and each such cause of action is separate. Thus, where it is desired to substitute two companies for the company originally named in the proceedings, only one of those can truly be 'substituted' for the party originally named. The other must be 'added' rather than substituted. However, it is also possible that a new party is substituted for an existing party in respect of one cause of

---

[73] *Horne-Roberts v SmithKline Beecham Plc* [2001] EWCA Civ 2006, [2002] 1 WLR 1662, 65 BMLR 79.
[74] [2005] EWCA Civ 134, [2005] 3 All ER 135, [2005] 1 WLR 2557.
[75] [2007] EWHC 1828 (Ch) Edward Bartley-Jones Q.C.
[76] At para.46.
[77] At para.22.
[78] [2007] EWCA 701.

action held by that party even though the original party remains in the proceedings in respect of a second cause of action which it also holds.

23.032   "(b) that the claim cannot properly be carried on by or against the original party unless the new party is added or substituted as claimant or defendant; or"

This is the broadest of the three heads in this rule. What is far from clear is what is meant by the word "properly". It is submitted that a narrow construction is likely—it does not extend to any case where the substitution is convenient; rather, it will be necessary to show that it would be procedurally improper to continue without the addition or substitution which is proposed.[79]

23.033   "(c) the original party has died or had a bankruptcy order made against him and his interest or liability has passed to the new party."

This would cover the case of substituting a personal representative or a trustee in bankruptcy.

Parsons v George[80] was a case of an application for a new tenancy under Pt II of the Landlord and Tenant Act 1954. After the expiry of the s.29(3) limitation period, the tenants applied to the court for an order substituting a new defendant. The 1954 Act contains no express provision for the substitution of parties, but the Court of Appeal held that CPR 19.5(1)(c) applied not only to enactments which expressly allowed a change of parties after the end of the relevant limitation period, but also to those which did not prohibit such a change. In effect, it is presumed that the power to substitute a party applies in any case where it is not expressly forbidden. Although the basis of the decision on the facts was disapproved by the Court of Appeal in *Morgan Est (Scotland) Ltd v Hanson Concrete Products Ltd*[81], the decision on which enactments are subject to CPR 19.5(1)(c) appears correct and is still good law.

Where a party who has previously brought an action on his own account wishes to amend that action so as to include a derivative claim, it cannot be said that the change is necessary in order to allow the action to be carried on.[82] An assignee of a cause of action does not sue in a different capacity from that of the assignor.[83]

23.034   It is to be noted that these provisions list exhaustively the circumstances in which a new party may be added after the expiry of the relevant period of

---

[79] Cited with approval by Lord Collins in *Roberts v Gill* [2010] UKSC 22 at para.62.
[80] [2004] EWCA Civ 912, [2004] 3 All ER 633.
[81] [2005] EWCA Civ 134, [2005] 3 All ER 135.
[82] *Roberts v Gill* [2010] UKSC 22 .
[83] *Finlan v Eyton Morris Winfield (a firm)* [2007] EWHC 914 (Ch), Blackburne J. See also *Haq v Singh* [2001] 1 WLR 1594.

limitation, apart from those cases within s.11 or 12 of the 1980 Act, as discussed above. Section 35(3) contemplates the addition of new causes of action out of time without leave in certain circumstances,[84] but there is no corresponding provision for the addition of new parties. Another important point is that there is no general or residual discretion for the court to allow the addition of a new party in these circumstances merely because it appears just to do so.

The only other case where a new party may be added after the expiry of the limitation period is where the court makes a direction under s.33 of the 1980 Act that s.11 or s.12 of the 1980 Act shall not apply, or where it orders the question of the application of s.11 or 12 to be determined at trial.[85] **23.035**

When amendment takes effect

In *Welsh Development Agency v Redpath Dorman Long Ltd*[86] the Court of Appeal held that an amendment authorised under s.35 cannot take effect before, at the earliest, the date when leave to amend is given. The amendment cannot be backdated to the date when the application for leave is made. Thus, where the application is made before the expiry of the limitation period, but the hearing does not take place until after the expiry of the limitation period, the court's power to grant leave to amend is subject to s.35. **23.036**

Application to third-party proceedings

Section 35(8) provides that s.35(4)–(7) shall apply to a new claim made in the course of third-party proceedings as if those proceedings were the original action, subject to any modifications which may be prescribed by rules of court. This rule is of great importance when considering the raising of set-offs or counterclaims in third-party proceedings. A party who is the defendant in the main action may already have made a counterclaim in that action. But for s.35(8) he would then be precluded from making any claim in the third-party proceedings. **23.037**

---

[84] See para.23.006.
[85] CPR r.19.5(4).
[86] [1994] 4 All E.R. 10, CA.; followed in *Furini v Bajwa* [2004] EWCA CIV 412, [2004] All ER (D) 56 (Apr), [2004] 1 WLR 1971.

Position in third-party proceedings

23.038 It is important to understand that third-party proceedings are treated quite differently from other forms of new claim under s.35. There is no back-dating, third-party proceedings are treated as commencing on the date on which they do actually begin and it is therefore necessary to comply with the basic time-limits in the 1980 Act, subject of course to any extensions of time permitted under Pt II of that Act. This rule makes it necessary to determine when third-party proceedings are in fact commenced. The procedure for commencing third-party proceedings, as provided by CPR Pt 20, is that, unless the defence has not yet been served, the leave of the court must first be obtained (the proposed third-party notice being annexed to the application), after which the person bringing the third-party proceedings must serve on the third party the third-party notice, a form for acknowledgment of service, a copy of the writ and a copy of any pleadings to date in the action. It is well known that in the case of originating process the date of commencement is the date when the writ is issued, and it might be thought that by analogy the vital date in third-party proceedings is the date when the third-party notice is issued. It is, however, unclear at present whether the vital date is that when leave is given or that when the proceedings are issued.

The rule that there is no backdating in third-party proceedings makes it unnecessary for s.35 to impose any restrictions on the addition of new claims by way of third-party proceedings—the ordinary Limitation Act rules ensure that no claim can be added once time has expired, though conversely another effect of this is that any number of third-party claims can be added within the limitation period.

MEANING OF "SET-OFF" AND "COUNTERCLAIM"

23.039 Section 35 frequently refers to claims being made by way of set-off or counterclaim, but it does not define these expressions, whose ambit must therefore be determined by reference to the case law. Since counterclaims and set-offs are treated identically for s.35 purposes, it is not necessary here to discuss in detail the differences between them.

In *Henriksens Rederi A/S v Rolimpex (T.H.Z.)*[87] Lord Denning gave a very detailed and learned account of the differences between counterclaim, set-off and defence. The case is worthy of close attention when seeking to understand the operation of s.35, and the facts also require to be stated in some detail. Shipowners (S) chartered a ship to charterers (C). Under the charterparty 80 per cent of the freight was due in advance, and this was

---

[87] [1974] Q.B. 233, CA.

duly paid by C. The remaining 20 per cent was due on delivery of the goods, but C refused to pay in full, alleging short delivery. The charterparty was governed by the Hague-Visby Rules, which allowed C one year in which to bring an action in respect of the short delivery. Those rules do not affect the action for freight, so that the limitation period in respect of a claim for freight was the ordinary six-year period applicable to contractual claims. Two years after the delivery of the goods S sued for the outstanding freight and C sought to plead short delivery as a defence. The first point to be made is that a defence, properly so-called, can never become time-barred; it was therefore necessary to decide whether the plea of short delivery was a defence or a counterclaim. The Court of Appeal held that this was properly a counterclaim; as such it was liable to become time-barred, and under the Hague-Visby Rules had done so by the time S's action was started. Had it not been barred at that time, s.35 would have allowed C to plead it as a counterclaim, notwithstanding that it was time-barred by the time it was pleaded.[88] On the more general question of categorisation Lord Denning said that "set-off" is limited to legal set-offs, i.e. those cases where the claims on both sides are liquidated debts or money demands which can be ascertained with exactitude at the time of pleading.[89]

A set-off must arise from a separate transaction from that on which the **23.040** claimant relies; if it arises from the same transaction, then it is properly described as a defence. "Counterclaim" is a broader expression. It is any claim which could be the subject of an independent action. It is not limited to money claims, and it need not relate to or be connected with the original subject of the cause or matter. If the counterclaim arises out of a separate transaction, then since 1939 the position is the same as for a set-off, but if it arises from the same transaction as that upon which the claimant relies it is simply a defence. With regard to counterclaims which are really defences it is helpful to distinguish further two classes of case. The first is where the counterclaim goes directly in diminution or extinction of the claimant's claim, as where there is a claim for the price of goods sold and the defendant alleges that by reason of a breach of warranty by the seller the goods are worth less then they should have been worth.[90] This is a defence at law. The second category is where the value of the goods is not reduced but the claimant causes some other damages to the defendant arising out of the same transaction. A claim of this kind is permitted by the Judicature Act 1873, but is more problematic because there is some confusion of terminology relating to it. It is variously described as an equitable set-off or an equitable defence. It will be seen that for s.35 purposes it is vital to know

---

[88] Note that this would not apply if the proceedings took the form of an arbitration as s.35 does not apply to arbitrations: *The Antares (No. 2)* [1986] 2 Lloyd's Rep. 633, Steyn J. see paras 16.028–16.029.

[89] *Hanak v Green* [1958] 2 Q.B. 9, CA; *Storke v Taylor* (1880) 5 Q.B.D. 569.

[90] *Mondel v Steel* (1841) 8 M. & W. 858; *Bright v Rogers* [1917] 1 K.B. 917, DC.

which of these terms is correct. Lord Denning indicates that for s.35 this is a defence—it does not come within his deliberately limited definition of set-off in this context. It will be apparent that close attention to these distinctions is vital—a defence is not in any way subject to the regime of s.35, but both set-offs and counterclaims are.

SECTION 35 AND SECTION 33

23.041 Section 35(3) expressly exempts cases within s.33 from the prohibition on allowing a new claim to be brought once the time for it has expired. Therefore, there may be an application under s.33 to add a second or subsequent defendant in a personal injuries case even though the time for bringing an action against that defendant has expired. Such an application is determined on the principles generally applicable to s.33 cases.[91]

EFFECT OF ADDING NEW PARTIES

23.042 There is a substantial body of authority on the question whether the addition of a party, once effected, is deemed to date back to the date when the original writ was issued, or whether it operates only prospectively. In *Liff v Peasley*[92] a motor accident occurred, injuring the plaintiff, who was a passenger in one of the cars involved. He sued one of the drivers, but that driver's insurers repudiated liability and conduct of the defence passed to the Motor Insurers' Bureau. After the primary limitation period had expired, a defence was served which cast the blame on to the other driver. The plaintiff and the first defendant applied ex parte to join the other driver as second defendant, and leave was eventually given for the necessary amendments of the writ and the statement of claim. The second defendant entered unconditional appearance to the writ, and accepted service of the statement of claim. He then pleaded limitation, and subsequently applied to be discharged from the action on the ground that he had been improperly joined within what is now CPR r.19.4.

23.043 The Court of Appeal found in favour of the second defendant on two grounds, either of which would alone have been sufficient to dispose of the case, and both of which merit consideration. First, it was held that he had been improperly joined, since the action against him was clearly time-barred (and s.35 could not save it, since it was not an original counterclaim). This misjoinder was not a mere irregularity of practice which could be cured by an unconditional appearance to the writ, since this would take

---

[91] *Walford v Richards* [1976] 1 Lloyd's Rep. 526, CA. Section 33 is considered in Ch.8.
[92] [1980] 1 W.L.R. 781, CA.

away an accrued right to plead limitation. Arguably the original joinder might at the time have been proper, since it was not then clear that the second defendant would exercise his right to plead limitation. However, he ceased to be a proper party at the latest at the time when he raised the limitation defence. Although the point is not addressed in the case, this last finding depends upon the fact that the limitation defence was obviously bound to succeed. Were there a question as to its validity, D2 would surely remain a proper party until that question had been resolved. The second ground of decision is concerned with the "relation back" theory. The Court of Appeal held that this theory is incorrect. The true position is that D2 becomes a party to the action only when the writ is amended, and his joinder does not date back to the issue of the original writ. Consequently, it would be wrong to order such joinder where the action is time-barred by the time of the application, since D2 could defeat this simply by pleading limitation.[93]

Some of these problems were also considered in *Liptons Cash Registers and Business Equipment Ltd v Hugin (G.B.) Ltd*.[94] The action against D1 was commenced in 1972; in 1978 leave was sought to join further defendants. The difficulty here was that it was arguable, but not certain, that the action against the additional defendants would have been barred at the date of the amendment. Whether this point was important depended in turn on the application of the "relation back" theory, and a suggestion was made that the uncertainty over limitation could be circumvented by allowing the joinder on terms that it was to operate only from the date of joinder. Judge Hawser held that there is an established rule that no new party will be added, either as claimant or as defendant, if such addition would deprive any party of the benefit of an accrued limitation defence. Such a rule makes no sense if the joinder is deemed to act retrospectively. Where it is unclear whether the limitation defence is valid or not, the correct procedure is to allow the joinder on terms that the proceedings involving the new party shall be deemed to have been commenced at the date of the amendment.[95] In *Leadbitter v Hodge Finance Ltd*[96] the plaintiff was injured in a motor accident. Initially he sued the manufacturers of the vehicle, but later obtained additional information which led him to believe that the local authority might be partly responsible. He sought to add the authority as second defendants. Much of the argument turned on the date of discoverability as regards his action against them,[97] but questions of procedure also

23.044

---

[93] As this was a case of personal injuries, the question of the s.33 discretion arose. On the facts the court declined to exercise this discretion in favour of P and D1.

[94] [1982] 1 All E.R. 595, Judge Hawser Q.C. as a High Court Judge.

[95] See also *Lovesy v Smith* (1880) 15 Ch.D. 655; *Re Bowden* (1890) 45 Ch.D. 444; *Sneale v Wotherton* [1904] 1 K.B. 295; *Attorney-General v Pontypridd Waterworks Co.* [1908] 1 Ch. 388.

[96] [1982] 2 All E.R. 167, Bush J.

[97] See Ch.8.

arose. Bush J. held that the vital time for determining whether this action was barred was the date when the application to amend the writ was heard. To issue a second writ and seek consolidation of the two actions was permissible but not mandatory. As a practical matter it may be observed that a second writ can be issued more quickly than an appointment for the hearing of an application to amend can be obtained. Bush J. suggests that this problem can be circumvented by applying ex parte for leave to amend. The decisions in *Liptons* and in *Leadbitter* still represent the law in cases to which the 1939 Act applies.[98] Section 35 of the 1980 Act deals expressly with the point for actions to which it applies by providing that the new action is to be deemed to have commenced on the same date as the original action. Therefore where the court grants leave to add the additional party, the effect is to override the limitation problem. It is for this reason that CPR r.19.5(3) limits so closely the circumstances in which such leave may be given.

DETERMINING THE LIMITATION ISSUE IN SECTION 35 CASES

23.045   In *Busby v Cooper*[99] the Court of Appeal considered an important procedural point about the application of s.35 in cases where the running of time depends on the claimant having knowledge of relevant facts. This was a latent damage case, where the defendant appeared to have an arguable case on limitation, so that, applying the test in *Welsh Development Agency v Redpath Dorman Long Ltd*[100] the correct course appeared to be to refuse leave to amend. However, the plaintiff sought to rely on the extended limitation period under s.14A of the 1980 Act. Whether such reliance was legitimate depended, of course, upon the date at which the plaintiff acquired the relevant knowledge. The Court of Appeal held that in these circumstances it is permissible to order the trial of a preliminary issue on the question of the date of knowledge.[101] The decision in *Welsh Development Agency v Redpath Dorman Long Ltd* was distinguished on the ground that in that case no question of ordering a preliminary issue arose, so that the circumstances of this case might properly be regarded as a gloss on those of the earlier case. Bearing in mind that an amendment does not take effect until actually made, there is no injustice in ordering the trial of a

---

[98]   i.e. actions which were commenced before May 1, 1981, the date in force for the 1980 Act. Actions which accrued before then, but for which proceedings were not commenced until after that date, are governed by the 1980 Act: see para.1.002.
[99]   *The Times*, April 15, 1996, CA, Unreported.
[100]   [1994] 4 All E.R. 10, CA.
[101]   See also *Davies v Reed Stock & Co. Ltd and Lovells Shipping and Transport Group Ltd*, July 26, 1984, CA, Unreported (a personal injuries case).

preliminary issue; if the action is found to be out of time, s.35 will be applied with full rigour. If it is found to be in time, s.35 has no relevance. In either case the additional information gleaned from the trial of the issue assists the court in doing justice.[102]

ACTIONS ON AWARDS

In *Government of the State of Kuwait v Sir Frederick Snow & Partners*[103] the plaintiffs sued on an arbitral award. They sought to add additional defendants to the action, but this was done more than six years after the making of the award. Mocatta J. held that such joinder would be improper as it would deprive these defendants of an accrued limitation defence.   **23.046**

COMMENCING A NEW ACTION

Where a claimant anticipates some difficulty in obtaining leave to join an additional party to the action, he may choose instead to commence a new action (assuming, of course, that he is still within the limitation period for doing so). The question may then arise whether this is a proper form of proceeding or whether the new action should be struck out as an abuse of process. In *Sybron Corporation v Barclays Bank Plc*[104] Scott J. declined to strike out such an action. CPR r.19.5 does not deal with this situation, but his Lordship held that any procedural safeguard available under the CPR or s.35 in respect of the first action would continue to be available in the new action.   **23.047**

REMOVAL OF PARTIES FROM THE ACTION

As a general rule, joinder of an additional party or of a new cause of action will not be permitted where this would have the effect of depriving a party of an accrued defence under the 1980 Act.[105] This follows from the principles which have been explained above. A party who has been joined to the action in defiance of this principle may apply under CPR r.19.2(3) to be   **23.048**

---

[102] This decision, like that in *Welsh Development Agency v Redpath Dorman Long Ltd*, is inconsistent with the view of the Court of Appeal in *Kennett v Brown* [1988] 2 All E.R. 600, which was expressly overruled in the latter case.

[103] [1981] 1 Lloyd's Rep. 656, Mocatta J.

[104] [1985] 1 Ch. 299, Scott J.

[105] CPR Pts 17 and 19; and see *Lucy v W.T. Henleys Telegraph Works Co. Ltd* [1970] 1 Q.B. 393, CA.

removed from it. In *Leicester Wholesale Fruit Market Ltd v Grundy*[106] the principles applicable to such an application fell to be considered.[107] The plaintiff in the action had joined a second defendant, relying on s.35, and that defendant now applied to be removed from the action. Before the Registrar and Otton J. argument centred on whether the applicant must show a clear case that the action against him was time-barred or merely an arguable case, with the Registrar opting for the former test and Otton J. for the latter.[108] The Court of Appeal approached the matter in a way that pays more attention to general principle. There is already authority on the position where the plaintiff issues a separate writ against the second defendant instead of joining him to the first action.

23.049   The leading case is *Ronex Properties Ltd v John Laing Construction Ltd*,[109] where it was held that an action should not normally be struck out as disclosing no cause of action merely because limitation is pleaded, though in a very clear case it may be appropriate to strike it out as an abuse of process. In the present case the Court of Appeal applied this principle by analogy to the case where the second defendant has been added pursuant to s.35. Accordingly it will only very rarely be possible for a defendant to be discharged from the action at this early interlocutory stage, though of course this does not prevent him from relying on the limitation point at the trial. The issue was considered again in *Holland v Yates Building Co. Ltd*,[110] where it was reiterated that the correct test is whether a fresh action on those facts started at that time would properly have been dismissed as an abuse of process.

NEW PARTIES AND CONTRIBUTION

23.050   A new party may be joined by a defendant, either as a co-defendant or as a third party for the purposes of making a contribution claim. The relationship between contribution claims and the law of limitation is considered in detail in Ch.15.

---

[106] [1990] 1 W.L.R. 107, CA.
[107] Although this was a case under the old rules, it is suggested that the approach of the court should not materially differ under the CPR—*International Distillers and Vintners Ltd v Hillebrand*, December 17, 1999, David Foskett Q.C.
[108] Otton J. relied here on *Grimsby Cold Store Ltd v Jenkins Potter* (1985) 1 Const.L.J. 362.
[109] [1983] Q.B. 398; strictly speaking this is a case about bringing in a third party, but the same principles must logically apply to any case of adding a new party.
[110] *The Times*, December 5, 1989, CA.

THE LAW COMMISSION'S PROPOSALS

The Consultation Paper gives relatively little attention to the very complex **23.051** issues considered in this chapter, since its emphasis is on substantive rather than procedural matters. Its one proposal in this area does, however, appear to represent something of a change in the law. It is that new claims should be permitted provided they are sufficiently related to the original cause of action, even where time has expired. The Commission observes that the present very narrow and very technical rules can have the effect of preventing the court from doing justice. It therefore suggests a more general discretion along the lines indicated above. Examination of the case law on the present s.35 certainly supports the claim that the existing law is too technical. It may well be that the range of cases that can arise simply cannot be adequately encapsulated in a blanket rule, and that discretion is the least unsatisfactory answer.

CHAPTER 24

The Merchant Shipping Act 1995

The Maritime Conventions Act 1911 (MCA 1911) applied to claims **24.001** against a vessel or her owners or any person responsible for her in respect of any damage or loss to another vessel, her cargo or freight, or any property on board her, or damages for loss of life or personal injuries suffered by any person on board her, caused by the fault of the former vessel, or in respect of any salvage services. The law recognises a lien for damages against the vessel in these circumstances,[1] and prior to the passage of the MCA 1911 no statute of limitation applied to an action in respect of this right.[2] The legislation is now to be found in s.190 of the Merchant Shipping Act 1995 (MSA 1995), but the wording has not changed. Inevitably, most of the cases dealt with in this chapter were decided under the old legislation. Section 190 of the Act imposes a time-limit of two years on the bringing of such claims. Time runs from the date on which the damage is caused or from the date on which the salvage services are rendered, according to the basis of the claim. There are therefore a number of different claims which may be brought under this MSA 1995, and the relevant limitation period may start at different times.

AMBIT OF THE ACT

Meaning of "vessel"

This question was considered by Steyn J. in *Steedman v Scofield*.[3] The **24.002** plaintiff was riding a jetski off Brighton beach when he was run down by the defendant in a speedboat. It was argued that the MCA 1911 applied to

---

[1] *The Bold Buccleugh* (1851) 7 Moo. P.C. 267, approved by the House of Lords in *Currie v McKnight ("The Dunlossit")* [1897] A.C. 97.
[2] *The Kong Magnus* [1981] P. 223.
[3] [1992] 2 Lloyd's Rep. 163.

this case, but Sheen J., noting that the applicable definition of "vessel" is that in the Merchant Shipping Act 1894,[4] held that a jetski is not a vessel for these purposes. That definition states that a vessel includes any ship or boat or other craft used in navigation. The concept of being "used in navigation" requires that the structure concerned be used to convey persons or property to an intended destination. This is obviously not the purpose of a jetski. Nor can a jetski properly be described as either a boat or a vessel.[5] It may be noted that a hovercraft is a vessel for these purposes.[6]

In *The Norwhale*[7] the plaintiff's vessel sank after the defendant's much larger ship discharged so much water onto it that it capsized. Proceedings were commenced more than two years later, and the plaintiffs argued that the MCA 1911 did not apply because the damage did not arise from any fault in navigation on the part of the defendants. Brandon J. rejected this argument. The Act is of general application, extending to any case where the damage is caused "by the fault of" another vessel, and it is not necessary that the fault have anything to do with navigation. In *Navarro v Larringia Steamship Co. Ltd*[8] the plaintiff sued as executrix of her husband, a seaman who lost his life in a collision between two vessels. He sued the owners of the vessel in which he had been travelling, and the question was whether s.8 of the Act applied. Hewson J. held that it did not. Where an action is brought for personal injuries by a person on board a vessel, s.190 applies only if the action is against the other vessel involved. This may appear to be an odd lacuna in the Act, but it follows inevitably from the wording of s.190.

There is a conflict of authority on the question whether the Act applies to an action in personam against an individual allegedly responsible for a collision at sea. In HMS *Archer*[9] it was held that the Act applied, but in *The Danube II*[10] the contrary conclusion was reached. It is submitted that the latter conclusion is correct, at least where the proposed defendant is not the master of the vessel concerned, since he will not then be a person responsible for the vessel within the meaning of s.190.

FATAL ACCIDENTS ACTS

24.003 Further difficult questions arise in connection with claims under the Fatal Accidents Acts by dependants of those who have lost their lives in maritime

---

[4] s.742.
[5] [1992] 2 Lloyd's Rep. 163 at 165.
[6] Hovercraft (Civil Liability) Order 1979 (S.I. 1979 No. 305).
[7] [1975] Q.B. 589, Brandon J.
[8] [1965] 3 W.L.R. 573, Hewson J.
[9] [1919] P. 1.
[10] [1921] P. 183.

accidents. The first is whether the appropriate time-limit is that imposed by the MSA 1995 or that imposed by the Fatal Accidents Acts. In *The Caliph*[11] it was held that the MSA 1995 prevailed, and it is submitted that this is the correct conclusion, since that Act is expressed to cover any action of the kind mentioned. The second question here is when time starts to run. The choice is between the date of the accident and the date on which the deceased dies. These may be the same, but need not be so. As a matter of general principle the answer ought to be that time runs from the date of death, since it is only then that the dependants definitely have a cause of action. There appears to be, however, no reported case on the point.

SALVAGE SERVICES

Salvage services fell under s.8 of the 1911 Act. The 1995 Act[12] makes the **24.004** relevant limitation period part of the Salvage Convention, to which the Act gives the force of law, but no point of substance turns upon this. In a salvage claim, time runs from the date on which the salvage services are rendered. This may cause problems where services are rendered on more than one day. In *The Katcher I*[13] the plaintiffs refloated the defendants' vessel, which had run aground. After towing it back to harbour they also manned it for some time while it was in harbour. Their claim for salvage initially relied only on the refloating, and they later sought leave to amend the statement of claim out of the time in order to include the later manning of the vessel. Brandon J. held that this was to be regarded as all one claim, with the result that the amendment did not amount to adding a new cause of action. The question of the date of accrual did not then directly arise, but it is submitted that the plaintiffs' cause of action in this case arose as soon as the first salvage services were performed, since they were immediately in a position to sue. This is simply the well-known situation of the plaintiff acquiring a right to sue but being able to add further items of claim at a later stage. Had the writ been issued more than two years after the date of the refloating, but less than two years after the date of the subsequent services, it is submitted that the plaintiffs could have recovered for the latter but not for the former.

---

[11] [1912] P. 213.
[12] S.224.
[13] [1969] P. 65; [1968] 3 All E.R. 344, Brandon J.

ACCRUAL OF CAUSE OF ACTION

24.005 The cause of action accrues and time begins to run when injury is suffered by the claimant, not, if earlier, at the time of the incident. So far as property damage is concerned the relevant time is when the damage is 'caused' [14] but in the case of personal injury or death time runs from when the injury is 'suffered'.[15] So in a case where the claimant suffered psychiatric injury which did not manifest itself for some time after the accident, time ran from the later date when the injury became apparent.[16]

EXTENDING TIME

24.006 The MSA 1995 allows for the extension of the two-year limit under two possible limbs. The first arises where the court is satisfied that there has not, during the two-year period, been any reasonable opportunity of arresting the vessel within the jurisdiction of the court or within the territorial waters of the country to which the claimant's ship belongs or in which the claimant resides or has his principal place of business. In these circumstances the court must extend time to an extent sufficient to give such reasonable opportunity.[17] Thus there is here an obligation to give an extension of time, but it is left to the discretion of the court to decide how long an extension is required in order to give the reasonable opportunity of which the statute speaks. It is a question of fact whether there has been such reasonable opportunity, and there cannot be opportunity to serve the claim form before it has been issued.[18] CPR r.7.6 allows the court, subject to the statutory limitations, to extend time even if the application to extend is not made until after the time has expired.[19] The second limb of the jurisdiction to extend is a more general one, allowing the court to extend the two-year period to such extent and on such conditions as it thinks fit. This limb is merely permissive. It gives the claimant no right to an extension of time. This discretion has been considered in a number of reported cases, beginning shortly after the passage of the MCA 1911. Various possible relevant factors have been considered, and these are discussed in the following paragraphs.

---

[14] S.190(3)(a).
[15] S.190(3)(b).
[16] *Sweet v RNLI*, January 22, 2002, Unreported, Tomlinson J.
[17] But see paras 24.017–24.018 for the position of the Crown in this respect.
[18] The *"Baltic Carrier"* and *"Flinterdam"* [2001] 1 Lloyd's Rep. 689, David Steel J.
[19] The *"Baltic Carrier"* and *"Flinterdam"* [2001] 1 Lloyd's Rep. 689, David Steel J.; see also *The Hai Hing* [2000] 1 Lloyd's Rep. 300.

Burden on claimant

In *The Kashmir*[20] Hill J. said:

24.007

"I think there is no doubt as to what the Act means, that the action is not to be maintained unless the person who is out of time satisfies the burden of showing the court that there is some good and substantial reason for the exercise of the court's discretion in favour of allowing the action to proceed."[21]

Need for good reason to be shown

In *The Hesselmoor* and *The Sergeant*[22] Willmer J. refused to extend time for the plaintiff's claim against a defendant where it appeared that the defendants, if successfully sued, would wish to claim indemnity from the second defendants, and that claim also would be out of time.[23] The learned judge reiterated the principle that leave will not be granted in the absence of special circumstances. He alluded to the prejudice which would obviously be caused to the first defendant if time were extended, and also drew attention to the reputation of the Admiralty Court for resolving disputes speedily. Such reputation would be detrimentally affected if time were routinely extended in cases of this kind. The very strict approach adopted in this case was not followed by Steyn J. in *The Zirje*.[24] In that case it was held that the claimant does not have to show exceptional circumstances, but merely good reason why the time-limit should be extended. This conclusion was reached in part by way of an analogy with the decision of the House of Lords in *Waddon v Whitecroft-Scovill*.[25] Although that decision was concerned with extending the validity of a writ under RSC, Ord.6, r.8, rather than with extending the time for commencing proceedings, it was approved in the context of s.8 by the Court of Appeal in *S.S. "Malindron" (Owners) v S.S. "Igman" (Owners)*.[26] Where a conscious decision has been taken not to include a particular party as a claimant, it is most unlikely that leave will later be given to that party to bring an action or join in an existing action out of time.[27]

24.008

---

[20] [1923] P. 85.

[21] [1923] P. 85 at 147; see also the decisions of Hill J. in *The Llandovery Castle* [1920] P. 119, *The P.L.M. 8* [1920] P. 236 and *H.M.S. Archer* [1919] P. 1.

[22] [1951] 1 Lloyd's Rep. 146.

[23] The potential second defendants had indicated to the first defendants that they would take the limitation point should any action be brought against them.

[24] [1989] 1 Lloyd's Rep. 493, Sheen J.

[25] [1988] 1 W.L.R. 309.

[26] May 27, 1993, CA, Unreported.

[27] *The "Lu Shan"* [1991] 2 Lloyd's Rep. 386, Sheen J.

Very short delay

24.009 In *The Zirje*[28] the writ was issued three days late, and it was proved that this was caused partly by the defendants' failure to reply promptly to telexes addressed to them and partly by their inappropriate insistence on a mutual extension of time although they had no possible claim to bring against the plaintiffs. Steyn J. granted the necessary extension of time. On the other hand, in *The Gaz Fountain*[29] Sheen J. refused an extension where the writ was issued 16 days late. In *The Al Tabith and Alanfushi*[30] the same judge refused an extension where the writ was issued 17 days late because the plaintiffs' solicitor was under the mistaken impression that the defendants were likely to grant an extension of time.

Fault of claimant

24.010 In *The Albany and Marie Josaine*,[31] Sheen J. listed as one factor to be taken into account in deciding whether to grant a discretionary extension of time the degree of blameworthiness to be attached to the plaintiff's failure to issue proceedings in time. It is not an adequate explanation to say that failure to protect the running of time by issuing a writ is due to an oversight—that is the usual situation.[32] Nor is it sufficient to show that the plaintiff wrongly expected the defendant to agree to grant an extension.[33]

Prejudice to claimant

24.011 It is not sufficient to show that because of the expiration of time the plaintiff will be deprived of his claim.[34] That is the necessary consequence of the time-limit. This principle is a salutary reminder of the importance of adhering to time-limits, and its explicit restatement is to be welcomed.

Prejudice to defendant

24.012 There is inevitably prejudice to the defendant when the limitation period is overridden, but the defendant should not be regarded as having an absolute

---

[28] Above fn.24.
[29] [1987] 1 F.T.L.R. 423, Sheen J.
[30] [1993] 2 Lloyd's Rep. 214, Sheen J.
[31] [1983] 2 Lloyd's Rep. 195, Sheen J.
[32] *The Gaz Fountain*, above, fn.29.
[33] *The Al Tabith* and *Alanfushi* [1993] 2 Lloyd's Rep. 214, Sheen J.
[34] *The Al Tabith* and *Alanfushi* [1993].

right to a limitation defence, notwithstanding the comments of Sheen J. in *The Gaz Fountain*.[35]

Solicitors' negligence

Where the failure to issue proceedings in time is apparently due to the negligence of the claimants' solicitors, it may be argued that the proper course is to leave the claimant to sue the solicitors. This argument is of some weight, though it is not conclusive,[36] and care is needed in drawing analogies between this situation and cases under s.33 of the Limitation Act 1980.[37]   **24.013**

Defendants' conduct

In *The Gaz Fountain* it was suggested that the court should not extend time unless the claimant can show special circumstances[38] and that these will nearly always arise as a result of the defendant's conduct.[39] This is probably too broad a statement, since there may be other factors pointing towards an extension. It is instructive to consider the Scottish case of *Thomson v Duggie*.[40] This was an action against the widow of the master of a ship involved in a collision. The widow was not the deceased's personal representative, and the action was ultimately dismissed as incompetent on this ground. The relevance of the case for the purposes of s.8 is that the master had died only a few weeks before the end of the two years, and the pursuers had been unable to discover in time the names of the personal representatives (and the widow had refused to tell them). Lord Birnam indicated that these facts were probably irrelevant to any question of the discretion under s.8 (though of course the point did not arise for decision). It might be argued that the pursuers would not have found themselves in this position had they issued proceedings at an earlier date, as they could perfectly well have done. Nevertheless, the factors present in this case are such as would   **24.014**

---

[35] [1987] 1 F.T.L.R. 423, Sheen J.

[36] *S.S. "Malindron" (Owners) v S.S. "Igman" (Owners)*, May 27, 1993, CA, Unreported.

[37] *S.S. "Malindron" (Owners) v S.S. "Igman" (Owners)*; for s.33, see Ch.8.

[38] On this general point see the case cited in the previous paragraph.

[39] *Bartlett v Admiralty* [1959] 2 Lloyd's Rep. 480, Merriman P. Neither the claimant's lack of funds nor any procedural difficulties arising from a foreign law will be sufficient reason to grant an extension (*The Sunoak* [1960] 2 Lloyd's Rep. 213, Hewson J.).

[40] (1949) 83 Lloyd's Rep. 44, Court of Session (Lord Birnam); for present purposes Scots law appears to be identical with English law, so that the case may legitimately be considered in the context of English law.

have justified an extension of time had a prompt application been made once the identity of the personal representatives was discovered.[41]

Defendants' knowledge

24.015 It does not assist the claimant to show that the defendant was aware of the existence of the claim, or could easily have discovered it.[42]

Length of the delay

24.016 This was stated to be a relevant factor by Sheen J. in *The Albany and Marie Josaine*.[43] Whatever delay has occurred needs to be adequately explained.[44]

Counterclaims

24.017 In *The Fairplay XIV*[45] the plaintiff's action had been started 11 days before time expired, and the defendant was slightly out of time in instituting his counterclaim. Merriman P. held that the Act does apply to counterclaims[46] and that this was an appropriate case for allowing an extension, since the delay was only a short one and appeared to have been caused partly by the plaintiff's own tardiness in instituting his claim. More recently, in *S.S. "Malindron" (Owners) v S.S. "Igman" (Owners)*[47] the plaintiffs had issued a writ in rem against the vessel, having obtained an undertaking from the original owners' insurers to accept service. However, the vessel had meanwhile changed hands, and the two-year limit had expired without judicial extension. The defendants' writ in the action was issued in time. The Court of Appeal held that the desirability of allowing a proper counterclaim was a factor which could be taken into account when deciding whether to grant a belated extension of time.[48]

---

[41] In the light of the points discussed at paras 24.001–24.002 it is open to question whether the MCA 1911 had any application to this case, but the point was not considered by the Court.

[42] *The Gaz Fountain*, above, fn.29.

[43] [1983] 2 Lloyd's Rep. 195, Sheen J.

[44] A delay of five weeks beyond the two-year period may be fatal if the claimant cannot give an adequate explanation for it (*The Vadne (No. 2)* [1960] 1 Lloyd's Rep. 260, Karminski J.

[45] [1939] P. 57, Merriman P.

[46] Confirmed in a modern context in *Gold Shipping Navigation Co SA v Lulu Maritime Ltd* [2009] EWHC 1365 (Admlty) Teare J.

[47] May 27, 1993, CA, Unreported.

[48] See below for the other issues in this case.

APPLICATION TO CROWN

Where the action is brought against one of Her Majesty's ships, s.30 of the **24.018**
Crown Proceedings Act 1947 applies to modify the provisions of s.190 of
the MSA 1995. Section 30 deletes from s.8 in such cases the provision for
mandatory extension of the two-year time-limit if there has been no reasonable opportunity to serve process. The discretionary limb for the
extension of time is unaffected, however, so that the court always has
discretion to extend the limit in an action against one of Her Majesty's
ships, but is never obliged to do so.

SISTER SHIPS

Section 3 of the Administration of Justice Act 1956 effected a significant **24.019**
change in the law by allowing a writ to be issued against the ship alleged to
be at fault and any of her sister ships. Such a writ can then validly be served
on any one of the ships which it names, and any one of them can be arrested
in order to enforce the claim. The 1956 Act did not deal with the relationship between this new method of proceeding and s.8 of the MCA 1911.
A number of problems in this area fell to be considered by Mocatta J. in
The Preveze.[49] The original writ in this case named only one ship. It was
not served within the 12-month period of its validity because there was no
reasonable opportunity to do so. Renewal of the writ was accordingly
granted, but at the same time an amended writ was lodged, which also
named nine sister ships of the defendant vessel. The amended writ was
subsequently served on a sister ship, and the question which arose directly
for decision was whether that service was valid. Mocatta J. held that it was
not, since there was not sufficient justification for allowing the amendments
to the original writ (without which the sister ship was not a named
defendant). However, the renewal of the unamended writ was ordered to
stand. Mocatta J. pointed out that there is no statutory provision which
expressly makes the bringing of the action against the sister ship subject to
the two-year limit imposed by the MCA 1911. However, if that period did
not apply, then it appeared that no period of limitation would apply, a
result which the learned judge regarded as unacceptable. Consequently, he
assumed that it must have been Parliament's intention to make the action
subject to the two-year period and that this must be treated as having been
done by implication since it clearly had not been done expressly. This is
obviously a sensible conclusion, though it involves a bold piece of judicial
legislation.

---

[49] [1973] 1 Lloyd's Rep. 202.

FAILURE TO SERVE THE CLAIM FORM IN TIME

24.020 A claim form in an action of this kind may be renewed at the discretion of the court. The general principles applicable to the renewal of claim forms are considered at paras 22.004–22.019. For the most part the same considerations apply to claim forms in Admiralty cases, but it is instructive to consider the decision of Sheen J. in *The Salviscount and Oltet*.[50] Sheen J. suggested that in considering whether to renew an Admiralty claim form the court should consider three matters:

(a) was there an agreement between the parties to defer service of the claim form?

(b) was the conduct of the defendants such as to lead the plaintiff's solicitors that service was unnecessary and an unjustifiable expense?[51]

(c) to what extent (if any) did the claimant have chance to serve the claim form, or would he have had such chance if he had pursued the matter with reasonable diligence?

24.021 These observations precede the decisions of the House of Lords in *The Myrto (No. 3)*[52] and *Waddon v Whitecroft-Scovill Ltd*,[53] which authoritatively explain the general principles applicable to the renewal of claim forms,[54] but they are nevertheless still useful. The general principle is that the claimant must show good reason for the renewal, and these observations may be regarded simply as pointing to the criteria which are most likely to be of relevance in Admiralty cases (though no doubt they cannot be exhaustive). However, two points of distinction must be made between the normal case of renewal of a claim form and the case of renewal of an Admiralty claim form. First, under s.8 of the MCA 1911 the court always has a discretion to extend the time for the bringing of the action, and an application for the exercise of that discretion will often have the same effect as the renewal of an existing claim form. Therefore it is sensible to try to harmonise the principles upon which extensions of time are given with those upon which claim forms are renewed. The discretion to extend time is

---

[50] [1984] 1 Lloyd's Rep. 164.
[51] Renewal was granted on this ground in *The Prins Bernhard* [1964] P. 117, Hewson J. and *The Owenbawn* [1973] 1 Lloyd's Rep. 56, Brandon J.
[52] [1987] A.C. 597.
[53] [1988] 1 All E.R. 996.
[54] It appears that these principles have largely survived the changes in the period of validity of writs; as to this, see further paras 22.009-22.010.

entirely unfettered,[55] though principles have been developed in the case law, as discussed above.[56]

Secondly, if the claim form in an Admiralty action is not extended, the issue of a second claim form in rem may be impossible even within the primary limitation period. This situation will occur where ownership of the vessel has changed hands since the original claim form was issued. Therefore, the consequences of refusal to renew within the primary limitation period may be more serious in an Admiralty case, and this may well be a factor pointing to a more lenient approach to the granting of extensions, at least in those cases where ownership of the vessel has changed.

THE LAW COMMISSION'S PROPOSALS

The MSA 1995 would not fall within the Commission's proposed core regime, since it is a statute that expressly provides for its own limitation period. Given that the Act implements an international convention to which the UK is party, this seems an inevitable outcome.   **24.022**

---

[55] This discretion is even wider than that under s.33 of the 1980 Act in respect of personal injury claims, since the MCA 1911 gives no guidance at all as to the factors to be taken into account.
[56] See paras 24.005–24.015.

CHAPTER 25

The Foreign Limitation Periods Act 1984

HISTORY AND PURPOSE

The Foreign Limitation Periods Act 1984 (FLPA 1984) was passed in order   **25.001**
to deal with a particular problem in the conflict of laws. In *Huber v Steiner*[1]
it was held that an action on a French promissory note, which was
admittedly governed by French law, could be maintained in the English
courts, notwithstanding that an action in the French courts would have
been time-barred under the relevant French enactment. The action was not
barred under the Limitation Act, and the court held that it was the English
law of limitations that was relevant. However, it was not in every case that
the foreign limitation period would be disregarded. In *Huber v Steiner* it
was assumed that there was a fundamental distinction between those cases
where the expiry of the period merely barred the claimant's remedy and
those cases where it had the further effect of extinguishing his right.[2] In the
former the foreign period would be ignored, whereas in the latter no action
could be brought in the English court once the foreign period had expired.
The ignoring of the foreign period in the former case extended to prohibiting actions which were time-barred under the English rule but not under
the relevant foreign rule.

The Foreign Limitation Periods Act 1984 fundamentally alters these rules   **25.002**
of the common law. Section 1 of the FLPA 1984 provides that where in any
action the law of a foreign country is to be taken into account in determining any matter, the law of that other country relating to limitation shall
apply to that matter to the exclusion of the English limitation rules.[3] This
exclusion of the domestic rules does not apply to matters in determining

---

[1] (1835) 2 Bing.N.C. 202.
[2] For the operation of this distinction in English law, see paras 2.012 et seq.
[3] For the meaning of "law relating to limitation", see FLPA 1984 s.4 and paras 25.023–
25.025.

which both the law of England and the law of some other country are to be taken into account.[4] The wording of s.1 requires careful examination. So long as the foreign law is to be taken into account, even partly, the foreign limitation rules apply. Where the law of England is also to be taken into account the result is that both sets of limitation rules apply. The most important class of case where this rule will apply is that of an action in tort, where the "double actionability" rule laid down in *Phillips v Eyre*[5] required that the tort be actionable both under the law of the place of commission and under English law. In such cases the effect of s.1(2) is that the action can be maintained only if neither the domestic limitation period nor the foreign limitation period has expired.[6]

The double actionability rule was abolished by s.10 of the Private International Law (Miscellaneous Provisions) Act 1995, but that rule still applies in relation to the determination of issues arising in any defamation claim.[7]

25.003   However, the double actionability rule gives rise to a further difficult problem, neatly illustrated by the case of *Gotha City (A Body Corporate) v Sotheby's (An Unlimited Company); Federal Republic of Germany v Sotheby's*,[8] whose facts require to be narrated at some length. The case concerned a painting called *The Holy Family with Saints John and Elizabeth*, painted in 1603 by Joachim Wtewael. At the end of the Second World War this painting disappeared from the collection in the gallery of the Ducal Family of Saxe-Coburg-Gotha in the city of Gotha. It was smuggled from Moscow in the mid 1980s, emerged briefly in West Berlin in 1987, and disappeared, only to reappear when offered for sale by Sotheby's in 1992.

The claimants claimed the return of the painting in conversion against a Panamanian Corporation, *Cobert Finance SA ("Cobert")*. An earlier action brought by the City of Gotha against Sotheby's was consolidated with this action. The Federal Republic of Germany claimed ownership of the painting. The City of Gotha asserted a possessory title to it. The claimants claimed declaratory relief, an order for delivery up and/or damages on the grounds that Cobert converted the painting by taking constructive delivery of it in March 1989, by consigning it to Sotheby's for sale at that time, by offering it for sale through Sotheby's to the City of Gotha in October 1991 and/or by demanding its return from Sotheby's in August 1993.

The cases came down to two central questions, namely whether the Federal Republic of Germany could establish title to the painting, and, if so, whether its claim was time-barred under the German law of limitation.

---

[4] FLPA 1984 s.1(2).
[5] (1870) L.R. 6 Q.B. 1; see also Boys v Chaplin [1971] A.C. 356, HL.
[6] Dicey & Morris, *The Conflict of Laws* at p.187.
[7] S.13.
[8] *The Times*, October 8, 1998, Moses J.

The limitation question involved the following issues:

Whether as a matter of fact the painting was misappropriated by a subsequent possessor after it had been stolen from Gotha (not considered here as it raises no issue of general importance);

Whether the German limitation period was relevant pursuant to s.1 of the Foreign Limitation Periods Act 1984;

Whether, if German law was relevant, the right to recovery was statute-barred under German law;

Whether pursuant to s.2(1) of the Foreign Limitation Periods Act 1984 the court should disapply German law, if it barred the claim, on the grounds that it conflicts with English public policy (as to this point see paras 25.010–25.011 below).

The dispute as to whether the German limitation period applied turned on the proper interpretation of s.1 of the 1984 Act. From that section it followed that the Act had no application unless German law was, in accordance with the rules of English private international law, to be taken into account "in the determination of any matter".   **25.004**

The claim under s.2(1) of the Torts (Interference with Goods) Act 1977 was a restitutionary proprietary claim.[9] It was a claim to protect and enforce rights deriving from the plaintiffs' ownership of the painting. Assertion of those rights depends upon the plaintiffs' assertion of title, which plainly had to be determined under German law. However, it was argued on behalf of the claimant that a distinction had to be made between the issues relating to title and limitation. German limitation law was not relevant to the issue whether the Federal Republic of Germany can trace its title by establishing the painting was expropriated or that title passed on dissolution of the Art Foundation. Once it had successfully traced its title to the painting, title could no longer be in issue and German law would no longer be relevant. The sole issue remaining would be one of English law relating to the conversion of a painting in England.[10] German law applied to the question of title because English conflict rules apply the lex situs, but it had no application in relation to limitation.

Wright J. observed that at the core of the 1984 Act lies the principle that the period of limitation applicable under the lex causae should be applied.[11] But that requires the court to decide what the "causa" was.

The problem arises because s.1(1) appears to suggest that any law which   **25.005**

---

[9] Goff and Jones, *The Law of Restitution* (7th edn 2006), pp.75–76.
[10] It would have been open to the court to find that title was established but that there had been no conversion.
[11] See The Law Commission's Report, *Classification of Limitation in Private International Law* (1982), No. 114, paras 4.3 and 4.11.

is to be applied on any substantive issue should also apply to limitation, thus giving rise to many cases where s.1(2) would apply. Several laws would be applicable to various aspects of a dispute.[12] In relation to contract it is clear that the Law Commission's intention was to apply the proper law of the contract to limitation questions,[13] but of course this approach cannot help in the context of tort claims. Only by saying that the causa was only the claim for wrongful interference with the painting and not the issue of title would it be possible to avoid the conclusion that s.1(2) governed the action and both German and English limitation law applied. It would obviously have been desirable to identify one law as governing the issue to be determined rather than two. There would be no great difficulty in adopting that approach in a case such as the present, where the German law of limitation was merely procedural and did not affect the plaintiffs' title to the painting. There would be far greater difficulty if the foreign law of limitation was substantive, in other words if the foreign law extinguished property rights. In such a case it would be difficult to say that there were not two laws governing the matter in issue.[14] If there may be two leges causae where the foreign limitation law is substantive, then it becomes necessary for a court in this country to consider whether the foreign law is procedural or substantive. That would run counter to one of the fundamental purposes of the 1984 Act, which is to avoid the necessity for making such decisions. Accordingly Wright J. rejected the claimant's arguments on this point and held that s.1(2) applied. The laws of both Germany and England governed the matter before the court. After a detailed consideration of the German law in this area, Wright J. held that the claimant's claim was not time-barred.

25.006   In *Chagos Islanders v AG*[15] an attempt was made to argue that this Act could in some circumstances lead a court to disapply the English law of limitation on public policy grounds. This was a misconceived argument and was rightly rejected.

It is the foreign law on limitation, which, if otherwise applicable, can be disapplied for reasons of public policy including hardship. Section 1 disapplies English law subject to exceptions set out in both subsection (2) and in s.2(1). As the judge observed, the language of the 1984 Act might be thought a trifle muddled in s.2, as to what parts of s.1 are to be disapplied but a little thought makes it tolerably clear. Evans J held in *Arab Monetary Fund v Hashim*[16] that the relevant hardship was that caused by the application of the section, that is the application of the foreign law. That assessment involves a comparison of the relevant competing laws on lim-

---

[12] For criticism of this solution, see P.A. Stone [1985] L.M.C.L.Q. 497.
[13] Law Com. 114, paras 3.9, 4.4 and 4.6.
[14] See also Waterhouse J. in *The Cintas Foundation Inc. v Sotheby's Unlimited and Fondarm International Establishment*, February 11, 1995, Unreported.
[15] [2003] EWHC 2222 (QB), [2003] All ER (D) 166 (Oct) Ouseley J.
[16] [1993] 1 Lloyd's Rep 543 592.

itation. Besides, it is obvious that Parliament did not consider that the English laws on limitation were contrary to its public policy or created hardship, or did only so when compared to foreign law.

COMMENCEMENT OF PROCEEDINGS

Limitation periods normally require that an action be brought within the specified time. One consequence of this is that it is necessary to have rules for determining whether and, if so, when proceedings have been commenced. Clearly these rules may differ from one country to another, and s.1(3) of the FLPA 1984 deals with the resulting problem of choice of law on this question. It subjects such questions to determination by the law of England. This rule has been justified as a matter of practical convenience,[17] but it is in fact fraught with difficulty. English law recognises a number of ways of commencing proceedings, such as the issue of a writ or an originating summons, but apparently does not recognise any others, at least in a domestic context. If a foreign system of law were to recognise some other means of commencing proceedings, or even to have an entirely different notion of what is involved in commencing proceedings, it is hard to see how s.1(3) could sensibly be applied to the question whether proceedings have been commenced, since the inevitable result will be a finding that no step has been taken which English law recognises as effective for this purpose. This appears to be a fundamental difficulty in the drafting of this statute, and it is hard to see how statutory interpretation can resolve the problem. What is needed is surely the adoption of the converse of this rule, namely that the foreign law determines whether proceedings have been issued under that foreign law.

25.007

Careful attention is also needed when dealing with the second part of s.1(3), which makes the question of when proceedings have been commenced subject to English law. The particular problem here, to which s.1(3) alludes, relates to s.35 of the 1980 Act. This section, which is extensively examined in Ch.23, allows certain new claims in pending proceedings to be treated as having been commenced on the same date as the original action, notwithstanding that they were in fact commenced significantly later. Whether the foreign law rule would produce the same result is a matter of chance, and it is necessary to remember that it is s.35 that is to be applied. The problem of differing procedures noted in the previous paragraph can also arise here, though it is likely to be less serious in this context. Section 35 speaks mostly of "new claims", a phrase which is general enough to cover most ways of proceeding in making such a claim but the section also refers to "third-party proceedings", and it is by no means clear how this

25.008

---

[17] Carter (1985), 101 L.Q.R. 68 at 74.

phrase can be made to make sense in the context of foreign legal systems. Again, the proper solution must be to make the timing of the commencement of proceedings subject to the rules of the foreign law.

25.009   Further difficulties may arise where there is some doubt as to whether the proposed new claim is time-barred under the relevant foreign law. In *Welsh Development Agency v Redpath Dorman Long Ltd* [1994] 4 All ER 10, [1994] 1 WLR 1409 it was held by the Court of Appeal that the correct approach was that where there was an issue as to whether the new claim was time-barred, the court should not resolve that issue at the stage of the application for permission to amend but should refuse permission unless the party seeking permission could show that the other party did not have a reasonably arguable case that the new cause of action was time-barred.[18]

EXERCISE OF DISCRETION

25.010   By making the foreign limitation rules applicable, s.1(1) of the FLPA 1984 raises the possibility that an English court will have to exercise a discretion (for example to extend a limitation period) which the foreign law confers on its own courts. Section 1(4) of the Act provides that in such cases the English court is to endeavour, so far as possible, to exercise that discretion in the same way as would the courts of the foreign country. This general submission to the principles of the foreign law must, however, be read subject to s.2, which, as is explained below, allows the court to disapply s.1 on grounds of public policy.[19]

RENVOI

25.011   The difficult private international law doctrine of renvoi causes further problems in this context. Section 1(5) of the FLPA 1984 provides that, for the purposes of s.1, "law" in relation to any country shall not include rules of private international law applicable by the courts of that country. The first issue here is to determine what is meant by the phrase "rules of private international law". This phrase ought to be limited to rules of a law other than the lex fori, and ought not to extend to cases where the lex fori makes special provision for cases with an international element, such as the various English statutes which deal with the international carriage of goods.[20] The second issue is more directly related to renvoi. The intention of s.1(5)

---

[18] See also *Goode v Martin* [2001] 3 All ER at 569 to 570 and *BP Plc v AON Ltd* [2005] EWHC 2554 (Comm), Colman J. at para.56.
[19] See paras 25.014–25.017.
[20] These statutes are examined in Ch.26.

appears to be to exclude renvoi. Therefore, if the proper law applicable to a contract case is French law, then it is the French limitation provisions which are to apply, even if the French court would have applied the limitation rules of another country (including England). This follows the approach adopted on substantive law, since English law does not operate the doctrine of renvoi in contract.[21] The application of s.1(5) is more problematic in cases where English law does operate renvoi, such as cases of real property, where the appeal to the lex situs is normally seen as involving a reference to whichever law the courts of the lex situs would apply.[22]

What is unclear is whether the possible further reference to a third system   25.012
of law is an application of the private international law rules of the lex situs or an application of English private international law rules. Carter[23] argues for the latter view, and this is undeniably more convenient, since it ensures that the limitation rules to be applied will always be those of the system of law which is being applied to the substantive issues. Support for this view may be found in *Bank of America National Trust and Savings Association v Epidavros Gulf Shipping Co. SA, ("The Cape Sounion").*[24] In this case the relevant foreign law was Greek law. It appeared that Greek law would regard questions of limitation as matters of procedure rather than of substance. Hobhouse J. assumed, without detailed consideration, that this did not affect the rule that it is the foreign limitation period which is to be considered.

"In relation to any country"

A further drafting point is that the words "in relation to any country" in   25.013
s.1(5) must be treated as meaning "in relation to any country other than England", since even the application of English private international law rules would otherwise be prohibited, and this would undermine the whole scheme of the Act.

EXCEPTIONS TO SECTION 1 OF THE FLPA 1984

The application of s.1 of the Act is subject to s.2. Section 2(1) provides that   25.014
in any case where the application of s.1 would conflict with public policy, that section shall to the extent of such conflict not apply. Section 2(2) provides that the application of s.1 in any given case shall be treated as conflicting with public policy to the extent that its application would cause

---

[21] Re *United Railways of Havana and Regla Warehouses Ltd* [1960] Ch. 52, CA.
[22] *Re Ross* [1930] 1 Ch. 377.
[23] (1985) 101 L.Q.R. 68 at 73–74.
[24] [1990] 2 Lloyd's Rep. 329, Hobhouse J.

undue hardship to a person who is or might be made a party to the action or proceedings. Section 2(1), however, makes clear that this is not an exhaustive definition of the notion of public policy for these purposes, but provides no further explanation.

The concept of public policy is inherently a vague one. In *Durham v T & N Plc*[25] the Court of Appeal observed, obiter:

"It would in our judgment be wrong to treat a foreign limitation period as contrary to English public policy simply because it is less generous than the comparable English provision in force at the time . . . "

The logic of this observation is undeniable. As between nations there must be a reasonable willingness to recognise that different limitation periods can reasonably be adopted for particular types of action. At the same time there must be limits to this principle of mutual recognition. In the present case the Court of Appeal also said:

"If the law of Quebec provided, as English law once did, that a limitation period ran from the date of sustaining personal injury irrespective of whether a claimant did, or even could, know of his injury at that time, it would be strongly arguable that such a rule would cause a plaintiff undue hardship and so conflict with English public policy."

In *Connelly v Rio Tinto Plc*[26] it was held not to be contrary to public policy to enforce a Namibian limitation period which in a personal injuries action allowed a period of three years from the date of discoverability, but which did not contain any provision for discretionary extension of time once the three years had expired.

25.015   Clearly no precise rule can be laid down, not least since there is a substantial element of discretion in deciding what "public policy" requires or permits in any given case. The passage quoted above suggests that a court will have to form a view about what are at the relevant time the "objectives" of the English law of limitations, and that a provision which is inconsistent with these is likely to be regarded as contrary to public policy. Of course, the passage also shows the way in which these fundamentals can change over time—as the Court of Appeal admits, the hypothetical rule which it would have been willing to strike down was at one time part of the law of England.

25.016   The most detailed consideration of the public policy exception is to be found in the judgment of Wright J. in *Gotha City (A Body Corporate) v Sotheby's (An Unlimited Company); Federal Republic of Germany v*

---

[25] May 1, 1996, CA, Unreported.
[26] December 4, 1998, Unreported, Wright J.

Sotheby's,[27] the facts of which were set out above. Given that Wright J. held that the claim was not time-barred, he did not find it necessary to decide whether the German rules were contrary to public policy, but in recognition of the importance of the question, he offered some conclusions on the point.

"(1) Public policy should be invoked for the purposes of disapplying a foreign limitation period only in exceptional circumstances. Too ready a resort to public policy would frustrate our system of private international law, which "exists to fulfil foreign rights not destroy them".[28]

(2) Foreign law should only be disapplied where that law is contrary to a "fundamental principle of justice".[29]

(3) The fundamental principle of justice with which it is said foreign law conflicts must be clearly identifiable. The process of identification must not depend upon a judge's individual notion of expediency or fairness but upon the possibility of recognizing with clarity a principle derived from our own law of limitation or some other clearly recognised general principle of public policy.[30] English courts should not invoke public policy save in cases where foreign law is manifestly incompatible with public policy. The Law Commission expected that that approach would be adopted and thus did not recommend the use of the word "manifestly" in its proposed Bill.[31]

(4) The English law of limitation serves the purpose of providing protection for defendants from stale claims, encouraging claimants to institute proceedings without unreasonable delay and conferring on a potential defendant confidence that after the lapse of a specific period of time he will not face a claim.[32]

(5) A foreign limitation period will not be disapplied as being contrary to public policy merely because it is less generous than the comparable English provision.[33] Some reason other than mere length must be identified for invoking public policy (see Law Commission Report No. 114, paragraph 4.46)."

---

[27] *The Times*, October 8, 1998, Moses J.; above, para.25.003.

[28] See Law Com. 114, paras 3.2(ii) and 4.35, and Evans J. in *Arab Monetary Fund v Hashim* [1993] 1 Lloyd's Rep. 543 at 592 referring to the Law Commission's view that it should only apply "in most unusual circumstances" (para.4.39).

[29] See Law Com. 114, paras 4.43 and 4.44. In *The Estate of Fuld (Deceased) (No. 3)* [1968] p.675; [1965] 3 All E.R. 776, Scarman J. said: "an English court will refuse to apply a law which outrages its sense of justice or decency" (at 698 of the former report). In *Oppenheimer v Cattermole* [1976] A.C. 249; [1975] 1 All E.R. 538 the House of Lords refused to recognise racially discriminatory legislation on the grounds of public policy; so too our courts would refuse to recognise discriminatory limitation law.

[30] See paras 4.35 and 4.45 of Law Com. 114.

[31] See para.4.38 of Law Com. 114.

[32] See para.4.44 of Law Com. 114.

[33] See *Durham v T & N Plc*, above, n. 22, followed in *Harley v Smith* [2009] EWHC 56 (QB) Foskett J.

25.017   The claimants relied upon various features of the German limitation law: no account is taken of the plaintiffs' state of knowledge,[34] no account is taken of the fact that the painting was stolen,[35] the defendants were not bona fide purchasers and the defendants were guilty of deliberately and unconscionably concealing *Cobert's* identity and address.[36] Wright J. considered all these factors, but held that the only one which could be regarded as being contrary to English public policy was that time still ran in favour of a thief. In the other areas, although German law might be different from English law there was no discernible point of public policy requiring the rejection of the German law.

Wright J.'s analysis is undeniably very interesting, but it is submitted that he came to the wrong conclusion for at least two related reasons. The first, to which he alluded, is that the limitation period was 30 years, rather than the six years of English law. It is obvious that a legal system can trade off within its limitation rules between the length of the period and the events which cause time to start running. What German law has in effect done is to be unsympathetic to claimants in relation to the commencement of the limitation period, but generous to them in the length of the period. This fact ought to have weighed more with the judge than it in fact did. The second point is that there ought to be more respect for the policy choices made by other states, especially other members of the European Union. Limitation law is about balancing the interests of claimants and defendants, and different states may legitimately take different views about where the proper balance lies. Judges should be very slow indeed to substitute their views for the views of a foreign legislature.

UNDUE HARDSHIP

25.018   Another vague notion used in the Act is "undue hardship" in s.2(2). The first significant case on this provision was *Jones v Trollope Collis Cementation.*[37] The proper law in the case was Pakistani law, but it appeared that this would have imposed a 12-month time-limit, which had expired. The Court of Appeal held that this was an appropriate case to disapply the Pakistani limitation period, since its effect would be to cause undue hardship to the claimant. In this context "undue" merely means greater hardship than the circumstances of the case warrant.[38] The particular facts relied upon were that the plaintiff had been unable to issue proceedings

---

[34] For comparable English provisions, see ss.14, 14A and 32 of the 1980 Act.
[35] cf. ss.3,4 of the 1980 Act.
[36] cf. s.32(1)(b) of the 1980 Act.
[37] *The Times*, January 26, 1990, CA.
[38] See also *Arab Monetary Fund v Hashim*, February 1, 1996, CA, Unreported.

within the 12-month period. More recently, in *Harley v Smith*[39] it was said that undue hardship simply meant greater hardship than normal, and that the test does not involve any balancing exercise of the interests of the claimant and those of the defendant[40]. The latter point appears obviously correct, but the former is more problematic. 'Undue' is not the same as 'unusual', and the two concepts should not be confused. The earlier decision in *Jones* appears to be a more accurate reading of the text, though it must be admitted that on either view the provision is not free from difficulty. Concepts of fairness are not easily applied in limitation cases because one side's advantage is always the other side's prejudice. The intention of that Act was that in most cases the foreign limitation period should apply to the exclusion of its English counterpart. A further point which arises in connection with s.2(2) is that the period which it is sought to disapply may be shorter or longer than its English counterpart. The cases so far have involved limitation periods which English law regards as too short,[41] though that has not been the basis of the decisions. In other cases the court could face the problem of a very long limitation period. The wording of s.2(2) clearly implies that such a limitation period could be disregarded— the court must consider the question of undue prejudice to any party—but it remains to be seen whether English courts will in fact be prepared to protect actual or potential defendants in this way. It may also be possible to derive some assistance from a comparison with s.12 of the Arbitration Act 1996, which allows the court to extend the time-limit for an arbitration if satisfied that the original limit will cause undue hardship to the party affected by it,[42] but the somewhat different context of s.12 makes it inappropriate to rely too closely on the cases decided under it. Section 2(2) was considered in *Gotha City (A Body Corporate) v Sotheby's (An Unlimited Company); Federal Republic of Germany v Sotheby's.*[43] The additional circumstance upon which reliance is placed over and above the mere impact of a limitation period of 30 years is that the plaintiffs were the victims of theft and, between that theft and 1991, they had no means of discovering the facts which would have enabled them to identify the possessor of the painting and its whereabouts. But that additional fact could not justify invoking s.2(2) in circumstances where s.2(1) did not apply. Either the public-policy objection exists or it does not. If it does not, then all the plaintiffs are, in essence, complaining about is the length of the German limitation period. That by itself is not enough. This shows that the court must be astute not to allow what are really s.2(1) arguments to be reintroduced by way of s.2(2).

---

[39] [2009] EWHC 56 (QB) Foskett J.

[40] At para.94.

[41] Notwithstanding that the period of one year applied between 1893 and 1939 to actions against public authorities—Public Authorities Protection Act 1893 s.21.

[42] For consideration of s.12, see paras 16.016–16.021.

[43] *The Times*, October 8, 1998, Moses J.; above, para.25.003.

Action time-barred in foreign country

25.019 *Metall und Rohstoff AG v Donaldson Lufkin*[44] considers, inter alia, the application of the 1984 Act in relation to the private international law rules on actions in tort. The general principle is that an action for a tort committed out of the jurisdiction can be brought if, but only if, the acts complained of were actionable in the other jurisdiction and would have been actionable here if committed here.[45] The question when an act is to be regarded as "actionable" in the other jurisdiction has given rise to some difficulty. In the present case it appeared that the action would have been treated as time-barred in the other jurisdiction, though that jurisdiction would have regarded the acts as wrongful and actionable. Ultimately it was not necessary in this case for the Court of Appeal to decide whether the requirement of double actionability is satisfied when the action is time-barred in the other jurisdiction, since it was held that the torts in question had been committed here. However, Slade L.J. suggests that the "public policy" exception in s.1(2) of the Act was included to deal specifically with the double actionability rule in *Phillips v Eyre*. An alternative view would be that this is a problem with which the Foreign Limitation Periods Act 1984 does not deal, since that Act stipulates only which limitation period is to be applied once the English court has accepted jurisdiction. It is submitted that the truth lies somewhere between these two extremes. Section 1(2) is intended to deal with substantive choice of law questions, as well as with the double actionability rule, as is shown by *Jones v Trollope Collis Cementation*, considered above; but the Act applies where the law of any foreign country is to be taken into account in the determination of any matter (s.1(1)), and the exception provided by s.1(2) is an exception from s.1(1) and is therefore of equally general application. Consequently, where it is pleaded that the double actionability rule is not satisfied because the action is time-barred in the other jurisdiction, the proper course is for the court to decide whether that is indeed so, and, if it is, to consider whether the foreign period ought to be disapplied under s.1(2).

Absence from the jurisdiction

25.020 Section 4 of the FLPA 1984[46] provides that the law relating to limitation includes any provision for the extension of a limitation period or for the suspension of the running of time. Section 2(3) restricts the ambit of this by providing that in the application of s.1 the court must disregard any provision of the foreign law in so far as it provides for extension or suspension

---

[44] [1990] 1 Q.B. 391, CA.
[45] *Phillips v Eyre* (1870) L.R. 6 Q.B. 1; *Boys v Chaplin* [1971] A.C. 356.
[46] See paras 25.015–25.017.

on the ground of the absence of a party to the action from any jurisdiction or country. Therefore, if the relevant foreign law provides that time is not to run so long as the defendant is out of the jurisdiction, the English court, in applying the foreign law, must disregard this provision. This had the odd effect that only part of the relevant foreign law is being applied. The justification for this must presumably be that as a matter of English public policy such rules are considered entirely unacceptable.[47] It is to be noted that the foreign rule must relate to the absence of a party to the action. A rule which allowed for suspension of time on the grounds of the absence of a witness would apparently not infringe s.2(3), and the English court would therefore be obliged to give full effect to it.

FOREIGN JUDGMENTS ON LIMITATION POINTS

Section 3 is the only section of the FLPA 1984 that deals with the recognition of judgments, as distinct from choice of law. The need for it arises from the rule that a foreign judgment which is not a judgment on the merits of the case does not qualify for recognition in England either at common law[48] or under the Foreign Judgments (Reciprocal Enforcement) Act 1933,[49] and that a judgment based on a limitation rule which merely bars the claimant's remedy without extinguishing his right is not a judgment on the merits for these purposes. Section 3 reverses this latter rule: where any court outside England has determined any matter wholly or partly by reference to the limitation rules of any country, that determination is to be treated as a judgment on the merits for the purposes of the law relating to the effect to be given to that judgment in England.

25.021

Meaning of "the law relating to limitation"

Many provisions of the FLPA 1984 refer to the law of any country relating to limitation. This expression is defined in s.4 of the Act. The basic definition is:

25.022

"so much of the relevant law of that country as (in any manner) makes provision with respect to a limitation period applicable to the bringing of proceedings in respect of that matter in the courts of that country."

---

[47] Though it may be observed that the Limitation (Enemies and War Prisoners) Act 1945 made a provision of just this kind. See para.27.004.

[48] *Harris v Quine* (1868) L.R. 4 Q.B. 653.

[49] *Black-Clawson International Ltd v Papierwerke Walkhoff Ascaffenberg AG* [1975] A.C. 591, HL. Quite apart from the FLPA 1984, the rule would not now apply in countries which are signatories to the Convention on Jurisdiction and the Enforcement of Judgments in Civil and Commercial Matters (i.e. Member States of the European Union).

This is in part self-referential, since it defines limitation rules by reference to limitation periods, but it seems unlikely that this semantic problem will give rise to any practical difficulties. Generally, any provision which relates to time-limits for the bringing of an action will be part of the law of limitation for these purposes.[50] For the avoidance of doubt, paras (a) and (b) of s.4(1) go on to declare that the term includes any rules on the application, extension, reduction or interruption of the limitation period, as well as any rule to the effect that no time-limit applies to the bringing of a particular action. English law has no rules providing for the reduction of any of its periods of limitation, but there are provisions for extension in the case of personal injuries[51] and defamation.[52] Exceptionally, s.14 of the Arbitration Act 1996[53] permits the running of time to be suspended in certain cases.[54] The words "relevant law" in s.4(1) of the FLPA 1984 are explained by s.4(2) as referring to the procedural and substantive law applicable to the case, apart from any rules of private international law. Therefore, the private international law doctrine of renvoi cannot be used to make parts of the domestic law of foreign countries into part of the English law of limitation for these purposes.

25.023   Section 4(3) of the FLPA 1984 qualifies the ambit of law relating to limitation for these purposes by providing that the expression does not extend to any rules allowing the court a discretion to refuse relief on the grounds of acquiescence or otherwise. Therefore, any rules of this character are not excluded by the general principle in s.1 which excludes the English law of limitation in certain cases. This raises the question of the way in which an English court should apply those rules to a case to which s.1(1)(a) applies. Section 4(3) provides some guidance on this point by stipulating that the English court shall have regard in particular to the provisions of the foreign law which is rendered applicable by s.1. The effect of this appears to be that the English court must consider the operation of the foreign rules before deciding whether and how to exercise its own discretion. The implication seems to be that so far as possible the discretion should be exercised in accordance with the foreign rules. This implication is strengthened by the further restriction of this part of s.4(3) to cases where the relevant foreign limitation period has not expired. Therefore, where the relevant foreign period is still current the intention is that only in exceptional cases should any English discretion to refuse relief be exercised. By contrast, where the relevant foreign period has expired, the English court's discretion will not normally be relevant, since that limitation period will

---

[50] Compare also the definition of "limitation periods" adopted for the purposes of this book at para.1.001.
[51] 1980 Act s.33.
[52] 1980 Act s.4A, as added by Defamation Act 1996 s.5.
[53] Replacing s.34 of the Limitation Act 1980.
[54] See para.16.029. The Limitation (Enemies and War Prisoners) Act 1945 can also have this effect: see para.27.004. See also para.2.001, on the suspension of running of time generally.

provide a defence to the action to which the English court must give effect. This provision may perhaps best be understood by comparison with s.2 of the FLPA 1984, which allows the court to disapply s.1 on the grounds of public policy. Although s.4(3) does not mention the concept of public policy, the coherence of the scheme of the Act can be best maintained by construing the subsections as allowing the court to disregard the approach which the foreign court would take only where strong considerations of public policy mandate this approach.

One point of difficulty which arises from s.4 concerns terms in contracts governed by the law of some other country. For present purposes these terms may be of two kinds. They may require a party to commence proceedings within a certain time: the rules incorporated into charterparties under the Hague-Visby Rules[55] are the best example of this. Alternatively they may require a party to take some other step, such as notifying the existence of a claim to the other party, an act which in English law would not be sufficient to start proceedings. The problem with clauses of this kind is to know whether they are part of the law relating to limitation in the relevant country.[56] Clauses of the latter kind clearly cannot be part of the law relating to limitation, since they have nothing to do with the commencement of proceedings nor with any procedural steps required to be taken after proceedings have been commenced.[57] Clauses of the former kind are more difficult. They do relate to time-limits for the commencement of proceedings and they do have the force of law, but they achieve the latter only by virtue of the contractual agreement of the parties.[58] The question is whether the expression "the law relating to limitation" includes such provisions or is limited to provisions which are of general application and do not depend upon the parties.

25.024

The FLPA 1984 gives no guidance on the resolution of this question, and the best approach is to consider the purpose of the provision. Section 4 is designed to ensure that the English court approaches these issues in the same way, so far as is practicable, as would the foreign court. This objective is best achieved by allowing the court to take account of the same factors, as nearly as possible, with regard to time-limits for the commencement of proceedings, as would the foreign court, and this must obviously include contractual provisions of the kind here discussed. Accordingly it is submitted that such provisions do form part of the law relating to limitation for the purposes of s.4 of the Act.

25.025

---

[55] For the Hague-Visby Rules see paras 26.002–26.015.
[56] On this point see also P.A. Stone [1985] L.M.C.L.Q. 497.
[57] See the definition of "limitation" adopted for the purposes of this work at para.1.001, on commencement of proceedings.
[58] The incorporation of rules such as the Hague-Visby Rules into a contract is always a matter of the choice of the parties.

BURDEN OF PROOF

25.026 Where the defendant wishes to rely on the provisions of a foreign law relating to limitation, the burden is on him to plead the point and to adduce the necessary evidence.[59]

ARBITRATIONS

25.027 Section 5 of the Act deals with the application of the Act to arbitrations. Section 13 of the Arbitration Act 1996 makes the provisions of limitation enactments applicable to arbitrations in the same way as they apply to High Court actions,[60] and s.5 of the FLPA 1984 makes ss.1, 2, and 4 of the FLPA 1984 limitation enactments for these purposes. An important consequence of this is that s.34(5) of the 1980 Act, which allows in certain circumstances the suspension of the time period provided by any limitation enactment, must now be read as referring, in any case to which s.1 of the FLPA 1984 applies, as authorising the suspension of the relevant foreign limitation period which s.1 requires the English court to apply. The FLPA 1984 will apply in any arbitration action which is governed by English procedural law, even if the substantive law applicable to the case is that of another country.

APPLICATION TO CROWN

25.028 Section 6 of the Act makes the provisions of the FLPA 1984 applicable to actions involving the Crown in the same way as it applies to actions to which the Crown is not a party. Section 6(2) explains the meaning of actions involving the Crown for these purposes, and it is to be observed that the definition is the same as that found in s.37 of the 1980 Act for actions involving the Crown under the domestic law of limitation.

---

[59] *Zapita v ACT Group Plc*, February 11, 1993, CA, Unreported.
[60] For the rules relating to arbitrations, see Ch.16.

TRANSITIONAL PROVISIONS

Section 7 of the FLPA 1984 contains transitional provisions. By s.7(3)(a) **25.029** nothing in the Act is to affect any proceedings or arbitration commenced before the Act came into force.[61] Therefore, proceedings already extant at that day are determined on the common law rules, which were summarised at paras 25.001–25.002. By s.7(3)(b) the Act cannot apply in relation to any matter if, under the limitation period which would have been applicable to it in the absence of the Act, the action would have been barred (whether as to right or merely as to remedy) at the time when the Act came into force, i.e. the Act cannot operate to revive any cause of action which was previously barred. In view of the lapse of time since the Act came into force, the effect of these provisions is now largely spent.

THE LAW COMMISSION'S PROPOSALS

The topic of foreign limitation periods is not dealt with in the Report. **25.030** Foreign limitation periods are normally regarded as a discrete area of the subject, which scarcely interacts at all with the issues considered by the Commission.

---

[61] Though the Act does apply to proceedings commenced after the Act came into force, even where the cause of action occurred before that date: *Jones v Trollope Colls Cementations Overseas Ltd, The Times,* January 26, 1990, CA; see also para.25.011.

CHAPTER 26

The Carriage Statutes

GENERAL

There are a number of statutes in English law which incorporate into that **26.001** law the provisions of international conventions on various matters relating to the carriage (usually the international carriage) by various means of persons and/or property. These conventions generally have their own specified periods of limitation for the making of claims, and a common feature of such conventions is that they impose limitation periods rather shorter than would normally apply in English law for actions of this kind. It is also fair to say that these conventions display some common features in their general approach to the question of limitation, though there are also some differences of detail. The final text of an international convention inevitably includes some degree of compromise, and it will be seen that from an English law point of view the limitation provisions of some of these conventions are somewhat unhappily drafted, though admittedly these conventions (with the exception of the Hague-Visby Rules) have so far produced very little English authority. The more important of these conventions are dealt with in this chapter.

CARRIAGE OF GOODS BY SEA ACT 1971

This is the statute in this group which has attracted the greatest attention. It **26.002** follows the usual pattern for carriage statutes of including in its Schedule the relevant international rules. In this case these are the Hague-Visby Rules,[1] which apply to the carrier of goods in a contract for the international carriage of goods by sea in relation to the loading, handling, stowage, carriage, custody, care and discharge of such goods from the time when

---

[1] See the Schedule to the Carriage of Goods by Sea Act 1971.

they are loaded to the time when they are discharged from the ship.[2] It is to be observed that the Rules do not cover actions for hire or freight.[3] The loss or damage referred to must be loss or damage which is related to the cargo owner's goods.[4]

However, they do cover actions for misdelivery of cargo. This was established by the decision of the Court of Appeal in *Cia Portorafti Commerciale SA v Ultramar Panama Inc. ("The Captain Gregos")*,[5] where it was also held to be irrelevant that the action in question was or might have been framed in tort.[6] Similarly, the Rules do cover actions for economic loss arising from damage to goods as well as to the damage to the goods themselves.[7] Moreover, they apply to goods intended to be shipped but never shipped and to events happening before loading begins.[8] So long as the action is against a shipowner in respect of the carriage of goods by sea, the Rules apply. In *Borgship Tankers Inc v Product Transport Corporation Ltd*[9] the vessel had been chartered on the Shelltime 4 Form, which incorporated this rule. A claim was made for loss of freight under a sub-charter allegedly resulting from the unfitness of the vessel's cargo tanks, and the question was whether this fell within the scope of the rule. A clause in identical terms to cl.27 (c) (in a charter party on the Shelltime 4 form) had been considered in *The Stena Pacifica*[10], where Evans J. said:

"The phrase 'loss or damage to or in connection with goods' appears in art.III, r.8, and art.IV, r.5(a) and (h). Article III, r.6, in its original form, was differently worded, referring only to liability 'in respect of loss or damage', but even this was held to include financial loss 'related to the cargo-owners' goods', (*Goulandris Brothers Ltd. v B. Goldman & Sons Ltd.*, [1957] 2 Lloyd's Rep. 207 at p 222, col. 1; [1958] 1 QB 74, at p 105, where it was further held that the cargo-owners' liability to pay general average contribution was not closely enough related to the goods to come within the phrase; cf. *GH Renton & Co. Ltd. v Palmyra Trading Corporation of Panama*, [1956] 2 Lloyd's Rep. 379; [1957] AC 149). In these circumstances, the starting point, in my judgment, is the fact that the phrase used in cl.27(c)(ii) has a well-recognized meaning which

---

[2] Hague-Visby Rules, art. 1.

[3] *Interbulk v Ponte dei Sospiri Shipping Co. ("The Standard Ardour")* [1988] 2 Lloyd's Rep. 159, Saville J.

[4] *(Goulandris Brothers Ltd v B Goldman & Sons Ltd* [1958] 1 QB 74, [1957] 3 All ER 100 at p 105).

[5] [1991] 3 All E.R. 967, CA, reversing the decision of Hirst J. [1989] 2 Lloyd's Rep. 63.

[6] See also *Anglo Irish Beef Processors International v Federated Stevedores Geelong and Others* [1997] 1 Lloyd's Rep. 207, Victoria Court of Appeal.

[7] *Cargill International SA v CPN Tankers (Bermuda) Ltd ("The Ot Sonia")*, The Times, June 10, 1993, CA.

[8] *Linea Naviera Paramaconi SA v Abnormal Load Engineering Ltd* [2001] 1 Lloyd's Rep. 763, Tomlinson J.

[9] [2005] EWHC 273 (Comm), 2004 FOLIO NO 759 Cresswell J.

[10] [1990] 2 Lloyd's Rep 234.

encompasses most, though not all, of the claims which may be brought by a cargo-owner for breach of the carriers' obligations under the rules. The intention of cl.27(c)(ii) is that claims of this kind shall be subject to the rules as between the charterer (or any other Claimant) and the shipowner, even when governed by the charter-party terms. If the charterer himself is the goods owner, then clearly the rules will apply. It is equally clear that when the charterer alleges a breach of the charter-party and claims damages measured otherwise than by reference to cargo, then the charter-party exceptions set out in cl.27(a) will apply. The difficulty arises when the charterer alleges a breach of the charter-party, but measures the damages by reference to third party cargo interests. The question is whether in these circumstances the shipowner's liability is governed by the rules, in whichever form, pursuant to the charter-party, they ought to apply. This is a difficult question and I do not believe that any clear answer is possible. The apparent intention is that the shipowner's liability for what I will call generally 'cargo claims' shall be governed by the rules. They are to be 'subject to' the rules. This means, in my judgment, claims which the goods' owner may bring under the rules and which are of the kind referred to in cl.27(c)(ii).

So, in so far as the owner is alleged to have been in breach of his obligations under the rules, in my judgment the charterer's claim is made subject to the rules. But the position is different where the charterer alleges not a breach of the rules, but of some other term of the charter-party itself. Here, for example, an express warranty as to the capacity or performance of the vessel would not necessarily be co-extensive with the owner's obligations under the rules to provide and maintain a seaworthy ship and properly to discharge the cargo. If the charterer alleges that such a term has been broken, his claim is not one that can be made 'subject to' the rules, except in the narrow sense, that the shipowner might seek to apply the exceptions to his obligations under the rules to his charter-party undertakings. This would be one-sided and it is not, in my judgment, what was intended to be the effect of cl.27(c)(ii). I hold, therefore, that cl.27(c)(ii) applies, in so far as the plaintiffs may seek to allege breaches of the defendants' obligations which arise under or are co-extensive with his obligations under the rules. But it does not apply where the plaintiffs allege breaches of charter-party obligations which are independent of the rules. The claim, moreover, must be one which, for the purposes of the rules, is for 'loss of or damage to or in connection with the goods', including a claim for financial loss arising in relation to the goods."

Cresswell J. agreed with Evans J that cl.27 (c) (ii) is concerned with what would be regarded in the marine market as "cargo claims". It refers only to claims sufficiently connected with cargo, that is to say claims (whether original or derivative) of the sort which are normally brought by cargo-interests (bill of lading holders), claiming loss or damage arising in relation to the cargo and measured by reference to the cargo. Included in this category are claims for physical loss of cargo and claims for physical damage to cargo. Also included are claims for financial loss such as (by way of example) a fall in the value of a particular cargo or the costs of storing/transshipping a particular cargo. Although, strictly speaking, these observations relate only to the Shelltime 4 Form, it is submitted that they are clearly the correct approach to be adopted in the context of the rule generally.

ARTICLE III, RULE 6 OF THE HAGUE-VISBY RULES

26.003   Article III, r.6 reads:

> "The carrier and the ship shall in any event be discharged from all liability whatsoever in respect of the goods, unless suit is brought within one year of their delivery or of the date when they should have been delivered. This period may, however, be extended if the parties so agree after the cause of action has arisen."

SUBSTITUTE TONNAGE

26.004   Where a chartered vessel is unavailable to perform all or part of the charter, or where the charterer chooses to use an alternative vessel because of defects in the chartered vessel, there may be a claim for the costs of the alternative vessel. It was held in *Noranda Inc. v Barton (Time Charter) Ltd ("The Marinor")*[11] that such a claim is not "in respect of" the goods shipped on the substitute vessel; rather, it is in respect of the condition of the original vessel. Thus, art.III, r.6 has no application. By contrast, where the claim is in respect of loss of profit on the goods, perhaps because they arrive later than they otherwise would have done or because they arrive in a damaged condition as a result of a defect in the chartered vessel, that is in respect of the goods and art.III, r.6 does apply.[12]

---

[11] [1996] 1 Lloyd's Rep. 301, Colman J.
[12] *Mauritius Oil Refineries Ltd v Stolt-Nielsen Nederlands BV (The "Stolt Sydness")* [1997] 1 Lloyd's Rep. 273, Rix J.

When time starts to run

Time runs from the date on which the goods were delivered or, in a case 26.005
where the basis of the action is the non-delivery of the goods, from the date
on which they should have been delivered. It is a question of fact whether
there has been delivery under the contract of carriage. Where the port of
delivery is varied, the evidence may (but will not necessarily) lead to the
conclusion that the delivery has been under an entirely separate
agreement.[13]

The length of the period

The period of limitation applicable under the Hague-Visby Rules is one 26.006
year.

Extension of the period

The one-year limit may be extended by agreement between the parties after 26.007
the cause of action has arisen, or by estoppel,[14] but it appears that it is not
otherwise subject to extension even in the case of fraud on the part of the
carrier.

Shortening the period

Bills of lading sometimes provide for a shorter limitation period than that 26.008
laid down in the Hague-Visby Rules. The period of nine months is commonly chosen. In *Finagra (U.K.) Ltd v OT Africa Line Ltd*[15] Rix J. set out
the principles to be followed in such cases for deciding which of the two
limitation periods is to prevail. The essential rule is to treat the rules as set
out in the body of the contract in extenso but rejecting provisions which
were inconsistent with the incorporating document. The presence of a
repugnancy clause, whether the clause inherent in the rules in the form of
art.III, r.8 or a separate repugnancy clause in the contract itself, is always
relevant but neither its presence nor its absence is necessarily decisive. A
specifically negotiated clause is likely to take precedence over the merely
incorporated. In the case of inconsistency the clause in the incorporating
document takes precedence over the merely incorporated, and the bill of

---

[13] *Trafigura Beheer Bv v Golden Stavraetos Maritime Inc (The "Sonia")* [2003] EWCA Civ
664, [2003] 1 WLR 2340, [2003] 2 Lloyd's Rep 201.
[14] *The Stolt Loyalty* [1993] 2 Lloyd's Rep. 281, Clarke J.
[15] [1998] 2 Lloyd's Rep. 622, Rix J.

lading or charter may contain special language to indicate which clause is to prevail. One set of incorporated rules may in certain circumstances oust another set of incorporated rules, even the Hague-Visby Rules, entirely, where they were quite incompatible; but if the conflicting clauses could live together the court should seek to give effect to both of them. Clear words are needed for a time-bar so that in a case of doubt or ambiguity the conflict must be resolved in favour of a longer time-limit. On the facts it was held that the longer Hague-Visby Rules time-limit applied.

Effect of expiry

26.009　The decision of the House of Lords in *Aries Tanker Corporation v Total Transport Ltd*[16] establishes the very important point that in a charterparty governed by the Hague-Visby Rules the expiry of the one-year period for the bringing of a claim extinguishes the claimant's right as well as his remedy, notwithstanding the general principle of English law that, at least in the context of personal obligations, the expiry of time merely bars the remedy. Lord Wilberforce, delivering the leading speech in the House of Lords, said of art.III, r.6:

> "It is a time bar of a special kind, viz. one which extinguishes the claim not one which, as most English statutes of limitation and some international conventions do, bars the remedy while leaving the claim itself in existence."

The effect of this is that the claim can no longer be raised even by way of counterclaim or set-off. On the other hand the expiry of the limitation period does not affect any defence which might be available to any party.[17]

Substitution of parties

26.010　In *The Jay Bola*[18] the plaintiffs were unaware of a change in the ownership of a vessel whose owners they wished to sue, and the solicitors acting for the owners did not bring this to their attention until the writ was served (which was after the expiry of the one-year time-limit). The plaintiffs' attempt to have the writ amended to name the new owners as defendants failed on the ground that the action against the true owners was absolutely

---

[16] [1977] 1 W.L.R. 185.
[17] *Mediterranean Freight Services Ltd v BP Oil International Ltd* July 7, 1994, CA, Unreported.
[18] [1992] 2 Lloyd's Rep. 62, Hobhouse J.

extinguished by the expiry of the one-year limit. Similarly, in *The Leni*[19] there was confusion over which company should be the plaintiff. By the time the position was clarified the one-year limit had expired, and it was held (very reluctantly) that it was not possible to allow an amendment of the writ to name the right company as plaintiff, notwithstanding that the defendants had obviously not been prejudiced by the error.

Arbitrations

Where an earlier suit is brought in breach of an arbitration clause, the court will not regard that as a suit for the purposes of the time-bar under art.III, r.6.[20] A further difficulty, which is explored elsewhere in this work,[21] is the question whether provisions of s.12 of the Arbitration Act 1996,[22] which gives the court discretion to extend the time for commencing proceedings, are available where the claim no longer exists.[23]   26.011

Stopping the running of time

The requirement in art.III, r.6 is that "suit" must be commenced within that one-year period. The meaning of the term "suit" was considered by the Court of Appeal in *The Merak*.[24] In that case the Court of Appeal pointed out that the Hague-Visby Rules are intended to apply in many countries of the world; for this reason it is necessary for them to use generic words to describe the process of instituting proceedings. "Suit" is such a word, being intended to cover any recognised way of beginning an action; as such it can include the commencement of arbitration proceedings,[25] and is not limited to the issuing of a claim form. In *Transpetrol Ltd v Ekali Shipping Company Ltd ("The Aghia Marina")*[26] the charterparty provided for a reference to two arbitrators. One side nominated an arbitrator who initially accepted appointment, but then discovered that he was unable to act because of a conflict of interest; by the time this discovery was made, the one-year time-limit had expired and the other party declined to accept the nomination of a   26.012

---

[19] [1992] 2 Lloyd's Rep. 48, Judge Diamond Q.C.

[20] *Thyssen Inc. (A Body Corporate) v Calypso Shipping Corp. SA (A Body Corporate)* [2000] 2 Lloyd's Rep. 243, David Steel J.

[21] See paras 16.016–16.027.

[22] Replacing s.27 of the Arbitration Act 1950; see Ch.16.

[23] *Consolidated Investment and Contracting Co. v Saponara Shipping Co. Ltd ("The Virgo")* [1978] 1 W.L.R. 986, CA.

[24] [1965] P. 223, CA.

[25] Though apparently in some US jurisdictions the commencement of arbitration proceedings does not count as "suit" for these purposes: *Mauritius Oil Refineries Ltd v Stolt-Nielsen Nederlands BV (The "Stolt Sydness")* [1997] 1 Lloyd's Rep. 273.

[26] [1989] 1 Lloyd's Rep. 62, Evans J.

replacement arbitrator. Evans J. held that the initial nomination, having been made in good faith, was sufficient to constitute the bringing of suit for the purposes of the Hague-Visby Rules. However, the action brought must be a proper or competent one.[27] Thus the requirement of bringing suit is not satisfied where the proceedings brought are conducted in such a way that they are liable to be dismissed for want of prosecution.[28] Equally, proceedings brought in breach of an exclusive jusrisdiction clause are not properly brought for these purposes.[29]

Proceedings in another jurisdiction

26.013 In *The Nordglimt*[30] proceedings had been begun within the one-year time-limit of the Hague-Visby Rules, but in Belgium rather than in England. Hobhouse J. held, in accordance with the observations of Lord Wilberforce in *Aries Tanker Corporation v Total Transport Ltd*,[31] that the sufficiency of these proceedings to stop time running under the Rules depended upon the meaning of the words "suit brought" in art.III, r.6. His Lordship went on to hold that the phrase meant proceedings brought in a proper jurisdiction by a person having the competence to bring them. Where, as in this case, the foreign court has accepted jurisdiction to try the case, it must be assumed that the foreign court was a proper forum. If it can also be shown that the claimant was competent to bring the proceedings, then those proceedings are sufficient to stop the running of time. Hobhouse J. declined to follow the contrary decision of Roskill J. in *Cia Colombiana de Seguros v Pacific Steam Navigation Co.*[32] Given the radical effect of failure to bring proceedings in time (i.e. that the claim is entirely extinguished), it would be inappropriate to impose an absolute requirement that proceedings be commenced in this country.[33]

26.014 His Lordship felt able to distinguish the decision of the Court of Appeal in *The Merak*[34] on the ground that there were in that case two time-limits, one being the substantive time-limit under the Hague-Visby Rules and the other being the procedural time-limit under the arbitration clause, and because of the form which the proceedings took it was not necessary for the Court of Appeal to decide what the position would have been in the absence

---

[27] *Fort Sterling Ltd v South Atlantic Cargo Shipping NV ("The Finnrose")* [1994] 1 Lloyd's Rep. 559, Rix J.
[28] *Fort Sterling Ltd v South Atlantic Cargo Shipping NV ("The Finnrose")* [1994].
[29] *The Havhelt* [1993] 1 Lloyd's Rep 523, Rix J.; see also *Government of Sierra Leone v Marmaro Shipping Co. Ltd ("The Amazona")* [1989] 2 Lloyd's Rep. 130, CA; *Thyssen Inc. v Calypso Shipping Corp. SA* [2000] 2 Lloyd's Rep. 243, David Steel J.
[30] [1988] Q.B. 183, Hobhouse J.
[31] [1977] 1 W.L.R. 185, HL.
[32] [1964] 1 Q.B. 101.
[33] See also *The Kapetan Markos N.L.* [1986] 1 Lloyd's Rep. 211, CA.
[34] [1965] P.223.

of the procedural time-bar. Hobhouse J. accepted, as must obviously be the case, that the result would be different if the charterparty contained a clause giving the English courts exclusive jurisdiction. In that event the foreign court could not possibly be an appropriate forum for proceedings, and time would continue to run until proceedings were commenced in this country.

Proceedings by the wrong claimant

In *Transworld Oil (USA) Inc. v Minos Compania Naviera SA ("The Leni")*[35] the action was started within the one-year period but by the wrong company because of confusion over which company in a group had bought the oil in question. By the time the mistake was discovered the one-year period had expired. Judge Diamond Q.C. analysed the underlying principles of the Hague-Visby Rules, and said that in the absence of authority he would have held that the starting of the action was sufficient to protect the plaintiff, notwithstanding that it was started by the wrong plaintiff. However, on analysing the authorities discussed in the previous paragraph,[36] the judge concluded that in the present state of the law the opposite conclusion must be reached. For the moment, therefore, the position is that an action started by the wrong claimant does not stop the running of time under the Hague-Visby Rules.   **26.015**

Rule 6bis

Rule 6bis deals with actions for indemnity against a third party under the Hague-Visby Rules. It provides that such claims may be brought even outside the one-year period allowed for in those Rules, so long as they are brought within the period allowed by the domestic law of the country concerned. However, that period is not to be less than three months starting with the date when the person bringing the claim for indemnity has settled the claim or has been served with process in the action against himself. The only reported case in which this provision has been considered is *China Ocean Shipping Co. v Andros*.[37] The first problem in this case was that the action which the plaintiffs here had settled was not brought under the Hague-Visby Rules, and it was argued that r.6bis applied only where the main action also fell under those Rules. The Privy Council rejected this contention, holding that r.6bis was a rule that stood on its own and was not to be understood as subject to r.6. The second point concerned the reference in r.6bis to a three-month period. The Privy Council held that this is the   **26.016**

---

[35] [1992] 2 Lloyd's Rep. 48, Judge Diamond Q.C. sitting as a High Court Judge.
[36] Especially The Nordglimt, above, fn.30.
[37] [1987] 1 W.L.R. 1213, PC.

minimum period which the Rules allow the domestic legislation to grant, but that there is no implication that the period should not be longer. Consequently, under English law the relevant period is six years from the date on which the cause of action accrued. On the facts of the case it was unnecessary to consider when that period expired.[38]

CARRIAGE OF GOODS BY ROAD ACT 1965

26.017   The Carriage of Goods by Road Act 1965 incorporates into English law the text of the Convention on the Contract for the International Carriage of Goods by Road.[39] It applies to every contract for the carriage of goods by road in vehicles for reward, when the place of taking over of the goods and the place designated for delivery, as specified in the contract, are situated in two different countries, of which at least one is a party to the Convention.

When time starts to run (Article 32)

26.018   When time starts to run depends upon the nature of the claim. In the case of a claim for partial loss, damage or delay in delivery, time runs from the date of delivery. In the case of a claim for total loss, time runs from the 30th day after the expiry of the agreed time-limit for delivery. If there is no agreed time-limit, time runs from the 60th day from the date on which the goods are taken over by the carrier. In all other cases time starts to run three months after the making of the contract of carriage.

The length of the period

26.019   The limitation period under this Convention is one year. Article 41 of the Convention forbids the parties to derogate from it. It is not clear whether an agreement which contained a shorter limitation period would be a prohibited derogation, but in *International Distillers and Vintners Ltd v J.F. Hillebrand (U.K.) Ltd*[40] it was assumed (but not decided) that such a period was in principle capable of being valid.

---

[38] The difficulties surrounding the date of accrual of a right to indemnity are explored at paras 10.025–10.030.
[39] See the Schedule to the Carriage of Goods by Road Act 1965.
[40] *The Times*, January 25, 2000, David Foskett Q.C.

Extension of the period

The period is extended to three years in the case of wilful misconduct or such default as in accordance with the domestic law is considered as equivalent to wilful default. A case where a driver deliberately disobeys instructions as to the route to be followed is capable of amounting to wilful misconduct.[41] This expression is not further defined in the Convention, but the obvious analogy which may be drawn is with the possibility of extensions of time in the case of an action based on fraud or where the defendant has deliberately concealed some fact relevant to the cause of action from the claimant.[42] A distinction between these two grounds of extension in the domestic law is that the former relates to the events creating the cause of action, whereas the latter normally relates to subsequent events. It is wholly unclear whether the Convention is intended to refer to both these possibilities or only to one of them. It is submitted that both situations should be construed as being equivalent to wilful default for these purposes. The effect of such wilful default under the Convention is not the same as the effect of the application of s.32 of the 1980 Act under the domestic law. The running of time is not postponed until the default is discovered; rather, there is a single, finite extension of the limitation period.

26.020

Effect of expiry

There is no provision in the Convention that deals expressly with the question whether the expiry of the limitation period extinguishes the claimant's right or merely bars his remedy, though art.32(4) provides that a claim which is time-barred may not be relied upon by way of counterclaim or set-off. As a matter of English law the result of this should be that the expiry of time merely bars the remedy. It may be observed that this Convention, unlike the Hague-Visby Rules, does not speak of discharging the carrier from all liability.

26.021

The requirement to give notice

The consignee is required to give notice to the carrier of any claim. Such notice must be given immediately in the case of apparent loss, within seven days of receipt for loss which is not immediately apparent. Failure to comply with this requirement will not necessarily preclude the bringing of a claim, but will operate as prima facie evidence that the goods were received

26.022

---

[41] The meaning of this phrase was considered in *Laceys Footwear (Wholesale) Ltd v Bowler International Freight Ltd* [1997] 2 Lloyd's Rep. 367, CA.
[42] 1980 Act, s.32; see Ch.20.

in the condition described in the consignment note. In the case of an action for delay in delivery the consignee must give notice to the carrier within 21 days from the time when the goods are placed at his disposal. Failure to comply with this requirement does preclude the bringing of a claim for compensation for the delay.

Stopping the running of time

26.023 Article 32 of the Convention provides that the running of time is suspended where the claimant makes a written claim to the carrier,[43] even though no proceedings are started. This suspension will continue until the carrier rejects the claim. Further written claims cannot then operate to suspend the period again. A case decided under this article, but which may be of general importance in cases under the various carriage statutes discussed in this chapter (most of which have a similar provision) is *ICI Fibres Ltd and ICI France SA v MAT Transport Ltd*.[44] In that case it was held that the running of time could be suspended (or, more accurately, prevented) even before it had begun (because the 30- or 60-day time-limit had not expired) by written notice evincing an unequivocal intention to hold the carrier liable.

CARRIAGE BY AIR ACT 1961[45]

26.024 The Carriage by Air Act 1961 incorporates into English law the provisions of the Warsaw Convention on the Carriage of Goods by Air.[46] This applies to all international carriage of persons, baggage or cargo performed for reward and to gratuitous carriage by aircraft performed by an air transport undertaking. For the purposes of the Act a hot-air balloon is an 'aircraft'.[47]

When time starts to run

26.025 Time runs from the date on which the aircraft arrived at its destination or, in the case of non-arrival, from the date when it should have arrived, or from the date on which the carriage stopped.

---

[43] As discussed in the previous paragraph.

[44] [1987] 1 F.T.L.R. 145, Staughton J.

[45] This Act was amended by the Carriage by Air and Road Act 1979; Sch.1 to that Act inserts a new Sch.1 to the 1961 Act, reflecting amendments to the Warsaw Convention made by the Hague Protocol.

[46] See Sch.1 to the Carriage by Air Act 1961.

[47] *Laroche v Spirit of Adventure (UK) Ltd* [2008] EWHC 788 (QB) Eady J.

The length of the period

The limitation period under this Convention is two years.   26.026

Extension of the period

The Convention contains no provisions relating expressly to the possible   26.027
extension of the two-year period, but art.29 provides that the method of
calculating the running of time is left to the domestic law. It may be argued
that this serves to incorporate the domestic law rules on extension of time.
If that argument is accepted, the result must be that all the rules of the
domestic law on extension are incorporated, not just those relating to
fraud. It is submitted, however, that rules as to extension of time are not
properly described as rules on calculating the running of time. The only
rules which merit that description are those which determine, for example,
whether parts of a day are included in the calculation.[48]

Effect of expiry

Article 29 of the Convention provides that upon the expiry of the period the   26.028
claimant's right to damages is extinguished. It therefore appears that this
Convention operates in the same way as the Hague-Visby Rules, that is to
say that it extinguishes the claimant's right as well as barring his remedy.

The requirement to give notice

The claimant must give notice to the carrier forthwith and in any event   26.029
within seven days from receipt by the claimant in the case of damage to
baggage, within 14 days of receipt in the case of cargo. Where the complaint relates to delay in transit the notice must be given within 21 days
from the time when the baggage or cargo are placed at the claimant's
disposal. If these requirements as to notice are not complied with, then no
action lies against the carrier except in the event of fraud on his part. The
Convention is silent on the meaning of fraud in this context, but it is
submitted that the term should be interpreted as referring to such fraud as
would prevent the claimant from giving timely notice, as for example by
concealing facts relevant to the cause of action.

---

[48] For these rules in a domestic context, see paras 2.001–2.002.

Stopping the running of time

26.030   The making of a complaint does not stop the running of time, and it appears that time will continue to run until proceedings are brought. It is a question of fact whether a particular notice is sufficient.[49] Article 28 allows the bringing of proceedings in any contracting state where the carrier has a business presence, and it is submitted, by analogy with *The Nordglimt*,[50] that the bringing of proceedings in any appropriate jurisdiction will stop the running of time in England.

Scope of the Convention

26.031   In *Phillips v Air New Zealand* [51] Morison J. held that the Warsaw Convention became applicable when the passenger presented a valid ticket for travel, the ticket was accepted and a boarding pass issued: in other words, the carriage began when the passenger had successfully completed the check-in procedure. In *Adatia v Air Canada*[52] it was held that a passenger who has disembarked from an aircraft and is on the travelator heading for passport control is not "in the course of any of the operations of embarking or disembarking".[53] Consequently, a claim for injury suffered in these circumstances is not governed by the Convention, and the ordinary three-year limitation period for personal injury cases applies to it.

INTERNATIONAL TRANSPORT CONVENTIONS ACT 1983

26.032   The International Transport Conventions Act 1983 incorporates into English law the International Convention concerning the Carriage of Passengers and Luggage by Rail.[54] This governs the liability of the railway for damage caused to passengers[55] by an accident occurring on the territory of a state which is a party to the Convention. This formulation covers accidents with no international elements at all, and art.1 therefore allows contracting states to reserve the right not to apply the Convention to pas-

---

[49] *Western Digital Corp and Western Digital (Singapore) Ltd and Western Digital Netherlands BV v British Airways Plc*, May 12, 2000, Unreported, CA.
[50] [1988] 1 All E.R. 400, Hobhouse J.
[51] [2002] EWHC 800 (Comm), [2002] 1 All ER (Comm) 801.
[52] [1992] P.I.Q.R. 238, CA.
[53] Warsaw Convention, art. 17, as amended.
[54] See the Schedule to the Act.
[55] Passengers here includes attendants accompanying consignments of goods: ibid., art. 1.

sengers who are subjects of that state or have their usual residence there and who sustain an accident on the territory of that state.

When time starts to run

Time runs from the day after the accident or, where the claim is brought by the dependants of a passenger who has died, from the day after the passenger's death.

26.033

The length of the period

Where the action is brought by the passenger, the limitation period is three years. Where the action is brought by the dependants of a deceased passenger the limitation period is again three years, but there is a longstop which takes effect five years from the day after the accident.[56] One unfortunate consequence of this is that the dependants' action can become barred before it has even arisen. This will occur where the passenger brings no action on his own behalf and dies more than five years after the accident.

26.034

Extension of the period

Extension of the limitation period is declared by art.17(4) to be a matter for the domestic law. It is submitted that provisions which delay the commencement of the limitation period are not for this purpose provisions extending the limitation period. In English law, this refers to s.33 of the 1980 Act, which allows the court to extend the normal limitation period in accordance with certain specified criteria. It may therefore appear that in actions for damages for personal injury under this Convention, s.33 can be applied. The difficulty is that s.33 expressly states that it is available only where the disadvantage to the claimant arises from non-compliance with s.11 or s.12 of the 1980 Act, and, with relation to disapplication of the time-limit in s.12(1) (which relates to actions by dependants of a deceased), gives the example of a claimant prejudiced by the time-limit in the Carriage by Air Act 1961 as a case where the court may not use s.33. It is noticeable, though, that this prohibition applies to s.12, but is not expressly applied to s.11, and it is therefore submitted that the s.11 limit can be disapplied under this Convention in accordance with the criteria in s.33.

26.035

---

[56] Art. 17 of the Convention.

Effect of expiry

26.036 The Convention is silent on this point, and it is therefore submitted that the usual English law rule applies, namely that the expiry of the period bars the claimant's remedy but does not extinguish his right.

The requirement to give notice

26.037 The claimant is required to give notice of the injury to the defendant within three months of becoming aware of it, though the Convention is silent on the effect of non-compliance with this requirement.

Stopping the running of time

26.038 A written claim to the carrier will suspend the running of time until the carrier gives written notice of rejection of the claim and returns to the claimant any documents that were submitted with the claim.

CARRIAGE OF PASSENGERS BY ROAD ACT 1974

26.039 In this case the convention which is incorporated into English law is the Convention on the Contract for the International Carriage of Passengers and Luggage by Road.[57] This applies to every contract for the carriage of passengers in vehicles by road when the contract provides that the carriage shall take place in the territory of more than one state and that the place of departure or the place of destination, or both, shall be situated on the territory of a contracting state.

When time starts to run

26.040 In the case of claims for personal injury time runs from the later of the date of the injury and the date when the claimant becomes aware of that injury.[58] In the case of claims for damage to property time runs from the date on which the vehicle arrived at the passenger's destination, or from the date on which it should have arrived if it never in fact did so.

---

[57] See the Schedule to the Carriage of Goods by Road Act 1965.
[58] Art. 22 of the Convention.

The length of the period

In the case of actions for personal injury the limitation period is three years. **26.041**
However, this is subject to a longstop time-limit of five years from the date
of the accident. For cases not involving bodily injury the period is one year.

Extension of the period

Article 22(4) makes this a matter for the domestic law. The difficulties **26.042**
arising from such a provision were considered at para.26.019.

Effect of expiry

The Convention is silent on this point. It is therefore submitted that the **26.043**
expiry of time bars the claimant's remedy, but does not extinguish his right.

The requirement to give notice

Where the claim relates to damage to property the claimant must give **26.044**
notice of a claim to the carrier within seven days of delivery of the property
to him or, where the basis of the complaint is that the property has not been
delivered at all, within seven days of discovering the non-delivery.

Stopping the running of time

A written claim will suspend the running of time until the claim is rejected. **26.045**
Exceptionally among the conventions considered in this chapter, this one
provides that a further written claim will suspend time again if the carrier
agrees to consider it.

THE MERCHANT SHIPPING ACT 1979

The Merchant Shipping Act 1979 incorporates into English law the pro- **26.046**
visions of the Convention Relating to the Carriage of Passengers and their
Luggage by Sea, commonly known as the Athens Convention.[59] The
Convention applies to any international carriage if the ship is flying the flag
of or is registered in a state party to the Convention or if the contract of

---

[59] See Schedule 3 to the Merchant Shipping Act 1979.

carriage has been made in such a state or if the place of departure or destination, according to the contract of carriage, is such a state. The Convention makes the carrier liable for death or personal injury to a passenger and for loss of or damage to a passenger's baggage in the course of the carriage and due to the fault or neglect of the carrier, his servants or agents in the course of their employment.

When time starts to run[60]

26.047 The date on which time starts to run depends upon the nature of the claim. In the case of personal injury time runs from the date when the passenger disembarks. In the case of death occurring during carriage time runs from the date when the passenger should have disembarked. In the case of death occurring after the carriage has ended but caused by an injury suffered during carriage, time runs from the date of death, but this is subject to art.16(3),[61] which imposes an absolute prohibition on the bringing of an action more than three years after the date on which the passenger disembarked or, if later, the date on which the passenger should have disembarked. In the case of loss of or damage to luggage, time runs from the date of disembarkation or, if this is later, from the date when disembarkation should have taken place.

The length of the period

26.048 The limitation period under this Convention is two years.[62]

Suspension and interruption of the period

26.049 Article 16(3) provides that the question of suspension and interruption of the period is a matter for the lex fori. In *Higham v Stena Sealink Ltd*[63] it was held that this provision did not allow s.33 of the 1980 Act to be used to extend the limitation period. The purpose of s.33 is to disapply the effects of expiry of a limitation period which has entirely run its course, and this is not at all the same thing as suspending or interrupting the period. In any event s.33 is by its terms limited to cases where the claimant is prejudiced by the operation of earlier sections of the 1980 Act: it has no application where the prejudice is caused by the operation of some other statutory

---

[60] Art. 16 of the Convention.
[61] See below, "The effect of expiry".
[62] Art. 16.
[63] [1996] 3 All E.R. 660, CA.

provision. In addition, art.16(3) goes on to impose a longstop time-limit by providing that in no case shall any action be brought under the Convention more than three years after the date on which the passenger disembarked or should have disembarked, whichever is later.

The requirement to give notice

Article 15 of the Convention requires the passenger to give written notice of **26.050** a luggage claim to the carrier or his agent. In the case of apparent damage this notice must be given at or before the time of disembarkation for cabin luggage and at or before the time of redelivery for other luggage. In the case of non-apparent damage the notice must be given within 15 days of the date of disembarkation or redelivery, or of the date when redelivery should have taken place. The giving of such notice is not a condition precedent to the making of a claim, but failure to give such notice creates a presumption that the passenger received the luggage undamaged.

The effect of expiry

The Convention gives no express guidance on this question: Art.16 merely **26.051** states that the action shall be time-barred after the expiry of the relevant period. In English law this should properly be interpreted as meaning that the action is barred but the right is not extinguished, since the words are not sufficiently clear to extinguish the claimant's right entirely.

Stopping the running of time

Article 16(4) allows the running of time to be suspended by a declaration of **26.052** the carrier to that effect or by an agreement to that effect between the carrier and the passenger. It is to be observed that the making of the written claim specified in art.15 does not have the effect of suspending the running of time under this Convention.

In *Norfolk v My Travel Group Plc*[64] the Court had to consider the **26.053** application of the International Convention on the Carriage of Passengers and their Luggage 1974 (the Athens Convention). The claimant was injured on board ship while taking a cruise. She claimed against the tour operator under the Package Holidays and Package Tours Regulations, 1992 claiming damages for consequential losses, including losses for pain, suffering and loss of amenity, and also including loss of enjoyment of the rest of her

---

[64] [2004] 1 Lloyd's Rep 106 Judge Overend.

holiday on the basis that the tour operator was in breach of its duty to ensure proper performance of the obligations of all those providing services to her as part of the holiday. If this was a simple personal injuries claim, then the limitation period was three years, but under the Athens Convention it was two years. It was held that this was in substance a claim within the Convention, and that conclusion could not be circumvented by disguising the case as a claim for improper performance of the contract.

THE LAW COMMISSION'S PROPOSALS

26.054 This is another area untouched by the Law Commission's review. The explanation for this is twofold. First, the various provisions considered in this chapter would fall outside the core regime on the ground that they are contained in statutes which expressly impose their own limitation periods. Secondly, those limitation periods are established by international conventions to which the United Kingdom is a party, so it would not be possible to change them.

CHAPTER 27

Other Statutes

GENERAL

In addition to the Limitation Act 1980, the Latent Damage Act 1986 and **27.001**
the Consumer Protection Act 1987, there are a number of other statutes
that impose time-limits on the bringing of an action. The more important of
these are dealt with in this chapter. It should be observed that s.39 of the
Limitation Act 1980 declares the general provisions of that Act to be
subject to any specific provision in any other Act.[1] Consequently, all the
various provisions dealt with in this chapter take precedence over the 1980
Act in their own particular spheres of applicability. By contrast, certain of
the provisions of Pt II of the 1980 Act which allow for the extension of the
limitation period apply only to periods created by that Act. The two sections of the 1980 Act which are in point here are s.28 (disability)[2] and s.32
(fraud, concealment and mistake).[3]

WORKMEN'S COMPENSATION ACTS

The old system of compensation contained in the Workmen's Compensa- **27.002**
tion Acts 1897 to 1925 was repealed by the National Insurance (Industrial
Injuries) Act 1946, but successive consolidations have left the old system
continuing to apply to injuries suffered before July 5, 1948,[4] and it is for
that reason that these statutes are briefly considered in the present work.
Section 14 of the Workmen's Compensation Act 1925 required that the

---

[1] This applies also to actions involving the Crown for which some other limitation period
would be applicable if the action were between subjects: 1980 Act and see para.9.020.
[2] See Ch.19.
[3] See Ch.20.
[4] The present legislation in point is the Industrial Injuries and Diseases (Old Cases) Act 1975;
the effect of this statute must now be largely spent.

workman give notice of a claim promptly, and imposed a limitation period in respect of the making of a claim. It was a matter of controversy whether these requirements excluded the application of the periods under the Limitation Acts when dealing with cases of this kind. In *Leivers v Barber, Walker & Co. Ltd*[5] the Court of Appeal held, by a majority, that the Limitation Acts were excluded in such cases.

THIRD PARTIES (RIGHTS AGAINST INSURERS) ACT 1930

27.003 In *Lefevre v White*[6] the plaintiff brought a personal injuries action which was successful. The defendant became bankrupt, so the plaintiff sought to use the 1930 Act, but the writ against the insurers was issued more than six years after the personal injuries were suffered. The plaintiff argued that the writ against the defendant saved the running of time for the purposes of this action, and in the alternative that the cause of action against the insurers did not arise until the defendant became bankrupt. Both contentions were rejected. The action against the insurers accrues at the same time as the action against the defendant. The insurers accordingly succeeded in the limitation defence.

LIMITATION (ENEMIES AND WAR PRISONERS) ACT 1945

27.004 This statute was passed to deal with limitation problems arising out of the Second World War where one or other party to the action had become an enemy[7] so as to be an incompetent party in an action in the English court, or was resident in enemy territory, so as to be unable as a matter of practice to participate in any such action. In such cases, s.1 of the Act provides that the limitation period in respect of any civil action cannot expire until at least one year after the date when both parties are first free of these impediments (if the limitations period would have expired at a later date in the absence of the Act, then this later date was the one which applied). There is only one reported decision on the application of the Act, *The Atlantic Scout*,[8] where it was held that a French company could still be an enemy within the meaning of the Act although it would by that time no longer have been an enemy alien at common law. The Act is still in force,

---

[5] [1943] 1 All E.R. 386, CA.
[6] [1990] 1 Lloyd's Rep. 569, Popplewell J.
[7] Within the meaning of the Trading with the Enemy Act 1939; see Limitation (Enemies and War Prisoners) Act 1945 s.2(1).
[8] (1950) 84 Lloyd's Rep. 22, Willmer J.

but its practical importance is obviously very limited, since the United Kingdom is not presently at war. The very small number of reported cases on the provision also tend to suggest that the practical significance of the Act was never great.[9]

UNIFORM LAWS ON INTERNATIONAL SALES ACT 1967

Under the Uniform Laws on International Sales Act 1967 the parties to a contract may agree that the Uniform Law on the International Sale of Goods shall apply to their contract. The Uniform Law is the annex to a Convention relating to a Uniform Law on the International Sale of Goods, held at The Hague in 1964 and forms the Schedule to the 1967 Act. Under art.39 of the Uniform Law the buyer loses the right to rely on the fact that the goods do not conform to the contract description if he has not given the seller notice thereof promptly after he has or ought to have discovered the lack of conformity. In any event the right is lost two years from the date on which the goods are handed over, except where the lack of conformity amounts to a failure to conform with a guarantee covering a longer period. Article 39 is also subject to art.40, which precludes the seller from relying on lapse of time where the defect is one of which he was aware and which he failed to disclose. It is to be observed that arts 39 and 40 speak of the giving of written notice to the buyer. This is not the same thing as commencing an action, and art.49 of the Convention goes on to provide that the right to rely on lack of conformity is lost one year after the giving of written notice, unless the buyer has been prevented from exercising that right by the fraud of the seller. After the expiration of this one year the lack of conformity may not be relied upon, except as a defence to a claim for payment of the price. It is to be observed that these limitation provisions relate only to reliance upon lack of conformity of the goods with the contract description: they have no application to any other breach of contract, so that in all other cases the domestic limitation rules will apply.

27.005

EQUAL PAY ACT 1970

The provision of the Equal Pay Act 1970 that is relevant for present purposes governs the bringing of complaints concerning infringements of a term of the contract of employment which has been inserted or modified by the Act (which imposes the concept of equal pay for work of equal value).

27.006

---

[9] The Act was also considered in passing in *Chaplin v Chaplin* [1949] P. 72, CA; *A/S D/S Heimdal v Questier & Co. Ltd* (1949) 84 Lloyd's Rep. 452 and *Duncan v London Borough of Lambeth* [1968] 2 W.L.R. 88.

Such a complaint must be brought before the industrial tribunal within six months of the complainant leaving the employment in question,[10] which means the ending of the contract of employment, rather than leaving a particular position in the business to move to a new position.[11] A woman claiming breach of the equal access to pension requirements under the Equal Pay Act 1970, who was forced to retire on grounds of ill-health, must bring her complaint within six months of the termination of her employment. The fact that but for her ill-health she would have continued in employment, and that after cessation of employment she was in a receipt of a pension, does not change that requirement.[12] Section 2(5) of the Act further provides that arrears of pay are not to be awarded for periods more than two years before the presentation of the claim. In *Levez v T. H. Jennings (Harlow Pools) Ltd*[13] the Employment Appeal Tribunal referred to the European Court of Justice the question whether this restriction is compatible with European law. The decision of the ECJ was delivered on December 1, 1998 and was to the effect that Community law precludes the application of a rule of national law which limits an employee's entitlement to arrears of remuneration or damages for breach of the principle of equal pay to a period of two years prior to the date on which the proceedings were instituted, there being no possibility of extending that period, where the delay in bringing a claim is attributable to the fact that the employer deliberately misrepresented to the employee the level of remuneration received by persons of the opposite sex performing like work. Moreover, Community law precludes the application of a rule of national law which limits an employee's entitlement to arrears of remuneration or damages for breach of the principle of equal pay to a period of two years prior to the date on which the proceedings were instituted, even when another remedy is available, if the latter is likely to entail procedural rules or other conditions which are less favourable than those applicable to similar domestic actions. It is for the national court to determine whether that is the case. The matter was then referred back to the EAT to apply these principles. In *Levez v T.H. Jennings (Harlow Pools) Ltd (No. 2)*; *Hicking v Basford Group Ltd*[14] the EAT ruled that the two-year limitation on arrears of remuneration in s.2(5) of the Equal Pay Act 1970 is a breach of the European Community law principle of equivalence, in that it is less favourable than those governing similar claims such as for unlawful deduction from wages and unlawful discrimination on grounds of race or disability. The two-year back-pay limit is thus unenforceable as being incompatible with the United Kingdom's obligations under Community law. The six-year

---

[10] Equal Pay Act 1970 s.1.

[11] *National Power Plc v Nanette Young*, November 8, 2000, Unreported, CA.

[12] *Clarke v London Borough of Harrow and Conjoined Cases* UKEAT/0745/02/ILB, UKEAT/0746/02/ILB (Transcript).

[13] [1996] I.R.L.R. 499, EAT. The ECJ judgment is at [1998] E.C.R. I-7835.

[14] [1999] I.R.L.R. 764; [1999] 3 C.M.L.R. 715; [2000] I.C.R. 58.

time-limit in the Limitation Act from the date of commencement of proceedings applies to claims under the Equal Pay Act.

Claims under the Equal Pay Act on the one hand, and under the Race **27.007** Relations or Disability Discrimination Acts on the other, are effectively identical. In each case, the complainant is relying on a statute which gives the tribunal primary jurisdiction. In each case, the statute imposes upon the parties a requirement that the contract of employment should not discriminate on grounds of sex or race or disability. In each case, apart from discrimination on grounds of gender, any loss attributable to failure by the employer to pay in accordance with the agreed or imposed terms and conditions can lead to an award for a period of six years.

A claim for unlawful deduction from wages is also juridically the same as a claim for breach of the equality clause, in that the claimant in each case is asserting that he or she has been paid less than their contractual entitlement.

Section 2(5), therefore, represents a unique limitation on compensation which applies only when the applicant is relying upon an equality clause. There are no compensating advantages. Accordingly, s.2(5) is a restriction on the right to have a full and effective remedy for breach of art.141 (ex art.119) EC and the Equal Pay Directive (Directive 75/117). It is a breach of the principle of equivalence, and unenforceable.

Subsequently, in *Preston v Wolverhampton Healthcare NHS Trust*; **27.008** *Fletcher v Midland Bank Plc*,[15] some 60,000 part-time workers submitted applications to employment tribunals complaining that they were unlawfully excluded from occupational pension schemes because membership of the scheme was dependent upon an employee working a minimum number of hours each week. The claims followed the decision of the European Court of Justice in the *Vroege* ([1994] I.R.L.R. 651, ECJ) and *Fisscher* ([1994] I.R.LR. 662, ECJ) cases, which declared that the right to join an occupational pension scheme falls within the scope of art.141 of the EC Treaty (ex art.119) and that the limitation in time of the *Barber* ([1990] I.R.L.R. 240, ECJ) decision does not apply to the right to join an occupational pension scheme. The applicants claimed that the denial of access to part-time workers was indirectly discriminatory against women. After proceedings in the lower courts the House of Lords[16] referred the case to the European Court of Justice for a preliminary ruling. The European Court of Justice held as follows:

1. Community law precludes a national procedural rule, such as that in section 2(5) of the Equal Pay Act as amended, which provides that a claimant's entitlement to join an occupational pension scheme is limited to a period which starts to run two years prior to the commencement of proceedings in connection with the claim.

---

[15] Case 78/98 [2000] I.R.L.R. 506.
[16] [1998] I.R.L.R. 197.

2. Unlike the rules which, in the interests of legal certainty, merely limit the retroactive scope of a claim for certain benefits and do not therefore strike at the very essence of the rights conferred by the Community legal order, a procedural rule such as in section 2(5) and regulation 12 of the Occupational Pension Regulations, as held by the Court in the *Magorrian* ([1998] I.R.L.R. 86) case, renders any action by individuals relying on Community law impossible in practice. Even though it does not totally deprive the claimants of access to membership, the procedural rule prevented the entire record of service completed by those concerned from being taken into account for the purposes of calculating pension benefits. However, the fact that a worker can claim retroactively to join an occupational pension scheme does not allow him to avoid paying the contributions relating to the period of membership concerned.

3. Community law does not preclude a national procedural rule, such as that contained in section 2(4) of the Equal Pay Act, which requires that a claim for membership of an occupational pension scheme must be brought within six months of the end of the employment to which the claim relates, provided that that limitation period is not less favourable for actions based on Community law than for those based on domestic law.

4. The setting of reasonable limitation periods for bringing proceedings, in principle, satisfies the Community law principle of effectiveness, inasmuch as it constitutes an application of the fundamental principle of legal certainty, even if expiry of the limitation period results in the dismissal of the claimant's action.

5. Where there has been a stable employment relationship resulting from a succession of short-term contracts concluded at regular intervals in respect of the same employment to which the same pension scheme applies, Community law precludes a procedural rule, such as that contained in section 2(4) of the Equal Pay Act, which has the effect of requiring a claim for membership of an occupational pension scheme to be brought within six months of the end of each contract of employment to which the claim relates.

6. Setting the starting point of the limitation period at the end of each contract renders the exercise of the right conferred by Article 141 (ex Article 119) excessively difficult. There is no reason why that starting point should not be fixed as the date on which the sequence of such contracts has been interrupted through the absence of one or more of the features that characterise a stable employment relationship of that kind, either because the periodicity of the contracts has been broken or because the new contract does not relate to the same employment as that to which the same pension scheme applies.

7. An action alleging infringement of a statute such as the Equal Pay Act does not constitute a domestic action similar to an action alleging infringement of Article 141 (ex Article 119) of the Treaty. Therefore, the fact that the same procedural rules apply to both claims is not enough to ensure compliance with the principle of equivalence, since one and the same form of action is involved.

8. In order to determine whether the principle of equivalence has been complied with, the national court must consider whether the right of action available under domestic law is a domestic action similar to proceedings to give effect to rights conferred by Article 141 (ex Article 119) of the Treaty as regards their purpose, cause of action and essential characteristics.

The importance of the *Levez* and *Preston* cases taken together is **27.009** immense, both in employment law and in the law of limitation of actions. Only the latter aspect will be considered here. The cases show that every aspect of the law of limitation is subject to scrutiny by the European Court of Justice, and that the strongly teleological approach adopted by that court allows it, when it so chooses, to strike down procedural rules of domestic law which might traditionally have been regarded as arbitrary rules, no better or worse than any alternative limitation period that might have been imposed. On the evidence of these cases it is probably fair to say that the ECJ is more likely to strike down very short periods than very long ones, but all possibilities must be regarded as still being open. It is, of course, also true that some European element will be needed in a case before it can fall within the ECJ's jurisdiction, but the steady spread of EU legislation continues to widen the areas of activity that are subject to at least some European influence.

TAXES MANAGEMENT ACT 1970

The Taxes Management Act 1970 governs the administration of the tax **27.010** system. It imposes time-limits which apply generally both to actions by the Inland Revenue for unpaid tax and claims by the taxpayer for relief from or repayment of tax. The general rule is that the action must be brought within six years from the end of the chargeable period to which the claim relates.[17]

---

[17] Taxes Management Act 1970 ss.34 and 43. Taxpayers should also be aware of Extra Statutory Concession A19, which provides that where the taxpayer has given full information to the Revenue and no assessment has been raised, so that the taxpayer could reasonably believe that his tax affairs were in order, some or all of the tax will be remitted if a claim is subsequently made by the Revenue after the expiry of the year of assessment following that to which the claim relates. Extra Statutory Concessions are, however, not legally enforceable.

In the case of actions by the Inland Revenue this is modified where there has been any fraud by the taxpayer within that six-year period. Then, the claims may be pursued also for a period of six years preceding the year in which the fraud took place; discoveries of further fraud within that extended period will extend time for a further six years backwards. In the case of claims against the personal representatives of a deceased in respect of gains accruing before death, the time-limit is three years from the end of the year of assessment following that in which the death occurred.

27.011 By contrast, claims to recover National Insurance Contributions are subject to the normal six-year limitation period of the 1980 Act. However, where questions of principle are to be determined by the Special Commissioners of Taxation in a lead case, there is no reason why the case chosen should not be one where the right of recovery is time-barred, since the Special Commissioners will decide only the issue of principle and will not award any remedy.[18]

Land Compensation Act 1973

27.012 Part I of this Act allows claims for noise nuisance by those living near to a highway. The limitation period is a curious one. It is six years from the first claim day, which is the first anniversary of the relevant date. The relevant date is the day upon which a highway is first opened to public traffic.[19] In effect, therefore, the period is seven years from the day when the highway is first opened to public traffic. In *Price v Caerphilly County BC*[20] it was held that the question to be asked when determining the relevant date is when that part of the highway from which the noise arises was first opened to public traffic, rather than looking more broadly at the scheme of what that part of the highway formed part.

DEFECTIVE PREMISES ACT 1972

27.013 The Defective Premises Act 1972 applies in those cases where a dwelling-house has been built with certain specified types of defect. Its purpose is to impose liability on the builder of the premises to owners and occupiers, since, at the time when the Act was passed, liability was not thought to exist at common law. The position in this regard was, of course, altered by the decision of the House of Lords in *Anns v Merton London BC*,[21] and the importance of the Act was correspondingly reduced.

---

[18] *EDI Services Ltd v Revenue and Customs Commissioners*, SpC 515; [2006] STC (SCD) 60.
[19] Land Compensation Act 1973 s.19(2A)
[20] [2005] 1 EGLR 157 Lands Tribunal.
[21] [1977] 2 All E.R. 492; [1978] A.C. 728.

The Act creates[22] a limitation period of six years for actions brought under its provisions. However, time starts to run as soon as the building is completed.[23] By contrast, it is likely that in the overwhelming majority of cases, time, in respect of a common law action for the defective construction of a building, will not start to run until the somewhat later date when defects in the building come into existence.[24] The Latent Damage Act 1986 may also operate to extend the limitation period.[25] The Defective Premises Act may nevertheless be of importance in those cases where the common law action is not available. Since the first edition of this book the retreat from the high-water mark of liability reached in *Anns*, which began in cases such as *Tate & Lyle (Industries Ltd) v Greater London Council*[26] and *D. & F. Estates Ltd v Church Commissioners for England*,[27] has culminated in the decision of the House of Lords in *Murphy v Brentwood DC*,[28] which overrules *Anns*, at least as regards the position of local authorities. This is likely to lead to something of a revival in the importance of the Defective Premises Act.

SOLICITORS ACT 1974

The Solicitors Act 1974 governs, inter alia, the process of taxing a solicitor's bill of costs. Section 70 provides that the client's right to apply for taxation must be exercised not later than one year after the date on which the bill is paid. If this is not done the court has no jurisdiction in any circumstances, either under the Act or under its inherent jurisdiction,[29] to order such taxation. It may be noted that, despite this, an aggrieved client may still have a remedy, since he may make a charge of serious professional misconduct against the solicitor, and this may result in the Law Society referring the bill to a taxing master for consideration of possible reductions. As is usual in the case of limitation periods the only effect of the expiry of the period is to preclude any judicial remedy. The availability of remedies by other means is not affected.   **27.014**

---

[22] Section 1.
[23] Section 1(5).
[24] *Pirelli General Cable Works v Oscar Faber & Partners* [1983] 2 A.C. 1, HL; *Ketteman v Hansel Properties Ltd* [1987] 2 W.L.R. 312.
[25] See Ch.6.
[26] [1983] 2 A.C. 509, HL.
[27] [1988] 2 All E.R. 992, HL.
[28] [1991] 1 A.C. 398, HL.
[29] *Harrison v Tew* [1990] 2 A.C. 523, HL, disapproving *Symbol Park Lane Ltd v Steggles Palmer* [1985] 1 W.L.R. 668, CA.

MATRIMONIAL CAUSES ACT 1973

27.015 This Act, as amended by the Matrimonial and Family Proceedings Act 1984, governs the bringing of petitions for nullity of marriage and for divorce. There are two time-limits which require to be considered. First, a petition for nullity must be brought within three years of the date of the marriage. This rule is absolute, and is not subject to extension on grounds of fraud or non-discoverability. Secondly, a petition for divorce may not be brought before the expiry of one year from the date of marriage. This is one of the relatively few examples in English law of a limitation period which prescribes a minimum delay in bringing an action.[30]

INHERITANCE (PROVISION FOR FAMILY AND DEPENDANTS) ACT 1975

27.016 The Inheritance (Provision for Family and Dependants) Act 1975 confers upon the dependants of a deceased (as therein defined) certain rights to apply to court on the grounds that the disposition of the deceased's property produced by his will or by the operation of the intestacy provisions does not make sufficient provision for them. The time-limit for an action under it is six months from the date on which representation in respect of the deceased's estate is first taken out,[31] though the court has discretion to extend this limit if it sees fit to do so. In *Escritt v Escritt*[32] Mrs Escritt, a widow, had been promptly advised of her rights under the Act of 1975, had decided not to claim and then, four years later, had changed her mind. She was refused permission to claim out of time. In *Re Salmon (Deceased)*[33] it was held relevant to consider whether a refusal of permission would leave the claimant without redress against anybody.

27.017 In *Re The Estate of the Right Honourable Simon George Earl of Craven (Deceased) Wilson (A Minor, by Her Next Friend) v Ironside-Smith*[34] the court had to consider an application out of time on behalf of the illegitimate eight-year-old daughter of the deceased. The application was late because the child's mother had been reluctant to become involved in litigation. Applying the principle in *Re Salmon*, and mindful of the fact that the child herself could not be held responsible for the delay, Wilson J. gave leave to

---

[30] See also the Landlord and Tenant Act 1954, which is examined at paras 13.078–13.081, for another example.
[31] Inheritance (Provision for Family and Dependants) Act 1975 s.4.
[32] [1982] 3 F.L.R. 280.
[33] [1981] 1 Ch. 167 [1980] 3 All E.R. 532.
[34] [1995] 2 F.C.R. 689, Wilson J.; also reported [1995] 2 F.L.R. 24, sub nom. Re C (Deceased) (Leave to Apply for Provision).

apply even though the claim was brought three-and-a-half years after the death. In *Hannigan v Hannigan*[35] permission was given to proceed with such an action where the initial proceedings, issued shortly after the coming into force of the CPR, were defective in that:

(i) the claim had been issued in the wrong form;

(ii) the statement of case had not been verified by a statement of truth;

(iii) the Royal Court of Arms had been lacking from the form;

(iv) the first defendant had been incorrectly named as Andrew Cooke rather than Andrew Cooke Hannigan;

(v) the claimant's witness statement had been signed in the name of her solicitors' firm rather than by her personally;

(vi) the form failed to have the legend required by para.17.1 of CPR PD 32;

(vii) the form failed to have marginal notes and a 3.5cm margin as required;

(viii) the exhibit to the claimant's witness statement failed to have the correct legend, a front page setting out a list of documents, and failed to have the documents paginated; and

(ix) there had been a failure to serve an Acknowledgement of Service form.

The Court of Appeal heavily criticised the applicant's solicitors, but observed that the defendant had at all times been perfectly well aware of the case which he had to meet and had therefore not been prejudiced by these errors and omissions. It must be said that the deficiencies were of a somewhat technical character, and that it would have been harsh to preclude the claimant from continuing with her case on the basis of these matters.

ADMINISTRATION OF JUSTICE ACT 1982

Applications under s.20 of the Administration of Justice Act 1982 for rectification of a will have a six-month time-limit from the date on which representation in respect of the deceased's estate is first taken out. Where the application is made out of time, the principles are the same as those under the Inheritance (Provision for Family and Dependants) Act 1975.[36]   **27.018**

---

[35] May 18, 2000 Unreported, CA.
[36] *Re the Estate of Chittock*, *The Times*, April 5, 2000, David Donaldson Q.C.

SEX DISCRIMINATION ACT 1975 AND RACE RELATIONS ACT 1976

27.019 These two statutes are considered together because they categorise matters of complaint in the same way for limitation purposes and impose identical time-limits, the only difference being the obvious one that one statute deals with discrimination based on gender, whilst the other deals with discrimination based on race or ethnic origin. The categorisation adopted is:

(a) discrimination in respect of employment. The time-limit is three months from the act complained of;

(b) discrimination under Pt III of the Sex Discrimination Act, which covers discrimination in education and in the provision of goods, facilities, services and premises, six months from the act complained of. This is subject to one exception, as follows;

(c) discrimination in respect of education; here the time-limit is eight months from the act complained of;

(d) complaints in respect of discriminatory advertisements, instructions or pressure to discriminate. In these cases only the Equal Opportunities Commission or the Commission for Racial Equality has locus standi to bring the complaint. The procedure is first to bring an action to determine whether discrimination has taken place, then, if no satisfactory undertakings can be obtained, to bring further proceedings for an injunction to restrain further breaches. There is a time-limit of six months for the bringing of the first of these actions, and a time-limit of five years for the bringing of the second action. In both cases time runs from the date of the act complained of.

Discretion to extend

27.020 Both the Sex Discrimination Act and the Race Relations Act give the court or tribunal discretion to extend any of the above time-limits if satisfied that it would be just to do so in the circumstances of the particular case.[37] It has been said that this discretion is intended to be of general ambit, so that it would be wrong to give these words a technical construction.[38] In *Hawkins v Ball and Barclays Bank Plc*[39] it was held that the court's jurisdiction to grant an extension of time where it was "just and equitable" to do so was a

---

[37] Sex Discrimination Act 1975 s.76(5); Race Relations Act 1976 s.68(6).
[38] *Hutchinson v Westward Television* [1977] I.C.R. 279, EAT.
[39] [1996] I.R.L.R. 258.

broader discretion than under the "reasonably practicable" formula that applies in cases of unfair dismissal. Although there are obvious analogies between this provision and s.33 of the Limitation Act 1980,[40] courts in discrimination cases should not allow themselves to be bogged down in considering the many reported decisions on s.33, but should instead take a broad common-sense view of the situation.[41] The same point arose in *Taylor v Department of Environment Food & Rural Affairs*,[42] where it was said that Industrial Tribunals considering whether to extend time must consider the prejudicial effect on either party of either allowing or refusing the application to extend time.

One remarkable example of the application of the discretion in the context of sex discrimination occurred in *Foster v South Glamorgan HA*.[43] This was a case involving alleged discrimination in regard to pension rights. The action was brought out of time, but the reason why it was brought at all was the decision of the European Court of Justice in *Marshall v Southampton & South-West AHA*,[44] which declared certain of the existing provisions of English law in this area to be contrary to the Treaty of Rome. The plaintiff argued that this change in the law provided a sufficient reason for the tribunal to allow the action to be brought out of time and the tribunal accepted this argument.

27.021

It may be observed in passing that the European Court, like English courts, is not usually regarded as changing the law, but merely as declaring it. Nevertheless, the Act gives the tribunal a wide discretion to extend the limitation period, and it might well be argued that the decision in *Marshall* brought about so radical a change in the general understanding of the law on this point that the decision was justified.[45] A similar approach has since been adopted in *Rastall v Midlands Electricity Plc*.[46] It now appears that an action in respect of sex discrimination based on directly applicable provisions of European law will be subject to similar time-limits, which will be applied by analogy, even though there are no statutory time-limits in English law for bringing actions based on European law.[47]

---

[40] See Ch.8.
[41] *Foley v BICC Pyrotenax Ltd*, February 11, 1999, EAT; see also *Liburd v Hideaway Youth Project*, September 23, 1999, EAT, where the Industrial Tribunal was criticised for not looking beyond the s.33 criteria. *Biggs v Someset County Council* [1996] I.C.R. 364; [1996] I.R.L.R. 203.
[42] [2003] All ER (D) 80 (Oct).
[43] [1988] I.C.R. 526, EAT.
[44] Case 152/84 [1986] Q.B. 401.
[45] Since the decision, the House of Lords has held in *Kleinwort Benson v Lincoln CC* [1999] 2 A.C. 349 that money paid on the basis of a generally accepted understanding of the law which is later held to have been wrong can be regarded as having been paid under a "mistake of law". Although the context is very different, this may be regarded as providing further support to the Foster approach.
[46] [1996] I.C.R. 644, EAT.
[47] *W.B. Livingstone v Hepworth Refractories Plc* [1992] 3 C.M.L.R. 601, EAT. See also Ch.28 under "European law".

27.022   In a case where a police officer alleged that a policy or regime of institutional racism existed, it was held that she was entitled to rely on individual acts of discrimination outside the three-month limitation period for the presentation of complaints to an employment tribunal.[48]

RENT ACT 1977

27.023   Section 38 of the Rent Act 1977 allows an action by a tenant against his landlord for the recovery of rent which has been overpaid. The Act applies a limitation period of two years to such an action,[49] and time runs from the date of the overpayment. Presumably each fresh instance of overpayment creates a new cause of action, in respect of which time will run afresh, though this should not affect the running of time for any previous overpayment.

EMPLOYMENT RIGHTS ACT 1996

27.024   The Employment Rights Act 1996 (the successor in this area to the Employment Protection (Consolidation) Act 1978) is the statute which contains the more important of an employee's rights against an employer in respect of the contract of employment. Generally it imposes limitation periods much shorter than those allowed by the 1980 Act. The most usual period under this Act is three months.[50] This applies to complaints on such matters as failure to provide a written statement of the terms of employment and failure to pay maternity pay to which the employee was statutorily entitled, as well as claims for unfair dismissal. Exceptionally, in the case of a complaint about the employee's right to a redundancy payment the period is normally six months, though in *Greenwich HA v Skinner*[51] it was held that a claim by NHS employees for contractual redundancy payments attracted a six-year limitation period, since it was based on contract.

27.025   There is discretion to extend the three-month time-limit where it was not "reasonably practicable" for the employee to have presented the claim within the three months.[52] This is a narrower test than the "just and

---

[48] *The Commissioner of Police of the Metropolis v J. Hendricks*, November 5, 2001, Unreported, EAT.
[49] Rent Act 1977 s.38(3).
[50] ERA 1996 s.111.
[51] [1989] I.C.R. 220, EAT.
[52] Employment Protection (Consolidation) Act 1978 s.67(2).

equitable" test that applies in cases of sexual, racial and disability discrimination.[53]

Where an applicant seeks a discretionary extension of time on the basis **27.026** that she was misled by her union representative, the line of cases[54] recognising the possibility of such extension is irrelevant where the misleading does not occur until after the expiry of the period.[55]

An applicant who complains of a decision in relation to his employment suffers detriment when that decision is made, rather than when it is promulgated. However, a delay in promulgation may be a relevant factor in exercising the discretion to extend time, as may a failure on the part of the applicant's solicitors.[56]

Addition of party

An industrial tribunal has power to add a new party to an unfair dismissal **27.027** claim after the expiry of the limitation period.[57] More generally, the power to allow the admission of new claims is wider in employment law claims than under the CPR.[58]

MAGISTRATES' COURTS ACT 1980

The Magistrates' Court Act 1980 has its major application in criminal **27.028** cases, which are beyond the scope of the present work, but the magistrates do also have jurisdiction in a number of civil matters, most notably those relating to maintenance payments and to affiliation orders. Under the Magistrates' Courts Act the complainant must lay the relevant information before the magistrates within six months of the matter of complaint arising; this rule applies equally to civil and criminal matters within the jurisdiction of the magistrates. Where there is a six-month time limit for the laying of an information under this Act, the information is to be taken as being 'laid'

---

[53] *Cuckson v Taylor*, July 21, 1998, EAT; *Averns v Stagecoach in Warwickshire* UKEAT/ 0065/08/DA.

[54] *Hawkins v Ball* [1996] IRLR 258; *Chohan v Derby Law Centre* [2004] IRLR 685; *Baynton v South West Trains Ltd* [2005] UKEAT 0848/04; *Anderson v George S Hall Ltd* [2006] UKEAT 0631/05; *Chief Constable of Lincolnshire Police v Caston* [2009] UKEAT/0530/08/ JOJ.

[55] *Hunwicks v Royal Mail Group Plc* UKEAT/0003/07/ZT Underhill J.

[56] *Virdi v Commissioner of Police of the Metropolis* [2007] IRLR 24 EAT.

[57] *Drinkwater Sabey v Burnett* [1995] I.C.R. 328, EAT.

[58] *Lehman Brothers Ltd v Smith* UKEAT/0486/05/TM, (Transcript) EAT; for the position under the CPR see Ch.23.

when it is received by the relevant magistrates court. Such reception may be by fax.[59]

SOCIAL SECURITY ACT 1986

27.029   Where decisions are made concerning the right of a claimant to one or other of the benefits governed by the Social Security Act 1986, there is usually a right of appeal. The Act requires such appeal to be brought within 21 days, usually calculated from the date on which the decision is notified to the claimant.

PLANNING LAW

27.030   In the context of planning law the following limitation periods may be noted. Sections 171B and 172 of the Town and Country Planning Act 1990[60] deals with enforcement notices, which are the means by which a planning authority requires a person to desist from an activity which has been undertaken in breach of planning controls. There is no general time-limit on the making and serving of an enforcement order, but s.172(4) of the Act provides that in certain specified cases the notice must be served within four years of the commencement of the breach. These cases are:

(a) the failure to comply with any condition or limitation which relates to the carrying out of such operation and subject to which planning permission was granted for the development of that land;

(b) the failure to comply with a condition which prohibits or has the effect of preventing a change of use of a building to use as a single dwelling-house.[61]

Section 171B provides that where there has been a breach of planning control consisting in the carrying out without planning permission of building, engineering, mining or other operations in, on, over or under land, no enforcement action may be taken after the end of the period of four years beginning with the date on which the operations were substantially completed. Where there has been a breach of planning control consisting in the change of use of any building to use as a single dwelling-house, no enforcement action may be taken after the end of the period of four years

---

[59] *Department for Environment, Food and Rural Affairs v Rockall* [2007] EWHC 614 (Admin) [2007] 3 All ER 258.

[60] Replacing s.87 of the Town and Country Planning Act 1971.

[61] Paragraph (d) was introduced for the first time by the 1990 Act.

beginning with the date of the breach. Therefore, building work and change of use to a single dwelling-house can become established by time. In all other cases of breach of planning requirements, the authority may serve an enforcement notice without limit of time.

Appeals

An enforcement notice must specify the date on which it is to take effect.[62] **27.031**
An appeal against an enforcement notice must be lodged with the Secretary of State not later than that date.[63]

Compulsory purchase

Section 10 of the Compulsory Purchase (Vesting Declarations) Act 1981 **27.032**
applies where a notice to treat in respect of compulsory acquisition is deemed to have been served under Pt III of that Act. Any dispute over the amount of compensation payable in such a case is to be referred to the Lands Tribunal. Such reference must be made within six years of the date on which the person claiming compensation knew, or could reasonably have been expected to know, of the vesting of the interest in the acquiring authority under Pt III of the Act.

INTELLECTUAL PROPERTY

The Copyright Designs and Patent Act 1988 has introduced two new **27.033**
statutory limitation periods in respect of copyright[64] and the rights in performances.[65] In the case of civil actions for delivery up of material which infringes either right, the rule now is that the action must be brought within six years of the date when the infringing copy was made, though this period can be extended in the usual way on grounds of fraud of disability.[66] For criminal proceedings the period is again six years, but here there is no possibility of extension.[67] The Patents Act 1977 contains no comparable provision dealing with patent infringement.[68]

---

[62] Town and Country Planning Act 1990 s.172(5).
[63] Town and Country Planning Act 1990 s.174(3).
[64] Copyright Designs and Patent Act 1988 s.113.
[65] Copyright Designs and Patent Act 1988 s.203.
[66] Copyright Designs and Patent Act 1988 s.99 (copyright), s.195 (performance rights).
[67] Copyright Designs and Patent Act 1988 s.108 (copyright), s.199 (performance rights).
[68] For the complexities of the limitation period in relation to patents, see *Sevcon v Lucas* [1986] 1 W.L.R. 462, CA and para.5.059.

PROCEEDS OF CRIME ACT 2002

27.034 Section 288 of the Proceeds of Crime Act 2002 adds a new s.27A to the Limitation Act 1980. This provides that none of the time limits in Pt I of the 1980 Act applies to any proceedings under Ch.2 of Pt 5 of the Proceeds of Crime Act 2002 (civil recovery of proceeds of unlawful conduct)[69]. However, proceedings under that Chapter for a recovery order in respect of any recoverable property may be brought after the expiration of the period of twelve years from the date on which the cause of action accrued to the Director of the Assets Recovery Agency.[70] Proceedings under that Chapter are brought on the earlier of when a claim form is issued, or an application is made for an interim receiving order.[71] The Director's cause of action accrues in respect of any recoverable property, in the case of proceedings for a recovery order in respect of property obtained through unlawful conduct, when the property is so obtained, in the case of proceedings for a recovery order in respect of any other recoverable property, when the property obtained through unlawful conduct which it represents is so obtained.[72]

If a person would but for the preceding provisions of the 1980 Act (and in particular s.3) have a cause of action in respect of the conversion of a chattel, and proceedings are started under that Chapter for a recovery order in respect of the chattel, s.3(2) of this Act does not prevent his making an application under s.281 of the Proceeds of Crime Act 2002 (which provides for proceedings by persons from whom property is alleged to have been stolen) for an order that the property belongs to him, or the court making a declaration in his favour under that section.[73] If the court makes such a declaration, his title to the chattel is to be treated as not having been extinguished by s.3(2) of this Act.[74] The effect of this appears to be that a person who can obtain a declaration that property seized under the 2002 Act was stolen from him is given protection against the operation of s.3(2).[75] There is as yet no case law on this new section.

---

[69] S.27A(1).
[70] S.27A(2).
[71] S.27A(3).
[72] S.27A(4).
[73] S.27A(5).
[74] S.27A(6).
[75] For s.3(2) see Paras 12.003–12.007.

THE LAW COMMISSION'S PROPOSALS

These are of no relevance to the limitation periods considered in this **27.035** chapter—all would fall outside the core regime on the ground that they are expressly created by a statute other than the Limitation Act.

CHAPTER 28

European law

EUROPEAN UNION LAW

The development of the internal market within the European Union, **28.001** together with the ever-increasing progress of the EU more generally, brings with it an increased amount of European legislation which is directly applicable in the United Kingdom. Some of this legislation is capable of resulting in litigation, either before the domestic courts or before the European Court of Justice. This makes it necessary to examine the European dimension to the English law of limitation periods.

General principles

A fundamental distinction must be drawn between actions before domestic **28.002** courts in respect of rights conferred by Community law and actions before the European Court of Justice.

Domestic courts[1]

National procedural rules that govern actions based on national law and **28.003** actions based on European Community Law must ensure that European Community claims are not treated less favourably than pure domestic actions in relation to limitation of actions. The principal problem in this respect is the application of limitation periods to rights of action created by European Community legislation or emanations, which are enforced in domestic courts, where there is no prescribed limitation period. The approach of the English courts in these cases has been to apply statutory limitation periods under the Limitation Act 1980 to such European Com-

---

[1] See also [2002] 10 E.R.P.L. 261.

munity created actions by analogy. This approach is appropriate where the relevant actions are similar to but sufficiently different from existing actions under pure domestic law so as not to fall within the strict letter of a pre-scribed limitation period governing any analogous domestic action. The most authoritative consideration of these issues is to be found in *Arkin v Borchard Lines Ltd.*[2] In Case 33/76 *Rewe-Zentralfinanz EG and Rewe-Zentral HG LandwirtschaftsKammer fur das Saarland,*[3] the ECJ held that:

"In the absence of Community rules on this subject, it is for the domestic legal system of each Member State . . . to determine the procedural conditions governing actions at law intended to ensure the protection of the rights which citizens have from the direct effect of Community law, it being understood that such conditions cannot be less favourable than those relating to actions of a domestic nature.

In the absence of such measures of harmonisation the right conferred by Community law must be exercised before the national courts in accordance with the conditions laid down by national rules.

The position would be different only if the conditions and time-limits made it impossible in practice to exercise the rights which the national courts are obliged to protect. This is not the case where reasonable periods of limitation of actions are fixed."

In Case 45/76 *Comet BV v Produktschap voor Siergewassen,*[4] the ECJ emphasised that each Member State had to lay down relevant procedural rules where EC law was silent on the issue. However, this principle was subject to two EC law conditions: first, the principle of equivalence or non-discrimination, namely that any remedy or cause of action available to ensure that national law was observed should also be available to ensure that EC law was observed; secondly, the principle of practical possibility, namely that no national condition or procedure should make the exercise of an EC law right impossible or excessively difficult in practice.

28.004   *Local Authorities Mutual Investment Trust v Customs and Excise Commissioners*[5] concerned the rule that allowable deductions for VAT cannot be claimed more than three years after the right to deduct accrues. An attempt was made to argue that the right to recover the tax was a 'possession' within art.1 of the First Protocol in Pt II of the schedule to the Human Rights Act 1998; that peaceful enjoyment of that possession was a right within s.1(1) of that Act, and that the rule in question infringed the exercise of that right in a manner which was not necessary to secure the general interest. Not surprisingly, this argument was dismissed. As had

---

[2] [2000] Eu. L.R. 232.
[3] [1976] E.C.R. 1989.
[4] [1976] E.C.R. 2043.
[5] [2003] EWHC 2766 (CH), [2003] All ER (D) 309 (Nov).

been held in previous cases, in the absence of Community rules on the subject, it was for the domestic legal system of each member state to designate the courts having jurisdiction and to determine the procedural conditions governing actions at law, subject to the qualification that these conditions:

(i) could not be less favourable than those relating to similar actions of a domestic nature (the equivalence principle) and

(ii) could not make it impossible in practice to exercise the rights which the national courts were obliged to protect (the effectiveness principle).

It was not correct to argue that a three year time limit was disproportionate or prevented the effective exercise of directly effective rights, nor did it breach the principle of equivalence. Furthermore, there could have been no infringement of art.1 of the first protocol because:

(i) the right to reimbursement was always subject to the three year limitation period, the application of which would not amount to an interference with that right and

(ii) in any event, the limitation period was imposed for the purposes of legal certainty, which was a legitimate aim, and was proportionate to that aim.

Department for Environment, Food and Rural Affairs v Maltco 3 Ltd[6] 28.005
involved the construction of limitation periods laid down in Council Regulation (EC, Euratom) No.2988/95 and in particular the construction of provisions in that Regulation to which there is nothing even approximately similar in English law. The Regulation lays down a limitation period of four years, but adds:

In the case of continuous or repeated irregularities, the limitation period shall run from the day on which the irregularity ceases. In the case of multiannual programmes, the limitation period shall in any case run until the programme is definitively terminated.

The limitation period shall be interrupted by any act of the competent authority, notified to the person in question, relating to investigation or legal proceedings concerning the irregularity. The limitation period shall start again following each interrupting act.

However, limitation shall become effective at the latest on the day on which a period equal to twice the limitation period expires without the

---

[6] [2003] EWHC 469 (QB) Davis J.

competent authority having imposed a penalty, except where the administrative procedure has been suspended in accordance with art.6(1).

The period for implementing the decision establishing the administrative penalty shall be three years. That period shall run from the day on which the decision becomes final.

Instances of interruption and suspension shall be governed by the relevant provisions of national law.

28.006   Davis J. felt unable in the context of a preliminary hearing to reach a definite view about these matters, but commented that the second paragraph of art.3.1 of reg.2988/95 provides to the effect that the limitation period, in the case of continuous or repeated irregularities (plural), runs from the date on which the irregularity (singular) ceases. The third paragraph provides for "interruption" of the limitation period by any notified act of the kind there specified, with the consequence that the limitation period "shall start again" following "each interrupting act". The combination of the long-stop provision in the fourth paragraph, and the requirement to "implement" the decision within three years thereafter, thus gives rise (subject to art.3.3) to a potential total permitted period for the commencement of legal process of seven years: and potentially even (in the case of renewed interrupting acts) of eleven years. He added that the phrase "shall start again" is rather ambiguous. It might mean that the period starts afresh; or it might mean (consistently with the notion of interruption) that the period starts again as to the balance of the limitation period. The notion of interruption, in the context of limitation periods is a familiar one in Community law[7]: In the case of *LVM v Commission*[8] it was taken that the like phrase (in the French text, "Court à nouveau") in reg.2988/74 meant that the limitation period started afresh following each interrupting act.

28.007   The problem of the application of limitation periods to rights of action created by EC legislation which are enforced in domestic courts where there is no prescribed limitation period has been addressed by the English courts. In *Cannon v Barnsley Metropolitan BC*[9] it was held that English law was capable in such cases of evolving, if necessary by analogy to statutory periods, a time-limit for the bringing of these claims. This is so even where such actions were similar to, but sufficiently different from, existing actions under domestic law so as not to fall within the strict letter of the prescribed limitation period governing the analogous domestic action.[10]

28.008   The court in *Cannon*, however, failed to address how, and under what

---

[7] See, for example Bellamy & Child on *European Community Law of Competition* 5th edn at para.12–114; and Reg 2988/74.

[8] Case C-238/99P, 15 October 2002, see the decision of the Court at first instance, reported at 1999 ECR 11-931 in particular at para.1092 of the judgment.

[9] [1992] 1 I.C.R. 698.

[10] The Court in expressing this opinion also referred to common law periods of limitation as being applicable to actions, but this must be regarded as wrong since limitation is a creature of statute.

circumstances, limitation periods prescribed under English law would be applied to domestic actions created by EC legislation, where that legislation does not provide for limitation periods. It is in this specific area that *Arkin* is most significant.[11] The defendants were, in 1984, operators of container transport services to and from Israel and the United Kingdom and Europe. The parties were involved in various joint ventures and agreements. In July 1984 various agreements were entered into which formed the core of the action by the claimant. These agreements provided for the sharing of cargoes and the setting of a common tariff to be charged by all parties except *Borchard* and certain other members, who would be entitled to charge rates which varied from the tariff by up to an agreed maximum differential to be decided by an executive committee. The claimant alleged, inter alia, that the purpose of the July 1984 agreements was to eliminate competition between members of pre-existing conferences serving the relevant routes, on the one hand, and independent container service operators, on the other.

In early 1986 parties to the July 1984 agreements entered into a further arrangement, under that they introduced freight rates that varied according to whether a shipper or forwarder shipped the entirety of his containers with those parties. If he did, that party was to be charged the standard tariff, known as the contractor rate (CR), but if he shipped any part of their containers by an independent line, the party was to be charged the non-contractor rate (NCR), which would be 40 per cent higher than the CR for the same trade in which the party had used an independent line, and 20 per cent higher for any other trade operated by the parties to the July 1984 agreements. These differentials were subsequently reduced, but never eliminated. The claimant maintained that these agreements and arrangements amounted to concerted practices which had as their object or effect the prevention, restriction or distortion of competition within the European Union and which might affect trade between Member States, contrary to arts 81 and 82 of the EC Treaty (ex arts 85 and 86). The agreements and practices were a price-fixing cartel. It is clear that arts 81 and 82 have direct effect and therefore give rise to rights that can be enforced by individuals in their domestic courts.[12] The independent shipping services operated by the claimant through the management of a company, BCL, represented considerable competition for the defendants. They responded to these threats by various strategies and by forming a "fighting committee", to devise a means of excluding BCL from the market. BCL made a complaint to the EC Commission alleging that the parties to the July 1984 agreements, including all the defendants, were operating in breach of EC competition rules, in particular arts 81 and 82. No exemption was possible under Council Regulation 4056/86.

---

[11] See also the case of *R. v Secretary of State for Transport, ex p. Factortame (No. 6), The Times*, January 10, 2001, at para.28.024, below.

[12] See, e.g. *BRT v Sabam* [1974] E.C.R. 51.

28.009   Following this complaint, the parties to the 1984 agreements made various amendments to those agreements, intending to bring these arrangements within the terms of Regulation 4056/86. Notwithstanding these amendments, the Commission issued its statement of objections on November 5, 1991. The Commission concluded that the defendants as parties to the July 1984 agreements and subsequent arrangements had acted in breach of art.81(1) and were not protected by the block exemption in Reg.4056/86. It intended to impose fines on the recalcitrant parties. The Commission rejected the claim that there was any breach of art.82, and further stated that in view of the cessation of the rate-differential system in February 1991 and the fact that BCL had not sought to challenge the conduct of the defendants after that date, that any breaches of art.81(1) after that period were to be ignored. The Commission subsequently informed BCL that in view of the cessation of the rate-differential system in February 1991, the trades in question appeared to be open to competition.

The Commission regarded the question of redress as an issue for the national courts. The claimant, as the assignee of the rights of BCL, consequently instituted proceedings in the United Kingdom. It was common ground between the parties that any cause of action that arose before April 18, 1991 was time-barred, and that the conduct of the defendants which occurred before that date, and which resulted in actionable damage, could not form the basis of any claim. Both parties accepted that a limitation period applied to the action, and agreed upon its duration, on the basis of previous authority. These assumptions were, in view of the case law, not unfounded.

28.010   Coleman J. followed the authority of *Lloyd's Society v Clementson*[13] in determining the nature of the claimant's action. It held that a person who suffers loss as a consequence of a breach of either art.81 or 82 EC has a private right of action which is analogous to a claim for breach of statutory duty. The logical consequence of this case is that the courts may apply by analogy the terms of s.2 of the Limitation Act 1980 to any such action. The limitation period for an action governed by s.2 is six years from the date of accrual. A cause of action for breach of statutory duty accrues when a breach causes actionable damage to the claimant. Actionable damage is damage which is more than purely nominal, although it should be noted that the court did not use this term expressly. The application of these principles to actions based on art.81 and 82 E.C. is not, however, without its problems. These issues will now be considered.

28.011   The court first addressed the principal issue that if s.2 of the 1980 Act was to be applied to the action, albeit by analogy, then the determination of the accrual of the action was crucial, as was the consequential issue as to whether any actionable damage had occurred within the period of limita-

---

[13] [1995] 1 C.M.L.R. 693 at 711, per Sir Thomas Bingham M.R.

tion. The court sought to differentiate and to concentrate on the different ways in which a breach of statutory duty might cause actionable damage to a claimant, and therefore how the concept of actionable damage could be applied to the action before the court. This was entirely appropriate, since the parties did not contest the fact that damage had been sustained by BCL as a consequence of the defendants' actions and in view of the Commission's finding that they had been in breach of art.81. The court considered that an isolated event could constitute a breach of the duty imposed by virtue of art.81. It was accepted that such an event could cause a chain of damage starting when the effects of the breach first affect the claimant. The effects of this type of damage could continue for a considerable length of time. Nevertheless, the court held that if the period of the breach and consequential actionable damage occurs prior to any cut-off date for the purposes of a period of limitation (albeit applied by analogy), then the claim must prima facie be time-barred. In these circumstances, it is irrelevant that the damage continues to affect the claimant within the cut-off date.

In coming to this conclusion the court applied general principles of **28.012** limitation law as it applies to tortious actions governed by s.2 of the 1980 Act. The court also considered the situation where there are continuous or repeated breaches of a statutory duty, over an extended period. Breaches of duty under Arts 81 and 82 are also capable of being continuous or being repeated over an extended period. The court in considering the issues of limitation raised by these forms of breach of duty made reference to the commission of a nuisance, such as the unlawful emission of toxic fumes that continue to affect and injure those exposed to them over the whole period of that breach. In these cases, any breach of a statutory duty which causes damage or which takes place within the prescribed limitation period governing the action cannot be time-barred. It is irrelevant in these circumstances that the breach is continuous or repeated. In the former case, the offending act extends into the relevant limitation period, and the claimant can recover for damage occurring within that period. In essence, a fresh cause of action is regarded as accruing on each and every day that the continuous tort exists. In the case of repeated breaches of a statutory duty, even those acts or omissions which constitute the breach of duty occurring outside the period of limitation could result in actionable damage which first occurs within the period of limitation governing the action. That damage is recoverable by a claimant. Actionable damage occurring within the relevant period of limitation is not time-barred in either case. The court in coming to these conclusions relied on the cases of *Crumbie v Wallsend Local Board*[14] and *Darley Main Colliery Co. v Mitchell*,[15] a case concerning nuisance, a continuous tort. The court held that breaches of both

---

[14] [1891] 1 Q.B. 503 at 508, per Lord Esher.
[15] (1886) 11 App. Cas. 127. See also Ch.5.

arts 81 and 82 EC which the claimant relied on in his pleadings were of a continuing nature. The defendants having entered into the unlawful agreement or having taken a decision to carry out unlawful conduct, it followed that the implementation of the agreement or decision represented a continuing breach or series of breaches of the duty derived from the Articles. Accordingly, if the implementation commenced outside the limitation period and continued within the limitation period, and subsequently caused actionable damage to the claimant, then a claim in respect of that damage cannot be time-barred. The Court also found another ground of recovery for the claimant. It held that as a general principle, even where the implementation of the unlawful agreement or decision took place prior to the cut-off date, but that the relevant act only caused actionable damage within the prescribed limitation period, a claim in respect of that damage was not time-barred.

28.013   The *Arkin* case continues the practice of the English courts of applying principles of English limitation law to domestic actions, not otherwise subject to limitation, and which are created by European legislation. It seems to have settled the issues of the determination of the accrual and duration of actions taken under the aegis of arts 81 and 82 EC.[16] This authority, it is suggested, provides that the principles to be applied for the purposes of determining the accrual and the duration of an action are the same irrespective of whether the action is governed by the Limitation Act 1980, or is an action created by European legislation, to which the principles of limitation are applied. This issue was considered by Morritt V-C in *Phonographic Performance Ltd v Department of Trade and Industry*[17] where he said that the English principles of limitation in relation to EC matters will be applied directly rather than by analogy.[18] It is submitted that little turns on the distinction. This practice cannot but help to produce a cross-fertilisation with regard to limitation law between purely domestic actions, which will in general be governed by the Limitation Act 1980, and actions based on EC sources, but which are undertaken in the domestic courts. One practical consequence of the *Arkin* decision is that the equivalent actions taken under domestic law by virtue of the newly enacted Competition Act 1998 will be governed for limitation purposes by similar principles.

---

[16] And therefore of actions which are derived from European legislation, and which are regarded by the courts as being analogous to actions in respect of a breach of statutory duty under domestic legislation.

[17] [2004] EWHC 1795 (Ch).

[18] Disapproving the suggestion made in this paragraph in the 4th edition of this book.

Requirements of promptness

In *Uniplex (UK) Limited v NHS Business Services Authority*[19] the ECJ   **28.014**
considered a provision equivalent to Reg.32(4)(b) of the Public Services
Contract Regulations 1993 [20], which sought to implement Council Directive 89/665/EEC of 21 December 1989.[21] That Directive sets out procedures for the awarding of public works contracts and provides a procedure
by which an unsuccessful tenderer may challenge the decision on the basis
that the proper procedures have not been followed. Regulation 32(4)(b) of
the Regulations (not the Directive) provides that proceedings making such a
challenge must be brought promptly and in any event within three months
from the date when grounds for the bringing of the proceedings first arose
unless the Court considers that there is good reason for extending the
period within which proceedings may be brought.

Until the *Uniplex* case the English courts operated provisions in the   **28.015**
nature of reg.32(4)(b) on the basis that the primary obligation was to apply
"promptly" once the breach of procedures had taken place. That might
require the commencement of proceedings within a 3-month period. The
three-month period was a long-stop date[22], notwithstanding that a claimant
might not know of the infringement until more than three months had
passed. In order to mitigate possible unfirness resulting from this fact the
English courts applied the discretion so as to give that person an opportunity to challenge once he had become aware of the breaches.

In *Uniplex* the ECJ held that a limitation period defined by "promptness"   **28.016**
was not sufficiently certain to be justified and it would be wrong to allow a
limitation period to start before knowledge of the infringement was
obtained by the complainant. However, the fact that a candidate or tenderer learns that its application or tender has been rejected does not place it
in a position effectively to bring proceedings. Such information is insufficient to enable the candidate or tenderer to establish whether there has been
any illegality which might form the subject matter of the proceedings. That
information is obtained only once a concerned candidate or tenderer has
been informed of the reasons for its elimination from the public procurement procedure. So the time limit for bringing proceedings must run only
from the date on which the claimant knew, or ought to have known, of the
alleged infringement of those provisions. However, it is not necessary for
the claimant also to be aware that loss or damage has been suffered.[23]

As ever in dealing with EU legislation, it is for the national court, as far as   **28.017**

---

[19] C-406/08.
[20] SI 1993 No. 3228.
[21] Commonly known as the Public Procurement Directive.
[22] It will be recognised that this is very similar to the approach adopted in judicial review
cases, and considered at paras 9.004–9.009.
[23] Para.45 of the judgment.

is at all possible, to interpret the domestic provisions establishing the limitation period in a manner which accords with the objective of the Directive.[24] So the national court dealing with the case must, as far as is at all possible, interpret the national provisions governing the limitation period in such a way as to ensure that that period begins to run only from the date on which the claimant knew, or ought to have known, of the infringement of the rules applicable to the public procurement procedure in question.[25] If the national provisions at issue do not lend themselves to such an interpretation, that court is bound, in exercise of the discretion conferred on it, to extend the period for bringing proceedings in such a manner as to ensure that the claimant has a period equivalent to that which it would have had if the period provided for by the applicable national legislation had run from the date on which the claimant knew, or ought to have known, of the infringement of the public procurement rule.[26]

28.018   In *SITA UK Limited v Greater Manchester Waste Disposal Authority*[27], where a similar point arose, Mann J. held that the application of these principles by the English court involved the following steps[28]:

(i)   It is for the court to interpret the English legislation, but it should do so in the light of the wording and purpose of the Directive.

(ii)   The interpretation should, if possible, ensure that the limitation period runs from the date of knowledge or constructive knowledge (which is the term I will use to describe the "ought to have known" elements).

(iii)   If that is possible, then the national provision is compliant and can be given effect to.

(iv)   If such an interpretation is not possible, then any discretion available must be exercised so as to allow a limitation period equivalent to that provided by the legislation but starting from the date of knowledge or constructive knowledge.

(v)   If neither of those steps is possible, the actual national provision cannot be brought into line with the Directive and it must be disregarded.

28.019   It is submitted that Mann J.'s approach correctly gives effect to the letter and the spirit of the decision in *Uniplex*. Essentially, the court tries, first as a matter of construction, then as a matter of discretion, to bring the domestic

---

[24] Para.46.
[25] Para.47.
[26] Para.48.
[27] [2010] EWHC 680 (Ch).
[28] Para.29.

provision into lines with the Directive. But, crucially, if this cannot be done, then the domestic provision must fall because it does not correctly implement the Directive.

Non-implementation of Directives

Where a Member State has failed to implement a Directive correctly, time **28.020** for the bringing of an action allowed in pursuance of the Directive does not run. Only the correct implementation of the Directive can set the clock running. This principle was laid down in *Emmott v Minister for Social Welfare*,[29] a case from Ireland, where the applicant's disability pension had been reduced because she was a married woman. Single people and married men in identical circumstances received pensions at the higher rate. Mrs Emmott successfully contended that this was unlawful discrimination, but then faced a limitation problem because she had delayed in bringing the action. Part of the delay arose from the fact that the Irish Government had persistently refused to deal finally with her claim because of litigation as to the validity of such discrimination, which was pending. During this period the relevant Directive[30] had not been implemented, and the ECJ held that until this was done time could not run against Mrs Emmott for the purposes of an action under the domestic law.[31] The ECJ declined to follow fully the views of the Advocate-General, who would have added the further requirements that any limitation period imposed under the domestic law must be reasonable and that time for the purposes of that limitation period must run from the date of discoverability of the cause of action.

Where a claimant acquires a right to bring a claim for damages for failure **28.021** to implement a Directive correctly or on time (commonly referred to as a *'Francovitch claim')* time runs from the date when he suffers the loss against which the Directive required him to be protected, rather than from any later date when that loss is quantified by judicial or other order.[32]

The decision of the ECJ in *Emmott v Minister for Social Welfare*[33] to the effect that EU Law precludes the competent authorities of a Member State from relying on national rules of limitation to defeat a claim in respect of rights granted by a Directive until such time as the Directive has been properly transposed into national law (in other words, time can only begin to run following implementation of a directive[34]) is to be regarded as being

---

[29] [1991] E.C.R. I-4269.
[30] Directive 79/7.
[31] For the application of this principle in a domestic context, see *Cannon v Barnsley MBC* [1992] 2 C.M.L.R. 795, EAT.
[32] *Moore v Secretary of State for Transport* [2007] EWHC 879 (QB)Eady J.; affirmed [2008] EWCA Civ 750 in conjunction with *Spencer v Department for Work and Pensions*.
[33] [1991] ECR I-4269, [1991] 3 CMLR 894, [1991] IRLR 387.
[34] See para.23 of the judgment of the court.

confined to its own special facts in view of the conceptual and practical difficulties to which it gives rise and having regard to subsequent authorities.[35]

28.022   In a case where the ECJ had held that a transitional regime introduced by HM Revenue & Customs in relation to VAT repayment claims did not comply with EU law because the time limit which it provided for the making of claims was too short, the House of Lords declined to lay down an appropriate time limit, saying that this was the task of the legislature or the executive, rather than of the judiciary. Instead, the House simply declared that the time limit stipulated by HMRC did not apply.[36]

Statute incompatible with EU law

28.023   An action for damages based on a breach of EU law in the form of passing a statute that is incompatible with EU law is an action based on tort for limitation purposes.[37]

28.024   Subsequent decisions of the ECJ may be seen as having undermined somewhat the statements in *Emmott*. In *BP Supergas*[38] it was observed that the effect of *Emmott* should be limited to cases where the time-limit deprived the plaintiff of all possibility of relying on the Directive. The principle should not apply where it merely made reliance more difficult, such as where there was still time to bring the action after the implementation of the Directive, even though that time was shorter than it would have been if the Directive had been implemented at the correct time. In *Johnson*[39] and again in *Steenhorst-Neerings*[40] it was held that the *Emmott* principle did not apply in cases where the national rule imposed no limit on the date when an action might be brought, but limited recovery to the period of one year before the action was brought.[41] The distinction is somewhat artificial, since both types of rules limit the recovery which can be made—the only difference appears to be that in one case all recovery is

---

[35] *Poole v Her Majesty's Treasury* [2006] EWHC 2731 (Comm), Langley J. The subsequent authorities include *Steenhorst-Neerings v Bvd B* [1993] ECR I-5475, [1995] 3 CMLR 323, [1994] IRLR 244; *Johnson v Chief Adjudication Officer* [1994] ECR I-5483, [1995] All ER (EC) 258, [1995] IRLR 157; *Preston v Wolverhampton Healthcare Trust* [1997] 1 CR 899: *Fantask A/S v Industreministeriet* [1997] ECR I-6783, [1998] All ER (EC) 1, [1998] 1 CMLR 473 the ECJ held that a time-limit could begin to run before the Directive in issue had been properly implemented; *Secretary of State for Work and Pensions v Walker-Fox* [2006] EuLR 601.

[36] *Fleming (trading as Bodycraft) v Revenue and Customs Commissioners; Condé Nast Publications Ltd v Revenue and Customs Commissioners* [2008] UKHL 2 [2008] STC 324.

[37] *R. v Secretary of State for Transport, ex p. Factortame Ltd* (No.6), Queen's Bench Division (Technology and Construction Court) [2001] 1 W.L.R. 942; see also Ch.4.

[38] [1995] E.C.R. I-1883.

[39] [1994] E.C.R. I-5483.

[40] [1993] E.C.R. I-5475.

[41] For commentary see Szyszczak (1996) 21 E.L.R. 351.

excluded, whereas in the other it is not. However, in the later cases the ECJ appears to have been influenced by the fact that the claims were against state-run insurance schemes, which operated on the basis that each year's claims had to be matched by the payment in of the same year. Allowing a long period of claims for arrears would thus have tended to destabilise the schemes.

The three-year time limit for bringing a claim under the Untraced Drivers **28.025** Agreement 1972 between the Motor Insurers' Bureau and the Secretary of State for Transport does not comply with Community law, and the UK is thus in breach of its Community obligations. That Agreement imposes a time limit for the bringing of a claim of three years from the date of the event giving rise to the death or injury. However, in *Evans v Secretary of State for the Environment, Transport and the Regions*[42] the European Court of Justice ruled that the protection provided by the national scheme under Art.1(4) of the Directive in respect of the victims of uninsured or untraced drivers had to be equivalent to and as effective as the protection available under the national legal system to victims of insured drivers. The MIB procedure did not provide protection equivalent to or as effective as the protection provided by the common law in respect of insured drivers because of the disparity, in terms of the time bar for any claim, between clause 1(1)(f) of the 1972 Agreement and the relevant provisions of the Limitation Act 1980.[43]

EUROPEAN COURT OF JUSTICE[44]

Procedure before the European Court of Justice is determined by the rules **28.026** of that court. The Treaties creating the various Communities lay down limitation periods for a number of different forms of action. All these periods can be extended to take account of postal delays—a flat-rate extension of a specified number of days is given according to the country in which the litigant is resident.[45] There is also a more general discretion to extend in cases of unforeseeable circumstances, but this rests in the discretion of the court. The distinct concept of "excusable error" may also be used to extend time. This is more likely to apply where the plaintiff's error arises from the conduct of the respondent institution.[46] Generally, time will run from the day on which the act complained of is done, though in the case of decisions (which are necessarily addressed to particular individuals) time

---

[42] *(Case C-63/01) (The Times* December 9, 2003; [2005] All ER (EC) 763, [2004] RTR 534).
[43] *Byrne v Motor Insurers' Bureau* (2007), *The Times*, 15 June Flaux J.; [2008] EWCA Civ 574; affirmed [2008] EWCA Civ 574.
[44] For the best general account of this topic see John Usher, *European Court Practice* (1983).
[45] Ten days in the case of U.K. residents—Annex II to the Rules of Procedure of the ECJ.
[46] *Bayer AG v European Commission* [1993] 4 C.M.L.R. 30.

will not run until the decision has been notified to the party affected. Proceedings are effectively commenced (and time therefore ceases to run) once the necessary documents have been lodged with the court.

The limitation periods

28.027   The limitation periods are generally very much shorter than those applicable in English domestic law. This may reflect the fact that in most cases what is being challenged is some legislative act; clearly it is not desirable that the status of these should be uncertain for protracted periods. Perhaps the best analogy in English law is with the rules on judicial review, which impose time-limits calculated in months rather than years.[47] An action for the annulment of legislation under art.173 of the Treaty of Rome must be brought within two months of the making of the legislation.[48] Actions for failure to act under art.175 of the Treaty must be brought within two months of the failure of the relevant body to respond to a request to act. Actions against the Community for damages under art.215 of the Treaty of Rome have a limitation period of five years if the claim is non-contractual.[49] The effect of these provisions is that an individual with a claim under art.215 can stop the five-year period of limitation running against him by notifying the institution against whom the claim lies of its existence. The institution then has two months in which to act to remedy the claimant's complaint. If the institution fails to do so within that period it is established as being in default. The passage of the limitation period remains interrupted, however, unless and until the claimant makes a further demand for action under art.175 of the institution in question. If the institution then denies the claim, or allows a further period of two months to go by without reacting, the claimant has a further period of two months within which to bring his proceedings, failing which his claim becomes barred. It will be observed that no time-limit is specified within which a claimant must make his further demand for action on the institution pursuant to art.175. However, in the case of *The Netherlands v The Commission*,[50] decided under similar limitation provisions of the European Coal and Steel Treaty,

---

[47] CPR Pt 54; see paras 9.002–9.007.

[48] References in the text are to the Treaty of Rome (as amended), which is the treaty which created the EEC (now the EC). Unless otherwise noted the same limits apply under the ECSC Treaty and the Euratom Treaty.

[49] Art. 43 of the Protocol, which provides: "Any natural or legal person may, under the same conditions, institute proceedings against a decision addressed to that person or against a decision which, although in the form of a regulation or a decision addressed to another person, is of direct and individual concern to the former. The proceedings provided for in this Article shall be instituted within two months of the publication of the measure, or of its notification to the plaintiff, or, in the absence thereof of the day on which it came to the knowledge of the latter, as the case may be."

[50] [1971] E.C.R. 639.

it was held that the second demand must be made within a reasonable time of first notification of the claim to the institution. In the *Netherlands* case a period of 18 months before[51] the second demand was made was held to be too long and the action time-barred. If the claim is contractual (which will apparently happen only very rarely) then there is no period of limitation.

Transport and competition

Regulation 2988/74 provides for five-year periods of limitation in the case of actions relating to competition law (including the enforcement of sanctions by the Commission) and to matters relating to transport.   **28.029**

Pleading

Like the national courts of most Member States, the ECJ does not raise the question of limitation of its own motion—it must be pleaded by the defendant.[52]   **28.030**

Indirect enforcement

Even where a Community provision is no longer open to direct challenge, a litigant in a case before the domestic court still has the option of seeking a reference of the matter to the European Court under art.177 of the Treaty of Rome, and it appears that the European Court must accept such a reference, if made, notwithstanding that no claim could have been brought before that Court directly.   **28.031**

European Economic Interest Groupings (EEIG)

EEIGs, created by a Community Regulation,[53] are a form of business association bearing some resemblance to a partnership. They are intended to facilitate cross-border commercial co-operation within the Community. Their significance here is that art.37 of the Regulation deals with limitation periods for actions against former members of an EEIG arising out of the activities of that EEIG. Article 37 prescribes a limitation period of five years from the date when the fact of a member's departure from the EEIG is   **28.032**

---

[51] *J.J. Dent v National Farmers Union and Associated Actions*, June 17, 1999, Unreported, Evans-Lombe J.
[52] *James Joseph Cato v E.C. Commission* [1992] 2 C.M.L.R. 459, ECJ.
[53] Reg. 2137/85.

published in the appropriate national Gazette[54] or from the date when the EEIG is dissolved. This period is expressed to be in substitution for any longer period laid down by the national law, but art.37 does not say that it is in substitution for any shorter period laid down by the national law. So far as most activities of an EEIG are concerned, it is suggested that actions will normally be brought in contract (occasionally perhaps in tort). This will usually involve a six-year limitation period, and at first sight it therefore appears that the five-year period of art.37 will be substituted. The difficulty is that the five-year period may well expire later than the six-year period. The reason for this apparently odd statement is that in contract time normally runs from the date of the breach, which will frequently be well before the member's departure or the dissolution of the EEIG. On the wording it nevertheless seems that the applicable period is that provided by art.37.

28.033   A further complication that may be mentioned arises from cases such as *Betjemann v Betjemann*,[55] which held that in a partnership time does not run for the purposes of an action between the partners (or former partners) until the partnership is dissolved. The EEIG clearly has features in common with a partnership, though it is not a partnership within the meaning of the Partnership Act 1890,[56] and it is not impossible that an English court will wish to adopt this analogy when considering the running of time as between members of an EEIG. Such an approach, if ultimately adopted, would merely serve to reinforce the conclusion tentatively expressed here, namely that the relevant period will always be five years from the member's departure or the dissolution of the EEIG.

HUMAN RIGHTS

28.034   The coming into force on 2 October 2000 of the Human Rights Act 1998 has given new force to the question of the English law of limitation of actions with the European Convention on Human Rights Issues may arise in relation to the right to a fair trial under art.6 and in relation to the right to peaceful enjoyment of property under art.1 of the First Protocol to the Convention. The art.6 issue was considered in *Stubbings v United Kingdom*,[57] where it was held that limitation periods are as a general rule a matter for the domestic law, and that the periods in use have not been harmonised to the point where it would be appropriate to regard minimum

---

[54] In England, the London Gazette.

[55] [1895] 2 Ch.474.

[56] Art.3 of the Regulation creating the EEIG forbids it to be profit-seeking, whereas s.1 of the Partnership Act defines partnership as "The relationship which subsists between persons carrying on business in common with a view of profit".

[57] (1997) 23 E.H.R.R. 213.

or maximum periods as being matters within the Convention. Although it might be argued that this approach rules out the use of art.6 as a way of challenging limitation periods, it could also be argued that the decision applies only to the fixed six-year period which was held in *Stubbings v Webb*[58] to be applicable to actions for intentional trespass to the person. It should be remembered also that excessively long periods of limitation are in principle as amenable to challenge as excessively short periods, for either could, for quite different reasons, be regarded as being inimical to the prospect of a fair trial. An unduly short period may prevent a claimant from vindicating his rights, whereas an unduly long period may expose defendants to liability in circumstances where the poor quality of evidence makes a fair trial impossible.

So far as the right to peaceful enjoyment of property is concerned, attention is drawn to *Elena Carbonara v Italy*,[59] where it was held that the retrospective application by the Italian courts of the constructive-expropriation rule, coupled with the retrospective application of a five-year limitation period in relation to the applicants' consequential right to claim compensation, meant that the applicants had been unlawfully deprived of their land in breach of art.1 of the European Convention.

Section 7(5) of the Human Rights Act 1998 ("HRA") provides that proceedings by a person who claims that a public authority has acted in a way which is made unlawful by s.6(1) HRA because it has acted in a way which is incompatible with a Convention right must be brought before the end of (a) the period of one year beginning with the date on which the act complained of took place, or (b) such longer period as the court considers equitable having regard to all the circumstances. In a Scottish case[60] it was held that the time limit did not apply to a claim that the Act complained of was unlawful for reasons other than the fact that it infringed the HRA. **28.035**

The time limit created by s.7(5) is an ordinary limitation time limit and does not raise a question of jurisdiction.[61] Thus it is appropriate to raise it by pleading it as a defence. It does not have to be raised as a challenge to the jurisdiction under CPR 11.

The discretion to extend time was considered in *Hanifa Dobson v Thames Water Utilities Ltd (Water Services Regulation Authority (Ofwat) intervening)*.[62] The particular feature of that case was that there was a **28.036**

---

[58] [1993] A.C. 498, HL.
[59] May 30, 2000, ECHR.
[60] *Somerville (AP) (Original Appellant and Cross-respondent) v Scottish Ministers (Original Respondents and Cross-appellants) (Scotland); Blanco (AP) (Original Appellant and Cross-respondent) v Scottish Ministers (Original Respondents and Cross-appellants) (Scotland); Henderson (AP) (Original Appellant and Cross-respondent) v Scottish Ministers (Original Respondents and Cross-appellants) (Scotland); Ralston (AP) (Original Appellant and Cross-respondent) v Scottish Ministers (Original Respondents and Cross-appellants) (Scotland) (Consolidated Appeals)* 2007 Scot (D) 1/8.
[61] *M (a minor by his litigation friend LT) v Ministry of Justice* [2009] EWCA Civ 419.
[62] [2007] EWHC 2021 (TCC) Ramsey J.

group action, and the question was whether, in determining a limitation issue under s.7(5)(b) of the Human Rights Act 1998, the court should exercise its discretion by analogy with s.33 of the Limitation Act 1980 with regards to all the circumstances of the individual claimant, and/or, in a group action, with regard to all the circumstances of the group. Ramsey J's answer neatly combined the two possibilities by saying that the court should exercise its discretion, by analogy with s.33 of the 1980 Act, having regard to all the circumstances of the individual claimant. In doing so, one of those circumstances would be the circumstances of the group in a group action. Subsequently, in *Dunn v Parole Board*[63] the Court of Appeal held that it is not appropriate to lay down any general guidelines on how the very broad discretion of s.7(5)(b) should be exercised. However, in *Rabone v Pennine Care NHS Trust*[64] Simon J. commented as follows[65]:

"(1) The burden is on the Claimants to show that there are circumstances which make it 'equitable' that the trust should not be able to rely on the limitation provisions, see for example, *Cameron v Network Rail Infrastructure Ltd* [2006] EWHC 1133 (QB), [2007] 1 WLR 163, Sir Michael Turner at [47], and *A v Essex County Council* [2007] EWHC 1652 (QB), Field J at [120], who added that there will be few cases which will be decided on the burden of proof.

(2) The Court has a wide discretion in determining what is 'equitable'; and each case will turn on its own circumstances. Proportionality will generally be taken into account: see *Dunn v Parole Board* [2008] EWCA Civ 374, [2009] 1 WLR 728, Thomas LJ at [31-33].

(3) The reason why the time limits are shorter in HRA cases was explained by Lord Brown of Eaton-under-Heywood in the decision of the House of Lords in *Van Colle*.

As Lord Bingham pointed out in *R (Greenfield) v Secretary of State for the Home Department* [2005] UKHL 14, Convention claims have very different objectives from civil actions. Where civil actions are designed essentially to compensate claimants for their losses, Convention claims are intended rather to uphold minimum human rights standards and to vindicate those rights. That is why time limits are markedly shorter . . . it is also why section 8(3) of the Act provides that no damages are to be awarded unless necessary for just satisfaction.

(4) In cases concerning personal injury or death the Court may have regard to circumstances of the type listed in section 33(3) of the Limitation Act 1980 as being relevant when deciding whether to extend time, see Cameron (above) [43]."

---

[63] [2008] EWCA Civ 374.
[64] [2009] EWHC 1827 (QB).
[65] At para.121.

Although these observations do not amount to an exhaustive list of relevant features, they are obviously helpful and are likely to be relied on in future cases.

The UK law of limitation in relation to real property does not infringe **28.037** art.1 of the First Protocol to the ECHR. The Court of Human Rights so held in *JA Pye (Oxford) Ltd v United Kingdom.*[66]

An interference with the right to the peaceful enjoyment of possessions has to strike a "fair balance" between the demands of the general interest of the community and the requirements of the protection of the individual's fundamental rights. The current English law on the subject does so because it provides reasonable protection for dispossessed landowners to assert their rights and reasonable opportunities for those who have acquired possession of land.

---

[66] App no 4403/02.

INDEX